D1521337

HANDBOOK OF RABBINIC THEOLOGY

HANDBOOK OF RABBINIC THEOLOGY

Language, System, Structure

BY

JACOB NEUSNER

BRILL ACADEMIC PUBLISHERS, INC.
BOSTON • LEIDEN
2002

Library of Congress Cataloging-in-Publication Data

Neusner, Jacob, 1932–
    Handbook of rabbinic theology / By Jacob Neusner.
    p. cm.
    ISBN 0-391-04139-8
    1. Judaism—Doctrines.   2. Rabbinical literature—History and criticism.
3. Hebrew language—Grammar. I. Title.

BM602 .N48 2002
296.3—dc21

2002011457

ISBN 0-391-04139-8
Paperback ISBN 0-391-04178-9

PRINTED IN THE UNITED STATES OF AMERICA

HANDBOOK OF RABBINIC THEOLOGY

CONTENTS

PART THREE

THE THEOLOGICAL STRUCTURE OF RABBINIC JUDAISM: NORMS OF BEHAVIOR IN THE ISRAELITE SOCIAL ORDER

LIST OF ABBREVIATIONS

Biblical Books

Gen.	Genesis
Ex.	Exodus
Lev.	Leviticus
Num.	Numbers
Dt.	Deuteronomy
1 Sam.	1 Samuel
2 Chron.	2 Chronicles
Ps.	Psalm
Prov.	Proverbs
Qoh.	Qoheleth
Is.	Isaiah
Jer.	Jeremiah
Lam.	Lamentations
Ez.	Ezekiel
Dan.	Daniel
Hos.	Hosea
Zech.	Zechariah
Mal.	Malachi
Mt.	Matthew

Rabbinic Literature

A.Z.	*'Abodah Zarah*
B.	Bavli/Babylonian Talmud
Ber.	*Berakhot*
B.M.	*Baba Mesi'a*
Dem.	*Dema'i*
Hag.	*Hagigah*
Ker.	*Keritot*
M.	Mishnah
Neg.	*Nega'im*

San.	*Sanhedrin*
Shab.	*Shabbat*
T.	Tosefta
Tem.	*Temurah*
Ter.	*Terumot*
Toh.	*Tohorot*
Zeb.	*Zebahim*

OTHER

b.	ben
ch.	chapter
no.	number
R.	Rabbi

PREFACE

James Joyce is reputed to have said that if Dublin were destroyed, it could be reconstructed, brick by brick, from the pages of *Ulysses*. Along these same lines, I allege, if the Hebrew Scriptures of ancient Israel, the Written Torah, were lost, the main lines of the narrative of Israel's life with God and the consequent social vision could be reconstructed out of the details of the Halakhah, norms of conduct, and of the Aggadah, norms of conviction, that are set forth in the Oral Torah, that is, the canon of Rabbinic writings of late antiquity.

Here I show that the Rabbinic documents of the formative age of Judaism, the first six centuries c.e., make use of a generative theological grammar to set Scripture forth as a comprehensive, rational theological system of conviction and to construct a cogent theological structure of the social order—thus the "language, system, and structure" of the title.

This handbook presents in condensed form the results of three of my systematic works on the theology of Rabbinic Judaism, the Judaism set forth by Scripture as mediated by the Mishnah, Talmuds, and Midrash-compilations of late antiquity. The three titles here formed into a single coherent statement are *The Theological Grammar of the Oral Torah* I–III (1999), *The Theology of the Oral Torah: Revealing the Justice of God* (1999), and *The Theology of the Halakhah* (2001). The three were conceived to form a single continuous statement, covering the theological language, system of belief, and structure of behavior that animates the definitive documents and characterizes the age and thought of those that produced them.

Accordingly, in the principal parts of this reprise, I lay out [1] how the Rabbinic system speaks, [2] what it says, and [3] how it is embodied in the social order of the community for which it constructs its encompassing conception. Parts Two and Three turn to the functioning system and categorical structure. The former concerns how the theological corpus set forth in the Aggadah ("narrative"), the corpus of Scriptural interpretation, doctrine, ethics, and narrative actually functioned in explaining Israel's condition, the latter addresses how the Halakhah ("norms of behavior," "law") identified the building blocks of Israel's social order and defined in rules of conduct the consequences of the human condition set forth in mythic monotheism, a term defined presently. To state the matter simply: the Aggadah tells the story of mankind in relationship to God, then the Halakhah states what to do about the human situation.

The foundation of the work is the conviction that the Rabbinic canon is made up of intelligible, rational documents, coherent statements of viewpoints, not merely collections of episodic remarks about one thing and another. These documents—so I allege and demonstrate—re-present the Torah of Sinai with this implicit claim: if at Sinai God had chosen a different mode of thought and expression for conveying his will, here is what we should have as the Torah. Specifically, had he selected the modes of thought and expression of philosophy for the shaping of religion, had he preferred to set forth the Torah as theology and law validated by a self-evident rationality—rather than in the episodic rulings, framed in ad hoc narratives, and validated by notional prophecy such as Scripture sets forth—this is how he would have given the Torah.

Here is the system and structure that would have emerged in accord with the vocabulary, syntax, and semantics of God's language. By that I mean, as to God's self-manifestation in the Torah, this is [1] how his language works, [2] how his laws, narratives, and exhortations translate into a working theological system of conviction, and [3] how that system organizes the received revelation into coherent building blocks for the cogent conduct of society. Thus are the religious facts of the Torah of Sinai reshaped into a cogent theology of the social and cosmic order of the holy people that at Sinai entered God's kingdom by accepting the Torah.

The embodied theology encompasses other issues besides grammar, convictions, and conduct. Language, system, and structure constitute only the most important components of the Rabbinic theology. Three instances suffice to suggest what more remains. Rabbinic Judaism sets forth a theology of history. It contains within itself a theological hermeneutics, which defines the theological foundations of Rabbinic Midrash, or interpretation of Scripture. There is a theology of the social order that defines the Israelite individual and Israel as corporate community. Not only do those three issues receive sustained attention, but Rabbinic theology takes up the religious experience afforded by the Torah of Sinai. It comes to realization, also, in liturgy, in the rhythm of the synagogue year and its lections, and in other critical components of Judaism. I have worked on these and other special theological problems of description, analysis, and interpretation of systems of ideas. So the appended list of prior studies shows. The three treated here, however, strike me as the ones on which all else builds.

ACKNOWLEDGEMENTS

My thanks go to Dowling College Press/Global Publications for permission to condense my *Theological Grammar of the Oral Torah* I–III, and to McGill-Queen's University Press for permission to epitomize my *Theology of the Oral Torah: Revealing the Justice of God.*

I am grateful to Brill Academic Publishers for serving as my principal publisher for my main academic projects, and to its staff in both Leiden and Boston for their hearty encouragement in all things that I undertake. Joed Elich and Patrick Alexander embody all that is constructive in scholarly publishing, and fortunate are the scholars who get to work with them.

From day to day I discussed this project and the ones on which it is based with Professor William Scott Green, University of Rochester, always with good results.

For Part One of this Handbook further acknowledgements are called for. First, Professor David Aaron, Hebrew Union College, read the second, third, and fourth drafts of the Preface and the Introductions to *Theological Grammar* I–III and made important corrections to my framing of the metaphor, correcting needless error in my understanding of matters. I appreciate very much his taking time to read my drafts and contribute his learning to them. He gave me a better understanding of the project than I possessed to begin with.

Professor Stephen T. Katz, Boston University, read the third draft of the Preface and gave me the benefit of a first-class philosophical-critical reading, for which I am very grateful.

Professor Brevard Childs, Yale University, read the second draft of the Preface and guided me to important works that pursue theological matters in the way that I here try to do and that I otherwise should not have known.

In earlier phases of this project I consulted Professor Maurice

Wiles, Oxford University, and Dean Frances Young, University of Birmingham, both of whom answered my queries in a very helpful way. They guided me in ways they may not themselves have realized, and I found in their writings a standard to which to aspire.

JACOB NEUSNER

BIBLIOGRAPHY

Other books and monographs of mine that focus on theological problems include the following:

Dual Discourse, Single Judaism. The Category-Formations of the Halakhah and of the Aggadah Defined, Compared, and Contrasted. Lanham, 2000: University Press of America. Studies in Judaism Series.

The Halakhah and the Aggadah: Theological Perspectives. Atlanta, 2000: Scholars Press for South Florida Studies in the History of Judaism.

The Initial Phases of the Talmud's Judaism. Atlanta, 1995: Scholars Press for South Florida Studies in the History of Judaism. IV.

Jerusalem and Athens: The Congruity of Talmudic and Classical Philosophy. Leiden, 1997: E. J. Brill. Supplements to the *Journal for the Study of Judaism.*

Judaism as Philosophy. The Method and Message of the Mishnah. Columbia, 1991: University of South Carolina Press.

Judaism States its Theology: The Talmudic Re-Presentation. Atlanta, 1993: Scholars Press for South Florida Studies in the History of Judaism.

Judaism's Story of Creation: Scripture, Halakhah, Aggadah. Leiden, 2000: E. J. Brill. The Brill Reference Library of Judaism.

Judaism's Theological Voice: The Melody of the Talmud. Chicago, 1995: The University of Chicago Press.

The Presence of the Past, the Pastness of the Present. History, Time, and Paradigm in Rabbinic Judaism. Bethesda, 1996: CDL Press.

Rabbinic Judaism. Structure and System. Minneapolis, 1996: Fortress Press.

Rationality and Structure: The Bavli's Anomalous Juxtapositions. Atlanta, 1997: Scholars Press for South Florida Studies in the History of Judaism.

Recovering Judaism: The Universal Dimension of Jewish Religion. Minneapolis, 2000: Fortress Press.

Religion and Law: How through Halakhah Judaism Sets Forth its Theology and Philosophy. Atlanta, 1996: Scholars Press for South Florida Studies in the History of Judaism.

The Social Teaching of Rabbinic Judaism. I. *Corporate Israel and the Individual Israelite.* Leiden, 2001: E. J. Brill. Brill Reference Library of Judaism.

The Social Teaching of Rabbinic Judaism. II. *Between Israelites.* Leiden, 2001: E. J. Brill. The Brill Reference Library of Judaism.

The Social Teaching of Rabbinic Judaism. III. *God's Presence in Israel.* Leiden, 2001: E. J. Brill. The Brill Reference Library of Judaism.

Symbol and Theology in Early Judaism. Minneapolis, 1991: Fortress Press.

Theological Commentary to the Midrash. VIII. *Sifré to Numbers and Sifré to Deuteronomy.* Lanham, 2001: University Press of America. Studies in Judaism Series.

Theological Commentary to the Midrash. IV. *Leviticus Rabbah.* Lanham, 2001: University Press of America. Studies in Judaism Series.

Theological Commentary to the Midrash. IX. *Mekhilta Attributed to R. Ishmael.* Lanham, 2001: University Press of America. Studies in Judaism Series.

Theological Commentary to the Midrash. VI. *Ruth Rabbah and Esther Rabbah I.* Lanham, 2001: University Press of America. Studies in Judaism Series.

Theological Commentary to the Midrash. VII. *Sifra.* Lanham, 2001: University Press of America. Studies in Judaism Series.

Theological Commentary to the Midrash. I. *Pesiqta deRab Kahana.* Lanham, 2001: University Press of America. Studies in Judaism Series.
Theological Commentary to the Midrash. II. *Genesis Rabbah.* Lanham, 2001: University Press of America. Studies in Judaism Series.
Theological Commentary to the Midrash. III. *Song of Songs Rabbah.* Lanham, 2001: University Press of America. Studies in Judaism Series.
Theological Commentary to the Midrash: V. *Lamentations Rabbati.* Lanham, 2001: University Press of America. Studies in Judaism Series.
The Theological Foundations of Rabbinic Midrash. Leiden, 2002. E. J. Brill. The Brill Reference Library of Judaism. Paperback edition: Boston, 2002: E. J. Brill.
Theological Grammar of the Oral Torah. Binghamton, 1999: Dowling College Press/ Global Publications of Binghamton University [SUNY]. I. *Vocabulary: Native Categories.*
Theological Grammar of the Oral Torah. Binghamton, 1999: Dowling College Press/ Global Publications of Binghamton University [SUNY]. II. *Syntax: Connections and Constructions.* Epitomized. in *Handbuch of Rabbinic Theology,* below.
Theological Grammar of the Oral Torah. Binghamton, 1999: Dowling College Press/ Global Publications of Binghamton University [SUNY]. iii. *Semantics: Models of Analysis, Explanation and Anticipation.*
The Theology of Rabbinic Judaism. A Prolegomenon. Atlanta, 1997: Scholars Press for South Florida Studies in the History of Judaism.
The Theology of the Halakhah. Leiden, 2001: E. J. Brill. Brill Reference Library of Ancient Judaism.
Theology of the Oral Torah. Revealing the Justice of God. Kingston and Montreal, 1999: McGill-Queen's University Press and Ithaca, 1999: Cornell University Press.
The Unity of Rabbinic Discourse. Volume One. *Aggadah in the Halakhah.* Lanham, 2000: University Press of America. Studies in Judaism series.
The Unity of Rabbinic Discourse. Volume Three. *Halakhah and Aggadah in Concert.* Lanham, 2000: University Press of America. Studies in Judaism series.
The Unity of Rabbinic Discourse. Volume Two. *Halakhah in the Aggadah.* Lanham, 2000: University Press of America. Studies in Judaism series.
What, Exactly, Did the Rabbinic Sages Mean by "the Oral Torah"? An Inductive Answer to the Question of Rabbinic Judaism. Atlanta, 1999: Scholars Press for South Florida Studies in the History of Judaism.

INTRODUCTION

To introduce the work, the elements of the title take priority. For that purpose, "Rabbinic" requires a single sentence. Rabbinic Judaism is the Judaic religious system of the social order set forth in the Hebrew Scriptures, called "the Written Torah," as mediated by the Mishnah, Talmuds, Midrash-compilations, and related compilations, called "the Oral Torah." As to the historical and temporal setting, that one whole Torah, written and oral, took shape in the Land of Israel and in Babylonia in the first six centuries of the Common Era; it is with that canon and formative period that we deal in this book. Rabbinic theology undertakes to compose of the Torah's native category-formations and their data a working system of thought. It seeks to form a paradigm of all facts and so to accommodate new facts. In that way it undertakes to solve new problems as well. All accords with the generative logic that the religious tradition identifies for its own systematization, a logic embodied in the theological grammar of the language of the canonical statements of that tradition. Now to the other elements of this handbook's program.

I. What Is Theology?

Theology, broadly construed, is the science of the reasoned knowledge of God. Theology presents the system that results from philosophical analysis of the facts set forth by a religion. To specify what in the setting of a religion I conceive theology to do, I find a suitable definition for the work of theology in the definition of Ingolf Dalferth:

> [Theology] rationally reflects on questions arising in pre-theological religious experience and the discourse of faith; and it is the rationality of its reflective labor in the process of faith seeking understanding which inseparably links it with philosophy. For philosophy is essentially concerned with argument and the attempt to solve conceptual problems, and conceptual problems face theology in all areas of its reflective labors.[1]

---

[1] Ingolf U. Dalferth, *Theology and Philosophy* (Oxford: Blackwell, 1988), vii.

Theology devotes its analysis to revealed truths ("pre-theological religious experience," "discourse of faith"). It is comparable in method to philosophy, particularly in the rationality of its reflective labor. That is represented by its analytical argument and confrontation with conceptual problems. But theology starts with established facts, religious truths accorded special privilege, and revealed truths do not correspond to the data of philosophy. Philosophical data are subject to analysis free of special claims but commonly agreed upon by all reasonable persons. The upshot is simple. In mode of thought and analysis theology is like philosophy, but it is not the same thing as philosophy. Thus we distinguish theology of a religion from philosophy of religion.

In the case of Judaism knowledge of God is afforded by God's self-manifestation in the Torah. The theology of Judaism sets forth knowledge of God produced by rigorous reflection upon, generalization and universalization of, the hard facts of the Torah, written and oral. This comes about in two ways. The first is to know God through God's self-revelation in the Torah. This requires that we know what the Torah is. Then knowing how to define and understand the Torah affords access to God's self-revelation. The second is to know through that same self-revelation what God wants of Israel and how God responds to Israel and humanity at large.[2] That specific, propositional knowledge comes through reasoned reading of the Torah, oral and written. The hermeneutics governing these documents encapsulate that knowledge of reasoned explication. And the language of theology adumbrates that hermeneutics.

II. SYSTEM

The Rabbinic sages follow a cogent program, and so they construct a coherent system of thought. That encompassing intellectual system governs and animates all details. It furthermore processes new data

---

[2] I paraphrase Ingolf Dalferth, "The Stuff of Revelation: Austin Farrer's Doctrine of Inspired Images," in *Hermeneutics, the Bible and Literary Criticism* (ed. Ann Loades and Michael McLain; London: Macmillan, 1992), 71.

and shapes them into cogent components of the working system of ideas. The system begins with first principles and constructs upon a cogent account of God as Israel knows God in the Torah: what he wants, how he responds, what Israel is and is supposed to do. So at issue in the description of a theological system is not merely the presence of religious data of a theological classification, e.g., information about God and what he wants and does. No one has ever denied that the Rabbinic sages found in Scripture information about God's will and activities. How could he? But what cogent analytical program governs, actively and effectively shaping data that it chooses into compelling demonstrations of fundamental propositions about God and what he wants and does? And how does the outcome of that program impart sense to the transient world and Israel's destiny in it? The theological system of Rabbinic Judaism answers those questions and explains all things. The system is set forth through the details of the Aggadic components of the Rabbinic canon of late antiquity. Here I spell out that theological system.

III. STRUCTURE

The social entity of the theological system, "Israel" the holy community, forms not an abstraction but a concrete social world, one defined by the Torah that conveys God's will for humanity. A structure of category-formations concerning concrete conduct functions and imparts coherence to the details. That structure of normative rules of conduct, in Hebrew, Halakhah, corresponds to, and is partially concentric with, the Aggadah's theological system of normative conviction. That structure that transforms raw data into building blocks of the social order of the kingdom of priests and holy people is set forth through the category-formations of the Halakhic components of that same Rabbinic canon as encompasses the Aggadic documents of Scripture-interpretation and extension. Here I spell out that theological structure of the social order of Holy Israel that the Halakhah embodies.

IV. Category-Formations and Theological Norms

By a "category-formation" in the context of theology I mean a coherent classification of data that actively selects and holds together kindred facts in a cogent pattern of exposition. A category-formation thereby yields a proposition subject to generalization and validation against further pertinent data. A category-formation imposes cogency on discrete facts. It then turns facts into knowledge, knowledge into truth. The theological system and structure, Aggadah and Halakhah, are comprised not by random data on diverse topics but by active category-formations. By these category-formations the data of normative behavior and belief are not only classified but are shown to cohere. In that way the facts are joined to prove a fixed set of propositions—and rendered able to deal with data beyond the givens as well. The theological system and structure show the dynamics, the movement and working and dialectics, of category-formations.

Such a statement of facts transformed into theological truth is exemplified by this statement of the theological category-formations, Israel and the gentiles, and how they impart coherence to diverse data of the classifications, Israel and gentiles. What do the facts, properly interpreted, prove?

God loves Israel because Israel accepts his sovereignty in the Torah and rejects the gentiles because they practice idolatry.

That statement of the besought category-formation does not simply collect data on Israel and on the gentiles. It imparts structure and meaning to those data. And it accommodates further data within its theory of matters. It follows that a category-formation is not the same thing as a topic.

A "category-formation" should not be confused with a mere verbal classification, e.g., God or Torah or gentiles or Israel. Such a classification designates a theme but yields no cogent proposition concerning that theme, yielded by the data that fall within the thematic frame. The category-formation therefore treats the data as active, the verbal classification ("category") treats them as inert; the former asks the data to coalesce into generalizations encompassing the details and imparting context and order to data, the latter requires no more than topical congruence. The verbal classification, a.k.a., topic or category, thus suffices by collecting, without analysis, sayings about God or Torah or Israel, and without regard to what is said. A verbal classification serves for religious data. By contrast a category-formation transforms religious data into theological constructions. A simple statement of the outcome of a functioning category-formation is this: Religion becomes theology in the case of the Rabbinic reading of Scripture when from Scripture's story of exemplary persons the principles emerge that are embodied in said persons' actions.

How do we know that we have defined a valid native category-formation? The answer comes when we consider this question: Is the corpus of data that are assembled within a topic deemed to yield a category-formation consistent, coherent, and responsive to uniform reason throughout? The criteria by which to answer this question are three. Religious attitudes and ideas and opinions form a category-formation yielding a theological statement when they can be shown to be [1] consistent, [2] coherent, and [3] reasoned—not inconsistent, not incoherent, and above all, because bound by rules, not arbitrary. These broad claims add up to a single allegation: we can define the generative category-formations of Rabbinic Judaism. Its canon yields evidence of a theological system and structure embodied in the details of the Aggadah and the Halakhah. With reference to Rabbinic Judaism in its formative age and canon, we can speak of "theology," not just diverse opinion on religious subjects. How so?

V. How Can We Speak of Theology in the Context of Rabbinic Judaism?

A fair question immediately presents itself: to begin with, is it legitimate to address to Rabbinic Judaism the theological questions raised here? Many who devote their lives to the canonical documents of Rabbinic Judaism have maintained that "Judaism has no theology." Moreover, they have held that the Rabbinic sources cannot be systematized. The documents are commonly represented as random compilations of hopelessly confused facts, full of contradictions, insusceptible of regularization, utterly inaccessible to the ordering that theology requires, e.g., into native category-formations. How then can I speak of a pervasive theological grammar, of a system and a structure realized everywhere?

True, singleton sayings conflict with other singleton sayings. But, viewed whole, the formative canon of Rabbinic Judaism certainly exhibits the traits of rigorous thought about religious experience, and "the discourse of faith" (in Dalferth's term) goes forward in logical and rational ways. Differences of opinion yield consensus, and normative judgments on religious truth—Aggadic and Halakhic—are made. Whether in the Talmuds or in the Midrash-compilations, we everywhere confront the realization and upshot of "argument and the attempt to solve conceptual problems." That phrase defines the task of the documents at hand. That task is to order data so as to yield overriding generalizations. Thus there is no basis for doubting that the theological enterprise thrives in Rabbinic Judaism. That is so even though the media of theological expression go their own way and do not correspond to those of Christian or philosophical (Judaic or Christian) expression.

Despite the unconventional form imparted to its theology by its exegetical, not propositional, modes of Aggadic and Halakhic discourse, Rabbinic Judaism in both law and lore is rich in its dialectical arguments. Critical thinking about religious truth marks its quest for rigorous demonstration of propositions out of coherent data of Scripture and nature and history. Not only so, but that thinking is articulately organized in theological compositions and cast in native category-formations in the Midrash-compilations. Those who deny that theology forms an intellectual dimension of Rabbinic Judaism in its formative canon therefore bear the burden of explaining precisely what it is that they deny.

In line with the working definition—reasoned discourse about faith—we have now to ask, What is the religious experience that is subjected to the reasoned discourse of faith? In Rabbinic Judaism the Torah supplies the data, the facts of God's presence and activity among men. The sages adduce from those data generalizations, rules that may apply to other data. These they form into a coherent system of such generalizations about God and his self-manifestation in the Torah. The generalizations may be asked in detail to explain the present and illuminate the future. A large and encompassing structure ultimately accommodates all pertinent facts.

An account of theological foundations of a type of Rabbinic compilation, then, represents the systematic effort to identify, and account for the working of, the theological propositions—attitudes, convictions, affirmations and recommended emotions—set forth by the Midrash-compilations. As I have just now said, it is not only to identify them but to show how they cohere in cogent category-formations. These category-formations inductively emerge as the Rabbinic sages systematize, generalize, and criticize discrete religious data: the facts determined by verses of Scripture and their established facts about God with us. And that leads to the basic question: How do we know?

VI. How Do We Know What the Rabbis Thought?

In presenting the normative theology of Rabbinic Judaism in its formative documents, I claim to know what the rabbis thought when they are viewed as a collegium: the Aggadic and Halakhic views that represent their official doctrine. That is what is implicit in the description in these pages of the system and structure of thought that govern throughout all their distinctive writings. On what basis do I allege as representative the account that I set forth in the three parts of this book? Let me explain the criteria that permit me to identify as both representative and also normative a given set of views and to treat as schismatic other opinions, everywhere bypassed in silence.[3]

In describing norms of belief and behavior I speak of what is normative throughout. A single logic, in the encounter with a single canon, produces a uniform result, that which is portrayed here—so I allege. That claim to describe the prevailing system and structure, taking account of differences of opinion on unimportant details, renders irrelevant the issue of what proportion of sages held which opinion.

The political and sociological sense of "representative" also does not pertain. I furthermore do not allege that "the Jews" in general concurred with the Rabbinic norms of theology and law. We know very little about what Jews other than sages and disciples thought. What little we have hardly suggests correspondence between sages'

---

[3] Since I have studied and translated all of the documents of the Rabbinic canon set forth here, readers ought to be able to stipulate that a composition or composite that is not dealt with here, and that says something to contradict the opinions that are set forth, has not been ignored or neglected or simply missed but rejected as not representative. It is on that basis that I use the language, "the sages thought," and not simply this document recorded or that particular sage said. I claim that little, if anything, has been missed, in a corpus of writings all of which I have systematically translated.

and popular opinion. No one today imagines that the Rabbinic canon portrays the opinions of those who flourished outside of the circles that produced the documents of the Rabbinic canon, preserved, studied, and proposed to realize them in the common life. That is because, to exaggerate only slightly, every page of the Rabbinic writings of late antiquity attests to the tension and conflict between "our sages of blessed memory" and the rest of that holy Israel that, sages insisted, belongs within the Kingdom of Heaven and under the domain of God, made manifest in the Torah. So on what basis do I portray *the* sages and *their* beliefs and opinions?

By what is "representative" I mean not what stands for broadly held opinion, but rather the following: *What embodies the ubiquitous and governing modes of rational thought, on the one side, and what sets forth the necessary and sufficient and integral doctrines generated by that rationality, on the other.*

By that criterion of what is "representative," therefore, the former—the modes of thought—are alleged to define rationality, and the latter—the logically consequent propositions—are claimed to define the *logos*, the principle that pervades the whole. This takes both Aggadic and Halakhic form in the idea that creation reveals God's justice, defined in terms man[4] comprehends, and appears in many forms.

It is within that logic of structure and system that I invoke the claim of normativity. But within that definition, I go to the outer limit of matters. For by what is normative I mean the official position of the rabbis, viewed as a collegium and council in the model of the councils that declared Catholic and Orthodox Christianity.

How, then, are we to know what composition or composite[5] represents the whole and was deemed obligatory for all who practiced

---

[4] See *Rationality and Structure: The Bavli's Anomalous Juxtapositions* (South Florida Studies in the History of Judaism; Atlanta: Scholars Press, 1997).

[5] The distinction between composition and composite (of compositions) is fundamental to my literary analysis of the Rabbinic documents, see *Making the Classics in Judaism: The Three Stages of Literary Formation*. Atlanta, 1990: Scholars Press for Brown Judaic Studies; *The Rules of Composition of the Talmud of Babylonia. The Cogency of the Bavli's Composite*. Atlanta, 1991: Scholars Press for South Florida Studies in the History of Judaism; and *Sources and Traditions. Types of Composition in the Talmud of Babylonia*. Atlanta, 1992: Scholars Press for South Florida Studies in the History of Judaism.

the religion of "the whole Torah of Moses, our rabbi," that the world has long known as Judaism? I owe readers an account of the governing criteria here, by which they may form a judgment of whether I am right in my account of matters.

A. *Logical Coherence*

What represents the structure and system that sustain a variety of kindred writings emerges in positions that logically hold together among them all. These positions, whether concerning doctrine or correct modes of thought, will dictate not only what may be said but also what must not be said. And, more consequentially, they will form a tight fabric, of gossamer weight to be sure, spread over the whole, a thin, translucent tent that holds within everything that belongs and keeps out everything that does not. As with philosophy, so here too, consistency with the first-established givens, beginning with the principle of one, sole, omnipotent, just God, opens the way for inclusion; contradiction among parts, failure to form a seamless whole, excludes.

That inquiry into what represents the logic of the whole, what proves coherent to the principal doctrines of the whole, forms the subtext of my entire account, which claims only that the Rabbinic canon attests to its own integrity by the common criteria of reasoned thought. The fact that we can make sense of these writings attests to the validity for the writers of the document as much as for us, the readers here and now, of such criteria. By integrity, for example, we mean what they must have meant, because—all learning concurs, wherever that learning takes place—we can understand them. And the rest follows. So by "the logic of the whole" I therefore mean modes of thought that govern throughout, for instance, analysis through comparison and contrast, on the one side, paradigmatic thinking, on the other. Time and again I point to how conclusions are reached, not only to what they profess. By coherence I mean doctrines that fit in place and do not impose stresses or strains on the structure that encompasses them.

If, to take an obvious example, the one God who created all things is just, then that generative doctrine cannot accommodate cases of structural injustice. So the doctrine that the wicked (nonetheless) prosper cannot on its own find a place. Some solution to anomalies that confront the theologians has to accommodate reality to the system, and the system to reality. And it cannot be a solution that posits two gods, or no god, or a weak god, or an unjust god—that is an obvious instance of systemic coherence.

My account of the Rabbinic canon seen whole then underscores the pervasiveness of specific modes of thought and shows how conclusions reached here, there, and everywhere come about because people are thinking in one way, rather than in some other. I further include only those main beams of doctrine that form a tight fit with other main beams, beginning with the foundations, ending with the roof, in proper sequence of inclusion. Not only so, but—to complete the survey of what I think represents the whole—I allege that a given starting point, the place at which I begin, marks the ground zero of the structure and system—*the* theology of the Aggadah and the Halakhah viewed as a coherent corpus—and the order of topics, their definition and substantive formulation, must unfold in the sequence in which I present them. Any other order will yield chaos and produce an unintelligible gibberish of random thoughts.

Translating into the characterization of the whole these considerations of logic and consistency and the sole rational and therefore necessary sequence of thoughts presents no difficulty. I claim that what is representative is that corpus of convictions that fits, logically and doctrinally, and what does not is noted but excluded from the account of representative views. For to describe *theology* is to identify the *logos*, the logic, of religious ideas. This demands thinking philosophically about religion. The result of such thought sets forth in the correct and inexorable order, start to finish, the structure and system that order the whole, even making provision for the preservation of views that do not fit and modes of thought that jar.

As to the inviolable order of ideas, it suffices to say that the problems that are laid out systematically—world order, sources of disruption, means of restoration—become unintelligible in any other sequence than the one I follow. And within each unit, any other presentation of topics would not only disrupt but would corrupt the entire account.

As to modes of thought that pervade, a single example suffices. My discussions on eschatological components of the theology pick their way among diverse opinions; where opinion is contradictory, e.g., about the character of the world to come or the timing and sequence of the stages en route from here and now to there and then, I make no claim to know what stands for the structure and system, or, in more common language, that represents "the rabbis" as a whole. Where I can explain how conclusions are reached and show the harmony of the result in both correct order and integral, harmonious doctrine, I offer that as my account of the theology of eschatology. And so throughout.

B. *Anonymity and Schismatic, Attributed Opinion*

But sages themselves also signify what is normative, so in their behalf a simple response suffices. A fifteen-hundred-year-old tradition of learning, amplified in a few places just now, serves. Several indicators establish the normative view and mark the schismatic one.

First, it is a well-established principle in the legal (Halakhic) documents that a rule that is not attributed to a named authority ordinarily—all other things being equal—stands for all authority, and so sets the norm. A rule or conflicted opinion bearing a name may well be, and mostly is, schismatic (with the proviso that certain names carry within themselves signals as to normative status). That hermeneutics is stated explicitly in the earliest documents and is taken for granted in the composition of those that reached closure later on. It forms the premise of much analysis in the two Talmuds.

C. *Signals of Normativity*

A further trait of the documents, second, both of law (Halakhah) and of lore (Aggadah), as has been realized more recently but I think was always implicit from the very beginning, requires consideration. It is that the authors of a cogent composition, all the more so the framers of a composite, so set forth their accounts as to give a clear indication of the position they favor. They may announce the besought proposition at the outset and amass evidence to demonstrate it, or they may lead to it at the end, through assembling much evidence, most of it affirmative, some not. I have identified a number of composites that set down the coherent judgment of the compilers about a given topic or problem. These composites, as a matter of fact, either prove unique in the entire literature—the sole systematic presentation

of a topic—or turn out to be entirely coherent with other composites
on the same theme. I have relied heavily, therefore, on the givens of
composites. So much for compositions and composites.

D. *Premises of Discourse*

Third, along these same lines, there is the matter of self-evidence, that
is to say, indications within the documents of the Rabbinic canon of
principles that are taken for granted and that generate secondary
articulation along lines that said principles dictate. Sages have left no
doubt about the indicators of self-evidence. Let me briefly explain
what I mean. In the Rabbinic writings, particularly but not only in
the Talmud of Babylonia (Bavli), certain points of connection are
taken as self-evident, so that compilers of composites simply *know*
what native category "obviously" joins with what other one, and what
does not. Through what is taken for granted, the system makes its
statement of theological givens. For the Bavli, I have shown how odd
connections reveal premises as to what is self-evident.[6]

When, therefore, we can outline the principles of constructing
groups of categories into intelligible combinations, we find in those
principles the main lines of theological order and structure. When we
can state what emerges as self-evident when we join two other wise
distinct topics, we gain insight into the established laws of meaning
and order that govern a system of coherent thought. So in examining the rules for joining native categories, we identify those indicators
of correct usage that point toward the logic pervading the whole. At
many points in my exposition of what I conceive to be the normative
theology of the Rabbinic canon, I introduce evidence of self-evidence
in the form of connections that are drawn and conclusions that those
connections dictate.

E. *Juxtapositions*

Sages have supplied other signals as well. Fourth, even entire documents weigh in, for the compilers of a document, moreover, have

---

[6] See *Rationality and Structure: The Bavli's Anomalous Juxtapositions*. Atlanta, 1997:
Scholars Press for South Florida Studies in the History of Judaism.

been shown through extensive research to take positions on important questions. This they do by their selection and arrangement of materials, by their juxtapositions of topics beyond the dimensions of composites, and by other subtle editorial means. They leave little doubt as to the positions they deem authoritative. Anyone who has worked through and identified the hermeneutics of, for one example, *Genesis Rabbah*, or of the Mishnah for another, will understand that documents seen whole do convey coherent judgments. Most, though not all, of the documents of the Rabbinic canon set forth coherent statements, which through a systematic labor of comparison and contrast I have already identified. That makes possible the description of the theological system of the writings seen whole. That is because by definition, the statement on a given, fundamental topic that is made by a document within the Rabbinic canon, not contradicted by the statement made by any other document—and none is!—constitutes a reliable indicator of the theology of the Rabbinic canon viewed whole.

F. *The Four Principal Indicators*

On the basis of these facts characteristic of compositions, composites, and entire documents, by my presentation of the abstracts and my paraphrase of sources that I have chosen to reconstitute into this coherent tale, I mark as representative of the position of "the rabbis," or the entirety of the Rabbinic canon, all of the statements I make concerning a given issue. Where the documents contain opinion that contradicts my presentation of matters—and that is very seldom and nearly always schismatic in form—I omit it. For a bit of research will show, especially for the interested readers who wish to check, that what I present bears the mark of normative standing within the documents read all together and all at once. That is to say,

[1] ANONYMITY: it will be anonymous or, if assigned to a particular authority, at least entirely unchallenged,

[2] COHERENCE: it will prove coherent with other statements on the same subject,

[3] PREMISE IN MAKING CONNECTIONS: it will define the (self-evident) premise of making certain connections or it will emerge as a result of making said connection, and/or

[4] PRIVILEGED IN DRAWING CONCLUSIONS: it will be presented as the regnant opinion when conflicting opinions register, e.g., as the opening proposition, or as the climactic statement; or in some other significant way signals will be given to accord privilege to the statement cited or alluded to in these pages as representative of the structure and system of Rabbinic Judaism seen whole, in proportion, as a coherent statement.

When readers check the documents against my use of them, I am confident that they will find that exceptions to these simple rules will prove few and inconsequential.

That is why my picture of the theology of Rabbinic Judaism will be seen to represent the Rabbinic sages as a collegium. Through the media just now outlined, sages did set forth the orthodox and catholic position of the Torah as they framed matters, the Oral in relationship to the Written Torah. For the work of setting forth a coherent logic of the faith, a theological structure and system, they chose the instruments they had available: the instruments of intellect, proposition, evidence, argument, thought and the writing down of thought—consensus attained through persuasion. Like the Jewish people, so too the sages—*their* sages—had no better options. Thus just as the people Israel had no politics of consequence, so the sages could not work through political institutions. No emperor confirmed their views, no court enforced their judgments, no armies carried their doctrines to distant places. They met, if at all, only irregularly—except on the field of argument. And, as individuals, to have a say was to deny their own integrity, the logic of their definitive myth—that, after all, is the meaning of claiming to receive and hand on a tradition, as sages did when they spoke of the oral tradition of Sinai, the Oral part of the Torah.

Their counterparts in the equally complex world of Christianity did two things that sages did not, and could not do. They held world councils, sponsored by the Roman Empire, from Constantine's time forward, to work out positions to embody Orthodox and Catholic Christianity. And as individuals, they wrote books. No state, as I said, sponsored sages' ecumenical meetings, and sages held none. Nor did the logic of sages permit individuals to write books in their own names, as did every principal of Christianity beyond the founder himself.

But my claim in writing about Rabbinic theology is self-evident: had the sages of the Oral Torah met in world councils, as their counterparts in Christian theology did, these are the Aggadic and Halakhic positions they would have taken and set forth as normative—every one of them. If we have no counterpart, for Rabbinic Judaism, to the Nicene Creed, we could readily write one out of the table of contents of this book. That claim is what made possible my decision to focus my discussion on the governing logic and to investigate and unpack the principles of coherence and proportion that govern throughout. Each abstract from a source that I set forth, I claim, speaks for the collegium of the sages, represents the Rabbinic canon viewed whole, and coheres with all others.

VII. The Project Viewed Whole

Why treat the entire Rabbinic canon as systematic, in the manner of a systemic portrait, coherent in details and cogent in the aggregate? That is because an entire religious system—a generative theory of the world view and the way of life, as well as the theory of the social entity comprised by the faithful—comes to concrete expression in detail that repeats the message of the whole. Whether here and there, whether in this detail or that, always whole and complete, the detail recapitulates the main point of the whole. For the system repeats itself interminably and unashamedly. A few topics predominate, and a small number of propositions govern what is to be said about those topics. Then it must follow that it is not the system that recapitulates the documents, but the documents that recapitulate the system. The writings constantly refer back to, take for granted, acknowledge the presence of, the coherent, generative system, comprised by a set of interlocking paradigms. The theology I propose to describe comprises that modest corpus of coherent and encompassing truths that the system spins out in unlimited variation.

That is, a symbolic structure and a precipitating myth, a system of ideas that transcends the texts and forms the matrix of the texts demands articulation. Then what do we do when we ask the theological question of the writings? It is to undertake a search, beneath the surface of their particular messages, to uncover that statement that, all together and all at once, wherever and whenever the documents speak, the generative system sets forth in its own behalf. To ask a corpus of religious writings to reveal what holds those writings together and makes them cogent, then, we raise the question of theology. By theology, then, I mean, the interior logic of reasoned discourse about the knowledge of God. In the case of Rabbinic Judaism, knowledge of God comes to Holy Israel through God's self-manifestation in the Torah revealed by God to our rabbi, Moses, at Sinai, in two media, Oral and Written. Concretely, how are we to move from perception to proposition, from the encounter with God in the Torah to critical reflection upon the experience? We begin with language as a metaphor for religious experience, linguistics as a metaphor for theology.

PART ONE

THE GRAMMAR OF RABBINIC THEOLOGY: VOCABULARY, SYNTAX, SEMANTICS

CHAPTER ONE

PROLEGOMENON TO THE THEOLOGICAL LANGUAGE OF RABBINIC JUDAISM

I. Language as a Metaphor for Theology

Theology identifies the main frame, the cognitive structure, of a religion's authoritative doctrines: what holds them all together and defines the message of each one. But how to identify the comprehensive theological traits and principal components? Here I turn to linguistics to supply a metaphor guiding the description and analysis of the theological structure and system of Rabbinic Judaism. I ask how the theological language was correctly, that is, intelligibly, spoken, giving an account of [1] important words (head-nouns) treated as a metaphor for native categories (Chapter Two); [2] rules of turning words into combinations (syntax) (Chapter Three), treated as comparable to the modes of forming correct constructions of data and making connections between them; [3] laws permitting the formulation of a virtually unlimited repertoire of propositions immediately intelligible to speakers of the language (semantics) (Chapter Four), counterpart to the cognitive models that govern coherent expression of thought in the Rabbinic canon.

Since I compare describing a theological system to describing a language, the three questions that I deem fundamental to the theological description of the Rabbinic writings of late antiquity cover its [1] vocabulary, [2] syntax, and [3] semantics. The metaphor of a grammar serves, for by grammar is meant "an example of a discrete combinatorial system. A finite number of discrete elements (in this case, words) are sampled, combined, and permuted to create larger structures (in this case, sentences) with properties that are quite distinct from those of their elements."[1] At issue then are the rules of combination and permutation into larger structures—an ideal way of

---

[1] Steven Pinker, *The Language Instinct* (New York: HarperPerennial, 1995), 84.

surveying the work at hand. In this three-part grammar I systematically lay out

[1] theological categories that are native to those writings;
[2] cogent statements that can be made with them; and
[3] coherent propositions that those statements set forth and (within their own terms and framework) logically demonstrate as both true and self-evident.

Like a language, a theology then begins with [1] a vocabulary that permits the classification of religious knowledge (discrete data) and experience, the organization and categorization of that knowledge and experience into intelligible and cogent sense-units. Many things of one type will be covered by a single word, of another by a different word. So much for what is offered in a grammar that sets forth available vocabulary: the words that this language uses for these things.

The units [2] then combine and recombine in sentences. These rules of theological discourse concerning religious experience we may deem the counterpart of syntax: which words combine—or do not combine—with which other words, in what inflection or signaled relationship, and why. That accounts for the second aspect of a grammar, namely, its provision of the rules governing the joining of words.

The semantics [3] then dictates how to generate meaning.[2] Semantics is what dictates intelligibility.

The grammar of vocabulary, syntax, and semantics then describes how the language works, tells us that for which it can be made to work. Finite means available for infinite use,[3] the lexical concepts and grammatical rules, finite in themselves, then can address in proper semantics an infinite number of situations, making sense of, impose meaning upon, pretty much whatever comes up. And that is the point

---

[2] I find a comparable tripartite approach to the systematic analysis and reconstruction of complex data in Edward O. Wilson, *In Search of Nature* (Washington, D.C.: Island Press, 1996), 113: "Concepts, the most elementary clusters, are signaled by words or phrases. . . . Propositions are signaled by phrases (such as 'dogs' and 'hunt'), clauses or sentences expressing objects and relationships ('dogs hunt'). Finally, schemata are signaled by sentences and larger units of text (the 'technique of hunting with dogs')." The context for the paradigm is quite different from ours, but the divisions strike me as identical. I could as well have called the components "concepts, propositions, schemata" instead of vocabulary, syntax, and semantics, but I find the analogy of a grammar more provocative.
[3] Oliver Sacks, *Seeing Voices* (New York: HarperCollins, 1989), 80.

at which constructive theology commences, and systematic theology will find its language.

Viewed synchronically,[4] how do the assertions of the documentary components of the Rabbinic canon cohere? Theology responds to that question. By theology I refer specifically to the governing rationality, the rules of coherent discourse, of the foundation documents of Rabbinic Judaism. Hence I explore the promise of treating theology as the counterpart for religion to grammar for a language. For grammar in the description of a language defines the generative categories that dictate the description, analysis, and interpretation of the data of the language. So too in solving the problem of describing theology: the question before us is, How are we going to identify that governing and generative theology that systematically transforms into intellectually accessible terms and categories, subject to generalization and criticism, the attitudes and feelings and intangible but very real perceptions of the enduring religious encounter of holy Israel with God that are set forth in words by the Torah, written and oral?

On what basis do I undertake to address to the Rabbinic canon questions of cogency and coherence? The foundation of the claim that coherent thought, theology, sustains and imparts cogency to the Rabbinic canon and its writings comes to expression in a simple principle. I invoke a single fact of intellection: the documents examined here conduct a constant dialogue among themselves: the Talmuds with the Mishnah, the Midrash-compilations with Scripture, and sayings attributed to a given sage with other sayings assigned to the same sage. The documents' cogency and coherence are also held together by such external indicators as the appeal to common-named authorities and the treasured conviction that together the documents form one half of the Torah revealed by God to Moses. Within such a community of documents the determinite religious system of document is mirrowed in any other document of the same authoritative corpus.

To undertake theological description I appeal for a metaphor to the study of a language, within the linguistic theory that maintains

---

[4] The now-completed diachronic work is systematically set forth in my *The Transformation of Judaism: From Philosophy to Religion* (Champaign, Ill.: University of Illinois Press, 1992); *Rabbinic Judaism: The Documentary History of the Formative Age* (Bethesda, Md.: CDL Press 1994), and *Rabbinic Judaism: Structure and System* (Minneapolis: Fortress, 1996).

that language imparts structure to inchoate experience. It supplies categories and organizing principles to articulate the order and system of preverbal and even nonverbal encounter. So I describe the "logic" of God—theology—as we would the grammar of (a) language: its vocabulary, syntax, and semantics. In like manner I formulate a description of the theology of the Rabbinic canon, treating a language's vocabulary ("head-nouns") as counterpart to a theology's native categories; a language's syntax as comparable to a system's rules for forming constructions and making connections; and a language's semantics as comparable to a theological system's models of analysis of data, explanation of (the system's own) facts, and anticipation (among diverse types of rational statements).[5]

To state matters simply: *theology is to religion as language is to experience and perception.*[6] Just as language turns inchoate experience into propo-

---

[5] Clearly, I could have chosen models of any number of other fundamental intellectual constructions besides those governing the solution of problems of analysis, explanation, and anticipation, but these struck me as critical. Chapter Four also shows that the raw data are strikingly abundant. How these models form the counterpart to semantics is explained presently.

[6] I hasten to differentiate what is at issue here from the comparable conception of religion as an a priori of experience; that is not what I claim, my introduction of the metaphor serving for formal purposes only. See George A. Lindbeck, *The Nature of Doctrine. Religion and Theology in a Postliberal Age* (Philadelphia: Westminster Press, 1984), 30–45. Lindbeck defines religion in a way comparable to this definition of theology when he states, "A religion can be viewed as a kind of cultural and/or linguistic framework of medium that shapes the entirety of life and thought. It functions somewhat like a Kantian a priori . . . it is similar to an idiom that makes possible the description of realities, the formulation of beliefs, and the experiencing of inner attitudes, feelings, and sentiments. Like a culture or language, it is a communal phenomenon that shapes the subjectivities of individuals rather than being primarily a manifestation of those subjectivities. It comprises a vocabulary of discursive and non-discursive symbols together with a distinctive logic or grammar in terms of which this vocabulary can be meaningfully deployed" (p. 33). Clearly, in invoking the metaphor of language when proposing to identify the principal components of the theology of the Rabbinic canon, I come into the orbit of Lindbeck's thought. But there are fundamental differences, which render the present exercise quite remote in character, not only in focus, from Lindbeck's. Where Lindbeck speaks of religion, I speak of theology. Not only so, but I address documents that use a single, coherent language throughout, and so the theology by its very character functions within the framework of language. He views religions "as products of those deep experiences of the divine (or the self, or the world) which most of us are accustomed to thinking of as peculiarly religious." This leads him into analysis of the nature of religion in general. But my focus is not on religion in general, but solely on the Torah—God's self-manifestation—in particular, and when I refer to language, it is for a governing analogy. I seek an appropriate medium for describing the unitary character of the documents

sitions subject to general intelligibility in public discourse, so theology transforms into appropriate language—into intellectually accessible forms, terms and categories, subject to generalization and systematization—the attitudes and feelings and intangible but very real perceptions of the Torah and the self-manifestation of God conducted therein. Systematic, descriptive theology in the present context therefore finds its governing elements by comparing the relationship of theology to the religious encounter of the Torah—the meeting with God in the words of the Torah—with the relationship of grammar to the reality of the living language. By some definitions of language,[7] then, theology serves as the language of religion, what makes concrete, specific, and rationally accessible the experience of religious encounter. The upshot is simple: theology ascribes meaning to otherwise random experiences and events and images that life within the Torah provokes in the way in which semantics allows otherwise random sounds to become meaningful.

In the case of Rabbinic Judaism, that premise—religious experience is to theology as grammar is to language—proves remarkably congruent with the character of the record to begin with. A common language, governed by a single grammar—vocabulary, syntax, and semantics, to use the metaphor I have chosen—governs throughout the documents. That absolutely incontrovertible fact on its own validates the work of theological description[8] carried out by invoking the

---

that all together comprise the Torah. The use of the analogy drawn from language becomes obvious when the character of the Torah—the record of encounter with God set down in words of a propositional character—is taken into account. If in the Torah religious experience and knowledge are conveyed in words, sentences, and paragraphs, then language is the particular medium for religious encounter, and the rest follows. That is why I see no important points of intersection, then, between the mode of theological analysis followed here and the reflections on the nature of religion that Lindbeck sets forth in his very different context.

[7] The metaphor is amplified presently. As already indicated, I do not take a position on the controverted questions of linguistics, only use, as a metaphor, a particular position within that field, the position associated with the name of Noam Chomsky. For a prior venture into linguistics as a source of useful metaphors in the analysis of the documents of the Rabbinic canon, see my *A History of the Mishnaic Law of Purities*, vol. 21, *The Redaction and Formulation of the Order of Purities in the Mishnah and Tosefta* (Leiden: Brill, 1977).

[8] Systematic, not only notional, description, as well as analysis and interpretation, the second step in the presentation of *a functioning system* of thought, will follow in Part Two, below.

metaphor just now set forth, so examining the Torah's theology within the categorical structure of language: vocabulary, syntax, semantics. Exactly how do I propose to describe a theology in the model of
a language?

We turn first to the matter of vocabulary, for language, or native
categories, for theology. Every religion uses keywords, head-nouns, to
mark the beginning of declarative sentences, just as does a language.
These words constitute the religion's native categories, comparable to
the head-nouns or vocabulary of a language.

Second, a religious system will select a certain cluster of words to
serve in a manner particular to its needs, as a language uses a small
fraction of the phonemes available. These clusters correspond to the
syntax that approves the joining of words in one way and not in
another, or the joining of these particular words but not those other
words. To take an obvious example, "the wicked Mordecai and good
Haman" form an unintelligible construction, equivalent to a phoneme
lacking all sense, in the Rabbinic canon. That is to say, on the one
side religion in general may find available an unlimited range of
myths and symbols, attitudes and emotions, experiences and possible
formulations of concrete encounters with God. But, on the other side,
religions do make their choices. And that is just as languages make
their choices among the possible phonemes. A religion thus establishes its own rules of discourse—syntax or logic, forming constructions and making connections. Violating those rules excludes a
statement from the system, marking the statement of what cannot be
connected or joined in a common construction as unintelligible.

And, third, every theological system sets forth rules of semantics—
methods for delimiting meanings, preferring some, rejecting others.[9]
Available native categories or head-nouns, formed into theoretically-
intelligible clusters or syntactically-viable constructions, may or may
not bear meaning, make sense. To take a famous example, "Colorless
green sleeps furiously" uses valid words (not gibberish-words) and follows the correct structure (rules of grammar). But it is unintelligible.
Semantics dictates what head-nouns and combinations thereof set
forth intelligible statements, and which ones are not possible. The

---

[9] I owe this formulation to Professor David Aaron, Hebrew Union College (personal letter, February 11, 1997).

counterpart for the theology of a religion will present itself in the models of plausible, as against unintelligible, discourse.[10] What we see concerns the principles that underlie how chosen clusters of words are structured into statements, how clusters once entered into a certain structure yield meaning.

II. WHY APPEAL TO GRAMMAR IN QUEST FOR SYSTEMIC LOGIC?

Why use the form of a grammar (including instructions on rules of grammar and lessons on semantics) to begin raising constructive and synchronic questions of governing logic, cogency, and coherence? Since I invoke the metaphor of a language to describe a theology, I quite naturally pursue the implications of the metaphor by choosing a form for assembling data that serves well in describing a language. There is no simpler or more rigorous medium for describing a language than a grammar, with a syntax and lessons of semantics included. A grammar exposes the discipline of system and order, focusing upon the individual units that can serve a given language in any way that the rules of that language permit. A grammar constitutes a sustained work of factual description, systematically carried out. It turns facts into cases, and cases into the exemplifications of rules. The grammar form imposes its own discipline: comprehensive coverage, systematic review of all pertinent evidence, and clear, cogent presentation of succinct statements of the facts.

Grammars by their nature accord a cool welcome to sustained presentations of large-scale reconstructions, hypotheses as to what "really" matters and what counts above all. Those issues, presently resting upon subjective judgment, not objective data, will come in due course and, when they do, they too are going to demand their own form. Grammars require hard facts, properly instantiated—that alone. Matters of taste and judgment here find no legitimate place. What grammars promise, and what I deliver, is a reliable, factual, accurate answer to questions of fact, accessible in free standing entries, arranged in the simplest possible way, alphabetically and thoroughly

[10] The specific types of models I have chosen—models of analysis, models of explanation, and models of anticipation—are explained.

cross-referenced. These entries are comprised by the data themselves, pertinent statements portrayed in their own words. They exemplify rules and by their regularities, from one entry to the next, also show that rules do govern. At many entries I specify how I think a rule is instantiated; at others, I do not make the obvious explicit. I can think of no more efficient way of setting forth facts, within categories that have been properly defined, structures that have been identified in accord with a single criterion, repeatedly invoked, and cogent, working systems, able to deal with the movement and change of data, analyzed within one and the same descriptive model throughout.

What accounts for the order of the chapters—vocabulary, syntax, semantics? In terms of the logic of my metaphor, which treats theology as the effort to translate into coherent discourse the divine encounter preserved in religious writings, we move from [1] head-nouns among the principal parts of sentences to [2] noun-clusters among the components of paragraphs to [3] semantically-intelligible statements or theological compositions, whole statements of the type defined in Chapter Four. In the simplest terms, Chapter Two presents accounts of how the Rabbinic canon forms its statements, beginning with nouns that can serve as the subjects of a sentence; Chapter Three identifies the clusters of nouns that comprise sentences of the Rabbinic canon, how the several native categories cohere into cogent statements, form syllogisms, and similarly impart (and impose) structure on otherwise inchoate facts; and Chapter Four spells out the way in which its entire chapters of cogent thought take shape—exercises in explanation, demonstrations of meaning.

III. A Religion of Intellect, Creating a Language of Faith

Clearly, I have chosen a rather odd medium for the analysis of the systematic substrate upon which the documents of the Rabbinic canon are founded. Why undertake theological description within the framework of a grammar, treating the principal components of a theological system and structure as comparable to the principal parts of a language? It is because, in Rabbinic Judaism, religious encounter to begin with takes place in, and is handed on for generations to come through, the medium of words properly used. It is a religion of intellect, encompassing emotions within the conventions of rationality, a religion that knows God through the close analysis of what God says in so many words and in the breaths, the silences separating them. "An ignorant person cannot be pious," sages maintain. Torah-learning forms the antidote to ignorance. But more: proper learning forms an act of religious worship. God meets holy Israel in the school house more than in the synagogue, in study of the Torah more than in prayer—much more. That is the position of innumerable sayings of the sages themselves, and that points to the center of the religious experience they mean to make accessible and available. A religion that selects intellectual media for its principal encounter with God— in this case, its record of God's meeting with Israel to be played, and, through the study of the language of the record, to be heard, again and again through eternity—that religion of language surely invites the metaphor that reigns in this study.

To understand that answer—God is made manifest in the Torah,[11] therefore Israel meets God in the Torah, that is, through study of the Torah—we have to recall a striking fact. For its account of what it knows about God, this particular religion appeals to the documentary record of God's presence in humanity. Specifically, the Torah, Oral and Written, sets forth what holy Israel knows about God in the record of God's own self-manifestation. Pointing to God's presence in nature and in history, the Torah identifies the occasions of encounter and intervention. The Torah preserves and hands on the record of God's presence in this world. There, in those words, sentences, paragraphs—the media by which theology forms its vocabulary based on its thought preferences—Israel finds the record of encounter with God. And God is to be met whenever the words that preserve the encounter are contemplated, thus:

Tractate *Abot* 3:2C–D

R. Hananiah b. Teradion says, "Two who are sitting, and words of Torah do pass between them—the Presence [of God] is with them, as it is said, 'Then they that feared the Lord spoke with one another, and

---

[11] And, ultimately, only in the Torah. That is to say, all occasions of self-mani-festation beyond the limits of the Torah—in nature and in history, for example—take on consequence when placed into the context of what the Torah teaches. It is the Torah that designates events of a particular order as manifestations of God's will and plan, that calls attention to nature in a particular context as the echo of God's voice.

the Lord hearkened and heard, and a book of remembrance was written before him, for them that feared the Lord and gave thought to His name' (Mal. 3:16). I know that this applies to two. How do I know that even if a single person sits and works on Torah, the Holy One, blessed be he, sets aside a reward for him? As it is said, 'Let him sit alone and keep silent, because he has laid it upon him' (Lam. 3:28)."

Tractate *Abot* 3:6

Rabbi Halafta of Kefar Hananiah says, "Among ten who sit and work hard on Torah-study the Presence comes to rest, as it is said, 'God stands in the congregation of God' (Ps. 82:1) [and 'congregation' involves ten persons]. And how do we know that the same is so even of five? For it is said, 'And he has founded his vault upon the earth' (Amos 9:6). And how do we know that this is so even of three? Since it is said, 'And he judges among the judges' [a court being made up of three judges] (Ps. 82:1). And how do we know that this is so even of two? Because it is said, 'Then they that feared the Lord spoke with one another, and the Lord hearkened and heard' (Mal. 3:16). And how do we know that this is so even of one? Since it is said, 'In every place where I record my name I will come to you and I will bless you' (Ex. 20:24) [and it is in the Torah that God has recorded His name]."

Not only so, but it is through Torah-study that prophecy is nurtured:

Leviticus Rabbah XI:VII.3

"And it came to pass in the days of Ahaz" (Is. 7:1).

What was the misfortune that took place at that time?

"The Syrians on the east and the Philistines on the west [devour Israel with open mouth]" (Is. 9:12).

The matter [the position of Israel] may be compared to a king who handed over his son to a tutor, who hated [the son]. The tutor thought, "If I kill him now, I shall turn out to be liable to the death penalty before the king. So what I'll do is take away his wet nurse, and he will die on his own."

So thought Ahaz, "If there are no kids, there will be no he-goats. If there are no he-goats, there will be no flock. If there is no flock, there will be no shepherd. If there is no shepherd, there will be no world."

So did Ahaz plan, "If there are no children, there will be no disciples; if there are no disciples, there will be no sages; if there are no sages, there will be no Torah; if there is no Torah, there will be no synagogues and schools; if there are no synagogues and schools, then the Holy One, blessed be he, will not allow his Presence to come to rest in the world."

What did he do? He went and locked the synagogues and schools.

That is in line with the following verse of Scripture: "Bind up the testimony, seal the Torah [teaching] among my disciples" (Is. 8:16).

Stated in both propositional and narrative ways, the conviction is the same: in the words of the Torah, God speaks; hearing those words, Israel meets God—and finds guidance in where to look for God in nature and in history as well. Language, properly construed, therefore forms the principal medium of the revealed knowledge of God. Revealed speech also effects the direct encounter with God so far as that meeting can take place within the created world. Every meeting with God in time begins in the words of the Torah.[12] No wonder, then, that in the study and exegesis of the Torah over time Israel has met the Eternal.

Now to take up the thread of argument: the metaphor of comparing theology to a language thus proves especially appropriate in the study of Rabbinic Judaism, because the representation of its religious life and experience comes to us in the sole medium of a distinctive corpus of holy texts, and those texts exhibit remarkably uniform traits of linguistic formalization and expression.[13] So to begin with we take up a religion that uses disciplined language to set down in permanent form whatever it wishes to say about knowing God. These fundamental convictions of Rabbinic Judaism explain why any account of the theology of that Judaism is going to focus upon the modes of recording in words Israel's moments of meeting God, and God's actions of self-revelation. Here we deal with the particular component of that record of the divine-human encounter, the Rabbinic canon— the other half of the record, the half unique to Israel. That integral and necessary component of the one whole Torah revealed by God

---

[12] I find in *Sifra* in particular the explicit and systematic embodiment of that theological conviction that the words of the Torah convey not only what God wishes to say but how God chooses to formulate thought, hence God's mind and not only God's message. See my *Uniting the Dual Torah: Sifra and the Problem of the Mishnah* (Cambridge: Cambridge University Press, 1989).

[13] I have systematically conducted a form-analysis of each of the documents, which comes to expression in my translations and the reference system I have devised therein. My form-history is now complete in *The Documentary Form-History of Rabbinic Literature* (Atlanta: Scholars Press, 1998) for South Florida Studies in the History of Judaism, in seven volumes, fourteen parts in all, covering the Mishnah, two Talmuds, and the Midrash-compilations as well. The form-history is not random but built upon the freestanding testimony of the several documents, viewed discretely. I have found that forms cannot be examined in the abstract but only in documentary context. For a current review of this work see Edward Goldman, "Neusner Translating Talmud," in *Critical Review, 1997* (Atlanta: Scholars Press, 1998).

to Moses our rabbi at Sinai is set forth in vast documents. Their number, more than a score or more in all, scarcely conveys the enormous volume of words that all together comprise that part of the Torah. The Oral part of the Torah, like the Written part, records that encounter in its own distinctive language, which pervades the entire record. The theology of that part of the Torah becomes accessible when we know how to understand that language for what it is: the this-worldly record of the meeting of the Eternal in time with Israel.

IV. Vocabulary, Syntax, Semantics

No wonder, then, that in these pages I appeal to the construction of a language to serve as a metaphor for the construction of a theology. Transforming what is private and, by its nature, individual into what is public and by its purpose, shared, theology does for religion what language does for experience and perception. So theology constitutes the language of religious faith, knowledge, and experience. Theology sets forth the record of the encounter with God, doing so like language, in language, "with its lexicon and syntax, its capacity to generate an infinite number of propositions."[14] The lexicon encompasses the concepts as these stand on their own. What transform words into useful language are rules "by which coherent utterances—sentences, propositions—can be generated."[15] A theology properly set forth may then generate fresh propositions; people who can speak a language can say the hitherto unsaid, even the unthought, and rightly expect to find immediate comprehension—just like language. To extend the metaphor, theology forms the natural sounds of religion into intelligible speech.

Then to treat theology as the language of religion, we have to learn how to describe the vocabulary, syntax, and semantics that afford access to that language as it is spoken, that rationally embody the religion as it is lived. The task of describing the theology of a religion— in the present case, of a privileged collection of religious writings, deemed continuous with one another and held to form a cogent state-

---

[14] Sacks, *Seeing Voices*, 78.
[15] Sacks, *Seeing Voices*, 80.

ment—is to discover within the documents of the Rabbinic canon the counterpart to the generative grammar of a language, that is, to discern what dictates the flow of thought and imposes form upon it. That generative grammar of theology renders public, and subject to shared discourse, the religious faith and encounter of those that value and privilege the selected writings. Through that grammar we move from the surface use of the language in the documents of the Rabbinic canon to the deeper structures of the language, its formal structures and the formal operations, its rules of thought emerging from the laws of permitted expression.[16] To state matters simply, if we meet God in the Torah, what, in consequence, do we tell one another that we have learned, and how do we say it? In the case of the Judaism set forth here, what rules of intelligible discourse govern the speech that comes in consequence of the meeting?

Treating language as the governing metaphor for theology allows a link between the infinite possibilities of religious experience and encounter, on the one side, and the finite rules that govern intelligible discourse about that experience and encounter, on the other. More concretely, it is in language that religious encounter enters the cognitive part of the human mind, and, in line with Noam Chomsky's reprise of Schlegel, here too, "language, as an expression of the human mind rather than a product of nature, is boundless in scope and is constructed on the basis of a recursive principle that permits each creation to serve as the basis for a new creative act."[17] The experiment in progress here thus seeks to learn from the study of theological language something about the inherent properties of the religious system that comes to concrete expression in the diverse documents of the Rabbinic canon and that imparts coherence to them all.[18] To describe the theological system expressed within the

---

[16] I paraphrase Noam Chomsky, *Language and Mind* (New York: Harcourt Brace Jovanovich, 1962), 111: "We abstract away from conditions of use of language and consider formal structures and the formal operations that relate them . . . This process of abstraction . . . expresses a point of view . . . the working hypothesis that we can proceed with the study of 'knowledge of language' . . . in abstraction from the problems of how language is used."

[17] Chomsky, *Language and Mind*, 102.

[18] I paraphrase Chomsky, 103, "I am primarily intrigued by the possibility of learning something, from the study of language, that will bring to light inherent properties of the human mind."

writings that all together comprise the Rabbinic canon in its classical
statement, therefore, I investigate principal traits of that language. If
therefore this project comes to fruition, we ourselves shall know how
to speak the language of the Rabbinic canon, having mastered its
vocabulary, syntax, and semantics; and in accord with those rules of
the language, we shall be able to speak of whatever we wish that the
language can make intelligible to begin with.

Now to the details of the metaphor of language: how, exactly, does
that comparison dictate the character of this project? In the model of
language, this grammar is in three parts: vocabulary, syntax, semantics. What, exactly, do I mean by the tripartite description undertaken here in grammar form?

GRAMMAR: First comes grammar itself, the metaphor of the whole.
Defining matters for the purpose of the present analogy, Chomsky
uses this language: "The theory of grammar is concerned with the
question, What is the nature of a person's knowledge of his language,
the knowledge that enables him to make use of language in the normal, creative fashion? A person who knows a language has mastered
a system of rules that assigns sound and meaning in a definite way
for an infinite class of possible sentences." Chomsky elsewhere says,
"The grammar proposed by the linguist is an explanatory theory; it
suggests an explanation for the fact that . . . a speaker of the language
in question will perceive, interpret, form, or use an utterance in certain ways and not in other ways."[19]

VOCABULARY: By vocabulary or native categories I mean, those
keywords that form the subjects of consequential sentences, sentences
by which the system overall makes its statement. As I explain in the
Introduction to this part of the Grammar, "vocabulary" is comprised
by native categories, and how these are defined presents a range of
considerations. My lexicon covers scarcely three dozen native categories. There are others; these suffice.

SYNTAX: By syntax or indicators of construction and connection I
mean a set of rules regarding permissible combinations. A dictionary
definition gives, "the means of indicating the relations of words in a
sentence, the rules of employing these in accordance with established

---

[19] Chomsky, 27.

usage."[20] Syntax then should reveal the rules that constitute knowledge of a language, the principles that govern these systems.[21]

How does this pertain to our project? When we speak of the "syntax" of a theological language, as we do in Chapter Three, we mean, what are the rules that permit certain combinations to be made, by which a finite set of words may be formed and re-formed into a nearly unlimited set of sense-statements. The matters of connection and relation form critical considerations in theological discourse; they dictate how we make connections and draw conclusions, the very heart of the matter of God with us.

SEMANTICS: Here "semantics" serves as a metaphor for those rubrics that set forth fully comprehensible theological propositions, that exemplify the things that may be said—and the ways in which they are to be said. I introduce in this context the word "model," meaning the generative pattern to which people refer in undertaking certain types of intelligible, persuasive discourse: how would I say this, set forth a proposition of this kind, rather than of that kind? In the context of theological language, the rules that correspond to a language's semantics govern the combination and recombination of clauses and sentences into intelligible patterns of large-scale discourse ("paragraphs"). Intelligible patterns both organize and explain the facts we know, and also precipitate anticipation of the future that impends.

For a theological system, therefore, when we understand how sentences may be made into paragraphs, we know something about forming the models of propositional thought—the models of imparting intelligibility to experience, those of explanation of how things are and anticipation of what is then to happen. We move from the data of the theological language, then, to the rules of vocabulary, syntax, and semantics that permit discourse to range freely over the broad expanses of everyday religious experience and reflection: making sense of God with us, the system would say. In all we seek to understand the logic of combinancy, of the combinational structures.

---

[20] *Compact Edition of the Oxford English Dictionary* (Oxford: Oxford University Press, 1971), s.v. "grammar."
[21] Chomsky, 28.

Accordingly, theology in the present framing of the problem of description investigates the interior intellectual traits and prevailing logic of coherent discourse that animate a cogent body of religious writings.

V. Speaking the Theological Language of Judaism

Why do I insist that these documents set forth a language that may be described, learned, and mastered? The language at hand is fluent and repetitive, saying in some few ways the same thing about many things. Its rules of word choice, construction of intelligible statements, and composition of compelling and persuasive propositions ("paragraphs"), while never explicitly spelled out, prove blatant. And that is why for long centuries, to the present day, a great many sages of the Torah, written and oral, through these same documents inductively mastered that language and learned to speak it, saying in a fresh setting about new topics what that language permits to be said at any time about anything.

My appropriation of Chomsky's reading of natural language as the source of my governing metaphor therein finds its justification in the very character of the documents, because he helps me make sense of the single definitive fact of Rabbinic-Judaic theological discourse.

It is that the vocabulary, grammar, and semantics of the Rabbinic canon have made possible a vast range of discourse, on many subjects over long spans of recorded time and in diverse cultural settings, and continue in our own time to permit intelligible and coherent exchange on a nearly unlimited repertoire of subjects.

This is a living language of religious expression, a language spoken this very morning in rabbinical circles throughout the world. The sages used and their continuators now—today—use the available words of this language to form intelligible sentences in accord with its grammar and to set forth correct and compelling propositions. The documents we consider still define the program of learning; knowing what they say and how to speak in their language marks a learned person, and not knowing them stigmatizes someone as ignorant. Enter any authentic yeshiva in the world today, listen to the conversations of rabbis and their disciples, and you will hear that language, correctly spoken by literate, cultured masters of the speech. The principal Judaisms of the day, inclusive of Conservative and Reform

Judaism, continue the language as well. Rabbis learned in the Torah as a matter of fact will find it possible to say anything they wish, to invent and create whatever thought they choose, within the rules of language dictated by the theology of the Rabbinic canon. Understanding that fact in the living religion, Judaism, comprehending the media of thought that impart coherence and intelligibility to the writings of that religion—these define what is at stake in theological description.

So vocabulary, syntax, and semantics of expression matching reflected-upon experience, rational thought, and deep reflection—these work together to provide a language that can be learned, one that is appropriate to the experience of encounter with God through the Torah. It is a language that is to be set down and conveyed in a public and commonly-comprehended manner. In line with its models of persuasive composition, its rules of evidence and argument, language embedded in the documents accommodates not only recapitulation of the known but immediately intelligible expression of the unknown. In the world of that Judaism that is defined by the Torah, oral and written, in our own day, the language that I propose to describe is fluently spoken, producing a broad and creative range of public discourse. Many have learned it and many today speak it; the task at hand is only to identify the rationality that inductively is learned but ought articulately to be defined. When, therefore, we examine the documents, we too ought to be able to identify that theology as language: its systemic vocabulary, its rules of rational sentence construction, its models of rationality.

CHAPTER TWO

VOCABULARY: NATIVE CATEGORIES

I. Defining Vocabulary/Category

I regard as the vocabulary of the theological system the active categories of discourse of the Rabbinic canon. A "category" or "category-formation" imposes order on the chaos of inchoate data; it marks the first step toward rational description of matters. By category I mean a classification that holds together and treats as cogent a variety of data, e.g., facts of a given order, events of a common class, persons who fit the same model, and the like. These categories function for theology as the nouns or substantives function for a language, in that they identify and name that about which the theology will conduct discourse, as nouns identify and name that about which language will speak.

A language is made up of these components: the smallest parts, its governing logic, and its structures that allow for the discernment of meaning (semantics). The "smallest parts" or vocabulary correspond to the categorical structures of a theological system, and by asking the documents to dictate their own categorical structure, I follow the model of grammarians, who find the "smallest parts" within the language, not—self-evidently—beyond its own testimonies. The working tools of a language find their counterpart in the native categories of a theological system. Within some theories of language, words impose order on preverbal perceptions, both calling attention to and identifying data otherwise not accessible to notice (as in "the limits of my language are the limits of my world"). Along these same lines the categories of a theological system serve as the principal organizers of inchoate data, dictating how we classify data and impute meaning to them. These categories may emerge from the documents or they may take shape out of the program of questions brought to those documents; the documents may dictate their own categorical structure, or we may bring to them categories of interest to us, which we find remarkable in the document themselves.

In the model of linguistics, I classify these "smallest parts," or words, by how they behave, and that is in line with the formulation of Steven Pinker:

> A part of speech, then, is not a kind of meaning; it is a kind of token that obeys certain formal rules, like a chess piece or a poker chip. A noun, for example, is simply a word that does nouny things; it is the kind of word that comes after an article, can have an *'s* stuck onto it, and so on. There is a connection between concepts and part-of-speech categories, but it is a subtle and abstract one. When we construe an aspect of the world as something that can be identified and counted or measured and that can play a role in events, language often allows us to express that aspect as a noun, whether or not it is a physical object [whether or not it is a person, place or thing].[1]

The words that register here are those "that can play a role in events," and the native categories identify principal and critical players in the religious events recorded by the Rabbinic canon. Our native categories therefore constitute items that can be identified and play a role in events or supply the topic of a sentence, in more formal terms.

If not counted or measured ("person, place or thing"), the native categories of Judaism nonetheless form the foci of activity and concern: Israel and the gentiles; God and man; sanctification, atonement, intentionality, Kingdom of Heaven, repentance—powerful forces all! What we can say with these categories is governed by considerations that correspond to syntax—which words can combine, and which ones cannot—and what propositions emerge to form an intelligible account of matters finds definition in the semantics to be considered in due course. Models of explanation and anticipation form the counterpart, in theological language, to the intelligible statements afforded by the semantics of a language. Thus, like language, theology has its building blocks (vocabulary), its syntax (conventions of discourse), and its semantics (factors that limit potential meaning).[2]

---

[1] Pinker, *Language Instinct*, 106.

[2] Professor David Aaron, Hebrew Union College, frames matters in the following way (personal letter, February 11, 1997): "That domain we call 'semantics' is not so easily parsed as the other two parts of the quotient. When the parts (phonemes) are entered into relations with one another according to the governing logic (syntax rules), meaning may still not be altogether evident. That is, a statement may be

The corpus of words and other linguistic tools by which a language labels things corresponds, in a theological system, to the primary vocabulary that (formally) stands at the head of the declarative statements of that system and (categorically) defines its principal topics of cogent discourse: persons, places, principles, attitudes, ideas, affirmations. Each accomplishes the same end, in the present context, a theological one. Those media for the identification, definition, and organization of religious experience, for the naming of the actors and active powers of religious encounter with God as recorded in the Torah, oral and written, constitute the counterpart of the vocabulary of a language. What we see is how a given classification holds together a number of distinct but cognate religious experiences or conceptions; the cognitive rules of a language that govern relations of words, and thus provide the metaphor for the native categories of a theological system.

Not unlike nouns for persons, places, and things, the native categories therefore supply the name that classifies or categorizes the data of religion, whether concrete or abstract. Experiences, however discrete, of a given category are joined together, being differentiated, also, from experiences of another type. A single action may fall into more than one category, but the system will always dictate that category that pertains and exclude those that do not. These categories form that selection of the counterpart to a language's nouns, allowing us to identify as known and knowable, as subject to rational rules of relationship, the components of the otherwise-chaotic world of religious life that the theology discerns. Out of that vocabulary the religious system identifies the building blocks of thought, the topical components of its intelligible statements. That is what I mean when I propose that native categories in religious writing form the counterpart to the nouns or substantives of a language. Whether with the

---

perfectly 'logical' in terms of structure and the phonemes may all be discretely recognizable as legitimate words, but the statement may still make no sense. What gives it sense may not be limited to the language-act alone. Body language, intonation, common experiences, previous contexts may all contribute to a statement's potential meaning. But these aspects are also structured by those communicating, and, consequently, they also function according to certain rules . . . The elements that contribute to those meanings are loosely understood as belonging to what we call semantics." In our documents, the counterpart to thee other modes of communication is formed by the context, the governing problematic of discourse, the recurrent concerns that instruct a writer concerning the issues he must address.

nouns of a language or the native categories of a religion, knowing
the name that we call the data, we are able to make sense of those
data, organize and categorize—and therefore understand them. Our
vocabulary in both cases not only labels but creates the data. So much
for systemic categories as counterparts to a language's vocabulary.

II. Native Categories

From categories in general, we proceed to the critical point of
differentiation: "native category." A category encompasses in a single
rubric diverse data. The origin of the category bears no consequence.
But a native category in particular is one defined by, emerging from
(in the present context), the documents themselves, not invented by
us out of a later, alien system altogether. By "native category," therefore, I refer to a building block of thought and speech that in the documents of the Rabbinic canon is identified as imparting significance
or cogency to diverse data. A native category serves in the Rabbinic
canon to organize facts into intelligible compositions. Such a category may be, but is not necessarily a fact, but it always encompasses
and organizes facts. A native category ought ordinarily not to be
divisible or subject to classification within other categories, even
though data that fit within one native category may for other (taxonomic) reasons also fit within another. Thus, for example, a critical
native category, Land of Israel, also is irreducible and indivisible,[3] so
too repentance, or God, or Israel. Diverse data may find their way to
such native categories as these, but by definition and by usage "God"
classifies but cannot be further classified, and so with the other items.[4]

---

[3] I introduce these considerations only in the context of native category; they are
not borrowed from linguistics and have no place within the metaphor.

[4] Indeed, on the list of native categories belong the names of all principal players
in the written Torah, e.g., Moses and Sennacherib, Israel and Egypt, the Temple
and the destruction thereof—all events selected by the system as indicative within
that Torah, all locations that bear symbolic meaning. These are omitted here, forming the centerpiece for the analysis of a different problem. On the other hand, I
include as native categories abstract ones that the documents do not label, e.g., intentionality, as much as the ones that the documents do identify for us, e.g., Land of
Israel. The entries themselves validate this procedure and demonstrate that some
abstractions do belong as native categories, even though not named by the documents
themselves. The concluding section of this introduction amplifies this discussion.

How then do we know what belongs and what does not? A simple rule of thumb serves. If we want to test a hypothesis that a given classification serves as a native category—organizing data and imparting sense to them—we may ask about its opposite. The indicative trait of a native category is that we cannot ordinarily use its opposite in the way in which we use the native category. God is a native category, idol is not; Land of Israel is a native category, other lands (not differentiated, all unclean for instance) are not.

A constructive, positive statement meant to stand on its own and not depend upon other categories cannot be composed in the Rabbinic canon with "idol" at the head, or with "land of the gentiles" at the head, and so throughout. Idol will stand in a contrastive relationship to God, Land of the gentiles to Land of Israel, and so on. And then, God or Torah or Land of Israel can stand on their own and head—provide the organizing center for—a sentence, a set of sentences, a paragraph, a proposition, an entire composite. We may speak of God and Land of Israel without invoking idol or land of the gentiles, but the contrary is rarely[5] the case.

A second criterion is not excluded by the first. What is undifferentiated is not native, e.g., gentiles except in contradistinction to Israel, and what is differentiated is native, e.g., Israel—priests, Levites, Israelites, and the like. That trait of native categories is blatant and requires no amplification.

III. WHAT MAKES A NATIVE CATEGORY THEOLOGICAL?

Everyone knows that the documents of the Rabbinic canon on their own present nothing so systematic as to qualify as theology. They consist of sayings, stories, exegesis of received texts, and the like. So, as a matter of simple fact, theology in no way constitutes a native category of the writing of the Rabbinic canon. It represents my, not the sages', categorical principle. How then do we know the *theological* native categories in particular?

---

[5] My claim to characterize the whole always leaves room for exceptions, in a set of documents of such enormous dimensions, reaching us in a chain of tradition via manuscripts copied over many centuries. A single example cannot prove or disprove a proposition.

A phenomenological answer serves. A theological native category takes up a topic treated in an other-than-this-worldly or supernatural context, for example, the relationship to God of a particular type of human being, a holy person or saint or sage; or the character of an event in which God is represented as taking part, a miracle or revelation for example. Three examples suffice. "Commandment" transforms an ordinary, secular action into one that sanctifies, expressing the intent of the actor to serve and obey God. Kingdom of Heaven utilizes for a transcendent purpose a political metaphor. Messiah, prayer, redemption, atonement, repentance, resurrection—all conform to the simple definition just now given; each addresses a point at which man meets God, whether in time, or in gesture, or in aspiration or intention or attitude or expectation.

How in actuality do we know a native theological category when we see one? In the documents under study and subject to theological systematization here, we recognize a native theological category if a simple condition is met. Specifically, when a sizable exercise in definition and illustration is presented by one or more documentary components, e.g., a systematic exposition of a category, an elaborate instantiation of diverse items that fall into the same category, or a topical composite held together within a single category, then we identify a category. Introduce the encounter with God, show the coherence and cogency of the data that fall into the classification, and the category self-evidently falls into the classification of theology. And since the category emerges from an analytical reading of the documents of the Rabbinic canon, it is native, not artificial and imposed.

To give two examples: a householder is a native category, the subject of many predicates. He would enter the classification of a theological native category at those points at which his relationship to God forms the determinative consideration in a transaction that is represented by the law, in the exposition of the theology of the laws of the first division of the Mishnah, for example, on the agricultural rules of the Torah. Repentance is a native category of a theological character, since all of the usages of the category—all of the data assembled within it—involve God in the transaction. And so throughout: the data assembled for the native categories such as Israel, gentile, atonement, and sin. These invariably engage God's participation.

By contrast, such candidates as the Dead Sea, or a cow that gores, or an olive tree subject to conflicting claims (among thousands of candidates) do not qualify as theological categories, though under some circumstances they may serve as native ones, indeed as representative of items beyond themselves. The theological native categories then signal that the framers of the documents of the Rabbinic canon identify said classifications of experience or encounter as a given and deem their irreducibility as self-evident. How do we know? As I said, we test our identification of a given category as native by examining a topical composite and asking what is primary thereto, and what is subordinate; what organizes, what is organized.

Let me broaden the matter by appealing once more to the generative metaphor. Linguistics stresses function—how words work—and that is precisely my approach to identifying native categories. I identify and classify them by reference to the way in which they work. A native category will always form the unifying taxon: repentance or sin suffice to exemplify the matter. That is a characteristic of function or behavior; it is by how native categories work that I know them.

It is also by reference to the broader context formed by the documents themselves. A word that does not affect the use or meaning of other words is not a native category; it is just a word. A word that imposes its sense and order upon other words is a native category— "something that can be identified." Prayer, righteousness, repentance—these govern. They make things happen, accomplish things, serve as the subject of a sentence, as in "prayer, righteousness, repentance avert the evil decree." By contrast, nowhere in my reading of matters do places make a difference except in the instance of Land of Israel (and its type of place, that is, Jerusalem, temple, and so on). Everywhere else is nowhere in particular.

A native category will commonly serve as the subject of a predicate, as that which is modified, but uncommonly as the predicate, as that which modifies. "God will redeem" is a possible sentence in accord with the theological grammar of the Rabbinic canon, but "the power that redeems is God" is not. Such a sentence violates the rules of thought and so produces no intelligible statement. So a native category will encompass data and impart coherence to them. But, being irreducible, it will rarely be encompassed and seldom forced to cohere with other primary data, e.g., facts or systemic givens. A native category may interact with others; indeed, that is how the structure of categories transforms itself into a system of consequential statements. But such a category will ordinarily affect the combination but be in itself unchanged therein. Native categories enjoying self-evidence include such as God, Torah, Israel, Land of Israel. God's actions and teachings, the Torah's contents and implications, Israel's adherents and experiences, the active, participative role of the enchanted Land as an active player in the supernatural drama of Israel's and God's struggle—these form examples of those irreducible classifiers of facts that in this survey of the Rabbinic canon's documents we come to define as native categories.

IV. THE USES OF THE METAPHOR, VOCABULARY/NATIVE CATEGORIES

Now to return to the metaphor introduced in the Preface and invoked in the opening lines of this introduction. What, in particular, is it about the lexicon of a language—what we may call "the smallest parts" or phonemes—that supplies an illuminating metaphor for this effort to characterize the theological substrate of the several documents of the Rabbinic canon? The answer is implicit in what has already been said. It is the identification of head-words, the relations of words according to fixed rules, and the semantics that emerges from those relations, that allow rationality to be perceived. The way we form statements reflects the logic that governs our thought processes. Words and how they are arranged and used then manifest the process, the tools that change how we think into what we say. That is why I work backward from the words the theology uses to the processes of thought that govern, to try to find out something about how theology forms a vocabulary based on its thought preferences. The governing question then is, how does a theology establish its word choices, and then how does theology govern the discourse that results (Chapters Three and Four)?

Where does the vocabulary in particular enter in? The available theological words instantiate the power of a category to afford the possibility of generalization out of discrete data and reflection thereon. Take "redemption" for example. Israel finds itself in trouble; God intervenes, whether at the Reed Sea, whether at the crossing of the Jordan. The set of cases takes shape within a process of generalization and abstraction such as we should call analysis (what have these things in common, what rule governs them all), and explanation (how to make sense of this pattern), and, in the case of the Rabbinic canon, further generates the condition of anticipation (what do we learn from these facts about the future). In the case of theology, native categories bring about theological discourse upon religious encounter and experience. The categories of the Rabbinic canon provide an account of what takes place in meeting God in the Torah. In both realms—the head-words (a.k.a., nouns) of a language, the native categories of a theological corpus—the generative particles of language and the structural categories of religion alike impart meaning, order, and structure to otherwise inchoate, even impalpable, data: things of the world, experiences of religious encounter, respectively.

V. The Workings of the Process of Category-Formation: Assigning Nouns to Sets of Persons, Places, or Things

How, exactly, does the process of category-formation or naming—assigning nouns to sets of persons, places, or things, designating categories to encompass varied moments of religious realization—work for language? How does its counterpart, the process of category-formation, work for theology? A noun selects and labels data, imparting to those (in some ways diverse) data the qualities of cogency and coherence and so raising them to consciousness for intellectual recognition. The process would then yield possibilities of reflection, analysis, generalization for instance. Nouns make possible a process of *"proposition-ization,"* so to speak.

By their nature words not only label but homogenize, calling by the same word things that, in some ways, bear traits of differentiation as well, e.g., dog for the various breeds of dogs, man for diverse men, mountain for extrusions of various dimensions, match for a nearly unlimited number of sets of things that bear traits in common, or for diverse instruments for kindling a flame. At the same time, categories exclude by identifying traits that differentiate all things within from all things without: species of a genus from another genus altogether. From our perspective, category-formation marks the point at which the language of a vocabulary and the category-formation of religious writings such as the documents of the Rabbinic canon intersect. For both language and theology, the names that label things and differentiate one from another are what permit discourse of a general character, both encompassing and transcending the cases or specific instances. Such nouns or substantives are represented, e.g., by man, mountain, match, for a person, place, or thing, respectively.

The power to organize data, to classify and to categorize what is otherwise hopelessly disparate, then illuminates the world that language informs and the eternal encounter with God that theology rationally recapitulates. With correct vocabulary in the correct structure—my "native category"—theological meaning emerges. For linguistics, the cluster of words dictates potential structures. When we know which cluster yields which structure, we have precisely what I mean by "native category." In the present work, then, my native categories join diverse data into a single cluster of congruent meanings; the native category identifies a word (or cognate words) that functions in accord with specific rules of meaning. Data that exhibit the pertinent indicative traits—even, or especially, in polythetic classification—will be rendered cogent by being given the same name, that is, by being called by the same word.

Words then label in a single manner these (otherwise diverse) bipeds with proper qualities (whether physical, whether intellectual) which all fall into the category of man, also excluding the bipeds that do not; they call by the right name those aspects of the landscape, mountain, and the other traits—a stick that can kindle a flame—match, respectively. It becomes possible to generalize and explain, even to compare and contrast the diverse things that bear the same name, e.g., while one is large and another small, both fit into the same genus, and the traits of the genus in general pertain to the things that fall into that genus, even though these may be speciated in some other way. In this way we may transcend cases and discuss principles. For long centuries debates have addressed the proposition that the case is all we have, so that we have only things but not thing or that the name identifies what matters in the thing and gives it consequence (nominalism vs. realism). To that debate I have no contribution to make; I invoke language as a metaphor. The analogy serves to clarify, not to complicate, the work. Then to clarify the character of the counterpart to the vocabulary of the language in theology I hardly need to review centuries of philosophical reflection on the thing-ness of "Ideas," the names of things.

VI. The Vocabulary of Religious Experience
Afforded by the Torah

I have now to specify what I found in the documents of the Rabbinic canon to be comparable to the vocabulary of a language. It is my task to identify in the documents those points at which we find ourselves speaking about head-words (persons, places, or things) that make discrete data cohere—the counterpart to such words as man, mountain, and match that encompass diverse men, mountains, and matches. Just as by nouns or substantives we speak of the cases and impute to them all certain traits of cogency and coherence, so in the writings at hand, particular nouns or substantives serve. That is because they identify categories that impart form and structure and cogency to the religious experience recorded in those writings. Once a category identifies as one a range of cases, occasions, persons, or events, then the traits of the cases impart definition to the category and take the measure of its dimensions.

Accordingly, within the analogy and argument at hand, religious experience within the framework of the Torah comes to expression in certain words that give shape and structure to that encounter, not to the case in particular, but to the principle in general: the thing, not only the examples thereof, dog, not only yellow Labrador retriever; but only dog, not dogs, cats, and other household pets. These chosen words label categories, and, by reason of the method followed here— remaining within the limits of a specified body of documents—they signify native categories, categories defined within the data. These then speak of a finite body of data and select within those data the important cases subject to recapitulation in general terms: "God forgave Israel" represents the case, "God's mercy," the categorical principle, which then is capable of encompassing a variety of kindred cases. Then on our catalogue of vocabulary we include the words "mercy, divine."

An important qualification now enters. A variety of words will refer to a single category of phenomena, and we may supply the word, not only the translation of the documents' own word, as in the case of divine mercy or justice (*middat harahamim, middat haddin*). For instance, take the power of intentionality to dictate the outcome of a transaction. Here a word we supply—intentionality—will in fact correspond to a native category that emerges out of the documents of the

Rabbinic canon, covered by the word "intentionality"—our word for their well-defined phenomenon. The language of the documents, e.g., *kavvanah*, will not appear invariably to signal the presence of the category. But it is, nonetheless, a cogent one. One way or the other, within the corpus of words by which the language identifies out of things that happen the intelligible and consequential moments or transactions or participants, we find a limited number of such substantives or nouns. These are the ones capable of holding many things together as one thing, many cases as one governing principle.

VII. What Is at Stake? What Holds the Whole Together

Now let me specify what I conceive to be at stake: what do we gain if we take this view of matters? The answer is, we gain access to the theological system and structure that the writings of the Rabbinic canon presuppose and instantiate. By analyzing the components of the language common to them all, and by doing so in the manner suggested by one school of linguistics, I hope to identify what holds the whole together: the substrate of theological reflection, the system of theological inquiries, the structure of theological convictions, all together, all at once. It is not the propositions that surface hither and yon, but the language that everywhere governs consciousness, that yields an account of that system and structure: its native categories, the ways in which it assembles and reassembles those categories, the models of thought that impart sense to, and derive meaning from, those categories.

The problem contains within itself its own solution. It is a problem comprised by a specific set of writings—not the usage of a language in general, but the particular evidences of how it is used in some few writings. Then when we know how these writings work, how their categorical structure, modes of forming constructions and drawing connections, models of coherent analysis, explanation, and anticipation, take shape—then we can say what the structure comprises and what the system does. From the usages we work our way back to the principles that govern correct usage. From what people say, we find out how they are thinking, and in that way we can reconstruct their modes of thought even on problems not explicitly addressed. The analogy to language then proves quite exact: if we know the rules of a language, with perfect confidence that we shall be understood, we can think thoughts hitherto never contemplated, we can say what has never been said before. That accounts for the appeal to the metaphor used here: its exact correspondence to the situation before us.

I hope to find out what theological language serves them all, what dictionary affords access to every one, what category-formation prevails, whether on the surface or deep in the structure of thought. That accounts for the stress on vocabulary, syntax, and semantics, the components of the language throughout. Once more the chosen metaphor serves, now in a direct and unmediated manner: the limits of the language set forth in the documents of the Rabbinic canon set the bounds to the system and their traits of order and form adumbrate the logic and regularity thereof. They define what can be said and cannot be said. They place limits on what may be thought. In theology the categories that define the range of discourse themselves form a critical component of the system; they play an active role and bear much of the systemic structure. The generative, active categories recapitulate the systemic tensions and resolve them, time and again. They make possible the statement of one thing about many things. That about which we can and are to speak to begin with defines that structure, also excluding from discourse, eliminating from consideration, a vast range of candidates for inclusion.

The system identifies, and the documents replicate, the repertoire of head-words, nouns and substantives—persons, places, and things—that can stand at the head of propositions, serving as the subjects of sentences for example, or as objects of verbs. And what is at stake is obvious: when we know the native categories, we find ourselves at the very heart of the theological system that identifies those categories and defines and organizes religious reality in accord with them.

This leads us back to our metaphor. The active vocabulary, the words that time and again dictate the head-nouns—meaning, here, the topical program of a cogent set of sentences—these define the repertoire of native categories by which the Rabbinic canon organizes discourse and defines that which deserves rational consideration. Such a category must be deemed active in that it imposes upon the facts that fall within it a single set of rules, a governing signification. Thus "*shema*" (a prayer) and "*alenu*" (another prayer) would not constitute categories unto themselves, being taxonomically inert (within the present corpus of writing, active elsewhere), but together, and with other writings of the same order, they would fit into the category of "prayer." The native theological categories, the active, systemically-charged vocabulary of the Rabbinic canon, are what I list here.

VIII. The Source of Category-Formation

Whence the repertoire of categories? How do we know that a category-formation that we find indicative and active is native to the system, expressing its points of tension and recapitulation, and not imposed upon it by the onlooker out of another system? As I explain elsewhere,[6] the dogmatics of Protestant theology has conventionally assigned to and imposed upon the data of the theology of Rabbinic Judaism its own category-formation. The process has worked systematically and inexorably, producing a deeply Protestant category-formation for the consequently-formulated Judaism that is portrayed. If Protestant dogmatics set forth doctrines of justification, then justification should define a category of Rabbinic Judaism as well, so too, covenant, so too, soteriology, ethics, and on and on. That is, we know what we want to know, how we wish to organize our data, what we propose to discern therein, because the standard program of dogmatics tells us: God, ethics, salvation, and the like. The result is a profoundly Protestant Judaism, stopping short only of justification by faith alone.

Since that simple list will remind the reader how rich and dense a category-structure inheres in those enormous compilations, the question must arise: how do I know a theological category from a category-formation of some other order? That question belongs at just this point, because it brings us to a serious challenge to my insistence that I improve upon the Protestant theologians by ignoring their dogmatics—indeed, their systematics—in favor of the category-formation I insist the Rabbinic canon itself has framed.

First, I claim to utilize native categories. But in distinguishing holy from ordinary, theological from secular categories, I make a distinction that is certainly not native to the Rabbinic canon (among many

---

[6] *The Theology of Rabbinic Judaism. A Prolegomenon.* (South Florida Studies on the History of Judaism; Atlanta: Scholars Press, 1997).

representations of religion before nearly our own day)! For, clearly, the exposition of the law in the Mishnah, upon which rests the entire legal-exegetical corpus serving the Mishnah, knows sixty-two tractates, hence sixty-two topics, each of them functioning in exactly the way that I maintain categories function: organizing cogent data and offering generalizations that pertain thereto. Why then is "blessings" a theological category, but the wife accused of adultery (*Sotah*), or oaths (*Nedarim*), or animal offerings (*Zebahim*) or the susceptibility of utensils to cultic uncleanness (*Kelim*), not a theological category?

In the world portrayed by the Rabbinic canon there is no distinguishing what belonged to the realm of religion from what was secular. Sages used the word sanctification for the hallowing of the Sabbath and the designation of a woman as holy to a particular man, the one religious, the other secular, in our world but not in theirs. And the same then must pertain throughout. Hence pots and pans, marital relationships, oaths, and the resolution of civil conflict, represented issues of sanctity and occasions of sanctification, as much as convictions about God, Israel, the Torah, atonement, suffering, and the soul stood for the transcendent dimensions of life. Since, moreover, the sages found in the Written Torah the rules of sanctification, all of the categories of scriptural law as much as those of scriptural lore formed integral components of the category-formation of the Oral part of the Torah that sages constructed in completion and fulfillment of the Written part. So if the categories of tractate *Abot* fit well, then those of tractate *Nedarim* or *Zebahim* must too.

Second, while seeking categories native to the Rabbinic canon, I have brought to my reading of the document a fair number of categories no more native than are justification or soteriology (or ecclesiology for that matter, or Christology!). These equally alien categories are religion (as distinct from the secular), and, therefore, its intellectual byproduct, theology (as distinct from other systematizations of thought). And within the encompassing category, theology, I include categories that sages will have found no more theological, and no less theological, than the pots and pans concerning which they legislated so reflectively. The project, then, finds its definition and destination outside the limits of the documents of the Rabbinic canon, bringing to those documents points of differentiation not native to them at all.

How therefore do I claim to have improved on the Protestant dogmatic theologians' reconstructive reading of the same writings? It is in insisting that, within the shared premise that we may differentiate and give emphasis to what we deem religious and not secular in writings that make no such distinction, we may still identify in those writings categories that are native. My act of extrinsic differentiation takes place within the framework only of the documents' own category-formations. I introduce none of my own, though classifying the work as a whole in my way, not in the manner of the sages. Admittedly, sages will have produced a much, much longer and more elaborate account of the governing categories of their thought than mine—sixty-two large topics of halakhah—life lived in accord with the rules of sanctification—corresponding to the number of tractates of the Mishnah, to begin with. I maintain then that I set forth native categories, but admittedly, not all of the native categories that sages would have identified for me.

But the Rabbinic sages would have recognized and accepted all of mine. I know that that is the fact because every category-formation listed here emerges from the data of the documents themselves, organized as the documents organize them—and the documents have been repeatedly read whole and complete, not merely mined for sayings pertinent to subjects important in some context other than the documents. For reasons that strike me as self-evident, sages cannot have grasped critical categories of Protestant dogmatics—justification, soteriology—that the Protestant theologians bring to bear upon these writings, any more than they would have grasped other categories of Protestant dogmatics—ecclesiology, Christology—that they do not introduce. Or—still more important—they would have recognized those categories, but not to the proportion and position accorded to them, as in the instance of covenantal nomism. By contrast sages also would have readily acknowledged that all of the categories that enjoy prominence in these pages also enjoy prominence in their systemic discourse—God's justice, God's mercy, for instance, and so throughout.

IX. Why Insist on the Native Sources of Category-Formations?

What do we gain in imposing the limits—native categories, not alien ones—that define and constrict this study? I mean to make stick my critique of the use of alien category-formations that, up to the present time, have been imposed on, and so have distorted, descriptions of Judaism. Until now people have imposed the categories of Protestant dogmatic theology, so distorting their picture of the theology of the Rabbinic canon by laying emphasis upon matters of slight consequence therein and bypassing matters of central importance. To give a single instance, the category-formation of Protestant dogmatic theology contains no rubric for Halakhah or norms of behavior (other than ethical norms) and therefore allows no exploration of how Halakhah expresses in its own framework theological principles as fundamental as those contained by norms of belief or Aggadah.

Marshall Sahlins cites a passage of Foucault who himself cites a zoological classification system that Borges invented to capture the problem:

> Better to adopt the attitude of Foucault when presented by Borges with a zoological classification from a certain Chinese encyclopaedia, in which it is written that "animals are divided into (a) belonging to the Emperor, (b) embalmed, (c) tame, (d) suckling pigs, (e) sirens, (f) fabulous, (g) stray dogs, (h) included in the present classification, (i) frenzied, (j) innumerable, (k) drawn with a very fine camel hair brush, (l) et cetera, (m) having just broken the water pitcher, (n) that from a long way off look like flies." In the wonderment of this taxonomy, the thing we apprehend in one great leap, the thing that, by means of the fable, is demonstrated in the exotic charms of another system of thought, is the limitation of our own, the stark impossibility of thinking *that*.[7]

Protestant interest in justification and soteriology in Rabbinic Judaism proves as jarring to us as do the items joined in the odd Chinese zoological classification scheme. We find ourselves in a comparable position. Faced with the classification system that forms the foundation of the documents of the Rabbinic canon, our own system of thought—based as it has been on the categories of Protestant dogmatic theology—leads us to cognitive deadends. So we have to begin the work of theological description with a systematic and orderly account of the categories that govern in the writings of the Rabbinic canon themselves.

---

[7] Marshall Sahlins, *How "Natives" Think about Captain Cook for Example* (Chicago: University of Chicago, 1995), 163, citing Michel Foucault, *The Order of Things* (New York: Vintage Books, 1973), xv.

Two obvious problems left unsolved have rendered null the results of the Protestant construction of the theology of Rabbinic Judaism. First, important categories are missed, not bearing upon the Protestant program. Second, importance is assigned to categories that, in the Rabbinic canon, enjoy little or no importance, categories that play no systemic role, generate no tensions, resolve no points of stress. The resulting account of matters proves accurate but pointless and uncomprehending, an exercise in intellectual vacuity.

An example of the former—missing what matters—is the category Land of Israel, which is simply missed by the Protestant reading of Rabbinic Judaism but which enjoys enormous prominence in the Rabbinic canon and its organization of the world. The Rabbinic canon must be classed as a profoundly enlandised religious system, but the Protestant theological reconstruction of "Judaism" does not convey that governing fact.

An instance of the latter—distortion and disproportion in the representation of the whole—is the category covenant, specifically "covenantal nomism." Now that category takes an important part in the liberal Protestant apologetics in behalf of Rabbinic Judaism (or just "Judaism"). The laws are kept not as silly formalities but as expressions of the solemn covenant between Israel and God. True enough, and only a malicious person would doubt it. But that issue preoccupies no one in the entire Rabbinic canon; there the commandments are supposed to purify the heart, or keeping the commandments marks us as accepting God's dominion; but to no one does the conception of the Halakhah as an empty and merely formal exercise ever occur. Hence nomism/covenantal defines no native category, no systemic player. Indeed, in the documents themselves, "covenant" identifies a systemically-inert category, remarkable by its power to remain in the deep background of nearly the whole of the Rabbinic corpus. By "covenant" that corpus of writings ordinarily refers only to "circumcision." In my survey I found some important composites on the theme of circumcision, but no interesting category-formation emerged that I could define; no "word" capable of classifying but not itself subject to classification for example. True, the Written Torah's account of the covenants of God with the patriarchs and with Israel animates the whole, but so too does much else in that same component of the Torah. But in the documents in which "covenant" stands for "circumcision," in which covenantal theology

plays little systemic role, to impute centrality to covenantal considerations hardly yields an account of what the documents say, only of
the context that we impute to the message that they set forth.

The reason that prior scholarship has resorted to imported category-
formations in preference to the native ones lies in the orientation
and preparation of those who have done the work. Few ever concentrated on the documents of the Rabbinic canon in particular; picking and choosing sayings, few actually mastered them start to finish.
So while context ought to be everything, for those intent on filling up
the blank spaces on a questionnaire devised for their own survey,
the setting that imparted consequence to a saying meant nothing. The
saying by itself sufficed for its purpose, to fill a blank space on
the Protestant questionnaire. Motivated by other interests entirely, the
Protestant theologians then did not trouble to master the documents
in their own terms. Rather they went in search of sayings pertinent
to their predetermined program. No wonder they turned up sayings
that could be found in the documents but out of all context therein.
These they noticed, to them they gave heavy emphasis. Finding sayings that fit their scheme and ignoring their context produced
remarkable disproportions, on the one side, and obtuse omissions, on
the other.

What is to be done? When the documents speak for themselves,
using their language in their context to lay down their judgment upon
formations of their own devising, we may teach ourselves to hear
their language, in the words and music they find proper. Clearly,
defining native categories marks the starting point, because, before we
can proceed to the description of the theological structure that sustained the intellectual enterprise of Rabbinic Judaism, we have to
identify the building blocks. Once we do, the formations of meaning
constructed out of the joining of native categories require examination. So only then may we raise questions of how the blocks hold
together and form larger statements of order and meaning. That is
the point at which another complete pass through the entire corpus
of the Rabbinic canon will identify the theological paradigms that are
comprised by the native categories. Yet a third pass will then show
us how those paradigms function, that is, how the structure formed a
working system, able to function so as to accommodate the ongoing
intellectual adventure of Rabbinic Israel.

So to conclude: how then have I identified the nouns of the lexicon, the native categories of the Rabbinic canon? From start to finish, beginning with the Mishnah and ending with the Talmud of Babylonia, I simply read the documents of the Rabbinic canon, line by line, looking for recurrent nouns—persons, places, things, ideas, attitudes, affirmations—that repeatedly form not only the topics of discourse but the points of recurrent tension, loci of the generative problematic that precipitates thought. Repentance, atonement, resurrection, commandment, Israel, Land of Israel, righteousness, sin, and suffering—these words represent one type of native category, the rock-bottom, hard-core nouns that stand at the head of many, many sentences. How they work, what they mean, why they matter—to these questions the documents give rich, dense answers.

CHAPTER THREE

SYNTAX: CONNECTIONS AND CONSTRUCTIONS

I. Syntax: Identifying the Mystery of Self-Evidence

When we know what a body of writing accepts as self-evident, we penetrate into the deepest layers of the order and the structure that sustain that entire corpus at its foundation. Our quest for the superficial signs of the theological system and structure that form the substrate of the documents of the Rabbinic canon carries us to an inquiry into the marks of self-evidence: what native category "obviously" joins with what other one, and what does not? Through what is taken for granted, the system makes its statement of theological givens. When, therefore, we can outline the principles of constructing groups of categories into intelligible combinations, we find in those principles the main lines of theological order and structure. When we can state what emerges as self-evident when we join two otherwise distinct topics, we gain insight into the established laws of meaning and order that govern a system of coherent thought. So in examining the rules for joining native categories, we identify those indicators of correct usage that point toward the logic pervading the whole. That is why we examine the evidence, in detail, for two principal indicators: self-evidence in [1] making connections between, and [2] forming constructions of, native categories.

The selected metaphor borrowed from the description of a language through its grammar clarifies what is at stake. The rules of correct syntax—sentence construction, in familiar terms—are to vocabulary as the rules of making connections and building constructions are to the native categories of a theological structure and system. Each dictates how the smallest whole units join to form clusters of meaning. The coherent phrases and even cogent sentences of a language correspond to the conceptual composites, the building blocks and even propositions of a theological system. Certain words in a language, as certain native categories in the documents of the

Rabbinic canon, properly join together, forming intelligible clusters of meaning and even complete thoughts. Other words or native categories, when joined, jar. They yield gibberish.

When we know which words may join with which others, and which not, formulating the theological counterpart to the rules of syntax of a language, we know the inner logic of the system: how to set forth statements that make sense. We may even explain why in context they make sense. Native categories such as "God," "Israel," "Sinai," "Torah," for example, combine and recombine. While meanings may well shift in context, within a prescribed range of possibilities, "God" and "gentiles," "idolatry" and "love," rarely join, and when "Sinai," "Torah," and "gentiles" do, the negative (e.g., "why did the gentiles *not* accept . . .?") must make its appearance early and prominently.

So too, linking words that theological syntax deems unconnected and unavailable for connection—the (unthinkable) pairs, "the wicked Mordecai," "the good Haman," for instance—produce, for language, gibberish, and for theology, error, even blasphemy. Constructions of native categories that are not capable of locking together make no sense. When we know which words never join which others in cogent combinations—"an idol of God" or "a gentile who worships God alone," for instance—we may spell out the substrate of theological truths. These then dictate the details and map out the system as a whole. So too in grammar, violating syntactic rules yields what is unintelligible and beyond all rationality. And the theological connections and constructions—media of joining native categories into clusters of meaning—of the Rabbinic canon identify for us the counterpart to the rules of syntax of the grammar of a language. Learning from the details how to frame the governing rules of order and the laws of proper arrangement of native categories, equivalent to forming words into sentences, we gain access to the principles of thought that surface only in detail.

But how are we to locate those rules of thought and their necessary consequences in the established propositions of theological truth? It is not by assembling articulated theological generalizations. In the documents of the Rabbinic canon we find few theological generalizations. Among those that we do have, most are assigned to named authorities and therefore by definition prove particular to a given sage

and even schismatic.[1] And in that same small collection of theolo-
goumena of a conventional order one saying commonly contradicts
another, so that generalization and systematization, such as the quest
for theological rationality requires, prove unlikely. Consequently, for
the Rabbinic canon and its distinctive theological structure and system, important rules of theological thinking—the modes of thought
and propositional consequences thereof that pervade all of the documents—emerge only in an inductive analysis of how words form correct combinations to link up into intelligible statements.

Rather, in search of what lies beneath the surface we look at the
points of articulated joining of native categories. That is in line with
the chosen metaphor. In a grammar, syntactical rules dictate what
words may be constituted in intelligible statements: order, inflection,
signals of a word's position and purpose, and other matters of correct
usage. In the "grammar" of thought subject to study here, as I said
at the outset, syntax then is to vocabulary ("head-nouns") as a molecule is to (its) atoms and as native categories are to theological propositions. To extend the range of the metaphor introduced at the outset,
the molecule defines the atoms that it wants to join together (to
impute teleology to the inanimate), the besought fabric requires that
thread and no other, the building dictates the requirements, as to ten-
sile strength, of its beams. And, as a matter of fact, singleton native
categories do not commonly serve as the foundation of intelligible
statements. Rather, they ordinarily join with other native categories
to create the theological equivalent of grammatical phrases ("word
clusters") and even whole sentences.

---

[1] That is shown by the simple fact that most generalizations can be countered with
contrary generalizations or conflicting cases and exceptions. Hence formulating the
theological structure and system that characterize the entirety of the documents of
the Rabbinic canon cannot be achieved through close attention to assigned sayings,
on the one side, or generalizations, on the other. We need large aggregates of data,
all going over the same ground in the same way, to attest to the consensus of the
whole. The full meaning of attributing sayings to named authorities, and then collecting in a single document those attributed sayings, many of them conflicting with
juxtaposed sayings, has yet to be understood; these two distinctive and definitive traits
of the documents of the Rabbinic canon distinguish those documents from the writings of all other Judaisms of antiquity. That the named authorities derive traditions
ultimately from Sinai, through a process of discipleship and repetition of teachings
of sages, forms only one available explanation, and it is one that occurs only spo-
radically.

II. Designating Relevant Evidence

But how, then, are we to identify the relevant evidence of the theological counterpart to the syntax of a language? The answer is to examine evidence of two distinct types, each body of which shows us the givens of a theological system that are not articulated but that govern everywhere: not only the rules of thinking but the propositions that are to be thought in the abstract and expressed in concrete terms. That special trait of the documents, which is the absence of what we in the West deem conventional theological writing, necessitates devising the inductive inquiry at hand. If statements of generalization, joined to evidence and argument of an analytical character, prove rare in the Rabbinic canon, the results of theological thinking—the presence of a coherent theological structure and system—make their impact upon virtually every line. Then the form in which we have that structure and system presents the problem, for formulations of theological conviction only in mythic and symbolic language take a prominent place in most of the documents and prove common in the rest. We have then to find our way back from the combination of native categories to the rules of combination. But this is no different from writing a grammar of a language by regularizing the data of that language.

Let me make this concrete. If we have no disquisitions on the meaning of history equivalent to Augustine's *City of God*, we do find elaborate recapitulations of thinking about history so formed as to convey judgments of meaning. The counterpart emerges in Rabbinic theological syntax, but not in Rabbinic vocabulary. If we use a given word of the Rabbinic theological vocabulary, sense-statements do not self-evidently present themselves. But if we combine the right words, they do. Say "God" or "atonement" or "Land of Israel," and more often than not, no statement of a generalizing character follows, e.g., God is one and unique, or God loves Israel, or God forgives sin that the sinner atones for. But these messages emerge powerfully and unmistakably. Join God/atonement/Land of Israel, and Israel, and a variety of intelligible statements becomes possible, e.g., God will restore the Land of Israel to Israel when Israel's atonement is complete. And for Scripture (prophecy) and Rabbinic Judaism that forms a perfectly routine and commonplace sentiment. It is, moreover, not only self-evident but never contradicted in the Rabbinic canon. From that combination of words, moreover, we are able to construct those general propositions of which theological structures and the description of their working systems are composed.

So the character of theological discourse both conceals large-scale principles and also exemplifies and embodies those principles through concrete cases. That hardly surprises, for it is the mode of thought and expression equally characteristic of the Mishnah and the Halakhic writings generally. These generalize rarely, but supply the data of generalization—well-constructed lists, for example—as the principal medium of discourse. It is not surprising, therefore, to find the same mode of thought paramount in theological expression as well. The same authorities, educated in the same tradition, stand behind both a single mode of discourse for norms of behavior and norms of belief and that language of thought, standard for philosophy, of seeking generalizations out of detail and then of testing the viability of those generalizations. And the same disciplined cadres of masters and disciples, educated in the same documents through the same pedagogical methods, stand behind all the documents without distinction. That is why, just as in examining modes of Halakhic thought, we follow suit when we move from the detail to the generalization. In seeking the results of theological reflection of a systematic character, we find guidance in uniformities of detail to identify the main lines of reflection and results of thought.

The counterpart of syntax, accordingly, emerges for the case at hand in the rules of the correct system of thought and the true theological conviction that link "Land of Israel" to "God" and the set to "Israel" and then yield the condition that joins the whole: atonement (for sin). Indeed, as soon as we join the native categories "Land of Israel," "God," and "atonement," no other proposition becomes possible than the one just now stated. But we stand some distance from the goal of listing the necessary conclusions yielded by the correct combinations of native categories—counterpart to a systematic syntax of a grammar of a working language.

But how shall we identify the counterpart to syntax in the documents of the Rabbinic canon? At the present, primitive stage in the work of theological description, we cannot hope to uncover the complete repertoire of rules governing the formation of intelligible clusters of native categories that when combined yield meaning. Much that we can locate proves obvious and even banal. The present probe offers a basic thesis of matters and then systematic studies of two quite separate equivalents to the syntax of a language.

Here we consider the basic mode of thought of the documents, which, as I have said, is list-making. That is because all secondary developments of thought begin with the making of lists, the comparison and contrast of discrete data leading to their classification. That produces the articulation of the general rule that the list shows all the listed data. From the list we move to consider the kinds of data that can intersect, and the ones that cannot—that is, to examine the lists—in a process of comparison and contrast of whole lists. And, in a different direction altogether, in examining the relationships among the items on a list we proceed to the kinds of composites—constructions—we can conceive, as well as those we cannot contemplate. That is to say, we consider when a list becomes a series, extending itself beyond its original limits. The comparison of list to list yields a theory of connection.

In terms of the organization of the data examined here, we next deal with the echoes of self-evidence. Specifically, we pursue the question of the self-evidence of intersections—this category and that. We ask, what are the connections between one native category and another that documents deem self-evidently consequential? Why do the documents take for granted that when a given topic intersects with another, a specific conclusion is mandatory? The answers to questions of that order outline a part of the theological substrate of the documents. That is because, like a word-association exercise, what is deemed intuitive or self-evident leads us into the deepest parts of structure and system, what is not articulated but everywhere operates.[2]

III. List-Making

Lists gather and classify data, identifying the traits that diverse items have in common and (often implicitly) defining the law or rule to

---

[2] That then solves the problem of schism and contradiction: what the framers of the documents and authors of the compositions and composites they hold together all deem obvious and regard as beyond all necessity of demonstration must constitute the intellectual structure and system that sustain and animate the data of theological expression.

which those items, however otherwise differentiated, conform. The foundation document of the Rabbinic canon, the Mishnah, consists mainly of sequences of lists. The exegetical documents devoted to the Written Torah that supply much of the theological data rely heavily on list-making as well, though they register their propositions in other ways as well. The two modes for describing the theological counterpart to syntax that I have chosen appeal for their logic of cogency to the principles of list-making. Both connection-making and construction-building form species of the genus list-making. How do they do so?

When we identify a point of intersection between two otherwise unlike items (wheat and chaff, for example, or eternal life and death), we form them into a single list for the purpose at hand, showing how the two or more intersecting items affect and change one another at their point of connection; or drawing a conclusion from the meeting of the two or more items that, severally, none of the items yields. The upshot is that the sum of the parts exceeds the whole, or, stated less extravagantly, the meeting of the parts produces a conclusion that, on their own, the respective components of the composite do not yield.

The formation of a construction of free standing entries deemed to share common taxonomic traits constitutes nothing other than the making of a list, for a given purpose. The items may have a common quality and yield a shared rule—a construction that meets the definition of a conventional list. Or, as is often the case, the items that are collected may stand in striking contrast with one another, and, when juxtaposed, produce a conclusion that on their own does not pertain—another form of creating an intersecting of kindred facts and so of underscoring a connection. But this one is effected through comparison and contrast. So let us turn to the list in its own terms, asking how a list of theological facts produces a theological rule.

At stake in philosophical list-making accomplished in the natural history of the Mishnah and related documents is the ordering of the natural world: to what rules do its diverse phenomena conform? At stake in theological list-making is the supernatural world, the facts of which are preserved and set forth in the Written Torah and require analysis and classification too. The task of list-making remains the same, the quest for generalization and governing rule. But what is classified are the data deriving from the record of what God has done and how God has made himself manifest in this world. The data of the Torah therefore correspond to the data of nature, the list-making of the exegetical, theological compositions to the list-making of the Mishnah.

Let us first consider how theological, as much as philosophical, facts yield lists. That lists of items deemed to fall into a single class were composed to make theological statements of consequence, and that such list-making was subject to rules, is shown at Sif. Dt. I:X.4. There we find a debate on the meaning of a list of places, or events referred to by place-names, and the debate is explicit that at issue is whether or not the list bears one (supposedly self-evident) meaning or some other:

Sifré Deuteronomy I:X.4

A. R. Judah says, "Lo, Scripture states, 'In the wilderness, in the plain.'
B. "These are the ten trials that our fathers inflicted upon the Omnipresent in the wilderness.
C. "And these are they: two at the sea, two involving water, two involving manna, two involving quails, one involving the calf, and one involving the spies in the wilderness."
D. Said to him R. Yosé b. Dormasqit, "Judah, my honored friend, why do you distort verses of Scripture for us? I call to testify against me heaven and earth that we have made the circuit of all of these places, and each of the places is called only on account of an event that took place there [and not, as you say, to call to mind Israel's sin].
E. "And so Scripture says, 'And the herdsmen of Gerar strove with the herdsmen of Isaac, saying, "The water is ours." And he called the name of the well Esek, because they contended with him' (Gen. 26:29). 'And he called it Shibah' (Gen. 26:33)."

What is important here is that both parties to the dispute take for granted the validity of making a statement by collecting words that fall together and form intelligible clusters of meaning. At issue is the meaning of the items when joined together. The point of the list is to establish that ten trials were inflicted by the generation of the wilderness upon God, a list that, in the larger context of lists of tens, bears its own comparisons and contrasts. Yosé then rejects the very premise of the list, that the specified items represents venues at which Israel tried God's patience.

To make the matter of the list still more concrete let me refer to one important compilation of lists, of the sixth century C.E., contemporary with the Talmud of Babylonia, a compilation of exegesis of

Song of Songs called *Song of Songs Rabbah*. We may regard *Song of Songs Rabbah* as the counterpart, for theology, of the Mishnah for natural history. The reason is that, as in the Mishnah, it is through lists that that document sets forth a sequence of theological propositions; understanding how lists register theological points carries us a long way toward understanding the theological constructions that express the counterpart to the syntax of a language. Specifically, *Song of Songs Rabbah* presents a reading of the Song of Songs as a metaphorization of God's relationship of intense love for Israel, and Israel's relationship of intense love for God. In that document we find sequences, or combinations, of references to Scripture's persons, events, actions, and the like. These bear the rhetorical emblem, "another matter," in long lists of composites of well-framed compositions.[3] Each entry on a given list will be represented as "another matter," meaning, another interpretation of a given verse in the Song of Songs. As a matter of fact, however, that "other matter," one following the other, turns out to be the same matter in other terms. These constructions form lists out of diverse entries. When in *Song of Songs Rabbah* we have a sequence of items alleged to form a taxon, that is, a set of things that share a common taxic indicator, of course what we have is a list. The list presents diverse matters that all together share, and therefore also set forth, a single fact or rule or phenomenon. That is why we can list them, in all their distinctive character and specificity, on a common catalogue of "other things" that pertain all together to one thing.

What makes *Song of Songs Rabbah* remarkable is its power to reclassify data in categories that the data, on the surface, do not themselves fit. It is the originality of this process of reclassifying the theological givens of the Torah that renders the document principal for theological inquiry. That is to say, on these lists of kindred theological facts in *Song of Songs Rabbah* we find classified within a single taxon events, persons, places, objects, and actions naturally classified in groups of events, persons, places, objects, or actions, but not in single sets encompassing these five distinct types of facts. It is important to understand how they coalesce.[4] The rhetoric is the key indicator,

---

[3] I estimate that approximately eighty percent of the document in bulk is comprised of "another-matter" compositions. The list in this form defines the paramount rhetorical medium and logical structure of the document.

[4] The archaeological evidence of ancient synagogues yields counterpart "lists," that is to say, recurrent groups of iconic symbols that appear together, but with no

since it is objective and superficial. When we find the rhetorical formula "another matter," *davar aher*, what follows says the same thing in other words, or at least something complementary and necessary to make some larger point. That is why I insist that the constructions form lists.

In general, "another matter" signals "another way of saying the same thing"; or the formula bears the sense, "these two distinct things add up to one thing," with the further proviso that both are necessary to make one point that transcends each one. Not only so, but in *Song of Songs Rabbah* the fixed formula of the *davar aher* compilation points toward fixed formulas of theological thought: sets of coherent verbal symbols that work together. These "other things" encompass time, space, person and object, action and attitude, and join them all together, for instance, David, Solomon, Messiah at the end of time; this age, the age to come; the exodus from Egypt, Sinai, the age to come all may appear together within a single list. Let me give a single example of the list that makes it possible to redefine "event" into a category of quite ahistorical valence. Here is an example of that noteworthy shift in classification that *Song of Songs Rabbah*, among the documents of the Rabbinic canon, effects: the point at which theology emerges from principles of classification, which is to say, rules of joining native categories.

Song of Songs Rabbah to Song 1:5

V:i.1. A. "I am very dark, but comely, [O daughters of Jerusalem, like the tents of Kedar, like the curtains of Solomon]" (Song 1:5):
 B. "I am dark" in my deeds.
 C. "But comely" in the deeds of my forebears.
 2. A. "I am very dark, but comely":
 B. Said the Community of Israel, "'I am dark' in my view, 'but comely' before my Creator."
 C. For it is written, "Are you not as the children of the Ethiopians to Me, O children of Israel, says the Lord" (Amos 9:7):
 D. "as the children of the Ethiopians"—in your sight.
 E. But "to Me, O children of Israel, says the Lord."

---

other items, from one synagogue to another, e.g., the ram's horn, the palm branch, the candelabrum, are commonly grouped, but no other iconic symbols then appear in groups or what we should call "iconic lists." I have compared the iconic lists with the "another-matter-lists" in *Theology and Symbol in Judaism* (Minneapolis: Fortress Press, 1990).

3. A. Another interpretation of the verse, "I am very dark": in Egypt.
   B. "but comely": in Egypt.
   C. "I am very dark" in Egypt: "But they rebelled against me and would not hearken to me" (Ez. 20:8).
   D. "but comely" in Egypt: with the blood of the Passover offering and circumcision, "And when I passed by you and saw you wallowing in your blood, I said to you, In your blood live" (Ez. 16:6)—in the blood of the Passover.
   E. "I said to you, In your blood live" (Ez. 16:6)—in the blood of the circumcision.
4. A. Another interpretation of the verse, "I am very dark": at the sea, "They were rebellious at the sea, even the Red Sea" (Ps. 106:7).
   B. "but comely": at the sea, "This is my God and I will be comely for him" (Ex. 15:2).
5. A. "I am very dark": at Marah, "And the people murmured against Moses, saying, What shall we drink" (Ex. 15:24).
   B. "but comely": at Marah, "And he cried to the Lord and the Lord showed him a tree, and he cast it into the waters and the waters were made sweet" (Ex. 15:25).
6. A. "I am very dark": at Rephidim, "And the name of the place was called Massah and Meribah" (Ex. 17:7).
   B. "but comely": at Rephidim, "And Moses built an altar and called it by the name 'the Lord is my banner'" (Ex. 17:15).
7. A. "I am very dark": at Horeb, "And they made a calf at Horeb" (Ps. 106:19).
   B. "but comely": at Horeb, "And they said, All that the Lord has spoken we will do and obey" (Ex. 24:7).
8. A. "I am very dark": in the wilderness, "How often did they rebel against him in the wilderness" (Ps. 78:40).
   B. "but comely": in the wilderness at the setting up of the tabernacle, "And on the day that the tabernacle was set up" (Num. 9:15).
9. A. "I am very dark": in the deed of the spies, "And they spread an evil report of the land" (Num. 13:32).
   B. "but comely": in the deed of Joshua and Caleb, "Save for Caleb, the son of Jephunneh the Kenizzite" (Num. 32:12).
10. A. "I am very dark": at Shittim, "And Israel abode at Shittim and the people began to commit harlotry with the daughters of Moab" (Num. 25:1).
    B. "but comely": at Shittim, "Then arose Phinehas and wrought judgment" (Ps. 106:30).
11. A. "I am very dark": through Achan, "But the children of Israel committed a trespass concerning the devoted thing" (Josh. 7:1).

B. "but comely": through Joshua, "And Joshua said to Achan, My son, give I pray you glory" (Josh. 7:19).

12. A. "I am very dark": through the kings of Israel.

B. "but comely": through the kings of Judah.

C. If with my dark ones that I had, it was such that "I am comely," all the more so with my prophets.

V:ii.5. A. [As to the verse, "I am very dark, but comely"] R. Levi b. R. Haita gave three interpretations:

B. "'I am very dark': all the days of the week.

C. "'but comely': on the Sabbath.

D. "'I am very dark': all the days of the year.

E. "'but comely': on the Day of Atonement.

F. "'I am very dark': among the Ten Tribes.

G. "'but comely': in the tribe of Judah and Benjamin.

H. "'I am very dark': in this world.

I. "'but comely': in the world to come."

The contrast of dark and comely yields a variety of applications; in all of them the same situation that applies to the one also applies to the other, and the rest follows in a wonderfully well-crafted composition. What is the repertoire of items—native categories in the language of this study? Dark in deeds but comely in ancestry; dark in my view but comely before God; dark when rebellious, comely when obedient, a point made at nos. 3 for Egypt, 4 for the sea, 5 for Marah, 6 for Massah and Meribah, 7 for Horeb, 8 for the wilderness, 9 for the spies in the Land, 10 for Shittim, 11 for Achan/Joshua and the conquest of the Land, 12 for Israel and Judah.

But to witness the jarring shift in category-formation, look at what follows: the week as against the Sabbath, the weekdays as against the Day of Atonement, the Ten Tribes as against Judah and Benjamin, this world as against the world to come. Whatever classification these next items demand for themselves, it surely will not be that of events. Indeed, if by event we mean something that happened once, as in "once upon a time," then Sabbath as against weekday, Day of Atonement as against ordinary day form a different category; the Ten Tribes as against Judah and Benjamin constitute social entities, not divisions of time; and this age and the age to come form utterly antihistorical taxa altogether.

The lists in the document at hand form selections from a most limited repertoire of candidates. If we were to catalogue all of the exegetical repertoire encompassed by *davar aher* constructions in this document, we should not have a very long list of candidates for inclusion in any list. And among the candidates, events are few indeed. They encompass Israel at the Sea and at Sinai, the destruction of the first temple, the destruction of the second temple, events as defined by the actions of some holy men such as Abraham, Isaac, and Jacob (treated not for what they did but for who they were), Daniel, Mishael, Hananiah, and Azariah, and the like.

IV. Connections

We turn first to a phenomenon that corresponds to, but in form scarcely intersects with, the list, which is the making of connections. The composite documents of the Rabbinic canon encompass points at which the extensive treatment of an extraneous topic interrupts the flow of exposition and even argument. Then we are made to wonder what one thing has to do with another. In some instances, the sole answer we may identify is, nothing. But in numerous others the insertion of the disruptive item redefines its own context and recasts the ongoing discourse at hand. Then, it is clear, the intrusion represents a constructive initiative, an intended reshaping of the exposition altogether. When we ask what has this to do with that, and when we attempt a response, we find time and again that at the foundations of the jarring juxtaposition or not-to-be-predicted connection is a self-evident proposition. It follows that, by "connections" I mean points of self-evident meaning that are yielded in the (redactional) intersection between and among composites devoted to distinct topics, cases in which subjects are joined in the premise that they illuminate one another. And, within the same premise, they do so in an obvious way, yielding an inexorable result of theological truth. So far as, in a grammar of a language, syntax sets forth rules of turning words into combinations, we find in these points of self-evidence the theological counterpart to syntax: these join to allow us to say that; but they do not join for any other purpose.

The data happen to derive from the Talmud of Babylonia and emerge from an odd trait of redaction of that document. The framers of the Bavli not only composed exegetical exercises in clarification of the Mishnah and related law as well as systematic exegetical compositions on specific passages of the Written Torah, or drew upon available compositions assembled for that purpose. They also accom-

modated within their exposition enormous free-standing compositions
and even large-scale composites devoted to particular topics. These
form autonomous statements, not dependent for form or meaning
upon the exegetical program of the document—exegesis of the
Mishnah and of Scripture—as a whole. Now, in some settings, the
large-scale, free-standing composite belongs for formal reasons, e.g.,
as a composite of facts that supplement the discussion at hand, constituting the equivalent of a long footnote or even an appendix.

But in some instances these topical composites are so situated as to
form a gloss upon the exegesis of law or theology that the exposition
of the Mishnah in its own terms has provoked—a topical gloss that
changes everything. And here we find access to the self-evident connections that permit us to join what on the surface ought not to intersect with the base exposition at hand. That is where we ask what this
has to do with that, and find an illuminating answer to the question.
For us the jarring juxtapositions function like a word-association test,
telling us that topic A triggers an association with topic B, furthermore pointing to a new meaning gained by topic A (and even by
topic B in its own framework) from said association. Thus, to the
compilers of the Bavli a clear rationality guided the inclusion of the
exposition, a topical intersection, this and that, so no one has to ask
what this has to do with that. What appears to impede the work—
the topical appendices tend to run on, and the composites prove disruptive and tedious in places—enriches the Talmud's comprehensive
statement. It is for us to identify these anomalous constructions and
ask about what is taken for granted in the topical intersection that
they bring about.

The evidence briefly summarized here will enjoy immediate recognition from everyone who has studied a complete tractate or perhaps
even an entire chapter of the Bavli, start to finish. In such coherent
study two important traits of the writing prove blatant. The first is
the presence of large composites that do not serve the purpose of
commenting on the Mishnah, and the second the intrusion of such
composites into the very heart of the work of Mishnah-exegesis.
These miscellaneous composites of materials on a given topic, lacking all argument and proposition, not only intrude but disrupt. Not
only so, but it is not always easy to explain why a given composite is
inserted where it is; juxtapositions of Mishnah-exegesis and a topical
miscellany—a composite of materials on a given subject that the

Mishnah, for its part, has not introduced, or of materials that vastly exceed what is required for the explanation of a reference in the Mishnah—prove jarring. What has one thing to do with another— wheat with straw, so to speak? From the study of these jarring juxtapositions emerges another set of rules that correspond to syntax in language: a theory of rational connection. The counterpart to syntax in a language, when it comes to the insertion of topical composites, is an explanation of why they are inserted where they are, and what the framer of the document accomplished in including in his exposition of the Mishnah and its law rather formidable topical composites that bear no obvious relationship to the tasks of Mishnah-commentary.

Juxtapositions—the making of connections—that jar and disrupt turn out to bear an entirely pertinent, even urgent, message for the larger discourse in which they take their place. Indeed, these topical composites themselves commonly constitute a comment upon the paramount subject of the Mishnah tractate at the very point at which they find their position—if only by highlighting what belongs but has been omitted. Properly understood, the topical miscellanies do not jar and do not violate the document's prevailing rationality.

I therefore identify a representative sample of these anomalous constructions and propose a theory of why they are inserted where they are. I spell out what the framer of the document accomplished in including them. How the whole holds together at any one passage then is what requires explanation. And that means what one thing has to do with some other. Here, in acute detail, I explain how topics that on the surface do not intersect in fact fit together very nicely and by their juxtaposition convey a message in tandem that on their own the respective parts do not deliver or even adumbrate.[5]

---

[5] Certainly one of the critical problems in the study of the history of the formation of Judaism is the relationship of the two Talmuds' system to the Mishnah's, and that means, what do the Talmuds have to say about the topical program of the Mishnah when it does more than paraphrase and clarify the Mishnah's message: when is a Talmud talmudic? I struggled with that problem in my *The Talmud of the Land of Israel. A Preliminary Translation and Explanation* (Chicago: University of Chicago Press, 1983), vol. XXXV. *Introduction. Taxonomy*, and it is the subtext of my *The Documentary Form-History of Rabbinic Literature* (Atlanta: Scholars Press, 1997) for South Florida Studies in the History of Judaism, Volumes VI and VII. But it is explicitly dealt with for the Bavli in *Rationality and Structure: The Bavli's Anomalous Juxtapositions*.

What we shall see is that juxtapositions that jar and disrupt turn out to bear an entirely pertinent, even urgent, message for the larger discourse in which they take their place. That message is taken for granted, not demonstrated but rather insinuated as a given. Indeed, these topical composites themselves commonly constitute a comment upon the paramount subject of the Mishnah tractate at the very point at which they find their position—if only by highlighting what belongs but has been omitted. Properly understood, the topical miscellanies do not jar and do not violate the document's prevailing rationality: what it takes for granted as self-evident.

How does the making of connections in the manner indicated here guide us toward the theological description of the documents of the Rabbinic canon? The answer is obvious. Questions of theological system find their answer in the givens, the established facts, the points beyond all dispute. The items that are taken for granted then encompass the matters of rationality, principles of self-evidence, laws of list-making. These then concern the points of emphasis and current stress, the agenda that comes to expression in whatever topic is subject to analysis. By explaining the coherence of the whole through the identification of the parts and the systematic specification of what links one part to another, I gain access to one aspect of the theological system that sustains the writings as a whole. That system—like all enduring works of intellect—in a monotonous voice says the same thing about many things and changes the subject only to re-present the original subject itself.

V. CONSTRUCTIONS

A much larger and more consequential corpus of clusters of native categories, forming the counterpart of meaningful clusters of headwords, emerges from the inquiry into "constructions" in the documents of the Rabbinic canon. While connections prove episodic and yield only odds and ends of insight, deriving as they do only from a single document, these constructions encompass a large number of documents and provide ample data about givens of theological connection-making between and among the established native categories.

What, exactly, do I mean by "constructions"? I refer to joining of "things"—native categories. These are deemed all together to make a statement that, on their own, the individual words do not make. Constructions usually are made up of two or more sets of native categories attested by a document of the Rabbinic canon. The set is comprised of two or more lists, which are juxtaposed with self-evident results. A construction therefore combines sets of native categories—we already have called them lists—to make a point that the native categories (or distinct lists) thereof on their own cannot register. Only the joining of the lists of native categories establishes that point, in a powerful demonstration—hence the word-choice "construction."

In the case of a well-framed construction, the formation of native categories into lists and the amalgamation of lists may join opposites, or organize data in a way that leads to an unavoidable conclusion, as in the example to follow, and in the comparison and consequent contrast, an important fact may emerge. Before proceeding, let me give a single example of a representative construction. It involves two separate combinations, both natural to the documents: Abraham, Isaac, and Jacob on the one side, and old age, sickness, and death on the other. Putting the two together produces a conclusion that neither set on its own yields—all the less likely that any item on either set would generate. The proposition that the construction sets forth is that Abraham, Isaac, and Jacob are responsible for old age, suffering, and sickness:

Genesis Rabbah LXV:IX.1

A. "When Isaac was old, and his eyes were dim, so that he could not see, he called Esau his older son, and said to him, 'My son,' and he answered, 'Here I am'" (Gen. 27:1):

B. Said R. Judah bar Simon, "Abraham sought [the physical traits of] old age [so that from one's appearance, people would know that he was old]. He said before him, 'Lord of all ages, when a man and his son come in somewhere, no one knows whom to honor. If you crown a man with the traits of old age, people will know whom to honor.'

C. "Said to him the Holy One, blessed be he, 'By your life, this is a good thing that you have asked for, and it will begin with you.'

D. "From the beginning of the book of Genesis to this passage, there is no reference to old age. But when Abraham our father came along, the traits of old age were given to him, as it is said, 'And Abraham was old' (Gen. 24:1)."

E. "Isaac asked God for suffering. He said before him, 'Lord of the age, if someone dies without suffering, the measure of strict justice is stretched out against him. But if you bring suffering on him, the measure of strict justice will not be stretched out against him. [Suffering will help counter the man's sins, and the measure of strict justice will be mitigated through suffering by the measure of mercy.]'

F. "Said to him the Holy One, blessed be he, 'By your life, this is a good thing that you have asked for, and it will begin with you.'

G. "From the beginning of the book of Genesis to this passage, there is no reference to suffering. But when Isaac came along, suffering was given to him: his eyes were dim."

H. "Jacob asked for sickness. He said before him, 'Lord of all ages, if a person dies without illness, he will not settle his affairs for his children. If he is sick for two or three days, he will settle his affairs with his children.'

I. "Said to him the Holy One, blessed be he, 'By your life, this is a good thing that you have asked for, and it will begin with you.'

J. "That is in line with this verse: 'And someone said to Joseph, "Behold, your father is sick"' (Gen. 48:1)."

The construction joins the list comprised by the patriarchs to the list made up of the kindred events, old age, and suffering, and sickness, each point at the joining for a wise consideration. Listed one by one, the patriarchs' entries produce a pattern lacking a point. The analytical process—collecting and examining facts supplied by Scripture or invented, it hardly matters, as in the case of the colloquies before us—has identified with the name of each patriarch a trait that, in one detail or another, is common to all three of them. Then the reasoning for each item is shown congruent: the proper ordering of society, the provision for a medium of atonement through suffering, and the orderly provision of one's affairs prior to death. These three considerations all form details that one prepares in this world for what is coming at death and in the next world; that the social order should establish hierarchy based on age; that strict justice must be countered with an opportunity for atonement; and the like. The construction seen whole establishes its own larger conception as well. The entries on their own do not make the point that all of them together are able to register. Joining Abraham, Isaac, and Jacob does not establish the point, nor does linking old age, suffering, and sickness; linking the two sets leaves no room for speculation on the point that the compiler (here, clearly, an author) wishes to establish and express in a memorable manner.

Constructions of sets of native categories define the principal focus of the theological equivalent to syntax in the sample set forth here.

How, exactly, do I conceive a parallel to exist? The rules of syntax emerge from knowledge that diverse head-nouns, e.g., persons, places, things may join together. Others may not. In the item just now presented, for example, the corresponding list for Abraham, Isaac, and Jacob could not have been stupidity, vulgarity, and obtuseness; the counterpart to rules of syntax prohibits such a corresponding list from joining the list of the patriarchs to yield an intelligible construction. The theological counterpart to syntactical rules of joining head-nouns, the principles of coherence, of order, of self-evidence, then encompass the principle that Abraham, Isaac, and Jacob cannot be matched by a list of three negative traits, and the obvious theological corollary is that the patriarchs cannot stand for what the system does not respect; and it follows (to continue the exercise in banality), what the patriarchs stand for or inaugurate belongs to the systemic heart of the theological system at hand.

That theological conception hardly has to be articulated, being ubiquitous and obvious. What is important in the use of the analogy is to find a way of describing, analyzing, and interpreting these familiar data so that we better understand the workings of a system that we already know—equivalent to learning the rules of a language that we already speak. The rules themselves then form a layer of exegesis of data, and the rules that emerge (sickness, old age, and suffering form gifts of a wise and loving God) themselves are to be amplified and extended in a secondary process involving the exegesis of exegesis. So knowing the obvious rules of joining native categories permits a process of amplification, extension, innovation, and renewal. The language permits a vast number of unthought thoughts to be thought, makes provision for a long future of intelligible speech. But this it does as much by closing off, as by opening, possibilities—just like syntax for a language.

The expression of norms of behavior as much as belief makes use of the construction that is defined here; we deal with a mode of thought, not a medium of expression; and a mode of thought by definition can and should govern in diverse circumstances of thought. Accordingly, we deal with a mode of thought and expression that serves a variety of purposes, not only those involving what we define as theological ones. Among constructions are sets of instances or cases required by this-worldly discourse on ordinary matters, and sets of instances or cases that bear testimony to data of an other-than-this-worldly venue: religious meaning, theological message.

The former is illustrated, among thousands of possibilities in the law, by the following lists, a list but not a construction within the definition given here:

Mishnah Baba Batra 2:1

A. One may not dig (1) a cistern near the cistern of his fellow,

B. nor (2) a ditch, (3) cave, (4) water channel, or (5) laundry pool,

C. unless one set it three handbreadths away from the wall of his fellow,

D. and plaster it with plaster [to retain the water].

E. They set (1) olive refuse, (2) manure, (3) salt, (4) lime, or (5) stones three handbreadths from the wall of one's fellow,

F. and plaster it with plaster.

G. They set (1) seeds, (2) a plough, and (3) urine three handbreadths from a wall.

H. And they set (1) a hand mill three handbreadths from the lower millstone, which is four from the upper millstone;

I. and (2) the oven so that the wall is three handbreadths from the belly of the oven, or four from the rim.

However many times the numbered items on the several lists appear together, they do not form a construction that dictates sense and meaning in theological discourse. They form natural groupings— handmill or millstone vs. oven; cistern, ditch, cave, water channel, laundry-pool, and like catchments; olive refuse, manure, salt, lime, stones, and like nuisances.

VI. THEOLOGICAL SYNTAX IN LISTS OF EVENTS

Let us now turn, specifically, to the syntax that governs the choice of happenings that can combine and recombine and the exclusion of happenings that cannot. Here we see how the counterpart to syntax operates to govern combinations that can, and cannot, be made. What we see is so concrete and specific, and yet so clearly founded upon established, if not articulated, rules of combinancy and recombinancy, that we cannot doubt the presence of a theological syntax. Concretely, we ask for the counterpart to a syntactic rule by inquiring, What taxic indicator dictates which happenings will be deemed events and which not? What are listed throughout are not data of nature or history but of theology: God's relationship with Israel, expressed in such facts as the three events, the first two in the past, the third in the future, namely, the three redemptions of Israel, the three patriarchs, and holy persons, actions, events, what-have-you. These are facts that are assembled and grouped; as we have already noticed, in *Song of Songs Rabbah* the result is not invariably propositional at all, or, if propositional, then essentially the repetition of familiar propositions through unfamiliar data. What we have is a kind of recombinant theology, in which the framer (the "theologian") selects from a restricted repertoire a few items for combination, sometimes to make a point (e.g., the contrast of obedient and disobedient Israel we saw just now), sometimes not. What is set on display justifies the display: putting this familiar fact together with that familiar fact in an unfamiliar combination constitutes what is new and important in the list. The consequent conclusion one is supposed to draw, the proposition or rule that emerges—this is rarely articulated and never important.

True, the list and even the construction in *Song of Songs Rabbah* may comprise a rule, or it may substantiate a proposition or validate a claim; the making of connections among ordinarily unconnected things is then one outcome of construction-making. What we have is the restatement, through an infinite range of possibilities, of the combinations and recombinations of a few essentially simple facts (data). It is as though a magician tossed a set of sticks this way and that, interpreting the diverse combinations of a fixed set of objects. The propositions that emerge are not the main point; the combinations are. That seems to me an important fact of a syntactic character: the culture at hand has defined for itself a repertoire of persons and events and conceptions (e.g., Torah study), holy persons, holy deeds, holy institutions, has presented candidates for inclusion in constructions; and the repertoire, while restricted and not terribly long, made possible a scarcely-limited variety of lists of things with like taxic indicators. That is to say, the same items occur over and over again, but there is no pattern to how they recur. By a pattern I mean that items of the repertoire may appear in numerous constructions or not; they may keep company with only a fixed number of other items, or they may not. Most things can appear in a *davar aher* composition with most other things. To make this point concrete, here is a survey of sequences of components of such constructions that occur in *Song of Songs Rabbah*:

Joseph, righteous men, Moses, and Solomon;
patriarchs as against princes, offerings as against merit, and Israel as against the nations; those who love the king, proselytes, martyrs, penitents;
first Israel at Sinai; then Israel's loss of God's presence on account of the golden calf; then God's favoring Israel by treating Israel not in accord with the requirements of justice but with mercy;
Dathan and Abiram, the spies, Jeroboam, Solomon's marriage to Pharaoh's daughter, Ahab, Jezebel, Zedekiah;
Israel is feminine, the enemy (Egypt) masculine, but God the father saves Israel the daughter;
Moses and Aaron, the Sanhedrin, the teachers of Scripture and Mishnah, the rabbis;
the disciples; the relationship among disciples, public recitation of teachings of the Torah in the right order; lections of the Torah;
the spoil at the Sea = the Exodus, the Torah, the Tabernacle, the ark;
the patriarchs, Abraham, Isaac, Jacob, then Israel in Egypt, Israel's atonement and God's forgiveness;
the Temple where God and Israel are joined, the Temple is God's resting place, the Temple is the source of Israel's fecundity;
Israel in Egypt, at the Sea, at Sinai, and subjugated by the gentile kingdoms, and how the redemption will come;
Rebecca, those who came forth from Egypt, Israel at Sinai, acts of loving kindness, the kingdoms who now rule Israel, the coming redemption;
fire above, fire below, meaning heavenly and altar fires; Torah in writing, Torah in memory; fire of Abraham, Miriam, bush, Elijah, Hananiah, Mishael, and Azariah;
the Ten Commandments, show-fringes and phylacteries, recitation of the Shema and the Prayer, the tabernacle and the cloud of the Presence of God, and the mezuzah;
the timing of redemption, the moral condition of those to be redeemed, and the past religious misdeeds of those to be redeemed;
Israel at the sea, Sinai, the Ten Commandments; then the synagogues and school houses; then the redeemer;
the Exodus, the conquest of the Land, the redemption and restoration of Israel to Zion after the destruction of the first Temple, and the final and ultimate salvation;
the Egyptians, Esau and his generals, and, finally, the four kingdoms;
Moses's redemption, the first, to the second redemption in the time of the Babylonians and Daniel;
the litter of Solomon: the priestly blessing, the priestly watches, the sanhedrin, and the Israelites coming out of Egypt;

Israel at the sea and forgiveness for sins effected through their passing through the sea; Israel at Sinai; the war with Midian; the crossing
of the Jordan and entry into the Land; the house of the sanctuary; the
priestly watches; the offerings in the Temple; the sanhedrin; the Day of
Atonement;

God redeemed Israel without preparation; the nations of the world
will be punished, after Israel is punished; the nations of the world will
present Israel as gifts to the royal messiah, and here the base verse
refers to Abraham, Isaac, Jacob, Sihon, Og, Canaanites;

the return to Zion in the time of Ezra, the Exodus from Egypt in the
time of Moses;

the patriarchs and with Israel in Egypt, at the Sea, and then before
Sinai;

Abraham, Jacob, Moses;

Isaac, Jacob, Esau, Jacob, Joseph, the brothers, Jonathan, David,
Saul, man, wife, paramour;

Abraham in the fiery furnace and Shadrach, Meshach, and Abed-
nego, the Exile in Babylonia, now with reference to the return to Zion.

The upshot is simple. Construction formation presents interesting
combinations of an essentially small number of native categories, the
candidates for the exercise. But these are combined in a wide variety
of ways. So the theological system that animates the entire range of
documents has imposed criteria of selection, among a probably
infinite number of possible native categories, of a few items to be
closely examined and thoughtfully manipulated. But with these items,
a nearly unlimited range of possible constructions can be brought
about. Here again the analogy to the grammar of a language proves
illuminating. A language selects the phonemes it wishes to use, closing off a vast range of possibilities. But then the same language makes
provision for a vast number of choices in how to use the chosen
phonemes. And knowing the rules of combination (the syntax), we
can understand not only what we have heard, but even what we ourselves have never thought.

In the construction, we identify theological vocabulary ("things")
and form from that vocabulary intelligible combinations—names,
places, events, actions deemed to bear theological weight and to affect
attitude and action. The play is worked out by a reprise of available
materials, composed in some fresh and interesting combination.
When three or more such theological "things"—whether person,
whether event, whether action, whether attitude—are combined, they
form a theological structure, and, viewed all together, all of the theo-

logical "things" in a given document constitute the components of the entire theological structure that the document affords. The propositions portrayed visually, through metaphors of sight, or dramatically, through metaphors of action and relationship, or in attitude and emotion, through metaphors that convey or provoke feeling and sentiment, when translated into language prove familiar and commonplace. The work of the theologian in this context is not to say something new or even persuasive, for the former is unthinkable by definition, the latter unnecessary in context. It is rather to display theological "things" in a fresh and interesting way, to accomplish a fresh exegesis of the canon of theological "things."

The combinations and recombinations defined for us by our documents form events or persons or activities or objects into facts, sharing the paramount taxic indicators of a variety of other facts, comprising a theological structure within a larger theological structure: a reworking of canonical materials. An event or person or act or object is therefore reduced to a "thing," losing all taxic autonomy within the taxonomy we find natural—event, person, act, object—and now requiring no distinct indicator of an intrinsic order. It is simply something else to utilize in composing facts into knowledge; the event or act or object does not explain, it does not define, indeed, it does not even exist within its own framework at all.

The principle of selectivity—what is there to be formed into a combination—and the principle of construction—what do we do with the items we select for combinancy—point in their way, as much as the connections we deem self-evident point in their way, to a substrate of theological thinking, a theological system. The principle of selectivity is then one key to the system. For every Abraham, Isaac, and Jacob that we find, there are Job, Enoch, Jeroboam, or Zephaniah, whom we do not find; for every Sea/Sinai/entry into the Land that we do find, there are other sequences, e.g., the loss of the ark to the Philistines and its recovery, or Barak and Deborah, that we do not find. Ezra figures, Haggai does not; the Assyrians play a minor role, Nebuchadnezzar is on nearly every page. Granted, Sinai must enjoy a privileged position throughout. But why prefer Hananiah, Mishael, and Azariah, over other trilogies of heroic figures? So the selection is an act of choice, a statement of culture in miniature. But once restricted through this statement of choice, the same selected theological "things" then undergo combination and recombination with other theological things. If we know the complex set of rules in play here, we also would understand the system that makes this document not merely an expression of piety but a statement of a theological structure: orderly, well-composed and proportioned, internally coherent and cogent throughout.

VII. Theological Syntax Summarized

To summarize: two distinct bodies of data contribute the theological counterpart to syntactic rules: connections and constructions. Revealing word associations, or conception associations, in the deepest layers of systemic structure, lead us into the theological system's sources of self-evidence, the profoundly situated givens, of the system. These may involve connections between one thing and some other but not a third. Or they may present juxtapositions of discrete topics (and data) in such a way as to form connections between one thing and something else. These then produce a coherent conception emerging from the intersection. Constructions comprised by the joining of two or more native categories, for their part, provide glimpses at the equally self-evident character of the same theological structure's definitive components. The constructions commonly prove greater than the sum of the parts, for, when viewed separately, the components of the units bear no determinate sense or meaning; but when joined together, they do. And we shall see a great many such constructions, each leaving no doubt as to the meaning intended through the composite of native categories—a meaning we can always articulate and never find ambiguous.

Now, it is clear, fundamental to the approach to theological description taken here is a simple premise. Both types of compositions—constructions and connections—appeal to an unarticulated rationality, a logic everywhere in charge but nowhere signified. They adumbrate a substrate of thought of a coherent character. They show us the outline of a coherent theological system, one of simplicity and integrity. They point to the outlines of a corpus of self-evidently valid ways of joining native categories (whether mythic-narrative, whether legal-normative) into coherent discourse: the theological counterpart to syntactic rules of language.

By constructions I refer to groupings of head-nouns that produce sense and not nonsense—never "the evil Mordecai and the good Haman," but always "Abraham, Isaac, and Jacob." But the set of native categories by itself bears meaning only when joined to a proposition, a corresponding list, or some other point of definition *and limitation*. There—where native categories join—the meaning of the grouping emerges. These constructions form the counterpart to the rules of syntax; they tell us what word may join with what other word, and with what consequence in meaning.

Connections people deem self-evident offer a glimpse into the established structures of the theology that the documents invoke. Constructions adumbrate the working system that governs in the documents. These comprise, on the one side, the rationality of inserted discourses that seem to violate the rules of structure and order otherwise dominant throughout, and, on the other side, the structure and organization of a document. Questions of system encompass the matters of rationality, principles of self-evidence, laws of list-making. These then concern the points of emphasis and current stress, the agenda that comes to expression in whatever topic is subject to analysis. The framers of the composites that comprise the document pursue a uniform analytical program throughout. They never leave us in doubt as to what they wish to discover in connections they take for granted or demonstrate in constructions they invoke. Questions of structure pertain to how the document is put together and is so framed as to convey its framers' messages in consistent forms.

By explaining the coherence of the whole—self-evident connections of system, compelling constructions that find a place in a larger, also self-evident, structure—I mean to show the Rabbinic canon for what it is. And that is, a corpus of diverse documents that all speak the same language to say the same thing. And that language—like all enduring media of intellect—in a never-monotonous voice over and over again says in diverse and interesting ways the same thing about many things. It is a language of theology that changes the subject only to re-present the original subject itself. Among the diverse types of data that yield an account of the rules of forming intelligible sentences of a theological character, these are the two types that serve to establish the syntax of the Rabbinic theological grammar.

CHAPTER FOUR

SEMANTICS: MODELS OF ANALYSIS, EXPLANATION, AND ANTICIPATION

> The goal of generative linguistics theory is a description, in structure mode, of what a human being knows (largely unconsciously) that enables him to speak a natural language.
>
> —Jackendoff, *Semantics and Cognition*

I. Defining Semantics

In appealing to the metaphor of grammar to demonstrate the presence, in the Rabbinic canon, of system and order, logic about God, I pursue a sequence of questions that yield a continuous answer: What do people everywhere and always know a priori, that is, in this context, prior to formulating any statements they deem to make sense? And, more to the point, does this a priori system of thought exhibit those traits of cogency and coherence that we discern as logical within the framework of logic that defines our own understanding of matters? I here demonstrate that the documents of the Rabbinic canon appeal to a system of thought that everywhere defines matters and appeals to a self-evident logic of order, proportion, and balance that we can readily comprehend. David Aaron phrases matters in this language:

> A formal theory of theology must be expressive enough to account for the distinctions of meaning made by those people operating within that theological system. Such distinctions of meaning include the semantic relations—most importantly, inference—that speakers within that theology draw upon when they employ certain words, phrases, sentences. It must also provide the basis on which speakers relate words, phrases, and sentences to their understanding of non-linguistic meaning, so that they can make judgments of reference and truth. Theology is just that system. As to judgments of reference and truth, only certain judgments are intelligible given the semantics of the theological system. But a whole lot of apparatus (words, rules of syntax, rules governing how

meaning is derived) must be in place before those non-linguistic judgments can be executed.[1]

A theological system everywhere governs. Its inner logic is always presupposed. Its modes of thought and even specific propositions dictate the identification of data that await analysis, the character of problems that require explanation, and the implications that define what is to be anticipated. That explains the equation worked out here: semantics is to grammar as models of analysis, explanation, and anticipation are to theology. The one identifies what is implicit in intelligible discourse and therefore intuitive or presupposed, the other, what is implicit in the particulars of religious discourse and therefore definitive of the a priori theological system—one that makes possible an immediate understanding of a range of statements that have never been made before but, once made make sense.

Syntax declares what is possible and what is not, semantics makes judgments about the real world, crossing the boundary that separates the possible from the uniquely intelligible. If syntax dictates—among other things—how nouns form clusters of meaning,[2] semantics provides the rules for how they do not. That is to say, theoretically intelligible combinations of head-nouns, such as syntax yields, turn out to bear no meaning at all. Then semantics takes over and dictates out of the intelligible what is in fact plausible.

To turn to a concrete case, a theological counterpart, in the documents of the Rabbinic canon, to the famous example of syntactically correct but semantic gibberish, "Colorless green sleeps furiously" is "the Men of Sodom will have a share in the world to come." That sentence is composed of two available native categories, "Men of Sodom" and "world to come." The combination does not violate theological syntax by contradicting known laws of construction or connection such as we identified in Chapter Three, for we may form a set of word clusters out of the phrases "Men of Sodom" and "world to come." But the theological counterpart to semantics dictates that a word is missing. The "will have" totally violates the theological

---

[1] David Aaron, personal letter, May 26, 1997.
[2] Syntax concerns the structure of every aspect of a statement, including everything from nouns to verbs to prepositional structures, not just nouns. But for the present purpose only a single aspect of syntax pertains.

givens of the Rabbinic canon and is therefore unintelligible. The absence of "not" changes everything. Thus in terms of our governing metaphor, the sentence is semantically unintelligible. It is our task to find out why, to uncover some of the givens of rationality and inner logic that govern throughout. That carries us to the description of some of the rules of rational construction that transcend matters of vocabulary/native categories and syntax/connection and construction.

I have chosen three types of models for exposition of intelligible propositions in intelligible language: models of theological analysis, models of theological explanation, and models of theological anticipation. To describe each stereotype pattern, I collect from all of the documents of the Rabbinic canon that I have translated a random sample of instances. These are described, and then, at the end, I have a systematic summary of the generalizations as to method and system. The criteria for relevance to the common theology of the documents are easily stated. The first type of model—analysis of what is remarkable—will identify traits of God and God's self-manifestation in the Torah, broadly construed: what we know about the realm of the real and supernatural; the second—the explanation of the result of analysis—how we go about solving theological problems; the third—anticipation of the consequence of what we have learned for what is going to happen in the future—where we look when we wish to peer into the future and how we take the measure of that vision. So we go in quest of [1] theological facts, [2] the reasons that explain those facts, and [3] the outcomes that lend importance to those facts, what difference they make.

II. Models of Rationality

How does one identify the documents' models of rationality? It is by generalizing on cases, which is to say, forming a picture of the models—indicated by traits of regularity shared by cases—that dictate the traits of individual propositions and the formulations thereof. Through examination of sets of cases of clearly acceptable discourse—discourse characteristic of the documents—we uncover common traits of logic and cogency. Then we may describe some of the traits of coherence and sense that define the governing pattern: modes of thought, recurrent givens that govern how problems of detail are worked out. These yield the (hypothetical) rules that through the writings of the Rabbinic canon govern the making of intelligible statements of a given order and that identify unintelligible ones as well. The distinct categories of thought may be simply stated as follows: "what?" or analysis; "why?" or explanation; and "so what?" or anticipation. I have limited the inquiry to models of three kinds, which moreover connect to form a single enormous pattern of reasoned inquiry. I describe the Rabbinic canon's models of analysis, explanation, and anticipation: how problems are identified and solved, how the result is explained, and how the explanation affords extrapolation from past to present to future. These models govern the formulation of statements concerning how things are the way they are, why that is so, and what meaning and predictive possibility we derive from the patterns we discern.

At stake therefore is the answer to this question: How, through the formation of words into sentences and sentences into coherent paragraphs, do the framers of compositions (and even composites)[3] make intelligible and compelling statements? What we shall see through dozens of specific cases is that the cases persistently appeal to a set of rules, a definition of how matters are to be set forth: models.[4] Models discerned here rest on deep foundations of thought systematically conceived, a fundamental rationality. That is not to suggest the theological counterpart to semantics forms the only indicator of rationality. For syntax on its own may rule out of all intelligibility such statements as "the good Haman, the evil Mordecai." Even the native categories or head-nouns will eliminate a broad range of possible but unacceptable matters, e.g., "idolatry" cannot stand at the head of an affirmative sentence, nor can "gentiles," "gods," or a variety of other head-nouns that the system as a whole stigmatizes. But while both

---

[3] The distinction between composition and composite (of compositions) is fundamental to my literary analysis of the Rabbinic documents. See *Making the Classics in Judaism: The Three Stages of Literary Formation* (Brown Judaic Studies; Atlanta: Scholars Press, 1990); *The Rules of Composition of the Talmud of Babylonia: The Cogency of the Bavli's Composite* (South Florida Studies in the History of Judaism; Atlanta: Scholars Press, 1991; and *Sources and Traditions: Types of Composition in the Talmud of Babylonia.* (South Florida Studies in the History of Judaism; Atlanta: Scholars Press, 1992).

[4] "Patterns" or "paradigms" would have served equally well, but "model" seems more modest, because the word claims less and insists only upon recurrence of a few simple rules of procedure.

vocabulary and syntax in their theological counterparts carry a large part of the burden of rationality, it is to semantics that we turn for a metaphor for the ubiquitous rules of rational thought that govern the entirety of the Rabbinic canon, working themselves out through all of its documentary realizations. And when we have examined a suitable repertoire of models of intelligible discourse, we shall find possible the identification of rules of rationality that form the theological counterpart to semantic rules of language.

III. Semantics Is to Language as Models of Cogent Discourse Are to Theology

Semantics/language = *models of cogent discourse/theology.* Since semantics dictates intelligibility, our task, specifically, is to investigate the properties of the propositional thought that throughout the documents characterize theological compositions of the Rabbinic canon.[5] For implicit in each composition is the conviction of its authorship: the rules of cogent discourse (that is, the counterpart to semantics) of what is said, not only the language and pattern of formulation of the particular message, makes the point in intelligible and even compelling fashion. Hence the self-evidence of what by definition—inclusion in the authoritative writings—is deemed intelligible captures our attention. I have identified models of three types of discourse: how we describe data, or models of analysis; how we analyze data, or models of explanation; and how we interpret data, or models of anticipation—what we think we know that is useful, about what is going to happen for instance, on the basis of our description and analysis.

In sizable sets of samples we locate the traits of self-evidence out of the kinds of evidence adduced. These yield the rules governing the identification and organization and presentation of the very types of propositions, evidence, and arguments that are implicit, in the expo-

---

[5] I have conducted inquiries along these lines for principal documents, e.g., the Mishnah in *Judaism as Philosophy. The Method and Message of the Mishnah* (Columbia, S.C.: University of South Carolina Press, 1991); a principal Midrash-compilation in *Judaism and Scripture: The Evidence of Leviticus Rabbah* (Chicago: University of Chicago Press, 1986); and the Bavli in *Jerusalem and Athens: The Congruity of Talmudic and Classical Philosophy* (Supplements to the Journal for the Study of Judaism; Leiden: Brill, 1997). But, as is clear, this is my first effort to cut across documentary Lines.

sition of theological conviction. This will allow us to connect at the
substrate of modes of thought the two divisions of the Rabbinic canon
that form its native categories, Halakhah and Aggadah. How the one
relates to the other—the norms of law realizing in concrete ways the
norms of conviction that correspond—remains to be examined in a
systematic way. While efforts to show the correspondence of a law to
a detail of theology have had some success, no systematic foundations
have been laid that will allow us a comprehensive view of matters.
That can come only when the modes of thought in the theological
component of the Rabbinic canon have been identified as have those
of the Halakhic component in its fundamental statement, the Mishnah (with the Tosefta), and in its analytical continuation in the Bavli.[6]

In the documents of the Rabbinic canon, these rules emerge
through regularities; things are always said in one way rather than in
some other; proof of one type rather than another is adduced; arguments, commonly not articulated but treated as blatant, will dictate
the course of thought in one path rather than another. We can find
enough cases to validate these on the character of such rules. These
rules, when exposed at an appropriate level of abstraction and generalization, I call "models." And the models in theological discourse
form the counterpart to semantics within the grammar of a language.
What I wish to find out is, what are the choices in thought and its
expression that confronted a thinker and writer who wished to make
a point, solve a problem, set forth a proposition? The answers are
spread before us in the documents themselves. We then take up the
work of examining the data for regularity and order, yielding rules
that permit us to predict what cannot be said and explain why what
can make sense does make sense.

These answers form the results of the semantics of the grammar of
the theological language before us. With vocabulary properly identified and set forth in syntactic constructions, a language makes possible
the formulation of sequences of propositions of meaning—identifying

---

[6] Among my books see, for the Mishnah, *Judaism: The Evidence of the Mishnah*
(Chicago: University of Chicago Press, 1981) and *Judaism as Philosophy: The Method and
Message of the Mishnah*; for dialectical argument in the Talmud, *Talmudic Dialectics:
Types and Forms* (South Florida Studies in the History of Judaism 1 [*Introduction.
Tractate Berakhot and the Divisions of Appointed Times*] and 2 [*The Divisions of Damages and
Holy Things and Tractate Niddah*]; Atlanta: Scholars Press, 1995); and for a general
statement, *Jerusalem and Athens.*

also those propositions that violate the rules of language. These semantic rules make possible the formulation of a nearly unlimited number of intelligible statements but also indicate an unlimited number of unintelligible ones. With a clear account of types of vocabulary and sorts of syntax in hand, we turn to identify some of the rules for the construction of intelligible discourse: the semantics of the Rabbinic canon. We therefore ask the question, what, in theology, forms the counterpart to the semantics that governs distinguishing intelligible from unintelligible statements? Fully articulated models show how theological propositions are set forth: the vocabulary that is used, the connections that are drawn and the combinations that are made, yielding the propositions the formation of which proves not occasional but exemplary. Working from the cases outward, therefore, we shall find guidance in how the system as a whole defines its rationality: what can, and cannot, be said, therefore thought—with immediate and complete comprehension. I shall now give simple examples of how a theological system, nowhere articulated, everywhere anticipated, precipitates thought and defines intellection.

IV. MODELS OF ANALYSIS

A model of analysis will define [1] the types of facts that are assembled and examined, [2] the methods deemed self-evidently probative in producing knowledge out of those facts, and [3] the overall traits of the analytical process: what questions are asked, how are they probatively answered? The analytical model followed in the documents of the Rabbinic canon will find noteworthy either sets of facts that yield a pattern in Scripture or facts that violate such an anticipated pattern set forth by Scripture. It will note the irregularity or the unusual fact. It will find in that pattern or irregularity proof for, or challenge to, an established principle. So the analytical model will invoke and seek to test an established system and to confirm the validity of that system.

We start with the documents' identification of the sort of problems that require attention, which I have defined as "the what." By that I mean, what attracts attention and invites examination, what sort of data pose questions, and what sort of questions do they pose? What data are deemed neutral, requiring no inspection, producing no possibility of useful knowledge? In ordinary terms, when we ask how a set of kindred writings re-presents information as knowledge, we ask, [1] what kinds of data are deemed to constitute noteworthy (as distinct from inert) information?; [2] of what does the analysis of data consist? (That is to say, once facts have attracted attention, what questions do we address to them to produce useful answers?); and [3] what conclusions are drawn, generalizations proposed, propositions demonstrated, in the process of turning raw data into useful knowledge?

A model of analysis will show how diverse data—those of Scripture in particular—are assembled into an orderly and comprehensible pattern so as to yield a generalization, a conclusion, a rule that can encompass further data and sustain testing. Anomalies require analysis, and regularization defines the goal thereof. The way of analysis directs thought to the work of natural history: comparison and contrast of data in quest of the order that the data yield: generalization out of a selection of well-dissected, properly classified, therefore probative cases. In the documents of the Rabbinic canon attention focuses on the quest for regularity and order, the generalization that diverse data yield in common. An act that is noteworthy is then to be compared with another such act, the comparison then producing a generalization. Abraham saddles his own ass when taking Isaac to Moriah, Balaam saddles his own ass when journeying to curse Israel: love or hatred change the natural order of things—that forms an analytical syllogism. When confronted with established facts, the composer of a coherent unit of thought will most commonly ask what generalization holds these data (whether comparable or contrastive) together? The result then moves us onward to the second and third stages of thought: What do I learn from these facts that I can use in making sense of other facts? How from the known may I peer into the unknown, from past and present into future time? These define the analytical problem and prospect that are characteristic of the writings at hand.

Let us then find our way to the starting point; whence, first, the facts that await regularization and analysis? All analytical inquiry, then, commences in a fact or a set of facts that Scripture produces. Scripture forms a translucent overlay over everyday reality, imposing its lines of structure upon the ordinary and imparting shape to the workaday world. The books of Scripture—and only a selection thereof—persistently take the center of discussion, so that whatever they allege is so is taken as fact. Not only so, but selected passages of Scripture serve as the principal source of facts; those deriving from other sources, for example, nature not set forth in Scripture, or history and politics not deriving from Scripture, appear only very rarely. When they do, moreover, they turn out to replicate facts of nature, history, or politics that Scripture has already designed, e.g., the destruction of the second temple, the paragon of virtue or sanctity, the sage in the position of the prophet for example.

So Scripture, the counterpart of nature for philosophy's natural history, provides nearly all of the remarkable facts that demand attention. Scripture's are the data that demand regularization, comparison, and contrast. Scripture's are the facts that may contradict a hypothesis or demonstrate it, but it is rare that facts deriving from any other source prove a point and, once a hypothesis resting on Scripture's facts is set forth, facts deriving from some other source *never* come under consideration at all, except, perhaps, to form exceptions that can be explained by appeal to the rule established in Scripture's facts. To prove a point, it suffices to set forth three or more cases from Scripture; these establish a pattern, and the pattern is its own proof.

That work of examination of what is noteworthy does not exhaust the analytical process. Then, as I said, the method of comparison and contrast of facts takes over to produce a generalization, which may or may not require further testing against more facts. Not only so, but the second and third stages await. For once analysis has established a pattern, the work of explanation takes over, imputing intention and sense to the pattern; and from that point, the real intention enters in, which is to predict what is going to happen. The documents viewed whole form an exercise in the analysis of the present in quest of an explanation thereof which yields reliable knowledge of the future.

That quest, implicit even within the analytical process in its initial stages, emerges in a single example. In this case we see a large-scale project, the comparison of facts involving Abram with facts involving his descendants later on, yielding the proposition that Israel lives out the paradigm originally set by the life and actions of Abram. So the work of analysis involves identifying indicative actions of Abram and matching them with actions of the descendants that conform to the same indicative traits—comparison and contrast in the most blatant formulation. And the model shows how at stake at every point is the future and what is to be done to shape that future.

Abraham as Model of Israel, the People

We shall now see how, in the process of comparison and contrast and in the quest for patterns of intelligibility, facts are formed into—more accurately, made to conform to established—paradigms. Here, each statement about Abram at Gen. 12:10–20 finds a counterpart in the later history of Israel, whether Jacob or the children of Jacob. The analysis of the data will establish a fact that allows us to know what is going to happen in the future. (The explanation of the result of analysis will produce the same result, as we shall see presently.) The present case analyzes the facts pertinent to Abram's actions, matching what Abram did then with what Israel would do later on, setting up a list of the one and comparing that list with a comparable catalogue of actions of the other in time to come. The analysis then yields a single result. Whatever Abraham did Israel later on would do, and whatever was said about Abraham would find its counterpart in the later life of Israel:

Genesis Rabbah XL:VI.1ff.

A. "And for her sake he dealt well with Abram" (Gen. 12:16):

B. "And Pharaoh gave men orders concerning him, [and they set him on the way, with his wife and all that he had]" (Gen. 12:20).

C. R. Phineas in the name of R. Hoshaiah said, "The Holy One, blessed be he, said to our father, Abraham, 'Go and pave a way before your children.' [Set an example for them, so that whatever you do now, they will do later on.]

D. "You find that whatever is written in regard to our father, Abraham, is written also with regard to his children.

E. "With regard to Abraham it is written, 'And there was a famine in the land' (Gen. 12:10) In connection with Israel: 'For these two years has the famine been in the land" (Gen. 45:6).

F. "With regard to Abraham: 'And Abram went down into Egypt' (Gen. 12:10).

G. "With regard to Israel: 'And our fathers went down into Egypt' (Num. 20:15).

H. "With regard to Abraham: 'To sojourn there' (Gen. 12:10).

I. "With regard to Israel: 'To sojourn in the land we have come' (Gen. 47:4).

J. "With regard to Abraham: 'For the famine is heavy in the land' (Gen. 12:10).

K. "With regard to Israel: 'And the famine was heavy in the land' (Gen. 43:1).

L. "With regard to Abraham: 'And it came to pass, when he drew

near to enter into Egypt' (Gen. 12:11: 'When he was about to enter
Egypt').

M. "With regard to Israel: 'And when Pharaoh drew near' (Ex. 14:10).

N. "With regard to Abraham: 'And they will kill me but you will they
keep alive' (Gen. 12:12).

O. "With regard to Israel: 'Every son that is born you shall cast into
the river, and every daughter you shall save alive' (Ex. 1:22).

P. "With regard to Abraham: 'Say you are my sister, that it may go
well with me because of you' (Gen. 12:13).

Q. "With regard to Israel: 'And God dealt well with the midwives' (Ex.
1:20).

R. "With regard to Abraham: 'And when Abram had entered Egypt'
(Gen. 12:14).

S. "Israel: 'Now these are the names of the sons of Israel, who came
into Egypt' (Ex. 1:1).

T. "With regard to Abraham: 'And Abram was very rich in cattle, in
silver, and in gold' (Gen. 13:23).

U. "With regard to Israel: 'And he brought them forth with silver and
gold' (Ps. 105:37).

V. "With regard to Abraham: And Pharaoh gave men orders concerning him and they set him on the way' (Gen. 12:20).

W. "Israel: 'And the Egyptians were urgent upon the people to send
them out' (Ex. 12:33).

X. "With regard to Abraham: 'And he went on his journeys' (Gen.
13:3).

Y. "With regard to Israel: 'These are the journeys of the children of
Israel' (Num. 33:1)."

The analytical method requires system, and the mélange of data—an
orderly repertoire of verses involving Abram, diverse verses of
Scripture that pertain to Israel—is systematically ordered. What we
have are two lists brought into juxtaposition, a familiar mode of
ordering diverse data. The one list matched against the other, the former—Abram's acts, the known-to-be-orderly list—imposes order
upon Israel's acts, the chaos of the latter being reduced to rules, and
the match provides the demonstration that is besought. The upshot
of the comparison and contrast yields useful knowledge that both
explains Israel's present condition and instructs how matters are to be
affected in the future.

The analytical inquiry in fact promises to demonstrate a proposition, not merely investigate data that yield one, as in our time we
should understand the work. For the generative question that governs
throughout, What is going to happen to Israel, and what is Israel sup-

posed to do? derives not from the data, nor even from the problem of ordering the data, nor yet from the proposition that the work in the end yields. It derives rather from the system that calls attention to these data rather than some other, because these data will yield exactly what the system to begin with knows to be true. And that is, that Israel recapitulates the life and teachings of the patriarchs. More to the point, what the patriarchs did governs what Israel now endures. That matters because of what must come: prediction, or, in my language, explanation and anticipation. The system that works out its intellectual disciplines in the identification of what requires analysis, and in conducting analysis through a labor of comparison and contrast and generalization therefrom, means to set forth the principles that govern what happens to Israel in the future.

The hypothesis announced at the outset is turned into a theory. So much for what is accomplished. Now let us take note of what is not required in the analytical process. First, we identify no dissonant cases. The proposition is not tested. Actions of Abram that have no bearing upon the life of his children are not introduced. Events in the life of Israel that do not correlate with occasions in the life of Abram are never invoked. So however systematic the demonstration, the survey of evidence is determined by the proposition to be demonstrated. Second, no contrary proposition is proposed—let alone a null hypothesis! Third, no effort is made to explain the evidence by appeal to a hypothesis other than the one that is announced at the outset. Fourth, as noted, no data beyond Scripture are introduced, e.g., stories of everyday conduct in the present age, reference to events beyond those recorded in Scripture, appeal to the present condition of Israel. True, the method is that of natural history. But in classifying and making hierarchies, natural history investigates all the data of nature; sages have chosen instead the revealed facts of Scripture, those alone. An a prior system is here being served. To state matters differently, nature is to philosophy as Scripture is to the sages' theology.

The upshot is that a highly determinate corpus of data comes into view; what is worthy of note—remarkable in the simplest sense—to begin with is the corpus of Scripture, with special reference to the narrative in the Torah for Abram, and statements in the Prophets and (to lesser extent) Writings for Israel. The very presentation of matters contains no claim at undertaking a free standing inquiry, one comparable to the pursuit of knowledge as we know it. Rather, the composer of the composition has set forth to demonstrate the order that emerges within the finite corpus of facts supplied by Scripture and intends from the very outset to prove a point, not to investigate a problem. What we deal with is theological demonstration in the manner of natural history.

Time and again we shall determine that an encompassing, enormous but simple theological system animates discourse, start to finish. The composer did not pretend to approach the data in a spirit of mere curiosity; not a philosopher seeking the order of this, the natural world, he was a theologian, intending to set forth the logic of matters having to do with God's actions and intentions in this world, with Israel. The data that he examined presented facts supplied by God in the Torah, and the task he took for himself was to turn those facts into useful knowledge of God's plans and program for Israel in the world. In the language I have used, the composer drew upon a model of explanation that itself emerged from an established system, a construction of ideas that formed a given, that sustained all further thought and animated it. Then he knew exactly what he was going to find, which is what he set out to demonstrate: "Go and pave a way before your children."

What is at stake? It is an explanation of Israel's present condition, and still more urgent, identification of the operative reasons that will lead to viable hypotheses concerning Israel's future prospects. Here the systemic subtext shapes articulated thought: the present properly analyzed and explained contains within itself the entire past, the whole future, all together, all at once. We turn to Abram because we wish out of the past to know the future and because we take as fact that Israel's future recapitulates the past of Abram. God has laid out matters from beginning to end; Scripture not only records the past but provides the key, through patterns we can identify in the present, to the future. The premise of analysis then is, when we understand the facts in hand, we also can learn the rules. So in a world created in accord with the requirements of exact balance, proportion, correspondence, complementarity and commensurability—matters that will preoccupy us when we come to the third part of this project, models of anticipation—there are no mysteries, only facts not yet noticed, analyses not yet undertaken, propositions not yet proved.

To summarize the analytical process of the Rabbinic canon: the facts that are classified for purposes of finding a generalization derive from Scripture. That is an important (if obvious) fact, because at each point we shall want to know the source of the data that are examined and ordered and how the several sources of facts are themselves shown to relate. Where facts from one source may contradict those from another, the system will have a problem to work out. Here the actions of Abraham are paralleled out of the history of Israel. The demonstration is so detailed and exact that one could postulate a narrative intent, that is, an explicit effort to retell Abraham's story in terms of Israel later on. The analytical result is then compelling.

V. Models of Explanation

Once we know what requires explanation, we should like to find out what constitutes an adequate explanation of a noteworthy piece of knowledge. A model of explanation will take the results of analysis—the articulation of a general rule emerging from and validated by diverse cases—and provide a rational account of the cause and consequence of the regularities that have been identified. Analysis yields a rule. Explanation accounts for the rule by appeal to the system that the rule embodies and describes. That system, everywhere taken for granted and no where expressed in broad and abstract terms, rests upon Scripture but only asymmetrically. The system embedded within the deep structure of thought answers the question, to what do the composers appeal when they tell us why things are the way they are, e.g., why is it that Abram's children recapitulate his life? The answer embodies in detail the system, or the logic, that pervades the whole.

Here—at the sources of rational explanation systemically sustained—we reach logic or rationality particular to the documents of the Rabbinic canon. For what serves as a plausible explanation—what is logical and rational—obviously will vary from system to system. Everyone understands the variables of rational explanation and understands that from the character of a suitable explanation we gain entry into the inner structure of an entire cultural system. Yesterday's phlogiston is today's oxygen, and while for long centuries Ptolemaic astronomy adequately described the heavens, Copernicus's models of explanation of the same facts have taken over. Our task, then, is to identify the paradigm that defines reasons for things, the modes of logic and rationality that all together constitute self-evident explanation in the documents of the Rabbinic canon.

Clearly, theoretical description without attention to cases cannot serve. A concrete instance will open the way to a broader account of models of explanation. Here is a case. We raise the question of why matters are the way they are, and, as it happens, the case at hand connects directly to the foregoing: why is it that the lives of Abraham and his children, Israel, run in so strikingly parallel paths?

Ancestral Merit and Virtue

The virtue of the latter generations responds to the merit achieved by the ancestors:

Ruth Rabbah LXIV:I.4

A. [Supply: "So she held it, and he measured out six measures of barley and laid it upon her":]

B. Said R. Judah b. R. Simon, "It is on the merit [zekhut] of 'and he measured out six measures of barley and laid it upon her' that six righteous persons came forth from him, and each one of them had six virtues.

C. "[These are] David, Hezekiah, Josiah, Hananiah-Mishael-Azariah [counted as a single entry], Daniel, and the royal Messiah:

D. "David: 'Skillful in playing and a mighty man of valor, and a man of war, prudent in affairs, and a comely person, and the Lord is with him' (1 Sam. 16:18).

E. "Hezekiah: 'That the government may be increased and of peace there be no end, upon the throne of David and upon his kingdom, to establish it and to uphold it, through justice and through righteousness' (Is. 9:6). 'And his name is called wonderful, counselor, mighty, strong, everlasting father, prince of peace' (Is. 9:5)."

G. [Reverting to E:] "Josiah: 'For he shall be as a tree planted by waters, that spreads out its roots by the river' (Jer. 17:8).

H. "Hananiah, Mishael, and Azariah: 'Youths in whom there was no blemish but fair to look on, and skilful in all wisdom, and skilful in knowledge, and discerning in thought, and such as had ability' (Dan. 1:4).

I. "Daniel: 'A surpassing spirit, and knowledge and understanding, interpreting of dreams and declaring of riddles and loosing of knots were found in the same Daniel' (Dan. 5:12).

J. "... and the royal Messiah: 'And the spirit of the Lord shall rest upon him, the spirit of wisdom and understanding' (Is. 11:2)."

The actions of the ancestors, particularly those of uncoerced grace—here, the gift of generosity—produce effects for their descendants. A small act at the outset multiplies in its effects later on. The six measures yielded six righteous persons, each with six distinctive virtues, as indicated. Then the system that sustains the passage presupposes a variety of principles, which are to be specified. The substance of the explanation—the merit effected through Boaz's act of uncoerced generosity—appeals to the self-evidence of a world in which the past is ever present, and the present forms an integral part of the past. The character of the future is implicit throughout, the figure of the Messiah overshadowing all else.

Then rationality is established by appeal not to the given of Scripture but to the conviction that balanced opposites, proportion, order, complementarity, and commensurability—these traits of perfection characterize creation and the Creator. All things are subject to the rules of logic and order that man's own mind obeys, and explanation in the end must derive from the sources of nature and its laws and the Torah and its regularities, each recapitulating the mind and will of the loving and merciful and reasonable God, in whose image, after whose likeness, man is made.

VI. Models of Anticipation

Sages compared themselves to prophets and insisted that their knowledge of the Torah provided a key to the future. That is the polemic that pervades *Genesis Rabbah*, for example, and *Sifré Deuteronomy*. Knowing why noteworthy things take place provided them with that key. For a model of anticipation will extrapolate from the results of analysis and explanation those governing rules of an orderly world that define a useful hypothesis concerning the future. Having identified regularities and defined descriptive laws, then accounted for those rules by spelling out the systemic reasons behind them, sages had every reason to peer over the beckoning horizon. For their basic conviction affirmed the order and regularity of creation, its perfection. If, therefore, they knew the rules and how they worked (including remissions of the rules), sages insisted they could predict how the future would take shape as well.

That is why they could ask, Given what we know about past and present and the signals of Providence that explain the condition of

the world, what shall we anticipate for time to come? Like the
prophets before them but thinking along quite other lines, sages spoke
with certainty, therefore, about what Israel may expect in the future.
But there was this difference. Prophets invoked God's explicit statements about the future. Sages' messages, by contrast, took shape as a
result of the analytical soundings sages made and explained, the data
they formed into rules, the rules the logic of which they set forth by
way of explanation. Theirs was the way of the natural historian and
the philosopher. But for them the path carried them into Scripture,
not nature, and into the logic of God's plan for the world, not the
telos of nature's impersonal perfection.

These few generalizations suffice to carry us to an illustrative case,
out of which we may construct a model. Here is a case that specifies
what does, and does not, shape Israel's destiny. It is a fine example
of how the system provides the tools for explaining the present and
peering into the future. The system's basic categories, in this case,
Israel, and its self-evidently valid bases for forming constructions for
the purpose of comparison and contrast, in this case, Israel and the
stars, yield a problem. It is, do the stars govern Israel's affairs? The
answer sages give appears contradictory, some sages affirming, others
negating, that proposition. But the composite viewed whole—the
weight of opinion that is cited, the evidence that is adduced, the trend
of argument and the governing considerations—leaves no doubt as to
the normative opinion and its logic. Israel is not subject to astrologi-
cal influence, because Israel's future is decided by other considerations altogether: mainly its own *zekhut*, as we shall now see.

Astrology and Israel

How does Israel know what to anticipate? The answer is negative:
Israel is not subject to the influence of the stars.

Bavli *Shabbat* 24:3 III.9–12/156a–c

III.9 A. It has been stated:
       B. R. Hanina says, "One's star is what makes one smart, one's
           star is what gives wealth, and Israel is subject to the stars."
       C. R. Yohanan said, "Israel is not subject to the stars."
       D. And R. Yohanan is consistent with views expressed elsewhere,
           for said R. Yohanan, "How on the basis of Scripture do we

know that Israel is not subject to the stars? As it is said, 'Thus says the Lord, Do not learn the way of the gentiles, nor be dismayed at the signs of the heavens, for the nations are dismayed at them' (Jer. 10:2). They are dismayed, but the Israelites are not dismayed."

III.10 A. And so Rab takes the view that Israel is not subject to the stars, for said R. Judah said Rab, "How on the basis of Scripture do we know that Israel is not subject to the stars? As it is said, 'And he brought him forth outside' (Gen. 15:5). Said Abraham before the Holy One, blessed be He, 'Lord of the world, "Someone born in my household is my heir" (Gen. 15:3).' He said to him, 'Not at all. "But he who will come forth out of your own loins" (Gen. 1:4).' He said before him, 'Lord of the world, I have closely examined my star, and I have seen that I am destined to have no children.' He said to him, 'Abandon this astrology of yours—Israel is not subject to astrology. Now what's your calculation? Is it that Jupiter stands in the west [and that is your constellation]? I'll turn it back and set it up in the East.' And so it is written, 'Who has raised up Jupiter from the east? He has summoned it for his sake' (Is. 41:2)."

B. It is also the position of Samuel that Israel is not subject to the stars.

C. For Samuel and Ablat were in session, and some people going along to a lake. Said Ablat to Samuel, "That man is going but won't come back, a snake will bite him and he'll die."

D. Said to him Samuel, "Yeah, well, if he's an Israelite, he will go and come back."

E. While they were in session, he went and came back. Ablat got up and took of the man's knapsack and found in it a snake cut up and lying in two pieces.

F. Said Samuel to the man, "What did you do [today in particular]?"

G. He said to him, "Every day we tossed our bread into one pot and ate, but today one of us had no bread, and he was shamed. I said to him, 'I will go and collect the bread.' When I came to him, I made as if to go and collect the bread, so he shouldn't be ashamed."

H. He said to him, "You have carried out a religious duty."

I. Samuel went forth and expounded, "'But charity delivers from death' (Prov. 10:2)—not from a grotesque death, but from death itself."

III.11 A. It is also the position of Aqiba that Israel is not subject to the stars.

B. For R. Aqiba had a daughter. Chaldeans [astrologers] told him, "On the day that she goes into the bridal canopy, a snake will bite her and she'll die."

C. This worried him a lot. On that day she took a brooch and stuck it into the wall, and by chance it sank into the eye of a snake. The next day when she took it out, the snake came trailing along after it.

D. Her father said to her, "What did you do [today in particular]?"

E. She said to him, "In the evening a poor man came to the door, and everyone was busy with the banquet so no one could take care of him, so I took some of what was given to me and gave it to him."

F. He said to her, "You have carried out a religious duty."

G. R. Aqiba went forth and expounded, "'But charity delivers from death' (Prov. 10:2)—not from a grotesque death, but from death itself."

III.12 A. It is also the position of R. Nahman bar Isaac that Israel is not subject to the stars.

B. For to the mother of R. Nahman bar Isaac the Chaldean said, "Your son will be a thief." She didn't let him go bareheaded, saying, "Keep your head covered, so fear of Heaven may be upon you, and pray for mercy."

C. He didn't know why she said that to him. One day he was in session, studying under a palm tree. His head covering fell off. He lifted his eyes and saw the palm tree, and was overcome by temptation; he climbed up and bit off a cluster of dates with his teeth.

The difference of opinion concerns not the validity of astrology but the applicability of astrology to Israel in particular. The composite is so constructed as to set forth the weight of opinion, acknowledging difference, that Israel is subject to rules unique to Israel, and not to astrology. That is explicit in connection with none other than Abraham himself.

If Israel's destiny is shaped by the virtue of the ancestors, transmitted through a heritage of unearned grace for which the word *zekhut* stands in this context (that is, *zekhut abot*, the unearned grace credited to the fathers and bequeathed by them to the children of Israel), then to that destiny other forces, such as astrology represents, prove null. Evidence then derives from [1] Scripture; [2] the interpretation of Scripture through a contributed narrative (III.10.A); [3] concrete events that show that individual Israelites are subject to a person's own *zekhut* or reward for meritorious actions of uncoerced generosity or love (very frequently involving women). Evidence then derives from diverse sources, and all the evidence points in a single direction. No differentiation among the types of evidence assigns greater probative value to one over another type. And, we see, a single conception comes to concrete expression in three different settings: one rationality makes its way through diverse problems of thought.

From a particular case, let us turn to the principal results: how the documents of the Rabbinic canon formulate their vision of the future. Each case produces a generalization, and, when they are viewed all together, a single encompassing conception emerges. The system's premises shape the cases and their rules of prediction. The theological counterpart to semantics then emerges not so much from our cases and the models they adumbrate as from the conceptions that are taken for granted: the definition of perfection, the certainty of balance, regularity, and order. To state matters simply, before we can ask about rules, we must assume the presence of regularity yielding rules. The system of thought—the theology—is everywhere taken for granted but no where articulately invoked.

Here are the principal results for prediction: The future contains few mysteries, since knowledge of why things happen as they do bears within itself a clear picture of what is going to happen, that is to say, of the necessary consequences of the violation of inexorable laws. People therefore may find certainty concerning the future by examining their present actions and attitudes. They also may be certain that if in this world they suffer, they will enjoy an enduring reward in the world to come, while if the wicked prosper, they too will continue onward and pay the price for their activities. The balance, order, above all, essential justice characteristic of the world that the system describes thus require a clear doctrine of the world to come, what lasts therein, and what ends. The key point is that the individual continues life beyond the grave.

As with models of explanation, so the models of anticipation recapitulate the systemic givens: creation is without flaw, all things serve a purpose, and rationality governs. The principal traits of creation are order, balance, proportion, all within a purposeful framework. Opposites balance, components of the whole structure complement one another, and good order permits us, out of the rules the past sets forth, to explain the present and to discern the shape of the future as well. The models of anticipation go over these established principles and rework them to suit individual cases. That is why the system throughout proves so wholly rational that, its logic mastered, the system's message for any particular case is wholly predictable, its positions subject to a single, prevailing rationality.

VII. The Upshot

The system is at stake in the theological counterpart to semantics; the specifics of cogent discourse turn out to derive from a generative structure, encompassing both modes of thought and massive conceptions of a concrete order. These modes we uncover by noting regularities of analytical procedure and repeated appeals to a finite corpus of explanations of a very particular character. It is at the point of anticipation that the specificities of the generative system come to the surface—but these turn out fully to embody the givens of the intellectual disciplines that govern: find the counterpart, establish the balance, take the measure of appropriate proportion. What we see throughout is how the rules of thought translate into method, logic, and perspective into the convictions of the system that animates the entirety of the documents. Each case turns out to respond to a systemic datum, and all the cases together to conform in detail to the system's generalizations—*which we can identify and state.*

This grammar of theological semantics tells us the rules of coherent, intelligible discourse, the details time and again recapitulating for a case the pertinent element of the governing rule. If we know the grammar, how the language works, the vocabulary, syntax, and semantics, we ought to be able to use the language for intelligible speech. Now that we have identified the native categories, the connections and constructions, the modes of analysis, explanation, and anticipation, we realize that a system guides and governs the whole. Because the world is the way we conceive it—that is, orderly and purposeful for philosophy, rational and ultimately benevolent for sages' reading of the way Scripture defines it—we can identify anomalies and conduct analyses, explain the results rationally, and extrapolate from the order of the present the shape and structure of the future.

So we ought to be able to set forth the entire system, to accomplish for theology what the use of a language achieves for linguistics. The theology of the Oral Torah sets forth the Written Torah as the embodiment of orderly rules that both describe and govern a perfect world, God's world in God's own words, received and read rationally, meaning, as an orderly, balanced, proportionate, commensurate structure and system. Had Aristotle read the Written Torah and chosen the media of law, myth, and exegesis for his discourse, the documents of the Rabbinic canon are what he would have written.

The Rabbinic sages of the Oral Torah read the Written Torah as philosophers read the book of nature. Both valued perfection, signified by balance, proportion, order, regularity. For philosophers perfection took the form of mathematics, physics, or biology. For the sages of the Rabbinic canon, perfection in the beginning took the form of Adam in Eden, and, in the end, matched and balanced, of Israel in the Land, enduring eternally—a tale there to be told and heard and taken to heart, for feeding the heart with hope. We shall now see how the theological system of the Aggadic documents and the theological structure of the Halakhic ones realized that conception, how the details yielded a whole and comprehensive picture.

PART TWO

THE THEOLOGICAL SYSTEM OF RABBINIC JUDAISM:
NORMS OF BELIEF

CHAPTER FIVE

PROLEGOMENON TO THE THEOLOGICAL SYSTEM THAT ANIMATES THE AGGADAH

I. Theology in Aggadic Realization: A System and its Dialectics

Rabbinic Judaism in documents of exegesis, narrative ("Aggadah"), exhortation, extension, and amplification of Scripture, sets forth a system that translates into governing principles the implications of Scripture's narratives, laws, and prophecies. That system recasts Scripture's mythic monotheism—monotheism set forth through the narrative of Scripture—into a working theology for holy Israel's cosmic and social order. That system does more than define set doctrine; it shows how new data may find their place in the established framework, new issues sorted out and resolved. It possesses a dynamism that sustains a functioning dialectics and so accommodates change and challenge over time.

How does monotheism frame its theology and define the generative issues thereof? A religion of numerous gods finds many solutions to one problem, a religion of only one God presents one solution to many problems. That is because life is seldom fair. Rules work only sometimes. To explain the reason, polytheisms adduce multiple causes of chaos, a god per anomaly. Diverse gods, possessed of uneven capacities and responsibilities, do various things, so, it stands to reason, outcomes ordinarily conflict. Monotheism by nature explains many things in a single way. One God rules. Life is meant to be fair, and just rules are supposed to describe what is ordinary, all in the name of that one and only God. So in monotheism a simple logic governs to limit ways of making sense of things.

But that logic contains its own dialectics, contradictory principles that come into conflict and so produce movement and require resolution. If one true God has done everything, then, since he is God all-powerful and omniscient, all things are credited to, and blamed on, him. In that case, given the human condition, he can be either good or bad, just or unjust—but not both. Responding to the generative dialectics of monotheism, Rabbinic Judaism so reads Scripture systematically to reveal the justice of the one and only God of all creation. God is not only God but also good. Appealing to the facts of Scripture, the Written part of the Torah, in the documents of the Oral part of the Torah, the Rabbinic canon, sages in the first six centuries of the Common Era constructed a coherent theology. Implicit in the Aggadic component of the Rabbinic canon, that theology set forth a cogent structure and logical system, to expose the justice of God. In Chapters Six through Nine, in detail, I show how and with what result. I identify the *logos* of God—the theology seen whole in the Torah, Written and Oral.

The categorical structure comprising that theology encompasses the components God and man; the Torah; Israel and the nations. The working system of Rabbinic Judaism finds its dynamic in the struggle between God's plan for creation—to create a perfect world of justice—and man's will. That is where myth enters in, the myth of Scripture with its ordering of events to produce a clear theological outcome. That myth embodies in a single paradigm the events contained in the matched sequences, involving first Adam, then Israel, the following events: rebellion, sin, punishment, repentance, and atonement; exile and return; the disruption of world order and the restoration of world order. None of these categories and propositions is new; anyone familiar with the principal components of the faith and piety of Judaism, the Written Torah, the Oral Torah, and the liturgy of home and synagogue, will find them paramount. It is not in identifying but in forming them into a *logos*—a sustained, rigorous, coherent argument, that can be set forth in narrative-sequential form, a vigorously working system—that I make my contribution in this part of the Handbook.

Let me set forth a somewhat more elaborate synopsis of the same story in these few, still-simple propositions, by which I mean to define the four principles of the Rabbinic theological system:

> 1. Chapter Six: God formed creation in accord with a plan, which the Torah reveals. World order can be shown by the facts of nature and society set forth in that plan to conform to a pattern of reason based upon justice. Those who possess the Torah—Israel—know God and those who do not—the gentiles—reject him in favor of idols. What hap-

pens to each of the two sectors of humanity, respectively, responds to their relationship with God. Israel in the present age is subordinate to the nations, because God has designated the gentiles as the medium for penalizing Israel's rebellion, meaning through Israel's subordination and exile to provoke Israel to repent. Private life as much as the public order conforms to the principle that God rules justly in a creation of perfection and stasis.

2. Chapter Seven: The perfection of creation, realized in the rule of exact justice, is signified by the timelessness of the world of human affairs, their conformity to a few enduring paradigms that transcend change (theology of history). No present, past, or future marks time, but only the recapitulation of those patterns. Perfection is further embodied in the unchanging relationships of the social commonwealth (theology of political economy), which assure that scarce resources, once allocated, remain in stasis. A further indication of perfection lies in the complementarity of the components of creation, on the one side, and, finally, the correspondence between God and man, in God's image (theological anthropology), on the other.

3. Chapter Eight: Israel's condition, public and personal, marks flaws in creation. What disrupts perfection is the sole power capable of standing on its own against God's power, and that is man's will. What man controls and God cannot coerce is man's capacity to form intention and therefore choose either arrogantly to defy, or humbly to love, God. Because man defies God, the sin that results from man's rebellion flaws creation and disrupts world order (theological theodicy). The paradigm of the rebellion of Adam in Eden governs, the act of arrogant rebellion leading to exile from Eden thus accounting for the condition of humanity. But, as in the original transaction of alienation and consequent exile, God retains the power to encourage repentance through punishing man's arrogance. In mercy, moreover, God exercises the power to respond to repentance with forgiveness, that is, a change of attitude evoking a counterpart change. Since, commanding his own will, man also has the power to initiate the process of reconciliation with God, through repentance, an act of humility, man may restore the perfection of that order that through arrogance he has marred.

4. Chapter Nine: God ultimately will restore that perfection that embodied his plan for creation. In the work of restoration death that comes about by reason of sin will die, the dead will be raised and judged for their deeds in this life, and most of them, having been justified, will go on to eternal life in the world to come. The paradigm of man restored to Eden is realized in Israel's return to the Land of Israel. In that world or age to come, however, that sector of humanity that through the Torah knows God will encompass all of humanity. Idolators will perish, and humanity that comprises Israel at the end will know the one, true God and spend eternity in his light.

Now, recorded in this way, the story told by Rabbinic Judaism proves remarkably familiar, with its stress on God's justice (to which his mercy is integral), man's correspondence with God in his possession of the power of will, man's sin, and God's response.

II. MYTHIC MONOTHEISM:
IMAGINING EDEN AND RE-PRESENTING THE RESULT

Imagine Eden as a philosopher would: a world of pure reason, where all things serve their assigned purpose and stand in proper rank. Form a mental image of a world where all things cohere to a single inner logic and so are to be explained in an orderly way. Contemplate a social order in which whatever happens is for good and sufficient cause. Conceive of a kingdom so governed by a moral calculus that an ethical physics describes actuality: each action produces an equal and opposite reaction, a perfect match, a mirror of the deed in the responsive deed. And try to picture a world of peace, in which nothing happens to change the perfect, the acutely just balance of matters.

Contemplate in mind that here, in this perfect world of universal mind and self-evident rationality, is a steady-state world: do this and that will happen, do not do this and that will not happen—measure for measure in all matters. The rational intellect encompasses all, which is why everything is subject to such an exact, reasonable accounting of force and reaction thereto. Among the principles of intellect that inhere in this Eden the most important, the innate sense of justice, ultimately prevails. Fairness and equity rule, and that explains why with thought everything certainly makes sense. Then the task of intellect will be to uncover and reveal how all things are to be justified, that is, shown to be just to begin with.

Consider how, in this social cosmos conceived by men of reason who take up the task of justification, principles of order describe the final outcome of all transactions, all relationships. Well-ordered nature finds its match in well-construed society of humanity. And at the third dimension of existence, the anthropological, in addition to the natural and the historical, the very traits of man himself correspond to those of nature. The same rule that governs the tree governs me, the orderly mind maintains.

Change then defies imagining. In place comes the realization, in full maturity, of what one already is. The *telos*, the ultimate end and goal, of all things, present at the outset, explains and governs what happens, but nothing happens to violate that rational rule. The acorn grown up has not changed but has only realized its end. Teleology then takes the place of history as a mode of organizing existence. In such a world the future is present even now, the oak in the acorn. Inertia and stasis characterize the teleological universe, in accord with the rules that dictate cause and effect. Proportion and balance, complementarity and commensurability—these traits of the well-ordered world everywhere characterize the condition of men and nations, their relationships, and the destiny meted out to each and to all by the purposeful intellect that has made things just so, that philosophers name in diverse ways but most commonly, God.

That is why, in this imaginary world that philosophers alone can conceive (with God in their image, after their likeness), in such a purposeful realm rationality yields compelling explanations for all things, a single integral rationality or *logos* commands. Before the cosmic intellect that has conceived all things in a single reasonable, purposeful way there are no mysteries, neither about the past and what lies hidden, nor about the present and what comes into view, nor even about what lies over the distant horizon of the future. Since rules govern, reason suffices to explain the past, understand the present, and dictate what is going to come about in the future.

Not only public history but private life conforms to the same reasonable laws: do this and that will happen. The well-examined life of persons and their destinies recapitulate those rules of reason, so that, purposeful and properly ranked, private lives embody—and even match item for item—the principles of public order. All things come under the one orderly law of reason, for every thing its place, for every person a calling, for every event a purpose. And that is why those who master the givens of reality and reflect reasonably about them make sense of all being, all doing.

Then in mind—to continue for just a bit longer this exercise in imagining a society situated in utopian eternity—address the question of history, the disruptions of events, and you will understand how reason masters, how logic controls even the chaos of man's remarkable doings, the ones that destroy perfection. In line with the inner logic of the whole, time and change do not—or at least ought not—mar this Eden, where perfection consists in stability in proper balance and proportion. And when change (not just fulfillment of innate *telos*) marks time, change is a problem that requires explanation. And time is subject to the requirement of accountability: how come? If rationality consists in the meting out of measure for measure, so that good is responded to with good, and evil with evil, then that of which history consists—what is remarkable by reason of its sheer illogic—finds no place but must be explained (away). For in this domain of contemplation of what is, or can be made, perfect, men know the rules and how they work and are applied. Consequently, through knowing the regularities of eternity that supersede the random moments of time, the past yields its secrets of how things really work. The present rehearses the rules in the here and the now. The future promises only more of that same regularity and certainty. The categories past, present, and future lose all currency.

So to conclude this fantasy constructed six inches above the level plane of the everyday and the here and now, events take place, but history—change, movement—does not happen. Events now stand not for that which disrupts, but for that which embodies rules or actualizes potentials, much as the well-conceived experiment in the laboratory allows the testing of hypotheses. And the same rules govern nations and families, social entities measured in multiples, or even the individual in his or her person and life. Public affairs and private ones match in conforming to the governance of order, purpose, reason. These virtues of the well-constructed intellect not only account for history and the course of nations in the unfolding of time but also prevail in the streets and marketplaces and households. There fairness and a balanced exchange in the marketplace of small affairs match in structure and proportion the workings of applied reason and practical logic in the relations of men and nations. In this philosophers' Eden, all things bear reasoned explanation, and there are no mysteries. Here then we discern the remarkable, hopeful vision, the fantasy world of intellectuals who conceive that ideas make all the difference, and minds command, and reason governs.

Now, if you can imagine such a world perfected by the tastes and aspirations of the rational mind, then you can enter into the world portrayed by the Rabbinic canon. The writings, read all together and all at once as a single coherent statement, portray the reason why things are now as they are. And they show the logic of that reason, revealing its integrity in the working of justice throughout. As sages portray the Written part of the Torah and set forth the Oral part, the Torah lays heavy emphasis upon the perfection of the timeless, flawless creation that God forms and governs in accord with wholly rational and accessible rules. If everything fits together and works coherently, it is because, as philosophers maintain in their realm of reflection, a single, unitary logic (*logos*), the logic of monotheism comprised by the one just, therefore reasonable and benevolent, God, prevails.

But for sages there was this difference: while philosophers uncovered the order of nature, employing mathematics abstractly to describe, and natural history comprehensively to organize, and reason to analyze, the facts of the world, it was into the facts of Scripture that sages pursued their comparable analysis. For all that I have asked as a supererogatory act of imagination—a world of pure reason, everything in place and in rank, all things serving an assigned purpose—encompasses the cosmic conception of sages as much as philosophers.

Sages produced out of Scripture a vision of the world comparable in its intellectual traits—the insistence upon the orderly and reasonable and purposeful character of all things, everything subject to a single logic, which is accessible to mind—to that conceived by philosophers. They accounted for things as they are and further instructed Israel on how to restore things to the state of grace that Eden had embodied. They then provided for moral regeneration and its consequences, set forth in the context of the eschatological theory of Rabbinic Judaism.

III. SAGES READ SCRIPTURE AS PHILOSOPHERS READ NATURE AND SOCIETY

What we see is a single, seamless story—and not a very complicated one at that. In these accounts, so far as is possible in their own words, I tell how sages portrayed the story of the world from start to finish: the rules that account for reality. And that story will strike the reader as remarkably familiar, its cogency sustained by its very commonplace quality: here is the story that we in the West who practice either Judaism or Christianity have been telling ourselves for so long as we have possessed Scripture. And, further, those who practice Judaism will find themselves entirely at home, because in the prayers recited three times a day they encounter the same tale that the sages of Rabbinic Judaism tell. That is because sages read Scripture—the facts it supplied or oral tradition contributed—as philosophers read nature. They thought philosophically about Scripture. The logic that they uncovered imparted that rationality and coherence to the theological convictions they set forth, to the system they devised to account for the unity of being, the conformity of all reality to the few simple rules of reason that God embodied in his works of creation.

To make this point more concrete: as philosophers sought to generalize out of the facts of nature, so sages brought system and order to the facts of Scripture, drawing conclusions, setting forth hypotheses, amassing data to them. Analytical principles comparable to those of natural history, specifically, guided them in their reading of the facts that Scripture provided. These involved, in particular, the classification and hierarchization of data in a taxonomical process of comparison and contrast: like followed like rules, unlike, opposite rules. And the rules that classify also hierarchize, e.g., what is classified as sanctified or as unclean will then possess the traits that signify sanctification or uncleanness, and these traits will also order themselves, this time at levels of intensity, for example (a case comes in a moment). The classification of matters and their hierarchization—the quest for generalizations, governing rules or principles— therefore comes prior to the identification of verses of Scripture that validate said classification.

What is primary is the governing conception of a prevailing logic, a governing reason articulated endlessly out of a few simple propositions of order and coherence. Throughout, a highly articulated system of classification is at work, one that rests on a deep theoretical foundation. The basic method involves a search for abstraction out of concrete data. A variety of cases deriving from Scripture is subjected to generalization, and the whole is then set forth in the form of a generalization sustained by numerous probative cases. The generalization, moreover, is itself elaborated. Cases that validate the generalization are selected not at random but by appeal to common taxonomic traits, and then the generalization not only derives from the cases but from a very specific aspect thereof. These cases are all characterized by sudden and supernatural intervention in a crisis, such as the situation under discussion now requires. Or a set of kindred propositions is established through a sequence of cases; no effort is made to order the cases in a compelling sequence. It is adequate to state the generalization and then adduce probative cases out of Scripture.

The whole represents the systematization of Scripture's evidence on a given topic, and it is the systematization of the data that yields a generalization. Scripture's facts are organized and sorted out in such a way as to present a generalization. Generalizations are to be formulated through that same process of collecting kindred facts and identifying the implication that all of them bear in common. But Scripture may also be asked to provide illustrative cases for principles that are formulated autonomously, as the result of analytical reasoning distinct from the sorting out of Scriptural precedents. Then Scripture is asked only to define in concrete terms what has been said abstractly. Successive propositions organize and rationalize a vast body of data, all of the facts pointing to the conclusions that are proposed as generalizations. The proof then lies once more in the regularity and order of the data that are collected. The balance and coherence of the opposed laws yield the besought generalizations. The method in no particular way would have appeared alien to elementary students of natural history or simple logic in the schools of certain ancient philosophical traditions.

So sages set forth the rational version of the myths of Scripture: creation and its flaws, Eden and the loss of Eden. But their logic, involving as it did the insistence on a perfect and unchanging world, sought out what complements and completes an account, modes of thought that will occupy us later on. Thus, they also taught how Eden is to be recovered. Adam and his counterpart, Israel, in the cosmic drama acted out every day, here and now, in the humble details of Israel's ordinary life, embodied the simple story of the world: unflawed creation, spoiled by man's act of will, restored by Israel's act of repentance. The rationality of an orderly and balanced world set forth in Rabbinic Judaism comes to full realization in the match of Eden and the Land of Israel, Adam and Israel, the paradise and paradise lost, with one difference. Adam had no Torah, Israel does. Adam could not regain Eden. But Israel can and will regain the Land. Sages' teleology imposed itself on eschatology, so forming a theory of last things corresponding to first things, in a theology of restoration, as we see in Chapter Nine.

Private life conformed; it too revealed that same flawless character that the world does—when reason takes over, and exception is explained (away). Exchanges of goods—scarce resources—likewise aimed at a perfect balance. Time, for sages, stood still, history bore no meaning, all things could be shown to exemplify rules and embody regularities. Scripture then conveyed lessons not of history and its admonitions but of logic—the logic of creation and its inner tension—and its inexorable result.

Here, we confront the actualization in mythic language of the philosophers' Eden, set forth in abstract terms. Sages in these proportionate, balanced, and measured components revealed a world of rules and exposed a realm of justice and therefore rational explanation. It was the kingdom of Heaven, so sages called it, meaning the kingdom of God. For that Eden in the abstraction of natural history that was invented by philosophy corresponds to the conception of the world and its perfection set forth by the theology of the sages. They accordingly conceived of a philosophical Eden out of Scripture's account—its authorized history of the world from Eden to the return to Zion. What the observed facts of nature taught philosophers, the revealed facts of Scripture taught our sages of blessed memory. Therein theology differs from philosophy—but, in Rabbinic Judaism in particular, the difference is there and there alone and nowhere else.

Working with the facts provided by Scripture and their own observations of nature, they cobbled together an account of the world, embedded in the written part of the Torah itself, that realized the philosophers' ideal of a world of reason and order, balance, and proportion, equity, and reliability. Others emerged from Scripture with quite different visions of the world from Eden onward, different perspectives on different realities. Those who framed the Authoritative History from Genesis through Kings certainly thought in a different way from sages, in a historical way. And others, who found in Scripture the secret of events to come, not to restore Eden but to transform creation altogether, took yet a third way, the apocalyptic one. We need not catalogue all of the diverse hermeneutics that Scripture was found by various groups to sustain or even require. Among the heirs of Scripture in late antiquity, sages alone approached Scripture as an exercise in rationality and emerged from Scripture with a world that followed accessible rules and realized a universal logic.

When they answered the question, Whence the knowledge of the rules of the ordered society, the world of balance and proportion in all things and of equitable exchange? sages took their leave of philosophers. Instead of reading nature, they read the Torah. Instead of searching for regularities of nature, they found patterns in the Torah. Instead of an abstract, natural teleology to be defined through systematic work of hierarchical classification, comparison, and contrast, they invoked the will of God. This will they showed to be dependable, regulated by rules man can discern, wholly rational, entirely just. Then, instead of an inquiry into natural history, guided by considerations of hierarchy, order, and ultimate purpose, sages contemplated the condition of Israel, explaining how those same principles of intent and order governed, the same modes of rational explanation functioned, the same media of reasoned thought in the form of applied reason and practical logic guided thought. That is what distinguished sages from philosophers and turned them into theologians: the privileged source of truth that the Torah constituted.

How, in concrete terms, did theology takes its leave from philosophy? It was through the appeal to revealed facts of the Torah in place of the discovered facts of nature. Further, sages' aesthetics required the recasting of those truths from the abstract language of generalization into the concrete myth form of a massive narrative, regularized and ordered into governing rules. Take, for example, the heart of the system of the dual Torah, the conviction of God's rule of a world of order that is to be explained by appeal to the principles of justice. Then events serve as the source of moral truth. Destiny is dictated by God, and God's hegemony realizes a morality defined by justice. So justice, not chance, governs Israel, specifically, God's plan. For God has a purpose in what he does with Israel.

IV. QUESTIONS OF SYSTEMIC DESCRIPTION, ANALYSIS, AND INTERPRETATION

Now we turn to blunt answers to fundamental questions of systemic description, analysis, and interpretation: If this is what we know, what else do we know? I deal with three questions that require specific answers.

[1] What is at stake? It is an explanation of Israel's present condition, and—I cannot over-stress—still more urgent, identification of the operative reasons that will lead to viable hypotheses concerning Israel's future prospects. Here the systemic subtext shapes articulated thought: the present properly analyzed and explained contains within itself the entire past, the whole future, all together, all at once. If, as we do, we repeatedly turn to Abram, it is because we wish out of the past to know the future and because we take as fact that Israel's future recapitulates the past of Abram. God has laid out matters from beginning to end; Scripture not only records the past but provides the key, through patterns we can identify in the present, to the future. The premise of analysis then is, when we understand the facts in hand, we also can learn the rules. So in a world created in accord with the requirements of exact balance, proportion, correspondence, complementarity, and commensurability there are no mysteries, only facts not yet noticed, analyses not yet undertaken, propositions not yet proved.

[2] How to explain the present? The sages' method of explanation will identify the rational principle that is involved. Scripture's facts do not suffice: the patriarchs asked. Reason is demanded: why did they value these experiences? Then rationality is established by appeal not to the given of Scripture but to the conviction that the familiar traits of perfection characterize creation and the Creator. That is to say, the conceptions that in general the paramount method of classical philosophy in its account of nature—teleology joined to order—govern here as well. That is why applied reason and practical logic and not the given and revealed of Scripture alone everywhere sustain thought. Sages do not paraphrase or recapitulate Scripture and its narrative, they transform Scripture into facts to be analyzed and reconstructed. The results yield the self-evidently valid doctrines. These prove to be few but paramount: the perfection of creation, the centrality of the Torah as a source of established facts, the subservience of God—therefore creation and history—to the same reason that animates the mind of man. All things are subject to the rules of logic and order that man's own mind obeys, and explanation in the end must derive from the sources of nature and its laws, and the Torah and its regularities, each recapitulating the mind and will of the loving and merciful and reasonable God, in whose image, after whose likeness, man is made.

[3] What of the future? Sages compared themselves to prophets and insisted that their knowledge of the Torah provided a key to the future. Knowing why noteworthy things take place provided them with that key. For a model of anticipation will extrapolate from the results of analysis and explanation those governing rules of an orderly world that define a useful hypothesis concerning the future. Having identified regularities and defined descriptive laws, then accounted for those rules by spelling out the systemic reasons behind them, sages had every reason to peer over the beckoning horizon. For their basic conviction affirmed the order and regularity of creation, its perfection. If, therefore, they knew the rules and how they worked (including remissions of the rules), sages insisted they could predict how the future would take shape as well.

Given what we know about past and present and the signals of Providence that explain the condition of the world, what shall we anticipate for time to come? Like the prophets before them but thinking along quite other lines to reach comparable conclusions, sages spoke with certainty, therefore, about what Israel may expect in the future. But there was this difference. Prophets invoked God's explicit statements about the future. Sages' message, by contrast, took shape as a result of the analytical soundings sages made and explained, the data they formed into rules, the rules the logic of which they set forth by way of explanation. Theirs was the way of the natural historian and the philosopher. But for them the path carried them into Scripture, not nature, and into the logic of God's plan for the world, not the *telos* of nature's impersonal perfection.

V. From Philosophy to Theology in the Framework of Scripture

That explains why what sages produced in the manner of philosophers is not philosophy but theology. Philosophy discovered the rules of the natural world, theology, the sages those of the realm of the supernatural. The same principles of reasoned inquiry into factual regularities and rational explanations based on those descriptive laws of how things are governed both inquiries. Analyzing nature and Scripture, respectively, philosophy and theology worked in the same way and produced matching results. Because the world is the way we

conceive God made it—that is, perfect, therefore, orderly and purposeful for philosophy, rational and ultimately benevolent for sages'
reading of the way the Torah defines it—we can identify anomalies
and conduct analyses, explain the results with rational explanations,
and extrapolate from the order of the present the shape and structure
of the future. That systematic exegesis of the world in accord with the
hermeneutics of the Torah defines the theology of Rabbinic Judaism:
its focus and the source of its coherence and cogency. Had The
Philosopher, Aristotle, read the Written Torah and chosen the media
of law, myth, and exegesis for his discourse, his lectures would have
recapitulated the results set forth by the sages. May we claim that the
documents of Rabbinic Judaism are what he would have written?
Working with the particular facts ordered by sages, he would have
done something quite akin in method and in modes of thought and
points of insistence, if not in form let alone in particular doctrine.

Israel's actualities contradicted sages' theology. For the world realized by natural Israel, whether in Aristotle's time, in the fourth century B.C.E., or in the time of our sages of blessed memory, the first
six centuries C.E., testified to the absurdity of the vision of rationality
and order, within the framework of God's logic, that the Torah portrayed. In no way did the natural world of Israel in actual history ever
validate sages' account of the theological world of mythic, holy Israel.
Instead of an imaginary world of balance, match, complementarity,
and proportion, Israel lived in a real world of disproportion, where
the wicked prospered and the righteous suffered.

Absurdity piled onto absurdity into the ultimate climax of space
and time, the temple mount ploughed over, the only offerings in those
days the flesh and blood of the Israelite martyrs themselves. That
is the everyday world confronted by the second-century sages who
produced the Mishnah and its concomitant traditions. A repressed
minority competing with Israel over the true message of the shared
Scriptures, the Christians two hundred years later found themselves
rulers of the world-empire, Rome. That is the (to them) utter absurdity faced by the fourth and fifth century sages who produced the
Talmud of the Land of Israel, *Genesis Rabbah*, and *Leviticus Rabbah*,
among other foundation-documents of Rabbinic Judaism. The world
they confronted in no way validated their fiercely-held convictions
about the ultimate rationality of all things. If everything is subject to
a reasonable explanation by appeal to regularities that wisdom may
discern, then why are things the way they are?

How then did sages construct this fantasy world of theirs, so vastly unlike the everyday world in which they lived out the life of Israel in a politics of triviality amid kingdoms and empires not called "Israel"— one empire, Iran, pagan and, heirs of Ahasuerus, by no means benign, the other, now-Christian Rome, laying claim to the same noble lineage, but now as Israel after the spirit on the authority not of the Torah of Sinai, Written and Oral, but of the Bible, Old and New Testaments alike? Specifically, what convictions, resting on what evidence, led them to the conclusions that, in their comprehensive account of theology, they set forth?

The answer is clear from what has already been said: Scripture, the written Torah, set forth a corpus of unassailable and generative facts, out of which all else was to be, and was, discovered and reconstructed (or, in more descriptive language, fabricated). So to understand the theology of Rabbinic Judaism, we must take as our starting point that theology's sources of the conviction of the orderly character of all being. We commence with the starting point of all else: the rule of justice, therefore also of law, that governs all else. How do sages find in the facts of Scripture that generative principle of their logic?

CHAPTER SIX

SOURCES OF WORLD ORDER

I. How (on the Basis of Scripture)
Do We Know That God Is Just?

In sages' view, which animates every line in the Rabbinic canon, the
will of the one unique God, made manifest through the Torah, governs, and, further, God's will, for both private life and public activity,
is rational. That is to say, within man's understanding of reason,
God's will is just. And by "just," sages understood the commonsense
meaning: fair, equitable, proportionate, commensurate. In place of
fate or impersonal destiny, chance, or simply irrational, inexplicable
chaos, God's plan and purpose everywhere come to realization. So
Rabbinic Judaism identifies God's will as the active and causative
force in the lives of individuals and nations.

How do sages know that God's will is realized in the moral order
of justice, involving reward and punishment? For reasons amply
spelled out, sages turned to Scripture for the pertinent facts; that is
where God makes himself manifest. But of the various types of scriptural evidence—explicit commandments, stories, prophetic admonitions—that they had available to show how the moral order prevailed
in all being, what type did they prefer? The one bearing the greatest probative weight derived from the exact match between sin and
punishment. Here is their starting point; from here all else flows
smoothly and in orderly fashion. World order is best embodied when
sin is punished, merit rewarded.

That body of evidence that Scripture supplied recorded human
action and divine reaction, on the one side, and meritorious deed and
divine response and reward, on the other. It was comprised by consequential cases, drawn from both private and public life, to underscore sages' insistence upon the match between the personal and the
public, all things subject to the same simple rule. That demonstration
of not only the principle but also the precision of measure for measure, deriving from Scripture's own record of God's actions, takes pri-

ority of place in the examination of the rationality of sages' universe. That is because it permeates their system and frames its prevailing modes of explanation and argument. The principle that all being conforms to rules, and that these rules embody principles of justice through exact punishment of particular sin, precise reward of singular acts of virtue, defined the starting point of all rational thought and the entire character of sages' theological structure and system.

That is why, without appeal to that fundamental principle of a just order, no question sages investigate, no dilemma their inquiry produces, no basic challenge to the absolute given of their world view makes any sense at all. Whatever they propose to account for the situation of Israel in public or the individual in private, whether the resolution of the historical crisis in the coming of the Messiah and the nations' standing in judgment by the criterion of the Torah or the advent of the world to come and individuals' standing in judgment by the same criterion—all of these massive presences in sages' thinking about the here and now, the past and the future, rested on the same foundation of conviction. That was that an exact, prevailing justice explained the meaning of all things. Of that principle all thought formed a systematic exegesis, first of Scripture for the explanation—*Midrash* is the word sages might use—of the here and the now, then of the workaday realities to be shaped into a *Midrash* upon Scripture—an extension, amplification, realization of Scripture. It was a reciprocal process because the same reasonable justice ruled small and great transactions without distinction. Not only so, but for sages, that conviction required an act not of faith but of rational inquiry into the record of reality, Scripture.

The teleological theory of natural history of philosophy here finds its counterpart. Sages' confidence in the sense, order, and the reasonable, because just, character of all reality matched philosophers' conviction that all things serve, each its assigned purpose. We might conceive that philosophy asked the teleological question of purpose, and theology responded with the revealed answer: to achieve a just world order. The one posited a goal or end, the other defined what that purpose was: all things serve the purpose of taking part in a just and equitable order.

So sages defined reason and rationality—despite the contrary evidence of everyday reality, beginning with Israel's own situation, subordinated as it was after its loss of great wars to Rome in the first and second centuries. That bedrock certainty identified as the fact of every life and the building block of every society the moral order of a world founded on justice. Sages deemed it a fact that man lived in a world in which good is rewarded and evil punished. Since the world in which they lived knew better, and since sages framed a system that coheres solely as an explanation of why, though justice is supposed to prevail, present matters are chaotic, we may take for granted that the sages too knew better, so far as knowing formed a secular act. It was their theology—the logic of God, systematically expounded—that taught them to see matters as they did.

That is why we seek to identify the sources for their conviction of the order of society, natural and supernatural alike. Since few in the history of humanity have offered as a simple fact of everyday reality such a principle of natural justice, but many have found the opposite, we are forced to ask why our sages conceived matters as they did. Exactly what endowed our sages of blessed memory with certainty that they along with all Israel lived in a trustworthy world of reason and order defined by justice? What we shall see is that their own systematization of the facts of the Written Torah nourished that conviction. Concurring on the teleological character of creation—everything with its goal and end—sages found in Scripture that pervasive purpose in the rule of justice, resting on reason and on equity. From that generative principle—a fact of revealed Scripture really—all else followed. Then the structure stood firm, the system worked.

What captures our interest therefore is not the conviction but the way in which sages set forth that conviction. What they found to overcome the doubt that everyday life surely cast upon their insistence upon the governing of a moral order was the facts of Scripture as they ordered those facts. Now, were we on our own to open Scripture and locate pertinent evidence that God is just and the world he made conforms to rules of equity, we should find Scripture states it in so many words. It is not merely that when God contemplated the world that he had made, he pronounced it good as Yannai says, specifically referring to the righteous. That surely represents a subjective judgment that can refer to anything, not only to what Yannai thought self-evident. Scripture leaves no doubt about God's definitive trait of justice, justice understood as man does, in a different context altogether.

It is that when man—Abraham—undertook to dispute God's decision and construct an argument against it, that God bound himself by the same rule of commonsense equity that Abraham deemed self-evident: "Will you sweep away the innocent along with the guilty? Far be it from you to do such a thing, to impose death upon the innocent as well as the guilty, so that innocent and guilty fare alike. Far be it from you! Shall not the Judge of all the earth deal justly?" (Gen. 18:23, 25). Then God does not reply, he merely responds by accepting Abraham's premise and proceeding to the negotiation. Silence bears assent: God is not only answerable, but he is answerable on exactly the counts that man deems consequential: justice, reason, commonsense rationality. Sages did not have to search deeply into obscure traditions or difficult passages to uncover the evidence of God's justice. Wherever in Scripture they looked, they found ample testimony, especially in the premise of Job's complaint!

Perhaps in that paradigmatic moment before Sodom sages identified the principle of the moral order that sustained the world: justice distinguishes the innocent from the guilty and punishes the guilty alone. But that is not how they demonstrated the validity of that principle. They had their own approach, which required them to establish proof through patterning well-analyzed facts, compared and contrasted. Like natural historians, they assembled evidence of a like kind—in this case, the administration of exact justice through appropriate, proportionate reward and punishment—and they then compared and contrasted the evidence they assembled. The concrete evidence on its own, properly arrayed, then established as fact what to begin with was entered as a postulate or hypothesis to be demonstrated—with no given axiom except the facticity of Scripture.

It is at this point that we turn directly to the method and the message of the governing theology of Rabbinic Judaism in particular. What we want to know is not how *we might find* in Scripture the basis for a position sages maintained, but how *sages did find that basis*. What satisfied them as necessary and sufficient demonstration of that fact of world order? While their theology systematically expounded the results of their disciplined study of the Written Torah—we might call the process their exegesis of, or *Midrash* upon, the Written Torah—the concrete and particular types of proof alone reveal to us the workings of their minds viewed as a single, cogent intellect: theological system.

To answer the question of the source of probative evidence for the principle that the world is reliable and orderly by reason of justice, we turn to the concrete evidence that they believed demonstrated their point. Now when sages opened Scripture to find out how, in the detail of concrete cases, the Judge of all the world bound himself by the rules of justice and systematically does justice, like philosophers in natural history they looked not for the occasional but the enduring: not for the singular moment but the routine pattern. Exegesis without a guiding hermeneutics bore little appeal to them. Single proof texts mattered less than governing paradigms. Sages were theologians before they were exegetes, and they were exegetes because they were theologians. So proof from specific texts they showed emerge from details, but hermeneutics holds details together in a single coherent whole. That is why they composed their account of the workings of the principle of measure for measure—whether for divine punishment or for divine reward—out of cases in which God does not intervene, but in which the very nature of things, the ordinary course of events, showed the workings of the principle.

What would suffice, then, to make a point that—we must assume—people in general deem counterintuitive? For who from Job onward—no one had to wait for Voltaire's *Candide*—ever assumed that the ordinary course of everyday events proves the justice (and the goodness) of God? More lost the faith because the here and now violated the rule of justice than gained the faith because it did. So, to begin with, sages framed for themselves what we might call a null hypothesis, that is to say, a hypothesis that they would test to prove the opposite of what they sought to show. They asked themselves this question: If justice did not govern, how should we know it? The answer is, we should find not a correlation but a disproportion between sin and consequent result, or penalty, between crime and punishment.

The null hypothesis framed the question of order through justice in its most palpable, material form. It is not enough to show that sin or crime provoke divine response, that God penalizes them. Justice in the here and now counts. The penalty must fit the crime, measure must match measure, and the more exactly the result corresponds to the cause, the more compelling the proof of immediate and concrete justice as the building block of world order that the sages would put forth out of Scripture. That is the point at which justice is transformed from a vague generality—a mere sentiment—to a precise and measurable dimension of the actual social order of morality: how things hold together when subject to tension, at the pressure points of structure, not merely how they are arrayed in general. Here, in fact, is how God made the world, what is good about the creation that God pronounced good, as Yannai says.

That is why, when sages examined the facts of Scripture to establish that principle of rationality and order in conformity to the requirements of justice and equity, what impressed them was not the inevitability but the precision of justice. Scripture portrays the world order as fundamentally just and reasonable, and it does so in countless ways. But Scripture encompasses the complaint of Job and the reflection of Qoheleth. Sages for their part identified those cases that transcended generalities and established the facticity of proportionate justice, treating them as not only exemplary but probative. They set forth their proposition and amassed evidence in support of it.

Let us turn to a systematic statement of the starting and main point: when God judges and sentences, not only is the judgment fair but the penalty fits the crime with frightening precision. But so too, when God judges and awards a decision of merit, the reward proves equally appropriate. These two together, the match of sin and penalty, meritorious deed and reward, then are shown to explain the point and purpose of one detail after another, and, all together, they add up to the portrait of a world order that is fundamentally and essentially just—the starting point and foundation of all else.

Here is the sages' account of God's justice, which is always commensurate, both for reward and punishment, in consequence of which the present permits us to peer into the future with certainty of what is going to happen, so M. *Sot.* 1:7ff. What we note is sages' identification of the precision of justice, the exact match of action and reaction, each step in the sin, each step in the response, and, above all, the immediacy of God's presence in the entire transaction. They draw general conclusions from the specifics of the law that Scripture sets forth, and that is where systematic thinking about cases takes over from exegetical learning about cases, or, in our own categories, philosophy from history:

Mishnah *Sotah* 1:7

A. By that same measure by which a man metes out [to others], do they mete out to him:

B. She primped herself for sin, the Omnipresent made her repulsive.
C. She exposed herself for sin, the Omnipresent exposed her.
D. With the thigh she began to sin, and afterward with the belly, there-
    fore the thigh suffers the curse first, and afterward the belly.
E. But the rest of the body does not escape [punishment].

We begin with the sages' own general observations based on the facts
set forth in Scripture. The response of the woman accused of adultery to her drinking of the bitter water that is supposed to produce
one result for the guilty, another for the innocent, is described in
Scripture in this language: "If no man has lain with you . . . be free
from this water of bitterness that brings the curse. But if you have
gone astray . . . then the Lord make you an execration . . . when the
Lord makes your thigh fall away and your body swell; may this
water . . . pass into your bowels and make your body swell and your
thigh fall away" (Num. 5:20–22). This is amplified and expanded,
extended to the entire rite, where the woman is disheveled; then the
order, thigh, belly, shows the perfect precision of the penalty. What
Scripture treats as a case, sages transform into a generalization, so
making Scripture yield governing rules.

When it comes to Israel, the principle of commensurate response
to each action extends also to God's response to Israel's atonement.
Israel is punished for its sin. But when Israel repents (of which we
shall hear more later) and God forgives Israel and restores the holy
people's fortunes, then that same principle that all things match takes
over. Hence we should not find surprising the logical extension, to the
character of God's forgiveness and comfort of Israel, of the principle
of measure for measure. When, specifically, Israel sins, it is punished
through that with which it sins, but it also is comforted through that
with which it has been punished.

If sages had to state the logic that imposes order and proportion
upon all relationships—the social counterpart to the laws of gravity—
they would point to justice: what accords with justice is logical, and
what does not is irrational. Ample evidence derives from Scripture's
enormous corpus of facts to sustain in sages' view that the moral
order, based on justice, governs the affairs of men and nations.
Critical to the argument is a different claim altogether. I maintain
that that defines the first principle, the governing logic, of their system. By that claim I allege that all else takes its leave from the conviction that by "good" God characterizes creation as just, that an

entire system of the social order coheres as amplification and exegesis of that principle, and that justice dictates the primary point of self-
evidence: the system's unmoved mover, the point before which there
is no appeal, and beyond which, no point is unaffected, no refuge
exists for the irrational. How to show that that conviction is not only
normative but generative? It is by asking about what sages deem to
require attention and explanation, and what they take for granted.

Let me express the matter of the a priori priority of justice as the
first principle of all things in a simple but probative way: *In sages' discourse, justice never requires explanation, but violations of justice always do.*

When what happens does not conform to the systemic givens but
violates the expectations precipitated by them, then sages pay close
attention and ask why. When what happens does conform, they do
not have to ask: their unarticulated conviction of self-evidence is
embodied, therefore, in the character of their discourse: not only the
speech but the silence.

Justice therefore defines the rational, and injustice the irrational. It
is now my task to proceed from the self-evidence of justice as the governing logic of all being to the self-evidence of injustice as the challenge to logic: the irrational that requires rationalization in the fullest
sense of that word. To sages the principal intellectual task is—in the
exact meaning of the word—to *justify* the condition of society by reference to conduct therein, both public and personal. That is, sages
want to explain the sense and meaning, account for the coherence
with justice of what defies the expectations that strict justice would
lead us to anticipate. The numerous cases we have considered in the
end prove episodic. We have now to turn to the systemic data: What
do sages define as the central issues, the critical tensions, when they
speak of Israel in its context within all of humanity? And how, further, do they frame the issues of private life? These matching categories now demand attention. Specifically, the same principle now
fully spelled out—that everything that happens responds to just
cause—has to be shown to define the very problematic of sages' discourse concerning public and personal Israel. That is, justice must
dictate what defines sages' interest when they speak of Israel and the
Israelite.

To begin with, then, we have to know what sages meant by
"Israel," and how the moral order was to come to realization within
Israel; then how sages made sense of "the gentiles," and what sort of

justice governed in Israel's relationship with them. That then carries us to sages' explanation of the irrationality of the personal order, phrased through time in many ways but in a single motif: Why do the wicked prosper and the righteous suffer? The premise of the question, whether addressed to Israel and the gentiles, or to the righteous and the wicked, remains the same, namely, the conviction that the moral order of justice governs. That is the conviction that defines the generative question sages raise at the most profound levels of their discussion of the public order and of the personal situation of households and individuals as well.

II. The Political Order: Israel and the Torah

Politics marks the starting point of this encompassing account of creation ordered by justice that, in my view, sages' systematically formulate through all of their documents. The theory of the political order that is set forth in the documents of the Rabbinic canon rests on a simple logic of balanced relationships. We begin with the fundamental fact that all humanity is divided into two sectors, the part that knows God through the Torah and the part that does not know God at all but instead worships idols. The former is called Israel, the latter, the gentiles. God rules as sovereign over all mankind, but the two sectors thereof compete and one, the gentiles, presently dominates the other, Israel. It follows that to make sense of, to justify, the political order, sages had to find the rational principle that accounted for two political entities and their relationships. To spell out the several components of that rationale I explain the Torah's political theology of Israel, then the Torah's political theology of the gentiles. What that theology says about Israel, *mutatis mutandis*, it says also about the gentiles.

Power relationships between the two respond to three rules. First, as the prevailing theory of world order maintains in its definition of justice, each action provokes an equal and commensurate reaction. Second, God responds to the attitude as much as to the action of the human actor, especially prizing humility over arrogance. Third, God's special relationship to those who know him through the Torah may require him to use the gentiles to penalize Israel for disobedience, to encourage their return to a proper attitude and consequent action. For the Rabbinic canon, within those three rules the political order of mankind plays itself out. In combination, they respond to the critical issue of Israel's public life: Why do the gentiles prosper while Israel languishes? Where is the justice in the political order of mankind?

Sages' doctrine of the political order of the world is comprised by these convictions. First, because Israel accepted the Torah, God loves Israel. The Torah therefore defines Israel's life and governs Israelites' welfare. Second, in genus, Israel does not differ from the gentiles, deriving from the same ancestry, sharing the same origin in Abraham. In species, matters are otherwise. Distinguished by the Torah, Israel is alone in its category (sui generis), proved by the fact that what is a virtue to Israel is a vice to the nations, life-giving to Israel, poison to the gentiles. Third, Israel's condition of weakness comes about by reason of its own sin, which God justly and reasonably punishes through, among others, political means. Still, fourth, if Israel sins, God forgives that sin, having punished the nation on account of it. Such a process has yet to come to an end, but it will and in time is going to culminate in Israel's complete regeneration and consequently the restoration of Eden, now in Israel's framework. Meanwhile, fifth, Israel's assurance of God's love lies in the many expressions of special concern, in his provision of numerous commandments for Israel to carry out for its own sanctification. This is expressed in the following explicit way:

Mishnah *Makkot* 3:16

A. R. Hananiah b. Aqashia says, "The Holy One, blessed be he, wanted to give occasions for attaining merit to Israel.
B. "Therefore he gave them abundant Torah and numerous commandments,
C. "as it is said, 'It pleased the Lord for his righteousness' sake to magnify the Torah and give honor to it'" (Is. 42:21).

The means for Israel's sanctification extend to even the humblest and most ordinary aspects of the national life: the food the nation eats, the sexual practices by which it procreates. These life-sustaining, life-transmitting activities draw God's special interest, as a mark of his general love for Israel. Israel then is supposed to achieve its life in conformity with the marks of God's love. That, in theory, forms the moral order that justifies Israel's existence through all time.

Now to the context in which that theory takes shape. The generative problematic of sages' theory of the political order—what captured attention as irrational and required rationalization—presented itself every day an Israelite in the Land of Israel walked out the gateway of his courtyard and confronted the reality of Roman rule, whether pagan, whether Christian. If an Israelite in Iranian-ruled Babylonia encountered an agency of the Sasanian state, inclusive of the priests of the established religion of Ahura Mazda ("Zoroastrianism"), he too had every reason to ask, Why them, not us? The gentiles thrive in this world and in this age, and Israel deteriorates, dying a slow, long-term death of dignity: loss of sovereignty and power, loss of the Land, and loss of even the means of serving God as the Torah had specified, through the offerings of the produce of the Land, wheat, wine, grain, oil, and meat. The matter is easily set forth in the sages' own language: God passionately loves Israel. The commandments express that passion. Then Israel's political condition—its standing in the power relationships of the nations—defies rationality and disrupts the moral order of the world.

In this protracted argument concerning theology of the sages, why identify politics as the first occasion for the demonstration that at the heart of theology is the integrating principle that God governs the world with justice? When sages addressed issues of the moral order, they turned first to public policy and political order because the Written Torah, Scripture, left them no choice. Its building block of world order is public, acts of a total community, people, nation, and society. The community bore responsibility for the acts of the individual—Israel being represented by every Israelite—so that if private persons sinned, everybody suffered.

That is because no one imagined the construction of world order out of disconnected individuals, a concept that would make its appearance only many centuries later and in a very different world. None conceived as consequential in its own terms the private preserve of the isolated individual, apart from family, household, village, people, or nation. The Torah's imperative of sanctification is phrased in the plural you, and God acts, as recorded in the Torah, upon that plural you. For in the account of the Written Torah God first addressed the community of Israel, only then the individual members thereof. Nearly the whole of the Written Torah's narrative concerns how Israel as a collectivity is to become a kingdom of priests and a holy people, a nation in the image of God, made up of individuals worthy of belonging thereto. As to the individual, Achan, in Joshua, typified the position of everybody: all Israel paid the price of one Israelite's sin against God. But issues of national life—sanctifying God, possessing the Holy Land, preventing individual sin from corrupting the public welfare—take priority.

It is not surprising, therefore, that the systematic exposition of the principle of the moral order of justice should focus upon politics, defined conventionally: who legitimately exercises violence against whom, what on-going entities control large-scale social aggregates through the regular (institutional) and valid (legitimate) exercise of force. In their consideration of the rationality of the political order, sages applied to the world of power that principle of rationality that God governs within moral rules. Because of the way in which they organized humanity into hierarchized categories, no component of the larger construction of world order occupied a more central position in their minds. Specifically, they saw the world as comprised by enduring political entities, peoples or nations that through enduring institutions collectively exercised legitimate violence (to review the initial definition). To sages it followed logically that the relationships among nations ought to take priority in the realization of the moral order of the world. Who legitimately does what to whom should provide probative evidence of God's government.

Then who is the "who" of politics, the head-noun of intelligible sentences (in the setting of Part One of this book)? Answering that question requires defining the actor, the subject of the sentence, *who* does what to whom? The political entities that exercised legitimate violence and so were empowered, and that also demanded from sages a place in an account of how things cohere, as I said at the outset, were two: Israel on one scale, all the nations of the world on the other. These are best represented visually: Israel holding to the Torah on the one side, the nations with their idols on the other. For sages could only imagine either one with its indicative emblem. By "Israel," sages meant many things, but all definitions concur that Israel is Israel by reason of the Torah. Israel's relationship to the Torah governs all else: God's attitude toward Israel, Israel's understanding of itself, and Israel's conduct of its affairs. And, to turn matters around, to be an Israelite was to know God through the Torah. And the nations were undifferentiated; they were what they were by reason of one indicative trait, which was idolatry, and that is to say, not possessing the Torah. To be a gentile found definition in idolatry. A collectivity defined by a negative trait, the nations' idolatry dictated God's attitude toward them, which, to sages, was all that mattered.

That definition of political actors then carries with it the principle of logic and order that the prevailing justice should embody. God rules. In a rational world ordered by the principle of justice, therefore, Israel, by reason of knowing God through the Torah, will exercise legitimate violence. The nations, by reason of idolatry, will subordinate themselves. But everyone knew that the nations, and particularly the world empires, exercised hegemony. I say "particularly" because sages persistently spoke not of "the nations" so much as the four that mattered: Babylonia, Media, Greece, and Rome, successive world empires; and sages in numerous ways insisted that the fifth and last would be Israel, when God's government would commence. In the logic of sages, therefore, Israel, few in number and scattered in location, took its place in the sequence of, commensurate with, the four known cosmopolitan empires. So the gentiles' governance of the world, their power and priority, dictated the first and most disruptive fact of the prevailing order, the starting point for the entire process of making sense of, finding the order in, how things are that sages made manifest, in their ultimate statement, in the Rabbinic canon.

How in sages' theology did Israel and the nations relate? To answer that question, as to deal with all others of a profound character, sages, like philosophers, turned to the simple logic of classification: comparison and contrast in a process of hierarchical classification. Israel in no way constituted what we should label a secular category, that is, a people or nation like any or all others—even an empire like Rome. Their understanding of "Israel" as a category would rather correspond to Christianity's "church" (in its various formulations) or Islam's *ummah*. For by "Israel" sages understood the blessed Israel of whom Scriptures speak, that is, the supernatural social entity called into being by God. To elect, sanctified Israel, the nations in no way compared except in one: they too found definition in their relationship to God. By the nations, which is to say, everyone else, sages understood idolaters, those who come under negative definitions: they do not know and worship the one and only true God, they worship no-gods.

Then why invoke the category of politics at all? While "church" and "ummah" and "Israel" at various times and places sustained this-worldly definitions, all three of them also constituted other-than-worldly entities as well. Certainly for the first three centuries of Christianity, "church" bore anything but a political meaning; no Christian at the end of the third century could have foreseen the Christian dominance of the Roman world such as was realized by the end of the fourth. But why insist that the politics of Israel and the nations forms the first step in the recapitulation of sages' theology?

The reason is that, since Scripture's "Israel" constituted a political entity, empowered legitimately to exercise violence to accomplish the common goals that God set for the holy society, sages naturally regarded the "Israel" of their own time as, by its nature and calling, a political entity. They did not have to take account of the long history of Israel's political autonomy and even independence, down to 70 C.E., to come to such a conception. For it was in the beginning of Israel that Moses had been commissioned to turn a class of powerless slaves into a kingdom of priests and a holy people. He exercised political, not merely cultic or pedagogical or even prophetic functions. In Scripture's account of Moses's activities and the Torah's law, moreover, the government of civil affairs takes priority. In that regard, however, the nations manifestly formed political entities too, exercising power, indeed, a great deal more power than Israel did. So for sages, the political order of the world was comprised on the one hand by the political entity unlike all others, Israel, which also formed a social order and a cultic community, and on the other hand by counterpart entities.

How to justify the comparison and contrast of entities of a single genus but not a common species? In sages' view individuals always represented the political entity with which they were identified, e.g., idolaters with the wicked empire, individual Israelites with God's people Israel. And that helps us to understand why, though Israel was sui generis, Israel also was to be treated as comparable to the nations. Because sages did not see Israel as a conglomerate of distinct individuals, but as a social entity that began whole and encompassed the parts, they also did not see the nations as a mass of idolaters, counted one by one, but as political entities, collective enterprises. That is why, by "everyone else," the sages' logic of world order understood not only idolaters viewed as individual sinners, but idol-worshipping nations, comparable to, and balanced against, Israel.

Having established the grounds for comparison, in what way Israel and the nations are alike, then, we may ask about the results of the necessary companion of comparison, which is contrast. Let us first take up the contrastive definition, Israel/not gentile. The components already are familiar. In this context Israel is defined both negatively and positively. Israel means not gentile, and one prominent antonym for Israel, unsurprisingly, is gentile. Gentiles worship idols, Israel worships the one, unique God.

But "Israel" in the Rabbinic canon stands also for the individual Israelite, so another antonym for Israel is Adam. These persons, Israel and Adam, form not individual and particular, but exemplary, categories. Israel is Adam's counterpart, Israel is the other model for man, the one being without the Torah, the other being with it. Adam's failure marked the occasion for the formation of Israel. Israel came into existence in the aftermath of the failure of creation with the fall of man and his ultimate near-extinction; in the restoration that followed the flood, God identified Abraham to found in the Land the new Eden, a supernatural social entity to realize his will in creating the world. Called, variously, a family, a community, a nation, a people, Israel above all embodies God's resting place on earth. I hardly need add that this definition of Israel cannot be confused with any secular meanings attributed to the same word, e.g., nation or ethnic entity, counterpart to other nations or ethnic groups.

The Scriptural record places Israel in the same line as all the rest of humanity, from Adam through Noah to Abraham. So does Israel not form part of a common humanity with the gentiles, all deriving from Noah and ultimately from Adam? Israel to begin with does not differ from the gentiles. But the election of Israel, beginning with God's call to Abraham and Abraham's response, distinguished Israel from the gentiles and so marked gentiles for what they are. If, as we see time and again, Israel is Israel by reason of the Torah, then gentiles are gentiles also by reason of the Torah, that is, not having the Torah, not accepting it. That point emerges. Israel's special status and relationship to God derive not from intrinsic qualities—though, as we shall see, sages imputed to Israel palpable qualities that marked them off from the nations and found in the Torah the source of those qualities—but from the record of right attitudes and right deeds.

On what basis is that special relationship founded? Here again, the nations had every opportunity that was given to Israel. Specifically, they could have received the Torah. But God found only Israel truly worthy to receive the Torah. Scripture offers a variety of explanations for the election of Israel, but the Rabbinic canon presents only one: Israel accepted the Torah, and the nations rejected it. So it was by an act of will on both parties that matters worked out in opposed ways. A function of God's own self-manifestation through the Torah, election is particular to the one that is chosen: God examined all the nations and chose Israel, all generations and chose the generation of the wilderness to receive the Torah, and so on:

Leviticus Rabbah XIII:II.1

1. A. R. Simeon b. Yohai opened [discourse by citing the following verse:] "'He stood and measured the earth; he looked and shook [YTR = released] the nations; [then the eternal mountains were scattered as the everlasting hills sank low. His ways were as of old]' [Habakkuk 3:6].
   B. "The Holy One, blessed be he, took the measure of all the nations and found no nation but Israel that was truly worthy to receive the Torah.
   C. "The Holy One, blessed be he, further took the measure of all generations and found no generation but the generation of the wilderness that was truly worthy to receive the Torah.
   D. "The Holy One, blessed be he, further took the measure of all mountains and found no mountain but Mount Moriah that was truly worthy for the Presence of God to come to rest upon it.
   E. "The Holy One, blessed be he, further took the measure of all cities and found no city but Jerusalem that was truly worthy in which to have the house of the sanctuary built.
   F. "The Holy One, blessed be he, further took the measure of all mountains and found no mountain but Sinai that was truly worthy for the Torah to be given upon it.
   G. "The Holy One, blessed be he, further took the measure of all lands and found no land but the Land of Israel that was truly worthy for Israel.
   H. "That is in line with the following verse of Scripture: 'He stood and took the measure of the earth.'"

The question that is answered is, Why did God choose Israel, the generation that received the Torah, Moriah, Sinai, the Land of Israel, and so on? The answer is, There was no better, more worthy choice, because of Israel's willingness to receive the Torah, just that generation, just that location being added.

What is at stake at Sinai explains all that follows. At Sinai God

announced, "I am the Lord your God who brought you out of the
Land of Egypt, out of the house of bondage. You shall have no other
gods before Me." In so stating, and through all that followed, God
revealed himself through the Torah. Then in accepting the Torah,
Israel responded as God wanted, but could not coerce, them to do.
The act of obedience requires a context of free choice, just as the
tragedy of Eden showed. So the Torah joins God to man through
Israel by introducing God to man through Israel. That accounts for
the election of Israel.

Above all, the right attitude receives the greatest emphasis. God
commands, but commands only man, because in all creation man
alone enjoys the free will to choose to obey or to choose to rebel.
Then the exercise of free will, embodied in proper intentionality, will
dictate all else. How does this shape thinking about Israel? Only
Israel was suitable to receive the Torah, not because of Israel's intrinsic character but because of Israel's attitude and actions. Specifically,
as we shall see time and again, it is the Torah that makes Israel into
Israel, meaning, Israel's acceptance of the Torah as its meeting place
with God makes all the difference:

Sifré Deuteronomy CCCXI:I.1

A. "... when the Most High gave nations their homes [and set the
   divisions of man, he fixed the boundaries of peoples in relation to
   Israel's numbers. For the Lord's portion is his people, Jacob his own
   allotment]" (Dt. 32:7–9):
B. Before our father Abraham came along, it was as if the Holy One,
   blessed be He, judged the world in accord with the principle of
   mere cruelty.

Now comes the familiar trilogy: generation of the flood, people of the
tower of Babylon (generation of the dispersion), and men of Sodom:

C. When the generation of the flood sinned, he extinguished them like
   sparks on water.
D. When the people of the tower of Babylon sinned, he scattered them
   from one end of the world to the other.
E. When the people of Sodom sinned, he drowned them in brimstone
   and fire.

Abraham breaks the sequence of sinners:

F. But when our father, Abraham, came into the world, he had the
   merit of receiving suffering [rather then utter extinction] which
   began to come along.

G. So it is said, "And there was a famine in the land and Abram went down to Egypt" (Gen. 12:10).

H. Now if you should say, "On what account do sufferings come," it is because of love for Israel:

I. "he fixed the boundaries of peoples in relation to Israel's numbers."

Sifré Deuteronomy CCCXI:II.1

A. Another teaching concerning the verse, ". . . when the Most High gave nations their homes":

B. When the Holy One, blessed be He, gave the Torah to Israel, he went and gazed and scrutinized, as it is said, "He stands and shakes the earth, he beholds and makes the nations tremble" (Hab. 3:6).

C. But there was no nation among the nations that was suitable to receive the Torah except for Israel:

D. ". . . and set the divisions of man, he fixed the boundaries of peoples in relation to Israel's numbers."

Readers may stipulate that passages such as these fill the documents of the Rabbinic canon: the gentiles were unworthy of receiving the Torah, shown by the fact that they rejected it; Israel was elected because it was worth of election, shown by the fact that they accepted the Torah. Below we shall see exactly how sages represent the gentiles' rejection of the Torah.

What about Israel's sin? That question brings us to the center of the structure built upon the election of Israel and carries within itself the answer to the anomaly of Israel's condition among the nations. God's response to Israel's sin produces the probative mark of divine love for Israel, God's capacity to bear with, even to forgive Israel. Israel tested God ten times, and God forgave them ten times:

Bavli 'Arakhin 3:5 II.3/15a–b

A. It has been taught on Tannaite authority said R. Judah, "Ten trials did our ancestors impose upon the Holy One, blessed be he: two at the shore of the sea, two in the water, two in regard to the manna, two in regard to the quail, one in regard to the [golden] calf, one in the wilderness of Paran."

The systematic collection of facts and analysis and reconstruction of them into probative propositions now commences. Scripture yields ample evidence of God's unlimited capacity to forgive Israel, so that the relationship between God and Israel is ordered by the principles of love and forbearance, shown by God through all time. So much for the election of Israel and the inner dynamics of that transaction.

But that—Sinai—was then and this—the world governed by the
pagan empire—is now. So it is time to ask, Who and what, exactly
is Israel in sages' logic? How about a this-worldly, political definition?
First let me eliminate the most conventional answer. The secular
sense of "Israel" and even "the Jews" occurs only very rarely in the
Rabbinic canon. I cannot point to the use of "Israel" to refer solely
to the nation in the context of other nations of the same genus, for
instance, the comparison of Israel's king and pagan kings; rather,
what are compared are Israel's prophets and the pagan prophets. In
the Rabbinic canon "Israel" bears these three meanings, which we
have already noted and have now to systematize:

[1] holy family, that is, a social entity different from the nations
    because it is formed by a common genealogy;
[2] holy nation among nations but holy among profane, a rose
    among thorns, sustained by a common root but yielding a differ-
    ent fruit;
[3] unique Israel, sui generis, different not in contingent, indicative
    traits but categorically, that is to say, in its very category from all
    other nations.

Scripture to sages told the story of "Israel" a man, Jacob. His children therefore are "the children of Jacob." That man's name was also
"Israel," and, it followed, "the children of Israel" comprised the
extended family of that man. By extension upward, "Israel" formed
the family of Abraham and Sarah, Isaac and Rebecca, Jacob and
Leah and Rachel. "Israel" therefore invoked the metaphor of genealogy to explain the bonds that linked persons unseen into a single
social entity; the shared traits were imputed, not empirical. That
social metaphor of "Israel"—a simple one, really, and easily
grasped—bore consequences in two ways. First, children in general
are admonished to follow the good example of their parents. The
deeds of the patriarchs and matriarchs therefore taught lessons on
how the children were to act. Of greater interest in an account of
"Israel" as a social metaphor, "Israel" lived twice, once in the patriarchs and matriarchs, a second time in the life of the heirs as the
descendants relived those earlier lives. The stories of the family were
carefully reread to provide a picture of the meaning of the latter-day
events of the descendants of that same family. Accordingly, the lives
of the patriarchs signaled the history of Israel.

While Israel was sufficiently like the gentiles to sustain comparison with them, Rome being treated as a correlative family to Israel, but descended from the wrong side, Israel also contrasted with the gentiles. In the end, despite all that has been said about Israel and the nations sharing a common genus, still Israel was to be seen as sui generis. Israel also found representation as beyond all metaphor. Seeing "Israel" as sui generis yielded a sustained interest in the natural laws governing "Israel" in particular, statements of the rules of the group's history viewed as a unique entity within time. The historical-eschatological formulation of a political teleology in that way moved from an account of illegitimate power to a formulation of theory of the inappropriate victim, that is to say, of Israel itself. That explains why, as we have already seen, sentences out of the factual record of the past formed into a cogent statement of the laws of this "Israel"'s destiny, laws unique to the social entity at hand.

Second, the teleology of those laws for an Israel that was sui generis focused upon salvation for individual Israelites—resurrection and judgment—and redemption for all Israel at the end of history, that is, an eschatological teleology formed for a social entity embarked on its own lonely journey through time. We shall ultimately see how the gentiles pass from the scene at the last, when the dead are raised, the Land regained, and Eden restored. Then all the living will form one Israel, that is, all mankind will recognize the rule of the one and only God.

The conception of "Israel" as sui generis, third, reaches expression in an implicit statement that Israel is subject to its own laws, which are distinct from the laws governing all other social entities. These laws may be discerned in the factual, scriptural record of "Israel's" past, and that past, by definition, belonged to "Israel" alone. It followed, therefore, that by discerning the regularities in "Israel's" history, implicitly understood as unique to "Israel," sages recorded the view that "Israel," like God, was not subject to analogy or comparison. Accordingly, while not labeled a genus unto itself, Israel is treated in that way. Theory of Israel as sui generis produced a political theory in which Israel's sole legitimate ruler is God, and whoever legitimately governs does so as God's surrogate. Theory of legitimate sanctions then is recast into a religious statement of God's place in Israel's existence, but retains its political valence when we recall that the sage, the man most fully "in our image, after our likeness," governs in accord with the law of the Torah. But how do sages translate into concrete, practical terms a theory of the political order formed by Israel?

This brings us to theology of politics contained within the image, Kingdom of Heaven. Here and now Israel forms the realm of God in this world, where God takes up presence, in synagogues and in school houses, where prayers are recited and the Torah studied, respectively. God's kingdom, unlike the kingdoms of this world and this age, is not locative, and it is also not tangible. It is a kingdom that one enters by right attitude, through accepting the government and laws of that king and undertaking to obey his rules, the commandments. To be Israel in the sages' model means to live in God's kingdom, wherever one is located and whenever, in the sequence of the ages, one enjoys this-worldly existence. God's kingdom forms the realm of eternity within time. Death marks not an end but an interruption in life with God; the individual is restored to life at the end, within that larger act of restoration of Adam to Eden, meaning Israel to the Land, that Israel's repentance will bring about. Various religious activities represent a taste even now of what is coming, the Sabbath, for example, affording a sixtieth of the taste of the world to come. Embodying God's kingdom by obeying God's will, Israel was created to carry out religious duties and perform good deeds. These are what differentiate Israel from the gentiles-idolaters.

What this means, concretely, is that God rules now, and those who acknowledge and accept his rule, performing his commandments and living by his will, live under God's rule. We recall the observation that, to single out Israel, God sanctified the people by endowing them with numerous commandments. Carrying out these commandments, then, brings Israel into the Kingdom of Heaven, as they acknowledge the dominion of God. That merging of politics and theology emerges in the language of the formula for reciting a blessing before carrying out a commandment or religious duty, "Blessed are you, Lord our God, king of the world, who has sanctified us by his commandments and commanded us to. . . ." That is the formula that transforms an ordinary deed into an act of sanctification, a gesture of belonging to God's kingdom.

Then the urgent question presents itself: how to account for the anomaly of Israel's condition in the world? Embodying virtue, unconditionally loved by God, encountering God through God's own self-revelation in the Torah, forgiven all its sins and faults, Israel ought to enjoy this world while anticipating eternal life. But that expectation conflicts with the sad reality that Israel does not enjoy this world and sees only a long, sad way from now to the end of time. Sages' account of the moral order appealed to justice to explain what is not an anomaly at all: Israel prospers when they do God's will, and they suffer when they do not do God's will. In this simple statement we find that account for reality that shows the prevailing order of all things, beginning with the most disruptive fact of all, Israel's condition:

Mekhilta Attributed to R. Ishmael XXX:I.12

A. Another interpretation of the phrase, "[Your right hand, O Lord,] glorious in power:"

B. When the Israelites carry out the will of the Omnipresent, they turn the left into the right: "Your right hand, O Lord, glorious in power, your right hand, O Lord, shatters the enemy."

C. But when the Israelites do not do the will of the Omnipresent, they turn the right hand into the left: "You have drawn back his right hand" (Lam. 2:3).

D. When the Israelites do the will of the Omnipresent, there is no sleep before him: "Behold the one who watches Israel dos not slumber or sleep" (Ps. 121:4).

E. But when the Israelites do not do the will of the Omnipresent, then, as it were, sleep comes to him: "Then the Lord awakened as one asleep" (Ps. 78:65).

F. When the Israelites do the will of the Omnipresent, there is no anger before him: "Fury is not in me" (Is. 27:4).

G. But when the Israelites do not do the will of the Omnipresent, then, as it were, anger is before him: "And the anger of the Lord will be kindled" (Dt. 11:17).

H. When the Israelites do the will of the Omnipresent, he does battle for them: "The Lord will fight for you" (Ex. 14:14).

I. But when the Israelites do not do the will of the Omnipresent, then, he fights against them: "Therefore he was turned to be their enemy, the Lord himself fought against them" (Is. 63:10).

J. Not only so, but they make the merciful God into a sadist: "The Lord has become as an enemy" (Lam. 2:5).

The answer appeals to a self-evident principle, which is that God rules and is responsive to Israel; hence if Israel does God's will, it prospers, and if not, it suffers. Then the condition of Israel itself validates the system's principal convictions.

The definition of who and what is Israel emerges in the following, through a simple manipulation of the opening statement: "All Israelites have a share in the world to come," meaning, they will be resurrected, stand in judgment, and then live forever. This passage defines who fit into the category of "all Israelites."

Mishnah *Sanhedrin* 10:1

A. All Israelites have a share in the world to come,
B. as it is said, "Your people also shall be all righteous, they shall inherit the land forever; the branch of my planting, the work of my hands, that I may be glorified" (Is. 60:21).

We may manipulate the opening declaration, reversing the subject and predicate, as follows: all who have a share in the world to come are Israelites. And all who do not cannot fall into the category "Israelites," as framed in that same sentence.

At the most profound level, therefore, to be "Israel" means to be those destined to rise from the dead and enjoy the world to come. Specifically, the definition of Israel is contained in the identification of "all Israel," as those who maintain that the resurrection of the dead is a teaching of the Torah, and that the Torah comes from heaven. The upshot is, to be "Israel" is to rise from the dead to the world to come. Gentiles, by contrast, are not going to be resurrected when the dead are raised, but those among them who bear no guilt for their sins also will not be judged for eternal damnation, so Yerushalmi *Shebi'it* 4:10 IX: "Gentile children who did not act out of free will and Nebuchadnezzar's soldiers who had no choice but to follow the orders of the evil king will not live after the resurrection of the dead but will not be judged for their deeds." If at the end of time Israel is comprised by those who will rise from the dead, in the interim "Israel" finds its definition in those who live the holy life and so imitate God, those who are, so far as they can be, "like God." For Israel to be holy means that Israel is to be separate, and if Israel sanctifies itself, it sanctifies God:

Sifra CXCV:I.2–3

1. A. "And the Lord said to Moses, Say to all the congregation of the people of Israel, You shall be holy, [for I the Lord your God am holy]" (Lev. 19:1–4):
2. A. "You shall be holy":
   B. "You shall be separate."

3. A. "You shall be holy, for I the Lord your God am holy":
   B. That is to say, "if you sanctify yourselves, I shall credit it to you as though you had sanctified me, and if you do not sanctify yourselves, I shall hold that it is as if you have not sanctified me."
   C. Or perhaps the sense is this: "If you sanctify me, then lo, I shall be sanctified, and if not, I shall not be sanctified"?
   D. Scripture says, "For I . . . am holy," meaning, "I remain in my state of sanctification, whether or not you sanctify me."

The final trait of God's kingdom—the Kingdom of Heaven—then comes to the fore: its utopian character. To be "Israel" is personal and collective but utopian, not locative. The dead will rise wherever located. While the Land of Israel is elect along with the people of Israel, to be Israel does not mean to live in the Land but to live by the Torah.

Now to make sense of the nations, those who do not imitate the sanctity of God but worship idols and who for that reason will die and not then rise from the grave, but who govern here and now—what is the logic there?

III. THE POLITICAL ORDER: THE GENTILES AND IDOLATRY

Gentiles by definition are idolaters, and Israelites by definition are those who worship the true God, the One who has made himself known in the Torah. In the Rabbinic canon, that is the difference—the only consequential distinction—between Israel and the gentiles. Still, there is one other: Israel stands for life, the gentiles for death. To state matters in more general terms, in the theology of the Rabbinic canon, the category gentiles or nations, without elaborate differentiation, encompasses all who are non-Israelites, that is, who do not belong to Israel and therefore do not know and serve God. That category takes on meaning only as complement and opposite to its generative counterpart, having no standing—self-defining characteristics—on its own. That is, since Israel encompasses the sector of humanity that knows and serves God by reason of God's self-manifestation in the Torah, the gentiles consist of everybody else, those placed by their own intention and active decision beyond the limits of God's revelation. Guided by the Torah, Israel worships God; without its illumination gentiles worship idols. At the outset, therefore, the main point registers: by "gentiles" sages mean God's enemies, and by "Israel" sages mean those who know God as God has made himself known, through the Torah. In no way do we deal with secular categories, but with theological ones.

Why does the chapter of the Rabbinic canon's theology have to encompass not only Israel but its antonym, gentiles? Because to reveal the justice of God, sages must devote a considerable account to the challenge to that justice represented by gentile power and prosperity, Israel's subordination and penury. For if the story of the moral order tells about justice that encompasses all creation, the chapter of gentile rule vastly disrupts the account. Like its counterpart, the anomalies represented by the chaos of private life, gentile rule forms the point of tension, the source of conflict, attracting attention and demanding explanation. For the critical problematic inherent in the category Israel is that its anti-category, the gentiles, dominate. So asking what rationality of a world ordered through justice accounts for the world ruled by gentiles represents the urgent question to which the system must respond. And that explains why the systemic problematic focuses upon the question, How can justice be thought to order the world if the gentiles rule? That formulation furthermore forms the public counterpart to the private perplexity, How is it that the wicked prosper and the righteous suffer? The two challenges to the conviction of the rule of moral rationality—gentile hegemony and the prosperity of wicked persons—match. First, let us focus upon explaining the prosperity of the gentiles, defined as idolaters, and then take up the counterpart dilemma provoked by the palpably dubious conviction that, by rights and all rationality, people get what they deserve.

The initial exposition of how things are, set forth in Genesis, tells how God made the world, recognized his failure in doing so, and corrected it. Through Abraham and Sarah a new humanity came into being, ultimately to meet God at Sinai and to record the meeting in the Torah. But then the question arises, what of the rest of humanity, the children of Noah but not of the sector of the family beginning with Abraham and Sarah, their son and grandson? The simple logic of the story responds: the rest of humanity, outside the holy family and beyond the commanding voice of Sinai, does not know God but worships idols. These are, today, the gentiles. And the gentiles, not Israel, govern the world. And how to resolve that tension imparts dynamism and movement to the story, which then is given an end, therefore also a beginning and a middle. That is Scripture's story, and that also is the story sages tell in their own idiom and manner. Scripture resorts to a sustained narrative, such as we call "history," that proceeds from beginning to end. That is not how sages describe and explain the world, for sages think paradigmatically, rather than historically. So to tell the same tale as Scripture does, they work out their ideas in a process of category-formation, in this case, the comparison and contrast of categories and their hierarchization.

Who, speaking categorically not historically, indeed are these "non-Israelites," called gentiles ("the nations," "the peoples," and the like)? The answer is dictated by the form of the question, Who exactly is a "non-Israelite"? Then the answer concerning the signified is always relative to its signifier, Israel. Within humanity-other-than-Israel, differentiation articulates itself along gross political lines, always in relationship to Israel. If humanity is differentiated politically, then it is a differentiation imposed by what has happened between a differentiated portion of humanity and Israel. It is, then, that segment of humanity that, under given circumstances, has interacted with Israel: [1] Israel arising at the end and climax of the class of world empires, Babylonia, Media, Greece, Rome; or [2] Israel against Egypt; or [3] Israel against Canaan. That is the point at which Babylonia, Media, Greece, Rome, Egypt, or Canaan take a place in the narrative, become actors for the moment, but never givens, never enduring native categories. Then, when politics does not impose its structure of power relationships, then humanity is divided between Israel and everyone else.

What then is the difference between the gentile and the Israelite, individually and collectively (there being no distinction between the private person and the public, social, and political entity)? A picture in cartographic form of theological anthropology of the Rabbinic canon would portray a many-colored Israel at the center of the circle, with the perimeter comprised by all-white gentiles; since, in the Halakhah, gentiles are a source of uncleanness of the same virulence as corpse-uncleanness, the perimeter would be an undifferentiated white, the color of death. The law of uncleanness bears its theological counterpart in the lore of death and resurrection, a single theology animating both. Gentile-idolaters and Israelite worshippers of the one and only God part company at death. Israelites die and rise from the grave, gentiles die and remain there. The roads intersect at the grave, each component of humanity taking its own path beyond. Israelites—meaning those possessed of right conviction—will rise from the grave, stand in judgment (along with some gentiles, as we shall see in a moment), but then enter upon eternal life, to which no one else will enjoy access. So, in substance, humanity viewed whole is divided between those who get a share in the world to come and who will stand when subject to divine judgment and those who will not.

While gentiles as such cannot inherit the world to come, because they are, by definition, idolaters, they too can enter the status of Israel, giving up idolatry in favor of worship of the one true God, in which case they join Israel in the world to come. And that is precisely what sages expect will happen. This the gentiles will do in exactly the way that Israel attained that status to begin with, by knowing God through his self-manifestation in the Torah, therefore by accepting God's rule as set forth therein. In this way theology of the Rabbinic canon maintains its perfect consistency and inner logic: the Torah determines all things. That point is made explicit: If a gentile keeps the Torah, he is saved. But by keeping the Torah, the gentile has ceased to be gentile and become Israelite, worthy even of the high priesthood. First comes the definition of how Israel becomes Israel, which is by accepting God's dominion in the Torah.

Sifra CXCIV:ii.1

1. A. "The Lord spoke to Moses saying, Speak to the Israelite people and say to them, I am the Lord your God":
   B. R. Simeon b. Yohai says, "That is in line with what is said else-where: 'I am the Lord your God [who brought you out of the land of Egypt, out of the house of bondage]' (Ex. 20:2).
   C. "'Am I the Lord, whose sovereignty you took upon yourself in Egypt?'
   D. "They said to him, 'Indeed.'
   E. "'Indeed you have accepted my dominion.'
   F. "'They accepted my decrees: "You will have no other gods before me."'
   G. "That is what is said here: 'I am the Lord your God,' meaning, 'Am I the one whose dominion you accepted at Sinai?'
   H. "They said to him, 'Indeed.'
   I. "'Indeed you have accepted my dominion.'
   J. "'They accepted my decrees: "You shall not copy the practices of the land of Egypt where you dwelt, or of the land of Canaan to which I am taking you; nor shall you follow their laws."'"

I cite the passage to underscore how matters are defined, which is by appeal to the Torah. Then the true state of affairs emerges when the same definition explicitly is brought to bear upon the gentiles. That yields the clear inference that gentiles have the power to join themselves to Israel as fully-naturalized Israelites, so the Torah that defines their status also constitutes the ticket of admission to the world to come that Israel will enter in due course. Sages could not be more explicit than they are when they insist that the gentile ceases to be in the status of the gentile when he accepts God's rule in the Torah.

Sifra CXCIV:ii.15

15. A. ". . . by the pursuit of which man shall live":
    B. R. Jeremiah says, "How do I know that even a gentile who keeps the Torah, lo, he is like the high priest?
    C. "Scripture says, 'by the pursuit of which man shall live.'"
    D. And so he says, "'And this is the Torah of the priests, Levites, and Israelites,' is not what is said here, but rather, 'This is the Torah of the man, O Lord God'" (2 Sam. 7:19).
    E. And so he says, "'open the gates and let priests, Levites, and Israelites will enter it' is not what is said, but rather, 'Open the gates and let the righteous nation, who keeps faith, enter it' (Is. 26:2)."
    F. And so he says, "'This is the gate of the Lord. Priests, Levites, and Israelites . . .' is not what is said, but rather, 'the righteous shall enter into it' (Ps. 118:20).
    G. And so he says, "What is said is not, 'Rejoice, priests, Levites, and Israelites,' but rather, 'Rejoice, O righteous, in the Lord'" (Ps. 33:1).
    H. And so he says, "It is not, 'Do good, O Lord, to the priests, Levites, and Israelites,' but rather, 'Do good, O Lord, to the good, to the upright in heart'" (Ps. 125:4).
    I. "Thus, even a gentile who keeps the Torah, lo, he is like the high priest."

That is not to suggest God does not rule the gentiles. He does—whether they like it or not, acknowledge him or not. God responds, also, to the acts of merit done by gentiles, as much as to those of Israel. The upshot is, "gentile" and "Israel" classify through the presence or absence of the same traits; they form taxonomic categories that can in the case of the gentile change when that which is classified requires reclassification.

Having seen how the division of humanity into Israelites and gentiles is spelled out in principle, we have now to ask about the basis for the division. Like philosophers, sages in the documents of the Rabbinic canon appeal to a single cause to account for diverse phenomena; the same factor that explains Israel has also to account for the opposite, that is, the gentiles; what Israel has, gentiles lack, and that common point has made all the difference. Idolatry is what angers God and turns him against the gentiles, stated in so many words at B. *A.Z.* 1:1 I.23/4b: "That time at which God gets angry comes when the kings put on their crowns on their heads and prostrate themselves to the sun. Forthwith the Holy One, blessed be He, grows angry." That is why it is absolutely forbidden to conduct any sort of commerce with gentiles in connection with occasions of idolatrous worship, e.g., festivals and the like, so M. *A.Z.* 1:1: "Before the festivals of gentiles for three days it is forbidden to do business with them, (1) to lend anything to them or to borrow anything from them, (2) to lend money to them or to borrow money from them, (3) to repay them or to be repaid by them." Gentiles' deeds—idolatry, rejection of God—and not their genealogy are what define them as non-Israel. Proving that point is critical to this account of theological anthropology of the Rabbinic canon.

Nothing intrinsic distinguishes Israel from the gentiles, only their attitudes and actions. Opinion coalesces around the proposition that Israel and the gentiles do form a single genus, speciated by the relationship to God and the Torah. So in the end, a ferocious Israelite or a forbearing gentile represent mere anomalies, not categorical imperatives. Sufficient proof derives from the explicit statement that, when Israel acts like gentiles, it enters the classification of gentiles; if Israel conducts itself like the gentiles, Israel will be rejected and punished as were the gentiles, with special reference to Egypt and Canaan. This matter is spelled out in another formally perfect composition.

Sifra CXCIII:I.1–11

1. B. "The Lord spoke to Moses saying, Speak to the Israelite people and say to them, I am the Lord your God":
   C. "I am the Lord," for I spoke and the world came into being.
   D. "I am full of mercy."
   E. "I am Judge to exact punishment and faithful to pay recompense."
   F. "I am the one who exacted punishment from the generation of the Flood and the men of Sodom and Egypt, and I shall exact punishment from you if you act like them."

First comes Egypt:

2. A. And how do we know that there was never any nation among all of the nations that practiced such abominations, more than did the Egyptians?

B. Scripture says, "You shall not copy the practices of the land of Egypt where you dwelt."

C. And how do we know that the last generation did more abhorrent things than all the rest of them?

D. Scripture says, "You shall not copy the practices of the land of Egypt."

E. And how do we know that the people in the last location in which the Israelites dwelt were more abhorrent than all the rest?

F. Scripture says, ". . . where you dwelt, you shall not do."

G. And how do we know that the fact that the Israelites dwelt there was the cause for all these deeds?

H. Scripture says, "You shall not copy . . . where you dwelt."

Now we deal with the Canaanites, following the given form:

3. A. How do we know that there was never a nation among all the nations that did more abhorrent things than the Canaanites?

B. Scripture says, "You shall not copy the practices . . . of the land of Canaan [to which I am taking you; nor shall you follow their laws]."

C. And how do we know that the last generation did more abhorrent things than all the rest of them?

D. Scripture says, "You shall not copy the practices of the land of Canaan."

E. And how do we know that the people in the place to which the Israelites were coming for conquest were more abhorrent than all the rest?

F. Scripture says, ". . . to which I am taking you."

G. And how do we know that it is the arrival of the Israelites that caused them to do all these deeds?

H. Scripture says, "or of the land of Canaan to which I am taking you; nor shall you follow their laws."

Now the two cases are expounded in the same terms, and the specific type of laws that Israel is not to follow is defined:

7. A. If "You shall not copy the practices of the land of Egypt . . . or of the land of Canaan,"

B. might one think that they are not to build their buildings or plant vineyards as they did?

C. Scripture says, "nor shall you follow their laws":

    D. "I have referred only to the rules that were made for them and for their fathers and their fathers' fathers."

    E. And what would they do?

    F. A man would marry a man, and a woman would marry a woman, a man would marry a woman and her daughter, a woman would be married to two men.

    G. That is why it is said, "nor shall you follow their laws."

8. A. ["My rules alone shall you observe and faithfully follow my laws":]

    B. "my rules": this refers to laws.

    C. ". . . my laws": this refers to the amplifications thereof.

    D. ". . . shall you observe": this refers to repeating traditions.

    E. ". . . and faithfully follow": this refers to concrete deed.

    F. ". . . and faithfully follow my laws": it is not the repetition of traditions that is the important thing but doing them is the important thing.

At stake in differentiating Israel from the gentiles is life in the world to come; the gentiles offer only death:

9. A. "You shall keep my laws and my rules, by the pursuit of which man [shall live]":

    B. This formulation of matter serves to make keeping and doing into laws, and keeping and doing into rules.

10. A. ". . . shall live":

    B. in the world to come.

    C. And should you wish to claim that the reference is to this world, is it not the fact that in the end one dies?

    D. Lo, how am I to explain, ". . . shall live"?

    E. It is with reference to the world to come.

11. A. "I the Lord am your God":

    B. faithful to pay a reward.

Here we find the entire doctrine of the gentiles fully exposed. God judges Israel and the gentiles by a single rule of justice; to each is meted out measure for measure. Israel is not elect by reason of privilege; Israel is elect solely because Israel accepts the Torah and so knows God. The same punishment exacted from the generation of the flood, the Sodomites, the Egyptians, and all others will be exacted from Israel if Israel acts like them. At that point, Israel becomes gentile. It is the Torah that differentiates. And, at the end, the stakes are exactly what the reading of Mishnah tractate *Sanhedrin* 10:1–2 sets forth implicitly: entry into the world to come, as we noted earlier.

Since, we note time and again, the generative transaction involves intention and attitude, which form the source of the system's dynamism, we cannot find surprising the focus, here too, upon intention. It is, specifically, upon how the idolater regards matters, rather than upon what he actually has done in making and worshipping the idol. The attitude of the idolater governs God's disposition of matters. God hates idolaters more than he hates the idol itself, for, all parties concur, in any case there is no substance in idolatry itself. The idolater rejects God and so makes the idol. So what is at issue in idolatry is the attitude of the idolater, that is, his rejection of the one true God, made manifest in the Torah. The idolater by his attitude and intention confers upon the idol a status that, on its own the idol cannot attain, being inanimate in any event. So the logic that governs distinguishes the actor from the acted upon, the cause from that which is caused, and the rest follows.

Having established that idolaters subject themselves to God's hatred by reason of their attitudes and consequent actions, we ask about the matter of fairness. To explain, we turn to an account of how things came about—a reason we should call historical but sages would classify as paradigmatic. That is, the sages' explanation, framed in terms of a narrative of something that happened, turns out to be a picture of how things now are—a characterization of the established facts as these are realized under all circumstances and at any time, the tenses, past, present, or future making no difference. So when we ask why to begin with gentiles have entered the category of death, and why it is just that they should not enjoy life eternal, we take up a tale that casts in mythic-narrative form what constitutes an analysis of characteristic traits. Not only so, but the narrative explicitly points to the enduring traits, not a given action, to explain the enduring condition of the gentiles: that is how they are, because that is how they wish to be.

So now the question becomes urgent: How has this catastrophic differentiation imposed itself between Israel and the gentiles, such that the gentiles, for all their glory in the here and now, won for themselves the grave, while Israel, for all its humiliation in the present age, inherits the world to come? And the answer is self-evident from all that has been said: the gentiles reject God, whom they could and should have known in the Torah. They rejected the Torah, and all else followed. The proposition then moves in these simple steps:

[1] Israel differs from the gentiles because Israel possesses the Torah and the gentiles do not;

[2] because they do not possess the Torah, the gentiles also worship idols instead of God; and

[3] therefore God rejects the gentiles and identifies with Israel.

And where do considerations of justice and fairness enter in? Here, at a critical turning, the system reaches back into its fundamental and generative conception, that the world is ordered by justice. The Rabbinic canon then has to demonstrate that the same justice that governs Israel and endows Israel with the Torah dictates the fate of the gentiles and denies them the Torah. And, predictably, that demonstration must further underscore the justice of the condition of the gentiles: measure for measure must play itself out especially here.

The gentiles deprived themselves of the Torah because they rejected it, and, showing the precision of justice, they rejected the Torah because the Torah deprived them of the very practices or traits that they deemed characteristic, essential to their being. That circularity marks the tale of how things were to begin with and in fact describes how things always are; it is not historical but philosophical. The gentiles' own character, the shape of their conscience, then, now, and always, accounts for their condition—which, by an act of will, as we have noted, they can change. What they did not want, that of which they were by their own word unworthy, is denied them. And what they do want condemns them. So when each nation comes under judgment for rejecting the Torah, the indictment of each is spoken out of its own mouth, its own self-indictment then forms the core of the matter. Given what we know about the definition of Israel as those destined to live and the gentiles as those not, we cannot find surprising that the entire account is set in that age to come to which the gentiles are denied entry.

When they protest the injustice of the decision that takes effect just then, they are shown the workings of the moral order, as the following quite systematic account of the governing pattern explains.

Bavli ʿAbodah Zarah 1:1 I.2/2a–b

A. R. Hanina bar Pappa, and some say, R. Simlai, gave the following exposition [of the verse, "They that fashion a graven image are all of them vanity, and their delectable things shall not profit, and their own witnesses see not nor know" (Is. 44:9)]: "In the age to come the Holy One, blessed be He, will bring a scroll of the Torah and hold it in his bosom and say, 'Let him who has kept himself busy with it come and take his reward.' Then all the gentiles will crowd together: 'All of the nations are gathered together' (Is. 43:9). The Holy One, blessed be He, will say to them, 'Do not crowd together before me in a mob. But let each nation enter together with [2B] its scribes, 'and let the peoples be gathered together' (Is. 43:9), and the word 'people' means 'kingdom': 'and one kingdom shall be stronger than the other'" (Gen. 25:23).

We note that the players are the principal participants in world history: the Romans first and foremost, then the Persians, the other world-rulers of the age.

C. "The kingdom of Rome comes in first."

H. "The Holy One, blessed be He, will say to them, 'How have you defined your chief occupation?'

I. "They will say before him, 'Lord of the world, a vast number of marketplaces have we set up, a vast number of bathhouses we have made, a vast amount of silver and gold have we accumulated. And all of these things we have done only in behalf of Israel, so that they may define as their chief occupation the study of the Torah.'

J. "The Holy One, blessed be He, will say to them, 'You complete idiots! Whatever you have done has been for your own convenience. You have set up a vast number of marketplaces to be sure, but that was so as to set up whorehouses in them. The bathhouses were for your own pleasure. Silver and gold belong to me anyhow: "Mine is the silver and mine is the gold, says the Lord of hosts" (Hag. 2:8). Are there any among you who have been telling of "this," and "this" is only the Torah: "And this is the Torah that Moses set before the children of Israel'" (Dt. 4:44). So they will make their exit, humiliated.

The claim of Rome—to support Israel in Torah study—is rejected on grounds that the Romans did not exhibit the right attitude, always a dynamic force in theology. Then the other world rule enters in with its claim:

K. "When the kingdom of Rome has made its exit, the kingdom of Persia enters afterward."

M. "The Holy One, blessed be He, will say to them, 'How have you defined your chief occupation?'

N. "They will say before him, 'Lord of the world, We have thrown up a vast number of bridges, we have conquered a vast number of

towns, we have made a vast number of wars, and all of them we
did only for Israel, so that they may define as their chief occupation the study of the Torah.'

O. "The Holy One, blessed be He, will say to them, 'Whatever you
have done has been for your own convenience. You have thrown
up a vast number of bridges, to collect tolls, you have conquered a
vast number of towns, to collect the corvée, and, as to making a
vast number of wars, I am the one who makes wars: "The Lord is
a man of war" (Ex. 19:17). Are there any among you who have
been telling of "this," and "this" is only the Torah: "And this is the
Torah that Moses set before the children of Israel"' (Dt. 4:44). So
they will make their exit, humiliated.

R. "And so it will go with each and every nation."

As native categories, Rome and Persia are singled out, "all the other
nations" play no role, for reasons with which we are already familiar.
Once more theology reaches into its deepest thought on the power of
intentionality, showing that what people want is what they get.

But matters cannot be limited to the two world empires of the present age, Rome and Persia, standing in judgment at the end of time.
Theology values balance, proportion, seeks complementary relationships, and therefore treats beginnings along with endings, the one
going over the ground of the other. Accordingly, a recapitulation of
the same event—the gentiles' rejection of the Torah—chooses as its
setting not the last judgment but the first encounter, that is, the giving of the Torah itself. In the timeless world constructed by the
Rabbinic canon, what happens at the outset exemplifies how things
always happen, and what happens at the end embodies what has
always taken place. The basic thesis is identical—the gentiles cannot
accept the Torah because to do so they would have to deny their very
character. But the exposition retains its interest because it takes its
own course.

Now the gentiles are not just Rome and Persia but others; and of
special interest, the Torah is embodied in some of the ten commandments—not to murder, not to commit adultery, not to steal;
then the gentiles are rejected for not keeping the seven commandments assigned to the children of Noah. The upshot is that the reason that the gentiles rejected the Torah is that the Torah prohibits
deeds that the gentiles do by their very nature. The subtext here is
already familiar: Israel ultimately is changed by the Torah, so that
Israel exhibits traits imparted by their encounter with the Torah. So

too with the gentiles: by their nature they are what they are; the Torah has not changed their nature.

So much for the gentile component of theological anthropology of the Rabbinic canon. Now that we have a clear picture of how humanity is constituted, we turn to the urgent question of the contemporary condition of Israel among the nations. The now-routine question, which the system identifies as critical, requires no elaboration: Why, for all that, do the gentiles rule Israel? The answer is, that is how God has arranged matters, and at every point the divine plan to impose justice is realized. The key proposition contains two elements: God has decided to do things in just this way, and God's plan accords with the requirements of the just governance of world order. It is the second of the two components that is elaborated, provoking the question natural to this theology: What has Israel done to deserve its punishment? And why this punishment in particular?

When we recall that, within this theology, world history orbits about Israel, we cannot find surprising that the present arrangement of world politics responds to Israel's condition, specifically, its sinfulness. The reason the gentiles rule is that Israel sinned. When Israel repents, they will regain dominion. This simple proposition comes to expression in so many words in the following statement:

Esther Rabbah XI:i.11

A. Said R. Aibu, "It is written, 'For the kingdom is the Lord's and he is the ruler over the nations' (Ps. 22:29).

B. "And yet you say here, 'when King Ahasuerus sat on his royal throne'?

C. "In the past dominion resided in Israel, but when they sinned, its dominion was taken away from them and given to the nations of the world.

D. "That is in line with the following verse of Scripture: 'I will give the land over into the hand of evil men'" (Ez. 30:12).

F. [Continuing D:] "In the future, when the Israelites repent, the Holy One, blessed be he, will take dominion from the nations of the world and restore it to Israel.

G. "When will this come about? 'When saviors will come up on Mount Zion'" (Obadiah 1:21).

Israel controls its own condition, its attitude governs its own fate. Because Israel sinned, gentiles rule; when Israel by an act of will repents, then Israel will regain dominion over itself. The nations serve as instruments of God's wrath; nothing that they do comes about by

their own volition, but only by consequence of Israel's. Israel is justly
punished for its own sins, and its present condition demonstrates the
working of God's justice. All things are foreseen, but free will is
accorded to Israel, and within those two principles is located a clear
and reasonable explanation for the enormous anomaly that idolaters
rule God's people. That turns out to be not anomalous but wholly
coherent with the principle of the rule of justice.

But if Israel is in control, why should punishment take the particular form of subjugation to idolaters? The reason is that Israel's condition responds not only to its own actions and intentions, which
ought to have subjected Israel to the penalty meted out to Adam
for his act of rebellion. Israel enjoys also the protection and intervention of the founders of Israel, the patriarchs. They establish the
point of difference between Adam and Israel: God's intervention, his
identification of the patriarchs as the means by which he will ultimately make himself known to humanity. Hence the very formation
of Israel bears within itself the point of differentiation between Adam
and Israel. As to the dominion of the gentiles, entailing also exile
from the Land of Israel, that penalty for sin represents a choice made
by Abraham. Foreseeing all that would come about through time,
God set forth the four constituents of Israelite being: the gentiles,
Gehenna, the sacrifices, the Torah. They formed a balance: if Israel
practices the commandments and studies the Torah, they will be
spared gentile rule and Gehenna; that is, they will thrive under the
dominion of the Kingdom of Heaven, on the one side, and they will
inherit the world to come, on the other. But God knows that Israel
will sin, so to begin with, Abraham is offered the choice of penalties.
He chooses the lesser of the two penalties, the dominion of the gentiles, reserving for Israel the greater of the two alternatives, life eternal. The system at each point recapitulates its main principles. Here
is how the matter is spelled out.

Pesiqta Rabbati XV [= *Pesiqta deRab Kahana* V]:II.1

1. A. "Great things have you done, O Lord my God; your wonderful
      purposes and plans are all for our good; [none can compare with
      you; I would proclaim them and speak of them, but they are
      more than I can tell]" (Prov. 40:5):

Now begins the process of the justification of subjugation to the
nations; whatever happens, happens for the good of Israel:

B. R. Hinenah bar Papa says two [teachings in respect to the cited verse]: "All those wonders and plans which you made so that our father, Abraham, would accept the subjugation of Israel to the nations were for our good, for our sake, so that we might endure in the world."

C. Simeon bar Abba in the name of R. Yohanan: "Four things did the Holy One, blessed be he, show to our father, Abraham: the Torah, the sacrifices, Gehenna, and the rule of the kingdoms.

D. "The Torah: '. . . and a flaming torch passed between these pieces' (Gen. 15:17).

E. "Sacrifices: 'And he said to him, Take for me a heifer divided into three parts' (Gen. 15:9).

F. "Gehenna: 'behold a smoking fire pot.'

G. "The rule of the kingdoms: 'Lo, dread, a great darkness' (Gen. 15:12)."

Here is the principal message: Torah and sacrifice preserve Israel, the subjugation to the nations and Gehenna penalize Israel for failing to maintain Torah study and sacrifice:

H. "The Holy One, blessed be he, said to our father, Abraham, 'So long as your descendants are occupied with the former two, they will be saved from the latter two. If they abandon the former two of them, they will be judged by the other two.

I. "'So long as they are occupied with study of the Torah and performance of the sacrifices, they will be saved from Gehenna and from the rule of the kingdoms.

Israel's failure is foreseen, if not foreordained, and now Abraham is offered a choice for his descendants' future:

J. "'But [God says to Abraham] in the future the house of the sanctuary is destined to be destroyed and the sacrifices nullified. What is your preference? Do you want your children to go down into Gehenna or to be subjugated to the four kingdoms?'"

All this conformed to Abraham's wishes:

K. R. Hinena bar Pappa said, "Abraham himself chose the subjugation to the four kingdoms.

L. "What is the scriptural basis for that view? 'How should one chase a thousand and two put ten thousand to flight, except their rock had given them over' (Deut. 32:30). That statement concerning the rock refers only to Abraham, as it is said, 'Look at the rock from which you were hewn' (Is. 51:1).

M. "'But the Lord delivered them up' (Deut. 32:30) teaches that God then approved what he had chosen."

Once more working out their own narratives in response to Scripture's, we now have an account of Abraham's thinking when he made the fateful choice:

> 2. A. R. Berekhiah in the name of R. Levi: "Now Abraham sat and puzzled all that day, saying, 'Which should I choose, Gehenna or subjugation to the kingdoms? Is the one worse than the other?'
>
>   B. "Said the Holy One, blessed be he, to him, 'Abraham, how long are you going to sit in puzzlement? Choose without delay.' That is in line with this verse: 'On that day the Lord made a covenant with Abram saying'" (Gen. 15:18).
>
>   C. What is the meaning of, saying?
>
>   D. R. Hinena bar Pappa said, "Abraham chose for himself the subjugation to the four kingdoms."
>
>   E. We have reached the dispute of R. Yudan and R. Idi and R. Hama bar Haninah said in the name of a certain sage in the name of Rabbi: "The Holy One, blessed be he, [not Abraham] chose the subjugation to the four kingdoms for him, in line with the following verse of Scripture: 'You have caused men to ride over our heads, we have been overcome by fire and water' (Ps. 66:12). That is to say, 'you have made ride over our heads various nations, and it is as though we went through fire and through water'" (Ps. 66:21).

Since Israel lives out the patterns originally set by the patriarchs, to understand Israel's condition we have to examine the deeds of Abraham and his selected son and grandson. But those deeds embodied the fundamental truths of the system. Torah and sacrifices preserve Israel from Gehenna and the rule of the kingdoms (the one personal, the other communal, in both instances). Faced with the choice of Gehenna or subjugation, Abraham chose the latter.

From these specific points of correlation, we turn to the more general, consequential claim of the Rabbinic canon, that God foresaw all that has come upon Israel. The importance of that conviction comes to the surface when we see the corollary:

[1] the Kingdom of Heaven continues to encompass Israel, even while it is ruled by the gentiles, and that

[2] the anomaly and injustice of gentile hegemony will ultimately come to an end, by reason of Israel's own act of will.

The prophets called the gentiles the instruments of God's wrath. Sages took the same view. They explained that the gentiles do not act on their own but carry out God's will. What happens to Israel therefore reassures Israel that the holy people continues to live in the kingdom of Heaven, and the very fact of the anomaly of pagan rule turns out to guarantee God's rule and Israel's role. Israel has not lost its position in the unfolding of the story of creation of a just world order set forth in the revelation of Sinai. Israel is now writing, and will continue to write, its own chapter of that story. Not only so, but Israel is not subordinate to the world empires but their equal, standing in its assigned position at the end and climax of that part of the story of creation that the gentile empires are assigned to write. These convictions come to express in systematic expositions that utilize the first three of the four principal media of expression of the Rabbinic canon—exegesis, mythic-narrative, even the symbolization of discourse through list-making and the amplification of lists, and Halakhah—to make a systematic statement.

We commence with the main point. The dominance of the gentiles, particularly in the form of the standard cluster of the succession of four world empires, guarantees that the just pattern that God has foreordained will impose structure and order upon history. That pattern leads inexorably from one gentile kingdom to the next in order, but finally to the rule of holy Israel, defined as those who know God. Israel will be the fifth and final monarchy, inaugurating God's rule and the end of Israel as a sector of humanity altogether. Sages maintained that world order is not only just and proportionate, but also regular and balanced. Hence they conceived that patterns reproduce themselves, because order governs.

What sages prove on the foundations of Scripture is that God foresaw all that would come about. Having brought Israel into being and given Israel the Torah, God gave Israel free will to obey or to suffer punishment for disobedience. He then realized what would come about and determined an appropriate punishment, one of a different order altogether from that inflicted on the generation of the flood. It would be a punishment appropriate to the sin. Since Israel did not accept the dominion of God, living in the Land of Israel, Israel would have to suffer the rule of world empires, and would live in exile from the Land of Israel. Then Israel would repent of its sin, recognize the error of submitting to pagan rule, which was cruel, rather than the rule of God, which is benevolent. And, as we shall see in due course, all the rest would follow.

Now, all of this was foreseen. In response to the participation of the patriarchs, particularly Abraham and Jacob, God not only chose exile as the penalty for Israel's disobedience of God's will set forth in the Torah. He even identified the particular nations that would subjugate Israel. These nations would be world rulers, as we already have noted, and thus appropriate in stature to the status of the nation they would rule. They would come in orderly succession, so indicating that a single plan covered all of world politics, and it would be clear to all concerned that the penultimate and greatest of the nations, Rome, would ultimately give way to the ultimate nation, holy Israel itself. Exegesis yielded these propositions. At the same time, numerous stories also served to bear elements of the same tale. But, as is clear, the entire complex of convictions forms a continuous story, beginning with creation, passing by Sinai, and ending up with the end of time as we now know it.

The just world order is comprised by the division of humanity into Israel with the Torah, and the gentiles with their idols. The one is destined to life eternal with God, the other to the grave, there to spend eternity. World order then finds its center and focus in Israel, and whatever happens that counts under Heaven's gaze takes place in relationship to Israel. That division yields rich and dense details but only a simple story, easily retold. In a purposeful act of benevolence, the just God created the world in so orderly a way that the principle of justice and equity governs throughout. Fair rules apply equally to all persons and govern all circumstances. God not only created man but made himself known to man through the Torah. But man, possessed of free will, enjoys the choice of accepting and obeying the Torah, therefore living in the kingdom of Heaven, or rejecting the Torah and God in favor of idolatry and idols.

Now we realize the full potentiality contained in the simple doctrines with which we began: that those who accept the Torah are called Israel, and the others are called gentiles. The gentiles hate Israel because of the Torah, and they also hate God. But the world as now constituted is such that the gentiles rule, and Israel is subjugated. Where is the justice in that inversion of right, with God's people handed over to the charge of God's enemies? Israel has sinned, so rebelled against God, and the gentiles then form God's instrument for the punishment of Israel. God's justice governs, the world conforms to orderly rules, embedded in the very structure of creation. Israel's own condition stands as the surest testimony of the world's good and just order. That guarantee is for now and all time to come.

So much for the large abstractions: justice worked out in the world-encompassing dimensions of the relationship of the two vast components of humanity, Israel and the gentiles. We now turn from macrocosm to microcosm, to that other dimension of order, the humble one that takes the measure of the workaday world. What logic, what justice, governs a world in which—as the marketplace and household attest—the wicked prosper and righteous suffer and no logic of justice demonstrably governs, but only happy accident for the fortunate, and misery for everybody else?

IV. Ordering the Ultimate Anomaly: Private Lives

The same premises that guided sages' thinking about Israel and the Torah, the gentiles and idolatry, required deep thought indeed on the ultimate anomaly of a logic animated by the principle of God's rational justice: the actualities of everyday life. That God orders the world through justice accessible to human reason confronts the everywhere acknowledged obstacle: justice prevails only now and then. Man's fate rarely accords with the fundamental principle of a just order but mostly discredits it. But if the human condition embodied in Israelites' lives one by one defies the smooth explanations that serve for justifying the condition of Israel in the abstract, then the entire logic of the Rabbinic canon fails.

How then reveal God's justice in the chaotic, scarcely-manageable detritus of private lives? It is through articulation of the doctrine of reward and punishment, the insistence on the justice of God in whatever happens. Because sages constructed a single coherent theology, encompassing every dimension of existence, they had to show the justice of a single principle of explanation for private and public affairs alike. Then how to hold together, within a unitary rule of order, explaining in the same way the abstract situation of an imagined nation and the concrete circumstance of ordinary people near at hand? When sages reflected upon the complex problem of how a world order of justice governs private lives, three principles set bounds to their speculation. These principles responded, in logical sequence, to three questions:

[1] Can the individual be at all distinguished from all Israel?
[2] If not, then on what basis does the individual matter at all? and
[3] Can the same explanation that necessarily accounts for the condition of Israel sufficiently serve also for that of Israelites, and if not, what further components does the encompassing rationalization of Israelite existence require?

What we shall now see is that sages maintained that the category "Israel" covered the holy people as a collectivity, and also encompassed every individual therein, referring to a private person by the same word as applies to the nation all together. But they did accord to the individual an autonomous standing, apart from the community. And they vastly expanded their thinking beyond the limits of the categories Israel and the gentiles. Rather, they composed a complex, many-sided theory of the way in which order consisting of justice explained private lives too.

The logic of system-building that covered category-formation offered no alternative but to invoke a single principle to cover the undifferentiated category "Israel," meaning both the collectivity and the individual. The alternative, one rule for the nation, another for the private person, violated the very premise of all thought within the monotheist framework, which found the ground of all being, the explanation of all things, in one God, the benevolent and just creator of heaven and earth. So sages' systematic reflection insisted that individual Israelites cannot be thought about in a manner separate from all Israel. Consequently, the same rules that apply to all Israel— the rule of justice, the appeal to the self-evident rationality expressed by the equation of measure for measure—explain what happens to individuals.

That principle closed off one possible way of solving the problem of evil confronting monotheism. Sages could not resolve the conflict between faith and personal fate by distinguishing between Israel, which plays out its history in a world of justice and fairness, and the individual Israelite, whose private life has no bearing upon public policy in God's dominion. In fact, sages took for granted the very opposite: to be an Israelite was to embody Israel in the here and now. The fate of the individual is wrapped up in the destiny of all Israel; the same calculus describes both. That is why monotheism's requirement of systemic coherence by nature produced an endless sequence of anomalous cases.

How then did the union of public and private Israel take place? Here the justification of Israel's fate at the hands of the nations serves. Take the case of martyrdom, which represents the ultimate joining of holy Israel and the private person's act of sanctifying God's name. Then the individual gives his life for the Torah shared by all. But even here we differentiate Israel and Israelite. For individuals enjoy the option, which, by definition, the community as a whole does not, of changing their private situation, improving it by joining the idolaters. It is at that point that the anomaly of unjust or unfair results emerges most sharply: How long are you going to do good deeds on his account, for him alone, while he pays you back with evil? And so the alternative presented by idolaters of good will: join us and we shall treat you well.

Here is how the united faith of Israel and the Israelite recapitulates the problem of evil in one concrete statement:

Song of Songs Rabbah LXXXIX:i.9, 11–12

A. ["Return, return, O Shulammite, return, return that we may look upon you. Why should you look upon the Shulammite, as upon a dance before two armies?" (Song 6:13)] "Return that we may look upon you:"

B. The nations of the world say to Israel, "How long are you going to die for your God and devote yourselves completely to him?"

C. "For thus Scripture says, 'Therefore do they love you beyond death' (Song 1:3).

D. "And how long will you be slaughtered on his account: 'No, but for your sake we are killed all day long' (Ps. 44:23)?

E. "'How long are you going to do good deeds on his account, for him alone, while he pays you back with bad things?

F. "Come over to us, and we shall make you governors, hyparchs, and generals,

G. "'That we may look upon you': and you will be the cynosure of the world: 'And you shall be the look out of all the people'" (Ex. 18:21).

So is set forth the gentile challenge. Now comes the Israelite response:

H. And the Israelites will answer, "'Why should you look upon the Shulammite, as upon a dance before two armies':

As usual, Scripture's facts are systematized and formed into general rules, as the philosophical sages transform Scripture into natural philosophy:

> I. "In your entire lives, have you ever heard that Abraham, Isaac, and Jacob worshipped idols, that their children should do so after them? Our fathers did not worship idols, and we shall not worship idols after them.
>
> J. "But what can you do for us?
>
> K. "Can it be like the dance that was made for Jacob, our father, when he went forth from the house of Laban?"

We now turn to instances of Israel's redemption, at the sea and in the time of Elisha:

> 11. A. [Continuing 9.K:] "Or can you make a dance for us such as was made for our fathers at the sea? 'And the angel of God removed . . .' (Ex. 14:19).
>
> B. "Or can you make a dance for us like the one that was made for Elisha: 'And when the servant of the man of God was risen early and gone forth, behold a host with horses and chariots was round about the city. And his servant said to him, Alas, my master, what shall we do? And he answered, Do not be afraid, for they who are with us are more than those who are with them. Forthwith Elisha prayed and said, Lord, I pray you, open his eyes that he may see. And the Lord opened the eyes of the young man, and he saw, and behold, the mountain was full of horses and chariots of fire around about Elisha' (2 Kgs. 6:15).

And finally comes the end time, to which the gentiles will not come anyhow:

> C. "Or can you make a dance for us like the one that the Holy One, blessed be He, will make for the righteous in the age to come?"

The passage continues with the exposition of God at the last as lord of the dance.

The question confronts individuals, as the dance or as death is a most private act: How long are you going to die for your God and give him the last full measure of devotion? And there is no dance without individual dancers. But death is public, and there also is no dance without a shared rhythm and gesture. The problem carries along its own solution: at the end of time the individual Israelite joins all Israel in the eschatological dance to be lead by the Lord of the dance, God himself. Here then we find a fine metaphor to make the systematic statement of the problem of evil formulated in both communal and individual terms: each dancer dances on his own, but all do the same step, stamping together in the same rhythm—predictably, within this theological system, with God leading the way.

That brings us to the second question: What difference do the state and fate of the individual make, if the individual Israelite finds himself subjected to the same fate as all other Israelites who constitute all Israel? And why do individual persons come under the purview of the theological system at hand? A single explanation, the one governing all Israel, ought to serve for the complaint of private persons at the injustice of what is meted out to them. But that is not the position that sages' theology adopts. Rather, they find particular purpose in the identification of the category of free-standing individual, defined in his own terms and in the framework of his own existence, not only within all Israel. The word "Israel" does refer to persons, Israelites one by one, not only to the people. So a dialectic, not to be resolved, takes shape between the public and the private. Each individual enjoys his own justice. But individuals suffer along with all Israel. All Israel designs its own destiny by its attitude and consequent actions. But all Israel is shaped by the actions and attitude of individuals one by one—a complex dialectic indeed, in which justice may well be obscured.

Individuals matter, on their own, not only within the collectivity of Israel. On what basis do sages construct their doctrine of individual worth? Sages themselves hardly valued for its own sake the perpetuation of the individual's name. In their normative statements, the law followed the anonymous, not the assigned ruling. One who wished to make a long-term contribution, therefore, had to seek to submerge his private views within a public consensus. Eternity for one's contribution demanded anonymity for one's person, much as, to save a child, a parent will willingly give up life itself. But sages did recognize that for worthy purposes the individual could be distinguished.

That brings us to the third question: Can we invoke the same explanation for private lives that serves in accounting for the public condition of all Israel? The answer is affirmative, but with important qualifications. The fundamental affirmation, pertaining to public Israel and private Israelite alike, maintains that exact justice governs. No anomalies will persist past the resurrection, the last judgment, and the world to come. But the application of that principle yields a much thicker layer of instantiation and application, far more diversity in the range of explanation, than in the case of the condition of Israel subjugated by the nations.

Private matches public. If the nations are responsible for their condition, so is Israel, so are Israelites. So too is the rule of justice, and justification, for private lives. Everything begins with the insistence that people are responsible for what they do, therefore for what happens to them, as much as Israel dictates its destiny by its own deeds. Justice reigns, whatever happens. The reason that man (therefore, groups formed by men) is responsible for his own actions is that he enjoys free will. Man is constantly subject to divine judgment; he has free choice, hence may sin. God judges the world in a generous way; but judgment does take place:

Tractate *Abot* 3:15

A. R. Aqiba says, "Everything is foreseen, and free choice is given. In goodness the world is judged. And all is in accord with the abundance of deeds."

B. He would say, "(1) All is handed over as a pledge, (2) and a net is cast over all the living. (3) The store is open, (4) the storekeeper gives credit, (5) the account book is open, and (6) the hand is writing.

C. "(1) Whoever wants to borrow may come and borrow. (2) The charity collectors go around every day and collect from man whether he knows it or not. (3) And they have grounds for what they do. (4) And the judgment is a true judgment. (5) And everything is ready for the meal."

God may foresee what is to happen, but man still exercises free will. His attitude and intentionality make all the difference. Because man is not coerced to sin, nor can man be forced to love God or even obey the Torah, an element of uncertainty affects every life. That is the point at which man's will competes with God's. It follows that, where man gives to God what God wants but cannot coerce, or what God wants but cannot command—love, generosity, for instance—there, the theology of the Rabbinic canon alleges, God responds with an act of uncoerced grace. But in all, one thing is reliable, and that is the working of just recompense for individual action. Expectations of a just reward or punishment, contrasting with actualities, therefore precipitate all thought on the rationality of private life: what happens is supposed to make sense within the governing theology of a just order.

But that expectation rarely is met. How then do sages justify—meaning, "show the justice of"—what happens in private lives? Let us first consider how sages explained private fate as a consequence of individual behavior. Their first principle, predictably, is that, as Israel defines its own fate, so individuals bear responsibility for their own condition. A person is responsible for his own character. Even though one is surrounded by wicked people, he may still remain righteous, and vice versa. A measure of righteousness is not to conduct oneself in the manner of one's wicked neighbors. Not only so, but the righteous son of a wicked father enjoys much admiration but bears no burden of responsibility for his ancestry, and so for the contrary circumstance.

Sifré to Numbers CXXXIII:II.1

A. "[Then drew near the daughters of Zelophehad] the son of Hepher son of Gilead son of Machir son of Manasseh:"

B. Scripture thus informs [us] that just as Zelophehad was a first-born, so all of them were first-born [daughters] [to their mothers]; that all of them were upright women, daughters of an upright man.

C. For in the case of whoever keeps his [worthy] deeds concealed, and his father's deeds are concealed, Scripture portrays a worthy genealogy, lo, this was a righteous man son of a righteous man.

D. And in the case of whoever keeps his [unworthy] deeds concealed, and his father's deeds concealed, Scripture portrays a disreputable genealogy, lo, this is a wicked man son of a wicked man.

But who bears responsibility when an infant dies, or a woman in childbirth, or a man before his appointed time (prior to age sixty in the Talmud's estimation)? And how do sages reasonably explain the anomalies round about, those manifested by Scripture and embodied in the here and now of everyday life? Several distinct explanations serve, depending on the circumstance. In one, the individual's fate is bound up with that of the group, Israel, or of the generation, of which he is part; in the second type of explanation, a specific sort of malady or affliction is bound up with a particular sort of sin. Since old age, sickness, suffering, and death come to all; moreover, sages will be seen not to concede the status, as punishment for sin, of these common mediators of man's fate.

Let us take up the first, that individuals suffer as part of Israel.

What happens to this one or that one may make sense within the story of what happens to Israel collectively. Sages thereby concede that, in an exact sense, life is not, cannot be, fair; we are not responsible for the fact that we are born into interesting times, though we become responsible for how we respond to those points of interest. But while sages do accord the moral role to the individual, they never conceive of the individual as utterly isolated, free-standing in any time or place; the individual is not necessarily party to the sin of his generation, but he is always part of the community that God has identified as the principal actor in the drama of human events, Israel. Haman hated Israel because of Mordecai. Moses was set adrift in the river because Pharaoh feared mighty Israel. It made no difference whether the individual or the group precipitated the crisis. But that meant, once the angel of death unleashed his scythe, everyone would be caught on its blade.

The second approach to justification of what happens to private persons forms a variation on the first. Just as individual Israelites are caught up within the fate of Israel, so they are party to what happens in their own day and age. That involves not so much temporal as circumstantial considerations: it is good to be a contemporary of righteous persons, and it is unfortunate to live in the age or place of wicked ones. Whatever happens comes about by reason of the character of a given generation and the presence of the righteous or the wicked. The righteous bring goodness to the world, and when they die, retribution follows; the wicked bring retribution to the world, and when they die, goodness returns. This is spelled out in so many words:

Tosefta *Sotah* 10:1–11:2

10:1 A. When righteous people come into the world, good comes into the world and retribution departs from the world.
    B. And when they take their leave from the world, retribution comes into the world, and goodness departs from the world.
10:2 A. When bad people come into the world, retribution comes into the world, and goodness departs from the world.
    B. And when they depart from the world, goodness comes back into the world, and retribution departs from the world.

The individual forms a moral arena of his own, but he also participates in the life and fate of Israel, on the one side, and his own generation, on the other. Scripture provides ample evidence of that fact.

So it is in the nature of things that the individual cannot claim exact justice in the here and now; circumstances intervene, and, when it comes to God's government, what happens to the holy people or to the community at large takes priority over the fate of the individual. That admission reaffirms the essential rationality of the divine rule, the justice that prevails overall, even while accepting that individuals may present anomalies. But these anomalies will work themselves out in another way, and the program of justification takes account of yet other, available solutions to the problem of evil. The individual may suffer in his generation, but that is only for the moment; at the end of days, when the dead return to life, the individual will be judged on his own and accorded a portion of the world to come commensurate with his virtue in this life.

A third approach addresses the individual in his own terms and framework and states in so many words that, just like the community of Israel, so too individuals suffer by reason of the result of their own deeds. We have already considered penalties for specific actions. The doctrine of reward and punishment is spelled out in close detail. First let us take up the matter of punishment for specific sins or crimes. Here is a clear statement that the individual brings his fate upon his own head, in the context of a specific disaster. The person afflicted with the imaginary ailment described at Lev. 13–14, here translated as "plagues," or "plague of leprosy," has brought the illness upon himself by gossiping, and Scripture contains ample proof of that fact.

Sifra CLV:i.8

A. ". . . saying" (Lev. 14:35)—
B. The priest will say to him words of reproach: "My son, plagues come only because of gossip [T. 6:7], as it is said, 'Take heed of the plague of leprosy to keep very much and to do, remember what the Lord God did to Miriam' (Deut. 24:80).
C. "And what has one thing to do with the other?
D. "But this teaches that she was punished only because of gossip.
E. "And is it not an argument *a fortiori*?
F. "If Miriam, who did not speak before Moses' presence, suffered so, one who speaks ill of his fellow in his very presence, how much the more so?"

Then one who gossips is penalized by an attack of whatever disease, if any, is represented by the word "plagues," or by the skin ailment under discussion here. God has spelled out in the Torah both sins and the penalty attaching to them. So what happens to the individual will naturally be explained as a consequence of what he has done.

But if some are virtuous and some commit sin, everyone dies. The fortunate reach old age. The common folk encounter sickness. How accommodate man's fate to God's benevolent, just providence? Accordingly, from the ordinary and everyday, we turn to other dimensions of the complex corpus of doctrines on how the just world order accounts, also, for what happens in all ordinary lives: death, sickness, old age, suffering, not to mention disappointment in its myriad forms.

Before proceeding, let us briefly review what we have established to this point. In our examination of how theology deals with the individual in his own terms, we have now established that destiny is justice, what happens to individuals in one way or another is susceptible to explanation by appeal to God's just intent. Astrology and impersonal fate dismissed, chance and accident co-opted, what still requires theological justification is man's fate: sickness, suffering, death.

Let us start with premature death. As we have noted along the way, sages treat death before one's "time" as a divine penalty for certain types of sin or crime. The penalty inflicted by Heaven is extirpation, the premature death of the felon or sinner. That accomplishes the expiation of the felony or the sin. Then the felon or sinner enters that right relationship with Heaven that allows life to go forward "in the world to come." Clearly, then, just as execution by the court corrects matters, so execution by Heaven does the same. The counterpart to the death penalty inflicted by the earthly or by the heavenly court is one and the same: atonement yielding life eternal. Sin and crime are for the here and now; but life eternal beyond the grave is for all Israel, defined as those who worship God and live in his kingdom.

So the sages mounted their theodicy in argument after argument. They framed and found scriptural bases for their doctrine. All this was to try to persuade themselves that somehow the world conformed to rationality defined by justice. True, the claim that anguish and illness, premature death and everyday suffering fit under the rules of reasonable world order; that insistence that when the wicked prosper, justice still may be done—these propositions, necessary to the system, may well have transcended the here and now and conformed to a higher reality. But still, when all is said and the day is done, the doctrine of suffering could not encompass all cases, let alone persuade everybody who raised the question, Why me? Why now? Nor did sages so frame matters as to suggest that they found theology's Panglossian solutions, if necessary, wholly sufficient let alone compelling. True, suffering is to be accepted as a mark of God's grace, a gift, an occasion, a mode of atonement and reconciliation with God. True, the patriarchs found much good in man's fate and asked God to arrange matters as they are. And yet the fact remains that some folk suffer more than others, and not uncommonly the wicked prosper and the righteous do not.

So the doctrine of suffering on its own could not, and did not, complete the Rabbinic canon's account of the confrontation with the key dilemma of sages' theology of world order, the anomalies that manifestly flaw private lives, viewed in comparison and contrast with one another. Say what they would, sages in the end had to complete the circle: some do not get what they deserve, whether for good or for ill, and, if their time is replicated in our own, those some were very many. To that protean problem sages found in their larger theology a commensurate and predictable response.

Sages identified with the Torah the promise of life eternal, with idolatry the extinction of being. This would come about at the last days, which will correspond with, and complete, the first days of creation. Justice will be done only when the world is perfected. With that conviction forming the foundation of their very definition of world order, divided between those who will overcome the grave, Israel with the Torah, and those who will not, the gentiles with idolatry, sages found in hand a simple solution. The righteous suffer in this world and get their just reward in the world to come, but the wicked enjoy this world and suffer in the world to come. Since theology of the Rabbinic canon to begin with distinguished the Torah and life from idolatry and death, what happens in this world and in this life does not tell the whole story. And when that entire story is told, the received formulation of the problem of evil no longer pertains, and the final anomalies are smoothed out.

That theology further contemplated a world beyond the grave—the world to come, in which individuals would resume the life they knew, but now for eternity. That conviction, critical to the system as a whole, also provided a solution to the problem of the prosperity of the wicked and the misery of the righteous. By insisting that this world does not tell the whole story of a private life, sages could promise beyond the grave what the here and now denied. The simplest statement of that position is as follows:

Bavli *Horayot* 3:3 I./11a

6. A. Expounded R. Nahman bar Hisda, "What is the meaning of the verse of Scripture, 'There is a vanity that occurs on the earth, for there are the righteous who receive what is appropriate to the deeds of the wicked, and there are the wicked who receive what is appropriate to the deeds of the righteous' (Qoh. 8:14).
   B. "Happy are the righteous, for in this world they undergo what in the world to come is assigned as recompense for the deeds of the wicked, and woe is the wicked, for in this world they enjoy the fruits of what is assigned in the world to come to the deeds of the righteous."

The righteous will enjoy the world to come all the more, and the wicked will suffer in the world to come all the more; the one has saved up his reward for eternity, the other has in this transient world already spent such reward as he may ever get. But that still raises a question:

   B. Said Raba, "So if the righteous enjoy both worlds, would that be so bad for them?"

Raba acts in the model of Abraham facing God before Sodom! But he has a better solution, making a still more radical claim:

   C. Rather, said Raba, "Happy are the righteous, for in this world they get what is set aside for the [meritorious] deeds of the wicked in this world, and woe to the wicked, for in this world they get what is assigned for the deeds of the righteous in this world."

Raba's solution takes account of theory of atonement through suffering. The righteous atone in the here and now; that is why they suffer. Then the world to come is all the more joyful. Now follows a story that shows how disciples of sages enjoy in this world such benefit as the wicked ought to have had in the world to come, and the rest follows.

D. R. Pappa and R. Huna b. R. Joshua came before Raba. He said to them, "Have you mastered such and such tractate and such and such tractate?"

E. They said to him, "Yes."

F. "Have you gotten a bit richer?"

G. They said to him, "Yes, because we bought a little piece of land."

H. He recited in their regard, "Happy are the righteous, for in this world they undergo what in the world to come is assigned as recompense for the deeds of the wicked."

To grasp how, in massive detail, ultimate justice pervades the here and now, the premise of this passage should not be missed. It is that of a steady-state moral economy: a finite store of rewards and punishments awaits the righteous and the wicked alike, so what comes to the one is denied the other. In due course we shall encounter again the sages' powerful yearning for a world of stability and hierarchical order, in which fair exchange assures that nothing much changes. There, not surprisingly, we shall once more address the dialectics of Torah versus land ownership, wealth in the transcendent and mundane planes of reality. Here it suffices to note that world order defined by reasoned justice serves to justify—show God's justice in— even humble, everyday experience. It follows that the rules that govern and account for everyday experience are supposed to make sense of the nonsense of the present age.

But sages were no fools, and hope for the at-present-intangible future did not dim their dark vision of the ordinary experience of life, its nonsense, its anomalies. While pursuing philosophical modes of thought, in the end sages valued sagacity beyond reason, however compelling. For all their insistence upon the rule of God through a just order, sages accepted that beyond the known and reasonable lay the unknowable, the realm of God beyond the part set forth in the revealed Torah. They affirmed, in the end, their own failure, which makes them plausible and human in their claims to account for much, if not all, of the anguish of which private lives even of the most holy of men are comprised. In the end we all die, and who knows how long the interval until the resurrection? So the sages' last word on the reasonable rule of the just order consists of a single imperative: humility, the gift of wisdom, not of wit.

Here is a passage that many generations of Talmud students have found sublime, the statement of all things, all in all:

Bavli *Menahot* 3:7 II.5/29b

5. A. Said R. Judah said Rab, "At the time that Moses went up on high, he found the Holy One in session, affixing crowns to the letters [of the words of the Torah]. He said to him, 'Lord of the universe, who is stopping you [from regarding the document as perfect without these additional crowns on the letters]?'

   B. "He said to him, 'There is a man who is going to arrive at the end of many generations, and Aqiba b. Joseph is his name, who is going to interpret on the basis of each point of the crowns heaps and heaps of laws.'

   C. "He said to him, 'Lord of the Universe, show him to me.'

   D. "He said to him, 'Turn around.'

   E. "He went and took a seat at the end of eight rows, but he could not grasp what the people were saying. He felt faint. But when the discourse reached a certain matter, and the disciples said, 'My lord, how do you know this?' and he answered, 'It is a law given to Moses from Sinai,' he regained his composure.

   F. "He went and came before the Holy One. He said before him, 'Lord of the Universe, How come you have someone like that and yet you give the Torah through me?'

   G. "He said to him, 'Silence! That is how the thought came to me.'

   H. "He said to him, 'Lord of the Universe, you have shown me his Torah, now show me his reward.'

   I. "He said to him, 'Turn around.'

   J. "He turned around and saw his flesh being weighed out at the butcher-stalls in the market.

   K. "He said to him, 'Lord of the Universe, 'Such is Torah, such is the reward?'

   L. "He said to him, 'Silence! That is how the thought came to me.'"

God rules, and man in the end cannot explain, account for the rationality of, everything that God decrees. Sages offer more than reasonable explanations for the perceived violation of justice. They offer also the gift of humility in the form of silence. That forms the barrier before the ultimate terror—not understanding, not making sense of things.

Accordingly, sages placed humility before God above even the entire theological enterprise with its promise of the explanation, understanding, and justification. But the last word must register: that God decrees, however inexplicable those decrees might be to the mind of man, bears the comforting message that God cares. And since the premise of the mystery of suffering is formed by the conviction of God's justice (otherwise why take note of the case at hand as an anomaly?), that God cares also means that God loves. And it is a love for man, taken care of one by one, a love so deep as not to leave anybody ever unattended—even Aqiba in his martyrdom, but especially ordinary folk, when they suffer, when they bleed, when they die, as all do. Now to the dream of perfection: the sages' account of how the world ought to be made to conform to God's plan for an orderly, justified creation.

CHAPTER SEVEN

PERFECTING WORLD ORDER

I. HOW DO WE SHOW THAT THE WORLD
GOD CREATED IS PERFECT?

The Rabbinic sages revealed the perfection of world order through an other-than-historical mode of thought. They organized experience through a mode of thought I call paradigmatic, identifying enduring patterns to account for how things were, are, or will be, rather than appealing to the sequence of happenings—first came this, then came that—to explain why the present is what it is. So the Rabbinic sages framed a world beyond time and deemed null the sequence of events, judging as null the illogical proposition that merely because one thing happened before another, therefore the one thing caused the other (post hoc ergo propter hoc). Here is the one critical point at which the Rabbinic sages in the Oral Torah part company from the Written Torah, so far as people deem the Written Torah to make its statement through historical narrative, as conventionally understood. In our terms the Rabbinic sages were not historians but social philosophers, we might say, or social scientists.

In the Rabbinic sages' world beyond time as historically understood, we deal with a realm in which the past is ever present, the present a recapitulation and reformulation of the past, and the future embedded in the here and now. To understand their mode of thought, at least as I represent it, requires a bit of effort, for we have to abandon what, in our time and circumstance, is the given of social explanation: appeal to history. But history's time is rigidly differentiated into past, present, and future, and history's events are linear and sequential. History may yield patterns, but history transcends those patterns.

II. Time and Paradigm

Now consider the Rabbinic sages' view of time and paradigm. When people recapitulate the past in the present, and when they deem the future to be no different from the remote long ago and far away, they organize and interpret experience in a framework that substitutes patterns of enduring permanence for models of historical change. Instead of history with its one time, unique events to be read in a singular manner, thought proceeds through the explanation of paradigms, events being recast as exemplars, then interpreted by the criterion of the likenesses or unlikenesses of things set forth in an original and generative pattern. That is why the familiar modes of classifying noteworthy events, the long ago and the here and now, lose currency. What is lost to us children of the Enlightenment is the gift of memory as the medium of interpretation of the social order; historical thinking as a mode of explanation of the social order ceases to serve. Universal paradigms govern instead, against which all things, now, then, anytime, are compared. That is why events lose all specificity and particularity.

The Rabbinic canon formulates its conception of world order in enduring paradigms that admit no distinction between past, present, and future. Its narrative of the life of its "Israel" and the meaning of that life transcend time and change. All things take form in a single plane of being; Israel lives not in historical time, moving from a beginning, to a middle, to an end, in a linear plan through a sequence of unique events. Nor does it form its existence in cyclical time, repeating time and again familiar cycles of events. Those familiar modes of making sense out of the chaos of change and the passage of time serve not at all. Appealing to a world of timeless permanence that takes shape in permanent patterns, the Oral Torah accounts for how things are not by appeal to what was and what will be, but by invoking the criterion of what characterizes the authentic and true being of Israel.

Paradigms respond to the question, If not change in linear sequence of unique events then what? The pattern that controls recapitulates the paradigmatic lives of the patriarchs and matriarchs, or the tale of Eden and Adam, or the story of Israel and the Land, or the model of the temple built, destroyed, and rebuilt, to take principal sources of paradigmatic construction. Therein the Rabbinic sages find the models of the perfection of a changeless world, that a set of established patterns governs. Here history gives way to not eternity but permanence, the rules of the paradigm telling us not how to make sense of what was or how to predict what will be, but only what it is that counts. It is this conception of a timeless perfection, attained at the beginning, restored at the end, that accounts for the Rabbinic sages' design for death, resurrection, judgment, and the world to come.

Paradigmatic thinking, and the particular paradigms at hand, frame a world order that is fully realized and stable, a world beyond the vagaries of time. The Rabbinic sages, like philosophers, conceived order to require a world at rest. Perfection entailed stasis, all things in place in a timeless realm of stability. So they thought about past, present, and future in a manner different from the familiar historical one. To the Rabbinic sages, then, change marked by linear time signified imperfection, a symptom that things continue in an incomplete process of realization, falling short of realizing their goal. In a completed state of order, the balanced exchanges of justice set the norm. All things in place and proportion, each will have achieved its purpose.

In this world of stasis, governed by propositions of a uniform and ubiquitous reason, men meet in a timeless plane of eternity. They are able to exchange thoughts, conduct debates, without regard to considerations of anachronism. It is a shared logic that makes possible their encounter in debate. We have already found Moses listening to Aqiba, and, more to the point, throughout the Rabbinic canon, the Rabbinic sages construct conversations between people of widely separated periods of history; moreover, they insert on their own conversations that, by their reason, people ought to have had. Indeed, the formidable proportion of the documents that is taken up by fabricated dialogue attests to one prevailing assumption. Reason is timeless, right thinking transcends circumstance. Therefore, whenever or wherever people lived, they can confront one another's ideas and sort out their differences by appeal to a common mode of thought and a shared rationality. Paradigmatic thinking then comes to expression every time a sage tells a story with an ample selection of what "he said to him . . . he said to him . . .," indeed, at every occasion at which a sage imputes a speech to God himself. All of this forms the consequence of that timeless, perfect world that the Rabbinic sages find in

Scripture and propose in their setting to recapitulate as well. That is only possible, only conceivable, when time stands still.

Accordingly, a just order attains perfection—an even and proportionate balance prevailing—and therefore does not change. To the Rabbinic sages, the entire Torah, Oral and Written, portrayed a world that began in perfection at rest, an eternal Sabbath, but then changed by reason of sin. The world preserved within itself the potentiality of restoration to a state of rest. The truly orderly world is then represented by the Sabbath, when God completed creation and sanctified it in its perfection. The weekly Sabbath, celebrating creation perfected and accordingly at rest, thus affords a foretaste of the world to come, one sixtieth of the Garden of Eden that awaits, the Talmud says.

In the Rabbinic canon the concept of history, coming to expression in the categories of time and change, along with distinctions between past, present, and future, therefore surrenders to an altogether different way of conceiving time and change as well as the course of noteworthy, even memorable social events. The past takes place in the present. The present embodies the past. And there is no indeterminate future over the horizon, only a clear and present path within a different paradigm, to be chosen if people will it. With distinctions between past, present, and future time found to make no difference, and in their stead, different categories of meaning and social order deemed self-evident, the Rabbinic canon transforms ancient Israel's history into the categorical structure of eternal Israel's society, so that past, present, and future meet in the here and now. Two basic propositions defined the Rabbinic sages' doctrine of time and change, one negative, the other positive.

First comes the negative: time, divided into eras, or epochs, or periods, bears no relationship to paradigms that organize into a single plane of eternity the past, present, and future. To the Rabbinic sages time is neither linear nor cyclical but unremarkable, that is, not kept. It is a minor detail, a contingency made congruent with the critical paradigms—Israel and the nations being the one we now have in hand—that the theology devises in a single model. Time subject to a paradigm yields a pattern that differentiates one period from some other. Events removed from linear, sequential time, bear their own, other-than-time-bound signification of the meaning and consequence of a given period. Thinking through paradigms, with a conception of time that elides past and present and removes all barriers between them, in fact governs the reception of the Written Torah by the Oral Torah.

To extend that the matter of how a paradigm replaces historical time, we see how the Rabbinic sages recognized no barrier between present and past. To them, the present and past formed a single unit of time, encompassing a single span of experience. That is why the liturgy, too, can say, "In all generations an Israelite is to regard himself as if he too were redeemed from Egypt." Why was that so? It is because, to them, times past took place in the present too, on which account the present not only encompassed the past (which historical thinking concedes) but took place in the same plane of time as the past (which, to repeat, historical thinking rejects as unintelligible). How come? It is because the Rabbinic sages experienced the past in the present. What happened that mattered had already happened; an event then was transformed into a series; events themselves defined paradigms, yielded rules. A simple formulation of this mode of thought is as follows:

Mishnah *Ta'anit* 4:6

A. Five events took place for our fathers on the seventeenth of Tammuz, and five on the ninth of Ab.
B. On the seventeenth of Tammuz
    (1) the tablets [of the Torah] were broken,
    (2) the daily whole offering was cancelled,
    (3) the city wall was breached,
    (4) Apostemos burned the Torah, and
    (5) he set up an idol in the Temple.
C. On the ninth of Ab
    (1) the decree was made against our forefathers that they should not enter the land,
    (2) the first Temple and
    (3) the second [Temple] were destroyed,
    (4) Betar was taken, and
    (5) the city was ploughed up [after the war of Hadrian].
D. When Ab comes, rejoicing diminishes.

We mark time by appeal to the phases of the moon; these then may be characterized by traits shared in common—and so the paradigm, from marking time, moves outward to the formation of rules concerning the regularity and order of events.

In the formulation just now given, we see the movement from

event to rule. What is important about events is not their singularity but their capacity to generate a pattern, a concrete rule for the here and now. That is the conclusion drawn from the very passage at hand:

Mishnah *Ta'anit* 4:7

A. In the week in which the ninth of Ab occurs it is prohibited to get a haircut and to wash one's clothes.
B. But on Thursday of that week these are permitted,
C. because of the honor owing to the Sabbath.
D. On the eve of the ninth of Ab a person should not eat two prepared dishes, nor should one eat meat or drink wine.
E. Rabban Simeon b. Gamaliel says, "He should make some change from ordinary procedures."
F. R. Judah declares people liable to turn over beds.
G. But the Rabbinic sages did not concur with him.

Events serve to define paradigms and therefore, also, to yield rules governing the here and now: what we do to recapitulate. Here is how diverse events are shown to fall into a single category, so adhere to the same rule, thus forming a paradigm through the shared indicative traits, but then losing that very specificity that history requires for events to make sense.

When we speak of the presence of the past, therefore, we raise not generalities or possibilities but the concrete experience that generations actively mourning the temple endured. When we speak of the pastness of the present, we describe the consciousness of people who could open Scripture and find themselves right there, in its record. They found themselves present not only in Lamentations, but also in prophecy, and, especially in the books of the Torah. Here we deal not with the spiritualization of Scripture, but with the acutely contemporary and immediate realization of Scripture; Scripture in the present day, the present day in Scripture. This is what we mean when later on we shall observe that the Rabbinic sages read from Scripture to the present, while their competition, in Christianity, would read from the present back to Scripture (from the "New" to the "Old" Testament, in their language). That is why it was possible for the Rabbinic sages to formulate out of Scripture a paradigm that imposed structure and order upon the world that they themselves encountered.

To generalize: unlike the mode of telling time familiar in the secular West, for the Rabbinic sages time is not marked off in a sequence of singular, unique, one-time events. Rather, time forms an entity, like space, like food, like classes of persons, like everything, meant to be differentiated and classified, hierarchized. The world perfected and at rest does not tell time through an account of what came first and then what happened, a clock that measures the movement of time and change. Therefore history, with its clear division established between past, present, and future, linked through sequences of singular events, does not apply. Rather, the Rabbinic sages defined the world by ages or periods, with no link to sequential division of past, present, and future but rather differentiated by indicative traits. Events exemplify indicative traits of the social order in relationship to God.

What, then, of the narrative of Scripture, particularly the Authorized History, Genesis through Kings, which bears the traits of history as defined in a secular way: past, present, future, the changing aspects of one-time linear and sequential events teaching lessons of history? Considerations of temporal sequence play no role in the Torah. That statement, in so many words, demonstrated by the usual assembly of probative cases, simply dismisses the historical mode of thought as irrelevant to Scripture (as philosophers would find it irrelevant to natural history):

Mekhilta Attributed to R. Ishmael XXXII:I.1–7

   A. "The enemy said, ['I will pursue, I will overtake, I will divide the spoil, my desire shall have its fill of them. I will draw my sword, my hand shall destroy them']:"

   B. This [statement was made] at the outset of the sequence of events, and why then was it stated here?

   C. It is because considerations of temporal sequence play no role in the Torah.

2. A. Along these same lines: "And it came to pass on the eighth day that Moses called" (Lev. 9:1).

   B. This [statement was made] at the outset of the sequence of events, and why then was it stated here?

   C. It is because considerations of temporal sequence play no role in the Torah.

3. A. Along these same lines: "In the year that king Uzziah died" (Is. 6:1).

   B. This [statement was made] at the outset of the sequence of events, and why then was it stated here?

   C. It is because considerations of temporal sequence play no role in the Torah.

4. A. Along these same lines: "Son of man, stand on your feet" (Ez. 2:1).

   B. Some say, "Son of man, put forth a riddle" (Ez. 17:2).

    C. This [statement was made] at the outset of the sequence of events, and why then was it stated here?

    D. It is because considerations of temporal sequence play no role in the Torah.

5. A. Along these same lines: "Go and cry in the ears of Jerusalem" (Jer. 2:2).

    B. This [statement was made] at the outset of the sequence of events, and why then was it stated here?

    C. It is because considerations of temporal sequence play no role in the Torah.

6. A. Along these same lines: "Israel was a luxuriant vine" (Hos. 10:1).

    B. This [statement was made] at the outset of the sequence of events, and why then was it stated here?

    C. It is because considerations of temporal sequence play no role in the Torah.

7. A. Along these same lines: "I, Qoheleth, have been king over Israel in Jerusalem" (Qoh 1:12).

    B. This [statement was made] at the outset of the sequence of events, and why then was it stated here?

    C. It is because considerations of temporal sequence play no role in the Torah.

The atemporality of Scripture's narrative is further illustrated in a still more striking statement:

Mekhilta Attributed to R. Ishmael XXII:I.24

    A. R. Yosé the Galilean says, "When the Israelites went into the sea, Mount Moriah had already been uprooted from its place, with the altar of Isaac that was built on it, and with the array of wood on it, and Isaac was as if bound and set on the altar, and Abraham as though his hand were stretched out, having taken the knife to sacrifice his son.

    B. "Said the Omnipresent to Moses, 'Moses, my children are in trouble, with the sea shutting the way before and the enemy pursuing, and you are standing and protracting your prayer!'

    C. "Moses said to him, 'And what am I supposed to do?'

    D. "He said to him, 'Lift up your rod [and stretch out your hand over the sea and divide it, that the people of Israel may go on dry ground through the sea].'

    E. "'You should now exalt, give glory, and praise, and break out in songs of praise, exaltation, praise and glorification of the One who possesses war.'"

But even if the matter were not made explicit, we should find ample evidence of the Rabbinic sages' ahistorical mode of thought on nearly every page of the Rabbinic canon, for every time the Rabbinic sages speak as though Abraham and David were contemporaries of theirs, they announced their conviction that the Torah was timeless.

The only way to validate the striking proposition that temporal considerations do not affect the narrative of Scripture, which pays no attention to the order in which events took place, is through examples of atemporality. The examples of the first composition show that the Torah cites later in its narrative what in fact took place earlier, and these shifts validate the claim made at the outset. The second composition makes the same point in a very different way, by claiming that the binding of Isaac was taking place at the very moment at which Israel was tested at the sea. The events then correspond and take place in the same indeterminate moment. And the third proceeds to another probative example of the same.

To say that the Rabbinic sages rejected historicism imposes upon them the burden of difference from our norm. But what about the positive side of matters, and how does the Rabbinic sages' antihistoricism produce a constructive result? The positive side of the same proposition bears a large burden of hermeneutics. Since historical time does not measure the meaning of Scripture, a philosophical one does, that is to say, that quest for regularity and order that we considered at some length. That quest for the rules of the social order is advanced when the Torah narrates not history—past, present, future—but rather an enduring paradigm, as I said at the outset. Accordingly, portraying a timeless world in which the past forms a principal part of the present, and the present takes place within an eternity of contemporaneity, yields an intellectually formidable reward.

If Abraham, Aqiba, and Ashi live within the same uniform plane of existence as do you and I, then we gain access to the orderly unfolding of the rules of a well-ordered world, with special emphasis upon the social rules of Israel's life instead of upon the physical rules of the natural world. That is why for the Rabbinic sages it was self-evident that, when the Israelites descended into the sea, Moriah was uprooted from its place, with Isaac bound on the altar and Abraham's hand poised with the knife, lessons are to be learned for their Israel too. No wonder that Moses then recapitulates Abraham's gesture (at *Mekhilta* XXII:I.24)—and the rest follows. This conception of events as patterned—here the gesture is what joins the one scene to the other—defies the historical notion of events as singular, sequential, linear.

With the past very present, the present an exercise in recapitulation of an enduring paradigm, therefore, time and change signify nothing but imperfection, as much as permanence beyond time and change signifies perfection. And that carries forward that quest for the perfection of the world order that the Rabbinic sages anticipate will justify—show the justice, meaning here, the perfection, of—God's work. That is why, as I said, time in a system of perfection can be neither linear nor cyclical; time in historical dimensions simply is not a consideration in thinking about what happens and what counts. Instead, paradigms for the formation of the social order of transcendence and permanence govern, so that what was now is, and what will be is what was and is.

It follows that the two conflicting conceptions of social explanation—the historical and the paradigmatic—appeal to two different ways of conceiving of, and evaluating, time. Historical time measures one thing, paradigmatic time another, though both refer to the same facts of nature and of the social order. For its exposition of the cogency and meaning of Israel's social experience, for its part the Oral Torah possesses no concept of history and therefore produces as its statements of the sense of the life of the people neither sustained historical narrative nor biography. Rather, the Oral Torah presents exemplary moments, significations of paradigm, and exemplary incidents in lives of saints, also indicators of a prevailing pattern. These stories yield chapters, not "lives."

To be "Israel"—God's portion of humanity—therefore means to conform to a pattern of actions and attitudes set forth for all time and without distinction in time. That pattern, or paradigm, comes to definition in the lives of the patriarchs and matriarchs. It is then recapitulated in a social world that knows not change but conformity to paradigm—or nonconformity. Since the paradigm endures, we explain happenings by appeal to its rules, and the event is not what is singular and distinctive but what conforms to the rule. We notice what is like the paradigm, not what diverges from it. To the paradigm, matters of memory and hope prove monumentally irrelevant, because they explain nothing, making distinctions that stand for no important differences at all.

That is why, when in the Oral Torah the Rabbinic sages want to explain what it means to be "Israel," they appeal not to time and change but to eternity and permanence. Or rather, the conception of the category, time—what is measured by the passage of the sun and moon in relationship to events here on earth—altogether loses standing. In place of distinguishing happenings through the confluence of time, measured by the passage of the sun and moon, and event, distinguished by specificity and particularity, paradigmatic thinking takes another route. It finds an event in what conforms to the paradigm, what is meaningful in what confirms it. In paradigmatic thinking we examine the norms for an account of how things ought to be, finding the rule that tells us how things really are. Then past, present, and future differentiate not at all, the pattern of an eternal present taking over to make sense of the social order.

It follows that in the paradigmatic mode of thinking about the social order, the categories of past, present, and future, singular event and particular life, all prove useless. In their place come the categories defined by the actions and attitudes of paradigmatic persons, Abraham and Sarah, for instance, or paradigmatic places, the temple, or paradigmatic occasions, holy time, for instance. We identify a happening not by its consequence ("historical") but by its conformity to the appropriate paradigm. We do not classify events in accord with their paradigms as past, present, or future, therefore, because to the indicators of eventfulness—what marks a happening as eventful or noteworthy—time and change, by definition, have no bearing at all. Great empires do not make history; they fit a pattern.

What they do does not designate an event, it merely provides a datum for classification within the pattern. To this point in the exposition, we have seen numerous examples of such a procedure. To this way of thinking, Scripture's apocalypse, with its appeal to symbol to represent vast forces on earth, makes its contribution; but paradigmatic and apocalyptic thinking about Israel's social being scarcely intersect. The paradigmatic excludes the historical, the indicative, the categorical pattern, the possibility of noteworthy change. Matters are just the opposite. Indeed, paradigmatic thinking accommodates historical thinking not at all, since the beginning of history, in the notion of the pastness of the past, contradicts the generative conception of the paradigm: the very paradigmatic character of the happening that bears meaning.

In that context, therefore, the governing categories speak not of time and change, movement and direction, but of the recapitulation of a given pattern, the repetition of the received paradigm. Being then moves from the one-time, the concrete, the linear and accumulative, to the recurrent, the mythic, and the repetitive; from the historical to the paradigmatic. These modes of identifying a happening as consequential and eventful then admit no past or present or future subject to differentiation and prognostication, respectively. Time therefore bears no meaning, nor the passage of time any consequence. If, therefore, the historical mode of organizing shared experience into events forming patterns, its identification of events as unique and persons as noteworthy, of memory as the medium for seeking meaning, and narrative as the medium for spelling it out, paradigmatic thinking will dictate a different mode of culture.

It is one in which shared experience takes on meaning when the received paradigms of behavior and the interpretation of the consequence of behavior come to realization once again; the paradigm recapitulated is the paradigm confirmed. What takes place that is identified as noteworthy becomes remarkable because today conforms to yesterday and provokes, too, tomorrow's recapitulation as well. We notice not the unlike—the singular—event but the like, not what calls into question the ancient pattern but what reviews and confirms it. If, then, we wish to make sense of who we are, we ask not where we come from or where we are heading, but whom we resemble, and into which classification of persons or events we fit. The social order then finds its explanation in its resemblances, the likenesses and the unlikenesses of persons and happenings alike.

Let me make this point concrete. The meaning of shared experience, such as history sets forth in its categories of past, present, and future, and teleology through narrative of particular events or through biography of singular lives, emerges in a different way altogether. In the formulation of the social order through paradigm, past, present, and future, the conception of time in general, set forth distinctions that by definition make no difference. Events contradict the paradigm; what is particular bears no sense. Then remarkable happenings, formed into teleology through history writing, or noteworthy persons' lives, formed into memorable cases through biography, no longer serve as the media of making a statement bearing intelligible, cultural consequence.

Paradigmatic thinking is never generalized, it only is meant to yield generalizations (a very different thing). Specific paradigms come into play. They define the criteria for the selection as consequential and noteworthy of some happenings but not others. They further dictate

the way to think about remarkable events, so as to yield sense concerning them. They tell people that one thing bears meaning while
another does not, and they further instruct people on the self-evident
meaning to be imputed to that which is deemed consequential. The
paradigms are fully as social in their dimensions, entirely as encompassing in their outreach, as historical categories. We deal not with
the paradigms of universal, individual life, taking the place of those
of particular social existence, such as history posits, with its unique,
one-time, sequential and linear events. The result of paradigmatic
thinking is no different from that of the historical kind.

For before us is not a random sequence of entirely personal recapitulations of universal experiences, for instance, birth, maturing,
marriage, love, and death; these modes of permanence in change,
these personal paradigms that form a counterpoint to one-time, public moments play no role in the formation of what endures, whether
past, whether past, whether future, in the eternal now. The definition
of the consequential, permanent paradigms that replace the conception of history altogether will emerge in due course. At the outset
what is at stake must be clear. The shift from historical to paradigmatic thinking represents a movement from one kind of thinking
about the social order to another kind. The particularity of history
finds its counterpart in the particularity of the paradigm of thought.

This leads directly to the kind of thinking—paradigmatic, ahistorical, and I claim, utterly anti-historical and dismissive of particularities
of time or circumstance but rather philosophical and generalizing—
that characterizes the Rabbinic canon's theological structure and system. Here the past is present, the present is past, and time contains
no delineative future tense at all. Eschatological teleology gives way
to paradigmatic teleology, and—it goes without saying—biography
abdicates in favor of highly selective paradigms of exemplarity in the
lives of persons, events in favor of patterns. Sustained narrative is
abandoned because it is irrelevant; biography, because it is filled with
useless information. The concept of organizing the facts (real or fabricated) of the social world of Israel into history as the story of the
life and times of Israel, past, present, and future, is succeeded by
the concept of organizing the received and now perceived facts of
the social world of Israel into the enduring paradigm in which past,
present, and future fuse into an eternal now.

When recapitulative paradigms of meaning obliterate all lines between past, present, and future, so that the past forms a permanent presence among the living, and the present recapitulates the paradigm of the past, the conception of history, with a beginning, middle, and end, a linear and cumulative sequence of distinct and individual events, is lost. And writing too changes in character, for with the loss of historical thinking perish three kinds of writing. These are, first, narrative, the tale of a singular past leading to the present and pointing toward the future, the concretization therefore of teleology. The second kind of writing is biography, the notion of an individual and particular life, also with its beginning, middle, and end. The third is formulation of events as unique, with close study of the lessons to be derived from happenings of a singular character.

And the loss of these three types of writing, commonplace in the standard history, Genesis through Kings, of the Hebrew Scriptures, signals a shift in categories, from the category of history, resting on the notion of time as a taxonomic indicator, to a different category-formation altogether. For the concept of history generates its conception of time, made concrete through the writing of narrative and biography, the formulation of things that have taken place into the formation of consequential, singular events, comparable to the identification of particular persons as events of consequence, worthy of preservation; time starts somewhere and leads to a goal, and lives begin, come to a climax, and conclude as well.

With the end of linear, cumulative, and teleological-historical thinking, the realization of history in narrative, event, and biography loses currency. Narrative strings together one-time events into meaningful patterns, with a beginning, middle, and end; that is the medium of history, and that medium bears history's self-evident messages. Biography then does for individuals what narrative accomplishes for remarkable moments in the existence of the social entity; the narrative takes its measure in different dimensions, but the mode of thought is identical, and the medium for explanation the same. So too the conception of time, that is, a sequence of distinct moments, whether cyclical, following a pattern of recurrence, or linear, pursuing a single line from start to finish, also loses all self-evidence. In place, the passage of the fixed stars and planets, the moon and sun, cease to mark off ages and signify periods in human events—this year, this event, next year, that event—and instead measure something else altogether. Just as the passage of a person's life from birth

to death takes place outside of historical, that is, public, shared, eventful time, only rarely intersecting with the historical and the consequential, so the paradigms marked off something other than the
cumulative passing of public time, or of any time that people ordinarily would measure at all.

In accord with the governance of paradigmatic instead of historical thinking, the rationality of a fixed order of events gives way. Now
events are reversible; no fixed order governs. That is why Abraham
and Isaac at Moriah are coincident with Moses at the shore of the
Red Sea, the raised hand of Abraham and the raised hand of Moses
forming a single pattern, coinciding in a single result. The logic of
sequence—first this, then that, therefore this caused that—plays no
role. Had we put Moses' raised hand before Abraham's, there would
be no loss of sense or meaning. Here the science of society shades
over into the imagination of art.

Under such conditions, explaining the world as it is by reference
to the past is impossible because, in an exact sense, it is unthinkable;
it simply cannot be thought. That is to say, by means of thinking with
principles such as we shall now examine, history—a mode of accounting for the social order by appeal to how things have been—in the
simplest and most conventional definition then cannot be conceived.
If history cannot identify that dividing point between past and present, it also cannot project that linear sequence of events, singular and
irreversible, that forms its second premise. For if past flows smoothly
into present, then the reverse also commands plausibility, the present
flowing into the past (as indeed we see in the paradigmatic mode of
analyzing human events followed by the Rabbinic sages).

Now that we recognize a different way of thinking about time past,
present, and future, we come to the question: What, exactly are the
paradigms through which the Rabbinic sages set forth the world
order they proposed to discern? In their view the written part of the
Torah defined a set of paradigms that served without regard to circumstance, context, or, for that matter, dimension and scale of happening. A very small number of models emerged from Scripture,
captured in the sets [1] Eden and Adam, [2] Sinai and the Torah,
[3] the land and Israel, and [4] the temple and its building, destruction, rebuilding. Within these paradigms nearly the whole of human
experience was organized. These paradigms served severally and
jointly, e.g., Eden and Adam on its own but also superimposed upon

the Land and Israel; Sinai and the Torah on its own but also superimposed upon the Land and Israel, and, of course, the temple,
embodying natural creation and its intersection with national and
social history, could stand entirely on its own or be superimposed
upon any and all of the other paradigms. In many ways, then, we
have the symbolic equivalent of a set of two- and three- or even four-
dimensional grids. A given pattern forms a grid on its own, one set
of lines being set forth in terms of, e.g., Eden, timeless perfection, in
contrast against the other set of lines, Adam, temporal disobedience;
but upon that grid, a comparable grid can be superimposed, the Land
and Israel being an obvious one; and upon the two, yet a third and
fourth, Sinai and Torah, temple and the confluence of nature and
history.

By reference to these grids, severally or jointly, the critical issues of
existence, whether historical, whether contemporary, played themselves out in the theology of the Oral Torah. I identify four models
by which, out of happenings of various sorts, consequential or meaningful events would be selected, and by reference to which these
selected events would be shown connected ("meaningful") and explic-
able in terms of that available logic of paradigm that governed both
the making of connections and the drawing of conclusions.

[1] How shall we organize (mere) happenings into events? On the
largest scale the question concerns the division into periods of not
sequences but mere sets of happenings. Periodization involves explanation, of course, since even in a paradigmatic structure, once matters are set forth as periods, then an element of sequence is admitted
into the processes of description and therefore of analysis and explanation.

[2] How Israel relates to the rest of the world. This involves
explaining not what happened this morning in particular, but what
always happens, that is, defining the structure of Israel's life in the
politics of this world, explaining the order of things in both the social,
political structure of the world and also the sequence of actions that
may occur and recur over time (the difference, paradigmatically,
hardly matters).

[3] How to explain the pattern of events, making connections and
drawing conclusions from what happens. Paradigmatic thinking, no
less than historical, explains matters. But the explanation derives from
the character of the pattern, rather than the order of events, which

governs historical explanation. Connections that then are drawn between one thing and something else serve to define a paradigm, rather than to convey a temporal explanation based on sequences, first this, then that, therefore this explains why that happened. The paradigm bears a different explanation altogether, one that derives from its principle of selection, and therefore the kinds of explanations paradigmatic thinking sets forth, expressed through its principles of selection in making connections and drawing conclusions, will demand rich instantiation.

[4] How to anticipate the future history of Israel. That concerns not so much explaining the present as permitting informed speculation about what will happen in the future. And that speculation will appeal to those principles of order, structure, and explanation that the paradigm to begin with sets forth. So future history in historical thinking and writing projects out of past present a trajectory over time to come, but future history in paradigmatic thinking forms projects along other lines altogether.

The purpose of paradigmatic thinking, as much as historical, thus points toward the future. History is important to explain the present, also to help peer into the future; and paradigms serve precisely the same purpose. The choice between the one model and the other, then, rests upon which appeals to the more authentic data. In that competition Scripture, treated as paradigm, met no competition in linear history, and it was paradigmatic, not historical, thinking that proved compelling for a thousand years or more. The future history of Israel is written in Scripture, and what happened in the beginning is what is going to happen at the end of time. That sense of order and balance prevailed.

The restorationist theology that infuses the Rabbinic sages' expression of paradigmatic thinking with its structure and system comes to expression in a variety of passages, of which a severely truncated selection will have to suffice:

Genesis Rabbah XLII:II

2. A. Said R. Abin, "Just as [Israel's history] began with the encounter with four kingdoms, so [Israel's history] will conclude with the encounter with the four kingdoms."
   B. "'Chedorlaomer, king of Elam, Tidal, king of Goiim, Amraphel, king of Shinar, and Arioch, king of Ellasar, four kings against five' (Gen. 14:9)."

  C. "So [Israel's history] will conclude with the encounter with the
    four kingdoms: the kingdom of Babylonia, the kingdom of
    Medea, the kingdom of Greece, and the kingdom of Edom."

Another pattern serves as well, resting as it does on the foundations
of the former. It is the familiar one that appeals to the deeds of the
founders. The lives of the patriarchs stand for the history of Israel;
the deeds of the patriarchs cover the future historical periods in
Israel's destiny.

A single formulation of matters suffices to show how the entire history of Israel was foreseen at the outset:

Pesiqta deRab Kahana XXI:V

1. A. R. Hiyya taught on Tannaite authority, "At the beginning of the
   creation of the world the Holy One, blessed be He, foresaw that
   the Temple would be built, destroyed, and rebuilt."
  B. "'In the beginning God created the heaven and the earth' (Gen.
   1:1) [refers to the Temple] when it was built, in line with the
   following verse: 'That I may plant the heavens and lay the
   foundations of the earth and say to Zion, You are my people'
   (Is. 51:16)."
  C. "'And the earth was unformed'—lo, this refers to the destruction, in line with this verse: 'I saw the earth, and lo, it was
   unformed' (Jer. 4:23)."
  D. "'And God said, Let there be light'—lo, it was built and well
   constructed in the age to come."

A single specific example of the foregoing proposition suffices. It is
drawn from that same mode of paradigmatic thinking that imposes
the model of the beginning upon the end. In the present case the
yield is consequential: we know what God is going to do to Rome.
What God did to the Egyptians foreshadows what God will do to the
Romans at the end of time.

We have now to ask why the Rabbinic sages rejected the linear
sequence of unique events that Scripture sets forth in the Authorized
History in favor of the kind of paradigmatic thinking that has now
been amply instantiated. Historical thinking yielded an unintelligible
result, paradigmatic thinking a rational one. The reason is that historical thinking—sequential narrative of one-time events—presupposes
order, linearity, distinction between time past and time present, and
teleology, among data that—for the Rabbinic sages, struggling with
the secular facts of Israel's condition—do not self-evidently sustain

such presuppositions. Questions of chaos, disorder, and disproportion naturally intervene; the very possibility of historical narrative meets a challenge in the diversity of story lines, the complexity of events, the bias of the principle of selection of what is eventful, of historical interest, among a broad choice of happenings: why this, not that. Narrative history first posits a gap between past and present, but then bridges the gap; why not entertain the possibility that to begin with there is none? These and similar considerations invite a different way of thinking about how things have been and now are, a different tense structure altogether.

A way of thinking about the experience of humanity, whether past or contemporary, that makes other distinctions than the historical ones between past and present and that eschews linear narrative and so takes account of the chaos that ultimately prevails, now competes with historical thinking. Paradigmatic thinking, a different medium for organizing and explaining things that happen, deals with the same data that occupy historical thinking, and that is why when we refer to paradigmatic thinking, the word "history" gains its quotation marks: it is not a datum of thought, merely a choice. Contradicting to its core the character of paradigmatic thinking, the category then joins its opposite, paradigm, only by forming the oxymoron before us: paradigmatic thinking about "history."

What Scripture yields for the Rabbinic canon, therefore, is not one-time events, arranged in sequence to dictate meaning, but models or patterns of conduct and consequence. These models are defined by the written Torah. No component of the paradigm we have reviewed emerges from other than the selected experience set forth by Scripture. But the models or paradigms pertain not to one time alone—past time—but to all times equally—past, present, and future. Then "time" no longer forms an organizing category of understanding and interpretation. Nor does nature, except in a subordinated role. The periods marked out by moon and sun and fixed stars bear meaning, to be sure. But that meaning has no bearing upon the designation of one year as past, another as present. The meaning imputed to the lunar and solar marking of time derives from the cult, on the one side, and the calendar of holy time, on the other: seven solar days, a Sabbath; a lunar cycle, a new month to be celebrated, the first new moon after the vernal equinox, the Passover, and after the autumnal, Tabernacles. The Oral Torah tells time the way nature does and only in that way; events deemed worth recording in time take place the way events in nature do. What accounts for the difference, between history's time and paradigmatic time as set forth here, I maintain, is a conception of time quite different from the definition of historical time that operates in Scripture: the confluence of the nature's time and history's way of telling time; two distinct chronographies brought together, the human one then imposed upon the natural one.

Israel kept time with reference to events, whether past or present, that also were not singular, linear, or teleological. These were, rather, reconstitutive in the forever of here and now—not a return to a perfect time but a recapitulation of a model forever present. Israel could treat as comparable the creation of the world and the exodus from Egypt (as the liturgy commonly does, e.g., in connection with the Sabbath) because Israel's paradigm (not "history") and nature's time corresponded in character, were consubstantial and not mutually contradictory. And that consubstantiality explains why paradigm and natural time work so well together. Now, "time" bears a different signification. It is here one is not limited to the definition assigned by nature—yet also not imposed upon natural time but treated as congruent and complementary with nature's time. How so? Events— things that happen that are deemed consequential—are eventful, meaningful, by a criterion of selection congruent in character with nature's own. To understand why, we must recall the character of the Torah's paradigms:

[1] Scripture set forth certain patterns which, applied to the chaos of the moment, selected out of a broad range of candidates some things and omitted reference to others.

[2] The selected things then are given their structure and order by appeal to the paradigm, or described without regard to scale.

[3] That explains how some events narrated by Scripture emerged as patterns, imposing their lines of order and structure upon happenings of other times.

And this yields the basis for the claim of consubstantiality:

[4] Scripture's paradigms—Eden, the Land—appealed to nature in another form.

The upshot, then, is that the rhythms of the sun and moon are celebrated in the very forum in which the Land, Israel's Eden, yields its
celebration to the Creator. The rhythmic quality of the paradigm
then compares with the rhythmic quality of natural time: not cyclical, but also not linear. Nature's way of telling time and the Torah's
way meet in the temple: its events are nature's, its story a tale of
nature too. Past and present flow together and join in future time too
because, as in nature, what is past is what is now and what will be.
Out of that presence of eternity in time, the world is ordered in perfection, quietly singing in its perfect orbit a hymn of praise to the
creator.

III. WORLD WITHOUT CHANGE

The Rabbinic sages maintained that, in a world without change, justice required that each person should emerge from a transaction
exactly as he entered it. A perfect world—one beyond time—also is
a world wholly at rest, in a steady state so far as wealth is concerned,
and for the same reason. Perfection entails stasis, permanence, transcending both time and change alike. That is why, with all things in
proper place, hierarchically arrayed, exact justice requires that in all
exchanges, no one's circumstance should shift upward, no one's
downward. All should preserve the status quo, possessing at the end
the same value as at the start of the transaction. Since the Rabbinic
sages took it as their task to reveal the perfection of justice in all
dimensions of the world that God made, they naturally turned to
questions of a material order. The Rabbinic sages' theology of the
commonwealth, of political economy, forms the equivalent of the
principle of measure for measure in establishing justice for crime and
sin, but it applies to everyday affairs. For in the Rabbinic sages' theology of justice, enduring stability is to characterize the perfection of
all relationships in Israel as in Eden.

Not only intellectuals but men of standing and political responsibility—politicians in this world, not only teachers in an intangible
heavenly academy—the Rabbinic sages therefore encompassed within their theology a theory of political economy. That is because, as
much as the sages, to accomplish their theological purpose, had to
form an account of Israel and the nations, they also could make their

theological statement whole and complete only through a doctrine of economics. But, not surprisingly, their theory of the rational disposition of scarce resources—that is, their economics—encompassed transactions of both this-worldly and other-worldly venues. This meant, as we shall see, a theory of both stability in what represents permanent value in this world, meaning real estate, and also unlimited riches in what is of supernatural worth. This yielded two complementary positions. The Rabbinic sages first held that all transactions among men, to attain the standard of justice, have to preserve the steady state of wealth in concrete terms. But there is value that is not limited to a specific amount or volume—the opposite of a scarce resource—but susceptible of infinite increase, and that is Torah-learning. So when dealing with what is finite, the law (Halakhah) that served as theological medium so arranged matters as to assure the equitable transfer of true value between both parties to an exchange.

At the same time, second, the law treated what was infinite—Torah-learning—as counterpart to what was finite—in context, real estate. So when dealing with what is infinite, the lore (Aggadah) of the Oral Torah took the position that wealth was freely fungible and infinitely transferable, without regard to balance or proportion, because everyone could make himself rich if he wished.

Accordingly, addressing the stability of the social order, theology of political economy provided an account of the rules for the rational management of scarce resources, and, as we shall see, also the rational increase of the authentic goods of Heaven. This world was not to change, but Israel lived in an order of being able to sustain unlimited increase. The riches of this world were to be preserved in a steady state, but the wealth of Heaven was there for all to attain without limit. These two matching principles, the one of economics in a conventional sense, the other of a categorical counterpart to economics, together coalesced to portray that world without change but with infinite potential for increase to which the Rabbinic sages aspired. Here is a very critical chapter in the demonstration of the justice of God in every dimension of creation and the world of man.

It follows that the Rabbinic sages' theory of political economy expressed in material terms and, as we shall see, in the language of the Halakhah, the same theology of a just world order that in other components was set forth in exegetical, or narrative, or abstract terms. Given the subject-matter, we cannot find surprising that the theology of a steady-state political economy took shape in rules governing how actual transactions are to be conducted. Law as much as lore served as an appropriate medium of theological discourse. The statement the Rabbinic sages set forth through law insured that, in any given transaction, fairness governed, so that no one emerged the richer, none the poorer, from the exchange. An exact transfer of true value was meant to take place.

Let us first take up the this-worldly economy, consisting of land and exchanges of real property. Then we shall identify the equivalent and counterpart to land, which is Torah-study. Forming a bridge to counterpart economics, a noteworthy passage will tell us that real estate and Torah-study form a single category, the one a scarce resource of uncertain reliability, the other an abundant resource of enduring value. From that point we shall see how a counterpart economics states the other half of the design of that perfect world at rest, subject to the Torah, that the Rabbinic sages portray as God's perfect accomplishment.

The Rabbinic sages set forth a fully-articulated and systematic economics, answering questions concerning the definition of wealth; a theory of money, property, production and the means of production; ownership and control of the means of production; the determination of price and ("true") value and the like. That statement cannot be treated as mere moralizing, for it vastly transcended the requirements of episodic sayings about mercy to the poor, recommendations of right action, fairness, honesty, and the like. These honorable sentiments, commonplaces in religions, do not by themselves add up to an economics. Issues of the rational disposition of scarce resources are treated in a sustained and systematic, internally coherent theory that in an encompassing way explains why this, not that, and defines market in relationship to ownership of the means of production. We have then a systematic account, an economics.

To understand the economic principle of the Rabbinic sages' theology of a practical world without change we must take note of the difference between two economic systems, the market economics with which we are familiar, and distributive economics. In market economics merchants transfer goods from place to place in response to the working of the market mechanism, which is expressed in price. In distributive economics, by contrast, traders move goods from point to point in response to political or theological or other commands independent of market pressures. In market economics, merchants make the market work by calculations of profit and loss. In distributive economics, there is no risk of loss on a transaction.[1] In market economics, money forms an arbitrary measure of value, a unit of account. In distributive economics, money gives way to barter and bears only intrinsic value, as do the goods for which it is exchanged. It is understood as "something that people accept not for its inherent value in use but because of what it will buy."[2] The idea of money requires the transaction to be complete in the exchange not of goods but of coins. The alternative is the barter transaction, in which, in theory at least, the exchange takes place when goods change hands. In distributive economics money is an instrument of direct exchange between buyers and sellers, not the basic resource in the process of production and distribution that it is in market economics.

The Rabbinic sages' this-worldly economics at every point opted for the principles of distributive economics. That is because, in their reading of matters, God in the Torah had dictated the principles of distribution. Community, self-sufficiency, and justice—these formed the foci of economic thinking. In the Rabbinic sages' theology, society is neatly organized by households, defined in relationship to the control of the means of production—the farm, for the household is always the agricultural unit. The Rabbinic sages maintained the conception of a simple world of little blocks formed into big ones: households into villages. Community, or village (*polis*) is made up of households, and the household (*bayit/oikos*) constituted the building block of both society or community and also economy. It follows that the household forms the fundamental, irreducible, and of course, representative unit of the economy, the means of production, the locus and the unit of production. The Rabbinic sages therefore saw Israel as made up, on earth, of households and villages. The economic unit also framed the social one, and the two together composed, in conglomerates, the political one, hence a political economy (*polis, oikos*), initiated within an economic definition formed out of the elements of production.

---

[1] W. I. Davisson and J. H. Harper, *European Economic History* (New York: Appleton-Century-Crofts, 1972–), 130.
[2] *Ibid.*, 131.

In the Rabbinic sages' political economy the village or *polis* comprising the household or *oikos*, therefore is orderly, with all things in relationship and in proper order and proportion. True, the political economy encompassed other economic entities, in particular, craftsmen and traders, both of them necessary for the conduct of the household. But each was placed into relationship with the household, the one as a necessary accessory to its ongoing functioning, the other as a shadowy figure who received the crops in volume and parceled them out to the market. The relationships between householder and craftsman, or between householder and hired hand, are sorted out in such a way as to accord to all parties a fair share in every transaction. Responsibilities of the one as against the other are spelled out. The craftsman or artisan, to be sure, is culpable should he damage property of the householder, but that judgment simply states the systemic interest in preserving the present division of wealth so that no party to a transaction emerges richer, none poorer.

In everyday transactions as the Rabbinic sages sorted them out, they proposed to effect the vision of a steady-state economy, engaged in always-equal exchanges of fixed wealth and intrinsic value. Essentially, the law as medium of theology aimed at the fair adjudication of conflict, worked out in such a way that no party gained, none lost, in any transaction. The task of Israelite society, as the Rabbinic sages saw it, is to maintain perfect stasis, to preserve the prevailing situation, to secure the stability of not only relationships but status and standing. That in the end reinforces the results of hierarchization, leading downward in the social order from God, the one, at the top, to the many distributed below. That is why, in the interchanges of buying and selling, giving and taking, borrowing and lending, transactions of the market and exchanges with artisans and craftsmen and laborers, it is important to preserve the essential equality, not merely the proximate equity, of exchange.

Fairness alone does not suffice. Status quo ante forms the criterion of the true market, reflecting as it does the exchange of value for value, in perfect balance. That is the way that, in reference to the market, the systemic point of urgency, the steady state of the polity, therefore also of the economy, is stated. The upshot of their economics is simple. No party in the end may have more than what he had at the outset, and none may emerge as the victim of a sizable shift in fortune and circumstance. All parties' rights to and in the stable and unchanging political economy are preserved. When, therefore, the condition of a person is violated, the law will secure the restoration of the antecedent status.

In framing matters in this way, the Rabbinic sages carried forward the conception of the Priestly authorship of Leviticus that the ownership of the land is supposed to be stable, so that, if a family alienates inherited property, it reverts to that family's ownership after a span of time. The conception of steady-state economy therefore dominated, so that, as a matter of fact, in utter stasis, no one would rise above his natural or inherent standing, and no one would fall either. And that is the economy they portray and claim to regulate through their legislation. In such an economy, the market did not form the medium of rationing but in fact had no role to play, except one: to insure equal exchange in all transactions, so that the market formed an arena for transactions of equal value and worth among households each possessed of a steady-state worth. Since, in such a (fictive) market, no one emerged richer or poorer than he was when he came to market, but all remained precisely as rich or as poor as they were at the commencement of a transaction, we can hardly call the Mishnah's market a market mechanism in any sense at all.

This brings us to the centerpiece of the Rabbinic sages' conception of the exchange of goods and services outside of the market mechanism, which is the notion of inherent or true worth. In market economics true value bears no clear meaning. The market mechanism— willing seller, informed buyer—dictates value, without the mediation of other considerations. In distributive economics, people know precisely what it means. In line with this conception prices must accord with something akin to true or intrinsic value, so the market simply facilitates the reasonable exchange of goods and services by bringing people together. The market provides no price-setting mechanism that operates on its own, nor is the market conceived as an economic instrument, but rather, as one of (mere) social utility in facilitating barter, encompassing, of course, barter effected through specie or money. In the following dispute, we see what is at issue:

Mishnah *Baba Batra* 5:1

A. If one sold the wagon, he has not sold the mules. If he sold the mules, he has not sold the wagon. If he sold the yoke, he has not sold the oxen. If he sold the oxen, he has not sold the yoke.

    B. R. Judah says, "The price tells all."
    C. How so? If he said to him, "Sell me your yoke for two hundred zuz," the facts are perfectly clear, for there is no yoke worth two hundred zuz.
    D. And the Rabbinic sages say, "Price proves nothing."

The Rabbinic sages hold that the purchaser can have set a higher value on the yoke than people ordinarily do; perhaps he saw some special use or need for it. Judah's view is that there is an intrinsic value, against which the market does not operate. This notion of true value, though in the minority in the case at hand, in fact dominates in the Rabbinic sages' thought about the market mechanism. The notion that true value inheres in all transactions, so that each party remains exactly as he was prior to the engagement, comes to concrete expression in a variety of circumstances.

Since the Rabbinic sages maintain that there is a true value, as distinct from a market value, of an object, we may understand the acute interest of our authorship in questions of fraud through overcharge and not only misrepresentation. The Halakhah therefore maintains that, if a purchaser pays more than a sixth more than true value, or if a seller receives a sixth less than that amount, in the form of an overcharge, fraud has been committed. The sale is null. The defrauded party has the choice of getting his money back or of keeping the goods and receiving only the amount of the overcharge. The notion of true value logically belongs together with the conception of money as an item of barter or meant merely to facilitate barter, because both notions referred to the single underlying conception of the economy as a steady-state entity in which people could not increase wealth but only exchange it. We take up both matters of Halakhah in the same discussion, therefore, just as the Mishnah presents them.

The governing conception is that money, by itself, does not effect an exchange and acquisition of the purchased item. Only a symbolic act of barter does so, and that fact (not unique to the law of the Mishnah, to be sure) tells us that, within this system, theory of money is set aside by theory of barter, and the market is simply a mechanism for barter. The principles that all transactions are really acts of barter, that money has no meaning other than an instrument of barter, and, consequently, that money (e.g., silver, gold) is merely another commodity—all these conceptions express in detail the substitute, within distributive economics, for the notion of the market as the mechanism of exchange.

Mishnah *Baba Mesi'a* 4:1–2

A. (1) Gold acquires silver, but silver does not acquire gold.
B. (2) Copper acquires silver, but silver does not acquire copper.
C. (3) Bad coins acquire good coins, but good coins do not acquire bad coins.
D. (4) A coin lacking a mint mark acquires a minted coin, and a minted coin does not acquire a coin lacking a mint-mark.
E. (5) Movable goods acquire coins, and coins do not acquire movable goods.
F. This is the governing principle: All sorts of movable objects effect acquisition of one another.

The commodity of lesser value effects acquisition of the commodity of greater value. The mere transfer of funds does not effect transfer of ownership. The actual receipt of the item in trade by the purchaser marks the point at which the exchange has taken place.

Barter of commodities, not exchange of (abstract) money, is what characterizes the exchange of things of value. Money is an abstraction. It does not merely represent something of value nor is it something itself of value. The entire notion of trade other than as an act of barter of materials or objects of essentially equal worth is rejected. Trade now is merely a way of working out imbalances when one party has too much of one thing but needs the other, while the other party has too much of the other thing but needs what the former has in excess. Since money does not effect a transaction, we have to determine that sort of specie which is (functionally) deemed to constitute currency, and that which is regarded as a commodity. In general, the more precious the metal, the more likely it is to be regarded not as money or ready cash, but as a commodity, subject to purchase or sale, just as much as is grain or wine. This notion is expressed very simply: "Gold acquires silver," meaning, gold is a commodity, and when the purchaser has taken possession of the gold, the seller owns the silver paid as money for it. But if the exchange is in the reverse—someone paying in gold for silver—the transaction is effected when the seller has taken possession of the gold. In an exchange of copper and silver, copper is deemed money, silver is now the commodity.

When the Rabbinic sages, as we shall see, compare the scarce resources of land with the unlimited resources of Torah-learning, they dealt with two media of sanctification, holy land, holy learning. That is the basis of equivalence, so far as I can discern. Accordingly, we must keep in mind, wealth and ownership of "land" speak of a very particular acreage, specifically, the territory known to the Rabbinic sages as the land of Israel, that alone. And, in this same context, only Israel is subject to wealth, because it is only when an Israelite owns land in the Land of Israel that God shares in the ownership and cares about his share of the crop (to go, as we shall see, to his scheduled castes, the priests, Levites, and poor, or to the support of the city, Jerusalem). It follows that land in the Land of Israel that is liable to sacerdotal taxes must be owned by an Israelite. Gentiles are not expected to designate portions of their crop as holy, and if they do so, those portions of the crop that they designate as holy nonetheless are deemed secular.

Let us dwell on the transcendent character of scarce resources (wealth) for which the Rabbinic sages legislated. We have an exceedingly specific set of conditions in hand, an economics of a remarkably particular, indeed, of an awry, character. Wealth for the Halakhah is not ownership of land in general, for example, land held by Jews in Babylonia, Egypt, Italy, or Spain. It is ownership of land located in a very particular place. And wealth for that same system is not wealth in the hands of an undifferentiated owner. It is wealth in the domain of an Israelite owner in particular.

Wealth therefore is ownership of [1] land in the Land of Israel [2] by Israel[ites].

That is meant in two senses, both of them contained within the italicized words. "Israel" then forms the key to the meaning of wealth, because it modifies persons and land alike: only an Israel[ite] can possess the domain that signifies wealth; only a domain within the land called by the name of "Israel" can constitute wealth. It is in the enchanted intersection of the two Israels, people and land, thus ownership of the land, ownership by the people, that wealth in the Halakhah becomes, in a this-worldly sense, real and tangible.

Wealth is conceived as unchanging and not subject to increase or decrease, hence, by the way, the notion of true value imputed to commodities. For if we imagine a world in which, ideally, no one rises and no one falls, and in which wealth is essentially stable, then we want to know what people understand by money, on the one hand, and how they identify riches, on the other. The answer is very simple. For the Halakhah, wealth constitutes that which is of lasting value, and what lasts is real property in the land of Israel, that alone. As I said, real estate in the land of Israel does not increase in volume, it is not subject to the fluctuation of the market, it was permanent, reliable, and, however small, always useful for something. True enough, we find more spiritual definitions of wealth, for example, Mishnah tractate *Abot* 4:2: "Who is rich? He who is happy in what he has." So too, one can become rich through keeping or studying the Torah, e.g., "He who keeps the Torah when poor will in the end keep it in wealth" (Mishnah tractate *Abot* 4:9). So too we find the following, "Keep your business to a minimum and make your business Torah" (Mishnah tractate *Abot* 4:10). But these sayings have no bearing upon a single passage of the Halakhah in which a concrete transaction in exchange of material goods takes place, nor does anyone invoke the notion of being satisfied with what one has when it comes to settling scores.

For the Rabbinic sages, since scarce resources are preserved in a steady state, profit or interest violate the norm; if I collect more than the true value of a piece of land or a cloak, I end up richer than before, and the buyer, poorer. And if, moving to the abstract, I treat money as subject to increase or decrease, I do the same. Hence, in the distributive economics of the Oral Torah, which sets squarely and symmetrically on the counterpart judgment of the Written Torah, profit-making and usury cannot be tolerated. If I lend a denar, I should get back a denar; if I lend a kor of wheat, I should get back a kor of wheat. Waiting for my money yields no gain to me, the use by the other no charge to him. And if a kor of wheat costs more when I get it back than when I lent it, that makes no difference, wheat remains wheat.

To the matter of usury: by usury the Rabbinic sages meant any payment for waiting on the return of something of value, but as the matter is fully explicated, usury became equivalent to profit of any sort. Here is the classical definition of the matter:

Mishnah *Baba Meṣiʿa* 5:1

A. What is interest, and what is increase [which is tantamount to taking interest]?
B. What is interest?
C. He who lends a *sela* [which is four *denars*] for [a return of] five *denars*,
D. two *seahs* of wheat for [a return of] three—
E. because he bites [off too much (NW'SK)].
F. And what is increase (TRBYT)?
G. He who increases (HMRBH) [profits] [in commerce] in kind.

H. How so?

I. [If] one purchases from another wheat at a price of a golden *denar* [25 *denars*] for a *kor*, which [was then] the prevailing price, and [then wheat] went up to thirty denars.

J. [If] he said to him, "Give me my wheat, for I want to sell it and buy wine with the proceeds"—

K. [and] he said to him, "Lo, your wheat is reckoned against me for thirty *denars*, and lo, you have [a claim of] wine on me"—

L. but he has no wine.

The meaning of interest is clear as given. Usury involves a repayment of 25 percent over what is lent in cash, or 50 percent over what is lent in kind (once more, we have no definition of the span of time involved).

Since God owns the land of Israel, God—represented by, or embodied through, the temple and priesthood, the Levites and the poor—joins each householder who also owns land in the land of Israel as an active partner, indeed, as senior partner, in possession of the landed domain. God not only demands a share of the crop, hence comprises a householder. God also dictates rules and conditions concerning production, therefore controls the householder's utilization of the means of production. Furthermore, it goes without saying, God additionally has provided as a lasting inheritance to Israel, the people, the enduring wealth of the country, which is to remain stable and stationary and not to change hands in such wise that one grows richer, the other poorer. Every detail of the distributive economics therefore restates that single point: *the earth is the Lord's*. That explains why the householder is partner of the Lord in ownership of the land, so that the Lord takes his share of the crop at the exact moment at which the householder asserts his ownership of his portion. All land was held in joint tenancy, with the householder as one partner, God as the other.

So much for the rational disposition of scarce resources, aimed, as we see, at the establishment of a steady-state economy, a world in perfect order and without change. But the Rabbinic sages treated as equal in standing real estate and Torah-learning. In that way they also took up the opposite of the notion of scarce resources, insusceptible of increase, such as real estate in the Land of Israel. They contemplated the conception of resources susceptible of infinite increase. In doing so, they accomplished the redefinition of scarce and valued resources in so radical a manner that the concept of value, while remaining material in consequence and character, nonetheless took on a quite different sense altogether. Issues such as the definition of wealth, the means of production and the meaning of control thereof, the disposition of wealth through distributive or other media, theory of money, reward for labor, and the like—all these questions found their answers in systematic discussion of another "scarce resource," another currency. Specifically, the definition of wealth changes from land to Torah. Why was such a transvaluation of value found plausible? Land produced a living; so did Torah. Land formed the foundation of the social entity; so did Torah.

When Torah-learning was deemed counterpart to land ownership, an economics concerning the rational management and increase of scarce resources worked itself out in such a way as to answer, for things of value quite different from real property or from capital such as we know as value, precisely the same questions that the received economics addressed in connection with wealth of a real character: land and its produce. The utter transvaluation of value finds expression in a jarring juxtaposition, an utter shift of rationality, specifically, the substitution of Torah for real estate. In the following statement in a fifth-century document in the name of first-century authorities, Tarfon thought wealth took the form of land, while Aqiba explained to him that wealth takes the form of Torah-learning. That the sense is material and concrete is explicit: land for Torah, Torah for land.

Thus, to repeat the matter of how Torah serves as an explicit symbol to convey the systemic worldview, let us note the main point of a now-familiar passage.

Leviticus Rabbah XXXIV:XVI

1. B. R. Tarfon gave to R. Aqiba six silver *centenarii*, saying to him, "Go, buy us a piece of land, so we can get a living from it and labor in the study of Torah together."

   C. He took the money and handed it over to scribes, Mishnah-teachers, and those who study Torah.

   D. After some time R. Tarfon met him and said to him, "Did you buy the land that I mentioned to you?"

   E. He said to him, "Yes."

   F. He said to him, "Is it any good?"

   G. He said to him, "Yes."

   H. He said to him, "And do you not want to show it to me?"

   I. He took him and showed him the scribes, Mishnah teachers, and people who were studying Torah, and the Torah that they had acquired.

J. He said to him, "Is there anyone who works for nothing? Where is the deed covering the field?"

K. He said to him, "It is with King David, concerning whom it is written, 'He has scattered, he has given to the poor, his righteousness endures forever' (Ps. 112:9)."

If, as we have seen, the Rabbinic sages framed an economics to provide for a world without change, we must wonder how this shift in the meaning of value accomplishes their goal, as, we see, it does.

The stress in the story at hand is on the enduring character of righteousness, meaning, in this context, support of masters and their disciples. That establishes the stability of wealth, marking it for eternity. So the theory of the rational disposition of scarce resources now encompasses the rational increase of resources that, by an act of will, the Israelite can make infinitely abundant—an anti-economics. How does theological goal, the formulation of a steady-state economy, follow? When it comes to land, a finite resource, one's gain marks another loss. But when it comes to Torah, a renewable resource, everyone gets richer when anyone acquires more; all Israel is enhanced. It follows that the Rabbinic sages' theory of a just society of permanent stability opens out onto a supernatural world of ever-increasing abundance. Only when we keep in mind, at every line of the discussion here, the supernatural character of holy Israel and the promise of the Torah as God's medium of self-revelation can we see how a single account of a perfect world at rest is set out here. That comes when we grasp how both the distributive economics of the Halakhah and its counterpart-economics in the Aggadah work together to form a coherent statement. That takes place when they are viewed in the larger theological context here under construction.

Now ownership of land, even in the Land of Israel, contrasts with wealth in another form altogether, and the contrast that was drawn was material and concrete, not merely symbolic and spiritual. It was material and tangible and palpable because it produced this-worldly gains, e.g., a life of security, comfort, ease, as these too found definition in the systemic context of the here and the now. It follows that it is an economics of scarce resources defined as something other than particular real estate. Whether thinking about real estate or Torah-learning, the Rabbinic sages deal with the rules or theory of the rational management of scarce resources, their preservation and increase. What the Aggadah changes here is the definition of resources of value, the rationality involved in the management of scarcity. In a word, while real estate cannot increase and by definition must always prove scarce, the value represented by Torah could expand without limit. Value could then increase indefinitely, resources that were desired and scarce be made ever more abundant, in the transformed economics of the successor system.

For at stake is not the spiritualization of wealth, that is to say, the representation of what "wealth" *really* consists of in other-than-material terms. That would represent not an economics but a theology. For example, the familiar saying in tractate *Abot*, "Who is rich? One who is happy in his lot," simply does not constitute a statement of economics at all. Like sayings in the Gospels that denigrate wealth, this one tells nothing about the rational management (e.g., increase) of scarce resources, it merely tells about appropriate moral attitudes of a virtuous order—how life is worth living—not answering an economic question at all. On the other hand, the tale that contrasts wealth in the form of land and its produce with wealth in the form of Torah (whatever is meant by "Torah") does constitute a statement of economics. The reason is that the storyteller invokes precisely the category of wealth—real property—that conventional economics defines as wealth. Let me state with heavy emphasis what holds the two theories of wealth together and places both in the same category:

If I have land, I have wealth, and I can support myself; if I have Torah, I have wealth, and I can support myself.

Those form the two components of the contrastive equation before us. But then wealth is disenlandised, and the Torah substituted for real property of all kinds.

Why do I insist that these kinds of stories deal with scarce resources in a concrete sense? Because in both cases cited to this point the upshot of the possession of Torah is this-worldly, concrete, tangible, and palpable. The rewards are not described as "filling treasuries in the heart," nor do they "enrich the soul," nor are they postponed to the world to come (as would be the case in a kind of capitalistic theology of investment on earth for return in heaven). The tale concerning Aqiba and Tarfon insists upon precisely the same *results* of the possession of wealth or value in the form of "Torah" as characterize wealth or value in the form of real estate. The key language is this: "Go, buy us a piece of land, *so we can get a living from it* and labor in the study of Torah together." Tarfon assumes that owning land buys leisure for Torah-study; Aqiba does not contradict that assumption, he steps beyond it. In Tarfon's mind, therefore, real (in theological sense) value is real (in the economic sense) wealth, that is, real estate, because if you own land, you can enjoy the leisure to do what you really want to do, which (as every philosopher understood) is to study (in the Rabbinic sages' case) the Torah together. But to Aqiba, in the tale, that is beside the point, since the real (in theological sense) value (in the economic sense, that is, what provides a living, food to eat for instance) is Torah (study), and that, in itself, suffices. The sense is, if I have land, I have a living, and if I have Torah, I have a living, which is no different from the living that I have from land—but which, as a matter of fact, is more secure.

Owning land involved control of the means of production, and so did knowing the Torah. But—more to the point—from land people derived a living, and from Torah people derived a living in *precisely* the same sense—that is to say, in the material and concrete sense— in which from land they could do so. That is alleged time and again, and at stake then is not the mere denigration of wealth but the transvaluation of value. Then the transvaluation consisted in [1] the disenlandisement of value from land, and [2] the transvaluation of (knowing or studying) the Torah, the imputation to Torah of the value formerly associated with land. And that is why it is valid to claim for Torah the status of a counterpart category: the system's economics, its theory of the way of life of the community and account of the rational disposition of those scarce resources that made everyday material existence possible and even pleasant: an economics of wealth, but of wealth differently defined, while similarly valued and utilized. So the concept of scarce resources was linked to the conception of Torah and took on altogether fresh meanings, but in exactly the same context and producing exactly the same material consequences, e.g., having food to eat and a dwelling for shelter, with the result that we have to redefine that which serves the very category "economics" altogether.

Now one can sell a field and acquire "Torah," meaning, in the context established by the exchange between Tarfon and Aqiba, the opportunity to gain leisure to (acquire the merit gained by) the study of the Torah. That the sage has left himself nothing for his support in old age makes explicit the material meaning of the statement, and the comparison of the value of land, created in six days, and the

Torah, created in forty days, is equally explicit. The comparison of knowledge of Torah to the merchandise of the merchant simply repeats the same point, but in a lower register. So too does the this-worldly power of study of the Torah make explicit in another framework the conviction that study of the Torah yields material and concrete benefit, not just spiritual renewal.

It is because economics deals with scarce resources, and the disenlandisement of economics in favor of Torah-learning has turned upon its head the very focus of economics: scarcity and the rational confrontation with scarcity. To land, rigid limits are set by nature, to the Holy Land, still more narrow ones apply. But to knowledge of the Torah no limits pertain. So we find ourselves dealing with an economics that concerns not only the rational utilization of scarce resources, but also the very opposite: the rational utilization and increase of what can and ought to be the opposite of scarce. In identifying knowledge and teaching of the Torah as the ultimate value, the Rabbinic sages have not simply found of value something other than what had earlier been valued; it has redefined economics altogether. It has done so, as a matter of fact, in a manner that is entirely familiar, by setting forth in place of an economics of scarcity an economics of abundant productivity. In so doing, the Rabbinic sages take a position consistent with their generative conception about Torah as distinguishing Israel from the nations. Torah serves, then, to form the point of differentiation in every detail, inclusive of the matter of value: the nations value land, Israel values Torah-learning; the nations know scarcity and have to learn the rules of estate management we call economics; Israel knows only abundance, on the condition that it choose abundance.

So much for the components of world order comprised by how people mark time and distribute wealth, both aimed at perfecting the just creation. But stasis in the distribution of scarce resources, like adhering to the unchanging present in keeping time—both stand for negative indicators of perfection. They say what must not happen, which is change. We now turn to the indicators of perfection that appeal to positive traits of creation: the complementarity of things and the correspondence, in a well-ordered world, of heaven and earth, such as the language of the Qaddish invokes: *He who makes peace in the heavens on high will bring peace for us and for all Israel.*

IV. COMPLEMENTARITY

Complementarity characterizes the way in which God and man relate, correspondence, the way in which God and man reach ultimate definition. They so act as to complement one another; they correspond in that they are like one another, man in God's image, after God's likeness. Here we reach the heart of world order: what is man, and who is God, and how and why they need each other. Let me explain, accounting also for the treatment just here, just now, of these two modes of relationship.

The negative dimensions of the Rabbinic sages' theology showed that world order exhibited no flaws. When, therefore, the Rabbinic sages insisted that time stands still in a steady-state social order, they explained that creation and society were unimpaired by change, whether marked by the passage of historical time or indicated by revisions in social relationships. So, in a negative mode, the Rabbinic sages demonstrated how world order attained stasis and therefore perfection. I have stressed how world order bore no flaws, the absence of change indicating a world at perfect rest. In their doctrines of marking time and of economics the Rabbinic sages emphasized what does not or should not happen, history on the one side, inequitable exchange on the other. Rather, humanity lives in a timeless present, the past and future belonging to the here and now. And a command economics assured that no change in value or status would result from material transactions, while providing for an endless increase in values that counted. But these indicative traits of perfection, both in design and in execution of the just world order, while necessary, were insufficient. Two positive ones would have to complete the picture of the design and its execution. Let me explain.

In this analysis of the system and structure of the theology animating the documents of the Rabbinic canon, I discern four indicative qualities of mind and method, each of which precipitates sustained thought on the message and the doctrine of the system seen whole, two negative, two positive. We have now identified two of the four principal traits that characterize the whole. The two now-familiar negative ones stress the absence of indications of flaws. God's plan for a just and perfect order involves a timeless world of lasting, rational traits of social organization, called here "paradigms." That aspect of perfection dictated the Rabbinic sages' doctrine of history, their denial of historical modes of thinking, such as Scripture afforded, in favor of the analytical modes that we today find common in social science. God's plan further is realized in a world of stasis, in which scarce resources of a worldly order, such as real estate, continue in enduring patterns, governing the holdings of households, for all time. At the same time, the Rabbinic sages made provision for an increase in wealth of a supernatural order, in which everyone participated in the benefits. In both components of the Rabbinic sages' theology, dealing with history and political economy, the Rabbinic sages framed doctrines, therefore, that declared God's plan flawless by reason of the absence of traits deemed negative.

But the Rabbinic sages claimed much more in behalf of the perfection of God's ordering of creation. They set forth two further characteristics of perfection, characteristics involving other qualities of mind, which in turn shaped other fundamental components in the Rabbinic sages' larger structure. The two affirmative ones, which highlight the presence of the positive marks of perfection, complete the Rabbinic sages' theology. Just as the principle of perfection attested by transcending time, balance shown by overcoming changes in the material relationships of the players in the social order, yielded a doctrine of history and of political economy, so we shall now examine two other principles of systemic perfection and the doctrines consequent upon them, traits of God (theology narrowly construed), and traits of man (theological anthropology), respectively.

What are those qualities of mind and message besides the traits of stasis in time and in resources? They involve considerations of balance, proportion, and coherence indicated by the prevalence of certain positive relationships. A single, simple logic, treating as self-evidently rational the relationship, between principal components, of complementarity, and the dynamics, between the major theological principals, God and man, of correspondence, governs throughout. Complementarity and correspondence form two sides of the same coin. Components of the social order—whether classes of persons or types of virtue or qualities of mind—fit together into a coherent whole, one class or type without the other being incomplete, unable to achieve its teleological task. The soul and the body present a principal theological case of complementarity; and that spills over into the matter of theological doctrine, God's relationship to the world being compared with the soul's relationship to the body. Some entities furthermore correspond with one another, not only matching static qualities, but intersecting in dynamic ones. Among these, one relationship makes all the difference, the one between God and man, man in God's image. Once more, theological doctrine emerges from modes of thought and argument characteristic of a complete and governing system, a logic, a theology.

What are some of the necessary and sufficient complementary relationships, public and private, that attest by their presence to the perfection of world order defined through justice? In public the logic of complementarity is discerned in the encounter of Heaven and earth, nature and super-nature, justice and mercy, and the pair now in hand, soul and body. The Land, standing for the natural world, the transcendent God, and Israel come together to complement and complete the processes of sustaining life. All are necessary, none alone sufficient. God, Israel, and the Land meet, specifically, in the temple, whence all of life is nourished and blessed. In private, in the inner lives of men, God's transactions of free grace respond to, are complemented by, man's actions of uncoerced generosity.

World order exhibits perfection because in any orderly, unflawed arrangement, whether of aesthetics, sociology, or architecture—flowers, social classes, or buildings—all things hold together in proportion, each with its sustaining counterpart and complement. That is what provides stability and strength. The principal systemic components or categories, then, do not stand in isolation, but require the balance of an other to form a coherent whole. Complementarity then points to that same logic that seeks to show the match of matters. Indeed, it is a principle comparable to the logic that deems justice to require the meting out of measure for measure, this sin or crime, that compensating penalty; this act of obedience to the Torah, that beneficent response in the order of society or desired result in nature. But in place of exchange, this for that, complementarity speaks of coherence, this together with that, above all, *this impossible without that.*

A single example suffices. As we shall see in a moment, the Rabbinic sages insist that, without mercy, justice cannot function. They also hold that categorically unrelated matters, such as creation and nature, Israel and society, and justice cannot endure in separation from one another, but nature, Israel, and justice converge and work together; so the Rabbinic sages state explicitly. That is where the principle of complementarity is invoked, maintaining that, in world order, the one is necessary to the other. Accordingly, complementarity positively indicates the completion and perfection of world order, yet another mark of everything in place, with no loose ends to disrupt either the natural or the social order.

To identify what is at stake, then, in the logic of complementarity, we turn first to a simple example of how, for perfection to come about, two traits must join together with one another. That same insistence upon the just match leads to the quest for other points at which world order comes to completion through the same just match. If we can show how one matter complements and completes another—mercy, justice, for example, or sanctification, election—then we can reveal the architectonic perfection of categories viewed in their relationships, their ultimate balance. The principle of complementarity is best illustrated by the Rabbinic sages' insistence that justice without mercy is incomplete. God created the world with the attribute of mercy and also of justice, so that in complementary balance the world might endure:

Genesis Rabbah XII:XV.1

A. "The Lord God [made earth and heaven]" (Gen. 2:4):

B. The matter [of referring to the divinity by both the names, Lord, which stands for mercy, and God, which stands for justice] may be compared to the case of a king who had empty cups. The king said, "If I fill them with hot water, they will split. If I fill them with cold water, they will contract [and snap]."

C. What did the king do? He mixed hot water and cold water and put it into them, and the cups withstood the liquid.

D. So said the Holy One, blessed be he, "If I create the world in accord with the attribute of mercy, sins will multiply. If I create it in accord with the attribute of justice, the world cannot endure."

E. "Lo, I shall create it with both the attribute of justice and the attribute of mercy, and may it endure!"

F. "Thus: The Lord [standing for the attribute of mercy] God [standing for the attribute of justice] [made the earth and heavens]" (Gen. 2:4).

Just as too much justice will destroy the world, but too much mercy ruin its coherence, so throughout, each set of traits achieving complementarity must be shown, like dancers, to move in balance one with the other. Then, and only then, are excesses avoided, stasis in motion attained. That brings about the world of justice at rest that the Rabbinic sages deemed God to have created in the beginning, to have celebrated on the original Sabbath, and to intend to restore in the end. Success in that inquiry into how this complements that

imparts integrity and coherence to the components of theology, in the
present case justice and mercy. That is why, when we can show complementarity, we identify the affirmative indicators of a well-crafted
world. That is a world in which each component links in one way or
another to others, one set to another, all parts holding together in a
single coherent statement. In this instance, the statement declares the
work of the Creator just and reliable.

The natural world without the embodiment of the just moral order,
and the moral order without full realization in Israel, and Israel
divorced from nature and the nurture of justice—all three prove
incomplete, indeed if not chaotic then in any case inchoate. Only
when joined before God do the three attain each its full realization
in the others. And that takes place in the elect abode of Israel, in the
Land of Israel, the chosen of all lands as we have seen, in Jerusalem,
the chosen of all cities, and in the temple, the highest of all mountains. All three form the setting for the perfect union of creation,
Israel, and the moral order. Complementarity attests to perfection,
then, in the conduct of the cult. The character of the offerings, the
representation of the vestments of the priest, the very inanimate furniture of the temple—all complete the union of man and nature in
the service of God. These are the propositions we shall now see
spelled out in so many words, the result of an interior logic that holds
together creation, Israel, and justice.

First comes creation in relationship to the temple cult. As we shall
now see, creation reaches its climax in the cult, where the blessings
of the natural world are offered up to God in Heaven. Second comes
Israel, the complement and counterpart to the world of nature, and
partner of God in creation. That brings us to the first match in the
trilogy of mutually complementary components of world order, the
natural order, the social order embodied in Israel, and the cult. Here
is the way that the Rabbinic sages show how creation is embodied in
and celebrated by the offerings of the temple in Jerusalem. The
sacrificial cult is celebrated as a memorial to creation, and the Psalms
that the Levites sing identify the particular aspect of creation that
took place on a given day of the week. So the selected Psalm set the
stage for the offering that celebrated what took place in creation on
that day:

Bavli *Rosh Hashanah* 4:4A–E I.2/31A

A. It is taught on Tannaite authority [at Mishnah tractate *Tamid* 7:4]:
R. Judah says in the name of R. Aqiba:

B. "On the first day what did they sing? [Ps. 24, which begins]: 'The
earth is the Lord's and the fullness thereof, [the world and they who
live therein].' [This psalm was used] because [on Sunday God] took
possession and gave possession and was ruler over his world [with-
out the heavenly hosts, who were created on the second day]."

C. "On the second day what did they sing? [Ps. 48, beginning]: 'Great
is the Lord and highly to be praised [in the city of our God, even
upon his holy hill].' [This psalm was used] because [on Monday
God] divided that which he created [into the upper and lower
worlds] and was sovereign over them."

D. "On the third day they did sing [Ps. 82, which begins]: 'God stands
in the congregation of God, [he is a judge among the gods].' [This
psalm was used] because [on Tuesday God] revealed the dry land
in his wisdom and prepared the earth for his congregation."

E. "On the fourth day they did sing [Ps. 94, which begins]: 'Lord God
to whom vengeance belongs, [you God to whom vengeance belongs,
show yourself].' [This psalm was used] because [on Wednesday
God] created the sun and moon and was destined to exact punishment from those who serve them."

F. "On the fifth day they did sing [Ps. 81, which begins], 'Sing aloud
to God our strength, [make a joyful noise to the God of Jacob].'
[This psalm was used] because [on Thursday God] created birds
and fish, which bring glory to his name."

G. "On the sixth day they did sing [Ps. 92, which begins], 'The Lord
reigns; he is robed in majesty.' [This psalm was used] because [on
Friday God] finished his work and ruled over all [he created]."

H. "On the seventh day they did sing [Ps. 92, which begins], 'A Psalm,
a song for the Sabbath day'—[a psalm] for the day that is wholly
Sabbath rest [for eternity]."

So the temple cult celebrates the natural order. We shall presently
note the correspondence between the priests' garments and the sins
that are atoned for by the wearing of those garments, and that egre-
gious match, in fact precipitated by substantive points of contact, will
bring the social order too within the framework of complementarity
and completion. Here the invocation of Psalms to be sung in the temple that correspond to events in the creation of the world underscores
that same sense of the integrity of all reality, natural and social.

When we turn to the complementarity between the sacred and the
profane, we come to the temple and its offerings. There this world

meets the transcendent when Israel designates as holy, and then in conditions of sanctification, offers up what was profane but now is holy to God, the gifts of nature particular to the Land of Israel, wine, wheat, oil, meat of domesticated non-carnivorous beasts. We here address an elect locus, locative sanctification.

The temple, where God and holy Israel meet, is the highest point in earth; there God receives his share of the natural gifts of the Holy Land—meat, grain, wine, and olive oil; and where, through the presentation of these gifts, the Israelite fulfills his obligations to God, inclusive of atoning for sin. Concomitantly, prayers are to be recited in the direction of the temple, for instance, Mishnah tractate *Berakhot* 4:6A: If he was travelling in a ship or on a raft, he should direct his heart towards the Chamber of the Holy of Holies. The priority of the Land of Israel over all other lands, and Jerusalem over all other places, and the temple over the rest of Jerusalem, is expressed in this language at Tosefta tractate *Berakhot* 3:15. Those who are outside the Land turn toward the Land of Israel. Those who are in the Land of Israel turn toward Jerusalem. Those who are in Jerusalem turn toward the temple. Those who are in the temple turn toward the chamber of the Holy of Holies and pray. "It turns out that those standing in the north face south, those in the south face north, those in the east face west, and those in the west face east. Thus all Israel turn out to be praying toward one place, the Temple mount."

The stakes in temple worship prove cosmic, for the welfare of the natural world as well as of Israel rests upon the temple service:

Abot deRabbi Natan IV:IV.1

B. So long as the Temple service of the house of the sanctuary went on, the world was blessed for its inhabitants and rain came down in the proper time.

C. For it is said, "To love the Lord your God and to serve him with all your heart and with all your soul that I will provide the rain of your land in its season, the former rain and the latter rain . . . and I will provide grass in your fields for your cattle" (Dt. 11:13–14).

D. But when the Temple service of the house of the sanctuary ceased to go on, the world was not blessed for its inhabitants, and rain did not come down in the proper time,

E. as it is said, "Take heed to yourselves lest your heart be deceived . . . and he shut up the heaven so that there shall be no rain" (Dt. 11:16–17).

The temple cult then sustained life, and its offerings of the gifts of creation to the Creator brought the response of renewed blessing of nature. But, representing the world of creation, the temple is incomplete. The temple requires the complement of Israel.

The components on which we have concentrated, creation, the just moral order, and Israel, in no way match categorically, and that is the challenge to complementarity. The Rabbinic sages for their part claim not only that within the world order of justice that God thought up and made, principal parts coexist in harmony. They further allege a quality of complementary relationship that transcends mere harmony, the absence of conflict. The Rabbinic sages maintain that the parts fit *only* when they function in perfect union. That is not an easy claim to sustain. For the natural world and the social order define their own categories, but do not intersect: what has a lamb to do with a city? And how does the particular social entity, Israel (or its categorical equivalent, the gentiles), match a cloud, on the one side, and an abstract category of thought (whether philosophical or legal or theological), justice, on the other. And yet, in the quest for showing how the generative categories (creation, society, justice) complement one another, the theology of the Oral Torah finds its answer in that hierarchy established by Land of Israel, Jerusalem, Temple Mount, priesthood, sacrifice. Only within the intellectual framework defined by the principle of complementarity can the remarkable statements about the union of nature and supernature, the social order and Israel, attain their full significance.

And yet, for this theological statement to make sense within its givens and its logic, it must encompass the principal, not only the secondary, players. And the principals are God and man (its being taken for granted that under discussion is Israelite man). For as we have already noted, once the Torah has announced God's intent in making man, "Let us make man in our image, after our likeness," and further specified God's act in actually doing so, "And God created man in his image, in the image of God he created him, male and female he created them" (Gen. 1:26–27), from the perspective guiding this discussion an urgent question arises: In what way are God and man complementary, meaning, how and why is the one completed in and by the other? Wherein—within theory of complementary relationships that is meant to justify world order—does God need man as complement?

Since God has commanded love, "You will love the Lord your God with all your heart, and with all your soul, and with all your might" (Dt. 6:4), God himself has announced that aspect in which he is incomplete, identifying what he requires but does not possess. And that is the love of man. God then at the very moment of the declaration of his uniqueness pronounces what he yet needs for completion, man's entire devotion. But, by its nature, that love cannot be commanded or coerced, only beseeched on God's part, freely given on man's. And reciprocally, it hardly need be added, what man requires but cannot gain through coercion or manipulation or fixed exchange is God's favor and love. So, in the ineffable exchange of love, in the transaction of the will, each party to the drama of creation seeks in the other its own complement, completion, and wholeness. When that exchange takes place, Eden is regained, Israel restored to the Land of Israel. When it does not take place, man's intentionality takes the form of arrogance, which leads to sin, which disrupts world order. So, in the relationship of complementarity, love surpasses even justice. The exposition of how through the concept of *zekhut* that relationship of complementarity is fully set forth in the Rabbinic canon will require a systematic exposition of how a single word encompasses a principal theological component of an entire system.

The Oral Torah finds in a very particular transaction the working out of this relationship of complementarity between God and man. That transaction it identifies in the performance of acts of will consisting of offerings of love to Heaven. Such acts take on a particular quality, which we shall see in a moment. But the principle they embody is this: What we cannot by will impose, we can by will evoke. What we cannot accomplish through coercion, we can achieve through submission. God will do for us what we cannot do for ourselves, when we do for God what God cannot make us do. In a wholly concrete and tangible sense, that means to love God with all the heart, the soul, the might that we have. In that way we enter a relationship of complementarity with God, freely and unconditionally contributing what we have and control, which is our capacity to love, and so completing that unity that God aspires to enjoy with us.

To define matters more concretely, we turn to stories that embody the ultimate, and perfect transaction of complementarity: giving God what he cannot coerce, receiving from God what we cannot compel or inveigle. In all three instances that follow, the deeds of the heroes of the story make them worthy of having their prayers answered, which is a mark of God's response. These are, in particular, deeds that transcend the strict requirements of the Torah, and even the limits of the law altogether. The keyword in some of the stories, *zekhut*, which may be translated "the heritage of supererogatory virtue and its consequent entitlements," stands for the empowerment, of a supernatural character, that derives from the virtue of one's ancestry or from one's own virtuous deeds of a very particular order. These are, concretely, deeds not commanded but impelled by utter generosity of the heart. These are deeds that make a difference only when they are done without hope, let alone prospect of, recompense and without pressure of any kind except the kind that wells up from within. It is, then, an indicator of one's inner quality and character. No single word in American English bears the same meaning, nor can I identify even a synonym for *zekhut* in the canonical writings, only the antonym, which is sin. Sin represents an act of rebellion, *zekhut* an act of humble, willing, and gratuitous submission, so the two represent binary opposites, and complements of another order, as we shall see in due course.

To illustrate the transaction, or relationship, of *zekhut*, we turn not to such familiar media as composites setting forth a systematic exposition in exegetical form, or even to compositions exposing an argument in propositional form enriched with the anticipated parables, but to some simple stories. Here the language of *zekhut* figures, and the meaning of that language is then conveyed in context. In the opening text, when the beggar asks for money, he says, literally, "acquire *zekhut* through me," referring in context to the action he solicits. But the same word, as noun or verb, in other contexts takes on other meanings, always with the same deeper significance of a relationship of grace, unearned, uncoerced love, that is besought. The difficulty of translating a word of systemic consequence with a single word in some other language (or in the language of the system's documents themselves) tells us that we deal with what is unique.

Yerushalmi *Ta'anit* 1:4.I

> F. A certain man came before one of the relatives of R. Yannai. He said to him, "Rabbi, attain *zekhut* through me [by giving me charity]."

G. He said to him, "And didn't your father leave you money?"

H. He said to him, "No."

I. He said to him, "Go and collect what your father left in deposit with others."

J. He said to him, "I have heard concerning property my father deposited with others that it was gained by violence [so I don't want it]."

K. He said to him, "You are worthy of praying and having your prayers answered."

The point of K, of course, is self-evidently a reference to the possession of entitlement to supernatural favor, and it is gained through deeds that the law of the Torah cannot require but does favor: what one does on one's own volition, beyond the measure of the law. Here I see the opposite of sin. A sin is what one has done by one's own volition beyond all limits of the law. So an act that generates *zekhut* for the individual is the counterpart and opposite: what one does by one's own volition that also is beyond all requirements of the law.

L. A certain ass driver appeared before the rabbis [the context requires: in a dream] and prayed, and rain came. The rabbis sent and brought him and said to him, "What is your trade?"

M. He said to them, "I am an ass driver."

N. They said to him, "And how do you conduct your business?"

O. He said to them, "One time I rented my ass to a certain woman, and she was weeping on the way, and I said to her, 'What's with you?' and she said to me, 'The husband of that woman [me] is in prison [for debt], and I wanted to see what I can do to free him.' So I sold my ass and I gave her the proceeds, and I said to her, 'Here is your money, free your husband, but do not sin [by becoming a prostitute to raise the necessary funds].'"

P. They said to him, "You are worthy of praying and having your prayers answered."

The ass driver clearly has a powerful lien on Heaven, so that his prayers are answered, even while those of others are not. What did he do to get that entitlement? He did what no law could demand: impoverished himself to save the woman from a "fate worse than death."

Q. In a dream of R. Abbahu, Mr. Pentakaka ["Five sins"] appeared, who prayed that rain would come, and it rained. R. Abbahu sent and summoned him. He said to him, "What is your trade?"

R. He said to him, "Five sins does that man [I] do every day, [for I am a pimp:] hiring whores, cleaning up the theater, bringing home their garments for washing, dancing, and performing before them."

S. He said to him, "And what sort of decent thing have you ever done?"

T. He said to him, "One day that man [I] was cleaning the theater, and a woman came and stood behind a pillar and cried. I said to her, 'What's with you?' And she said to me, 'That woman's [my] husband is in prison, and I wanted to see what I can do to free him,' so I sold my bed and cover, and I gave the proceeds to her. I said to her, 'Here is your money, free your husband, but do not sin.'"

U. He said to him, "You are worthy of praying and having your prayers answered."

Q moves us still further, since the named man has done everything sinful that one can do, and, more to the point, he does it every day. So the singularity of the act of *zekhut*, which suffices if done only one time, encompasses its power to outweigh a life of sin—again, an act of *zekhut* as the mirror image and opposite of sin. Here again, the single act of saving a woman from a "fate worse than death" has sufficed.

The critical importance of the heritage of virtue together with its supernatural entitlements emerges in a striking claim. Even though a man was degraded, one action sufficed to win for him that heavenly glory to which rabbis in lives of Torah-study aspired. A single remarkable deed, exemplary for its deep humanity, sufficed to win for an ordinary person the *zekhut* that elicits supernatural favor enjoyed by some rabbis on account of their Torah-study. *Zekhut* represents a power that only God can ultimately grasp: the power of weakness. It is what the weak and excluded and despised can do that outweighs what the great masters of the Torah—impressed with the power of the ass driver to pray and get his prayers answered—have accomplished. *Zekhut* also forms the inheritance of the disinherited: what you receive as a heritage when you have nothing in the present and have gotten nothing in the past, that scarce resource that is free and unearned but much valued.

The systemic statements made by the Rabbinic sages concerning *zekhut* speak of relationship, function, the interplay of humanity and God. One's store of *zekhut* derives from a relationship, that is, from one's forebears. That is one dimension of the relationships in which one stands. *Zekhut* also forms a measure of one's own relationship with Heaven, as the power of one person, but not another, to pray and so

bring rain attests. What sort of relationship does *zekhut*, as the opposite of sin, then posit? It is one of autonomous grace, for Heaven cannot force us to do those types of deeds that yield *zekhut*, and that, story
after story suggests, is the definition of a deed that generates *zekhut*:
doing what we ought to do but do not have to do. But then, we cannot coerce Heaven to do what we want done either, for example, by
carrying out the commandments. These are obligatory, but do not
obligate Heaven.

A simple answer now is demanded to the question, why does *zekhut*
form the centerpiece in the Rabbinic sages' doctrine of how God and
man require one another? Whence—in mythic language—then our
lien on Heaven? A few words contain the response: God needs man's
love, man needs God's grace, and neither can coerce the other to give
what, by definition, cannot be coerced at all. The relationship of complementarity is realized through man's deeds of a supererogatory
character—to which Heaven responds by deeds of a supererogatory
character.

That defines the heart and soul of the Rabbinic sages' theology of
man's relationship to God. Self-abnegation or restraint shown by
man precipitates a counterpart attitude in Heaven, hence generating
zekhut. The complementary relationship measured by *zekhut*—Heaven's
response by an act of uncoerced favor to a person's uncoerced gift,
e.g., act of gentility, restraint, or self-abnegation—contains an element of unpredictability for which appeal to the *zekhut* inherited from
ancestors accounts. So while one cannot coerce Heaven, he can
through *zekhut* gain acts of favor from Heaven, and that is by doing
what Heaven cannot require but only desire. Heaven then responds
to man's attitude in carrying out what transcends his duties. The
simple fact that rabbis cannot pray and bring rain, but a simple ass
driver can, tells the whole story. That act of pure disinterest—giving
the woman his means of livelihood—is the one that gains for him
Heaven's deepest interest. And we must not miss the starting point of
the transaction, the woman's act of utter and tangible self-sacrifice in
behalf of her husband, which wins the ass driver's empathy and provokes the action to which Heaven responds.

"Make his wishes yours, so that he will make your wishes his. . . .
From anyone from whom people take pleasure God takes pleasure"
(tractate *Abot* 2:4). These two statements hold together the two principal elements of the conception of the relationship to God that in a

single word *zekhut* conveys. Give up, please others, do not impose
your will but give way to the will of the other, and Heaven will
respond by giving a lien that is not coerced but evoked. By the rationality of discipline within, we have the power to form rational relationships beyond ourselves, with Heaven; and that is how the system
expands the boundaries of the social order to encompass not only the
natural but also the supernatural world. The conviction that, by dint
of special effort, I may so conduct myself as to acquire an entitlement
of supernatural power turns my commonplace circumstance into an
arena encompassing Heaven and earth. God responds to holy Israel's
virtue, filling the gap that one leaves when he forebears, withdraws,
and gives up his space, his selfhood. Then God responds; man's
sacrifice evokes memories of Abraham's readiness to sacrifice Isaac.

We observe at the end that order is ultimately attained by transcending the very rules of order. In order to establish the moral order
of justice, therefore, God breaks the rules, accords an entitlement to
this one, who has done one remarkable deed, but not to that one,
who has done nothing wrong and everything right. So a life in accord
with the rules—even a life spent in the study of the Torah—in
Heaven's view is outweighed by a single moment, a gesture that violates the norm, extending the outer limits of the rule, for instance, of
virtue. And who but a God who, like us, not only thinks but also feels,
responds to impulse and sentiment, can be portrayed in such a way
as this?

> "So I sold my ass and I gave her the proceeds, and I said to her, 'Here
> is your money, free your husband, but do not sin [by becoming a pros-
> titute to raise the necessary funds].'" They said to him, "You are wor-
> thy of praying and having your prayers answered."

No rule exhaustively describes a world such as this. We are in God's
image, after God's likeness, because we not only through right thinking penetrate the principles of creation, but also through right attitude replicate the heart of the Creator. Humanity on earth incarnates
God on high, the Israelite family in particular, and, in consequence,
earth and Heaven join—within.

This brings us back to the principle of complementarity. What is
asked of Israel and of the Israelite is godly restraint, supernatural
generosity of soul that is "in our image, after our likeness"; that is
what sets aside all rules. The bounds of earth have now extended to

Heaven. God dwells with Israel, in Israel: "today, if you will it," a phrase we shall meet when we ask when the Messiah is going to come. The Rabbinic sages portray a social order in which, in relationship to God, Israelites and Israel alike control their own destiny. This they do by ceasing to exercise control and submitting to God's will and purpose. In the end both the nation and the individual had in hand the power to shape the future. How was this to be done? It was not alone by keeping the Torah, studying the Torah, dressing, eating, making a living, marrying, procreating, raising a family, burying and being buried, all in accord with those rules. That life in conformity with the rule, obligatory but merely conventional, did not evoke the special interest of Heaven. Why should it? The rules describe the ordinary.

But "God wants the heart," and that is not an ordinary thing. Nor is the power to bring rain or hold up a tottering house gained through a life of merely ordinary sanctity. Special favor responded to extraordinary actions, in the analogy of special disfavor, misfortune deemed to punish sin. And just as culpable sin, as distinct from mere error, requires an act of will, specifically, arrogance, so an act of extraordinary character requires an act of will. But, as mirror image of sin, the act would reveal in a concrete way an attitude of restraint, forbearance, gentility, and self-abnegation. A sinful act, provoking Heaven, was one done deliberately to defy Heaven. Then an act that would evoke Heaven's favor, so imposing upon Heaven a lien that Heaven freely gave, was one that, equally deliberately and concretely, displayed humility.

Now to look ahead to what must follow. Complementarity shades over into correspondence. For in stressing the complementarity of God and man, we ought not to miss their correspondence at the deepest levels of sentiment and emotion and attitude. The one completes the other through common acts of humility, forbearance, accommodation, a spirit of conciliation. For one thing, Scripture itself is explicit that God shares and responds to the attitudes and intentionality of human beings. God cares what humanity feels—wanting love, for example—and so the conception that actions that express right attitudes of humility will evoke in Heaven a desired response will not have struck as novel the authors of the Pentateuch or the various prophetic writings, for example. The Written Torah's record of God's feelings and God's will concerning the feelings of humanity leaves no room for doubt.

Before turning from the relationship of complementarity to the closely similar relationship of correspondence between man and God, let us fix firmly in mind the results of this inquiry:

[1] the conception that acts of omission or commission expressing an attitude of forbearance and self-abnegation generate *zekhut* in particular;

[2] the principle that *zekhut* functions in those very specific ways that the system deems critical: as the power to attest to human transformation and regeneration, affording that power inhering in weakness, that wealth inhering in giving up what one has, that in the end promise the attainment of our goals.

When we deem the attitude of affirmation and acceptance, rather than aggression, and the intentionality of self-abnegation and forbearance, to define the means for gaining *zekhut*, what we are saying is contrary and paradoxical. It is this: if you want to have, then give up. If you want to impose your judgment, then make the judgment of the other into your own. If you want to coerce Heaven, then evoke in Heaven attitudes of sympathy that will lead to the actions or events that you want, whether rain, whether long life, whether the salvation of Israel and its hegemony over the nations. So too, to rule, be ruled by Heaven; to show that Heaven rules, give up what you want to the other.

Embodying all of these views in a single, protean concept, *zekhut* results: the lien upon Heaven, freely given by Heaven in response to one's free surrender to the will and wish of Heaven. And by means of *zekhut*, whether one's own, whether one's ancestors', the social order finds its shape and system, and the individual his or her place within its structure.

V. CORRESPONDENCE

Man not only complements God, he also is like God. When the Rabbinic sages read in the Torah that man is created in God's image, they understood that to mean, God and man correspond, bearing comparable traits. These have now to be examined. The theological anthropology of the Oral Torah, treating the study of man as a chapter in the knowledge of God, in whose image man is made, defined correspondence between God and man in three ways:

[1] intellectually, sharing a common rationality;

[2] emotionally, sharing common sentiments and attitudes, and

[3] physically, sharing common features.

That is why, to begin with, God and Israel relate. They think alike. They feel the same sentiments. And they look alike. Like God, man is in command of, and responsible for, his own will and intentionality and consequent conduct. The very fact that God reveals himself through the Torah, which man is able to understand, there to be portrayed in terms and categories that man grasps, shows how the characteristics of God and man prove comparable. The first difference between man and God is that man sins, but the one and the just God, never; connecting "God" and "sin" yields an unintelligible result. And the second difference between creature and Creator, man and God, is that God is God.

Let us start with the most startling point, that correspondence encompasses not only intangible, but material qualities. How do God and man compare in physical presence? Because the theology of Judaism in its later, philosophical mode has long insisted on the incorporeality of God, we take up in some detail the Oral Torah's explicit claim that God and man look exactly alike, being distinguished only by actions performed by the one but not the other.

Genesis Rabbah VIII:X.1

A. Said R. Hoshayya, "When the Holy One, blessed be he, came to create the first man, the ministering angels mistook him [for God, since man was in God's image,] and wanted to say before him, 'Holy, [holy, holy is the Lord of hosts].'"

B. "To what may the matter be compared? To the case of a king and a governor who were set in a chariot, and the provincials wanted to greet the king, 'Sovereign!' But they did not know which one of them was which. What did the king do? He turned the governor out and put him away from the chariot, so that people would know who was king."

C. "So too when the Holy One, blessed be he, created the first man, the angels mistook him [for God]. What did the Holy One, blessed be he, do? He put him to sleep, so everyone knew that he was a mere man."

D. "That is in line with the following verse of Scripture: 'Cease you from man, in whose nostrils is a breath, for how little is he to be accounted' (Is. 2:22)."

Man—Adam—is in God's image, interpreted in a physical way, so the angels did not know man from God. Only that man sleeps distinguishes him from God.

The message derives from the verse that states, ". . . in our image, after our likeness" (Gen. 1:26). While this passage is not cited in the present construction, *Genesis Rabbah* VIII:X simply carries forward the concluding entry of *Genesis Rabbah* VIII:IX, in which the relevant verse is cited. Accordingly, "In our image" yields two views, first, that the complete image of man is attained in a divine union between humanity—man and woman—and, further, that what makes man different from God is that man sleeps, and God does not sleep.

Beyond the words of the Torah, God makes himself manifest to man in many ways, most of them corporeal. It is quite proper, in the Rabbinic sages' view, to imagine God in human form; God makes himself manifest in the ways in which man can comprehend, and God becomes accessible to man by taking on forms that man can grasp.

Pesiqta deRab Kahana XII:XXV

1. A. Another interpretation of "I am the Lord your God [who brought you out of the land of Egypt"] (Ex. 20:2):
   B. Said R. Hinena bar Papa, "The Holy One, blessed be he, had made his appearance to them with a stern face, with a neutral face, with a friendly face, with a happy face."
   C. "with a stern face: in Scripture. When a man teaches his son Torah, he has to teach him in a spirit of awe."
   D. "with a neutral face: in Mishnah."
   E. "with a friendly face: in Talmud."
   F. "with a happy face: in lore."
   G. Said to them the Holy One, blessed be he, "Even though you may see all of these diverse faces of mine, nonetheless: 'I am the Lord your God who brought you out of the land of Egypt' (Ex. 20:2)."

So far we deal with attitudes. As to the iconic representation of God, the following is explicit:

2. A. Said R. Levi, "The Holy One, blessed be he, had appeared to them like an icon that has faces in all directions, so that if a thousand people look at it, it appears to look at them as well."
   B. "So too when the Holy One, blessed be he, when he was speaking, each and every Israelite would say, 'With me in particular the Word speaks.'"

   C. "What is written here is not, I am the Lord, your [plural] God,
   but rather, 'I am the Lord your [singular] God who brought you
   out of the land of Egypt' (Ex. 20:2)."

That God may show diverse faces to various people is now established. The reason for God's variety is made explicit. People differ,
and God, in the image of whom all mortals are made, must therefore
sustain diverse images—all of them formed in the model of human
beings:

3. A. Said R. Yosé bar Hanina, "And it was in accord with the capac-
      ity of each one of them to listen and understand what the Word
      spoke with him.
   B. "And do not be surprised at this matter, for when the mana
      came down to Israel, each and every one would find its taste
      appropriate to his capacity, infants in accord with their capaci-
      ty, young people in accord with their capacity, old people in
      accord with their capacity.
   C. "infants in accord with their capacity: just as an infant sucks
      from the tit of his mother, so was its flavor, as it is said, 'Its taste
      was like the taste of rich cream' (Num. 11:8).
   D. "young people in accord with their capacity: as it is said, 'My
      bread also which I gave you, bread and oil and honey' (Ez.
      16:19).
   E. "old people in accord with their capacity: as it is said 'the taste
      of it was like wafers made with honey' (Ex. 16:31).
   F. "Now if in the case of mana, each and every one would find its
      taste appropriate to his capacity, so in the matter of the Word,
      each and every one understood in accord with capacity."

The individuality and particularity of God rest upon the diversity of
humanity. But, it must follow, the model of humanity—"in our
image"—dictates how we are to envisage the face of God.

   But first comes shared rules of intellect, which render God and
man consubstantial. God and man intellectually correspond in the
common logic and reason that they share. That is in two aspects.
First, like Abraham at Sodom, the Rabbinic sages simply took for
granted that the same rationality governs. God is compelled by arguments man finds persuasive, appeals to which man responds: "Will
not the Judge of all the world. . . ." Second, meeting God through the
study of the record of God's self-revelation, the Torah, the Rabbinic
sages worked out their conviction that man's mind corresponded to
God's, which is why man can receive the Torah to begin with. That
man can study the Torah proves that man has the capacity to know

God intellectually. That explains why they maintained that God is to be met in the study of the Torah, where his presence will come to rest. God's presence, then, came to rest with those who, in an act of intellect, took up the labor of Torah-learning:

Tractate *Abot* 3:6

A. R. Halafta of Kefar Hananiah says, "Among ten who sit and work hard on Torah the Presence comes to rest,

B. "as it is said, 'God stands in the congregation of God' (Ps. 82:1).

C. "And how do we know that the same is so even of five? For it is said, 'And he has founded his group upon the earth' (Am. 9:6).

D. "And how do we know that this is so even of three? Since it is said, 'And he judges among the judges' (Ps. 82:1).

E. "And how do we know that this is so even of two? Because it is said, 'Then they that feared the Lord spoke with one another, and the Lord hearkened and heard' (Mal. 3:16).

F. "And how do we know that this is so even of one? Since it is said, 'In every place where I record my name I will come to you and I will bless you' (Ex. 20:24)."

But there is more. The Rabbinic sages took as their task not only passive learning of the Torah but active and thoroughly critical participation in the inquiry into the meaning of the Torah. It is one thing to absorb the Torah, quite another to join in the processes of thought, the right way of thinking, that sustain the Torah.

Through their critical, analytical inquiry into the Torah and its law, the Rabbinic sages thought to gain access to the modes of thought that guided the formation of the Torah. This involved, for instance, dialectical argument concerning comparison and contrast in this way, not in that, identification of categories in one manner, not in another.

In their delineation of correct hierarchical logic, the Rabbinic sages maintained that they uncovered, within the Torah (hence by definition, written and oral components of the Torah alike) an adumbration of the working of the mind of God. That is because the premise of all discourse is that the Torah was written by God and dictated by God to Moses at Sinai. Here is the point at which the correspondence of man and God bears profound theological meaning. It is one thing to absorb the Torah, oral and written, and it is quite another to join in the processes of thought, the right way of thinking, that sustain the Torah. That is what the Rabbinic sages maintained that they did. In their study they proposed to gain access to the modes of thought that guided the formation of the Torah, oral and written alike: comparison and contrast in this way, not in that, identification of categories in one manner, not in another. Since those were the modes of thought that, in the Rabbinic sages' conception, dictated the structure of intellect upon which the Torah, the united Torah, rested, a simple conclusion is the sole possible one. In their analysis of the deepest structures of intellect of the Torah, the Rabbinic sages supposed to enter into the mind of God, showing how God's mind worked when God formed the Torah, written and oral alike. For their minds, like God's, penetrated reality through the same paths. The Rabbinic sages, in insisting that man's and God's minds correspond, claimed for themselves a place in that very process of thought that had given birth to the Torah. They could debate about the Torah because, knowing how the Torah originally was written, they too could write (though not reveal) the Torah. That is, man is like God, but God is always God.

That view of man's capacity to join his mind with God's is not left merely implicit. God not only follows and joins in the argument of the laws of the Torah conducted by the Rabbinic sages. God is party to the argument and subjects himself to the ruling formed by the consensus of the Rabbinic sages—and says so. God not only participates in the debate but takes pride when his children win the argument over him. The miracles of nature cast God's ballot—which does not count over man's reason. God's judgment, as at Sodom, is outweighed by reason, which man exercises, and which takes priority in the reading of the Torah's laws even over God's judgment!

In the following story, we find an explicit affirmation of the priority of reasoned argument over all other forms of discovery of truth:

Bavli Baba Meṣi'a 59A–B

A. There we have learned: If one cut [a clay oven] into parts [so denying it its normal form as an oven] but put sand between the parts [so permitting it to function as an oven]

B. Eliezer declares the oven [broken-down and therefore] insusceptible to uncleanness. [A utensil that is broken and loses the form in which it is useful is deemed null, and so it cannot receive the uncleanness that pertains to whole and useful objects.]

C. And the Rabbinic sages declare it susceptible [because while it is formally broken it is functionally useful, and therefore retains the status of an ordinary utensil].

D. And this is what is meant by the oven of Akhenai [Mishnah tractate *Kelim* 5:10].

Up to this point we have examined only the statement of the issue, which, as we see, concerns in practical terms the theoretical problem of what defines an object, form or function. When an object loses its ordinary form, it ceases to belong to its category, so the one side. But so long as an object accomplishes that for which it is made, its teleology, it remains within its category, so the other side. No philosopher will have found the dispute a difficult problem to follow. But what has God to do with all this? Now comes the answer:

E. Why [is it called] the oven of Akhenai?

F. Said R. Judah said Samuel, "It is because they surrounded it with argument as with a snake and proved it was insusceptible to uncleanness."

G. It has been taught on Tannaite authority:

Here come God's ballots, the miracles, and the Rabbinic sages' rejection of them in favor of arguments devised by man:

H. On that day R. Eliezer produced all of the arguments in the world, but they did not accept them from him. So he said to them, "If the law accords with my position, this carob tree will prove it."

I. The carob was uprooted from its place by a hundred cubits—and some say, four hundred cubits.

J. They said to him, "There is no proof from a carob tree."

K. So he went and said to them, "If the law accords with my position, let the stream of water prove it."

L. The stream of water reversed flow.

M. They said to him, "There is no proof from a stream of water."

N. So he went and said to them, "If the law accords with my position, let the walls of the school house prove it."

O. The walls of the school house tilted toward falling.

P. Joshua rebuked them, saying to them, "If disciples of the Rabbinic sages are contending with one another in matters of law, what business do you have?"

Q. They did not fall on account of the honor owing to R. Joshua, but they also did not straighten up on account of the honor owing to R. Eliezer, and to this day they are still tilted.

R. So he went and said to them, "If the law accords with my position, let the Heaven prove it!"

S. An echo came forth, saying, "What business have you [contending] with R. Eliezer, for the law accords with his position under all circumstances!"

T. R. Joshua stood up on his feet and said, "'It is not in heaven' (Dt. 30:12)."

Here is the point at which God is told the rules of engagement: the Rabbinic sages' reason rules, and miracles do not matter. How does God take it?

U. What is the sense of, "'It is not in heaven' (Dt. 30:12)"?
V. Said R. Jeremiah, "[The sense of Joshua's statement is this:] For the Torah has already been given from Mount Sinai, so we do not pay attention to echoes, since you have already written in the Torah at Mount Sinai, 'After the majority you are to incline' (Ex. 23:2)."
W. Nathan came upon Elijah and said to him, "What did the Holy One, blessed be he, do at that moment?"
X. He said to him, "He laughed and said, 'My children have overcome me, my children have overcome me!'"

Here man is not only like God but, in context, equal to God because subject to the same logic. God is bound by the same rules of logical argument, of relevant evidence, of principled exchange, as is man. So man can argue with the mere declaration of fact or opinion—even God's, beyond the Torah, must be measured against God's own reason, set forth, we see, within the written part of the Torah. That is why the (mere) declaration of matters by Heaven is dismissed. Why? Because God is bound by the rules of rationality that govern in human discourse, and because humanity in the person of the sage thinks like God, as God does; so right is right, and nature has no call to intervene, nor even God to reverse the course of rational argument.

How then are we to take the measure of man's and God's correspondence with one another? To answer that question, we have to systematize the place of God in the coherent theological system that animates the documents of the Oral Torah. These yield four categories that organize what in the Torah man is told about God. In the Oral Torah God takes up a position as [1] premise, [2] presence, [3] person, and [4] personality. It is at the fourth category, the representation of God as a personality, that man and God meet. In the first three, God takes up a position to which man does not aspire; for, as I said, God is always God.

By God as premise, I refer to passages in which an authorship reaches a particular decision because that authorship believes that God created the world and has revealed the Torah to Israel. God as presence stands for yet another consideration. It refers to God as part of a situation in the here and now. God's law governs, but when present, God does not always participate; the law of the Torah fully suffices. When an authorship speaks of an ox goring another ox, the law does not appeal to God to reach a decision and does not suggest that God in particular has witnessed the event and plans to intervene. But God may make his presence known, especially when needed. For example, when the law speaks of a wife's being accused of unfaithfulness to her husband, by contrast, that law's authority expects that God will intervene in a particular case, in the required ordeal, and so declare the decision for the case at hand. In the former instance, God is assuredly a premise of discourse, having revealed in the Torah the rule governing a goring ox. In the latter, God is not only premise but very present in discourse and in making a decision. God furthermore constitutes a person in certain settings, not in others. But these do not form points of correspondence between God and man. It is when the Rabbinic sages envisage God as a "you," that is, as a presence, that God enters into relationship with man. But in such settings God is not always represented in ways that correspond to traits of man.

The correspondence of God and man—the point when the image that they share in common registers—emerges when God is portrayed as a vivid and highly distinctive personality, actor, conversation partner, hero. It is in references to God as a personality, for example, that God is given corporeal traits. God looks like God in particular, just as each person exhibits distinctive physical traits. Not only so, but in matters of heart and mind and spirit, well-limned individual traits of personality and action alike endow God with that particularity that identifies every individual human being. These correspondences present no surprise, for the Written Torah for its part portrays God in richly personal terms: God wants, cares, demands, regrets, says, and does—just like man. God is not merely a collection of abstract theological attributes and thus rules for governance of reality, nor a mere person to be revered and feared. God is not a mere composite of regularities, but a very specific, highly particular personality, whom people can know, envision, engage, persuade, impress.

The Written Torah establishes that Abraham is prepared to contend with God through reasonable argument. The occasion was the destruction of Sodom. Matching God's contention over destroying the gentile city with his conduct in destroying Israel's Jerusalem, the Oral Torah constructs a counterpart dispute. God is represented as accepting accountability, by the standards of humanity, for what he does. And Abraham is represented as forcing this point in an implacable argument.

Bavli Menahot 5:1 I.4/53b

A. Said R. Isaac, "When the temple was destroyed, the Holy One, blessed be he, found Abraham standing in the Temple. He said to him, 'What is my beloved doing in my house?'

B. "He said to him, 'I have come because of what is going on with my children.'

C. "He said to him, 'Your children sinned and have been sent into exile.'

D. "He said to him, 'But wasn't it by mistake that they sinned?'

E. "He said to him, 'She has wrought lewdness' (Jer. 11:15)."

Now comes an echo of the exchange before the destruction of Sodom.

F. "He said to him, 'But wasn't it just a minority of them that did it?'

G. "He said to him, 'It was a majority' (Jer. 11:15).

H. "He said to him, 'You should at least have taken account of the covenant of circumcision [which should have secured forgiveness despite their sin]!'

I. "He said to him, 'The holy flesh is passed from you' (Jer. 11:15)."

Why did God not wait for Israel to repent?

J. "'And if you had waited for them, they might have repented!'

K. "He said to him, 'When you do evil, then you are happy' (Jer. 11:15).'

L. "He said to him, 'He put his hands on his head, crying out and weeping, saying to them, God forbid! Perhaps they have no remedy at all!'

M. "A heavenly voice came forth and said, 'The Lord called you "a leafy olive tree, fair with excellent fruit"' (Jer. 11:16).

The matter is resolved only at the advent of the restoration, the world to come, with the return of the exiles to the Land.

N. "'Just as in the case of an olive tree its, future comes only at the end [that is, it is only after a long while that it attains its best fruit], so in the case of Israel, their future comes at the end of their time.'"

God relates to Abraham as to an equal. That is shown by God's implicit agreement that he is answerable to Abraham for what has taken place with the destruction of the temple. God does not impose on Abraham silence, saying that that is a decree not to be contested but only accepted. God as a social being accepts that he must provide sound reasons for his actions, as must any other reasonable person in a world governed by rules applicable to everyone. Abraham is a fine choice for the protagonist, since he engaged in the argument concerning Sodom. His complaint is expressed at B: God is now called to explain himself. At each point, then, Abraham offers arguments in behalf of sinning Israel, and God responds, item by item. The climax, of course, has God promising Israel a future worth having. God emerges as both just and merciful, reasonable but sympathetic. The transaction attests to God's conformity to rules of reasoned transactions in a coherent society.

Among the available models for the comparing of man to God—warrior, teacher, young man—the one that predominated entailed representation of God as sage. That is hardly surprising in the Oral Torah. The sage in the Oral Torah embodied the teachings of the Oral Torah, did the deeds that the Torah required, such as Torah-study, and so conformed to God's image of man as set forth in the Torah. In this connection we recall that God is represented as a schoolmaster: "He sits and teaches school children, as it is said, 'Whom shall one teach knowledge, and whom shall one make to understand the message? Those who are weaned from milk' (Is. 28:9)" (Bavli tractate '*Abodah Zarah* 3b). But this is not the same thing as God as a master-sage teaching mature disciples, that is, God as rabbi and sage.

The point of correspondence of greatest consequence concerns attitudes, feelings, and emotions. Our consideration of the matter of *zekhut* has prepared us for that result, the point at which complementarity shades over into correspondence. God and man are consubstantial, above all, at heart. A systematic statement of the matter comes to us in tractate *Abot*, which presents the single most comprehensive account of religious affections. These turn out to pertain as much to God's as to man's feelings. The reason is that, in that document above all, how we feel defines a critical aspect of virtue. A simple catalogue of permissible feelings comprises humility, generosity, self-abnegation, love, a spirit of conciliation of the other, and eagerness to please. A list of impermissible emotions is made up of envy, ambition, jealousy, arrogance, sticking to one's opinion, self-centeredness, a grudging spirit, vengefulness, and the like. People should aim at eliciting from others acceptance and good will and should avoid confrontation, rejection, and humiliation of the other. This they do through conciliation and giving up their own claims and rights. So both catalogues form a harmonious and uniform whole, aiming at the cultivation of the humble and malleable person, one who accepts everything and resents nothing.

What we see therefore is an application of a large-scale, encompassing exercise in analogical thinking—something is like something else, stands for, evokes, or symbolizes that which is quite outside itself. It may be the opposite of something else, in which case it conforms to the exact opposite of the rules that govern that something else. The reasoning is analogical or it is contrastive, and the fundamental logic is taxonomic. The taxonomy rests on those comparisons and contrasts we should call parabolic. In that case what lies on the surface misleads, just as we saw how the Rabbinic sages deem superficial the challenges to God's justice that private lives set forth. Conceding the depth of human suffering, the Rabbinic sages also pointed out that sometimes suffering conveys its own blessing. And so throughout, what lies beneath or beyond the surface—there is the true reality. People who see things this way constitute the opposite of ones who call a thing as it is. Self-evidently, they have become accustomed to perceiving more—or less—than is at hand.

God and man correspond in the call from the One to the other for forbearance, patience, humiliation, self-abnegation. God, disappointed with creation, challenged by the gentiles with their idolatry, corresponded with Israel, defeated and subjugated, challenged by the worldly dominance of those who rejected the Torah. Both, the Rabbinic sages maintained, dealt with failure, and both had to survive the condition of defeat. But if, we cannot remind ourselves too often, God and man correspond, God is always God, man, man, Creator and creature.

We conclude the matter of theological anthropology exactly where we ended our account of the ultimate anomaly, man's condition in the world order of justice, with the insistence that, all things having been said, man's ultimate task is silence in the face of the tremendum.

Bavli *Menahot* 3:7 II.5/29b

5. A. Said R. Judah said Rab, "At the time that Moses went up on high, he found the Holy One in session, affixing crowns to the letters [of the words of the Torah]. He said to him, 'Lord of the universe, who is stopping you [from regarding the document as perfect without these additional crowns on the letters]?'"

B. "He said to him, 'There is a man who is going to arrive at the end of many generations, and Aqiba b. Joseph is his name, who is going to interpret on the basis of each point of the crowns heaps and heaps of laws.'"

C. "He said to him, 'Lord of the Universe, show him to me.'"

D. "He said to him, 'Turn around.'"

E. "He went and took a seat at the end of eight rows, but he could not grasp what the people were saying. He felt faint. But when the discourse reached a certain matter, and the disciples said, 'My lord, how do you know this?' and he answered, 'It is a law given to Moses from Sinai,' he regained his composure.'"

F. "He went and came before the Holy One. He said before him, 'Lord of the Universe, How come you have someone like that and yet you give the Torah through me?'"

G. "He said to him, 'Silence! That is how the thought came to me.'

H. "He said to him, 'Lord of the Universe, you have shown me his Torah, now show me his reward.'"

I. "He said to him, 'Turn around.'"

J. "He turned around and saw his flesh being weighed out at the butcher-stalls in the market.'"

K. "He said to him, 'Lord of the Universe, 'Such is Torah, such is the reward?'"

L. "He said to him, 'Silence! That is how the thought came to me.'"

The Rabbinic sages had in mind to construct man in God's image, not God in man's.

So much for the doctrines that systematically and coherently set forth the theology of a world order regulated by God's justice, an order in which reward and punishment proportionately and exactly responded to man's deeds, an order in God that responded according to reliable rules to both Israel and the Torah, gentiles and idolatry, an order that encompassed both public affairs and private life. This perfect world, unchanging and beyond time, brought God together with man in relationships of a complementary character, endowing Israel and God with corresponding traits, so that the one could understand and rely upon the other. But if the Oral Torah's theology of a just world order could account for how things are and are supposed to be, how, in a manner coherent with their doctrines of justice and rationality and coherence, did the Rabbinic sages make sense of what ought not to happen, which is the way things have come about in the here and now? To the sources of disruption and the causes of chaos, the true challenges to the Rabbinic sages' theology of prevailing justice in the public order and private condition as well, we now turn.

CHAPTER EIGHT

SOURCES OF WORLD DISORDER

Most devious is the heart, it is perverse, who can fathom it?
"I the Lord probe the heart, search the mind—
to repay every man according to his ways,
with the proper fruit of his deeds"
                                            —Jeremiah 17:9–10 (trans. JPS Tanakh)

I. WHAT DISRUPTS EDEN?

The theology of the Rabbinic canon realizes in its fullness the theological anthropology set forth in the relationships of complementarity and correspondence. Here that theology explains, at just this turning in the unfolding of the system, its logic that explains who man is. Complementary with God in some ways, corresponding in others, man bears a single trait that most accords with the likeness of God. It is his possession of free will and the power of the free exercise thereof. In his act of will God makes just rules, and in his, man will-fully breaks them.

Man matches God in possessing freedom of will. And therein sages found the source of world disorder. Man's will was the sole power in the world that matched the power of God. And it is that variable in creation that accounts for the present imperfection of creation. To understand why, we recall that by his act of will God created the orderly world of justice, one that exhibits abundant, indicative marks of perfection. Then whence chaos embodied by disorder and dissonance? And, when the rules that embody rationality—that guarantee measure for measure above all—cease to describe the everyday experience of mankind and the here and now of Israel, where shall we find the reason? In the logic of a world order based on exact justice, in the Torah God accords to man a statement of his own will, a commandment, and the one who issues a command both wants the command to be obeyed but also accords to the other the power to disobey. That is the very premise of commandments.

For the sages, therefore, it was man's rebellion, beyond God's control but within God's dominion, that explains change. And change, imperfection, the ephemerality of affairs—these signal the actualities of disorder in a world meant for perfection, stasis, balance throughout. God proposes, man disposes. Chaos begins not in God but in man, in that trait of man that endows man with the same power that the Creator has, to conceive and to do. Since God has made an orderly world, only his counterpart on earth, man, can account for the disruption of world order. For the sole player in the cosmic drama with the power to upset God's plans is man. He alone is like God, "in our image, after our likeness." In their penetrating reflection on the power of intentionality, sages explain chaos, and that prepares the way for their investigation of sin and its remedy.

That is why, explaining the imperfection of change, the advent of time in the historical sense, the inequality of exchange, the theology of the Rabbinic canon finds in the opposite of the indicators of perfection the sources of disruption. And change comes about principally because man by an act of will corrupts perfection. Accordingly, the Rabbinic canon takes as its critical problem the generative tension between the word of God and the will of man, in full recognition that God judges what man does by reason of the exercise of free will. Set forth in many ways, the simplest statement is made when Aqiba says, "Everything is foreseen, and free choice is given; in goodness the world is judged; and all is in accord with the abundance of deeds" (tractate *Abot* 3:15A).

Free will, moreover, reaches concrete expression in the deeds a man does by reason of the plans or intentions that he shapes on his own. The high value accorded by God to man's voluntary act of accepting God's dominion, the enthusiastic response made by God to man's supererogatory deeds of uncoerced love and uncompelled generosity, the heavy emphasis upon the virtues of self-abnegation and self-restraint—these emblematic traits of the coherent theology attest to the uncertainty of man's response that, from the beginning, God has built into creation. For the one power that lies beyond the rules of reason, that defies predicting, is man's power to make up his own mind.

Now how to show how these convictions form the center of the theological structure and system set forth in the Rabbinic canon? Commensurate with the claim just now set forth, that intentionality defines the center of the system, the demonstration must adduce evidence of a systemic and systematic character. For that purpose, sayings, however demonstrably typical, and episodic stories or exegeses of verses of Scripture, however probative in character, do not match the task. Turning, rather, to norms of behavior, we seek evidence in the authority of required, enforced law. This is of two kinds.

First, the Rabbinic canon designs enduring structures, institutions for the governance of Israel as a godly realm. If I can show that in its very doctrine of how holy Israel is governed, intentionality forms the critical point of differentiation even of institutional politics—the power legitimately to inflict violence—then my claim concerning the centrality of intentionality in explaining world order and its corruption will find commensurate demonstration.

Second, the Rabbinic canon makes its theological statement not only in apodictic sayings, such as the one of Aqiba cited just now, or in exegesis of Scripture, or in tales of sages and exemplary stories. It speaks also, and especially, through specific norms of conduct. My task is to show how intentionality governs actualities of behavior, not of mere belief. We shall see how the consideration of the will of man preoccupies sages when they define the norms of everyday conduct.

To accomplish the task of showing the normative and paramount power of intentionality or the act of will, I have selected sages' theoretical account of the working of the enduring institutions of holy Israel, the theological politics of their system. When they describe the government of holy Israel, they carry out a labor of differentiation of power, indicating what agency or person has the power to precipitate the working of politics as legitimate violence at all. And, as we shall see through the provisions that they make for various institutional foci of power to carry out diverse tasks, it is at the point of intentionality, with the story of Eden in hand, that sages accomplish their goal. Were we to ignore Eden, we could make no sense of their concrete provisions for holy Israel's government. When, therefore, we understand the differentiating force of intentionality at the most practical level of sages' theory of the social order, the power of the human will that imparts to politics its activity and dynamism, we shall grasp what everywhere animates the structures of the politics and propels the system. That is why I have chosen as a principal part of my account of intentionality the sages' theological politics.

Politics concerns legitimate violence, the functioning of sanctions.

Specifically, we analyze the mythic foundations of sanctions that sages assign to various authorities, on earth and in Heaven. And when we move from sanctions to the myth expressed and implicit in the application and legitimation of those sanctions, we see a complex but cogent politics sustained by a simple political theology. This survey of sanctions and their implications had best commence with a clear statement of what we shall now uncover. The encompassing political framework of rules, institutions, and sanctions is explained and validated by appeal to God's shared rule. That dominion, exercised by God and his surrogates on earth, is focused partly in the royal palace, the king, partly in the temple, the priesthood, and partly in the court and its sages. For us, the issue here is, which part falls where and why? Helpfully, the political myth explains who exercises legitimate violence and under what conditions, and furthermore specifies the source for differentiation. The myth consequently serves a particular purpose—which is to answer that particular question. Indeed, the sages' political myth comes to expression in its details of differentiation, which permit us to identify, and of course to answer, the generative question of politics.

Moving from the application of power to the explanation thereof, we find that the system focuses upon finding answers to the question of who imposes which sanction, and why. And those answers contain the political myth, nowhere expressed, everywhere in full operation. Through the examination of sanctions, we identify the foci of power. At that point we ask how power is differentiated. In spelling out what the reader may now find somewhat enigmatic, I have skipped many stages in the argument and the examination of the evidence. So let us begin from the very beginning. How, exactly, do I propose to identify the political myth of the Dual Torah? And precisely what data are supposed to attest to that myth?

Institutions of political persuasion and coercion dominate not only through physical but also through mental force, through psychological coercion or appeal to good will. So my inquiry's premise is not far to seek. I take as a given that a political myth animates the structure of a politics. But the authorship of the Mishnah, upon the politics of which we concentrate for the present analysis, has chosen other media for thought and expression than narrative and teleological ones. It is a philosophical, not a historical (fictive) account; it is conveyed through masses of detailed rules about small things. While the Mishnah through its cases amply informs us on the institutions of politics, the mythic framework within which persuasion and inner compliance are supposed to bring about submission to legitimate power scarcely emerges, remaining only implicit throughout.

But it is readily discerned when we ask the right questions. If we were to bring to the authorship of the Mishnah such questions as "who tells whom what to do?" (or "who can do what to whom, and for how long?") they would point to the politics' imaginary king and its equally fictive high priest, and its court comprised by sages, all with associated authorities and functionaries. Here, they would tell us, are the institutions of politics—represented in personal rather than abstract form, to be sure. But if we were to say to them, "And tell us the story (in our language: the myth) that explains on what basis you persuade people to conform," they would find considerable difficulty in bringing to the fore the explicit mythic statements made by their writing.

How then are we to identify, on the basis of what the Mishnah does tell us, the generative myths to which the system is supposed to appeal? A myth explains the exercise of legitimate power. Now, we know that power comes to brutal expression when the state kills or maims someone or deprives a person of property through the imposition of legal sanctions for crime or sin. In the absence of a myth of power, we therefore begin with power itself. We shall work our way back from the facts of power to the intimations, within the record of legitimately violent sanctions, of the intellectual and even mythic sources of legitimation for the exercise and use of that legitimate violence. For it is at the point of imposing sanctions, of killing, injuring, denying property, excluding from society, that power operates in its naked form. Then how these legitimate exercises of violence are validated will set before us such concrete evidence of the myth. And, so far as there is such evidence, that will identify the political myth of the Dual Torah that commences with the Mishnah. The relevance to the centrality of intentionality in the theology of the Dual Torah will become transparent by the end, even though it is obscure at this point.

Since the analysis of sources will prove somewhat abstruse, let me signal in advance the main line of argument. Analyzing myth by explaining sanctions draws our attention to the modes of legitimate violence that the system identifies. There we find four types of sanctions, each deriving from a distinct institution of political power, each bearing its own mythic explanation.

[1] The first comprises what God and the Heavenly court can do to people.
[2] The second comprises what the earthly court can do to people. That type of sanction embodies the legitimate application of the worldly and physical kinds of violence of which political theory ordinarily speaks.
[3] The third comprises what the cult can do to the people. The cult through its requirements can deprive people of their property as legitimately as can a court.
[4] The fourth comprises conformity with consensus—self-imposed sanctions. Here the issue is, whose consensus, and defined by whom?

Across these four types of sanction, four types of coercion are in play. They depend on violence of various kinds—psychological and social as much as physical. Clearly, then, the sanctions that are exercised by other than judicial-political agencies prove violent and legitimately coercive, even though the violence and coercion are not the same as those carried out by courts.

On this basis we can differentiate among types of sanctions—and hence trace evidences of how the differentiation is explained. Since our data focus upon who does what to whom, the myth of politics must explain why various types of sanctions are put into effect by diverse political agencies or institutions. As we shall see, the exercise of power, invariably and undifferentiatedly in the name and by the authority of God in Heaven to be sure, is kept distinct. And the distinctions in this case signal important differences which, then, require explanation. Concrete application of legitimate violence by

[1] Heaven covers different matters from parts of the political and social world governed by the policy and coercion of
[2] the this-worldly political classes. And both sorts of violence have to be kept distinct from the sanction effected by
[3] the community through the weight of attitude and public opinion. Here, again, we find a distinct set of penalties applied to a particular range of actions.

When we have seen the several separate kinds of sanction and where they apply, we shall have a full account of the workings of politics as the application of power, and from that concrete picture we may, I think, identify the range of power and the mythic framework that has to have accommodated and legitimated diverse kinds of power.

Our task therefore is to figure out on the basis of sanctions' distinct realms, Heaven, earth, and the mediating range of the temple and sacrifice, which party imposes sanctions for (in modern parlance) what crimes or sins. Where Heaven intervenes, do other authorities participate, and if so, what tells me which party takes charge and imposes its sanction? Is the system differentiated so that where earth is in charge, there is no pretense of appeal to Heaven? Or do we find cooperation in coextensive jurisdiction, such that one party penalizes an act under one circumstance, the other the same act under a different circumstance? A survey of the sanctions enables us to differentiate the components of the power structure before us. So we wonder whether each of these three estates that enjoy power and inflict sanctions of one kind or another—Heaven, earth, temple in between—governs its own affairs, without the intervention of the others, or whether, working together, each takes charge in collaboration with the other, so that power is parceled out and institutions simultaneously differentiate themselves from one another and also intersect. The survey of sanctions will allow us to answer these questions and so identify the myth of politics and the exercise of power that the Rabbinic canon promulgated through the institutional arrangements set forth by the law of the Mishnah.

Clearly, simply knowing that everything is in accord with the Written Torah and that God wants Israel to keep the laws of the Torah does not reveal the systemically active component of the political myth. On the one hand, the propositions are too general; on the other hand, they do not address the critical question. The sequence of self-evident premises that runs [1] God revealed the Torah, [2] the political institutions and rules carry out the Torah, and therefore [3] people should conform, hardly sustains a concrete theory of *just* where and how God's authority serves the systemic construction at hand. The appeal to Scripture, therefore, reveals no incisive information about the Rabbinic canon's validating myth as set forth in the laws of the Mishnah.

In the Rabbinic canon the manipulation and application of power, allowing the impositions of drastic sanctions in support of the law for instance, invariably flow through institutions, on earth and in Heaven, of a quite concrete and material character. "The kingdom of Heaven" may be within, but violate the law deliberately and wantonly and God will kill you sooner than you should otherwise have had to die. And, as a matter of fact, the Mishnah's framers rarely appeal in the context of politics and the legitimate exercise of violence to "the kingdom of Heaven." When we considered the same matter earlier, we noted that Israel's acceptance of the dominion of the kingdom of Heaven involved acts of worship and obedience, but at no point invoked coercion in a this-worldly framework.

Indeed, from the Pentateuchal writings, we can hardly construct the *particular* politics, including the mythic component thereof, that operates. First of all, the Written Torah does not prepare us to make sense of the institutions that the politics of the sages for its part designs—government by king and high priest, rather than, as in the Pentateuch, prophet. Second, and concomitantly, the Pentateuchal myth that legitimates coercion—rule by God's prophet, governance through explicitly revealed laws that God has dictated for the particular occasion!—plays no active and systemic role whatsoever in the formulation and presentation of the Mishnah's theological politics. Rather, of the types of political authority contained within the scriptural repertoire, the Mishnah's philosophers reject prophetic and charismatic authority and deem critical the authority exercised by the sage's disciple, who has been carefully nurtured in rules, not in gifts of the spirit. The authority of sages in their theological politics does not derive from charisma (revelation by God to the sage who makes a ruling in a given case, or even from general access to God for the sage). The myth we shall presently explore in no way falls into the classification of a charismatic myth of politics.

The data to which we now turn will tell us who does what to whom and why, and, in the reason, we shall uncover the political myth we seek. At the very heart of matters we shall uncover the determinative power of intentionality. But the process by which we reach that conclusion is what counts, since that requires us to sift the evidence meant by sages to dictate the very governance of holy Israel, the institutions, procedures, and sanctions of government on earth and in Heaven. And out of the result we shall see a clear, powerful, and normative statement of the meaning of intentionality, how man's and God's acts of will bear equal weight. Predictably, when we work our way through sanctions to recover the mythic premises thereof, we begin with God's place in the institutionalization and execution of legitimate violence. Of course, the repertoire of sanctions does encompass God's direct intervention, but that is hardly a preferred alternative or a common one. Still, God does commonly intervene when oaths are violated, for oaths are held to involve the person who invokes God's name and God. Further, whereas when faced with an insufficiency of valid evidence under strict rules of testimony, the earthly court cannot penalize serious crime, the Heavenly court can and does impose a penalty. Clearly, then, God serves to justify the politics and account for its origin. Although God is never asked to join in making specific decisions and effecting policy in the everyday politics of the state, deliberate violation of certain rules provokes God's or the Heavenly court's direct intervention. Thus obedience to the law clearly represents submission to God in Heaven. Further, forms of Heavenly coercion such as we shall presently survey suggest a complex mythic situation, with more subtle nuance than the claim that, overall, God rules, would indicate. A politics of rules and regulations cannot admit God's ad hoc participation, and this system did not do so. God joined in the system in a regular and routine way, and the rules took for granted God's part in the sages' theological politics.

Now come the data of real power, the sanctions. We may divide sanctions just as the authorship of the Mishnah did, by simply reviewing the range of penalties for law infraction as they occur. These penalties, as we mentioned above, fall into four classifications:

[1] what Heaven does,
[2] what political institutions do,
[3] what religious institutions do, and
[4] what is left to the coercion of public opinion, that is, consensus, with special attention to the definition of that "public" that has effective opinion to begin with. The final realm of power, conferring or withholding approval, proves constricted and, in this context, not very consequential.

Let us begin with the familiar, with sanctions exercised by the earthly court as they are fully described in Mishnah tractates *Sanhedrin* and *Makkot*. Here is covered the imposition of sanctions as it is represented by the earthly court, the temple, the heavenly court, the sages.

This review allows us to identify the actors in the system of politics—those with power to impose sanctions, and the sanctions they can inflict. Only from this perspective will the initial statement of the sages, the Mishnah, in its own odd idiom, be able to make its points in the way its authorship has chosen. When we take up the myth to which that statement implicitly appeals, we shall have a clear notion of the character of the evidence, in rich detail, on which our judgment of the mythic substrate of the system has been composed.

How to proceed? By close attention to the facts of power and by sorting out the implications of those facts. A protracted journey through details of the law of sanctions leads us to classify the sanctions and the sins or crimes to which they apply. What precisely do I think requires classification? Our project is to see who does what to whom and, on the basis of the consequent perception, to propose an explanation for that composition. For from these sanctions of state, that is, the legitimate exercise of coercion, including violence, we may work our way back to the reasons adduced for the legitimacy of the exercise of coercion, which is to say, the political myth. The reason is that such a classification will permit us to see how in detail the foci of power are supposed to intersect or to relate: autonomous powers, connected and related ones, or utterly continuous ones, joining Heaven to earth, for instance, in the person of this institutional representative or that one. What we shall see is a system that treats Heaven, earth, and the mediating institution, the temple, as interrelated, thus, connected, but that insists, in vast detail, upon the distinct responsibilities and jurisdiction accorded to each. Once we have perceived that fundamental fact, we may compose for ourselves the myth, or, at least the point and propositions of the myth, that accounted for the political structures contemplated by the Rabbinic canon and persuaded people to obey or conform even when there was no immediate threat of penalty.

A survey of [1] types of sanctions, [2] the classifications of crimes or sins to which they apply, and [3] who imposes them, now yields a simple and clear fact, and on the basis of that simple fact we may now reconstruct the entire political myth of the Rabbinic canon. This myth accounts for the differentiation among penalties and institutions that impose them, and from the facts we reach backward to the myth that explains them. The basis for all conclusions, let me emphasize, is this fact: *Some of the same crimes or sins for which the Heavenly court imposes the penalty of extirpation are those that, under appropriate circumstances (e.g., sufficient evidence admissible in court) the earthly court imposes the death penalty.*

That is, the Heavenly court and the earthly court impose precisely the same sanctions for the same crimes or sins. The earthly court therefore forms down here the exact replica and counterpart, within a single system of power, of the Heavenly court up there. This no longer looms as an empty generalization; it is a concrete and systemically active and indicative detail, and the system speaks through its details.

But this is not the entire story. There is a second fact, equally indicative for our recovery of the substrate of myth. We note that there are crimes for which the earthly court imposes penalties, but for which the Heavenly court does not, as well as vice versa. The earthly and Heavenly courts share jurisdiction over sexual crimes and over what I classify as serious religious crimes against God. The Heavenly court penalizes with its form of the death penalty religious sins against God, in which instances a person deliberately violates the taboos of sanctification.

And that fact calls our attention to a third partner in the distribution and application of power, the temple with its system of sanctions that cover precisely the same acts subject to the jurisdiction of the Heavenly and earthly courts. The counterpart on earth is now not the earthly court but the temple. This is the institution that, in theory, automatically receives the appropriate offering from the person who inadvertently violates these same taboos of sanctification. The juxtaposition involves courts and temple, and the upshot is that both are equally matters of theory. In the theory at hand, then, the earthly court, for its part, penalizes social crimes against the community that the Heavenly court, on the one side, and the temple rites, on the other, do not take into account at all. These are murder, apostasy, kidnapping, public defiance of the court, and false prophecy. The earthly court further imposes sanctions on matters of particular concern to the Heavenly court, with special reference to taboos of sanctification (e.g., negative commandments). These three institutions, therefore, exercise concrete and material power, utilizing legitimate violence to kill someone, exacting penalties against property, and inflicting pain. The sages' modes of power, by contrast, stand quite apart, apply mainly to their own circle, and work through the intangible though no less effective means of inflicting shame or paying honor.

The facts we have in hand draw us back to the analysis of our differentiation of applied and practical power. In the nature of the facts before us, that differentiation tells us precisely for what the systemic myth will have to give its account. Power flows through three distinct but intersecting dominions, each with its own concern, all sharing some interests in common.

[1] The Heavenly court attends to deliberate defiance of Heaven.
[2] The temple pays attention to inadvertent defiance of Heaven.
[3] The earthly court attends to matters subject to its jurisdiction by reason of sufficient evidence, proper witnesses, and the like, and these same matters will come under Heavenly jurisdiction when the earthly court finds itself unable to act.

Accordingly, we have a tripartite system of sanctions—Heaven cooperating with the temple in some matters, with the court in others, and, as noted, each bearing its own distinct media of enforcing the law as well. What then can we say concerning the systemic myth of politics? The forms of power and the modes of mediating legitimate violence draw our attention to a single political myth. The unity of that myth is underlined by the simple fact that the earthly court enters into the process right alongside the Heavenly court and the temple; as to blasphemy, idolatry, and magic, its jurisdiction prevails. So a single myth must serve all three correlated institutions. It is the myth of God's authority infusing the institutions of Heaven and earth alike, an authority diffused among three principle foci or circles of power, Heaven's court, the earthly court, and the temple in between.

Each focus of power has its own jurisdiction and responsibility, Heaven above, earth beneath, the temple in the position of mediation—transmitting as it does from earth to Heaven the penalties handed over as required. And all media of power in the matter of sanctions intersect at some points as well: a tripartite politics, a single myth drawing each component into relationship with a single source and origin of power, God's law set forth in the Torah. But the myth has not performed its task until it answers not only the question of why, but also the question of how. Specifically, the details of myth must address questions of the details of power. Who then tells whom to do what? And how are the relationships of dominion and dominance to compliance and obedience made permanent through myth?

We did not require this sustained survey to ascertain that God through the Torah has set forth laws and concerns. Nor on the surface did this considerable exercise claim a place in any account of the role of intentionality in the cosmic order. So God's place in transactions of power requires explanation, and the primacy of intentionality has now to be set forth. Specifically, it is where power is differentiated and parceled out that we see the workings of the political myth, and there we should find the facts that we seek. So we ask, how do we know who tells whom to do, or suffer, what sanction or penalty? It is the power of myth to differentiate that defines the generative question. The key lies in the criterion by which each mode of power, earthly, mediating, and Heavenly, identifies the cases over which it exercises jurisdiction. The criterion lies in the attitude of the human being who has done what he or she should not: did he act deliberately or unintentionally?

I state the upshot with heavy emphasis, as we identify the point of relevance to our inquiry: *The point of differentiation within the political structures, supernatural and natural alike, lies in the attitude and intention of a human being.*

We differentiate among the application of power by reference to the attitude of the person who comes into relationship with that power. A person who comes into conflict with the system, rejecting the authority claimed by the powers that be, does so deliberately or inadvertently. The myth accounts in the end for the following hierarchization of action and penalty, infraction and sanction:

[1] If the deed is deliberate, then one set of institutions exercises jurisdiction and utilizes supernatural power.

[2] If the deed is inadvertent, another institution exercises jurisdiction and utilizes the power made available by that same supernatural being.

A sinner or criminal who has deliberately violated the law has by his action challenged the world order of justice that God has wrought. Consequently, God or God's surrogate imposes sanctions—extirpation (by the court on high), or death or other appropriate penalty (by the court on earth). A sinner or criminal who has inadvertently violated the law is penalized by the imposition of temple sanctions, losing valued goods. People obey because God wants them to and has told them what to do, and when they do not obey, a differentiated political structure appeals to that single hierarchizing myth. The components of the myth are two: first, God's will, expressed in the law of the Torah, second, the human being's will, carried out in obedience to the law of the Torah or in defiance of that law.

Since the political myth has to explain the differentiation of sins or crimes, with their associated penalties or punishments, and so sanctions of power, I have to find that story in the Torah that accomplishes that labor of differentiation. And given the foci and premises of the present study of the governing theology of the Rabbinic canon, that story must pertain to the nature of things and concern beginnings. And in Scripture there is a very precise answer to the question of how to differentiate among sins or crimes and why to do so. Not only so, but, in the framework of the present chapter of that theology, the point of differentiation must rest with one's attitude or intentionality. And, indeed, I do have two stories of how the power of God— the power to command—conflicts with the power of humanity—the power to obey or to rebel—in such wise as to invoke the penalties and sanctions in precisely the differentiated modes we have before us. Where do I find such stories of the conflict of wills, God's and humanity's, captured by the words, "will" or "intentionality"?

The first such story of power differentiated by the will of the human being in communion or conflict with the word of the commanding God comes to us from the Garden of Eden. We cannot too often reread the following astonishing words.

Genesis 2:15ff.

> The Lord God took the man and placed him in the garden of Eden . . . and the Lord God commanded the man, saying, "Of every tree of the garden you are free to eat; but as for the tree of knowledge of good and bad, you must not eat of it; for as soon as you eat of it, you shall die."
>
> . . . When the woman saw that the tree was good for eating and a delight to the eyes, and that the tree was desirable as a source of wisdom, she took of its fruit and ate; she also gave some to her husband, and he ate. . . .
>
> The Lord God called out to the man and said to him, "Where are you?"
>
> He replied, "I heard the sound of You in the garden, and I was afraid, because I was naked, so I hid."

Then He asked, "Who told you that you were naked? Did you eat of the tree from which I had forbidden you to eat?"
. . . And the Lord God said to the woman, "What is this you have done!"
The woman replied, "The serpent deceived me, and I ate."
Then the Lord said to the serpent, "Because you did this, more cursed shall you be than all cattle. . . ."
So the Lord God banished him from the garden of Eden. . . .

Now a reprise of the exchange between God, Adam, and Eve tells us that at stake was responsibility: who has violated the law, but who bears responsibility for deliberately violating the law. Each blames the next, and God sorts things out, responding to each in accord with the facts of the case: whose intentionality matches the actual deed?

"The woman You put at my side—she gave me of the tree, and I ate."
"The serpent duped me, and I ate."
Then the Lord God said to the serpent, *"because you did this. . . ."*

The ultimate responsibility lies with the one who acted deliberately, not under constraint or on account of deception or misinformation, as did Adam because of Eve, and Eve because of the serpent.

True enough, all are punished, the serpent, but also woman, "I will make most severe your pangs in childbearing," and Adam, "Because you did as your wife advised and ate of the tree about which I commanded you, 'you shall not eat of it,' cursed be the ground because of you." Thus all then are punished—but the punishment is differentiated. Those who were duped are distinguished from the one who acted wholly on his own. The serpent himself is cursed; the woman is subjected to pain in childbearing, which ought to have been pain-free; because of man, the earth is cursed—a diminishing scale of penalties, each in accord with the level of intentionality or free, unco-erced will, involved in the infraction. Then the sanction applies most severely to the one who by intention and an act of will has violated God's intention and will.

To establish what I conceive to be the generative myth, I turn to a second story of disobedience and its consequences, the tale of Moses's hitting the rock.

Numbers 20:1–13

The community was without water, and they joined against Moses and Aaron. . . . Moses and Aaron came away from the congregation to the entrance of the Tent of Meeting and fell on their faces. The Presence of the Lord appeared to them, and the Lord spoke to Moses, saying, "You and your brother Aaron take the rod and assemble the community, and before their very eyes order the rock to yield its water. Thus you shall produce water for them from the rock and provide drink for the congregation and their beasts."

Moses took the rod from before the Lord as He had commanded him. Moses and Aaron assembled the congregation in front of the rock; and he said to them, "Listen, you rebels, shall we get water for you out of this rock?" And Moses raised his hand and struck the rock twice with his rod. Out came copious water, and the community and their beasts drank.

But the Lord said to Moses and Aaron, "Because you did not trust me enough to affirm My sanctity in the sight of the Israelite people, therefore you shall not lead this congregation into the land that I have given them."

Those are the waters of Meribah, meaning that the Israelites quarreled with the Lord—through which He affirmed His sanctity.

Here we have not only intentional disobedience, but also the penalty of extirpation. Both this myth and the myth of the fall make the same point. They direct attention to the generative conception that at stake in power is the will of God over against the will of the human being, and in particular, the Israelite human being.

What we see is quite striking. The political myth of the Rabbinic canon emerges in the Mishnah in all of its tedious detail as a reprise—in now-consequential and necessary detail—of the story of God's commandment, humanity's disobedience, God's sanction for the sin or crime, and humanity's atonement and reconciliation. The Mishnah omits all explicit reference to myths that explain power and sanctions, but invokes in its rich corpus of details the absolute given of the story of the distinction between what is deliberate and what is mitigated by an attitude that is not culpable, a distinction set forth in the tragedy of Adam and Eve, in the failure of Moses and Aaron, in the distinction between murder and manslaughter that the Written Torah works out, and in countless other passages in the Pentateuch, Prophetic Books, and Writings. Then the Mishnah's Halakhah sets forth a politics of life after Eden and outside of Eden. The upshot of the matter is that the political myth of the Rabbinic canon sets forth the constraints of freedom, the human will brought to full and unfettered expression, imposed by the constraints of revelation, God's will made known.

Since it is the freedom of humanity to make decisions and frame intentions that forms the point of differentiation among the political media of power, we are required, in my view, to return to the paradigmatic exercise of that same freedom, that is, to Eden, to the moment when Adam and Eve exercise their own will and defy God. Since the operative criterion in the differentiation of sanction—that is, the exercise of legitimate violence by Heaven or by earth or by the temple—is the human attitude and intention in carrying out a culpable action, we must recognize that the politics before us rehearses the myth of Adam and Eve in Eden—it finds its dynamic in the correspondence between God's will and humanity's freedom to act however it chooses, thus freely incurring the risk of penalty or sanction for the wrong exercise of freedom.

At stake is what Adam and Eve, Moses and Aaron, and numerous others intend, propose, plan, for that is the point at which the politics intervenes, making its points of differentiation between and among its sanctions and the authorities that impose those penalties. For that power to explain difference, which is to say, the capacity to represent and account for hierarchy, we are required, in my opinion, to turn to the story of the fall of Adam and Eve from Eden and to counterpart stories. The reason is that the political myth derives from that same myth of origins its points of differentiation and explains by reference to the principal components of that myth—God's and humanity's will and power—the dynamics of the political system at hand. God commands, but humanity does what it then chooses, and in the interplay, each power in its own right, the sanctions and penalties of the system apply.

Power comes from two conflicting forces, the commanding will of God and the free will of the human being. Power expressed in immediate sanctions is also mediated through these same forces, Heaven above, human beings below, with the temple mediating between the two. Power works its way in the interplay between what God has set forth in the law of the Torah and what human beings do, whether intentionally, whether inadvertently, whether obediently, whether defiantly. That is why the politics of the Rabbinic canon is a politics of Eden. True, we listen in vain in the creation myth of Genesis for echoes resounding in the shape of the institutions such as those the theology of politics actually invents. But the points of differentiation of one political institution from another will serve constantly to

remind us of what, in the end, distinguishes this from that, to set forth
not a generalized claim that God rules through whoever is around
with a sword. At every point we are therefore reminded of the most
formidable source of power, short of God, in all. That always is the
will of the human being. And that is why only man has the power to
disrupt that world order so painstakingly created and maintained by
God. Only man is sufficiently like God to possess the utterly free will
to corrupt perfection.

The theology of Rabbinic Judaism, like its law, therefore identifies
free will as the principal point of correspondence between God and
man, the point at which God's image makes its deepest mark upon
man's visage. Just as God freely chooses, so does man. In man God
has made, and therefore has met, his match. Man has the power to
violate the rules of order; the rationality of justice then dictates the
result. When man rebels against God, rejecting God's dominion
instead of loving God, that sin disrupts world order. Punishment
"with the proper fruit of his deeds" follows. But, as we shall see,
man's free will in response may inaugurate the process by which
world order is restored, creation renewed. And that process leads to
the last things of all, eternal life embodied in the resurrection of the
dead and the world to come. So the theology of the Rabbinic canon
accounts for life, death, and life restored. We return to this matter in
Chapter Twelve, section I, where I encompass these results in my theology of the Halakhah.

II. Sin

Sin explains the condition of Israel. The governing theory of Israel,
that had Israel kept the Torah from the beginning, the Holy People
would never have had any history at all but would have lived in a
perfect world at rest and balance and order, is now invoked. There
would have been nothing to write down, no history, had Israel kept
the Torah. I can imagine no more explicit statement of how the
world order is disrupted by sin, and, specifically, sinful attitudes, than
the following:

Bavli *Nedarim* 3:1 I.14ff./22a–b

I.18 A. Said R. Ada b. R. Hanina, "If the Israelites had not sinned, to
them would have been given only the Five Books of the Torah
and the book of Joshua alone, which involves the division of
the Land of Israel. How come? 'For much wisdom proceeds
from much anger' (Qoh. 1:18)."

Adam ought to have stayed in Eden. With the Torah in hand, Israel,
the new Adam, ought to have remained in the Land, beyond the
reach of time and change, exempt from the events of interesting
times. Sin ruined everything, for Adam, for Israel, bringing about the
history recorded in Scripture—not a very complicated theodicy.

That the theology of the Rabbinic canon spins out a simple but
encompassing logic makes the character of its treatment of sin entirely
predictable. First, the system must account for imperfection in the
world order of justice; sin supplies the reason. Second, it must explain
how God remains omnipotent even in the face of imperfection. The
cause of sin, man's free will corresponding to God's, tells why. Third,
it must allow for systemic remission. Sin is so defined as to accommodate the possibility of regeneration and restoration. And, finally,
sin must be so presented as to fit into the story of the creation of the
perfect world. It is.

Defined in the model of the first sin, the one committed by man
in Eden, sin is an act of rebellion against God. Rebellion takes two
forms. As a gesture of omission sin embodies the failure to carry out
one's obligation to God set forth in the Torah. As one of commission, it constitutes an act of defiance. In both cases sin comes about
by reason of man's intentionality to reject the will of God, set forth
in the Torah. However accomplished, whether through omission or
commission, an act becomes sinful because of the attitude that
accompanies it. That is why man is responsible for sin, answerable to
God in particular, who may be said to take the matter personally, just
as it is meant. The consequence of sin is death for the individual,
exile and estrangement for holy Israel, and disruption for the world.
That is why sin accounts for much of the flaw of creation.

Since sin represents an act of rebellion against God, God has a
heavy stake in the matter. It follows that sin in public is worse than
sin in private, since in public one's sin profanes God's name.

Bavli *Qiddushin* 1:10 I.10/40a

A. Said R. Abbahu in the name of R. Hanina, "It is better for someone to transgress in private but not profane the Name of Heaven in
public: 'As for you, house of Israel, thus says the Lord God: Go,
serve every one his idols, and hereafter also, if you will not obey me;
but my holy name you shall not profane' (Ez. 20:39)."

B. Said R. Ilai the Elder, "If someone sees that his impulse to sin is
overpowering him, he should go somewhere where nobody knows
him and put on ordinary clothing and cloak himself in ordinary
clothing and do what he wants, but let him not profane the Name
of Heaven by a public scandal."

Sin therefore defines one important point at which God and man
meet and world order is affected. The just arrangement of matters
that God has brought about in creation can be upset by man's intervention, for man alone has the will and freedom to stand against
God's plan and intention for creation.

It follows, as we now realize, that the consequences of the correspondence of God and man account for all else. If the one power in
all of creation that can and does stand against the will of God is
man's will or intentionality, then man bears responsibility for the
flawed condition of creation, and God's justice comes to its fullest
expression in the very imperfection of existence, a circularity that
once more marks a well-crafted, severely logical system. But free will
also forms the source of remission; God's mercy intervenes when
man's will warrants. Specifically, God restores the perfection of creation through his provision of means of atonement through repentance. That presents no anomaly but conforms to the encompassing
theory of matters. For repentance represents yet another act of
human will that, like the transaction that yields *zekhut*, is countered
with a commensurate act of God's will. The entire story of the world,
start to finish, therefore records the cosmic confrontation of God's
will and man's freedom to form and carry out an intention contrary
to God's will. The universe is not animate but animated by the
encounter of God and, in his image, after his likeness, man—the
story, the only story, that the Rabbinic canon recapitulates from, and
in completion of, the Written Torah.

The moral order, we have seen, encompasses exactly commensurate penalties for sin, the logic of a perfectly precise recompense forming the foundation of the theory of world order set forth by the

Rabbinic canon. But knowing the just penalty tells us little about the larger theory of how sin disrupts the perfection of the world created by the one just God. Since sin is deemed not personal alone but social and even cosmic, explaining sin carries us to the very center of the theology that animates the Rabbinic canon. What is at stake in sin is succinctly stated: it accounts for the deplorable condition of the world, defined by the situation of Israel. But sin is not a permanent feature of world order. It is a detail of an orderly progression, as God to begin with had planned, from chaos, which gave way to creation, to the Torah, which after the flood through Israel restored order to the world, and onward to the age of perfection and stasis. To understand that doctrine, we have first to examine the place of sin in the unfolding of creation. In the Rabbinic canon the history of the world is divided into these three periods, indicated by Israel's relationship with God.

Bavli *'Abodah Zarah* 1:1 II.5/9a
[= Bavli *Sanhedrin* 1:1 I.89/97a]

A. The Tannaite authority of the household of Elijah [stated], "The world will last for six thousand years: two thousand years of chaos, two thousand years of Torah, two thousand years of the time of the Messiah. But because of the abundance of our sins, what has passed [of the foreordained time] has passed."

The "two thousand years of chaos" mark the period prior to the giving of the Torah at Sinai, as God recognized the result of creating man in his image and the consequence of the contest between man's will and God's. Then come the two thousand years of Torah, which is intended to educate man's will and endow man with the knowledge to want what God wants. Then comes the time of the Messiah. Now the persistence of sin has lengthened the time of the Torah and postponed the advent of the Messiah. It follows that, to understand how sages account for the situation of the world in this age, revealing God's justice out of the elements of chaos in the here and now, we have to pay close attention to the character of sages' doctrine of sin.

What has already been said about sin as an act of rebellion bears the implication that an act may or may not be sinful, depending upon the attitude of the actor, a view that our inquiry into intentionality has adumbrated. In fact only a few actions are treated as *eo ipse* sinful. Chief among them are, specifically, murder, fornication, and idolatry.

Under all circumstances a man must refrain from committing such actions, even at the cost of his own life. These represent absolute sins.

Genesis Rabbah XXXI:VI.1

A. Another matter: "For the earth is filled with violence" (Gen. 6:13):
B. Said R. Levi, "The word for violence refers to idolatry, fornication, and murder.
C. "Idolatry: 'For the earth is filled with violence' (Gen. 6:13).
D. "Fornication: 'The violence done to me and to my flesh be upon Babylonia' (Jer. 51:35). [And the word for 'flesh' refers to incest, as at Lev. 18:6].
E. "Murder: 'For the violence against the children of Judah, because they have shed innocent blood' (Joel 4:19).
F. "Further, the word for 'violence' stands for its ordinary meaning as well."

Since these were the deeds of the men of the generation of the flood that so outraged God as to bring about mass destruction, they form a class of sin by themselves. The children of Noah, not only the children of Israel, must avoid these sins at all costs. But there is a sin that Israel may commit that exceeds even the cardinal sins. Even those three are forgivable, but rejection of the Torah is not:

Yerushalmi *Hagigah* 1:7/I:3

A. R. Huna, R. Jeremiah in the name of R. Samuel bar R. Isaac: "We find that the Holy One, blessed be he, forgave Israel for idolatry, fornication, and murder. [But] for their rejection of the Torah he never forgave them."
B. What is the scriptural basis for that view?
C. It is not written, "Because they practiced idolatry, fornication, and murder," but rather, "And the Lord said, 'Because they have forsaken my Torah.'"
D. Said R. Hiyya bar Ba, "'If they were to forsake me, I should forgive them, for they may yet keep my Torah. For if they should forsake me but keep my Torah, the leaven that is in [the Torah] will bring them closer to me.'"
E. R. Huna said, "Study Torah [even if it is] not for its own sake, for, out of [doing so] not for its own sake, you will come [to study it] for its own sake."

Still, that the classification of an action, even of the most severe character, depends upon the intentionality or attitude of the actor governs even here.

An Israelite's rejection of not God but the Torah is forthwith set into the context of will or intentionality. God does not object to insincerity when it comes to study of the Torah, because the Torah itself contains the power to reshape the will of man (as framed succinctly by sages elsewhere, "The commandments were given only to purify the heart of man," "God craves the heart," and similar formulations). The very jarring intrusion at D, developing C but making its own point, underscores that conviction. God can forgive Israel for forsaking him, because if they hold on to the Torah, they will find their way back. The Torah will reshape Israel's heart. And then, amplifying that point but moving still further from the main proposition, comes Huna's sentiment, E, that studying the Torah does not require proper intentionality, because the Torah in due course will effect the proper intentionality. Two critical points emerge. First, intentionality plays a central role in the discussion of principal sins. Second, sin ordinarily does not form an absolute but only a relative category, which is to say, an action that is sinful under one set of circumstances, when the intent is wicked, is not sinful but even subject to forgiveness under another set of circumstances.

That the variable of sin is man's intentionality in carrying out the action, not the intrinsic quality of most sinful actions (though, as we saw, not all), emerges in a striking formulation of matters. Here we find a position that is quite remarkable, yet entirely coherent with the principal stresses of the theology of the Rabbinic canon. Sages maintain that it is better sincerely to sin than hypocritically to perform a religious duty; to "sin bravely" sages would respond, "No, rather, sincerely!" It would be difficult to state in more extreme language the view that all things are relative to attitude or intentionality than to recommend sincere sin over hypocritical virtue:

Bavli *Horayot* 3:1–2 I.11/10b

11. A. Said R. Nahman bar Isaac, "A transgression committed for its own sake, in a sincere spirit, is greater in value than a religious duty carried out not for its own sake, but in a spirit of insincerity."

B. "For it is said, 'May Yael, wife of Hever the Kenite, be blessed above women, above women in the tent may she be blessed'" (Judges 5:24).

C. "Now who are these women in the tent? They are none other than Sarah, Rebecca, Rachel, and Leah." [The murder she committed gained more merit than the matriarchs' great deeds.]

The saying shocks and is immediately challenged:

> D. But is this really true that a transgression committed for its own sake, in a sincere spirit, is greater in value than a religious duty carried out not for its own sake, but in a spirit of insincerity. And did not R. Judah say Rab said, "A person should always be occupied in study of the Torah and in practice of the commandments, even if this is not for its own sake [but in a spirit of insincerity], for out of doing these things not for their own sake, a proper spirit of doing them for their own sake will emerge"?
>
> E. Say: it is equivalent to doing them not for their own sake.

Now we revert to the view that insincere Torah-study and practice of the commandments still have the power to transform a man:

> 12. A. Said R. Judah said Rab, "A person should always be occupied in study of the Torah and in practice of the commandments, even if this is not for its own sake [but in a spirit of insincerity], for out of doing these things not for their own sake, a proper spirit of doing them for their own sake will emerge."

Now comes a concrete case of blatant insincerity's producing a reward; the Messiah himself is the offspring of an act of hypocrisy on the part of Balak, the king of Moab, the ancestor of Ruth, from whom the scion of David, the Messiah, descends:

> B. For as a reward for the forty-two offerings that were presented by the wicked Balak to force Balaam to curse Israel, he was deemed worthy that Ruth should descend from him.
>
> C. For said R. Yosé b. R. Hanina, "Ruth was the granddaughter of Eglon, the grandson of Balak, king of Moab."

The upshot is, as we already realize, intentionality is everything; sin is rarely absolute but ordinarily conditioned upon the attitude of the actor; and sincerity in sin exceeds in merit hypocrisy in virtue.

So much for sages' general theory of sin and its cause, an act of rebellion. But they formulate the theology of sin within a larger theory of the character of man. Responding to the question, if man is like God, then theological anthropology must explain, how is it that man's will does not correspond with, but rebels against, the will of God? Here man's free will requires clarification. Man and God are possessed of free will. But man's free will encompasses the capacity to rebel against God, as we know, and that comes about because innate in man's will is the impulse to do evil, *yeser hara* in Hebrew. So here we extend theological anthropology to encompass a more complex theory of man than I suggested: man corresponds to God, but is complex, comprised as he is by conflicting impulses, where God is one and unconflicted.

Here is the crux of the matter: man by nature is sinful, and only by encounter with the Torah knows how to do good. That explains why the gentiles, with idolatry in place of the Torah, in the end cannot overcome their condition but perish, while Israel, with Torah the source of life, will stand in judgment and enter eternal life. The key to man's regeneration lies in that fact that Israel, while part of humanity and by nature sinful, possesses the Torah. That is how and where Israel may overcome its natural condition. Herein lies the source of hope. Gentiles enjoy this world but have no hope of regeneration in the world to come. Here three distinct components of the theology of the Rabbinic canon, [1] theological anthropology, [2] the doctrine of sin, and [3] eschatology intersect to make a single coherent statement accounting for the destiny of the whole of humanity, all in accord with the account of world order set forth at the very outset. When at the outset I alleged that when we examine the theology of sin we see that the Rabbinic canon spins out a simple but encompassing logic, so framing a single, coherent theology, I did not exaggerate.

What are the costs of sin to holy Israel? Sages' view of the costs of sin then fits tightly with their larger theory of the world order of justice that God has established. Because Israel has sinned, it has lost everything. Exile forms a particularly appropriate mode of punishing the entirety of holy Israel. Israel suffers in exile in the way in which gentiles do not, because their religious duties isolate them, and their poverty degrades them and weakens them:

Lamentations Rabbah XXXVII.i.1–2

1. A. "Judah has gone into exile."
   B. Do not the nations of the world go into exile?
   C. Even though they go into exile, their exile is not really an exile at all.
   D. But for Israel, their exile really is an exile.
   E. The nations of the world, who eat the bread and drink the wine of others, do not really experience exile.
   F. But the Israelites, who do not eat the bread and drink the wine of others, really do experience exile.
   G. The nations of the world, who travel in litters, do not really experience exile.

H. But the Israelites, who [in poverty] go barefoot—their exile
   really is an exile.
I. That is why it is said, "Judah has gone into exile."
2. A. Here Scripture states, "Judah has gone into exile,"
   B. and elsewhere, "So Judah was carried away captive out of his
      land" (Jer. 52:27).
   C. When they went into exile, they grew weak like a woman,
   D. so it is said, "Judah has gone into exile."

The Torah, which defines Israel and sanctifies the people, also
accounts for Israel's isolation among the gentiles. Israel is not suited
to exile, because it cannot assimilate with the gentiles. Exile weakens
Israel and tries the people.

Beyond exile, sages go so far as to attribute to Israel's own failings
the fall of Jerusalem and the cessation of the animal offerings of
atonement to God. Just what these failures were is subject to the sort
of dispute at which sages excel, that is to say, dispute that underscores
the iron consensus on the main principle. Once sages concur that sin
explains the fall of Jerusalem, they are free to differ to their hearts'
content on the identity of that sin; then they do not even have to state
the generative principle at all, it is simply taken as self-evident.

Bavli *Shabbat* 16:2 II.42ff./119b–120a:

II.42 A. Said Abbayye, "Jerusalem was ruined only because they vio-
       lated the Sabbath therein: 'And they have hidden their eyes
       from my Sabbaths, therefore I am profaned among them'
       (Ez. 22:26)."

From the Sabbath, we turn to the rejection of the yoke of the kingdom of Heaven, signified by the failure to recite the *Shema*:

B. Said R. Abbahu, "Jerusalem was ruined only because they
   stopped reciting the *Shema* morning and evening: 'Woe to
   them that rise up early in the morning, that they may follow
   strong drink . . . and the harp and the lute, the tabret and the
   pipe and wine are in their feasts, but they do not regard the
   works of the Lord,' 'Therefore my people have gone into cap-
   tivity for lack of knowledge' (Is. 5:11–13)."

Now comes neglect of Torah-study:

C. Said R. Hamnuna, "Jerusalem was ruined only because they
   neglected the children in the schoolmaster's household: 'pour
   out . . . because of the children in the street' (Jer. 6:21). Why
   pour out? Because the children are in the streets."

The specific sins review religious obligations—Sabbath, recitation of the *Shema*, Torah-study, improper social mores, and, inevitably in the Rabbinic canon, humiliation of sages. The details hardly matter.

The heaviest cost exacted by sin, however, is neither individual nor communal but cosmic. Sin separated God from man. Man's arrogance, his exercise of his will to confront the will of God, brings about sin and ultimately exiled Israel from the Land of Israel. That same act of attitude estranges God from Israel. If sin cuts the individual off from God and diminishes him in the world, then the sin of all Israel produces the same result. The costs of sin to Israel have proved catastrophic. Just as Israel was given every advantage by reason of accepting the Torah, so by rejecting the Torah, death, exile, and suffering took over. When Israel accepted the Torah, death, exile, and suffering and illness no longer ruled them. When they sinned, they incurred all of them. That is because God himself went into exile from the temple, the City, the Land. We begin with the penalty of alienation from God, marked by the advent of death.

Leviticus Rabbah XVIII:III.2ff.

2. A. "Yet the harvest will flee away (ND)" (Is. 17:11).
   B. You have brought on yourselves the harvest of the foreign governments, the harvest of violating prohibitions, the harvest of the angel of death.
   C. For R. Yohanan in the name of R. Eliezer, son of R. Yosé the Galilean, said, "When the Israelites stood before Mount Sinai and said, 'All that the Lord has said we shall do and we shall hear' [Ex. 24:7]. At that very moment the Holy One, blessed be he, called the angel of death and said to him, 'Even though I have made you world ruler over all of my creatures, you have no business with this nation. Why? For they are my children.' That is in line with the following verse of Scripture: 'You are the children of the Lord your God'" (Dt. 14:1).
   D. And it says, "And it happened that when you heard the voice out of the midst of the darkness" (Dt. 5:20).
   E. Now was there darkness above? And is it not written, "And the light dwells with Him" (Dan. 2:22)?
   F. That (D) refers to the angel who is called, "Darkness."

At Sinai, for the brief moment from the mass declaration, "We shall do and we shall obey," death died. But when Israel rebelled as Moses tarried on the mountain, sin took over, and the process of alienation from God got under way. Later on, we shall learn when and how death again will die, marking the end of time and change that commenced with Adam's sin. But the main point is clear. Death, exile, suffering, and illness do not belong to the order of nature; they have come about by reason of sin. Israel was exempt from them all when they accepted the Torah. But when they sinned, they returned to the natural condition of unredeemed man. A basic rationality then explains the human condition: people bring about their own fate. They possess the power to dictate their own destiny—by giving up the power to dictate to God.

But there is more to the costs of sin, the cosmic charge. Since God now finds himself alienated, he has abandoned not only Israel but the temple, the City, the Land—the world altogether. The estrangement of God from Israel is set forth in concrete terms, as a series of departures. This is set forth in a set of remarkably powerful statements, narratives of profound theological consequence. In one version, God's presence departed in ten stages, as God abandoned the people of Israel and they were estranged from him, and the sanhedrin was banished in ten stages as well.

Bavli *Rosh Hashanah* 4:4A–F I.6/31A–B

[A] Said R. Judah bar Idi said R. Yohanan, "The divine presence [Shekhinah] made ten journeys [in leaving the land and people of Israel prior to the destruction of the first Temple]. [That is, "The Divine Presence left Israel by ten stages." [This we know from] Scripture. And corresponding to these [stages], the Sanhedrin was exiled [successively to ten places of banishment]. [This we know from] tradition."

[B] The divine presence [Shekhinah] made ten journeys [in leaving the people, Israel, prior to the destruction of the first Temple]. [This we know from] Scripture: [It went]
(1) from the ark-cover to the cherub;
(2) and from the cherub to the threshold [of the Holy-of-Holies];
(3) and from the threshold to the [Temple-] court;
(4) and from the court to the altar;
(5) and from the altar to [Temple-] roof;
(6) and from the roof to wall;
(7) and from the wall to the city;
(8) and from the city to the mountain;
(9) and from the mountain to the wilderness;
(10) and from the wilderness it ascended and dwelled in its place [in heaven]—as it is said [Hos. 5:15]: "I will return again to my place, [until they acknowledge their guilt and seek my face]."

The systematic proof, deriving from Scripture, shows how God moved by stages from the inner sanctum of the temple; but the climax comes at C.10, pointing toward the next stage in the unfolding of the theology of the Rabbinic canon: the possibility of reconciliation and how this will take place. The language that I have supplied contains the key.

The next phase in the statement before us expands on that point: God hopes for the repentance of Israel, meaning, as we shall see, its freely-given act of acceptance of God's will by a statement of a change in attitude, specifically, regret for its act of arrogance. This is articulated in what follows:

> [D] Said R. Yohanan, "For six months, the divine presence waited on Israel [the people] in the wilderness, hoping lest they might repent. When they did not repent, it said, 'May their souls expire.' [We know this] as it says [Job 11:2]: 'But the eyes of the wicked will fail, all means of escape will elude them, and their [only] hope will be for their souls to expire.'"

God's progressive estrangement in Heaven finds its counterpart in the sequence of exiles that Israel's political institution suffered, embodying therein the exile of all Israel from the Land:

> [E] "And corresponding to these [stages through which the divine presence left Israel], the Sanhedrin was exiled [successively to ten places of banishment; this we know from] tradition." [The Sanhedrin was banished] (1) from the Chamber of Hewn Stone [in the inner court of the Temple] to the market; and (2) from the market into Jerusalem [proper], and (3) from Jerusalem to Yabneh, [31b] and (4) from Yabneh to Usha, and (5) from Usha [back] to Yabneh, and (6) from Yabneh [back] to Usha, (7) and from Usha to Shefar, and (8) from Shefar to Beth Shearim, and (9) from Beth Shearim to Sepphoris, and (10) from Sepphoris to Tiberias.
>
> [F] And Tiberias is the lowest of them all [below sea-level at the Sea of Galilee, symbolic of the complete abasement of the Sanhedrin's authority]. [We know of the lowered physical location and reduced status of the Sanhedrin] as it is said [Is. 29:4]: 'And deep from the earth you shall speak.'

So much for estrangement from Israel in particular.

But this same mode of thinking about God and man in the context of man's sin yields a quite separate account. The same matter of God's progressive alienation is stated, moreover, in relationship to humanity at large, rather than the temple, City, and Land. But if the alienation from sinning humanity forms the motif, then Israel takes a different position in the journey; Israel in this account forms the medium for bringing God back into the world. That stands to reason, for it is through Israel that God relates to all humanity, and only to Israel that God has given the Torah; indeed, Israel is defined as those who have accepted the Torah. Hence if God abandons Israel, it is not to take up a location in some other place of humanity, but to give up humanity. This then finds its localization in movement through the Heavens, rather than through the temple.

God's progress out of the created world is therefore set forth with seven movements, corresponding to the fixed stars (the visible planets) of the seven firmaments, out of, and back into, the world; the implication is that the present condition of Israel also comes about by reason of sin and will be remedied through attainment of *zekhut*.

Pesiqta deRab Kahana I:i.3, 6

3. A. R. Tanhum, son-in-law of R. Eleazar b. Abina, in the name of R. Simeon b. Yosni: "What is written is not, 'I have come into the garden,' but rather, 'I have come back to my garden.' That is, 'to my canopy.'

   B. "That is to say, to the place in which the principal [presence of God] had been located to begin with.

   C. "The principal locale of God's presence had been among the lower creatures, in line with this verse: 'And they heard the sound of the Lord God walking about' (Gen. 3:8)."

6. A. [Reverting to 3.C,] the principal locale of God's presence had been among the lower creatures, but when the first man sinned, it went up to the first firmament.

   B. The generation of Enosh came along and sinned, and it went up from the first to the second.

   C. The generation of the flood [came along and sinned], and it went up from the second to the third.

   D. The generation of the dispersion [came along] and sinned, and it went up from the third to the fourth.

   E. The Egyptians in the time of Abraham our father [came along] and sinned, and it went up from the fourth to the fifth.

   F. The Sodomites [came along], and sinned, . . . from the fifth to the sixth.

   G. The Egyptians in the time of Moses . . . from the sixth to the seventh.

Now God returns to the world through the founders of Israel.

H. And, corresponding to them, seven righteous men came along and brought it back down to earth:

I. Abraham our father came along and acquired merit, and brought it down from the seventh to the sixth.

J. Isaac came along and acquired merit and brought it down from the sixth to the fifth.

K. Jacob came along and acquired merit and brought it down from the fifth to the fourth.

L. Levi came along and acquired merit and brought it down from the fourth to the third.

M. Kohath came along and acquired merit and brought it down from the third to the second.

N. Amram came along and acquired merit and brought it down from the second to the first.

O. Moses came along and acquired merit and brought it down to earth.

P. Therefore it is said, "On the day that Moses completed the setting up of the Tabernacle, he anointed and consecrated it" (Num. 7:1).

God yearns for Israel, but Israel is estranged—why is that the case? The explanation appeals to Israel's sin. The same explanation, in more explicit language, emerges in the account of how God departed from the world. The estrangement took place by reason of the sins of one generation after another. Then the merit of successive generations of Israel brought God back to the world.

Both the question and the answer derive from the sustaining system. The two accounts—God leaves the world by reason of man's sin, is brought back through Israel's saints, God leaves the world by reason of Israel's sin but can be restored to the world by Israel's act of repentance—match. They conform to the theory of Israel as the counterpart to man, the other Adam, the Land as counterpart to Eden, and, now we see, the exile of Israel as counterpart to the fall of man. The first set—God abandons the temple—without the second story would leave an imbalance; only when the one story is told in the setting of the other does the theology make its complete statement.

God's fate is bound up with Israel's, just as God's inner life of affections and emotions is lived in response to Israel's feelings and attitudes.

Yerushalmi *Ta'anit* 1:1 II:5

A. It has been taught by R. Simeon b. Yohai, "To every place to which the Israelites went into exile, the presence of God went with them into exile.

First comes the archetypal exile, to Egypt.

B. "They were sent into exile to Egypt, and the presence of God went into exile with them. What is the scriptural basis for this claim? '[And there came a man of God to Eli, and said to him, Thus the Lord has said], I revealed myself to the house of your father when they were in Egypt subject to the house of Pharaoh' (1 Sam. 2:27).

Now follows the familiar pattern of the four kingdoms, Babylonia, Media, Greece, and Rome.

C. "They were sent into exile to Babylonia, and the presence of God went into exile with them. What is the scriptural basis for this claim? '[Thus says the Lord, your Redeemer, the Holy One of Israel]: For your sake I will send to Babylon [and break down all the bars, and the shouting of the Chaldeans will be turned to lamentations]' (Is. 43:14).

D. "They were sent into exile into Media, and the presence of God went into exile with them. What is the scriptural basis for this claim? 'And I will set my throne in Elam [and destroy their king and princes, says the Lord]' (Jer. 49:38). And Elam means only Media, as it is said, '[And I saw in the vision; and when I saw], I was in Susa the capital, which is in the province of Elam; [and I saw in the vision, and I was at the river Ulai]' (Dan. 8:2).

E. "They went into exile to Greece, and the presence of God went into exile with them. What is the scriptural basis for this claim? '[For I have bent Judah as my bow; I have made Ephraim its arrow]. I will brandish your sons, O Zion, over your sons, O Greece, [and wield you like a warrior's sword]' (Zech. 9:13).

F. "They went into exile to Rome, and the presence of God went into exile with them. What is the scriptural basis for this claim? '[The oracle concerning Dumah]. One is calling to me from Seir, "Watchman, what of the night? Watchman, what of the night?" Is. 21:11).'"

Now, in this systematic statement, what should not be missed is not only God's exile, but also what will bring God back to the Land, which is, Israel's return at the end of the reign of the fourth and final empire, Rome. Then Israel will govern, because all mankind will accept God and give up idolatry. So cosmic dimensions take the measure of what is at stake in sin.

If sages' theology builds upon the foundation of God's justice in creating a perfect world and accounts for the imperfections of the world by appeal to the conflict of man's will and God's plan, then, we must ask ourselves, What is the logical remedy for the impasse at which, in the present age, Israel and the world find themselves? Their explanation for flaws and transience in creation, sin brought about by the free exercise of man's will, contains within itself the systemic remission—that required, logical remedy for the human condition and creation's as well. It is an act of will to bring about reconciliation between God and Israel, God and the world. And that act of will on man's part will evoke an equal and commensurate act of will on God's part. When man repents, God forgives, and Israel and the world will attain that perfection that prevailed at Eden. And that is why death will die. So we come to the account of restoring world order. Here we begin to follow the unfolding of the restorationist theology of eschatology that completes and perfects the sages' theology set forth in the documents of the Rabbinic canon.

CHAPTER NINE

RESTORING WORLD ORDER

I. Repentance, Regeneration, and Renewal

The logic of repentance is simple and familiar. It is a logic that appeals to the balance and proportion of all things. If sin is what introduces rebellion and change, and the will of man is what constitutes the variable in disrupting creation, then the theology of the Rabbinic canon makes provision for restoration through the free exercise of man's will. What brings about disruption effects the restoration. That requires [1] an attitude of remorse, [2] a resolve not to repeat the act of rebellion, and [3] a good-faith effort at reparation, in all, transformation from rebellion against, to obedience to, God's will. So with repentance we come once more to an exact application of the principle of measure for measure, here will for will, each comparable to, corresponding with, the other. World order, disrupted by an act of will, regains perfection through an act of will that complements and corresponds to the initial, rebellious one. That is realized in an act of willful repentance (Hebrew *teshubah*).

Repentance, a statement of regret and remorse for the sin one has committed and hence an act of will, in the Rabbinic canon effects the required transformation of man and inaugurates reconciliation with God. Through a matched act of will, now in conformity with God's design for creation, repentance therefore restores the balance upset by man's act of will. So the act of repentance, and with it atonement, takes its place within the theology of perfection, disruption, and restoration, that all together organizes—shows the order of—the world of creation.

Apology does not suffice; an atoning act also is required. That is why repentance is closely related to the categories of atonement and Day of Atonement, and is integral to them. The one in the cult, the other in the passage of time, respond to the change of will with an act of confirmation, on God's part, that the change is accepted, recognized, and deemed effective. That is because, through the act of repentance, a person who has sinned leaves the status of sinner, but must also atone for the sin and gain forgiveness, so that such a person is no longer deemed a sinner. Self-evidently, within a system built on the dialectics of competing wills, God's and man's, repentance comes first in the path to reconciliation. That is because the act of will involves a statement of regret or remorse, resolve never to repeat the act, and, finally, the test of this change of heart or will (where feasible). Specifically, it is a trial of entering a situation in which the original sin is possible but is not repeated. Then the statement of remorse and voluntary change of will is confirmed by an act of omission or commission, as the case requires.

Followed by atonement, therefore, repentance commences the work of closing off the effects of sin: history, time, change, inequity. It marks the beginning of the labor of restoring creation to Eden, the perfect world as God wants it and creates it. Since the Hebrew word *teshubah* is built out of the root for "return," the concept is generally understood to mean returning to God from a situation of estrangement. The turning is not only from sin but toward God, for sin serves as an indicator of a deeper pathology, which is utter estrangement from God—man's will alienated from God's.

Teshubah then involves not humiliation but reaffirmation of the self in God's image, after God's likeness. It follows that repentance forms a theological category encompassing moral issues of action and attitude, wrong action and arrogant attitude in particular. Repentance forms a step in the path to God that starts with the estrangement represented by sin: doing what I want, instead of what God wants, thus rebellion and arrogance. Sin precipitates punishment, whether personal for individuals or historical for nations. Punishment brings about repentance for sin, which, in turn, leads to atonement for sin and, it follows, reconciliation with God. That sequence of stages in the moral regeneration of sinful humanity, individual or collective, defines the context in which repentance finds its natural home.

True, the penitent corrects damage actually carried out to his fellow man. But apart from reparations, the act of repentance involves only the attitude, specifically substituting feelings of regret and remorse for the arrogant intention that led to the commission of the sin. If the person declares regret and undertakes not to repeat the action, the process of repentance gets underway. When the occasion to repeat the sinful act arises and the penitent refrains from doing it again, the process comes to a conclusion. So it is through the will and attitude of the sinner that the act of repentance is realized; the entire process is carried on beyond the framework of religious actions, rites, or rituals. The power of repentance overcomes sins of the most heinous and otherwise unforgivable character. The following is explicit that no sin overwhelms the transformative power of repentance:

Bavli *Gittin* 5:6 I.26/57b

A. A Tannaite statement:
B. Naaman was a resident proselyte.
C. Nebuzaradan was a righteous proselyte.
D. Grandsons of Haman studied Torah in Bene Beraq.
E. Grandsons of Sisera taught children in Jerusalem.
F. Grandsons of Sennacherib taught Torah in public.
G. And who were they? Shemaiah and Abtalion.

Shemaiah and Abtalion are represented as the masters of Hillel and Shammai, who founded the houses of Hillel and Shammai that are dominant in many areas of the Halakhah set forth in the Mishnah and related writings. The act of repentance transforms the heirs of the destroyers of Israel and the temple into the framers of the redemptive Rabbinic canon. A more extreme statement of the power of any attitude or action defies imagining—even the fact of our own day that a distant cousin of Adolph Hitler has converted to Judaism and serves in the reserves of the Israel Defense Army.

As the prophets had said, God takes an active role in bringing about the restoration of the perfection of the world. This he does by goading man into an act of repentance—the purpose of punishment of sin being not so much retributive as redemptive. Aiming at bringing about repentance, God first penalizes property, then the person, in the theory that the first will arouse the man to reflect on what he has done, so a penalty exacted from the person himself will not be necessary, repentance having intervened.

Ruth Rabbah IX:i.1ff.

B. R. Huniah in the name of R. Joshua b. R. Abin and R. Zechariah son-in-law of R. Levi in the name of R. Levi: "The merciful Lord does not do injury to human beings first. [First he exacts a penalty from property, aiming at the sinner's repentance.]
C. From whom do you derive that lesson? From the case of Job: 'The oxen were plowing and the asses feeding beside them [and the

Sabaeans fell upon them and took them and slew the servants with the edge of the sword; and I alone have escaped to tell you' (Job 1:14). Afterward: 'Your sons and daughters were eating and drinking wine in their eldest brother's house, and behold, a great wind came across the wilderness and struck the four corners of the house, and it fell upon the young people, and they are dead' (Job 1:19).]"

D. Now were the oxen plowing and the asses feeding beside them? Said R. Hama b. R. Hanina, "This teaches that the Holy One, blessed be He, showed him a paradigm of the world to come.

E. "That is in line with the following verse of Scripture: 'The plowman shall overtake the reaper'" (Amos 9:13).

God warns before inflicting punishment, preferring repentance to imposing penalties for sin. It is a mark of his mercy. The proposition is demonstrated by four probative cases; these cases do not form a natural list but coalesce only in the matter at hand. The second, third, and fourth cases are presented in an unadorned way. No other point in common draws them together.

Two other media of atonement for sin are death, on the one side, and the advent of the Day of Atonement, which accomplishes atonement: "For on this day atonement shall be made for you to cleanse you of all your sins" (Lev. 16:30). Death marks the final atonement for sin, which bears its implication for the condition of man at the resurrection. Because one has atoned through sin (accompanied at the hour of death by a statement of repentance, "May my death be atonement for all my sins," in the liturgy in due course), when he is raised from the dead, his atonement for all his sins is complete. The judgment after resurrection becomes for most a formality. That is why "all Israel has a portion in the world to come," with the exception of a few whose sins are not atoned for by death, and that is by their own word. The Day of Atonement provides atonement, as the Written Torah makes explicit, for the sins of the year for which one has repented, and that accounts for the elaborate rites of confession that fill the day. Here is how the media of atonement of death, for a lifetime, and the Day of Atonement, for the year just past, are sorted out:

Mishnah *Yoma* 8:8–9
8:8

A. A sin offering and an unconditional guilt offering atone.
B. Death and the Day of Atonement atone when joined with repentance.

C. Repentance atones for minor transgressions of positive and negative commandments.
D. And as to serious transgressions, [repentance] suspends the punishment until the Day of Atonement comes along and atones.

8:9

A. He who says, "I shall sin and repent, sin and repent"—
B. they give him no chance to do repentance.
C. [If he said,] "I will sin and the Day of Atonement will atone,"—the Day of Atonement does not atone.
D. For transgressions done between man and the Omnipresent, the Day of Atonement atones.
E. For transgressions between man and man, the Day of Atonement atones, only if the man will regain the good will of his friend.

The first statement sorts out the workings of repentance, death, the Day of Atonement, and atonement. We see that repentance on its own serves for the violation of commandments, for that involves God; when another man is involved in a man's sin, then the this-worldly counterpart to repentance, which is reparation and reconciliation, is required. The formulation underscores the tight weaving of the several components of a single tapestry.

First comes inadvertent sin, acts that violate God's will but are not done intentionally. A sin offering in the temple in Jerusalem, presented for unintentional sins, atones, and therein we find the beginning of the definition of repentance. It lies in the contrast between the sin offering at A, that is, atonement for unintentional sin, and those things that atone for intentional sin, which are two events, on the one side, and the expression of right attitude, *teshubah*, returning to God, on the other. The role of repentance emerges in the contrast with the sin offering; what atones for what is inadvertent has no bearing upon what is deliberate. The willful sin can be atoned for only if repentance has taken place, that is to say, genuine regret, a turning away from the sin, after the fact therefore transforming the sin from one that is deliberate to one that is, if not unintentional beforehand, then at least, unintentional afterward. Then death, on the one side, or the Day of Atonement, on the other, work their benefits.

The act of repentance commences with the sinner, but then compels divine response; the attitude of the penitent governs, the motive—love, fear—making the difference. The power of repentance to win God over, even after recurring sin, forms the leading theme—

the leitmotif—of the composite. Israel's own redemption depends upon Israel's repentance. The concluding statement proves most concrete. Repentance takes place when the one who has sinned and declares his regret ("in words") faces the opportunity of repeating the sinful action but this time refrains. That we deal with the critical nexus in the relationship between God and humanity emerges in one composition after another, e.g., repentance overrides negative commandments of the Torah (the more important kind); brings redemption; changes the character of the already-committed sins; lengthens the life of the penitent. Not only so, but the power of repentance before the loving God of grace is such that mere words suffice. The upshot is, we deal with a matter of attitude that comes to the surface in concrete statements; but as to deeds, the penitent cannot repeat the sin, so no deed can be required. The penitent has a more difficult task: not to do again what he has done before.

But repentance is a far cry from loving and forgiving one's unrepentant enemy. God forgives sinners who atone and repent and asks of humanity that same act of grace—but no greater. For forgiveness without a prior act of repentance violates the rule of justice and also humiliates the law of mercy, cheapening and trivializing the superhuman act of forgiveness by treating as compulsive what is an act of human, and divine, grace. Sin is to be punished, but repentance is to be responded to with forgiveness, as the written Torah states explicitly: "You shall not bear a grudge nor pursue a dispute beyond reason, nor hate your brother in your heart, but you shall love your neighbor as yourself" (Lev. 19:18). The role of the sinful other is to repent, the task of the sinned-against is to respond to and accept repentance, at which point, loving one's neighbor as oneself becomes the just person's duty, so repentance forms the critical center of the moral transaction in a contentious and willful world.

The perfect balance between sin and repentance, mercy and forgiveness, emerges when we ask about the children of sinners. In the context of the Rabbinic canon, the question finds its meaning when we recall that, when the founders of Israel, Abraham, Isaac, and Jacob, performed acts of supererogatory love for God and exemplary service, the *zekhut* with which God responded to their attitude accrued to the advantage of their heirs, Israel in time to come. For sages, the antonym of *zekhut* is sin, and since the causative, to cause others *zekhut* (to endow others with *zekhut*) finds its opposite in the causative, to cause others to sin. So, in their language-world, even without the explicit statement of Ex. 20:5, ". . . visiting the sins of the parents upon the children, upon the third and fourth generations of those who reject me," it was natural to wonder about a heritage of not *zekhut* but guilt, unmerited favor matched by unearned penalty. This sages found it easy to reframe in terms of their prevailing logic. They did so when they maintained that God punishes the sons who continue the sins of the father, but not those who repent of the fathers' sins.

Sages do recognize limits to the power of repentance and atonement. They recognize that, in the world order, atonement does not always accomplish its goals, for with genuinely evil persons repentance on its own may not suffice to accomplish atonement. Specifically, they recognize that genuinely wicked people may repent but not for long, or their repentance in the end proves incommensurate to the affront against God that they have committed. The process of repentance and atonement therefore works only in a limited way. In this doctrine they are able in yet another way to account for the prosperity of the wicked.

The Fathers According to R. Nathan XXXIX:V.1

A. The repentance of genuinely wicked people suspends [their punishment], but the decree against them has been sealed.
B. The prosperity of the wicked in the end will go sour.
C. Dominion buries those that hold it.
D. Repentance suspends [punishment] and the Day of Atonement achieves atonement.
E. Repentance suspends [punishment] until the day of death, and the day of death atones, along with repentance.

The wicked enjoy this world, getting their reward now, but they do not gain the life eternal of the world to come. The righteous suffer now, atoning for their sins through suffering, but they will have a still more abundant life in the world to come.

The Fathers According to R. Nathan XXXIX:VII.1

A. They [immediately, in this world] pay off the reward owing to the wicked [for such good as they may do], while they credit to the righteous [the reward that is coming to them, but do not pay it off, rather paying them off in the world to come].
B. They pay off the reward owing to the wicked [in this world] as though they were people who had carried out the Torah ungrudgingly, in whom no fault had ever been found.

    C. They credit to the righteous [the reward that is coming to them, but do not pay it off, rather paying them off in the world to come], as though they were people lacking all good traits.

    D. They thus give a little bit to each party, with the bulk of the remainder laid up for them.

In these ways, the complementary doctrines of repentance and atonement are given nuance, fitting together with comparable doctrines to account for the condition of individuals in the here and now.

Clearly, then, what is at stake in repentance and atonement vastly transcends issues of this world. Time and again we have noted that repentance, along with atonement, forms the condition of the restoration of world order. Even in the here and now, Israel is able through repentance to reconcile itself with God, and in God's own time, the reconciliation—Israel's will now voluntarily conforming to God's word—will mark the end of the world as man knows it and the beginning of the time of restoration. That is why repentance forms the bridge between the analysis of the imperfection of world order and the account of the restoration of world order at the last. In so many words repentance is linked to the salvation of the individual Israelite and the redemption of Israel, for these mark the return to Eden.

And so we find, as I surmised earlier, that repentance is required if one is to be resurrected at the end of time and gain a portion in the world to come.

Yerushalmi Shebi'it 4:10 VI
(Translation by Alan J. Avery-Peck)

    A. Said R. Jonah in the name of R. Hama bar Hanina, "One who dies during the seven year [battle of] Gog [Ez. 38–39] [so as not to suffer fully the troubles of the nation] does not have a portion in the coming world.

    B. "The mnemonic sign for this is: 'One who takes part in the wedding preliminaries will [also] have a share in the wedding feast.'" {But whoever is not involved in the preliminaries does not have a part in the feast.}

    C. R. Yosé heard [this] and said, "Now, is this really true?

    D. "[For] there is always repentance [as a method of earning a place in] the world to come." [This applies even if the individual has not suffered along with the Israelite nation.]

The act of repentance then serves to secure the victory over death represented by resurrection and consequent entry into the world to come—a considerable result.

Once we ask about how repentance forms a principal requirement for the restoration of life over death, in resurrection, and the restoration of Israel over its condition of exile and alienation, we turn to the place of repentance in the end of the world as it now is. We begin with the figure of the Messiah, an important motif in all discussions of matters of eschatology: the resurrection of the dead, the advent of the world or age to come. We already realize that Israel's repentance is a precondition for salvation, hence for the coming of the Messiah. We should not find surprising, then, that the characterization of the Messiah should stress his humility, as much as the promise of his coming to raise the dead should rest upon Israel's conduct as well.

When Israel really wants the Messiah to come, he will come. But we are now aware of the special weight attached to the word "want" or "will." What Israel must want is only what God wants. What Israel must do is give up any notion of accomplishing on its own, by its own act of will, the work of redemption. It is only through the self-abnegation of repentance that Israel can accomplish its goal. Specifically, when Israel's will conforms to the will of God, then God will respond to the act of repentance by bringing about the time of restoration and eternal life. This is expressed in a colloquy that announces that the Messiah will come when all Israel keeps a single Sabbath. And that will take place when Israel wants it to take place. It requires only an act of will on the part of Israel to accept one of the Ten Commandments. Then, in a broader restatement of matters, the entire redemptive process is made to depend upon Israel's repentance.

Yerushalmi Ta'anit 1:1 II:5

G. The Israelites said to Isaiah, "O our Rabbi, Isaiah, What will come for us out of this night?"

H. He said to them, "Wait for me, until I can present the question."

I. Once he had asked the question, he came back to them.

J. They said to him, "Watchman, what of the night? What did the Guardian of the ages say [a play on 'of the night' and 'say']?"

K. He said to them, "The watchman says: 'Morning comes; and also the night. [If you will inquire, inquire; come back again]'" (Is. 21:12).

L. They said to him, "Also the night?"

M. He said to them, "It is not what you are thinking. But there will be morning for the righteous, and night for the wicked, morning for Israel, and night for idolaters."

Now comes the main point in the exchange: When will this happen? It will happen when Israel wants. And what is standing in the way is Israel's arrogance, to be atoned for by Israel's remorseful repentance:

N. They said to him, "When?"
O. He said to them, "Whenever you want, He too wants [it to be]— if you want it, he wants it."
P. They said to him, "What is standing in the way?"
Q. He said to them, "Repentance: 'come back again'" (Is. 21:12).

This is stated in the clearest possible way: one day will do it.

R. R. Aha in the name of R. Tanhum b. R. Hiyya, "If Israel repents for one day, forthwith the son of David will come.
S. "What is the scriptural basis? 'O that today you would hearken to his voice!'" (Ps. 95:7).

Now comes the introduction of the Sabbath as a test case.

T. Said R. Levi, "If Israel would keep a single Sabbath in the proper way, forthwith the son of David will come.
U. "What is the scriptural basis for this view? 'Moses said, Eat it today, for today is a Sabbath to the Lord; [today you will not find it in the field]' (Ex. 16:25).
V. "And it says, '[For thus said the Lord God, the Holy One of Israel], "In returning and rest you shall be saved; [in quietness and in trust shall be your strength." And you would not]'" (Is. 30:15). By means of returning and [Sabbath] rest you will be redeemed.

The main point, then, is the linkage of repentance to the coming restoration of Israel to the Land, the dead to life, by the Messiah. But the advent of the Messiah depends wholly upon Israel's will. If Israel will subordinate its will to God's, all else will follow.

We recall that, to hasten Israel's repentance, God promises to abrogate those conditions of prosperity that bring about excessive confidence in one's own power and therefore nurture arrogance. The Messiah will come when all Israel will keep a single Sabbath. The matter therefore depends upon Israel's own conduct, which expresses Israel's attitude and will. What is required therefore is repentance, an act of humility that removes the consequences of arrogance.

The Rabbinic system of theology of Judaism delivers a few simple messages, repeating them with great power of intricate variation, but in all with little substantive change. That is because, as we have already noted, sages adopt as their mode of thought the paradigmatic way of organizing and interpreting experience. They look for patterns that are simple but capable of sustaining endless applications, and they find in narrative and exegesis of narrative (whether their own or, more commonly, Scripture's stories) the ideal mode of making their statement. In this case, it is the story of how God created an orderly world but at the climax of creation made man, in his image, after his likeness.

Man both complemented and corresponded with God, and it was man's freedom, meaning his effective will and power of intentionality, that matched God's will. When these conflict, man's arrogance leads him to rebel against God, sin resulting. And from sin comes the imperfection of world order, change, inequity, imbalance. Punished and remorseful, man gives up his arrogant attitude and conforms his will to God's. God responds with mercy, freely accepting the reformation that is freely offered. Then, world order restored, that perfection effected at the outset is regained for Israel, which means for God's part of mankind. Eden, now the Land of Israel, is recovered, Adam, now embodied in Israel, is restored to his place. For the Israelite death dies, man rises from the grave to life eternal. For Israel the gentiles' rule comes to an end, and Israel regains the Land. Repentance then marks the recovery of the world as God wanted it to be, which is to say, the world in which Israel regains its promised place.

II. RESTORING PRIVATE LIVES: RESURRECTION

Throughout the Rabbinic canon the main point of the theological eschatology—the theory of last things—registers both negatively and affirmatively. Death does not mark the end of the individual human life, nor exile the last stop in the journey of Holy Israel. Israelites will live in the age or the world to come, all Israel in the Land of Israel; and Israel will comprehend all who know the one true God. The restoration of world order that completes the demonstration of God's justice encompasses both private life and the domain of all Israel. For both, restorationist theology provides eternal life; to be Israel means to live. So far as the individual is concerned, beyond the grave, at a determinate moment, man [1] rises from the grave in resurrection, [2] is judged, and [3] enjoys the world to come. For the entirety of

Israel, congruently: all Israel participates in the resurrection, which takes place in the Land of Israel, and enters the world to come.

Restorationist eschatology flows from the same cogent logic that has dictated theological doctrine from the beginning of this systematic account. The last things are to be known from the first. In the just plan of creation man was meant to live in Eden, and Israel in the Land of Israel in time without end. The restoration will bring about that long and tragically-postponed perfection of the world order, sealing the demonstration of the justice of God's plan for creation. Risen from the dead, having atoned through death, man will be judged in accord with his deeds. Israel for its part, when it repents and conforms its will to God's, recovers its Eden. So, the consequences of rebellion and sin having been overcome, the struggle of man's will and God's word having been resolved, God's original plan will be realized at the last. The simple global logic of the system, with its focus on the world order of justice established by God but disrupted by man, leads inexorably to this eschatology of restoration, the restoration of balance, order, proportion—eternity.

The two principal components of the Rabbinic canon's theology of last things—[1] resurrection and judgment, [2] the world to come and eternal life—as laid out in the several documents do not fit together seamlessly. In general, it would appear, the theology arranges matters in categorical sequence, individual then community. First comes the resurrection of individuals, and, with it, judgment of individuals one by one. Then, those chosen for life having been identified, "the world to come" takes place, and that final restoration of perfection, involving all Israel in place of Adam, lasts forever. Israel forms the cohort of those chosen for life, and Israelites are restored to life in the Land of Israel. That sequence suggests a single, uninterrupted narrative of last things, while, in general, passages that concern themselves with resurrection do not ordinarily join together with composites that deal with the world to come. While mutually complementary, each of the two components of eschatology in the Rabbinic canon bears its distinctive focus. Before we proceed, let us consider a cogent statement of what is at stake in all eschatological thinking in the Rabbinic canon.

Let us now address the resurrection of the dead in its own terms. That conviction is stated in so many words: in the end of days, death will die. The certainty of resurrection derives from a simple fact of restorationist theology: God has already shown that he can do it, so *Genesis Rabbah* LXXVII:I.1: "You find that everything that the Holy One, blessed be he, is destined to do in the age to come he has already gone ahead and done through the righteous in this world. The Holy One, blessed be he, will raise the dead, and Elijah raised the dead."

The paramount composite on the subject derives its facts, demonstrating the coming resurrection of the dead, from the Written Torah, which, as we realize, serves as counterpart to nature for philosophy, the source of actualities. Sages deem urgent the task of reading outward and forward from Scripture, and at the critical conclusion of their theological system the Rabbinic canon focuses upon Scripture's evidence, the regularization of Scripture's facts. But the doctrine of resurrection as defined by the principal (and huge) composite of the Talmud of Babylonia contains a number of components: [1] origin of the doctrine in the Written Torah; [2] the gentiles and the resurrection of the dead; [3] the distinction between the days of the Messiah and the world to come; [4] the restoration of Israel to the Land of Israel.

A sequence of virtues, properly carried out, will lead to the resurrection of the dead, which forms a natural next step beyond this world's life. No radical caesura interrupts the course of affairs, but this-worldly traits, for example, cleanness, abstinence, holiness, modesty, and the like, carry directly to other-worldly events, the encounter with the Holy Spirit, the resurrection of the dead, and onward.

Mishnah *Sotah* 9:15

> R. Pinhas b. Yair says, "Heedfulness leads to cleanliness, cleanliness leads to cleanness, cleanness leads to abstinence, abstinence leads to holiness, holiness leads to modesty, modesty leads to the fear of sin, the fear of sin leads to piety, piety leads to the Holy Spirit, the Holy Spirit leads to the resurrection of the dead, and the resurrection of the dead comes through Elijah, blessed be his memory, Amen."

Now, the ladder of virtue reaches the perfection of man, who, perfect in form in life ("in our image, after our likeness") will be resurrected in the same form beyond the grave. That seems to me to form the restorationist logic of the composition. That explains why there are stages in the road to resurrection, leading through the virtues of cultic cleanness to holiness, to the fear of sin, to piety, then the Holy

Spirit, the resurrection of the dead, a straight path for those that take it.

The first component of the doctrine of the resurrection of the dead—belief both that the resurrection of the dead will take place and that it is the Torah that reveals that the dead will rise—is fully exposed in a fundamental composition devoted by the framers of the Mishnah to that subject. The components of the doctrine fit together, in that statement, in a logical order. [1] In a predictable application of the governing principle of measure for measure, those who do not believe in the resurrection of the dead will be punished by being denied what they do not accept. Some few others bear the same fate. [2] But to be Israel means to rise from the grave, and that applies to all Israelites. That is to say, the given of the condition of Israel is that the entire holy people will enter the world to come, which is to say, will enjoy the resurrection of the dead and eternal life. "Israel" then is anticipated to be the people of eternity. [3] Excluded from the category of resurrection and the world to come, then, are only those who by their own sins have denied themselves that benefit. These are those who deny that the teaching of the world to come derives from the Torah, or who deny that the Torah comes from God, or who are hedonists. Exegesis of Scripture also yields the names of three kings who will not be resurrected, as well as four commoners; also specified are: the flood, the dispersion, and Sodom, the generation of the wilderness, the party of Korah, and the Ten Tribes:

Mishnah *Sanhedrin* 10:1
[= Bavli *Sanhedrin* 11:1]

A. All Israelites have a share in the world to come,
B. as it is said, "Your people also shall be all righteous, they shall inherit the land forever; the branch of my planting, the work of my hands, that I may be glorified" (Is. 60:21).

That single statement serves better than any other to define Israel in the Rabbinic canon. The details of judgment that follows resurrection prove less ample. The basic account stresses that God will judge with great mercy. But the Rabbinic canon presents no fully-articulated story of judgment.

How to stand in judgment, meaning, go through the process of divine review of one's life and actions and emerge in the world to come, restored to the Land that is Eden? Proper conduct and study

of Torah lead to standing in judgment and consequently the life of
the world to come, and not keeping the one and studying the other
deny entry into that life. What is striking is the appeal to Eden for
just this message about reentry into the Land.

Leviticus Rabbah XXXV:VI:1f.

1. A. Said R. Abba b. Eliashib, "[The reference at Lev. 26:3 to
statutes is to] statutes which bring a person into the life of the
world to come.
   B. "That is in line with the following verse of Scripture: 'And he
who is left in Zion and remains in Jerusalem will be called holy,
everyone who has been recorded for life in Jerusalem' [Is. 4:3]—
for he is devoted to [study of] Torah, which is called the tree of
life."

Now comes the reference to Eden in the context of the world to come.

2. A. It has been taught in the name of R. Eliezer, "A sword and a
scroll wrapped together were handed down from heaven, as if to
say to them, 'If you keep what is written in this [scroll], you will
be saved from the sword,
   B. "'and if not, in the end [the sword] will kill you.'
   C. "Whence is that proposition to be inferred? 'He drove out the
man, and at the east of the Garden of Eden he placed the cherubim, and a flaming sword which turned every way, to guard the
way to the tree of life' [Gen. 3:4].
   D. "The [first] reference to 'the way' refers to the rules of proper
conduct, and the second reference, '[the way to] the tree of life'
refers to the Torah."

The same message is given in a different framework.

3. A. It was taught in the name of R. Simeon b. Yohai, "A loaf and
a rod wrapped together were given from heaven.
   B. "It was as if to say to them, 'If you keep the Torah, lo, here
is bread to eat, and if not, lo, here is a staff with which to be
smitten.'
   C. "Whence is that proposition to be inferred? 'If you are willing
and obedient, you shall eat the good of the land; but if you refuse
and rebel, you shall be devoured by the sword'" (Is. 15:19–20).

The world to come, involving resurrection and judgment, will be
attained through the Torah, which teaches proper conduct. That simple doctrine yields the proposition here.

When it comes to the last judgment, we need hardly be reminded that God judges in a merciful manner. If the balance is equal, then God inclines the scale to forgiveness. Given that mercy complements justice, so that justice is not possible without mercy, that trait of God's judgment conforms to the logic that pervades the entire system. We deal first with the quality of justice, which involves measure for measure; and much of the judgment is worked out in this life, so that the world to come awaits those who suffer:

Yerushalmi Sanhedrin 10:1 I:2

H. If the greater part of his record consisted of honorable deeds, and the smaller part, transgressions, they exact punishment from him [in this world].

I. If the smaller part of the transgressions which he has done are of the lesser character, [he is punished] in this world so as to pay him his full and complete reward in the world to come.

J. If the greater part of his record consisted of transgressions and the lesser part of honorable deeds, they pay him off with the reward of the religious deeds which he has done entirely in this world, so as to exact punishment from him in a whole and complete way in the world to come.

K. If the greater part of his record consisted of honorable deeds, he will inherit the Garden of Eden. If the greater part consisted of transgressions, he will inherit Gehenna.

Now we reach the critical point at which mercy enters in.

L. [If the record] was evenly balanced—

M. Said R. Yosé b. Haninah, "'. . . forgives sins . . . ,' is not written here, but rather, '. . . forgives [a] sin' (Num. 14:18). That is to say, the Holy One, blessed be he, tears up one bond [recorded] among the transgressions, so that the honorable deeds then will outweigh the others."

N. Said R. Eleazar, "'And that to thee, O Lord, belongs steadfast love. For thou dost requite a man according to his work' (Ps. 62:13). 'His deed' is not written here, but 'like his deed'—if he has none, you give him one of yours."

Here is a further statement of the systemic realization of the future: the righteous will ultimately triumph, the wicked will ultimately suffer, in the age to come if not in this age. Then this age is the time in which the righteous atone for their sins, and in which the wicked do not. Then in the world to come the wicked will be punished, not having prepared and atoned. The systemic variable now allows God to intervene and help the righteous to attain the merit that they require.

III. THE MESSIAH: THEME, NOT CATEGORY-FORMATION

What of the Messiah? The Messiah figures at every point in the categorical structure of the Rabbinic canon's eschatological thinking: [1] troubles attendant upon the coming of the Messiah, which either do or do not bring about Israelite [2] repentance, as we have already seen, leading to [3] resurrection, as we shall see here, and a task then to be performed, [4] the world to come. But, important in two free-standing categories (resurrection, world to come) and a presence in the third (repentance), on its own account the Messiah theme simply does not coalesce into an autonomous category. That theme certainly does not define a categorical imperative in the way that Israel and the gentiles, complementarity and correspondence, and the eschatological categories, sin and atonement, resurrection and the world to come, all do. By contrast, to take a specific case, the gentiles and idolatry encompass a broad range of data, interact with other categories, form a focus of thought and a logical center; but they cannot then be reduced to some other categories, e.g., Israel and the Torah, private life, repentance. For its part the Messiah theme forms a subset of several categories and by itself does not take up an autonomous presence in the theology of the Rabbinic canon.

Does the Messiah bear responsibility for raising the dead? I do not identify that claim in so many words. And then, who bears responsibility for doing so? It is Israel, that point is made time and again when pertinent. Israel's own repentance will provide the occasion, and God will do the rest. It is when Israel has repented that the Messiah will come. It follows that the Messiah's advent and activity depend upon Israel, not on the Messiah's own autonomous decision, character, and behavior. Israel decides issues of its own attitude toward God and repents, God decides to respond to the change in will. But not being a comparable, categorical imperative, the Messiah only responds to Israel's decision on when he should make his appearance to signal the change in the condition of mankind, and the Messiah responds to God's decision, taking a part within that sequence that comes to an end with Elijah. The Messiah then plays a part in the resurrection of the dead, on the one side, and the restoration of Israel, on the other. But the Messiah doctrine clearly encompasses the view that the Messiah will not endure for the world to come but himself carries out the task assigned to him and then passes from the scene, a doctrine clearly indicated by the specification of the period of time assigned to the Messiah. How the Messiah figures in discussions of the age or world to come remains to be seen.

IV. RESTORING THE PUBLIC ORDER: THE WORLD TO COME

For us it is not easy to imagine a thought world in which patterns, rather than sequences of events treated as cause and effect, are asked to organize experience. Yet the theology of the Rabbinic canon sets forth a thought world in which at stake are not beginnings and endings in an ordinal or (other) temporal sense. At issue, rather, are balances and proportions, the match of this to that, start to finish, Eden and world to come. True, that mode of thought is not commonplace outside of the rule-seeking sciences of nature and society. These worlds of intellect do not tell the teleologically-framed story of a molecule or the history of a law of economics, but seek to formulate in abstract terms the concrete facts of molecules and enduring rules of economics that describe secular facts whatever the temporal context. But, I think it is now clear, that is precisely how sages think; they have in mind paradigms of relationship.

Specifically, when sages speak of the world to come, their language signifies a final change in relationship between God and man, a model of how God and man relate that marks the utter restoration of the world order originally contemplated. That is the way man and God conduct their cosmic transaction that God had intended from the beginning and for eternity—time having no place in his category-formation for ordering creation. The point, specifically, is that Israel enjoys a set of relationships with God that are not differentiated temporally and certainly not organized in causal patterns of sequence, in ordered, causative sequence through time, but in other ways.

How then are these relationships classified in this governing model? They are either rebellious or obedient, selfish and arrogant or selfless and humble, and so on, as we have seen at great length. Since at issue are patterns of relationship, the circumstance and context, whether temporal or singular in some other way, make no impact. That is because they make no difference, the relationship transcending circumstance. Therefore it is entirely reasonable that the world to come match the world that has been—why not? The one, like the other, will find its definition in how God and man relate. That is what I mean when I claim that we deal with modes of thought of an other-than-historical and temporal character. As I shall explain, that kind of thinking makes difficult the use of the word "eschatology" in reference to the world to come. The restorationist character of the theology of the Rabbinic canon explains what sages mean. That theology, by reason of the modes of thought that define its logic of making connections and drawing conclusions, requires that endings match beginnings, the relationships of God and man at the one point matching those at the other.

We should err if we invoked in this connection the word "cyclical" and supposed that sages contemplate a recurring cycle of existence, beginnings and endings and new beginnings, such as nature presents. Cyclical thinking is as alien to sages as historical thinking, because it presupposes an eternal return, an endless recapitulation of the pattern. But that is not what sages have in mind. They anticipate a one-time return, then an eternity of perfection. The perfection of world order leaves no alternative. Once man has repented and conformed his will to God's, that relationship, embodying measure for measure in a most just and merciful realization, attains perfection and, man's will and God's meeting, finality, complementarity, utter correspondence. That is why there is no room in the sages' system for an endless cycle of sin, punishment, atonement, reconciliation. I see, within the system, three embodiments: Adam loses Eden; Israel, the new Adam, loses the Land—two times; then Israel repents, the dead are raised, Israel is restored to the Land, and eternal life follows. In that model, with its stress on eternal life with God, no logical place opens up for the cyclical replay of the pattern. Paradigmatic thinking then finds its position between the historical-linear and ahistorical-cyclical kinds.

So here the story comes full circle that commences with God's creation of a perfect world defined by a just order. That world exhibits flaws, it is not perfect by reason of the character of man. But the world will be restored to perfection (requiring, then, eternity), man to Eden, Israel to the Land of Israel, through man's, and Israel's, act of repentance and reconciliation with God. That act of reconciliation, prepared for in countless lives of virtue and acts of merit, is realized in the world or age to come. Through its account of that world or age, therefore, that theology writes the last, but unending, chapter in the story of how God's justice establishes and ultimately restores the world order of perfection and equity.

The world to come concludes the eschatological series that is comprised by sequenced paradigms that cover [1] past, [2] present, [3] Israel's collective repentance, [4] the age (days) of the Messiah, [5] days of the war of Gog and Magog, [6] the resurrection of the dead, [7] the judgment, and onward to the last things at [8] the world to come. If resurrection concerns the individual Israelite, with some further implications for the whole of Israel, the world to come that follows encompasses all Israel. The one embodies salvation for the private person, the other redemption for the entire holy people, now at the end encompassing all of mankind within Israel. But what, exactly, when sages set forth their theological eschatology, do they mean by *'olam habba*, the world or the age that is coming? The world or the age to come (the Hebrew *'olam* may sustain either the locative, world, or the temporal-ordinal age) completes, and necessarily forms the final chapter, of the theology of the Rabbinic canon. The age that is coming will find Adam's successor in Eden's replacement, that is, resurrected, judged, and justified Israel—comprising nearly all Israelites who ever lived—now eternally rooted in the Land of Israel.

As we have seen, the governing theology sets forth its main components in a simple narrative, and very often, a single sentence captures the story. Here is such a version of the complete tale of the world to come in one short sentence: *When Israel returns to God, God will restore their fortunes*. The sentence remains brief enough with the added adjectival clause, *in the model of Adam and Eve in Eden*. Everything else amplifies details. That simple sentence is explicitly built on the verb-root for return, encompassing restore, *shub*, yielding *teshubah*, repentance as well as the causative form of the verb, *hashib*, thus return or restore. It thereby defines the condition, (intransitive) return or repentance, for the advent of the age to come, which encompasses the action, (transitively) to return matters to their original condition.

How, exactly, do sages envisage restoration? Predictably, because they think paradigmatically and not in historical (let alone cyclical) sequences, sages find models of the end in beginnings. That is why in this context they cluster, and systematically review, the two principal ones, liberation and restoration. First is the account of Israel's liberation from Egypt, the initial act of redemption, which will be recapitulated in the end. Second, as we have seen many times now, comes the story of Adam and Eden for their picture of the world to come, the return of Adam to Eden, now in the form of Israel to Zion. (A secondary motif in the latter paradigm contains the complementary category, Gehenna, to which gentiles—meaning, those who deny God—and Israelites who sufficiently sin are consigned when they are denied life.) In the latter case the important point for paradigmatic thinking is that there is no meaningful difference between the world to come and "the Garden of Eden." We go over, once more in so many words, an explicit statement that the two are not to be distinguished, here in a formulation that we shall more fully see again later in a different context.

Yerushalmi Pe'ah 1:1 XXXII.1

A. "He who performs mostly good deeds inherits the Garden of Eden, but he who performs mostly transgression inherits Gehenna."

Garden of Eden is the opposite of Gehenna, and the context explains the rest. Since Mishnah tractate Pe'ah at the outset speaks of the world to come, so inheriting the Garden of Eden in context bears precisely the meaning of inheriting the world to come; there is no difference, and the two, Eden and world to come, are interchangeable when sages speak of what happens after death, on the one side, or after resurrection and judgment, on the other. For man entering the world to come, on the other side of resurrection and judgment, marks a homecoming. At the moment of return to Eden, entry into the world to come, man returns to his original condition, in God's image, after God's likeness, complement and conclusion of creation. Here is the ultimate complementarity, the final point of correspondence.

Whatever model serves out of Scripture, that restorationist eschatology is stated in so many words in the following, which appeals to the rhetoric of return, restoration, and renewal.

Lamentations Rabbati CXLIII:I.1–4

A. "Restore us to yourself, O Lord, that we may be restored!:"
B. Said the Community of Israel before the Holy One, blessed be He, "Lord of the world, it all depends on you: 'Restore us to yourself, O Lord.'"
C. Said to them the Holy One, blessed be He, "It all depends on you: 'Return to me and I will return to you, says the Lord of hosts' (Mal. 3:7)."
D. Said the Community of Israel before the Holy One, blessed be He,

"Lord of the world, it all depends on you: 'Restore us, O God of our salvation' (Ps. 85:5)."

E. Thus it says, "Restore us to yourself, O Lord, that we may be restored!"

Israel insists that restoration depends on God, but God repays the compliment, and the exchange then is equal: God restores Israel when Israel returns to God, just as we learned when we examined the category of repentance and atonement.

Now we see a sequence of models of redemption. First, as anticipated, comes the explicit comparison of Adam's Eden with the coming restoration, part of a sequence of recapitulated paradigms.

2. A. "Renew our days as of old:"
   B. As in the days of the first Adam: "So he drove out the man and he placed at the east of the garden of Eden the cherubim" (Gen. 3:24). [The word for "east" and the word for "of old" using the same letters, the sense, is this: "Renew our days like those of him in connection with whom *kedem* is stated." After being driven out, Adam repented of his sin.]

The restoration involves the temple offerings as well, which later on are defined in particular; this is here too "as in the days of old":

3. A. Another interpretation of the phrase, "Renew our days as of old:"
   B. That is in line with this verse: "Then shall the offering of Judah and Jerusalem be pleasant to the Lord as in the days of old and as in ancient years" (Mal. 3:4).

But the restoration is multidimensional, since it involves also the figures of Moses and Solomon.

C. "as in the days of old": this refers to Moses: "Then his people remembered the days of old, the days of Moses" (Is. 63:11).
D. "and as in ancient years": this refers to the time of Solomon.

Noah and Abel, for reasons that are specified, now are introduced; they are necessary for the reason given at the end.

4. A. [Another interpretation of the phrase, "Renew our days as of old:"]
   B. Rabbi says, "'as in the days of old' refers to the time of Noah: 'For this is as the waters of Noah unto me' (Is. 54:9).
   C. "'and as in ancient years' refers to the time of Abel, prior to whose time there was no idolatry in the world."

Noah represents the moment at which God made his peace with man, even in man's flawed condition. Of intense interest for my analysis, within the restorationist pattern, Abel stands for the time before idolatry, so explicitly excluding idolators from the world to come. While Noah, representing all of humanity, and Abel, standing even for antediluvian humanity, make their appearance, the upshot remains exclusionary. The restoration to perfection involves the exclusion of imperfection, and so idolators cannot enter the new Eden. But, later on, we shall see other inclusionary dimensions that logically complete the doctrine of the gentiles in the world to come.

By "last things" sages' theology means the model of things that applies at the last, from now on, for eternity. By that, in the sages' case, they mean to say, *the last, the final realization or recapitulation of the ever-present and enduring paradigm(s)*, creation and exodus, for instance. That is, I cannot sufficiently stress, a paradigm organizes and classifies relationships, treats concrete events as merely exemplary. So the actualities of this one's conduct with, and attitude toward, that One are restated in generalizations, laws, or rules. "Love God" defines a relationship, and actions and attitudes that express that relationship then may be exemplified by incidents that show what happens when Israel loves God, or what happens when Israel does not love God. These further may be captured, many cases by a single pattern. In concrete terms that means intense interest will focus on the way in which the redemption of Israel from Egypt compares with the advent of the world to come. This point is made explicitly. The fall of the oppressor at the start of Israel's history and the fall of the nations at the end, character of the redemption of that time and of the coming time, will be matched by the fall of the other at the end and the traits of the redemption that is coming. To see how this is made concrete is to enter into the theological workshop of the sages.

Within the theory of paradigmatic thinking about the received facts of Scripture that is set forth here, a given paradigm should come to expression in a broad variety of exemplary cases (matched events, arrangements of symbols whether verbal or actual). In theory, therefore, once we fix upon a restorationist paradigm to account for the sages' classification of data and interpretation thereof, we should find more than a single case that embodies the paradigm. In fact, as we shall now see, a number of patterns is adduced to explain how the world to come will come about and to define its character. Our next case is a pattern that once more involves the liberation of Israel from Egypt, this time as the liberation is celebrated at the Passover Seder by the drinking of four cups of wine. These four cups drunk at the Passover Seder correspond to the redemption of Israel, four instances of the same pattern: the retribution carried out against Pharaoh, the retribution to be carried out against the Four Kingdoms, and the nations of the world generally, and the consolation of Israel; there is then a balance between Israel's and the nations' fate.

So much for the definition of the world to come in the other-than-temporal-historical terms that are required. The world to come marks the final condition of world order. It signifies the realization of correct and perfect relationships between God and man, God and Israel in particular. Those who reject God having been disposed of, we realize, the age to come finds its definition in the time of total reconciliation between God and man. It is the age when man loves God and accepts his dominion and completes the work of repentance and atonement for acts of rebellion. While, clearly, that reconciliation of God and man takes place in individual life, in which case, as already instantiated, we may use the language of salvation, it also governs the public life of Israel, in which case we may speak of redemption. That leads us to wonder what is at stake in the location of the theology's final chapter in what is clearly not a historical-eschatological setting but one that finds definition in intangibles of relationship: reconciliation, return, renewal, right attitude.

V. What Do the Sages Mean by "The World to Come"?

We reasonably ask, what indeed do sages have in mind when they speak of the world to come—concrete actualities, or intangible feelings and attitudes, impalpable matters of the spirit? May we suppose that we deal with a mere narration, in mythic form, of what in fact represents an inner, other-worldly, intangible and spiritual encounter? That is to say, if all that is at stake is abstract patterns of relationships that happen to come to expression in tales of the eschaton, one might suppose that the expression "the world to come" simply serves as another way of saying "man reconciled with God." Then, through paradigmatic thinking, sages should be represented as finding in the myth a vivid and palpable way of speaking of the inner life of intentionality and attitude. That is a possible reading of the character of the discourse at hand. But I think that that would drastically misrepresent the worldly reality, the concrete actuality, of the sages' account of matters, their intent to speak to the here and now—"today, if you will it"! We contemplate what is palpable and real in an ordinary, everyday sense, not what is intangible or merely "spiritual" in the vulgar sense.

First, while their Israel is the holy people, living in the plane of transcendence, their Israel truly lives in the trenchant world of marketplace and farm, and engages in the material and physical transactions of farming and love. Not a single line in the entire Rabbinic canon would sustain the reading of "Israel" as other than (in a different theology's language) "after the flesh." Sages found no cause to differentiate an "Israel after the spirit" from their "Israel after the flesh," since when they referred to Israel, they meant all those who know God as God made himself manifest, meaning, in the Torah, and at the end, that Israel, shorn of the handful of aliens (those who deny God, the resurrection of the dead, the resurrection of the dead as a fact set forth by God in the Torah, and so on), all together, in the flesh, sees God and enters eternal life.

Second, their Israel does constitute a political entity—this world's embodiment of the locus of God's rule—and as we have already noted, God's intervention at the very least will bring about a radical change in the politics of world order, Rome giving way to Israel. We have already found it possible to state the theology of intentionality that governs only by appeal to the theoretical politics that sages put forth as medium for their statement. Sages, like philosophers, were public intellectuals, undertaking the work of the community of holy Israel (sages) or the polis (philosophers). They thought about concrete, practical things, and at no point can we identify an area of the law or lore of the Rabbinic canon that has no bearing upon the everyday world of the here and now. That, indeed, is the very upshot of the point-by-point match of Halakhah and Aggadah, law and lore, that we have had occasion to review here and there.

Third, when they speak of the world to come, the sages mean a world that is public and shared, not private and inner-facing, and, as I have underscored many times, certainly not personal as distinct from public. It is not a world of relativities and relationships as these intangibles are concretely symbolized, but a world of real encounter. Sages know a palpable God who punishes arrogance and rewards humility, in both instances in worldly ways. Prayers are answered with rain or healing, virtue responded to with grace bearing material benefit, acts of generosity with miracles. Heaven intervenes in matters of health and sickness, in the abundance or scarcity of crops, in good fortune and ill. Sages insist upon an exact correspondence between practicalities and transcendent relationships.

Thinking paradigmatically, rather than historically, sages envisaged matters not temporally but through epochs divided by the indicative traits of Israel's relationship with God, as we noted at Yerushalmi tractate *Megillah* 2:1 I:2. There, we saw, "past" is marked by Israel's exodus from Egypt; "present" by God's mercy as a mark not of Israel's desserts but God's own love; the days of the Messiah as God's responding to Israel's supplication; the days of Gog and Magog as the embodiment of the verse, "[The Lord is God, and he has given us light.] Bind the festal offering with cords [up to the horns of the altar!]" (Ps. 118:27), and the age to come as the age of thanks to God for being God. The same matter is made still more explicit. Egypt, Sinai, Gog and Magog, and Messiah—locations, events, moments, persons—mark the four epiphanies of God to Israel.

Sifré Deuteronomy CCCXLIII:VII.1

A. "He appeared from Mount Paran [and approached from Ribeboth-kodesh, lightning flashing at them from his right, lover, indeed, of the people, their hallowed are all in your hand]":
B. There are four epiphanies.
C. The first was in Egypt: "Give ear, O Shepherd of Israel, you who leads Joseph like a flock, you who are enthroned on the cherubim, shine forth" (Ps. 80:2).
D. The second at the time of the giving of the Torah: "he shone upon them from Seir."
E. The third in the days of Gog and Magog: "O Lord, you God to whom vengeance belongs, you God to whom vengeance belongs, shine forth" (Ps. 94:1).
F. And the fourth in the days of the Messiah: "Out of Zion the perfection of beauty, God has shown forth" (Ps. 50:2).

The list of these native categories on its own suffices to register the intent, which is to identify, compare, and contrast, the epiphanies.

Just as God was at Egypt and Sinai with Israel, so God will be at the eschatological war and at the climactic moment of the Messiah as well. And, it goes without saying, in the age or world to come, the final epiphany will find God and Israel at one, as we shall see, celebrating the beneficence of God, studying the Torah, enjoying dance and song and feasting, for all eternity. Thinking paradigmatically, these "events" represent relationships with God. Israel in the here and now and Israel at the age to come differ only in relationship with God.

The Messiah, whose advent marks the period before the resurrection of individuals, takes on a public task in the age to come, one already adumbrated. It is the reunion of Israel with the Land of Israel, such as brings about the resurrection of the dead, but now with attention to living Israel when the age to come dawns. For the task of the king-messiah is to gather the exiles and restore Israel to the Land of Israel. That is why the Messiah has an important task to perform not only in his own age, in raising the dead, but in the last age as well, though so far as I can discern, beyond that one action of restoring the exiles to the holy land, the Messiah plays no consequential part in the life of the age to come

Genesis Rabbah XCVIII:IX.2

2. A. Said R. Hanin, "Israel does not require the learning of the king-messiah in the age to come, as it is said, 'Unto him shall the nations seek' (Is. 11:1)—but not Israel.
   B. "If so, why will the king-messiah come? And what will he come to do? It is to gather together the exiles of Israel and to give them thirty religious duties: 'And I said to them, If you think good, give me my hire, and if not, forbear. So they weighed for my hire thirty-pieces of silver' (Zech. 11:12)."

The same point, that when the Messiah comes he will gather the exiles back to the land, occurs at *Song of Songs Rabbah* LII:ii.1ff.: "Said R. Hunia in the name of R. Justus, 'When the exiles returning to Zion when the Messiah brings them back reach Taurus Munus, they are going to say a Song.'"

This brings us to the actualities of the world to come, what people are supposed to be doing then. What is going to happen in the age to come? Israel will eat and drink, sing and dance, and enjoy God, who will be lord of the dance. What about the restored temple? The war of Gog and Magog having concluded, the dead having been returned to the Land and raised, the next stage in the restoration of world order requires the reconstruction of the temple, where, as we recall, God and man, Heaven and earth, meet.

Genesis Rabbah XCVIII:II.7

A. "Then Jacob called his sons and said, 'Gather yourselves together, that I may tell you what shall befall you in days to come":

B. R. Simon said, "He showed them the fall of Gog, in line with this usage: 'It shall be in the end of days . . . when I shall be sanctified through you, O Gog' (Ez. 38:165). 'Behold, it shall come upon Edom' (Is. 34:5)."

C. R. Judah said, "He showed them the building of the house of the sanctuary: 'And it shall come to pass in the end of days that the mountain of the Lord's house shall be established' (Is. 2:2)."

D. Rabbis say, "He came to reveal the time of the end to them, but it was hidden from him."

So in the now-familiar sequence of restoration, [1] final war, [2] advent of the Messiah and the resurrection and judgment, and [3] the age to come, next in sequence must be [4] the restoration of Israel to the Land, and [5] rebuilding the temple, destroyed by reason of Israel's sin.

The theology of the Rabbinic canon accordingly reaches its climactic statement as it turns from the transcendent situation of Israel in the age to come to Israel at this time, and there finds grounds for sublime hope. The theology contains the promise that, while now Israel grieves, in the end of days God will give them grounds for rejoicing, and that will be in a measure commensurate to the loyalty and patience shown in the interim. How do we know, and how long? The perfect justice of the one God comes to realization in the promises that have been kept, surety and guarantee of the promises that will be kept. A homely story captures the promise.

Tosefta Kippurim 2:7

A. Said R. 'Aqiba, "Simeon b. Luga told me, 'A certain child of the sons of their sons and I were gathering grass in the field. Then I saw him laugh and cry.

B. "'I said to him, 'Why did you cry?

C. "'He said to me, "Because of the glory of father's house, which has gone into exile.'"

D. "'I said to him, "Then why did you laugh?"

E. "'He said, "At the end of it all, in time to come, the Holy One, blessed be He, is going to make his descendants rejoice."'"

The exile guarantees the return, one promise kept, another is sure to be carried out. Now the story winds its way onward.

F. "'I said to him, "Why?" [What did you see to make you think of this?]

G. "'He said to me, "A smoke-raiser in front of me [made me laugh]."

H. "'I said to him, "Show it to me."'"

I. "'He said to me, "We are subject to an oath not to show it to anyone at all."'"

J. Said R. Yohanan b. Nuri, "One time I was going along the way and an old man came across me and said to me, 'I am a member of the house of Abtinas.

K. "'At the beginning, when the house of father was discreet, they would give their scrolls [containing the prescriptions for frankincense only] to one another.

L. "'Now take it, but be careful about it, since it is a scroll containing a recipe for spices.'

M. "And when I came and reported the matter before R. 'Aqiba, he said to me, 'From now on it is forbidden to speak ill of these people again.'"

N. On the basis of this story, Ben 'Azzai said, "Yours will they give you,

O. "by your own name will they call you,

P. "in your own place will they seat you.

Q. "There is no forgetfulness before the Omnipresent.

R. "No man can touch what is designated for his fellow."

Israel finds itself subjugated to the gentiles in a world flawed by the prosperity of the wicked and the suffering of the righteous. So it is a time of mourning—but one of remembrance of the future, which the past promises out of the pathos of the present. Given the condition of the world and of Israel in it, it is right to mourn—beginning after all with mourning for Israel's own failures. But those who mourn properly now will rejoice in time to come, the one serving as an act of faith for what is to be. Whoever mourns for Jerusalem now will merit rejoicing with her in the world to come.

What makes sages so sure of themselves? To them, what gives Israel hope even now is that the prophetic warnings about punishment for sin have come true, so the prophetic consolation about God's response to Israel's repentance also will come true. That is, for them, a natural result of a theology that finds perfection in balance, order, proportion, above all complementarity. Just as the prophets warned that Israel would be punished for its rebellion against God, so they insisted that Israel would attain reconciliation through its repentance to God. Now that the first of the two elements of the equation, punishment for arrogant sin, has been realized, sages find solid grounds for certainty in the ultimate fulfillment also of the promise of reconciliation in consequence of repentance in humility. The condition of the world today, sages held, contains within itself not only the past and its consequence but, as a matter of certainty, also the future and its consolation. All are present in the here and now, as the Rabbinic canon says, "Today, if you want."

It is appropriate that this account of the theology of the Rabbinic Aggadic documents should conclude with the sages' voice.

Lamentations Rabbati CXL:i.1–2

1. A. "for Mount Zion which lies desolate; jackals prowl over it":
   B. Rabban Gamaliel, R. Joshua, R. Eleazar b. Azariah, and R. Aqiba went to Rome. They heard the din of the city of Rome from a distance of a hundred and twenty miles.
   C. They all begin to cry, but R. Aqiba began to laugh.
   D. They said to him, "Aqiba, we are crying and you laugh?"
   E. He said to them, "Why are you crying?"
   F. They said to him, "Should we not cry, that idolators and those who sacrifice to idols and bow down to images live securely and prosperously, while the footstool of our God has been burned down by fire and become a dwelling place for the beasts of the field? So shouldn't we cry?"
   G. He said to them, "That is precisely the reason that I was laughing. For if those who outrage him he treats in such a way, those who do his will all the more so!"
2. A. There was the further case of when they were going up to Jerusalem. When they came to the Mount of Olives they tore their clothing. When they came to the Temple mount and a fox came out of the house of the Holy of Holies, they began to cry. But R. Aqiba began to laugh.
   B. "Aqiba, you are always surprising us. Now we are crying and you laugh?"
   C. He said to them, "Why are you crying?"
   D. They said to him, "Should we not cry, that from the place of which it is written, 'And the ordinary person that comes near shall be put to death' (Num. 1:51) a fox comes out? So the verse of Scripture is carried out: 'for Mount Zion which lies desolate; jackals prowl over it.'"

E. He said to them, "That is precisely the reason that I was laughing. For Scripture says, 'And I will take for myself faithful witnesses to record, Uriah the priest and Zechariah the son of Jeberechiah' (Is. 8:2).

F. "Now what is the relationship between Uriah and Zechariah? Uriah lived in the time of the first temple, Zechariah in the time of the second!

G. "But Uriah said, 'Thus says the Lord of hosts: Zion shall be plowed as a field, and Jerusalem shall become heaps' (Jer. 26:18).

H. "And Zechariah said, 'There shall yet be old men and old women sitting in the piazzas of Jerusalem, every man with his staff in his hand for old age' (Zech. 8:4).

I. "And further: 'And the piazzas of the city shall be full of boys and girls playing in the piazzas thereof' (Zech. 8:5).

J. "Said the Holy One, blessed be He, 'Now lo, I have these two witnesses. So if the words of Uriah are carried out, the words of Zechariah will be carried out, while if the words of Uriah prove false, then the words of Zechariah will not be true either.'

K. "I was laughing with pleasure because the words of Uriah have been carried out, and that means that the words of Zechariah in the future will be carried out."

L. They said to him, "Aqiba, you have given us consolation. May you be comforted among those who are comforted."

And that is exactly what the sages intended, to console and hearten Israel, for God's sake. That has remained the task of sages in age succeeding age. Bearing this compelling theology of one just God to account for all things, through the ages the sages have sustained Israel with a sufficiency of reasoned hope.

PART THREE

THE THEOLOGICAL STRUCTURE
OF RABBINIC JUDAISM: NORMS OF BEHAVIOR
IN THE ISRAELITE SOCIAL ORDER

CHAPTER TEN

PROLEGOMENON TO THE THEOLOGICAL
STRUCTURE OF RABBINIC JUDAISM REALIZED
IN THE HALAKHAH

> I will dwell among the people of Israel and will be their God. And they
> shall know that I am the Lord their God who brought them forth out
> of the land of Egypt that I might dwell among them; I am the Lord
> their God.

Exodus 29:38–46

To summarize the burden of this part of the Handbook in a few
words, let me specify the three points that I aim in Part Three to
establish as the theology of the Halakhah.

[1] As recapitulated by the Halakhah, Scripture's account of Eden
portrays not an event but a condition. "Eden" stands for man and
God dwelling together.

[2] Restoring that condition, the Halakhah sets forth the norms for
a society formed by Israel in the Land that is worthy of God's presence in this Eden.

[3] The Halakhah systematizes the laws of the sanctification of the
social order that God himself has revealed to Israel at Sinai in the
Torah, and theology states the result of reading those laws—that religion's story—philosophically.

These three statements capture what is at stake in the theology of
the Halakhah. They together answer the question, What exactly does
the Halakhah set forth to realize the conviction that if one follows its
many carefully-crafted regulations for the many dimensions of life,
God will dwell among Israel? Here, in quest of the modes of realizing the divine imperative, we take up the specificities of the law:
how working backward from details to that which the details actualize, the theology that animates the Halakhah is to be discerned and
characterized.

I. Adam and Israel, Eden and the Land

The theology of the Halakhah records the result of the Rabbinic
sages' systematic, generalizing, universalizing reading of the narratives, exhortations, and laws of Scripture. From their comprehensive
definition of those results in the form of practical norms for the construction of holy Israel's social order we derive this account of the
theological structure and system embodied therein. That structure of
category-formations of the normative law set forth in Scripture as
realized by the Mishnah, Tosefta, and two Talmuds, begins here. It
aims at the restoration of man to Eden through Israel in the Land.
In line with the Torah's narrative, Israel represents the new Adam,
God's way of correcting what went wrong in the initial creation.
The Land of Israel stands for the new Eden. Just as Adam entered a
perfect world but lost it, so Israel was given a perfect world—in
repose at the moment of Israel's entry—but, sinning against God, lost
it. The story told from Joshua through Kings matches the story told
in Genesis. Here is how the Rabbinic sages express the comprehensive structure of their narrative for the corresponding stories of Adam,
representing humanity, and Israel:

Genesis Rabbah XIX:IX.2

> R. Abbahu in the name of R. Yosé bar Haninah: "It is written, 'But
> they [Israel] are like a Man [Adam], they have transgressed the
> covenant' (Hos. 6:7).
> "'They are like a Man,' specifically, like the first Man.
> "'In the case of the first Man, I brought him into the garden of
> Eden, I commanded him, he violated my commandment, I judged
> him to be sent away and driven out, but I mourned for him, saying
> "How . . ."' [which begins the book of Lamentations, hence stands for
> a lament, but which, as we just saw, also is written with the consonants
> that also yield 'Where are you'].
> "'I brought him into the garden of Eden,' as it is written, 'And the
> Lord God took the Man and put him into the garden of Eden' (Gen.
> 2:15).
> "'I commanded him,' as it is written, 'And the Lord God com-
> manded . . .' (Gen. 2:16).
> "'And he violated my commandment,' as it is written, 'Did you eat
> from the tree concerning which I commanded you' (Gen. 3:11).
> "'I judged him to be sent away,' as it is written, 'And the Lord God
> sent him from the garden of Eden' (Gen. 3:23).

"'And I judged him to be driven out.' 'And he drove out the Man' (Gen. 3:24).

"'But I mourned for him, saying, "How . . .".' 'And he said to him, "Where are you"' (Gen. 3:9), and the word for 'where are you' is written, 'How. . . .'

"'So too in the case of his descendants, [God continues to speak,] I brought them into the Land of Israel, I commanded them, they violated my commandment, I judged them to be sent out and driven away but I mourned for them, saying, "How. . . ."'

"'I brought them into the Land of Israel.' 'And I brought you into the land of Carmel' (Jer. 2:7).

"'I commanded them.' 'And you, command the children of Israel' (Ex. 27:20). 'Command the children of Israel' (Lev. 24:2).

"'They violated my commandment.' 'And all Israel have violated your Torah' (Dan. 9:11).

"'I judged them to be sent out.' 'Send them away, out of my sight and let them go forth' (Jer. 15:1).

"'. . . and driven away.' 'From my house I shall drive them' (Hos. 9:15).

"'But I mourned for them, saying, "How. . . ."' 'How has the city sat solitary, that was full of people' (Lam. 1:1)."

I cannot imagine a more explicit statement of a massive theological construction than this detailed comparison of Israel and Adam in time and eternity. Its explicit comparison of the loss of Eden to the loss of the Land, its treatment of Israel as counterpart to Adam— these form the foundations of the system and structure of Rabbinic theology, to which all else forms a commentary and amplification. The key, then, is Israel's repentance, made possible by God's grace: "I mourned for them."

What is the difference between Adam and Israel? Israel has what Adam did not have, which is the Torah, a point that does not enter here except indirectly. The Torah's theory of who is man and what God wants of man leaves no unclarity. What God craves is man's willing accord with God's will, made known in the Torah, beginning with the drama, for which the Halakhah legislates, of the proclamation of God's unity and yearning for man's love, freely given: *Hear, Israel, the Lord is our God, the Lord is unique. And you shall love the Lord your God with all your heart, with all your soul, and with all your might.*

That is why it follows, through realizing the law of the Torah, that Israel regains Eden. This it will do in the Land that God had given it for its Eden but that had been lost to sin. And the Torah, setting forth the Halakhah, the rules for the social order of restored Eden, would reform Israel, even sinful Israel, ever so capable of rebellion against God's will just as Adam had been. Then Israel, a worthy occupant of the Eden that the Land was meant to be, had been for a brief moment, and would once again become, would rise from the grave to eternal life. That would take place in the Land that is Eden. Divine justice would be fully realized. For death had come about through sin, but at the end, standing in judgment, those who acknowledge God and the Torah overcome sin, which is rebellion. What next? Risen from the dead, having atoned through death, man will be judged in accord with his deeds. Israel for its part, when it repents and conforms its will to God's, recovers its Eden.

So, the consequences of rebellion and sin having been overcome, the struggle of man's will and God's word having been resolved, God's original plan for creation will be realized at the last. The Halakhah, viewed from its minute details to the construction of the whole, by its category-formations read in logical sequence, tells this story. That is what I shall show in detail in this third and final part of my account of Rabbinic theology.

II. THE HALAKHIC REALIZATION, IN ISRAEL'S SOCIAL ORDER, OF THE MYTHIC MONOTHEISM OF SCRIPTURE

How Israel is like Adam, man, spelled out by the exposition of Abbahu in the name of Yosé bar Haninah, captures the heart of the Halakhic structure of category-formations. That is because, as we shall see in Chapter Eleven, the themes of creation and Eden with the climax on the first Sabbath, play themselves out in concrete, detailed norms of conduct. These actualize for everyday life moments in the drama portrayed by Scripture. So the theology of the Halakhah begins in the sages' exposition of the parallel stories of man (Adam and Eve) and Israel. God created man "in our image, after our likeness." Failing to accomplish his purpose through Adam and Eve, God tried again with Israel, only to be disappointed once more. The stories for a time run parallel: Adam and Eve, exercising their free will to rebel and so losing Eden, form the pattern recapitulated by Israel's gaining the Eden that the Land was meant to be, only through sin to lose the Land.

The Halakhic theology makes provision for the restoration. That, spelled out in Chapter Twelve, comes about in Israel's public life and civil order, in the here and now of Eden, by the will and act of repentant, regenerate man. In line with Scripture's plain message, the Halakhah, specifically, explores the requirements of the restoration within the social formation of Israel in the Land of Israel. Accordingly, there is this difference. Educated by the Torah to exercise freedom of will to accord with God's will, repentant, regenerate Israel may regain Eden. That is both now, temporally, on sacred occasions, and also in the end of days.

But the struggle between life and death, begun with man's exile and the advent of death, goes on, as Chapter Thirteen explains, from now to the end of days. It is embodied in the material forces of pollution marshaled by death, opposed by the Israelite in a constant state of alertness to contamination round about. Israel struggles for purity and against death. In the end, then, those who know God as self-manifest in the Torah, in its entirety (encompassing the oral and written parts), will rise from the grave and triumph over death, stand in judgment, and regain eternal life in Eden (Chapter Fourteen, Choosing Life in the Kingdom of God). Israel then is that portion of humanity destined for eternal life by reason of its realization, within its social order in the here and now, of the Torah, wherein God is made known, his will made concrete for humanity. And the Halakhah, both in the Land and beyond its limits, guides Israel's encounter with God, both in the present hour and in the age to come.

The Halakhah, accordingly, takes up the story of the perfection of Eden (Chapter Eleven, in my exposition of the theology therein), then addresses the situation implicit in that story of man's disobedience (Chapter Twelve), and finally takes up the theme of the here-and-now embodiment of God's kingdom, the encompassing theological motif embodied in that story (Chapters Thirteen and Fourteen). Embedded in the norms of public conduct, then, the theology embodied by the Halakhah portrays Scripture's account of the meaning of man in the meeting with God, what I call mythic monotheism. Thinking philosophically about religion, focusing upon the data set forth by the stories that Scripture tells, the rules that it sets forth, and the exhortations that bear its message, the Rabbinic sages produced theology in an unconventional idiom. That is because the theology is expressed and realized in norms of behavior that actualize norms of belief. It is our task to work back from behavior to belief, but in a systematic and comprehensive framework.

The Halakhah then is comprised by not just random rules but a wholly coherent system and structure embodied in concrete, detailed rules. That system, as we have now seen in Part Two, recapitulates Scripture. So too, the Halakhic structure of actualized category-formations perfectly realizes, in the norms of Israel's social order, Scripture's full truth about the human condition.

III. The Halakhah in Theological Context: Judaism's Theological Anthropology

The Halakhah, accordingly, weaves in the intangible threads of daily deeds a tapestry, a portrait of what it means to be man in God's image, after God's likeness. Seen from this perspective, in theological context the Halakhah takes its place alongside the great exercises of reflection, both remorseful and hopeful, in western civilization, upon the Torah's account of who, and what, is man. Like the Apostle Paul's masterpiece, his Letter to the Romans, with its tragic vision (". . . as sin came into the world through one man and death through sin . . .," reminiscent of Fourth Ezra's "Oh Adam, what hast thou done!"), like Augustine's *City of God*, like Michelangelo's *Last Judgment* in the Sistine Chapel, and like John Milton's *Paradise Lost*—to name just four counterparts to the Halakhic meditation on the story of man that begins in Eden—the Halakhah addresses the central problem of western civilization as defined by the Torah. To all the heirs of Scripture Genesis records the nature and destiny of man and sets the issues for reflection. But among all scripturally-founded constructions out of the vision of man's tragedy the Oral Torah's stands quite by itself. That is because the Halakhah provides for the formation of an entire society in the image, after the likeness, of Scripture's account of how matters are supposed to be. Augustine and Milton wrote, Michelangelo painted, but the Rabbinic sages undertook to create in a unique medium: the conduct of man's life, the construction of the order of man in society.

That response to Eden and its aftermath is unique in context, because of the Halakhah's immediacy and practicality. The Halakhah embodies the unique mode of thought conducted by the great sages of Judaism in its formative age, its concreteness, its insistence upon deed as the medium of deliberation. The Judaic sages thought deeply but valued thought only by reason of its practical power to change man: "study of the Torah takes priority, because study leads to concrete deed," they decided. That is why the Halakhah—much of it a matter of theory at the time at which it was given the canonical formulation we now have—forms an account of how the very social fabric of man embodied by Israel may be formed of a tapestry of right deeds to yield Eden within the very material of the ordinary. The Halakhah endows the ordinary life of everyday Israel with cosmic consequences.

For sages deliberation alone did not suffice, though, as we shall see, their account of deeds to be done in the quest for human regeneration rests upon deep layers of profound reflection, indeed upon the Scriptural account of man in God's image, but sinful by reason of his free will to love or to rebel. Like Plato, in the *Republic*, the sages conducted their thought through legislating the design of Israel's social order. Unlike Plato, they actively aimed to realize in everyday affairs the principles of their utopian theory of matters. Augustine told the story of the social order through history, Scripture's history. For their part the Judaic sages wrote their *City of God* in the Halakhah's details, certain that those formed of the parts would intuit the whole. When the Rabbinic sages contemplated issues strikingly congruent to those addressed in the salvific program of Paul in Romans, it was through not theoretical theological reflections but practical rulings on the construction of the holy society that they conducted their inquiry into the logic of man's fate and what is required for his redemption. And, in the nature of their writings, sages produced few word-pictures, though their Halakhic writings adhered to remarkably powerful aesthetics, both in form and in intellectual elegance.

Note the contrast. God addressed the social order of a kingdom priests and a holy people and commanded the plural "you": "You shall be holy, for I the Lord your God am holy," so calling for Israel's formation of a society worthy of serving as God's place on earth. The great theologians of Christianity, Paul and Augustine, produced profound reflection upon precisely the same story of man. The counterpart artists, Michelangelo and Milton, conveyed the fall through art and poetry, through eye and ear and intellect responding to the tragic moment of Eden and its aftermath. But none in the line of Israelite

Scripture but the Judaic sages conceived of responding to the generalities of the human condition by defining as the remedy to that condition the particular character of an entire social order, its norms of
conviction and conduct, its culture embodied in rules of behavior and
belief. In their mind, the very character of the community as constructed by concrete laws would form a commentary upon man and
the loss of Eden—a response to Eden but also a remedy for the rebellion that reduced man to his and her present estrangement from God.

Had they wished to argue that the salvation of man from the condition of the sin that brought about the fall would come about
through law—the laws of the Torah in particular—they could not
have framed a more compelling, and, in their context, a more eloquent statement than they did through the logic and exegesis of the
Halakhah. My governing thesis, briefly summarized, is that the sages
of the Halakhic, or legal, system for the practical conduct of holy
Israel's social order in the Mishnah and Talmuds defined as the remedy for the human condition revealed first at Eden the practicalities
of quotidian life of an entire community. In accepting God's rule
Israel would embody the City of God, for mankind the Israelite sector would accomplish corporately what for Paul's Christianity one
man is supposed to have done. In the Torah, as they portrayed the
Torah, the system of norms of behavior meant to realize within the
social order the norms of belief set forth by the sages of Judaism
responded to the tragedy of the fall—the starting point of the entire
system—and the promise of restoration—the climax of its structure.
This they did by defining the labor of social renewal, relating the
rules of regeneration in the exact sense.

That theology holds together the details of the rules of concrete
behavior and frames of them a systematic statement. The formation
of the entire social order through legal norms to regain paradise represents the unique genius of the Rabbinic sages. Their vision of the
social order responding to God's imperative in the Torah forms the
counterpart to the exercises introduced just now—Paul, Augustine,
Michelangelo, and Milton. That observation vastly transcends generalities and rises to the specificities of ordinary affairs. Paul's insistence
upon the inadequacy of the law to deal with the condition of man's
sinfulness finds its answer here. For it was through the Halakhah that
the sages chose to show that, in the very context of the crisis of man's
fall, the Torah would bring about in the here and now of everyday

life that very regeneration that, in Paul's system, faith was meant to accomplish.

In light of the workaday world for which sages legislated, moreover, it was as if they had read the *City of God* and undertook to show the Bishop of Hippo how to accomplish in the visible and tangible world the realization of the promise of citizenship in an unseen city. And, were they to have spread forth before the poet the artful language that conveys the Halakhah in the Mishnah, they might have said to him, "Here, here is paradise recovered, these are its natural sounds, the Mishnah to be memorized like your poem" and to the artist, "Paint this—this picture of the world in repose, of man regenerate, of Eden restored; Paint what Balaam found himself impelled to see: 'For from the top of the mountain I see him, from the hills I behold him; lo, a people dwelling alone (Num. 23:9).'" Paul, Augustine, Michelangelo, Milton worked in solitary splendor to frame a vision. Only the sages of Judaism undertook to render palpable and tangible man's hope for his restoration in Eden in God's dominion. That is why, in my Halakhic portrait, we start with Eden and end in Israel in the village, aspiring to live in God's kingdom.

IV. The Topical Sequence of the Halakhic Re-presentation

The Halakhah sets forth what is to be done about man, by man, with the guidance of the Torah. To be sure, the Halakhah has rarely found itself represented as cogent to begin with—let alone as a surpassing vision of mankind in God's image, with a story to tell. But there is a reason that the parts have won detailed analysis, the whole has been lost sight of. The canonical documents themselves form the cause; their power, the capacity to translate theological anthropology into the details of the social order, defines their pathos, the stress on details. The Halakhah's natural disciplines of intellect favor atomistic exegesis, on the one hand, and episodic comparison and contrast, on the other. Generalizations are rare and always challenged. Only a few masters of the Halakhah, at widely separated times and places, undertook to portray matters whole and in a coherent way, and not all of these were up to the task; banality, sentimentality, and incomprehension always competed with the outcome of astute reflection. Not only so, but when the Halakhah has been set forth within a theory of cogency and coherence in detail, the character of the Halakhic theology has ordinarily been portrayed episodically, through cases and examples of we know not what. It has rarely been *systematically* represented, as I here undertake to do, in a cogent and continuous, coherent account. That intent explains the importance of the framework of the principal narrative of Scripture, the story that sages deem explicitly set forth from Genesis through Kings in two parts, as is now abundantly clear:

[1] the creation of mankind to enjoy bliss in Eden, in perfect repose, then his and her rebellion and loss of Eden; and

[2] the creation of Israel to enjoy the Land, then Israel's rebellion and loss of the Land.

I allege that that is the intent of Scripture and of sages alike, and the validity of the Halakhic structure of category-formations that I portray depends on whether readers concur in my reading of the story that Scripture tells as the tale that the Halakhah means to embody in the actions of Israel's social order.

What about the topical sequence of my exposition, in Chapters Eleven through Fourteen? In the Halakhah I discern the logic of [1] loss and restoration (Chapter Eleven), [2] sin and atonement (Chapter Twelve), then [3] death and life, embodied in uncleanness and purification, standing for judgment and return and ultimate resurrection of all Israel, followed here (Chapters Thirteen and Fourteen). That narrative, from beginning to end, precipitated by the tension of the beginning, moving toward resolution at the end, dictates the order of the presentation and the reading of the details. Here, I maintain, we see that the Torah's own hermeneutics—set forth in the narrative order from Genesis through Kings—turns out to guide the reading of the Halakhic component of the Torah as well. Step by step, followed within the necessary logic of that story, the chapters of the Halakhah unfold within the logic portrayed in this book, in inexorable sequence, to show how Israel restores the Land to its perfection, Israel to its perfect repose. But that is with the recognition that Israel, like man, sins by reason of rebellion, setting its will against God's. Then the Halakhah provides for the character of Israel and makes possible that atonement that reconciles Israel to God. So the theology of the Halakhah addresses the human condition, to which rebellion and willfulness come by nature.

How do I propose to demonstrate these claims of the Halakhah's systemic cogency and systematic character? It is through a reading of the principal components of the Halakhic structure, with constant attention to details. Everyone understands that the Halakhic documents portray the results of applied reason and practical logic. Then I propose to recover that reason and to recapitulate, retrace the steps of, that logic. The Halakhah comes to us in a set of native categories that organize these details and form of them coherent units. We follow the native categories, which correspond to the topical (often propositional) tractates that uniformly organize and so comprise the Mishnah, the Tosefta, the Talmud of the Land of Israel (Yerushalmi), and the Talmud of Babylonia (Bavli). All that I have done is set the native categories into a certain order and ask them a few questions of a religious character.

V. The Halakhic Canon and its Category-Formations

Besides the instructions concerning normative behavior set forth by the Torah, particularly the Pentateuch in Exodus, Leviticus, Numbers, and Deuteronomy, we find the Halakhah, in its initial statement, set forth in the Mishnah (closed ca. 200 C.E.), in the Tosefta (ca. 300 C.E.), the Yerushalmi (ca. 400 C.E.), or the Bavli (ca. 600 C.E.). The four Halakhic documents of late antiquity, the first a philosophical law code, the next an amplification and complement as well as a supplement thereto, and two commentaries to the law, organized in response to the code and supplement, all together form the statement. Specifically, they portray the Torah's norms of behavior, realizing the norms of belief. As to the category-formations that transform data into constructions of meaning, for the latter three of them the Mishnah defines the native category-formations, carried forward, selectively, by each.

The theological claim already set forth dictates how we proceed. We shall, therefore, have to engage with the native category-formations of the Mishnah-Tosefta-Yerushalmi-Bavli in the setting of the tripartite system formed of concentric circles of interiorities, that is, a

320 CHAPTER TEN

set of topical category-formations defined by [1] the relationships of God and Israel, or [2] Israel's transactions in the social order, or [3] the Israelite household's inner reconstruction in time, space, and circumstance.

We have now briefly to examine the topical program of the Mishnah, which is to say, the Mishnah-Tosefta-Yerushalmi-Bavli's native category-formations. The Mishnah's six thematic divisions encompass sixty-two tractates, of which sixty-one form topical expositions. The principal divisions and topical subdivisions are as follows:

1. AGRICULTURE (*Zeraʿim*): *Berakhot* (blessings); *Peʾah* (the corner of the field); *Demaʿi* (doubtfully tithed produce); *Kilayim* (mixed seeds); *Shebiʿit* (the seventh year); *Terumot* (heave offering or priestly rations); *Maʿaserot* (tithes); *Maʿaser Sheni* (second tithe); *Hallah* (dough offering); *ʿOrlah* (produce of trees in the first three years after planting, which is prohibited); and *Bikkurim* (first fruits).

2. APPOINTED TIMES (*Moʿed*): *Shabbat* (the Sabbath); *ʿErubin* (the fictive fusion meal or boundary); *Pesahim* (Passover); *Sheqalim* (the temple tax); *Yoma* (the Day of Atonement); *Sukkah* (the festival of Tabernacles); *Besah* (the preparation of food on the festivals and Sabbath); *Rosh Hashanah* (the New Year); *Taʿanit* (fast days); *Megillah* (Purim); *Moʿed Qatan* (the intermediate days of the festivals of Passover and Tabernacles); *Hagigah* (the festal offering).

3. WOMEN (*Nashim*): *Yebamot* (the levirate widow); *Ketubot* (the marriage contract); *Nedarim* (vows); *Nazir* (the special vow of the Nazirite); *Sotah* (the wife accused of adultery); *Gittin* (writs of divorce); *Qiddushin* (betrothal).

4. DAMAGES or civil law (*Neziqin*): *Baba Qamma, Baba Mesiʿa, Baba Batra* (civil law, covering damages and torts, then correct conduct of business, labor, and real estate transactions); *Sanhedrin* (institutions of government; criminal penalties); *Makkot* (flogging); *Shebuot* (oaths); *ʿEduyyot* (a collection arranged on other than topical lines); *Horayot* (rules governing improper conduct of civil authorities).

5. HOLY THINGS (*Qodoshim*): *Zebahim* (everyday animal offerings); *Menahot* (meal offerings); *Hullin* (animals slaughtered for secular purposes); *Bekhorot* (firstlings); *ʿArakhin* (vows of valuation); *Temurah* (vows of exchange of a beast for an already consecrated beast); *Keritot* (penalty of extirpation or premature death); *Meʿilah* (sacrilege).

6. PURITY (*Tohorot*): *Kelim* (susceptibility of utensils to uncleanness); *Ohalot* (transmission of corpse-uncleanness in the tent of a corpse);

Nega'im (the uncleanness described at Lev. 13–14); *Parah* (the preparation of purification water); *Tohorot* (problems of doubt in connection with matters of cleanness); *Miqvaot* (immersion-pools); *Niddah* (menstrual uncleanness); *Makhshirin* (rendering susceptible to uncleanness produce that is dry and so not susceptible); *Zabim* (the uncleanness covered at Lev. 15); Tebul Yom (the uncleanness of one who has immersed on that self-same day and awaits sunset for completion of the purification rites); *Yadayim* (the uncleanness of hands); *'Uqsin* (the uncleanness transmitted through what is connected to unclean produce).

Now to examine the program of the several category-formations. How do the tractates, as native-categories, coalesce into divisions and cohere in large ways?

The Division of AGRICULTURE treats two topics, first, producing crops in accord with the scriptural rules on the subject, second, paying the required offerings and tithes to the priests, Levites, and poor. The principal point of the division is that the Land is holy, because God has a claim both on it and upon what it produces. God's claim must be honored by setting aside a portion of the produce for those for whom God has designated it. God's ownership must be acknowledged by observing the rules God has laid down for use of the Land. In the temporal context in which the Mishnah was produced, some generations after the disastrous defeat by the Romans of Bar Kokhba and the permanent closure of Jerusalem to Jews, the stress of the division brought assurance that those aspects of the sanctification of Israel—Land of Israel, Israel itself and its social order, the holy cycle of time—that survived also remained holy and subject to the rules of Heaven.

The Division of APPOINTED TIMES carried forward the same emphasis upon sanctification, now of the high points of the lunar-solar calendar of Israel. The second division forms a system in which the advent of a holy day, like the Sabbath of creation, sanctifies the life of the Israelite village through imposing on the village rules on the model of those of the temple. The purpose of the system, therefore, is to bring into alignment the moment of sanctification of the village and the life of the home with the moment of sanctification of the temple on those same occasions of appointed times. The underlying and generative logic of the system comes to expression in a concrete way here. We recall the rule of like and opposite, comparison and contrast. What is not like something follows the rule opposite to that pertaining to that something. Here, therefore, since the village is the mirror image of the temple, the upshot is dictated by the analogical-contrastive logic of the system as a whole. If things are done in one way in the temple, they will be done in the opposite way in the village. Together the village and the temple on the occasion of the holy day therefore form a single continuum, a completed creation, thus awaiting sanctification. The village is made like the temple in that, on appointed times, one may not freely cross the lines distinguishing the village from the rest of the world, just as one may not freely cross the lines distinguishing the temple from the world. But the village is a mirror image of the temple. The boundary lines prevent free entry into the temple, so they restrict free egress from the village. On the holy day, what one may do in the temple is precisely what one may not do in the village.

So the advent of the holy day affects the village by bringing it into sacred symmetry in such wise as to effect a system of opposites; each is holy, in a way precisely the opposite of the other. Because of the underlying conception of perfection attained through the union of opposites, the village is not represented as conforming to the model of the cult, but of constituting its antithesis. The world thus regains perfection when, on the holy day, heaven and earth are united, the whole completed and done: the heaven, the earth, and all their hosts. This moment of perfection renders the events of ordinary time, of "history," essentially irrelevant. For what really matters in time is that moment in which sacred time intervenes and effects the perfection formed of the union of heaven and earth, of temple, in the model of the former, and Israel, its complement. It is not a return to a perfect time but a recovery of perfect being, a fulfillment of creation, which explains the essentially ahistorical character of the Mishnah's division on Appointed Times. Sanctification constitutes an ontological category and is effected by the creator.

This explains why the division in its rich detail is composed of two quite distinct sets of materials. First, it addresses what one does in the sacred space of the temple on the occasion of sacred time, as distinct from what one does in that same sacred space on ordinary, undifferentiated days, which is a subject worked out in Holy Things. Second, the division defines how for the occasion of the holy day one creates a corresponding space in one's own circumstance, and what one does, within that space, during sacred time. The division as a whole holds together through a shared, generative metaphor. It is the comparison, in the context of sacred time, of the spatial life of the temple to the spatial life of the village, with activities and restrictions to be specified for each, upon the common occasion of the Sabbath or festival. The Mishnah's purpose therefore is to correlate the sanctity of the temple, as defined by the holy day, with the restrictions of space and of action which make the life of the village different and holy, as defined by the holy day.

The Division of WOMEN defines the women in the social economy of Israel's supernatural and natural reality. Women acquire definition wholly in relationship to men, who impart form to the Israelite social economy. The status of women is effected through both supernatural and natural, this-worldly action. Women formed a critical systemic component, because the proper regulation of women—subject to the father, then the husband—was deemed a central concern of Heaven, so that a betrothal would be subject to Heaven's supervision (*Qiddushin*, sanctification, being the pertinent tractate). Documents, such as the marriage contract or the writ of divorce, drawn up on earth, stand also for Heaven's concern with the sanctity of women in their marital relationship; so too, Heaven may through levirate marriage dictate whom a woman marries. What man and woman do on earth accordingly provokes a response in heaven, and the correspondences are perfect. So women are defined and secured both in heaven and here on earth, and that position is always and invariably relative to men.

The principal interest for the Mishnah is interstitial, just as, in general, sanctification comes into play at interstitial relationships, those that require decisive classification. Here it is the point at which a woman becomes, and ceases to be, holy to a particular man, that is, enters and leaves the marital union. These transfers of women are the dangerous and disorderly points in the relationship of woman to man, and therefore, the Mishnah states, to society as well. The division's systemic statement stresses the preservation of order in transactions involving women and (other) property. Within this orderly world of documentary and procedural concerns a place is made for the disorderly conception of the marriage not formed by human volition but decreed in heaven, the levirate connection. Mishnah tractate Yebamot states that supernature sanctifies a woman to a man (under the conditions of the levirate connection). What it says by indirection is that man sanctifies too: man, like God, can sanctify that relationship between a man and a woman, and can also effect the cessation of the sanctity of that same relationship.

Five of the seven tractates of the division of Women are devoted to the formation and dissolution of the marital bond. Of them, three treat what is done by man here on earth, that is, formation of a marital bond through betrothal and marriage contract and dissolution through divorce and its consequences. The division and its system therefore delineate the natural and supernatural character of the woman's role in the social economy framed by man: the beginning, end, and middle of the relationship. The whole constitutes a significant part of the Mishnah's encompassing system of sanctification, for the reason that heaven confirms what men do on earth. A correctly prepared writ of divorce on earth changes the status of the woman to whom it is given, so that in heaven she is available for sanctification to some other man, while, without that same writ, in heaven's view, should she go to some other man, she would be liable to be put to death. The earthly deed and the heavenly perspective correlate. That is indeed very much part of larger system, which says the same thing over and over again.

The Division of DAMAGES comprises two subsystems, which fit together in a logical way. One part presents rules for the normal conduct of civil society. These cover commerce, trade, real estate, and other matters of everyday intercourse, as well as mishaps, such as damages by chattels and persons, fraud, overcharge, interest, and the like, in that same context of everyday social life. The other part describes the institutions governing the normal conduct of civil society, that is, courts of administration, and the penalties at the disposal of the government for the enforcement of the law. The two subjects form a single tight and systematic dissertation on the nature of Israelite society and its economic, social, and political relationships, as the Mishnah envisages them. The main point of the first of the two parts of the division is that the task of society is to maintain perfect stasis, to preserve the prevailing situation, and to secure the stability of all relationships. To this end, in the interchanges of buying and selling, giving and taking, borrowing and lending, it is important that there be an essential equality of interchange. No party in the end should have more than what he had at the outset, and none should be the victim of a sizable shift in fortune and circumstance. All parties' rights to, and in, this stable and unchanging economy of society are to be preserved. When the condition of a person is violated, so far as possible the law will secure the restoration of the antecedent status.

The goal of the system of civil law is the recovery of the prevailing order and balance, the preservation of the established wholeness of the social economy. This idea is powerfully expressed in the organization of the three tractates that comprise the civil law, which treat first abnormal and then normal transactions. The framers deal with damages done by chattels and by human beings, thefts and other sorts of malfeasance against the property of others. The civil law in both aspects pays closest attention to how the property and person of the injured party so far as possible are restored to their prior condition, that is, a state of normality. So attention to torts focuses upon penalties paid by the malefactor to the victim, rather than upon penalties inflicted by the court on the malefactor for what he has done. When speaking of damages, the Mishnah thus takes as its principal concern the restoration of the fortune of victims of assault or robbery. Then the framers take up the complementary and corresponding set of topics, the regulation of normal transactions. When we rapidly survey the kinds of transactions of special interest, we see from the topics selected for discussion what we have already uncovered in the deepest structure of organization and articulation of the basic theme.

The other half of this same unit of three tractates presents laws governing normal and routine transactions, many of them of the same sort as those dealt with in the first half. At issue are deposits of goods or possessions that one person leaves in safekeeping with another. Called bailments, for example, cases of such transactions occur in both wings of the triple tractate, first, bailments subjected to misappropriation, or accusation thereof, by the bailiff, then, bailments transacted under normal circumstances. Under the rubric of routine transactions are those of workers and householders, that is, the purchase and sale of labor; rentals and bailments; real estate transactions; and inheritances and estates. Of the lot, the one involving real estate transactions is the most fully articulated and covers the widest range of problems and topics. The three tractates of the civil law all together thus provide a complete account of the orderly governance of balanced transactions and unchanging civil relationships within Israelite society under ordinary conditions.

The Division of HOLY THINGS presents a system of sacrifice and
sanctuary. The division centers upon the everyday and rules always
applicable to the cult: the daily whole offering, the sin offering and
guilt offering which one may bring any time under ordinary circumstances; the right sequence of diverse offerings; the way in which the
rites of the whole, sin, and guilt offerings are carried out; what sorts
of animals are acceptable; the accompanying cereal offerings; the support and provision of animals for the cult and of meat for the priesthood; the support and material maintenance of the cult and its
building. We have a system before us, the system of the cult of the
Jerusalem temple, seen as an ordinary and everyday affair, a continuing and routine operation. That is why special rules for the cult,
both in respect to the altar and in regard to the maintenance of the
buildings, personnel, and even the whole city, will be elsewhere—in
Appointed Times and Agriculture. But from the perspective of Holy
Things, those divisions intersect by supplying special rules and raising extraordinary (Agriculture: land-bound; Appointed Times: time-
bound) considerations for that theme which Holy Things claims to set
forth in its most general and unexceptional way: the cult as something
permanent and everyday.

The Division of PURITIES presents a very simple system of three
principal parts: sources of uncleanness, objects and substances susceptible to uncleanness, and modes of purification from uncleanness.
So it tells the story of what makes a given sort of object unclean and
what makes it clean. Viewed as a whole, the division of Purities treats
the interplay of persons, food, and liquids. Dry inanimate objects or
food are not susceptible to uncleanness. What is wet is susceptible. So
liquids activate the system. What is unclean, moreover, emerges from
uncleanness through the operation of liquids, specifically, through
immersion in fit water of requisite volume and in natural condition.
Liquids deactivate the system. Thus, water in its natural condition is
what concludes the process by removing uncleanness. Water in its
unnatural condition, that is, deliberately affected by human agency,
is what imparts susceptibility to uncleanness to begin with. The
uncleanness of persons, furthermore, is signified by body liquids, or
flux in the case of the menstruating woman, and the *zab* (the person
suffering from the form of uncleanness described at Lev. 15:1ff.).
Corpse uncleanness is conceived to be a kind of effluent, a viscuous
gas, which flows like liquid. Utensils for their part receive uncleanness

when they form receptacles able to contain liquid. In sum, we have a system in which the invisible flow of fluid-like substances or powers serves to put food, drink, and receptacles into the status of uncleanness and to remove those things from that status. Whether or not we call the system "metaphysical," it certainly has no material base but is conditioned upon highly abstract notions. Thus in material terms, the effect of liquid is upon food, drink, utensils, and man. The consequence has to do with who may eat and drink what food and liquid, and what food and drink may be consumed in which pots and pans. These loci are specified by tractates on utensils and on food and drink.

VI. HALAKHIC INTERIORITIES

Now to return to the characterization of the native category-formations as a coherent construction of Israel's social order. With this information in hand, we have surveyed the topics that define the native category-formations of the Mishnah as these topics fall naturally into six divisions. It is self-evident from my account that the divisions are exclusive, affording no logical position for any tractate presently located in some other division; the tractates, examined in detail, will be shown equally exclusive, each one treating only the topic assigned to it, occasionally encompassing some secondary points of amplification. If the Aggadah takes up exteriorities, then what are the counterparts within the interior structure constructed by the Halakhah? A consideration of the divisions and most, though not all, tractates thereof shows the simple correlation set forth in section IV.

[1] BETWEEN GOD AND ISRAEL: the interior dimensions of Israel's relationships with God—the division of Agriculture, the division of Holy Things. The division of Agriculture defines what Israel in the Land of Israel owes God as his share of the produce of the Holy Land, encompassing also Israel's conformity to God's regulation on how that produce is to be garnered; the anomalous tractate *Berakhot* concerns exactly the same set of relationships. The division of Holy Things corresponds by specifying the way in which the gifts of the Land—meat, grain, oil, wine—are to be offered to Heaven, inclusive of the priesthood, as well as the manner in which the temple and its staff are supported and the offerings paid for. Two tractates, moreover, describe the temple and its rite, and one of them sets forth

special problems in connection with the same. The sole anomalous tractate, *Hullin*, which takes up the correct slaughter of animals for secular purposes, belongs, because its rules pertain, also to the conduct of the cult.

[2] WITHIN ISRAEL'S SOCIAL ORDER: the social order that is realized by Israelites' relationships with one another—the division of Damages. That division spells out the civil law that maintains justice and equity in the social order, the institutions of government and the sanctions they legitimately impose.

[3] INSIDE THE ISRAELITE HOUSEHOLD: DEATH AND LIFE. INTERIOR TIME, SPACE, AND CIRCUMSTANCE: The inner life of the household, encompassing the individual Israelite, with God—the division of Women, the division of Appointed Times, and the division of Purities, as well as some singleton tractates such as *Hullin*. The division of Women deals with the way in which relationships of man and woman are governed by the rules of sanctification enforced by Heaven, which takes an interest in how family relationships are formed, maintained, and dissolved, and the affects, upon the family, of invoking Heaven's name in vows. The division of Appointed Times addresses the affect upon the conduct of ordinary life of the advent of holy time, with special reference to the Sabbath and the pilgrim festivals (Passover, Tabernacles), the pilgrimage, and the intermediate days of festivals, the New Year and Day of Atonement, Fast Days, and Purim. While parts of some of these tractates, and nearly the whole of a few of them, concern conduct in the temple, the main point of the tractates is to explore the impact upon the household and village of the Appointed Times. The same interstitial position—between household and village, on the one side, and temple and cult, on the other— serves the division of Purity. The laws of the tractates concern mainly the household, since the cleanness rules spelled out in those tractates concern purity at home. But, it goes without saying, the same uncleanness that prevents eating at home food that is to be preserved in conditions of cultic cleanness also prevents the Israelite from entering the restricted space of the temple. But in the balance, the division concerns cleanness in that private domain that is occupied by the Israelite household.

A brief repertoire of concrete cases suffices at the outset to show what we may expect to uncover in due course in the project that begins here:

A. *Between Israel and God*

Israel engages with God in the possession of the Land of Israel in particular. That is where God's presence locates itself, in the temple. It is the gift of the Land to holy Israel that sets the conditions of Israel's relationship with God. Israel in the Land is a sharecropper, for example. In connection with tractate *Ma'aserot* and the general rules of tithing, for one example, we shall want to know how God and the Israelite farmer relate, when they intersect, and what precipitates their encounter in partnership—the general theory embodied by the details of the law. Israel returns to God, through the altar, the principal gifts in which the Land glories, wine, oil, grain, meat. The principal tractates of the two divisions that work out the details of how Israel relates to God, the first, on Agriculture, and the fifth, on Holy Things, embody in the details of the law a variety of religious principles. Here we learn about how God and man correspond, just as much as, within the theological anthropology set forth by the Aggadah, dimensions of that correspondence are set forth.

B. *Within Israel's Social Order*

In connection with the *Babas* (*Baba Qamma, Baba Mesi'a, Baba Batra*), which deal with the regulation of the social order, we shall want to identify those governing principles of equity that dictate the character of the details, both laws that deal with the imperfections of the social order, conflict for instance, and the ones that regulate the social order in all its balance and perfection, properly-conducted transactions, for example.

C. *Inside the Israelite Household*

And when we examine tractates *Shabbat* and *'Erubin*, out of the specific rules we shall ask for a general theory of the interplay of space and time in the grid defined by the advent of sanctified time with the coming of the Sabbath, for example: Where am I now, where am I then, and what dictates my condition? How, in holy time, do I continue the life-sustaining activities of nourishment? The sources of the rules at hand, not in a literary but in a metaphysical sense, will have to be located, the modes of thought that govern to be identified. Such a theory will form a component of an account of the situation, in world order, of the Israelite household, a focus of holiness comparable in its way to the locus of sanctification in the temple.

The Halakhah as set forth in its formative age aims to describe how in concrete terms holy Israel is to construct a social order in the Land of Israel to realize that just and perfect world order that God had in mind in creating the world. The Halakhah is so framed, its category-formations so constituted, as to yield an account of how man in paradise, Adam in Eden, ought to have lived. Speaking in monumental dimensions, the Halakhah makes a teleological, but not a messianic, statement. And the promise of the Halakhah speaks to not Israel's messianic so much as to its restorationist aspiration: to form Eden not in time past nor in time future but in the here and now of everyday Israel, but this time to do it right. And here is how—in the concrete detail to which we now turn.

CHAPTER ELEVEN

WHAT, WHERE, AND WHEN IS EDEN?

Thus the heavens and the earth were finished and all the host of them. And on the seventh day God finished his work that he had done, and he rested on the seventh day from all his work that he had done. So God blessed the seventh day and sanctified it, because on it God rested from all his work that he had done in creation.

—Genesis 2:1–3

I. REALIZING EDEN

Scripture begins with the original man, Adam and Eve in Eden, and so do we in our reading of the Halakhah. By "Eden" Scripture means that place whole and at rest that God sanctified. In the Halakhah "Eden" stands for creation in perfect repose, not a location but a situation to be restored at specified occasions, through designated attitudes and actions. In the Halakhah set forth in the native categories (specific tractates) of the Mishnah-Tosefta-Yerushalmi-Bavli, Eden stands for not a particular place but nature in a defined condition. That is realized at a particular moment defined by circumstance: creation in Sabbath repose, sanctified. Then if Eden is a place in repose, we reverse the predicate and the subject. What flows is a place in repose at the climax of creation, at sunset at the start of the seventh day, whole and at rest, the embodiment of Eden.

The Halakhah means to systematize the condition of Eden, to define Eden in its normative traits, and also to localize Eden within Israel. How does the Halakhah localize that place? Eden is the place—the condition—to the perfection of which God responded in the act of sanctification at the advent of the seventh day. Where is that place? Here as elsewhere, the Halakhah accommodates itself to both the enlandised and the utopian condition of Israel, the people. So, on the one hand, that place is or ought to be the Land of Israel. The Halakhah finds in Scripture ample basis for identifying with the Land of Israel that place perfected on the Sabbath. It is the Land

that, in the Written Torah's explicit account of matters, claims the
right to repose on the seventh day and in the seventh year of the
septennial cycle. But, as we shall see, on the other hand, the perfected
place also is the location of Israel wherever that may be at the advent
of sunset on the eve of the seventh day of the week of creation. But
when it comes to time—the seventh day—the perfection of creation
takes place, also, in the households of Israel, where the conditions of
the first Sabbath are replicated every seventh day.

We treat location before situation: the Land as comparable to
Eden. We begin with enlandised Israel, that is, the Land of Israel, at
the moment at which Eden was made real. When was that moment
of perfection? It was when Israel entered into the Land at the
moment of realization of God's plan for Israel, comparable to Adam's
entry into Eden at the moment of the realization of God's plan for
man. That moment recovered, Eden is restored—the correct starting
point, therefore, for a theology of the Halakhah that claims the whole
holds together as a systematically restorationist theology.

A. *Shebiʿit*

In Hebrew, *shabbat* stands for Sabbath, *shebiʿit* stands for "seven," and
shanah shebiʿit speaks of the seventh year in the seven-year cycle that
corresponds to the seven days of creation. That is the explicit position of the Halakhah of *Shebiʿit*, which elaborates the Written Torah's
commandment, at Lev. 25:1–8:

> When you enter the land that I am giving you, the land shall observe
> a Sabbath of the Lord. Six years you may sow your field and six years
> you may prune your vineyard and gather in the yield. But in the
> seventh year the land shall have a Sabbath of complete rest, a Sabbath
> of the Lord; you shall not sow your field or prune your vineyard. You
> shall not reap the aftergrowth of your harvest or gather the grapes of
> your untrimmed vines; it shall be a year of complete rest for the land.
> But you may eat whatever the land during its Sabbath will produce—
> you, your male and female slaves, the hired-hand and bound laborers
> who live with you, and your cattle and the beasts in your land may eat
> all its yield.

Sages thus find in Scripture the explicit correlation of the advent of
the Sabbath and the condition of the Land, meaning, "the land that I
am giving you," which is to say, the Land of Israel. After six years of
creation, the Land is owed a Sabbath, as much as is man. A second,

correlative commandment, at Dt. 15:1–3, is treated as well: "Every seventh year you shall practice remission of debts. This shall be the nature of the remission: every creditor shall remit the due that he claims from his neighbor; he shall not dun his neighbor or kinsman, for the remission proclaimed is of the Lord. You may dun the foreigner, but you must remit whatever is due you from your kinsmen."

The Torah represents God as the sole master of creation, the Sabbath as testimony to God's pleasure with the perfection, and therefore sanctification, of creation. The Halakhah of *Shebi'it* sets forth the law that in relationship to the Land of Israel embodies that conviction. The law set forth in the Mishnah-Tosefta-Yerushalmi systematically works through Scripture's rules, treating [1] the prohibition of farming the land during the seventh year; [2] the use of the produce in the seventh year solely for eating, that is to say, its purpose and function by its very nature; and [3] the remission of debts. During the Sabbatical Year, Israel relinquishes its ownership of the Land of Israel. So the Sabbath involves giving up ownership, a point to which we shall return later in this chapter when we encounter *Shabbat-'Erubin*, the climax of the Halakhic account of Eden in Israel's acutely present tense. At that time Israelites in farming may do nothing that in secular years effects the assertion of ownership over the land (Avery-Peck, *Yerushalmi Shebi'it*, 2). Just as one may not utilize land he does not own, in the Sabbatical year the farmer gives up ownership of the land that he does own.

What links the Sabbatical Year to Eden's restoration? The reason is clear: the Sabbatical Year recovers that perfect time—but we now prefer *condition*—of Eden when the world was at rest, all things in place. Before the rebellion, man did not have to labor on the land; he picked and ate his meals freely. And, in the nature of things, everything belonged to everybody; private ownership in response to individual labor did not exist, because man did not have to work anyhow. These then represent the Halakhah's provisions for the Seventh Year. Reverting to that perfect time, the Torah maintains that the land will provide adequate food for everyone, including the flocks and herds, even—or especially—if people do not work the land. But that is on condition that all claim of ownership lapses; the food is left in the fields, to be picked by anyone who wishes, but it may not be hoarded by the landowner in particular. Avery-Peck (Avery-Peck, *Yerushalmi Shebi'it*, 3) states this matter as follows:

Scripture thus understands the Sabbatical year to represent a return to a perfected order of reality, in which all share equally in the bounty of a holy land that yields its food without human labor. The Sabbatical year provides a model through which, once every seven years, Israelites living in the here-and-now may enjoy the perfected order in which God always intended the world to exist and toward which, in the Israelite world view, history indeed is moving . . . The release of debts accomplishes for Israelites' economic relationships just what the agricultural Sabbatical accomplishes for the relationship between the people and the land. Eradicating debt allows the Israelite economy to return to the state of equilibrium that existed at the time of creation, when all shared equally in the bounty of the Land.

The Priestly Code in Lev. 25:8–10 expresses that same concept when it arranges for the return of inherited property at the Jubilee Year to the original family ownership: "You shall count off seven weeks of years, so that the period of seven weeks of years gives you a total of forty-nine years . . . You shall proclaim release throughout the land for all its inhabitants. It shall be a jubilee for you; each of you shall return to his holding and each of you shall return to his family." The Jubilee year is observed as is the Sabbatical year, meaning that for two successive years the land is not to be worked. The Halakhah establishes that when land in the Land of Israel is sold, it is for the span of time remaining to the next Jubilee year. That then marks the reordering of landholding to its original pattern, when Israel inherited the land to begin with and commenced to enjoy its produce. So the object is restorative: recovering the perfection in the beginning, even in the division of the Land.

Just as the Sabbath commemorates the completion of creation, the perfection of world order, so does the Sabbatical year. So too, the Jubilee year brings about the restoration of real property to the original division. In both instances, Israelites so act as to indicate they are not absolute owners of the Land, which belongs to God and which is divided in the manner that God arranged in perpetuity. Avery-Peck states the matter in the following way (Avery-Peck, *Yerushalmi Shebi'it*, 4):

On the Sabbath of creation, during the Sabbatical year, and in the Jubilee year, diverse aspects of Israelite life are to return to the way that they were at the time of creation. Israelites thus acknowledge that, in the beginning, God created a perfect world, and they assure that the world of the here-and-now does not overly shift from its perfect character. By providing opportunities for Israelites to model their contemporary existence upon a perfected order of things, these commemorations further prepare the people for messianic times, when, under God's rule, the world will permanently revert to the ideal character of the time of creation.

Here we find the Halakhic counterpart to the restorationist theology that the Oral Torah sets forth in the Aggadah. Israel matches Adam, the Land of Israel, Eden, and, we now see, the Sabbatical year commemorates the perfection of creation and replicates it. (Later in this chapter we shall see that the same conception of relinquishing ownership of one's real property operates to facilitate everyday activities on the Sabbath.)

The Sabbatical year takes effect at the moment of Israel's entry into the Land, counterpart to Adam's and Eve's entering Eden on the sixth day of Creation. That repeated point of insistence then treats the moment of the entry into the Land as the counterpart to the moment of repose, of perfection at rest, of creation. Observing the commandments of the Sabbatical year marks Israel's effort at keeping the Land like Eden, six days of creation, one day of rest, and so too here:

Sifra CCXLV:I.2

A. "When you come [into the land which I give you, the land shall keep a Sabbath to the Lord]":
B. Might one suppose that the sabbatical year was to take effect once they had reached Transjordan?
C. Scripture says, "into the land."
D. It is that particular land.

Now comes the key point: the Sabbatical Year takes effect only when Israel enters the Land, which is to say, Israel's entry into the Land marks the counterpart to the beginning of the creation of Eden. But a further point will register in a moment. It is when Eden/the Land enters into stasis, each family receiving its share in the Land, that the process of the formation of the new Eden comes to its climax; then each Israelite bears responsibility for his share of the Land. That is when the Land has reached that state of order and permanence that corresponds to Eden at sunset on the sixth day.

E. Might one suppose that the sabbatical year was to take effect once they had reached Ammon and Moab?
F. Scripture says, "which I give you,"

G. and not to Ammon and Moab.

H. And on what basis do you maintain that when they had conquered the land but not divided it, divided it among familiars but not among fathers' houses so that each individual does not yet recognize his share—

I. might one suppose that they should be responsible to observe the sabbatical year?

J. Scripture says, "[Six years you shall sow] your field,"

K. meaning, each one should recognize his own field.

L. ". . . your vineyard":

M. meaning, each one should recognize his own vineyard.

N. You turn out to rule:

O. Once the Israelites had crossed the Jordan, they incurred liability to separate dough offering and to observe the prohibition against eating the fruit of fruit trees for the first three years after planting and the prohibition against eating produce of the new growing season prior to the waving of the sheaf of new grain [that is, on the fifteenth of Nisan].

P. When the sixteenth of Nisan came, they incurred liability to wave the sheaf of new grain.

Q. With the passage of fifty days from then they incurred the liability to the offering of the Two Loaves.

R. At the fourteenth year they became liable for the separation of tithes.

So much for the systematic exploration of the enlandisement of Eden in the Land of Israel, the formulation of Israel's relationship with God through Israel's use of the Land of Israel and its produce, in a way analogous to Adam's use of Eden—and abuse thereof.

God pays the closest attention to Israel's attitudes and intentions. God furthermore identifies the Land of Israel as the archetype of Eden and model of the world to come. That is why God treats the Land in its perfection just as he treats Eden, by according to the Land the Sabbath rest. He deems the union of Israel and the Land of Israel to effect the sanctification of the Land in its ascending degrees corresponding to the length of the term of Israel's possession. And, finally, God insists, as the ultimate owner of the Land, that at regular intervals the possession of the Land be relinquished, signaled as null, and that at those same intervals ownership of the produce of the Land at least in potentiality be equally shared among all its inhabitants.

B. 'Orlah

Devoted to the prohibition of the use of the produce of a fruit tree for the first three years after its planting and the restriction as to the use of that same tree's produce in the fourth year after its planting, the Halakhah of 'Orlah elaborates the Torah's commandment at Lev. 19:23–25: "When you come to the land and plant any kind of tree for food, you shall treat it as forbidden. For three years it shall be forbidden, it shall not be eaten. In the fourth year all its fruit shall be set aside for jubilation before the Lord, and only in the fifth year may you use its fruit, that its yield to you may be increased: I am the Lord your God." The produce of the fourth year after planting is brought to Jerusalem ("for jubilation before the Lord") and eaten there. But the main point of the Halakhah centers upon the prohibition of the fruit for the first three years.

In the Halakhah, the role of man in precipitating the effect of the prohibition takes priority. Man has a role in bringing about the prohibition of the law, but man cannot by his intentionality change the facts of the case. How does the Israelite farmer's intentionality govern? It is man's assessment of the use of the tree that classifies the tree as a fruit tree or as a tree of some other category, e.g., one meant for lumber. If man deems the tree planted for fruit, then the prohibition applies. But man cannot declare it as a fruit tree, so subjecting the produce to the prohibition for three years from planting, one that does not bear fruit at all. Man's actions reveal his original intentionality for the tree, e.g., how the tree is planted.

Here is an explicit statement, in connection with the exegesis of the Halakhah, that intentionality dictates whether or not a tree that can bear fruit actually is covered by the prohibition. Trees not used for fruit are not affected by the prohibition, so the farmer may use the lumber even in the first three years from planting; and parts of trees not intended for fruit are not subject to it either, so they may be pruned off and used for fuel. But intention cannot classify what nature has already designated for one or another category. In the following, Simeon b. Gamaliel refines the law by insisting that man's intention conform to the facts of nature. That is to say, if one planted a tree for lumber or firewood but it is not appropriate for such a use, then his intentionality is null.

7. A. ". . . trees for food":
   B. this excludes the case of planting trees for fence posts or lumber or firewood.
   C. R. Yosé says, "Even if he said, 'The side of the tree facing inward is to be used for food and the side outward is to be used as a fence, the side of the tree inward is liable to the laws of 'Orlah, and the side of the tree facing outward is exempt" [M. 'Orlah 1:1A–D].
   D. Said Rabban Simeon b. Gamaliel, "Under what circumstances? When he planted it as a fence for lumber or for firewood, a use appropriate for those trees. But when he planted it as a fence, for lumber, or for firewood in a case not appropriate for that species, the tree is liable to the laws of 'Orlah" [T. 'Orlah 1:1C–H].
   E. How do we know the law given just now?
   F. Scripture says, "all kinds of trees."

The matter of appropriateness will recur many times, since the intense interest of the Halakhah in the correct classification of things comes to expression in an interesting notion. A thing has its inherent, intrinsic purpose, and when it serves that purpose, it is properly used; when not, it is improperly used. How does that make a difference? What is edible is food, and produce that may serve for food or for fuel, if it is of a sacred status, cannot be used for anything but food. So intentionality meets its limits in the purpose that a thing is supposed to serve, that is to say, intentionality is limited by teleology.

The power of the metaphor of Eden emerges, we shall now see, in specificities of the law. These turn out to define with some precision a message on the relationship of Israel to the Land of Israel and to God. In *Sifra*'s reading of matters, our attention is drawn to a number of quite specific traits of the law of 'Orlah, and these make explicit matters of religious conviction that we might otherwise miss. The first is that the prohibition of 'Orlah fruit applies solely within the Land of Israel and not to the neighboring territories occupied by Israelites, which means that, once again, it is the union of Israel with the Land of Israel that invokes the prohibition.

Sifra CCII:I.1

A. "When you come [into the land and plant all kinds of trees for food, then you shall count their fruit as forbidden; three years it shall be forbidden to you, it must not be eaten. And in the fourth year all their fruit shall be holy, an offering of praise to the Lord. But in the fifth year you may eat of their fruit, that they may yield more richly for you: I am the Lord your God" (Lev. 19:23–25).]

B. Might one suppose that the law applied once they came to Transjordan?

C. Scripture says, ". . . into the land,"

D. the particular Land [meaning, the Land of Israel].

What that means is that some trait deemed to inhere in the Land of Israel and no other territory must define the law, and a particular message ought to inhere in this law.

First, as with *Shebi'it*, the law takes effect only from the point at which Israel enters the land. That is to say, the point of Israel's entry into the Land marks the beginning of the Land's consequential fecundity. In simpler language, the fact that trees produce fruit matters only from Israel's entry onward. To see what is at stake, we recall that the entry of Israel into the Land marks the restoration of Eden. The Land bears fruit *of which God takes cognizance* only when the counterpart moment of creation has struck. The Halakhah has no better way of saying that the entry of Israel into the Land compares with the moment at which the creation of Eden took place. In this way, moreover, the law of *Shebi'it* finds its counterpart. *Shebi'it* concerns telling time, marking off seven years to the Sabbath of creation, the one that affords rest to the Land. The Halakhah of *'Orlah* also means telling time. Specifically, *'Orlah*-law marks the time of the creation of produce from the moment of Israel's entry into the land. Israel's entry into the Land marks a new beginning, comparable to the very creation of the world, just as the Land at the end matches Eden at the outset.

Second, Israelite intentionality is required to subject a tree to the *'Orlah*-rule. If an Israelite does not plant the tree with the plan of producing fruit, then the tree is not subject to the rule. If the tree grows up on its own, not by the act and precipitating intentionality of the Israelite, the *'Orlah*-rule does not apply. If an Israelite does not plant the tree to produce fruit, the *'Orlah*-rule does not apply. And given the character of creation, which marks the norm, the tree must be planted in the ordinary way; if grafted or sunk as a root, the law does not apply.

Third, the entire issue of the Halakhah comes down to Israelite restraint in using the produce of the orchards. What is the counterpart to Israelite observance of the restraint of three years? And why should Israelite intentionality play so critical a role, since, *Sifra* itself notes, the *'Orlah*-rule applies to trees planted even by gentiles? The answer becomes obvious when we ask another question: Can we think of any other commandments concerning fruit trees in the Land that—sages say time and again—is Eden? Of course we can: "Of every tree of the garden you are free to eat; but as for the tree of knowledge of good and evil, you must not eat of it" (Gen. 2:16). But the Halakhah of *'Orlah* imposes upon Israel a more demanding commandment. Of *no* tree in the new Eden may Israel eat for three years. That demands considerable restraint. Israel must exceed the humble requirement of obedience in regard to a fruit tree that God assigned to Adam; the Land imposes obligations far in excess of those carried by Eden. And the issue devolves upon Israel's will or attitude, much as Eden turned tragic by reason of man's rebellious will.

That is because Israel's own intentionality—not God's—imposes upon every fruit-bearing tree—and not only the one of Eden—the prohibition of three years. That is the point of the stress on the effects of Israel's desire for the fruit. So once Israel wants the fruit, it must show that it can restrain its desire and wait for three years. By Israel's act of will, Israel has imposed upon itself the requirement of restraint. Taking the entry point as our guide, we may say that, from the entry into the Land and for the next three years, trees that Israelites value for their fruit and plant with the produce in mind must be left untouched. And, for all time thereafter, when Israelites plant fruit trees, they must recapitulate that same exercise of self-restraint, that is, act as though, for the case at hand, they have just come into the Land.

To find the context in which these rules make their statement, we must ask that details, not only the main point, carry the message. So we ask, why three years in particular? A glance at the narrative of creation provides the obvious answer. Fruit trees were created on the third day of creation. Then, when Israel by intention and action designates a tree—any tree—as fruit-bearing, Israel recapitulates the order of creation and so must wait for three years, as creation waited for three years. Then the planting of every tree imposes upon Israel the occasion to meet once more the temptation that the first Adam could not overcome. Israel now recapitulates the temptation of Adam then, but Israel, the New Adam, possesses, and is possessed by, the Torah. By its own action and intention in planting fruit trees, Israel finds itself in a veritable orchard of trees like the tree of knowledge of good and evil. The difference between Adam and Israel—permitted to eat all fruit but one, Adam ate the forbidden fruit, while Israel refrains for a specified span of time from fruit from all trees—marks what has taken place through Israel, in the Land of Israel, which is the regeneration of humanity. The enlandisement of the Halakhah bears that very special message, and I can imagine no other way of making that statement through law than in the explicit concern sages register for the fruit trees of the Land of Israel. No wonder, then, that 'Orlah-law finds its position, in the Priestly Code, in the rules of sanctification.

So when Israel enters the Land, in exactly the right detail Israel recapitulates the drama of Adam in Eden, but with this formidable difference. The outcome ought not to be the same. By its own act of will Israel addresses the temptation of Adam and overcomes the same temptation, not once but every day through time beyond measure. Adam could not wait out the week, but Israel waits for three years—as long as God waited in creating fruit trees. Adam picked and ate. But here too there is a detail not to be missed. Even after three years, Israel may not eat the fruit wherever it chooses. Rather, in the fourth year from planting, Israel will still show restraint, bringing the fruit only "for jubilation before the Lord" in Jerusalem. That signals that the once-forbidden fruit is now eaten in public, not in secret, before the Lord, as a moment of celebration. That detail too recalls the fall and makes its comment upon the horror of the fall. That is, when Adam ate the fruit, he shamefully hid from God for having eaten the fruit. But when Israel eats the fruit, it does so proudly, joyfully, above all publicly, before the Lord. The contrast is not to be missed, so too the message. Faithful Israel refrains when it is supposed to, and so it has every reason to cease to refrain and to eat "before the Lord." It has nothing to hide, and everything to show.

And there is more. In the fifth year Israel may eat on its own, the time of any restraint from enjoying the gifts of the Land having ended. That sequence provides fruit for the second Sabbath of creation, and so through time. How so? Placing Adam's sin on the first day after the first Sabbath, thus Sunday, then calculating the three forbidden years as Monday, Tuesday, and Wednesday of the second week of creation, reckoning on the jubilation of Thursday, we come to Friday, eve of the second Sabbath of creation. So now, a year representing a day of the Sabbatical week, just as Leviticus says so many times in connection with the Sabbatical year, the three prohibited years allow Israel to show its true character, fully regenerate, wholly and humbly accepting God's commandment, the one Adam broke. And the rest follows.

Here, then, is the message of the 'Orlah-Halakhah, the statement that only through the details of the laws of 'Orlah as laid out in both parts of the Torah, written and oral, the Halakhah could hope to make. By its own act of restraint, the New Adam, Israel, in detailed action displays its repentance in respect to the very sin that the Old Adam committed, the sin of disobedience and rebellion. Facing the same opportunity to sin, Israel again and again over time refrains from the very sin that cost Adam Eden. So by its manner of cultivation of the Land and its orchards, Israel manifests what in the very condition of humanity has changed by the giving of the Torah: the advent of humanity's second chance, through Israel. Only in the Land that succeeds Eden can Israel, succeeding Adam, carry out the acts of regeneration that the Torah makes possible.

C. *Kilayim*

An enlandised relationship, then, identifies the encounter between Israel and God with not only the right time and the right person but also the right place: the Land God has chosen for the people whom he has chosen. When it comes to the details, the Written Torah defines the conditions in which Israel is to work that particular Land, deriving its sustenance from the Land and its exceptional gifts. These are the rules of interior relationship that govern when, in God's presence and by his act, holy Israel and the Land are (re)joined together. These rules turn out to establish for the Land the order and system that characterize Eden: all things properly classified, species by species. The Halakhah of *Kilayim* elaborates upon Lev. 19:19, "You shall not let your cattle mate with a different kind; you shall not sow your field with two kinds of seed; you shall not put on cloth from a mixture of two kinds of material." Further, Dt. 22:9–11 figures: "You shall not sow your vineyard with a second kind of seed, otherwise the crop from the seed you have sown and the produce of the vineyard may not be used; you shall not plow with an ox and an ass together; you shall not wear cloth that combines wool and linen." Lev. 19:2 places into the context of the sanctification of Israel the considerations of meticulous division among classes or species of the animal and vegetable world that define the tractate's topic. Sanctification takes place in the context of Gen. 1:1–2:4, the orderly creation of the world, species by species. The act of sanctification of creation took place when all things were ordered, properly in place, each according to its kind. Creation takes place when chaos is brought under control and ordered, that is, when the world is made perfect and ready for God's act of sanctification. Mandelbaum observes, "The point of the laws of the Priestly Code in Leviticus . . . is to prevent the confusion of those classes and categories that were established at the creation. P thus commands man to restore the world from its present condition of chaos to its original orderly state, and so to make the world ready once again for sanctification."[1]

From one viewpoint *Kilayim* takes God's perspective on the Land, imagining the landscape as seen from on high. God wants to see in the Land an orderly and regular landscape, each species in its proper place. He wants to see Israel clothed in garments that preserve the distinction between animal and vegetable exactly where that distinction operates for fabrics. He wants to see animals ordered by their species, just as they were when Noah brought them into the ark (Gen. 7:14). What that means is that grapes and wheat are not to grow together, oxen and asses are not to be yoked together, and wool and linen—animal and vegetable fibers—are not to be worn in a single garment together.

But from another viewpoint, it is the perspective of not God but man, Israel in particular, that dictates matters. For who bears responsibility for restoring the perfection of creation? The Priestly Code wants the land to be returned to its condition of an unchanging perfection. But the Mishnah, Mandelbaum states, has a different view:

> The Mishnah underlines man's power to impose order upon the world, a capacity unaffected by historical events. In spite of the occurrence of catastrophes and disasters, man retains the ability to affect the world around him through such ordinary activities as sowing a field. While the Priestly Code thus has man confront confusion by reconstructing the ideal order of creation, the Mishnah regards man as imposing his own order upon a world in a state of chaos, and, so, in effect, as participating in the process of creation.[2]

---

[1] Irving J. Mandelbaum, *The Talmud of the Land of Israel*, vol. 4, *Kilayim* (Chicago Studies in the History of Judaism; Chicago: University of Chicago Press, 1987), 3.
[2] Mandelbaum, *Kilayim*, 4.

Man has the power to do in the Land of Israel what God did in creating the world at Eden, that is, establish order, overcome chaos, perfect the world for the occasion of sanctification. The law thus embodies in the topic at hand the view prevailing throughout the Halakhah, as formulated at M. *Kelim* 17:11: "Everything is according to the measure of the man." The Halakhah that elaborates the commandments on the present topic set forth in Scripture makes man God's partner in overcoming chaos and establishing order. It is man's perspective that governs, man's discernment that identifies chaos or affirms order.

Now if we ask ourselves, how in a religious system that deems man created in God's image, after God's likeness, do we account for the law's stress on man's view, an answer immediately presents itself. Man's perspective governs, how man sees the Land determines whether or not the law is obeyed, for two reasons. The first is that, with man created "in our image, after our likeness," man's and God's perspectives are the same. If man discerns the confusion of species, so would God, and if man does not, then neither would God. But when the Halakhah leaves matters relative to appearance to man, the actualities of mixed seeds no longer matter, or matter so much as appearances. And that requires a second reason as well. For if God cares that "you shall not sow your field with two kinds of seed and that you shall not sow your vineyard with a second kind of seed," surely the actuality, not the appearance, ought to prevail—unless another consideration registers. That consideration comes into play when we ask, how, through the shared engagement with the Land, do God and Israel collaborate, and to what end?

The answer to that question exposes the second, and I think, principal, explanation for the emphasis of the Halakhah upon how man sees things, Israelite man being the subject throughout. Israel is in charge of the Land. Israel not only bears responsibility for what happens in the land, but also bears the blame and the penalty when matters are not right. Israel relates to God through Israel's trusteeship of the Land. The tractates that deal with the enlandisement of the relationship of Israel to God, *Kilayim* and the others, present Israel as the trustee of the Land and, as we see in the present tractate, assign to Israel the task of cultivating the Land in a manner appropriate to the perfection of creation at the outset. No wonder, then, that Israel's view of matters must prevail, for Israel bears full responsibility on the spot for how things will appear to Heaven.

That fact—Israel's responsibility to farm the Land in accord with the orderly rule of Eden—makes Israel not only the custodian of the Land but also partner in that vast labor of reform that, in the end, will bring about the restoration of Adam to Eden. Adam was responsible only for not eating the produce of a single tree; he did not have to labor; for a harvest, he needed only reach up and pick the fruit. Israel for its part had to work the Land and bore responsibility for the appearance of the whole of it. For, we recall, it is God's plan at the end to bring to life all Israel and in the world or age to come to restore all Israel to the Land of Israel, completing the return to Eden but with the difference made by the Torah: Israel back to the Land of Israel compares to Adam in Eden in all but one aspect. Armed with the Torah, Israel will not rebel as Adam did. That is why, the restorationist teleology maintains, the world to come will endure: chaos overcome, order will prevail. How Israel cultivates the Holy Land entrusted to it then makes all the difference, field by field in its correct configuration.

The restoration of Adam to Eden takes place, at the end, in and through the restoration to the Land of Israel, of Israel, the particular embodiment of that part of Adam, or humanity, that knows God through the Torah. So all matters cohere. In assigning to Israel the task of farming the country in a manner appropriate to the principles of creation, therefore, the Halakhah asks Israel to do its concrete part in restorationist teleology: to make the end like the beginning, Eden recovered. Once God has assigned the Land to Israel and instructed Israel on how to attain and preserve its condition of perfection as at creation, then Israel's perspective, not God's, must govern, because, for Israel, the stakes are very high: the resurrection of the dead to life, the restoration of Israel to the Land. But the Halakhah concerns the here and now, and that brings us to the Sabbath of creation, which Israel celebrates, in the Land and otherwise, every seventh day.

D. *Shabbat-ʿErubin*

Aggadic sayings and Halakhic norms concur that, on the Sabbath, Israel gains a foretaste of paradise, which means, temporally regains

Eden. How does that take place within the Halakhic framework? To restore Eden by recapitulating its principal qualities, the Halakhah of *Shabbat-'Erubin* identifies the climactic time of Eden—the sanctification of creation in its perfection at the advent of the Sabbath—with the Sabbath day and the space of Eden with the Israelite household. Unlike the Halakhic outcomes of *Shebi'it, 'Orlah,* and *Kilayim,* however, the Sabbath is utopian, not enlandised, in its focus: a condition, not a location but an occasion.

So Eden forms the metaphor that governs the Israelite household on the seventh day. The lines of structure and order that organize the Israelite household's interior construction mark the confluence of time, space, and circumstance. At a particular time, the space encompassed by the household is closed off entirely so that the circumstance of the conduct of life therein is deeply affected. At that point the Israelite household comes to spatial realization, keeping within all who belong, walling off the rest. In concrete terms, on the Sabbath an invisible wall descends to differentiate the private domain of the household from public domain of marketplace and street—and other private domains—and to close off the one from the other. And, at that time, in that space, the ordinary foci of workaday activities—cooking and eating, working and resting—become radically reconfigured: no cooking, no working, only eating and resting in perfect repose. And that is paradise, or, as the sages say, one-sixtieth of the taste of the Garden of Eden.

The Israelite household at rest on the Sabbath day recapitulates the celebration of God at the moment of the conclusion and perfection of creation. Then the Israelite household, like creation at sunset marking the end of the sixth day, is sanctified, separated from the profane world and distinguished as God's domain. With all things in place and in order, at the sunset that marks the advent of the seventh day, the rest that marks the perfection of creation descends. The sanctification takes place through that very act of perfect repose that recapitulates the one celebrated at the climax of creation. Like God at the celebration of creation, now man achieves perfect, appropriate rest. That takes place when time, circumstance, but space too, come together. The advent of the Sabbath marks the time, the household, the space, and the conduct of home and family life, the circumstance. Sages then make through the Halakhah of the Sabbath the first and most important statement of their system. It is the statement that cel-

ebrates God's repose by bringing about the stasis of creation, the perfection of the Creator's work, all evoked every time the word
"Sabbath" resonated with the sounds of the beginnings, the melodies
of the restoration.

The issue of residence therefore becomes critical to an account of
how Israel meets God within the walls of the Israelite household,
because on the Sabbath one is to remain in place, meaning, within
the limits of private domain. But the transformation of private
domain—what is private, what is shared—on the Sabbath forms the
generative problematic of the Halakhah—that, and the meaning of
"eating in his place." Private domain defines the critical focus of the
Halakhah. To effect that shift in concern, bringing people within the
walls of the courtyards and alleyways in which they are imagined to
reside, realizes the intent of the Written Torah when it says, "Remain
every man of you in his place." Consequently, activities in public
domain are severely circumscribed by the prohibition against carrying therein, as well as by the one that prohibits unlimited travel.

The Halakhah formulates matters at two levels; on the surface it
attends to minutia of carrying from one domain to the other (*Shabbat*)
and to the detailed, richly instantiated definition of private domain
(*'Erubin*). But at the heart of matters profound reflection on the meaning of what is private and what is shared takes place. The tractate in
detail therefore addresses the problem, How can Israelites on the
Sabbath move about from one private domain to another, so arrang-
ing matters that shared and common ownership of private domain
secures for all parties the right to carry in the space held in common?
One answer is, since where one eats, there one resides, prepare a
symbolic, or fictive, meal, the right to which is shared by all. All
householders thereby commingle their property rights, so that will
then form of various private domains a single common estate.
Another answer is, establish a boundary around the entire set of private domains, one that like a wall forms of them all a single property.

The medium by which the one or the other procedure is carried
out is called an *'erub*, a medium of commingling, thus referring to
either the symbolic, shared meal or the equally fictive demarcation
line, as the case requires: a meal of commingling, or a boundary
marker for commingling ownership of private property. In play
throughout the exposition of the Halakhah of *'Erubin* are these propositions that have already come to full exposition in the Halakhah of

Shabbat: [1] one may not transport objects from private to public domain, but [2] there are types of domain that are neither the one nor the other, specifically, the courtyard linking a number of private properties, and the alleyway onto which a number of courtyards debouch. These may be formed into a single, commingled domain, if all of the householders relinquish ownership for the spell of the seventh day and form of the whole a jointly owned area, in the model of the Land of Israel in the Seventh Year.

The paramount question before us is, Why do sages devote their reading of the law of *Shabbat-ʿErubin* above all to differentiating public from private domain? All of *ʿErubin* and a fair component of *Shabbat* focus upon that matter, which stands at the head of the first of the two tractates (M. *Shabbat* Chapter One) and at the conclusion of the second. And, to revert to the Halakhah of *Shabbat* once more, the other principal focus, the definition of an act of labor that, when performed on the Sabbath, is culpable, defines yet another question that demands attention. Why do sages formulate the principle that they do, that the act of labor prohibited on the Sabbath is one that fully constitutes a completed act of labor—beginning, middle, and end—in conformity with the intentionality of the actor?

The answer to both questions derives from the governing theology of the Sabbath, the key to the restoration of Eden, first at regular, temporal intervals, and, ultimately, for all eternity. The Written Torah represents the Sabbath as the climax of creation. The theology of the Sabbath put forth in the Oral Torah's Halakhah derives from a systematization of definitions implicit in the myth of Eden that envelopes the Sabbath. Sages' thinking about the Sabbath invokes, in the formation of the normative law defining the matter, the model of the first Sabbath, the one of Eden. The two paramount points of concern—the systematic definition of private domain, where ordinary activity is permitted, and the rather particular definition of what constitutes a prohibited act of labor on the Sabbath—precipitate deep thought and animate the handful of principles brought to concrete realization in the two tractates. "Thou shalt not labor" of the Commandments refers in a generic sense to all manner of work; but in the Halakhah of *Shabbat*, "labor" bears very particular meanings and is defined in a quite specific, and somewhat odd, manner. We can make sense of the Halakhah of *Shabbat-ʿErubin* only by appeal to the story of creation, the governing metaphor derived therefrom, the sages' philosophical reflections that transform into principles of a general and universal character the case at hand.

Given the broad range of possible points of Halakhic emphasis that the Written Torah sustains—the dual formulation of matters in the Ten Commandments that make remarkably slight impact here, Dt. 5:12–15's version, with its emphasis upon rest for animals and slaves playing no role in the articulation of the law, we realize that sages made choices. Why the stress on space and activity? When approaching the theme and problem of the Sabbath, they chose to answer two questions: What does it mean to remain "in his place," and What constitutes the theory of forbidden activity, the principles that shape the innumerable rules and facts of the prohibition? Accordingly, we must ask a basic question: What is it about the Sabbath of creation that captures sages' attention?

The foci of their thinking are in what is implicit and subject to generalization in the story of creation. The Halakhah turns out to realize in detailed, concrete terms generalizations that sages locate in, and derive from, the story of creation. And what they find is a metaphor for themselves and their Israel, on the one side, and the foundation for generalization, out of the metaphor, in abstract terms susceptible to acute concretization, on the other. That is to say, the Sabbath of Eden forms the model: like this, so all else. And sages, with their remarkable power to think in general terms but to convey thought in examples and details, found it possible to derive from the model the principles that would accomplish their goal: linking Israel to Eden through the Sabbath, the climax of their way of life, the soul of their theological system.

Only when we know what is supposed to take place on the Sabbath—in particular in the model of the Sabbath that originally celebrated creation—to the exclusion of the model of the Sabbath that would focus the Halakhah upon the liberation of slaves from Egypt (Deuteronomy's version) or the cessation of labor of the household, encompassing animals and slaves (Exodus's version)—only then shall we find the key to the entire matter of the Sabbath of the Halakhah. Then we may identify the setting in which the rules before us take on meaning and prove to embody profound religious thinking. I find the Halakhah that presents the model of how sages think about the Sabbath and accounts for the topical program of their thought—the fully articulated source of the governing metaphor—is

Shebi'it. That tractate, as we have now seen, describes the observance of the Sabbath that is provided every seventh year for the Land of Israel itself. The Land celebrates the Sabbath, and then Israel in its model. The Land is holy, as Israel is holy, and the Priestly Code leaves no doubt that for both, the Sabbath defines the rhythm of life with God: the seventh day for Israel, the seventh year for the Land.

For both, moreover, to keep the Sabbath is to be like God. And, specifically, that is when God had completed the work of creation, pronounced it good, sanctified it—imposed closure and permanence, the creation having reached its conclusion. God observed the Sabbath, which itself finds its definition as the celebration and commemoration of God's own action. This is what God did, this is what we now do. What God did concerned creation, what we do concerns creation. And all else follows. The Sabbath then precipitates the imitation of God on a very particular occasion and for a very distinctive purpose. And given what we have identified as the sages' governing theology—the systematic account of God's perfect justice in creation, yielding an account and explanation of all else—we find ourselves at the very center of the system. The meeting of time and space on the seventh day of creation—God having formed space and marked time—finds its counterpart in the ordering of Israelite space at the advent of time, the ordering of that space through the action and inaction of the Israelites themselves.

'Erubin, with its sustained exercise of thought on [1] the commingling, symbolically, prior to the Sabbath, of ownership of private property for the purpose of Sabbath observance and [2] the commingling of meals to signify shared ownership of real estate domains via commensality, accomplishes for Israel's Sabbath what *Shebi'it* achieves for the Land's. On the Sabbath inaugurated by the Sabbatical Year, the Land, so far as it is otherwise private property, no longer is possessed *exclusively* by the householder. So too, the produce of the Land consequently belongs to everybody. It follows that the Halakhah of *'Erubin* realizes for the ordinary Sabbath of Israel the very same principles that are embodied in the Halakhah of *Shebi'it*. That Halakhah defines the Sabbath of the Land in exactly the same terms: the Land is now no longer private, and the Land's produce belongs to everybody. The Sabbath that the Land enjoys marks the advent of shared ownership of the Land and its fruit. Sharing is so total that hoarding is explicitly forbidden, and what has been hoarded

has now to be removed from the household and moved to public domain, where anyone may come and take it.

Here we find the Sabbath of creation overspreading the Sabbath of the Land, as the Priestly Code at Gen. 1:1–2:3 and at Lev. 25:1–8, cited above, define matters. The Sabbatical year bears the message that, on the Sabbath, established arrangements as to ownership and possession are set aside, and a different conception of private property takes over. What on ordinary days is deemed to belong to the householder and to be subject to his exclusive will on the Sabbath falls into a more complex web of possession. The householder continues to utilize his property but not as a sole proprietor does. The sole proprietor exercises his will without restraint; he alone dictates what is to be done with what he owns. But that is not the situation of the Israelite householder on the Sabbath. He gives up exclusive access thereto, and gains in exchange rights of access to other peoples' property. Private property is commingled; everybody shares in everybody's. The result is, private property takes on a new meaning, different from the secular one. So far as the householder proposes to utilize his private property, he must share it with others, who do the same for him. To own then is to abridge ownership in favor of commingling rights thereto, to possess is to share. And that explains why the produce of the Land belongs to everyone as well, a corollary to the fundamental postulate of the Sabbath of the Land.

What qualities of Eden then impress sages? With the Halakhah as the vast corpus of facts, we focus upon two matters: time as transformative of space, time as transformative of activity—just as at Eden. That is to say, the advent of sunset on the eve of the Seventh Day marked God's recognition of the perfection of the space that he had created, and that same moment precipitated the sanctifying activity of repose. How is space demarcated at the specified time, how is activity classified at that same time? The former works itself out in a discussion of where people may move on the Sabbath and how they may conduct themselves (carry things as they move). The latter finds its definition in the model of labor that is prohibited. How does Eden form the generative metaphor? With Eden as the model and the metaphor, we take a simple sighting on the matter. First, Adam and Eve are free to move in Eden where they wish, possessing all they contemplate. God has given it to them to enjoy. If Eden then belongs to God, he freely shares ownership with Adam and Eve. And—all the more so—the produce of Eden is ownerless. With the well-known exception, all the fruit is theirs for the taking. So we find ourselves deep within the Halakhah of *Shebi'it*.

For the Halakhah of *Shebi'it* sets forth in concrete terms what is implicit in the character of Eden. In the Sabbatical Year the Land returns to the condition characteristic of Eden at the outset: shared and therefore accessible, its produce available to all. The Sabbatical Year recovers that perfect time of Eden when the world was at rest, all things in place. Before the rebellion, man did not have to labor on the land; he picked and ate his meals freely. And, in the nature of things, everything belonged to everybody; private ownership in response to individual labor did not exist, because man did not have to work anyhow. Reverting to that perfect time, the Torah maintains that the land will provide adequate food for everyone, including the flocks and herds, even if people do not work the land. But that is on condition that all claim of ownership lapses; the food is left in the fields to be picked by anyone who wishes, but it may not be hoarded by the landowner in particular.

It is in this context that we read the Halakhah of *Shabbat-'Erubin*, with special reference to the division of the world into private and public domain, the former the realm of permitted activity on the Sabbath, the latter not. If we may deal with an *'erub* fence or an *'erub* meal, how are we to interpret what is at stake in these matters? It in both instances is to render private domain public through the sharing of ownership. The *'erub* fence for its part renders public domain private, but only in the same sense that private domain owned by diverse owners is shared, ownership being commingled. The *'erub* fence signals the formation, for purposes of the sanctification of time, of private domain—but with the ownership commingled. So what is "private" about "private domain" is different on the Sabbath from in secular time. By definition, for property to be private in the setting of the Sabbath, it must be shared among householders. On the Sabbath, domain that is totally private, its ownership not commingled for the occasion, becomes a prison, the householder being unable to conduct himself in the normal manner in the courtyard beyond his door, let alone in other courtyards in the same alleyway, or in other alleyways that debouch onto the same street. And the Halakhah, as we have seen, makes provision for those—whether Israelite or gentile—who do not offer their proprietorship of their households for commingling for the Sabbath.

What happens, therefore, through the 'erub fence or 'erub meal is the redefinition of proprietorship: what is private is no longer *personal*, and no one totally owns what is his. But then everyone (who wishes to participate, himself and his household together) owns a share everywhere. So much for the "in his place" part of "each man in his place." His place constitutes an area where ordinary life goes on, but it is no longer "his" in the way in which the land is subject to his will and activity in ordinary time. If constructing a fence serves to signify joint ownership of the village, now turned into private domain, or constructing the gateway, of the alleyway and its courtyards, what about the meal? The 'erub meal signifies the shared character of what is eaten. It is food that belongs to all who wish to share it. But it is the provision of a personal meal, also, that allows an individual to designate for himself a place of Sabbath residence other than the household to which he belongs.

So the Sabbath loosens bonds, those of the householder to his property, those of the individual to the household. It forms communities, the householders of a courtyard into a community of shared ownership of the entire courtyard, the individual into a community other than that formed by the household to which he belongs—now the community of disciples of a given sage, the community of a family other than that in residence in the household, to use two of the examples common in the Halakhah. Just as the Sabbath redefines ownership of the Land and its produce, turning all Israelites into a single social entity, "all Israel," which together possesses the Land in common ownership, so the Sabbath redefines the social relationships of the household, allowing persons to separate themselves from the residence of the household and designate some other, some personal, point of residence instead.

Israel on the Sabbath in the Land, like God on the Sabbath of Eden, rests from the labor of creation. And that brings us to the question, What about that other principle of the Sabbath, the one set forth by the Halakhah of *Shabbat?* The richly detailed Halakhah of *Shabbat* defines the matter in a prolix yet simple way. It is to be stated with emphasis: *On the Sabbath it is prohibited deliberately to carry out in a normal way a completed act of constructive labor, one that produces enduring results, one that carries out one's entire intention: the whole of what one planned, one has accomplished, in exactly the proper manner.*

That definition takes into account the essence of the Halakhah of *Shabbat* as set forth in the Mishnah tractate, and the amplification and extension of matters in the Tosefta and the two Talmuds in no way revise the basic principles. Here there is a curious, if obvious, fact: it is not an act of labor that itself is prohibited (as the Ten Commandments in Exodus and Deuteronomy would have it), but an act of labor of a very particular definition.

What is striking is that no prohibition impedes performing an act of labor in an other-than-normal way. In theory, one may go out into the fields and plough, if he does so in some odd manner. He may build an entire house, so long as it collapses promptly. The issue of activity on the Sabbath therefore is removed from the obvious context of work, conventionally defined. Now the activity that is forbidden is of a very particular sort, modeled in its indicative traits after a quite specific paradigm. A person is not forbidden to carry out an act of destruction, or an act of labor that produces no lasting consequences. He may start an act of labor if he does not complete it. He may accomplish an act of labor in some extraordinary manner. None of these acts of labor is forbidden, even though, done properly and with consequence, they represent massive violations of the Halakhah. Nor is part of an act of labor that is not brought to conclusion prohibited. Nor is it forbidden to perform part of an act of labor in partnership with another person who carries out the other requisite part. Nor does one incur culpability for performing an act of labor in several distinct parts, e.g., over a protracted, differentiated period of time. A person may not willingly carry out the entirety of an act of constructive labor, start to finish. The issue is not "why not?," since we know the answer: God has said not to do so. The question is, whence the particular definition at hand?

Clearly, a definition of the act of labor that is prohibited on the Sabbath has taken over and recast the commonsense meaning of the commandment not to labor on the Sabbath. For considerations enter that recast matters from an absolute to a relative definition. One may tie a knot—but not one that stands. One may carry a package, but not in the usual manner. One may build a wall, only if it falls down. And, as I have stressed, one may do pretty much anything without penalty—if he did not intend matters as they actually happened. The metaphor of God in Eden, as sages have reflected on the story of creation, yields the governing principles that define forbidden labor. What God did in the six days of creation provides the model.

Let us review the main principles item by item. They involve the three preconditions. The act must fully carry out the intention of the actor, as creation carried out God's intention. The act of labor must be carried out by a single actor, as God acted alone in creating the world. An act of labor is the like of one that is required in the building and maintenance of God's residence in this world, the tabernacle. The act of labor prohibited on the Sabbath involves two considerations. The act must be done in the ordinary way, just as Scripture's account leaves no doubt that God accomplished creation in the manner in which he accomplished his goals from creation onward, by an act of speech. And, weightier still, the forbidden act of labor is one that produces enduring consequences. God did not create only to destroy, but he created the enduring world. And it goes without saying, creation yielded the obvious consequences that the act was completely done in all ways, as God himself declared. The act was one of consequence, involving what was not negligible but what man and God alike deemed to make a difference. Sages would claim, therefore, that the activity that must cease on the Sabbath finds its definition in the model of those actions that God carried out in making the world.

What then takes place inside the walls of the Israelite household when time takes over space and revises the conduct of ordinary affairs? Israel goes home to Eden. How best to make the statement that the Land is Israel's Eden, that Israel imitates God by keeping the Sabbath, meaning, not doing the things that God did in creating the world but ceased to do on the Sabbath, and that to restore its Eden, Israel must sustain its life—nourish itself—where it belongs? To set forth those most basic convictions about God in relationship to man and about Israel in relationship to God, I can imagine no more eloquent, no more compelling and appropriate, medium of expression than the densely detailed Halakhah of *Shebi'it*, *Shabbat*, and *'Erubin*. Indeed, outside of the setting of the household, its ownership, utilization, and maintenance, I cannot think of any other way of fully making that statement stick. In theory implausible for its very simplicity (as much as for its dense instantiation!), in Halakhic fact, compelling, the Oral Torah's statement accounts for the human condition. Israel's

Eden takes place in the household open to others, on the Sabbath, in acts that maintain life, share wealth, and desist from creation.

The key words, therefore, are in the shift from the here and now of time in which one works like God, to the *then* and *there* when one desists from working, just as God did at the moment the world was finished, perfected, and sanctified. Israel gives up the situation of man in ordinary time and space, destructive, selfish, dissatisfied and doing. Then, on the Sabbath, and there, in the household, with each one in place, Israel enters the situation of God in that initial, perfected, and sanctified then and there of creation: the activity that consists in sustaining life, sharing dominion, and perfecting repose through acts of restraint and sufficiency. Then where is Eden? Eden is Israel, the holy people. And when does Eden take place? Eden takes place on the Sabbath—just as in the beginning. But then if the Land corresponds to Eden, Israel to Adam and Eve, then what relationships with God unfold in partnership? The particular issue that predominates is, How does Israel's will for the Land respond to God's—and God's to Israel's? Now the question of intentionality arises, just as it did when God told man what he wanted and man rebelled.

II. Who Owns Eden?

The Halakhic representation of the story of the creation of Eden now expands to encompass within the motif of the usufruct of Eden ("You may freely eat of every tree of the garden, but of the tree of the knowledge of good and evil you shall not eat," [Gen. 2:16–17]), the matters of ownership and possession. For the Halakhah attitude and intentionality form critical criteria for Israel's right relationship with God. And, not surprisingly, attitude and intentionality come to realization in the disposition of that concerning which man proposes, but God disposes: hence, ownership versus possession (usufruct). As before, these serve as media for the expression of the relationship between man and God. God accorded to Adam and Eve possession of nearly everything in Eden, retaining ownership, the right to govern according to his will, for himself. The right of ownership then is embodied in the prohibition of eating the fruit of a single tree out of all of paradise. There we identify the point of intersection, and conflict, between God's and man's will. The Halakhah takes as its task the realization of Israel's acceptance of God's will for God's Land, shared by Israel on generous terms. It provides occasions for Israel to exercise and exhibit its recognition that it lives in God's kingdom and obeys God's will in precisely those matters in which man had originally failed.

The key to the entire system of interaction between God and Israel through the Land and its gifts emerges in the Halakhah of *Ma'aserot* and its companions, which deal—along the lines of *Shebi'it* and *'Erubin*—with the difference between possession and ownership. God owns the world, which he made. But God has accorded to man the right of possession of the earth and its produce. This he did twice, once to man—Adam and Eve—in Eden, the second time to Israel in the Land of Israel. And to learn the lesson that man did not master, that possession is not ownership but custody and stewardship. Israel has to acknowledge the claims of the creator to the glory of all creation, which is the Land. This Israel does by giving back God's share of the produce of the Land at the time, and in the manner, that God defines. The enlandised components of the Halakhah therefore form a single, cogent statement of matters.

If there is a single obstacle to obedience to God's will, it is man's natural inclination to mistake possession for ownership. For it is the attitude expressed in the claim of entire right of ownership—"my power and the might of my hand have gotten me this abundance" (Dt. 8:17)—that conveys the arrogance motivating rebellion such as took place to begin with in Eden. Someone who can do anything that he wants with a given object or person or property owns that object, person, or property. Someone whose will therefor is limited by the will of another does not. Hence, for its part, the antidote to rebellion and sin, which is the Torah, would impose upon ownership of the Land the supererogatory obligation to acknowledge a divided right of ownership and possession, that is to say, a partner's claim. And for Israel in the Land, the partner is God. And at stake is Israel's demonstration that, this time around, man acts with correct intentionality, responding to God's will with obedience, not rebellion.

A. *Ma'aserot*

Ma'aserot, the tractate concerning tithes, the portion of the crop set aside for God's purposes, not the householder's, discusses the entire set of agricultural dues, viewed generically: what the Israelite owes God out of the produce of the Land. The point of the Halakhah, permeating all categories, is that when Israel asserts its rights of possession, God's interest in that same crop is provoked, and he lays claim to his share in the crop of Land, ownership of which is held in partnership between God and the Israelite farmer. Then the rest follows, a vast exercise in how the will of God and the will of the Israelite meet in concord, Israel obeying God's laws about the disposition of the abundance of the Land. The link to Eden is firm: Israel obeys laws concerning the disposition of the fruit of the Land in the way in which Adam did not obey those concerning the fruit of Eden.

The basic Halakhic principle concerns not only Israel's relationship with God but also the Israelite's correspondence to God. In concrete terms the Halakhah realizes the theological position of the Pentateuchal account, which makes explicit that God and Israel relate through the Land. That is where the conflict of wills—the free will of Israelite man, the commanding voice of the God who created all things—works itself out. And the point of conflict focuses upon the conduct of Israel in the Land. The Halakhah here too, as on the Sabbath in the Land, accords to Israel possession, but not ownership of the Land, which God alone retains. God asserts his ownership when Israel proposes to exercise its rights of usufruct: when the tenant takes his share of the crop, he must also hand over to the Landowner (and to those designated by him to receive his share) the portion of the crop that is owing. And until the tenant, in possession of the Land, does pay his rent, he may not utilize the crop, as owners may freely do.

The basic principle is that, when the produce is suitable for use by its owner, then it becomes subject to tithing and may not be used until it is tithed. The Halakhah then indicates the point in the growth of various species at which tithes may be removed. That is the moment at which the produce is deemed edible. If someone picks and eats unripe produce, that does not impose the obligation to tithe, since commonly people do not regard unripe produce as food and do not eat it. Only when people ordinarily regard the produce as edible does consideration of tithing arise. Then there are two stages in the process, votive and obligatory. Crops may be tithed when the produce ripens. Then the produce becomes useful, and it is assumed that the farmer values the produce. But crops *must* be tithed when the farmer claims the produce as his own.

So what makes the difference? It is not the condition of the produce at all, but, rather, the attitude toward the produce that is taken by the farmer who has grown it. That attitude takes effect through the farmer's act of ownership, beyond possession. Asserting ownership takes place when he brings untithed produce from the field to the courtyard or prepares it for sale in the market. At that moment, the farmer having indicated his claim to the produce and intent to use it for his own purposes, God's interest is aroused, his share then is due. God responds to man, specifically, God's attitudes correspond to those of man: when (Israelite) man wants to own the crop and dispose of it as he wishes, then God demands his share.

What is ownerless and thus not possessed by a particular farmer as his private property simply is not liable to tithing. The second (now familiar) one is, the obligation to tithe pertains once the crop has ripened. There are some interstitial problems, e.g., the status of land in Syria, which is neither the Land of Israel nor the land of the gentiles. If the crop is purchased prior to ripening, in Syria the crop is exempt. But some opinion holds that Israelite ownership of land—not merely the crop—in Syria is the prerequisite for liability to begin with. And that underscores the critical issue at hand: the intersection of Israel, the Land of Israel, and the produce. When an Israelite in the Land of Israel possesses Land, his right of possession, but not ownership, is underscored by the restrictions that govern his disposition of the produce of the Land.

As in the account of Eden, God's will comes into conflict with man's, showing them to be emotionally consubstantial, so here too, God and man respond in the same way to the same facts. How is it that Israel and God relate in so concrete and specific a situation as is defined by the course of nature, the ripening of the crops? It is because, the Halakhah takes for granted, God and Israel bear the same attitudes, feel the same emotions, form corresponding intentions. God and man are alike not only in intellect—the same rules of reasoning applying to both—but also, and especially, in attitude and emotion, in virtue in the classic sense. God commands Israel to love him, therefore God values and prizes the emotion of love. Man is commanded to love God. But that is not the only emotion shared by man and God. In the biblical biography of God, the tragic hero, God, will despair, love, hope, feel disappointment or exultation. The biblical record of God's feelings and God's will concerning the feelings of humanity—wanting human love, for example—leaves no room for doubt. In this matter, the Rabbinic literature is explicit when it says, "the merciful God wants the heart." God commands that humanity love God with full heart, soul, mind, and might, because God feels and values that same emotion. God's heart, not only his rationality, corresponds to man's. In that context we take up the Halakhic position outlined in *Ma'aserot*. When the farmer wants the crop, so too does God. When the householder takes the view that the crop is worthwhile, God responds to the attitude of the farmer by forming the same opinion. The theological anthropology that brings God and the householder into the same continuum prepares the way for understanding what makes the entire Mishnaic system work.

B. *Terumot*

The agricultural dues to which *Ma'aserot* in general makes reference are assigned to God's dependents, specifically the sacerdotal castes, priests and Levites, and the poor; and they are further used to support the holy city, Jerusalem, by securing an enhanced supply of food and an increased flow of funds to the city. In addition, obligatory and votive offerings for the temple, both in specie (temple coin) and the produce of nature (animals, wine, and grain), support the temple buildings and the cycle of regular offerings that are maintained in the city. The upshot is, Israel in the holy Land, God's partners in the possession of the country and its abundance, give back to Heaven through designated castes, locations, and activities, God's share in the whole, and this the holy people do both in obedience to God's commandments and also on their own initiative.

The Halakhah of *Terumot* constitutes a vast exegesis of a single religious principle: the Israelite has the power by an act of will confirmed (where required) by a concrete deed to sanctify what is common. The Israelite then is accorded by God the remarkable power to designate as holy, by reason of the Israelite's own uncoerced will, what is otherwise ordinary and not sacred. Not the only category of the Halakhah to embody in concrete actions that considerable proposition, the Halakhah of *Terumot* nonetheless forms a remarkably apt medium for delivering that message. That is because of the stress in the Halakhah at hand on considerations of particularity: the householder's act of sanctification pertains to a very specific batch of produce, the consequence of sanctification invokes a very particular teleology inherent in the type of produce that has been sanctified. The upshot is, Israel's and God's purposes and power intersect. And, to revert to what we have learned in the Halakhah of *Ma'aserot*, here possession shades over, if not to ownership, then to responsibility; for that which is subject to one's will, one is responsible, and that means, specifically, one must conform to God's will that which is subject to one's own will.

A critical component of the Israelite's relationship to God is his responsibility for preserving the sanctification of what belongs to God and is designated for God's clients. It is the thought, confirmed by deed, of the Israelite that what is secular is made sacred. In his translation and commentary on *Terumot*, Alan J. Avery-Peck expressed that principle in the following language: "It is the common Israelite, the non-priest, who, while forbidden to eat holy produce, has the power to cause produce to be deemed holy." The active player in the designation and disposition of the portion of the crops to serve as heave offering for the priest therefore is the Israelite householder or farmer, not the priest, and not God (except through the working of chance). Once God's interest in the crop has made the crop liable to the separation of the various tithes and offerings, it is the householder who takes over, and by an act of deliberation and intentionality, imparts the status of holiness to the portion of the crop he designates for the priesthood. And he bears full responsibility, also, for what happens to the designated produce until it is handed over to the priest. Avery-Peck (Avery-Peck, *Mishnah*, p. 3) frames the matter in this way: "The common Israelite is central in the process of sanctification. The holy heave offering comes into being only if man properly formulates the intention to sanctify part of his produce and indicates that intention through corresponding words and actions." All else flows from that basic principle. The Israelite householder has the power to initiate the entire process of sanctification, to transform the classification of produce and to subject that produce to the logic that inheres in its very character, its own teleology. The householder then restores to God his share in the crop and imposes upon God's share the discipline required by the logical character of that particular crop.

A productive corollary insists that the intentionality of the Israelite pertain to a very specific, differentiated corpus of produce. While holiness does not inhere in a given batch, so that the heave offering of one batch may serve for several, nonetheless batches must be formed of like produce. That means that one's intentionality pertains to the species, not to the genus: olive oil, not olives in general, and so throughout. The particularity of the focus of intentionality cannot be overstated; the Halakhah stresses the matter in a wide range of cases, e.g., they may not separate oil as heave offering for olives which have been crushed, nor wine as heave offering for grapes which have been trampled but the processing of which has not yet been completed.

On the other hand, when it comes to the actual identification of the portion of the crop to serve as heave offering and so to be sanctified, the householder cannot act deliberately, choosing this part and not that, but must act in such a way that chance produces the selection. One cannot measure out or weigh out or count out the produce that is to be sanctified; rather, God indicates his choice through the workings of chance. That chance constitutes the expression of God's will is made explicit in various Aggadic passages, and here the Halakhah makes exactly the same statement. So man's intentionality arouses God's participation in the transaction, but God's role in making the selection then excludes man's participation in that chapter of the matter.

Man's intent for a given object bears the power to classify as sacred that particular object. God's intent in making that same object controls the legitimate use of the object that is sanctified. So the plan or attitude or program of each party to the transaction—the householder's, God's—governs. But that takes place for each party in his own way. Man's intentionality dictates the classification of the object as God's (that is, as sanctified) and then, God's, the disposition of the object now subjected to his ownership. That is where the teleology of things enters in. We may then say, once man has assigned ownership to God (through God's surrogates), God's plan in making an object, the teleology that inheres in that object, takes over. No wonder, then, that the Halakhah so emphasizes the specificity of the transaction: this particular object (batch of produce), serving the natural purpose that inheres in this particular object, forming the transaction at which man and God intersect.

That somewhat complicated calculus yields a quite simple and now obvious proposition. In assigning to the status of sanctification a portion of the crop, the householder gives up his possession of, thus his right to subject to his own will, a batch of produce and assigns that which he gives up to God's domain, therefore makes the produce subject to God's will. God's will then extends to Israel in its way, to nature in its context. Stated in this way, the transaction in heave offering represents an act of submission by man's to God's will that is very specific and concrete. The importance of the specificity of intentionality, on the one side, and the particularity of the teleology that governs the use of heave offering, on the other hand, now merges. Israel and nature relate to God in accord with the same rules, in the same way, but in quite different dimensions.

The Halakhah of *Terumot* returns us by a direct and smooth route to the issues of creation, once more realizing in concrete words and gestures the dynamics of the relationship between God and man—now: Israelite man possessed of a share in the Land, that is to say, the householder—in creation. God has created the realm of nature, Eden and the Land (to invoke the principal locative categories of the Aggadic-Halakhic system, respectively). He did so with a purpose, and in each component of creation inheres the Creator's plan for that thing. And, we may now say, [1] when, through man's initiative, a component of creation is declared sacred, that particular thing subject to the intentionality of man must then realize the distinct and specific plan or purpose that defines the attitude of man. When then [2] man assigns to God a portion of the crop, that act of sanctification places that portion of the crop under God's plan and purpose in carrying out the act of creation. The rules that dictate the disposition of heave offering therefore bring about a transaction in which wills work together, [2] God's and [1] man's, now to realize God's purpose in creation, on the one side, and demonstrate man's accord with that purpose, on the other.

Man by an act of will assigns to God his share in the produce of the Land, at which point that batch of produce becomes subject to God's will—meaning, the particular teleology of that produce, by species, not only genus. The act of sanctification then takes place when man by his act of will concerning what is subject to his possession declares subject to God's will that which, once made subject to God's will, must be utilized as God intended. Man then by the act of sanctification declares nature subject to God's initial purpose. In the setting of *Terumot*, which the system finds particularly appropriate for a statement of this character, Israelite man by an act of will declares subject to God's plan and program the produce of the Land that is God's share—a perfectly simple, rational, and right transaction reaffirming the order of nature. And that is a conception that the Halakhah of *Ma'aserot* has not set forth, but for which that Halakhah has prepared us. Israel in the Land has its role to play in restoring nature to its original perfection.

C. *Hallah*

When the householder takes possession of his share of the crops, he also designates God's portion. Within the household itself, the householder does the same, but not for the same reason. At issue is God's share of the bread. As soon as we know *when* God's interest is provoked, we also know *why*—that is to say, what man does that elicits God's participation. We start with the definition of bread: it is a baked food product that is made of flour that, upon being moistened and kneaded and fermented, rises. What derives from flour that does not leaven is not liable to dough offering and not classified as bread for purposes of Passover either.

Two criteria of liability to separate the dough offering coexist, one marking the beginning, the other the end, of the spell. Liability commences with the mixture of flour and water and the working of the two into a mass, and it is fixed with the conclusion of the same process. The upshot is, the span of susceptibility coincides with the process of fermentation: the activation of the enzyme, at the outset, then the cultivation of the fermentation process, and finally the realization of the goal of that process in the forming of a crust, the conclusion of fermentation. And, to address the third question briefly, dough offering must be presented out of dough made from grain that is eaten by Israel in the Land of Israel.[3] The Mishnah insists that the priests will not accept dough offering from bread prepared outside the Land.

---

[3] Not necessarily grown in the Land of Israel, but possibly from the interstitial territory of Syria, which in Halakhic theory is neither part of the Land of Israel nor part of the land of the gentiles.

We may say that the critical criterion is dough [1] that has incurred liability within the Land of Israel and [2] that is consumed by Israelites in the Land. So there is a very specific point of intersection that dictates which dough is liable to dough offering: [1] dough prepared from wheat and comparable flour, which, when mixed with yeast and water, has the power to ferment; [2] dough at the point at which the fermentation process has realized its goal. The upshot is that the derivation of the grain by itself bears no consequence. But the processing of the flour produced by the grain, and the location of the Israelites who consume the bread form the critical criteria.

Dough that has formed a crust within the Land of Israel is liable, whatever the origin of the flour. In the priests' view, dough offering may not be brought from outside of the Land of Israel, but that is not because considerations of cultic cleanness pertain, which would exclude the produce of foreign lands, unclean as they are by definition. Why the priests should reject dough offering brought by Israelites from abroad is clear: it is when Israelites in the Land of Israel prepare dough that liability takes effect. Then the actuality of Israel dwelling on the Land, not the origin of the grain, determines: Israelites living in the Land of Israel separate dough offering from the bread that they are going to eat, from the point at which the bread begins to ferment, and they are obligated to do so from the point at which the bread has ceased to ferment.

That the whole forms an exercise in thinking about the fermentation process is demonstrated, moreover, by the explicit insistence that, just as flour produces dough subject to dough offering only if a fermentation process is possible, so flour produces unleavened bread valid for Passover only if a fermentation process is possible but is thwarted. So the bread that the Israelites in the Land of Israel eat to which God establishes his claim is comparable in its traits to the bread that the Israelites leaving Egypt, or commemorating their exodus from Egypt, are required to eat—and that bread too is liable to dough offering, as a matter of fact. At stake, then, is the fermentation process itself.

Then God takes notice.

The process need not take place, but it must bear the potential to take place. So it may not affect the bread of the exodus—which is liable to dough offering—but it must affect the bread of Israel in the Land of Israel—also liable.

Having come this far, we may readily perceive the broad outlines
of a simple message: bread in which God takes an interest is bread
subject to living processes of nature, the life of the enzyme (as we
should express matters). Leavening then is the key to the definition of
bread. Taken as a natural process, leavening is animate, or is perceived as animate. It comes about (in contemporary language)
"through the action of gas bubbles developed naturally or folded in
from the atmosphere. Leavening may result from yeast or bacterial
fermentation, from chemical reactions or from the distribution in the
batter of atmospheric or injected gases."[4] Fermentation, required for
wine or beer as much as for bread, involves a process of frothing
brought about by microorganisms growing in the absence of air. That
sages grasped the main point—fermentation represents the animation
of the grain in its mixture with yeast and water—we need not doubt,
even though they would have used different language to describe the
process. How then draw conclusions from natural processes of fermentation, perceived as the animation of ingredients for food? The
calculus then is readily discerned: Israel's life in the Land of Israel is
nourished through the transformation of grain into bread, that is,
through the life-process that takes grain and makes it edible and life-
sustaining. Then and there God lays his claim to a share: when Israel
renews its life, meal by meal, its action in invoking the life-process of
fermentation, start to finish, provokes God's reaction. That is because
God too has a share in the transaction by which life is maintained—
but (as the priests clearly maintained) only in the transaction that
takes place between Israel and the Land of Israel, there alone.

To understand the next point, a fact is required. Sages read Lev.
11:34, 37 to mean that dry produce is insusceptible to cultic uncleanness, produce that has been wet down is susceptible. They further
maintained in the category of law, *Makhshirin*, that for dry produce to
become susceptible through contact with water (or other appropriate
liquid), the act of wetting down has to have taken place deliberately,
by an intentional act. So, the Halakhah holds, Israel becomes responsible for the cultic cleanness of the produce only by an act of intentionality, but—as we see here—Israel becomes liable to hand over
God's share of the produce willy-nilly. So it is with life. Why then

---

[4] Samuel A. Matz, "Baking and Bakery Products," *Encyclopaedia Britannica* 2:597.

does intentionality play no role in the liability of the dough to dough offering?

The reason becomes clear when we recall the critical role human intentionality plays in the Halakhah of *Makhshirin*, the counterpart and opposite of the Halakhah of *Hallah*. The fact is, while what is deliberately wet down is subject to uncleanness, what is accidentally wet down is not. Here, by contrast, the mixing of the flour, salt, yeast, and water inaugurates a process through which, at the end, liability to the offering is incurred—whether the process came about deliberately or accidentally. A simple formulation involves a concrete case. A householder takes flour, which is dry and has not been deliberately wet down. Why not? Because once wet down, the flour molders. The householder further takes yeast. And, putting the two together, the householder adds water. At that moment, when the process of kneading dough to bake bread commences (in contemporary language: with the irrigation of the yeast and the dough, the moment at which the dough congeals and the yeast buds and ferments, producing its sugar, its carbon dioxide, and its ethanol)—at that exact moment, the instant of animation, at which the bread begins to live, the householder goes on the alert for dangers to the bread—and so throughout.

The moment of wetting grain down defines the hour of conflict between life and death, yielding sanctification or uncleanness—and this in concrete ways. Then, at the very time, the act done with deliberation precipitates the conflict. But that is only if the householder cares. If the householder does not intend the dough to congeal and the yeast to rise, in regard to susceptibility to uncleanness nothing of consequence happens. It is the Israelite's will and intention and the act that realizes them that endow with consequence what by nature happens willy-nilly. But so far as the process itself, it does not depend upon the householder's intentionality. The fermentation process that animates the flour and produces bread goes forward whether or not the householder intended it to. Nothing he does can stop it once it has started, and no call upon his alertness to prevent uncleanness is issued. That is why God's claim on the dough, for the dough offering for the priesthood, does not depend upon man's intentionality—irrelevant to the process of animation, of bringing life to the inert flour—but upon God's own reason for engagement. That has to do with the maintenance of the processes of life, man's and nature's.

If I had to identify where the everyday meets the Eternal, I should

choose the here and now of petty obsessions with tiny events and
their intangible, animated histories, down to the moment of adding
water to the yeast and dough when making bread: when life renews
itself through the life-precipitating touch of water to the flour and the
yeast. Here considerations of uncleanness and those of sanctification
intersect. That is the point that precipitates concern with the forces
of death, the prime source of cultic uncleanness. Then, to preserve
purity, Israel goes on the alert for the danger of pollution, at the
moment when yeast, flour, and water ignite the processes of animation. So too for all of their counterparts: "if water be put on the
seed," take care. Now we see the other half of the story. Unclean or
otherwise, the dough congeals, the yeast ferments and yields gas, and
so life-processes have commenced, though death and its surrogates
threaten. Then the householder goes on the alert—if he cares, if by
an act of deliberation he has made life happen. And there too, by
sharing the outcome of the fermentation with God, the householder
acknowledges the opposite of death, which is life, embodied in the living processes by which the bread comes into being, and resulting in
the presence, within the dough, of a portion subject to sanctification:
donation to the priest in the present instance.

The particularity of dough offering should now register. It is paid
from bread made from grain from which the heave offering has
already been removed. So the critical point of differentiation—an
offering from the mixture of flour, yeast, and water, taken from when
fermentation starts to when it ends—takes on still greater consequence. Wine and beer ferment, but no counterpart offering from
wine, over and above the heave offering and tithes to which all produce is liable, is demanded, nor from beer. In the wine-olive-oil-
wheat-culture of the Land of Israel, it is only wheat, in the course of
its later processing, that becomes subject to a further offering of the
present kind, one linked to its life cycle. And that is because—so it
seems to me—bread stands for life, consumed to be sure with oil and
wine. Therefore it is the processing of flour into bread to sustain life
where fermentation represents life that particularly registers. That
marks the occasion for the affirmation of God's presence in all life-
forms and processes: God lays his claim to his share, because God's
claim upon the Israelite householder extends to the outer limits of
vitality. We find ourselves beyond the narrow limits of Eden as a

story, but well within the programmatic, the theological theme that Eden embodies in that story: the theme of the power of human will.

D. *Ma'aser Sheni*

The frontiers of Eden are crossed, also, when we introduce the comparable realm, the Land of Israel. The metaphor of Eden forms one localization of Israel's relationship with God, the key one, as we have seen. But once Eden serves as the counterpart to the Land, then the Land, in all its integrity and autonomy, enters in. But, defined in its own terms, the Land and its traits, carrying in their wake issues of relationship sorted out through enlandisement, impose their own logic upon that same relationship. With the Land, localization takes on the character of enlandisement, and a relationship that requires a certain kind of place gains a specific, very particular character for itself.

How does the metaphor of Eden cease to mark the outer limits of the theology of the Halakhah? Three settings within the Land differentiate, therefore localize the relationship of Israel and God: [1] the household of Israel, situated anywhere in the Land, [2] Jerusalem, and [3] the temple. These localizations of the relationship then involved the householder and the priesthood and other scheduled castes, the householder in the holy city, and the priesthood and God in the temple, respectively. So relationships unfold beyond those that link God to Israel through the disposition of the Land that is Eden.

That brings us to the first of two tractates on where and how Israel itself—not only the priesthood, not only the altar fires in God's behalf—may consume part of God's share of the produce of the Land. Here where the eating takes place, not what is eaten, defines the focus. God's food must be eaten in God's chosen locale, which is Jerusalem. *Ma'aser Sheni*, with its companion, *Bikkurim*, forms a bridge between the division of Agriculture and that of Holy Things, that is, between the sanctity of the Land and its produce, shared between Israel and God, and the sanctity of the holy house and its offerings, shared among Israel, the priests, and God. With the Halakhah of *Ma'aser Sheni* and *Bikkurim*, we undertake the journey from the provinces of the Land of Israel to the metropolis, Jerusalem, where, Scripture explicitly declares, God resides. Within the Land, Israel and God meet there in particular, and that is in several ways. First, in the holiest location in the Land, the highest point in Jerusalem, stands the temple, where God's Name abides, and there Israel provides God with meat, wine, oil, and bread. Second, God calls Israel to Jerusalem, there to eat a portion of the crop sanctified to him. So—within the framework of the theory of *Ma'aserot*—what belongs to God comes to the holy city, there to bring joy to the life of the holy people through the produce of the holy Land.

The way in which things become holy and cease to be holy forms the problem for sages, because in their view sanctification is a status conferred or removed, not a condition intrinsic to things. Scripture itself dictates the conception that the produce designated as second tithe, and so sanctified, may be turned into money and carried in that form to Jerusalem, there to be converted back into (other) produce for consumption in Jerusalem. The details of the rules then yield a variety of governing principles. And that fact reminds us of the distinction, critical to the Halakhah, between ownership and possession. First, the householder does not own this produce; he is assigned possession and enjoyment of it. The Halakhah thus teaches the lesson that even possession and usufruct ("of all the trees . . . eat") do not constitute ownership; the rules of sanctification intervene, imposing God's will upon the produce that the farmer in all practicality possesses and uses to his own advantage.

Second, from God's perspective as set forth in the Torah, Written yielding Oral, what is it that God's will for the relationship between himself and Israel concerns? What God wants, then, becomes critical, an indicator of the character of the relationship between Israel and God that comes to expression in the Halakhah. In Eden God wanted only for man to take pleasure in his, God's, creation. All God now asks is that the householder enjoy God's gift in God's presence, in Jerusalem. God calls Israel to gather in his city and provides food for their enjoyment there. No native category of the law makes a more explicit statement on what Israel's relationship to God comprises than this one, and its message is, to serve God. As the Aggadah requires that Israel love God, the Halakhah demands that Israel rejoice with God, in God's presence, by having a good meal of God's produce in Jerusalem. So the Halakhah orders that Israel relate to God through joy, finding in its act and occasion of rejoicing the realization of Israel's interaction with God. Eden has prepared us for such a conception of man's meeting with God.

What marks God's ownership, and Israel's mere possession, of the Land is God's laying claim to two matters. First is a share of the crop, on the one side. Second is a share of the outcome of particular life-processes that render the important part of the crop desirable, on the other. The one share represents God's response to man and is owing when man indicates by his action that he wishes to make his own the now-ripe crops, so God responds to man's will by laying claim to his portion. The other share forms God's response to nature and is owing when the natural processes of life have accomplished their task. Then God responds to the moment of fulfillment of his purpose, to which man's intentionality is irrelevant, and his share once more is owing. Man's intentionality, nature's teleology—both come to realization in God's laying claim to what is his. So requiring what is due him, God convenes with man when man's engagement defines the venue—the harvest in the field, the transport of the crop to the courtyard—and with nature when nature's processes do. It is all the same; God's purpose, not man's will or nature's way, governs.

But what, exactly, does God want for man? Answering that question brings us to the very remarkable Halakhic category before us, the share of the crop belonging to God that God assigns to the householder and his family. God thereby imposes his will upon the crop, but indicates that his will is for the householder and his family to attend upon God in God's abode itself, there to celebrate an occasion for rejoicing. So now we deal with the Israelite household, not only God's sharecropper but also God's beneficiary. Now what makes the transaction consequential is the condition of rejoicing: to share God's portion of the crop, the Israelite must leave his household altogether and go to God's house. Here we confront another act that underscores the transient nature of possession, but the enduring character of relationship. The Israelite householder brings these components of God's share to Jerusalem and consumes them there, as Scripture is explicit: "where God takes up an abode." Accordingly, when Israelites eat a portion of the crop that is set aside as holy and subjected to the special rules inherent in that status, they do so in the holy place, Jerusalem, where Israel and God convene. There, as the Halakhah underscores, the designated produce enters the condition of irrevocable sanctification, entering the city confirming the sanctification of the produce and making it permanent. That is because the produce has entered the location where his "Name" takes up an abode. Given the bearer of sanctification, the produce itself, we find no surprise that eating God's share of the crop in God's place defines the occasion for the encounter with God. As in Eden, the medium for sustaining life forms also the venue of the relationship between man and God.

Once again, the character of the relationship—the joy that is consequent upon humility and obedience—is made explicit. God in the Torah insists that in relating to God, Israel find occasion for rejoicing, and God explicitly declares, among the emotions or sentiments or attitudes that animate Israel's relationship with him, the experience of pure joy takes priority. When we deal with Israel's relationship with God, time and again we find Israel *required* to rejoice, and that takes place through eating God's food in God's place. This comes about through renunciation of ownership in favor of conditional possession. Israel leaves its own household and transfers to God's. Eating God's food in God's place accomplishes God's goal, which is for Israel to rejoice. Then, concomitantly, Israel should not find in its own enlandisement, in the household, the place of ultimate joy, but rather in God's locus. And the rest follows.

The meticulous designation of portions of the crop as tithes and heave offering forms a weighty matter of the Torah because, in disposing of the produce of the Land as God requires Israel to do, Israel recapitulates, with a different ending, that story of the beginning that closed in disaster. Adam could not refrain from one thing. Israel gives up many. Adam lost it all. Israel gains pure joy, and its relationship with God is one of utter happiness—bliss is not too strong a word. Representing the agricultural dues as a mere formality, an onerous tax, therefore misses the point of the Halakhah—both Scripture's and the Oral Torah's! Matters could not be stated more uncomprehendingly than in the language, "Woe to you, scribes and Pharisees, hypocrites! for you tithe mint and dill and cumin and have neglected the weightier matters of the law, justice and mercy and faith; these you ought to have done, without neglecting the others" (Mt. 23:23, RSV). That formulation frames the issue disproportionately. The Halakhah does not neglect the weightier matters of the law, making ample provision for justice and mercy. The Halakhah here concerns itself with Israel's relationship with God, which is one of bliss attained through obedience to God's always-benevolent will. To treat as opposites tithing and justice is to miss the point: tithing in its place, justice in its place, realize the undivided will of the one God. And primary to the acts of faith are those statements through deed that affirm God's ownership of the Land and Israel's covenantal, stipulative possession of it—just as the Written Torah insists from beginning to end. These acts of conformity to God's will in the disposition of the crops form a nexus in the relationship of Israel and God, because when Israel accepts God's will for the produce, Israel is accorded an occasion for rejoicing with God. And God rejoices too.

E. *Bikkurim*

Second tithe is not the only portion of the crop belonging to God that is assigned by God to the householder for eating in Jerusalem. Firstfruits, an offering presented in the temple to the priest by the householder out of the crops of his land, represents a different kind of agricultural presentation from heave offering, on the one side, and second tithe, on the other. Like heave offering, it belongs to the priest. Like second tithe, it must be conveyed to Jerusalem. But unlike heave offering, it must be presented to the priest in the temple itself. And unlike second tithe, it cannot be eaten by the householder, but only by the priest. So we deal with an aspect of Israel's relationship with God that encompasses other dimensions than those already treated. Now God calls the householder to the temple, but to receive for his designated beneficiary, that is, for himself, what the householder is obligated personally to deliver in kind, not to convert to specie and to reconvert to produce for consumption in the city. The specificity of the Halakhah matches the particularity of the sages' statement, conveyed thereby.

The entire statement made through the Halakhah responds to two questions: What is required? Who is obligated? What is required is firstfruits of those species in which the Land specializes. Who is obligated is the Israelite, who not only possesses a share in the Land but also derives from the Israel to whom the Land was initially handed over. The presentation of the firstfruits defines the occasion for declaring who is, and who is not, that Israel of whom Scripture speaks, the one to whom reference is made in the statement,

> A wandering Aramean was my father, and he went down into Egypt and sojourned there, few in number; and there he became a nation, great, mighty, and populous. And the Egyptians treated us harshly and

afflicted us and laid upon us hard bondage . . . and the Lord brought
us out of Egypt with a mighty hand and an outstretched arm, with great
terror, . . . and he brought us to this place and gave us this land, a land
flowing with the milk and honey. And behold, now I bring the first of
the fruit of the ground that thou, O Lord, have given me. (Dt. 26:3ff.)

Possession of the land forms the final act in the drama of Israel's wandering, descent, exodus, and entry into the Land. Presenting firstfruits
and reciting the declaration characterize one who is wholly Israel,
possessing both the Land by inheritance and the genealogy that mark
one as such. Converts, on the one side, and non-householders
(landowners), on the other, fall outside of the rite, the one presenting
firstfruits without a declaration, the other having no firstfruits to present. Those who cannot make that statement find themselves excluded from the Israel, possessed of the Land, who celebrate their
relationship with God in the rite at hand. The link to the Land via
Israel's history, moreover, is physical and personal.

The points of stress identify the particularity of the Land and the
singularity of genealogical Israel's possession thereof. The convert
who possesses a share in the Land presents the firstfruits; God wants
his share. He is equal to all other Israelites in his obligations to God.
But, while the convert's children may marry native Israelites and so
through ethnic and territorial assimilation enter into normative Israel,
the convert himself cannot fully participate in the rite. He may present his firstfruits to the priest, but he does so in silence. He enjoys
full equality as God's partner in the ownership of the Land; the priest
receives in God's behalf the firstfruits that he therefore presents. So
in practical terms the convert forms one with all Israel. But having
been Israel from the moment at which Israel set foot in the Land is
not the same thing as having become part of Israel later on. In the
end, the enchantment of the Land by the presence of Israel, the
imposition of the sanctity of the one upon the sanctity of the other—
these represent a dimension of being Israel that only time and future
genealogical integration may bring about: more time within Israel,
more time on the Land. So the reading of the language of the declaration that sages undertake requires them to reflect upon what it
means to live on the Land, be nurtured by the Land, and be changed
in the passage of time, in the intersection of the two sanctified entities, Land and People.

To identify the particular point that the Halakhah of *Bikkurim* registers, we have to classify the offering in relationship to others that are both like and unlike it. How do the firstfruits compare with other agricultural offerings? They are comparable to, but different from, produce that has been designated as heave offering and second tithe.

Firstfruits and heave offering both are consecrated to the priesthood and eaten only by them; both sanctify any unconsecrated produce with which they are mixed but can be neutralized in proper proportion; both are eaten in a state of cleanness. They are comparable to heave offering in that firstfruits are to be eaten by the priests and their families, not the householders who present them. They must be eaten in a state of cultic cleanness.

What about firstfruits and second tithe? They are comparable to second tithe in that firstfruits like second tithe must be presented in Jerusalem and involve the correct recitation; heave offering is presented without a declaration. Like second tithe, firstfruits must be removed at the designated point in the year. A person in mourning before the burial of the deceased may not eat either second tithe or firstfruits. Both represent occasions for rejoicing. Once in Jerusalem, considerations of neutralization no longer apply. Then the sanctity inheres and is indelible.

How do firstfruits stand alone? Unlike heave offering and second tithe, firstfruits do not render prohibited for consumption produce that has been completely processed; there is no prescribed volume that must be designated firstfruits; only the seven species are covered by the offering; the rite does not apply in the time in which the temple is in ruins; those who do not own the crops may not designate firstfruits from them. Not only so, but

[1] the status of produce as firstfruits may be designated even to what has not been harvested;

[2] an entire field may be donated;

[3] the householder must see to it that the produce is delivered and replace what is designated and then lost; and

[4] a temple rite is involved in the presentation (an ox for meat for the householder and his family as well as for the priesthood, a bird for a burnt offering, Levitical song, waving before the altar and

[5] in the temple rite, the householder participates. While the basket is still on his shoulder, he recites the entire confession of firstfruits,

beginning from the words "I declare this day to the Lord your God" (Dt. 26:3), and proceeding until he finishes the entire passage. In Judah's view, while the basket is on his shoulder, he recites only up to the second part of the confession, which begins with the words, "A wandering Aramean was my father" (Dt. 26:6). Once he has reached those words, he takes the basket down from his shoulder and holds it by its rim, and a priest puts his hand beneath the basket and waves it before the altar. And then the Israelite recites the second part of the confession. And then he places the basket beside the altar, bows down, and departs.

[6] The final requirement is the householder's remaining overnight in Jerusalem. To heave offering and second tithe these rulings do not pertain. Then these are the critical indicators of the Halakhic standing of firstfruits and tell us the statement that the Halakhah makes through its rules of firstfruits and through no other category of the Halakhah.

Firstfruits focus upon the Land as the particular medium for the celebration of life. Once again they draw the householder off the Land he tends as his own to God's place, there to explain his claim upon the nurturing Land. When God and Israel meet for Israel's presentation of the firstfruits of the Land, the new crops in hand, Israel comes to God's abode and speaks of its own: the Land they have in common. Israel sets forth its claim to possess the Land at the very moment of acknowledging God's ownership. It does so in the offering of the choice crop to the priesthood—not a mere random sample of the entire crop, such as is represented by heave offering, eaten by the priests wherever located, nor a tithe of the crop reserved for Israel's own enjoyment at God's abode. For the firstfruits the householder bears responsibility until the priest takes possession in God's behalf in the temple—just like the animal offerings the householder brings along. But, unlike the obligatory offerings presented out of public funds, the obligatory offerings presented out of personal funds in expiation of sin, firstfruits are both personal and public. They are personal, because—the declaration stresses—they represent the householder's individual and physical claim to presence and possession of the Land. They are public because they are obligatory and serve no individual aspiration of atonement.

Anyone may buy a beast or bird or cereal and designate it for a personal purpose. Only the householder presents firstfruits. Anyone may declare the classification of a beast or bird or cereal, e.g., a sin offering, a guilt offering, a freewill offering, a peace offering. Only the householder may classify the produce as firstfruits by an explicit designation. The householder's is a remarkable statement, bringing what he calls his own but merely possesses on God's sufferance, as we have seen time and again—and then speaking of himself and his fathers. The rite then defines the relationship of Israel and God in acutely personal terms, invoking the "I" and the "my," in giving back to God the first testimonies to God's ongoing benevolence. Firstfruits makes the relationship between God and Israel personal and immediate, familial and genealogical—wholly through the nexus of the Holy Land. Heave offering and tithe are presented whether or not the temple is standing and they are separated by sharecroppers, tenant farmers, holders of confiscated property, and by robbers. But firstfruits are presented, their purpose and standing explicated, only by the specific Israelite householder born to inherit the Land, out of crops raised on his own fields and presented to the priesthood only in the temple. Now, when the Halakhah wishes to state that Israel in its fleshly embodiment of families through genealogical ties relates to God at the temple through the gifts of grace presented by the Land, it can make no more particular and concrete statement than that.

F. Pe'ah

We come to yet another beneficiary of God's portion of the crop, the poor. Roger Brooks (*Yerushalmi Pe'ah*, 1) explains the matter in this language:

> ... all estate holders in the Land of Israel were responsible for the material welfare of the poor in their vicinity. Their [the sages'] view stemmed from the Rabbinic understanding of a few verses scattered throughout the Hebrew Bible. These passages specified constraints upon normal agricultural procedures, all designed to allow poor and indigent Israelites to eke out a living by gathering scraps of food from fields and orchards. Leviticus 19:9 commanded Israelites to leave a corner of their fields unharvested, so that poor people might reap a bit of grain; Leviticus 19:10 extended this provision by ruling that stalks of grain or clusters of grapes that accidentally fell to the earth were not to be gathered by the harvesters, but left behind for the poor.

Deuteronomy 26:19 ruled that produce that workers left behind in a
field, orchard, or vineyard, should be abandoned so that the poor, once
again, might gain some benefit of the Land's yield. And finally, Deuteronomy 26:12–13 described poorman's tithe, a portion of the yield set
aside during the third and sixth years of the Sabbatical cycle. These
various and scattered laws of the corner-offering (*Pe'ah*, from which the
Tractate takes its name), of grain-gleanings and separated grapes, of
forgotten produce, and of poorman's tithe, provide the entire foundation of Tractate Pe'ah.

It follows that the poor have (in Brooks's language) "a proprietary
entitlement" to part of the crop. Brooks (*Support for the Poor*, 17) further links the diverse claims of the poor to those of the priesthood:

> By placing the tractate in this context [that of Zeraim], Mishnah's
> redactors indicate that in their view the poor, and the poor-offerings
> due them, are in some way analogous to the priests and the priestly
> rations given them. In fact, Mishnah's framers make this analogy explic-
> it when they compare the poor with the priests (see M. 1:6, 4:6–8) and
> assert that just as the priestly caste receives tithes from each house-
> holder, so the poor should receive a part of each crop. God grants both
> an exclusive right to a portion of the crops grown on the Land of Israel.
> The poor, no less than the priests, seem to be counted as a distinctive
> caste of Israelite society. What conception stands behind this analogy
> between the poor and the priests? It is their common claim on God for
> protective support. Because neither group possesses a portion of the
> Land of Israel, neither can produce the food it needs. The priests, for
> their part, are forbidden by Scriptural law to own land (Dt. 18:1–5).
> Instead, they act as God's servants in the Temple and are accorded
> food on that account. Similarly, the poor have lost whatever portion of
> the Land they may have possessed and so are entitled to receive some
> of its yield. God supports both the priests and the poor because they
> neither own land nor attain the economic prosperity promised to all
> Israelites who live in the Land (Dt. 8:7–10).

Here, again, we see how Israel and God relate through the nexus of
the Land.

At stake in the support of the poor is a structure of an other-than-
secular, rather other-worldly character. The main rules express a theory of what it means for Israelite householders to possess the Land.
Support for the poor, like support for the priesthood and Levites,
underscores God's ownership and reinforces the provisional character
of the householder's possession. For the landless—the priesthood, the
Levites, and the poor—God sets aside what is coming to him from

the produce of the Land. That equalizes Israel in relationship to the Land. Some possess, others do not, portions of the Land, but all gain what they need from its produce; the householders then hold what they have on sufferance, covenantally. In that way those either not enlandised with Israel to begin with or dispossessed of their portion of the Land later on gain a position within that holy community that is nourished—and given definition—by the Land.

In linking the poor man's tithe with the second tithe—the one for its years of the Sabbatical cycle, the other for its years—the Halakhah makes a statement on a subject other than mere charity, support for those in need. For mere eleemosynary activities can hardly define what is at stake, when for four of the six years of the cycle the poor get nothing, Jerusalem everything. And, in fact, support for the poor is perpetual and annual, the poor getting their share of the crop and additional support from the community as well. The issue of economic entitlement takes a subordinate position. The food given out in the dole and soup kitchen serves a practical purpose and does not exhibit marks of God's intervention, as selection of produce for the gifts to the poor does. Merely to support the priesthood and the poor, the elaborate provisions of sanctification of the Land's produce hardly are required, as the Halakhah of the dole and the soup kitchen for the poor makes abundantly clear. Unlike the scripturally-indicated gifts to the poor, all of them marked off supernaturally by some trait or other, that food is not subject to divine selection nor removed from human ownership and even the significations of personal possession, as is the case with the food for the poor that is provided by the Halakhah out of the householder's crops.

The presence of the poor, rather, forms the occasion for the householder's giving a powerful signal of his relinquishing possession (not merely ownership) of the Land and subordinating his possession of it to God's ownership. The householder tastes landlessness by being disenlandised, on the one side, or by relinquishing what he has harvested but lost, on the other. In both classes of gifts to the poor, the upshot is the same: the householder no longer subjects to his will the produce of his own labor on his own land. Ownership is compromised, possession replaced by dispossession. For the Halakhah, excelling, as it does in the choice of particular media for a large and encompassing message, the occasion is very specific. It is the successive tithes of the Sabbatical cycle. Giving to the poor is like providing for pilgrimage to Jerusalem; giving to the poor at home for four out of six years then is equated with spending time with God in Jerusalem the other two. That on its own represents a mere formality: two types of offering on the same cycle. But the Halakhah dwells on other matters, from which, if we wish, we may infer substantive grounds for contemplating the equivalency of poor to pilgrimage—in more abstract language, occasion to location. To frame the question in simple terms: What, in the Halakhah, have the poor to do with the pilgrimage, occasion with location? Or, to state matters still more plainly, What have the poor to do with the possession of the Land and locative residence thereon?

This question carries us back to the issue of ownership and possession. God owns the Land, Israel possesses it—and Israel encounters God on occasions of dispossession, that is, relinquishing not only formal title but actual, physical possession. Brooks frames the matter in the present context in this language (*Support for the Poor*, 18):

> Each time the householder asserts his ownership of the Land's yield, God demands a portion for those under his protective care, the poor and the priests. God's interest in the crop is aroused at two distinct points, once in behalf of the poor, once in behalf of the priests. First, as the householder harvests the grain in his field, thereby claiming it for himself, God causes a portion to be set aside. This bit of food, separated seemingly at random, then is available for the poor alone. In the case of *Pe'ah* . . . the poor must wait for the householder explicitly to designate what God has set aside. Second, when the farmer later collects food at his threshing floor, God again asserts his ultimate ownership of the Land's yield by removing some for the priests.

What takes place, then, in both transactions—the one involving the priesthood, the other the poor—is that the condition of dispossession of God's dependents overtakes the householder himself; he enters into the situation of those that live in the Land but not on the Land. But then all are made equal—the produce for the poor is classified as ownerless, just as the produce of the seventh year is ownerless and free for all.

No wonder, then, that, as part of the cycle climaxing in the equalization brought about by dispossession—everything being declared ownerless for a year!—the householder and his family leave their land altogether and transfer to God's abode in Jerusalem. There they take up the position of guests, eating the Host's food—that very portion that in the third and sixth years of the cycle goes to the poor. The householder removed from his land within the Land enters the condition of the poor—and of the priesthood! He becomes God's client, just like them; he enters a relationship of dependency, just like them. The two landless classes of society, disenlandised throughout all the years of the Sabbatical cycle, the one at one side of the social spectrum, the other at the other, now are joined by the mass of householders. The upshot is, all Israel depends equally upon God's benevolence, depending on the Land as a gift, not as a given.

Imposing upon the crops of the Sabbatical Year the status of ownerless property therefore adumbrates the purpose of the seventh year—prefigured on the Sunday, Monday, Thursday, and Friday of the septennial cycle. What happened, in creation, Tuesday and Friday, the third and the sixth days of the cycle? On the third day vegetation ("plants yielding seed and fruit trees bearing fruit") were brought forth. On the sixth day came living creatures, cattle and beasts—and man. So in the third year the poor receive their share of the crops, meaning, the creation of the crops is meant for all, the enlandised and the disenlandised; and commemorating the sixth day of creation, in the sixth year of the cycle, the poor are given that tenth of the crop that helps them get ready for the Sabbatical Year that follows. The match, for both the third and the sixth days of creation and years of the Sabbatical cycle, proves fitting, just as we saw in connection with fruit of the fourth year after the planting of the orchard.

What about the other years? They speak to other concerns, besides the poor but congruent with those of the poor—the concerns of possession, ownership, and residence. In the first, second, fourth, fifth years—not to mention also the seventh year—of the Sabbatical cycle, the householder leaves his home and takes up residence in God's place instead. So, whether as guests in Jerusalem or evicted from possession of the crops altogether, as takes place in the seventh year, the householder must acknowledge that all he possesses he holds with open arms. This he signals in some years by moving out, in the climactic year by relinquishing all claim to dictate the disposition of the crops. In the third and sixth years the householder separates for the landless poor a share of the crop that in other years goes to the landless sacerdotal castes, the priests and the Levites. But every year, for every crop, by his own active intervention, God provides for the poor what he wishes.

So Israel—all Israel, householder and landless (whether rich, whether poor) alike—in the Land takes up the situation of Eden, the seven years of the Sabbatical cycle matching the seven days of creation, the elaborate instructions concerning the use of the otherwise free and available crops corresponding to the simple commandment to man concerning the fruit of the tree of knowledge. And if Eden testifies to man's situation, as beneficiaries of a benevolent Creator and Lord, the record of Eden also sets forth God's in relationship to man's situation. God enters into intense engagement with man, specifically concerning himself with how man makes use of the gift of creation that God has so thoughtfully shaped for man's enjoyment.

A second glance at this matter of the "accidental" character of God's intervention shows that to which God responds in man's disposition of the gifts of Eden, the donations of nature. What man neglects or forgets or does not value, God identifies, reserves, and secures for his particular dependents. As worthy as are the firstfruits, the choicest ones, as valued and protected the heave offering for the priesthood, so esteemed are the forgotten sheaf and the imperfect grape cluster.

The lessons then are not to be missed, and they form a coherent statement. Here we shift from man in Eden to Israel in the Land. What Israel values, Israel relinquishes, whether the crop, when claimed by the claim made liable for the designation of God's share, whether the occupancy of the private household to be suspended in favor of a pilgrimage to God's household, or whether the possession of the Land and disposition of its crops, abandoned every seventh year. So little that is "accidental" lies beyond systemic explanation. What Israel disregards, God finds noteworthy and claims. What Israel values, God reclaims. The forgotten sheaf, the imperfect stalk, the corner of the field, the gleanings, the separated grapes and defective clusters—they come about not by accident at all. The outcome of natural processes, whether human or otherwise, they mark God's provision for himself and his dependents out of what Israel disesteems. Israel's intentionality extends, then, even to what lies beyond Israel's ken: what Israel misses and, by inaction or action, neglects, God reserves for himself. That teaches one lesson. And, as we have noted, that in which Israel takes pride—the very possession of the Land itself—defines what Israel must give up, at regular intervals, not to the landless poor or the landless Levites and priesthood, but to the very condition Israel most dreads: dispossession altogether. That teaches the other lesson.

But while the householder relates to God through acts of obedience, with special reference to transforming claim to ownership into mere right of contingent possession, the poor, the priests, and the Levites relate through disenlandisement of the former, and un-enlandisement of the latter, in their ongoing life of reliance upon God. That reliance takes the form of their dependence on divine ownership of the Land for their share in its yield. The un-enlandised and the disenlandised then enter into their own framework of interaction with God—different from the householder's, and holier than that. That is because, unlike the householder, they own nothing and possess nothing in the Land. But among the sacerdotal castes, the poor reach the pinnacle: they not only do not possess a portion in the Land, but the very food that the Land yields to them itself bears no marks of individual ownership. They do not own even what they eat—and they also do not worry:

Bavli Besah 2:1 I.6/16A

A. It is taught on Tannaite authority:
B. They said concerning Shammai the Elder that all of the days of his [life] he would eat with an eye to the honor of the Sabbath.
C. [If] he found a fine animal, he would say, "This is for the Sabbath."
D. [If] he found a different animal, finer than the first, he would put aside the second [finer one for the Sabbath] and would immediately eat the first.
E. But Hillel the Elder had a different trait.
F. For all of his actions were for the sake of Heaven.
G. as it is written, "Blessed be the Lord day by day" (Ps. 68:19).

None more than the landless poor find more ample grounds to bless God day by day. Theirs (within the Halakhic theory) is the perfect faith that God provides, by reason of the obedient character of holy Israel, what everyone needs. The poor place their hope in God, confident of their share in the scarce resources made available to the Israelite social order by reason of God's ownership of all things. So the poor embody in their lives that perfect trust in God that all Israel owes, just as the priesthood and the Levites realize in the conduct of their lives that entire sanctification that all Israel is meant to attain. In the Halakhah of Pe'ah we see how the theological virtue of faith— the poor acknowledging God's reliability, the rich and enlandised

God's ownership—finds articulation in the Land and the disposition of its benefits among those that possess and those that do not possess land. The Land is everything: so much for Israel's relationship to God through the Land. Now to the final issue of the social relationship: the diversity of Israel before the one and only God.

G. *Dema'i*

How do we define that Israel that engages in life with God through the Land? Does that Israel encompass only those that conform to the Halakhah, or is Israel capable of sustaining the presence of diverse Israelites. Given the theological weight assigned to the social category Israel, we may phrase matters very simply: Are all Jews—such as the Romans would call them—Israelites? In the context of the Halakhah and its focus upon theological issues of God's commandments and Israel's response, God's yearning and Israel's love, we turn outward, toward the social realities that the legal system in theory chooses to address.

The Halakhah that we meet in the category-formation of *Dema'i* focuses attention upon a practical issue of the religious life: how to conduct relationships with God when holy Israel—meant to encompass pretty much all Jews—does not exhibit uniform traits or constitute a homogeneous body of faithful? That issue carries us beyond the framework of the householder and his disposition of the bounty of the Land and requires us to consider the condition of Israel in general, not just the enlandised part, or the impoverished part, or the sacerdotal, genealogically differentiated part. Here is where the broad swath of the population that did not own land, did not descend from priests, and did not live from day to day, plays its part: in the tithing of food purchased in the market in particular. So in the Halakhah at hand, we move from the household in relationship to God to the community at large in relationship to God.

Dema'i, produce concerning the tithing of which doubt exists, requires special treatment. Here we deal with the laws that dictate how a responsible person makes certain that what he purchases in the marketplace and eats, or gives to another to eat, will be properly tithed. All Israelites, the Halakhah takes for granted, separate heave offering. But the other pertinent agricultural offerings, first tithe—a tenth of the crop remaining when heave offering has been removed, given to the Levite, heave offering of the tithe, that is to say, a tenth removed from the Levite's tithe and given to the priest, and second tithe or poor man's tithe (depending on the year of the Sabbatical cycle, first, second, fourth, and fifth, or third and sixth, respectively)—are designated only by those faithful to the rule. The specific problem that provokes the formation of the Halakhah before us concerns the heave offering of the tithe given to the Levite, which heave offering further goes to the priest. If not removed, the heave offering of the tithe given to the Levite imparts the status of holiness to the produce in which it is mixed, even as would the heave offering of the entire crop that everyone is assumed to designate and remove.

The generative issue is how those who properly separate tithes are to relate, commercially and commensally, to those that do not: what is their responsibility for produce that they transfer to others, what is their obligation in regard to produce that they receive from others? The Halakhic problematic then defines the theological issue: how do Jews (using the term to refer to those deemed to belong to a common ethnic group) relate to Israel, meaning, the holy people whom God brought into being through the Torah at Sinai? And the answer that the Halakhah sets forth is, all Israel is Israel. What the Halakhah of *Demaʿi* emphatically registers is that the Israelites who do not observe cultic cleanness in the household intermarry with, and will respect the convictions and conduct of, those that do. Other components of the Halakhah stress that those who do not observe cultic cleanness in the household will not wantonly or deliberately impart cultic uncleanness to the secular food of that component of Israel that does so.

The premise of the Halakhah in both cases is one and the same: all Israel keeps some of the Halakhah, and some of Israel keeps it all—and all together, the two components form a single, holy Israel. That is why the Halakhah legislates for the situation that it treats here and in tractate *Tohorot*. And viewed as a matter of social policy, that conviction underscores the wisdom of the Halakhah in requiring the observant to make provision for the unobservant, doing so, however, without intruding into their affairs in a haughty or hostile manner. Of such intrusion in the spirit of holier-than-thou, in the Halakhah, I can identify not a trace. Who then forms that Israel that relates to God through the Land? While one might easily frame the question in terms of politics and sociology, in fact the Halakhah's recognition of the heterogeneity of Israel forms a religious judgment. Everyone is

Israel, responsible to God and for Israel equally. Specifically, the Halakhah here makes its statement on who is Israel, making as explicit as possible, in the very context of how Israel relates to God, that Israel forms an encompassing community, excluding no one, including everyone. Even Samaritans, even less observant Israelites, are assumed to exhibit integrity and good will, since they are held to keep the law correctly, as we noted: "He who leaves his tithed produce in the keeping of a Samaritan or an *'am ha'ares*—[the produce remains] in its presumed status with regard to tithes and with regard to Seventh-Year produce." Where they err, they err, where not, not.

Those who keep the tithing law relate to those who do not in three ways. First, they form a single community. Those deemed reliable do not aspire to segregate themselves in public life from others or expect to do so, though home-hospitality is another matter. But that underscores the public focus of the law: all Israel. And the Halakhah presupposes, as we noted, that Israelites (here including Samaritans) respect the convictions of those who keep the law differently, more strictly, than they do. So the more reliable may—the Halakhah rules as a matter of the norm, not merely of whim or will—rely upon the honesty of the less observant.

Second, they take precautions to preserve the integrity of their observance within the company of those who do not. They keep the rules among those who do not. That is why they can participate in public life, in the market or the synagogue for example. They properly tithe what they are given or give away. So the more reliable within Israel do make provision for the failure of the others to tithe in the correct manner; they do not adapt themselves to a lower requirement of the Torah but preserve their own integrity.

Third, the more observant take responsibility for the observance of those who do not observe. They regard themselves as their brothers' keepers. That is what is at stake in properly tithing all food that goes back into the market or passes into unknown hands. So far as they can correct the prevailing situation, they do so, tithing properly what they introduce into common usage, e.g., in the market or in transfer-payments through gifts.

Here then we find the balance between righteousness, for which, in its moderate and middle of the road way, the Halakhah provides, and self-righteousness. But that comes about not by reason of sound public policy. It is the consequence of a religious conviction concerning who is Israel, which is everyone who is born to Israel or accepts the Torah and joins Israel—enlandised or dispossessed, and, concomitantly, within the Land or in the realm of uncleanness and death, that is, the territory of the gentiles. So far as the Halakhah is concerned, that Israel that is sanctified by residence in the Land and that by its residence sanctifies the Land finds its definition in not minima of belief or behavior but its basic character, defined by birth or rebirth, as the case requires. And disembedding Israel from the Land opens the way toward the extension of Israel's sanctity not only to the local unenlandised or disenlandised but to the overseas Israelites as well.

If, therefore, we had to identify the religious principle that animates the Halakhah of *Dema'i*, it is with little discrimination to affirm the integrity of all Israel, to make a statement of the fundamental coherence of the Israelite community in the Land. The householder bears many particular obligations; but all Israelites now are shown to bear responsibility for themselves and others. Without regard to their situation in relationship to the Land, all engage with God. The householder does not stand nearer to God because he possesses a share in the Land. *Dema'i* has defined the structure that encompasses everyone within the framework of the same obligations that, to begin with, devolve upon the householder.

So the focus of the law yields this religious statement: everyone, not only the householder, bears responsibility to God for the disposition of the produce of the Land. All Israel enters into a covenanted relationship with God through possession (by only some) of the Land, and the conduct of all Israel upon the Land, in respect to its produce, bears heavily on Israel's enduring possession of the Land. So when it comes to doubtfully-tithed produce, the practice of all Israel is taken into account, and the condition of all Israelites registers. That is why, the Halakhah insists, the faithful shop in the same market as the less observant, diminishing so far as possible the occasions for the less faithful to misuse produce.

It is the very insistence of the Halakhah upon rules for dealing with the public square of Israel that makes the most eloquent statement: all Israelites, when it comes to relating to God through the produce of the Land, forms a single Israel before God. In the very center of its exposition of how Israel relates to God through the Land, the Halakhah disembeds that relationship from enlandisement, opening the way to Israel beyond the limits of the Land to participate. And when we come to the other focus of Israel's relationship with God, the temple and its cult, we shall see how sanctification overspreads Israel wherever situated. So much for man in Eden, Israel in the Land. What of Adam and Eve? When we ask about the principals, we enter into the domain of Israel's social order, lived out in public: Israel as a new moral entity.

III. ADAM AND EVE

Eden requires its Adam and Eve. For the Land of Israel, where is the corresponding figure? In Rabbinic theology Israel forms the counterpart to Adam and Eve, but only at a few points is the metaphor articulated. Rather, the narrative shifts its focus to Israel as the new moral entity, the anti-Adam. Then the paramount motif takes up the theme of the sanctification of Israel through acts of intentionality. The Halakhah of the family, covering the act of sanctification of a woman by a man (*Qiddushin*), the marriage agreement (*Ketubah*), vows and special vows, the disposition of a charge of unfaithfulness against a woman alleged to have violated her status of sanctification, and the severance of the marital bond of sanctification through a writ of divorce or death, invokes a different metaphor: Israel is comparable to that other animate being that is sanctified to God, the offering on the altar. The governing focus of the Halakhah is the act of sanctification, in the model of an animal for use at the altar, of a woman for the bed of a man.

How then does Eden figure in the relationships of Israelites to one another within the social order? The connection is made articulate by the liturgical framework in which the Halakhah plays itself out. There, in the liturgy of the marriage canopy, the act of creation of man is recapitulated, the bride and groom explicitly compared to Adam and Eve. Not only so, but the theme of the Land and Israel intervenes as well—two motifs we have found dominant in the Halakhic theology examined to this point. The operative language, defining the transaction, is contained in the blessings that are said over the cup of wine of sanctification, which are as follows:

Praised are You, O Lord our God, King of the universe, Creator of the fruit of the vine.

Praised are You, O Lord our God, King of the universe, who created all things for Your glory.

Praised are You, O Lord our God, King of the universe, Creator of Man [Adam].

Praised are You, O Lord our God, King of the universe, who created man and woman in his image, fashioning woman from man as his mate, that together they might perpetuate life. Praised are You, O Lord, Creator of the Man [Adam].

May Zion rejoice as her children are restored to her in joy. Praised are You, O Lord, who causes Zion to rejoice at her children['s return].

Grant perfect joy to these loving companions, as You did to the first man and woman in the Garden of Eden. Praised are You, O Lord, who grants the joy of bride and groom.

Praised are You, O Lord our God, King of the universe, who created joy and gladness, bride and groom, mirth, song, delight and rejoicing, love and harmony, peace and companionship. O Lord our God, may there ever be heard in the cities of Judah and in the streets of Jerusalem voices of joy and gladness, voices of bride and groom, the jubilant voices of those joined in marriage under the bridal canopy, the voices of young people feasting and signing. Praised are You, O Lord, who causes the groom to rejoice with his bride.[5]

At the new act of creation, represented by the formation of the Israelite household, covered by the Halakhah of *Qiddushin* and *Ketubot*, we recall Eden. The theme of ancient paradise is introduced by the simple choice of the word *Adam*, so heavy with meaning. The myth of man's creation is rehearsed: man and woman are in God's image, together complete and whole, creators of life, "like God." Woman was fashioned from man together with him to perpetuate life. And again, "blessed is the creator of Adam." The wedding canopy recapitulates the union of Adam and Eve. That is the starting point for our inquiry into the structure that sustains and imparts coherence to the Halakhah of the marriage and the family.

---

[5] Jules Harlow, ed., *A Rabbi's Manual* (New York: The Rabbinical Assembly, 1965), 45.

A. *Qiddushin*

The Written Torah leaves no doubt that God deems a matter of sanctification that Israel conduct its sexual life in the model of the sanctity of its cultic life. The formation of the family of the household begins with the act of betrothal, which, in the context of the Halakhah, means we deal with the sanctification of a woman to a particular man. When an Israelite wishes to present a particular animal to God as an offering in the temple, a comparable act of sanctification of the beast for that particular purpose takes place; at that point God through the temple acquires ownership of the beast, and any secular use of the beast is punished as sacrilege.

The act of betrothal forms a particular detail of the larger theory of how a man acquires title to, or possession of, persons or property of various classifications. That is the this-worldly side of the Halakhah. The transcendent part emerges with the result: the sanctification of the relationship between a particular woman and a particular man, so that she is consecrated to him and to no other. The upshot is, just as a farmer acquired a slave or an ox or real estate, so he effected possession of, gained title to, a woman. But while the slave or ox or field could never be called "consecrated" to that particular farmer, so that the language of sanctification never operates in such transactions, the act of acquisition of a woman also transformed the relationship of the woman not only to that man who acquired her but to all other men. The language that is used here, the language of sanctification, derives from the temple, and when we speak of sanctifying or consecrating a woman to a specific man, we are using the language of the altar, which speaks of sanctifying an animal to the altar for a particular purpose. It is the particularity of the designation—for this and no other, the altar and nothing else, the particular man (e.g., whose sins are to be atoned for through the blood of that beast) and no other men, no other sins—that constitutes the act of classification that is sanctification.

To state that Israel procreates in accord with rules of sanctification that pertain to the temple, as much as Israel sustains life in accord with (other) rules of sanctification that radiate outward from the cult, sages could have had no better medium than the Halakhah that is before us. The very categorical structure of the Halakhah, its language, its governing considerations—all bear the message of how the life force of the holy people flows through channels made sacred, table and bed alike forming extensions of the altar's governing principles, and (in the present case) the consecration of the offering, on the one side, the priesthood, on the other. Israel defines itself as holy in two ways: by nature, through birth; and by conviction, through adherence to the Torah. Sanctification by nature, the first of the two media for forming Israel realized in a given household, then, comes about when an Israelite man consecrates an Israelite woman who is available to him—not married or betrothed to someone else (the governing analogy being the consecration of the offering, as we shall note), and not forbidden to him by reason of incest taboos or caste regulations (the governing analogy being the consecration of the priesthood). Then sanctification by nature continues when that union produces offspring. Sanctification by conviction takes place when through those actions specified in connection with, e.g., food preparation, the Israelite sustains life as life is sustained at the altar.

But while bed and table come under the rules of sanctification that radiate from the altar, the generative principles that overspread altar and bed differ from those that join altar to table. Since the paramount analogy compares the woman to the offering, what follows? Here the governing principle focuses upon the specificity of the transaction of betrothal that is compared to one with the altar and the particularity of its effects. Now what is at issue is sanctifying a particular woman to a particular man, comparable to sanctifying a given beast to the Lord for a given, particular purpose, e.g., this animal for this classification of offering, and, in the case of a sin offering, for this specific sin committed inadvertently in particular. That is because in the Halakhah to sanctify means to select in a concrete way, for a distinctive purpose, not in a general way or for a generic purpose. The act of selecting a beast for sacrifice on the altar involves setting that beast aside from all others and designating it for the unique purpose of an offering for the sacrifier (the one who benefits, e.g., expiates sin, through the offering) carried out by the priest (the sacrificer). The animal must be designated ("consecrated") for an offering; it must be a specific type of offering, e.g., sin offering; and the particular sin that the sacrifier has in mind must be articulated, there being no such thing as a sin offering in general. So the act of sanctification finds its definition in the specificity of the selection, designation for a unique purpose, and performance of those rites that effect the selection and designation and carry out the purpose—out of which the transaction of sanctification produces a relationship of sanctity, God to this Israelite among all Israelites.

The difference between the consecrated offering for the altar and the consecrated woman for the marriage canopy, governing the entire process of sanctification of woman to man, lies in what distinguishes the human being, man or woman, from the beast: the freedom of will, the power of intentionality. The man may declare the woman sanctified, but if she objects, the act is null. If she is of age for the act of betrothal to be valid, the woman must willingly accept the tokens of betrothal, directly or through her agent. If not of age when she comes of age, she may reject an act of betrothal, even consummated, taken by others with control over her in her minority, her father if he is alive, her brothers if he is deceased. Then she simply ups and walks out, not requiring even a writ of divorce. No sanctification has ever taken place, the woman not having confirmed what has happened through the exercise of will of others with temporary jurisdiction over her. So the woman consecrated for her husband is like the beast sanctified for the altar, but with a formidable difference.

But the woman is unique and incomparable, as we see when we broaden the discussion by contrasting the power of the woman to effect an act of intentionality in the transaction of betrothal with the impotence of counterparts in her category, slaves and minors, to effect their will in any way. Along with slaves and minors, women form a classification of Israelites deemed not fully capable of independent will, intentionality, entire responsibility, and action and therefore subject not only to God's will but also to the will of another, the husband or father in the case of the woman, the master in the case of the slave, and the parent in the case of the child. Thus M. *Ber.* 3:3: Women, slaves, and minors are exempt from the recitation of the Shema and from the obligation to wear phylacteries, but are obligated to the recitation of the prayer, and to post a mezuzah, and to recite the blessing over the meal. But they do not form part of the community of holy Israel that is obligated to recite blessings publicly, thus M. *Ber.* 7:2: Women, slaves or minors who ate together with adult Israelite males—they may not invite others to bless on their account. While comparable to slaves and minors in forming a classification of persons of lesser powers of intentionality than the

Israelite man, the Israelite woman in the aspect of betrothal stands far above the others of her class.

The unique relationship of the woman to the man finds its counterpart in the unique relationship of the animal designated ("consecrated") to the altar by a farmer in expiation of a particular sin. That animal could serve only as a sin offering, and it could expiate only the particular sin the farmer had in mind to atone. But that intense specificity cannot characterize, e.g., possession of a given slave, who could be rented out to others, or title to a particular piece of real estate, available for sharecropping. The ox, the real estate, and the slave are transferred willy-nilly; no act of will on their part intervenes. But a woman can be consecrated to a particular man only by an act of agreement, her will forming the foundation of the entire transaction. So, while without an act of assent a lamb is consecrated by the farmer and so made holy to the altar, only her full and uncoerced agreement will consecrate a woman to a man. The woman is partner in the process of her own sanctification, in a way in which no other classification of persons or property participates in the process of his, her, or its transfer from ownership to ownership.

A woman is consecrated to a particular man, just as an animal is consecrated to the altar for the expiation of a particular inadvertent sin that has been carried out by a particular person. A sin offering consecrated for a particular person and a specific action he has inadvertently performed proves null if it is used for another offering than the designated class, another person, or another sin by the same person. A woman consecrated for a particular man is subject to exactly the same considerations of sanctification (*mutatis mutandis*). In both cases the relationship is one of consecration, meaning, differentiation from all secular purposes and designated for a sacred function or task. Just as the temple altar provides the governing comparison for the formation of the laws about the slaughter of animals for meat for the Israelite table, so the temple altar provides the pertinent analogy for the transaction that links a selected woman to a given man in a relationship of sanctity. What marks the woman as unique is that, when she is consecrated, she makes a choice of this circumstance, not that, so to effect her sanctification she assents in an act of will responding to the act of will of the counterpart to the sacrifier, the proposed groom. Then she is Isaac at Horeb, the archetype of the willing victim. But no one invokes that analogy; the governing conception is, Israel's life is extended, in procreation, and sustained, in nourishment, through acts of sanctification; it is threatened through acts of uncleanness, adultery on the one side, the forces of uncleanness analogous to death on the other.

B. *Ketubot*

The *ketubah*—marriage-agreement—provides for support for the wife by the husband and alimony in the event of divorce or the husband's death. This promises also restoration to the wife's family and patrimony of lands, goods, and capital brought by the wife into the marriage and reserved for her male children by that husband. The details of the law contribute to the main point: through this piece of writing, a woman becomes sacred to a particular man. Without the document (at least in implicit form), the relationship is not legitimated. What has the marriage document to do with the process of sanctification of the relationship of the wife to the husband; how is the woman transformed, in part, through this document and the procedures to which the contract is critical? We deal with something other than an ordinary legal document, e.g., a bill of sale of a piece of property or a will. Not all formulaic writings effect sanctification; this one does. And at specific points the Halakhah itself confirms the transformative power of the language and writing at hand. How come language exercises such power, and what analogies or models define the context in which to interpret the religious meaning of the Halakhah of *Ketubot?*

To answer that question, we recall the power of language to effect sanctification in the two other critical contexts of the Halakhah, the separation of heave offering from the crop, and the designation of an animal for the offering. When the farmer evinced the desire to utilize the produce, then God responded by imposing the requirement of separating his share. At that point, the crop became liable to tithing and the separation of other offerings. Then a portion of the crop shared by the farmer and God grown on land, ownership of which is invested in the farmer and God, was to be removed, leaving the rest free for the farmer's use. And the act of separation took the form of a statement, a formulaic act of transformation. To accomplish that end, the farmer recited a formula that serves to designate as holy to the priesthood a portion of the grain at the threshing floor. That part of the whole crop, called variously "heave offering" or "the priestly ration" enters into the status of sanctity—is sanctified—when the farmer says something along the lines of, "The heave offering of this heap [of produce] is in its northern portion" [M. *Ter.* 3:5C]. At that point, the designation portion of the grain enters the status of sanctity, with the result that a non-priest who eats that grain incurs severe punishment. Second comes the consecration of an animal for the altar. The householder who wishes to make an offering has first to designate an animal for the purpose of that offering, and that designation, the act of consecration, involves stating something along the lines of, "This lamb is a sin offering for such-and-such an inadvertent sin that I have committed." So too, if someone says, "This beast is instead of that beast, a sin offering," the beast to which he makes reference is consecrated, even while the one to which he made reference remains consecrated. And that language effects even parts of the beast, so M. *Tem.* 1:3: "he who says, 'The foot of this is a burnt offering'—the whole beast is a burnt offering." And the Halakhah of *Qiddushin* maintains, if a woman agrees when one who says, "Lo, you are sanctified to me on the strength of this coin," the formula, along with the woman's agreement, constitutes the act of consecration. She then is transformed, and if she violates the rules governing her status of sanctity, God expects the holy community to inflict appropriate punishment.

It is in that context that the *ketubah*, too, finds its place. Even though the Halakhah frames the topic in other than mythic language and terms, the *ketubah* forms an integral component in the process by which, through the evocation of certain language, a woman's status as to all men in the world radically shifts. Before the recitation of the correct formula, including (as in the case at hand) a written record, the woman was free to marry any appropriate Israelite (excluding male relatives); afterward she was not. The upshot is, the *ketubah* represents the formula of sanctification. That the document bears its own significance, beyond the language that is used in it, is shown by a simple, much-explored fact. The *ketubah*'s power is fully present even when the requisite language is not written and properly articulated, just as much as the formula of *Qiddushin* commences the process of sanctification, the formula of designating priestly rations changes the status of both the portion of the crop so designated and the remainder of the crop, no longer containing inherent sanctification, and the formula of designating an animal for the altar. The upshot is, in the transaction represented by, as much as in the language used in, the *ketubah* inheres the power of sanctification, such that the status of the woman is redefined and transformed. That explains why clauses take effect even when not written out. Before us is language that evokes conditions and establishes facts not through what is said, but through the transformative power of what is evoked.

But what defines Heaven's interest, and why should the use of the specified language attract Heaven's attention? Must the relationship of man to woman invariably involve documents that embody the sanctity of the relationship and effect sanctification? To understand the answer we have to ask, Is there a transformation that takes place in a woman's status as to sanctification to a given man? Can a woman's status in relationship to all men but one change without the provision of a particular document, meaning, without the recitation of a specified formula, properly witnessed? Of course there is, and of course it can. A particular man may be singled out as the sole man in the world to whom a given woman is available for marriage and procreation, and no documentary media for the transaction of transformation are required. I refer to the transaction covered by the levirate connection (Dt. 25:5–10), when a man dies and his childless widow forthwith becomes consecrated to a surviving brother. Before the man died, she was forbidden to the brother, and had the man had children, she would have remained forbidden to him. But now, by reason of the decedent's childlessness, she is automatically deemed to have entered into a consecrated relationship with her brother-in-law. On what basis? Heaven has imposed that relationship; then no document by man is required. And to respond to that relationship, one of two things must happen. Either the surviving brother states in advance his intention of entering into levirate marriage with the sister-in-law and then has sexual relations with her—the counterpart to the act of betrothal and the consummation of the marriage, respectively—or he goes through a rite of "removing the shoe," prescribed by Scripture to sever the levirate connection. In neither case is a document essential to the transaction.

What is the difference, and why is a document required, then, in the case of a betrothal and marriage and divorce in other-than-levirate circumstances but not in the levirate one? The answer is self-evident. What God does requires no documentary confirmation effected by man, what man does requires transformative language, whether or not in written form; and—more to the point—the actions of God find their counterpart in the documents of man. Specifically, God has established the levirate connection, and man merely proceeds through the rites that will either realize or sever that connection. The connection comes about because of the death of the childless husband. No document is called for. The woman is automatically restricted to the decedent's brother. God does it all, having created the conditions that transfer the woman from one man to another. In an ordinary act of betrothal and marriage, by contrast, man—the offer of the man, the acceptance by the woman—effects that other connection, the ordinary one between the man and the woman where no intervention on Heaven's part, e.g., in the form of childlessness and death, has taken place.

The upshot is that when Heaven intervenes, documents representing the enactment of formulary language of transformation play no role. When man acts on his own account and enters into a relationship of sanctity through an act of sanctification, then man must speak the words that articulate and realize—make real—his intention in that circumstance, for the object of his intentionality, whether grain, whether beast, whether woman. God acts by speaking, as in creation. Man speaks but then confirms in writing the announced intention: let there be. . . . Then the document lends palpability to the intention, not so much confirming it as realizing it in an exact sense of the word, just as much as the statement in connection with a specific animal accomplishes the same goal. Sanctity overtakes the animal of which man has spoken; no further documentation in the context of the cult is necessary. Sanctity overtakes the woman in the agreed-upon transaction of betrothal and marriage, but, in the context of the household, documents do play their part. In that context the *ketubah* or the *get* forms a statement, in material form, of the intentionality of the man, to consecrate the woman or to suspend and annul the status of consecration, as the case may be. The documents form concrete representations of intentionality. To those representations, to that intentionality, the conditions and clauses of the contract of marriage form mere details; they state the consequences of the realization of the intentionality to consecrate the woman to that particular man, or to release the woman to all men.

The *ketubah*, proclaimed (in the liturgy) at that very moment of the marital union under the marriage canopy serves to define the interior dimensions of Eden, explains what makes the groom into Adam and the bride into Eve, specifies the worldly meanings of paradise. Israel in the household realizes Eden through the relationships defined as norms by the Halakhah. The Halakhah declares, if you want to know Eden, come to the Israelite household, where the woman is fairly and considerately provided for, and where the man's obligation to found a household in Israel is diligently carried out by the wife. Of that Eden consists. To more than that let no man aspire, therein is the consecrated relationship realized. And, I need hardly stress, that message coheres with the statement of the Halakhah of *Shabbat-'Erubin*.

C. *Nedarim*

The Halakhah of *Nedarim* and its companion, *Nazir*, investigates the taxonomic power of language, namely, the capacity of a person through invoking the name of Heaven to affect the classification in which he or she is situated and so his or her concrete and material relationships with other people. That represents a very particular instance of the governing premise of the Halakhah: by the use of appropriate language, acts of consecration take place. When it comes to vows, what is consecrated is rendered prohibited to the designated party, much as the consecration of a woman renders her prohibited to all but the designated party. This is done by stating, "May what I eat of your food be prohibited to me as is a sacrifice prohibited to me," all conveyed in the word "Qorban." Having said that, the person may not eat the food of the other. The reason is that the other person's food has been declared by the individual who took the vow to be in the status of a sacrifice.

Language bears power even for purposes of which we (and Heaven) disapprove. Sages therefore warn: Watch what you say, hold your tongue and keep your temper, because in expressing intentionality, your words give effect to your will, and you will be unable to retract. That is because sages to begin with take a negative view of vowing. While of oaths taken in court with full deliberation, invoking the name of God, they approve, vows they despise. They are explicit on that matter: people who take vows show their weakness, not their strength. Vows represent the power of the weak and put-upon, the easy way to defend oneself against the importunities of the overbearing host, the grasping salesman, the tormenting husband or wife. But sages do not honor those who take the easy way, asking God to intervene in matters to which on our own we ought to be able to attend.

"Qorban," "*Nazir,*" and other effective language—these form a single classification, words that transform by reason of the intent with which they are spoken, which they realize because they are spoken. At stake in the vow and in the special vow of the Nazirite is the realization of intention brought about through the use of language. But language used for vows, so sages portray matters, does not sanctify, it contaminates. That language ought to express reflected-upon intentionality—like the designation of an animal to expiate an inadvertent, newly-realized sin—but it conveys the outcome of temper and frustration. Designating a beast as consecrated realizes a noble, godly intention; designating benefit one receives from one's spouse as "Qorban" uses the exalted language of the altar to embody a lowly and disreputable intention, one to humiliate and reject and disgrace the other. The sages' message registers that language is dangerous because it realizes—makes palpable the effects of—otherwise-mute intentionality, which had best, therefore, be expressed with probity and restraint. And these virtues form the opposite of the traits of mind and character of the vow-taking Israelite, wife or husband, host or guest, salesman or customer, as the exemplary cases of *Nedarim* have shown us.

The Halakhah deems language the mirror of the soul; the words expose the heart, articulate and give effect to intentionality. The key to the entire system comes to expression in the language: An act of consecration done in error is not binding. And from the viewpoint of the Torah's Halakhah, what we intend makes all the difference: God responds to what we want, more than to what we do, as the distinction between murder and manslaughter shows in an obvious way. For the critical dialectics of the Torah embodies the conflict between God's and man's will—the very heart of what happened in the tragedy of Eden. That focus upon the definitive, taxonomic power of intentionality explains, also, why if a man says to a woman, "Lo, you are consecrated . . .," and the woman acquiesces, the intentionalities matching, the woman is thereby sanctified to that man and forbidden to all others; the act of intention formulated in words bears the power of classification upon which the entire system builds. But—self-evidently—not all intentionality finds Heaven's approval, and that is so even though Heaven confirms and acquiesces therein. And that brings us to the vow, which realizes in words the intentionality of the person who takes the vow and imposes upon himself restrictions of various kinds. And, inseparable from the vow, in sequence comes the special vow of the Nazirite.

D. *Nazir*

The special vow of the Nazirite, described at Num. 6, like the vow in general, draws in its wake consequences for the life of the family of which that individual that takes the vow is (by definition) a key member: the householder, his wife, children, and slaves. Not drinking wine, not shaving the head, not contracting corpse-uncleanness are matters that are personal and impinge upon the household; they do not pertain in any weighty way to public life, on the one side, or to relations between the people, Israel, and God, on the other. The Nazirite cannot attend to the deceased, cannot drink wine with the family, and subjects himself to his own rule when it comes to his appearance. As is the priest to the family of Israel, so is the Nazirite to the household of Israel, a particular classification of persons, distinguished in consequential and practical ways as to nourishment and comportment.

What statement do sages make through the Halakhah of *Nedarim* and *Nazir*? People bear direct, personal responsibility for what they say, and while statements made in error are null, those made in jest bear real consequences. That is why euphemisms form so central a concern. There is no fooling around with God, no language exempt from God's hearing. Accordingly, the Halakhah of vows and the Nazirite vow finds an appropriate situation here because it is coherent in its generative problematics with the Halakhah of the household in general. For what makes the Nazirite vow effective is language that an individual has used, and it is the power of language to bring about profound change in the status of a person that forms the one of the two centers of interest of the Halakhah of life within the walls of the Israelite household—the focus of sanctification. That formal fact explains the topical pertinence.

Sages do not treat respectfully the person who takes vows. Vow-takers yield to the undisciplined will, to emotion unguided by rational considerations. But intentionality must (ideally) take form out of both emotion and reflection. Vows explode, the fuel of emotion ignited by the heat of the occasion. "Qonam be any benefit I get from you" hardly forms a rational judgment of a stable relationship; it bespeaks a loss of temper, a response to provocation with provocation. Right at the outset the Halakhah gives a powerful signal of its opinion of the whole: suitable folk to begin with do not take vows, only wicked people do. That explains in so many words why, if one says that something is subject to "the vows of suitable folk," he has said nothing. Suitable people make no vows at all, ever. A distaste for vowing and disdain for people who make vows then characterize the law. People who take vows are deemed irresponsible; they are adults who have classified themselves as children. They possess the power of intentionality but not the responsibility for its wise use. That is why they are given openings toward the unbinding of their vows; they are forced at the same time to take seriously what they have said. Vows are treated as a testing of Heaven, a trial of Heavenly patience and grace. Sanctification can affect a person or a mess of porridge, and there is a difference. Expletives, with which we deal here, make that difference; these are not admired.

But because the Halakhah begins and ends with the conviction that language is power, the Halakhah also takes account of the sanctifying effect of even language stupidly used. That is the message of the Halakhah, and it is only through the Halakhah that sages could set forth the message they had in mind concerning the exploitation and abuse of the power of language. It is a disreputable use of the holy. And language is holy because language gives form and effect to intentionality—the very issue of the Halakhah at hand! That is why we do admit intentionality—not foresight but intentionality as to honor—into the repertoire of reasons for nullifying vows, as we note in the Halakhah of *Nedarim*:

Mishnah *Nedarim* 9:1, 9

M. 9:1 In a matter which is between him and his mother or father, they unloose his vow by [reference to] the honor of his father or mother.

M. 9:9 They unloose a vow for a man by reference to his own honor and by reference to the honor of his children. They say to him, "Had you known that the next day they would say about you, 'That's the way of So-and-so, going around divorcing his wives,' and that about your daughters they'd be saying, 'They're daughters of a divorcée! What did their mother do to get herself divorced' [would you have taken a vow]?" And [if] he then said, "Had I known that things would be that way, I should never have taken such a vow," lo, this [vow] is not binding.

The normative law rejects unforeseen events as a routine excuse for nullifying a vow; foresight on its own ("had you known . . . would you have vowed?") plays a dubious role. But when it comes to the intentionality involving honor of parents or children, that forms a consideration of such overriding power as to nullify the vow.

Here, then, the Halakhah answers the question, How is Heaven mindful of man and woman on earth? The ornate essays into the trivialities of language and the use of language that we find in the Halakhah of *Qiddushin, Ketubot, Nedarim, Nazir,* and, as we shall see, *Gittin*—but not *Sotah,* for one set of reasons, and not *Yebamot,* for another set—respond to that question. The Halakhah speaks large and simple truths in conveying a remarkable vision of humanity in God's image. Man and woman are so like God as to be able through what they say to provoke, and even encumber, God's caring and concern. That is because man and woman know how to say the ordinary words that make an extraordinary difference on earth and in Heaven. The message of the Halakhah of the Oral Torah is, we are responsible for what we say—there is no such thing as "mere words"— because what we say brings to full articulation what we want, words bearing the burden of intentionality. After all, the first act of creation is contained in the statement, "And God said. . . ." God created the world through words, communicates his will through words, responds to acts of sanctification and deconsecration through words.

E. *Sotah*

If a woman is sacred to a particular man, as a sheep is consecrated to the altar of God, then her act of unfaithfulness offends against God, in the model of an act of sacrilege. The injustice done to the innocent wife, required, in line with Num. 5 by the husband's whim, to undergo the humiliating ordeal of the bitter water, serves as the Halakhah's occasion to make its definitive statement that God's justice is perfect: the wicked get their exact punishment, the righteous their precise reward. For the sages that statement becomes possible only here. For in their view it is not enough to show that sin or crime provokes divine response, that God penalizes evildoers. Justice in the here and now counts only when the righteous also receive what is coming to them. Scripture's casual remark that the woman found innocent will bear more children provokes elaborate demonstration, out of the established facts of history that Scripture supplies, that both righteous and wicked are subject to God's flawless and exact justice. Here, it is important to note, the metaphor of Eden does not impinge; the woman accused of unfaithfulness is never compared to Eve. God's justice infuses the Halakhah with its sense and structure.

If I had to summarize in a single sentence the main thrust of the Halakhah of *Sotah*, it is to create the conditions of perfect, unresolved doubt, so far as the husband is concerned, alongside perfect certainty of innocence, so far as the wife is concerned. Despite the humiliation that awaits, she is willing to place her marriage settlement on the line, so sure is she that she is innocent. His doubt is well-founded, but remains a matter of doubt, so uncertain is he of her status. Then, and only then, the ordeal intervenes to resolve the exquisitely balanced scale of her certainty against his doubt.

Here the Halakhah embodies the Aggadah, for we have already noted in Chapter Six how the Halakhic corpus of *Sotah* states the Aggadic principle, God's justice is effected through the careful balance: the penalty must fit the crime, measure must match measure, and the more exact the result to the cause, the more compelling the proof of immediate and concrete justice as the building block of world order that sages would put forth out of Scripture. That is the point at which justice is transformed from a vague generality—a mere sentiment—to a precise and measurable dimension of the actual social order of morality: how things hold together when subject to tension, at the pressure points of structure, not merely how they are arrayed in general. Here, in fact, is how God made the world, what is good about the creation that God pronounced good. And to make that point, sages select a rite that reeks of injustice, the case of the wife accused of adultery and the ordeal to which she is subjected. Their presentation of the rite, in the setting of home and family, is framed so as to demonstrate God's perfect justice—not only in the public life of Israel's social order, but in the here and now of home and family. It is hard to find a less likely candidate for service in demonstrating that proposition than the subject before us.

Justice begins in the adjudication of the affairs of men and women
in the Israelite household and from there radiates outward, to the
social order of Israel, and thence to the world order of the nations.
It is from the Halakhah before us that sages commence their exposition of God's perfect justice, in rewarding the innocent and punishing
the guilty, because only there could they state their deepest conviction concerning justice: all things start in the Israelite household, the
smallest whole social unit of creation: Adam and Eve.

F. *Gittin*

The sanctification of a woman to a particular man takes place when
the woman, available for that man, meaning not otherwise consecrated, and also not prohibited by rules of consanguinity or incest,
consents. Designating a woman as "holy" or set apart for a particular
man, requires the woman's participation through assent. The consecrated relationship thus involves affirmative intentionality on the part
of both parties. That is not so when it comes to the desacralization
of the relationship, at which point the woman is no longer consecrated to that particular man but becomes available to any other man
of her choice (within some obvious limitations defined by the Torah).
One of two parties—man or God, but not woman—intervenes. In
general, the husband acts to desanctify what he has sanctified. His initiative, resulting from his intentionality, is dissolved at his own will.
In special cases, Heaven intervenes; the husband dies, leaving the wife
free to remarry. In very unusual circumstances, as we shall see in our
reading of the Halakhah of *Yebamot*, Heaven intervenes to bring to a
conclusion one relationship of consecration but immediately to impose another.

Scripture does not contemplate a role for the woman in its account
of how the relationship of sanctification to a particular man is secu-
larized, that is, nullified. But even though only the husband may initiate the writ of divorce and have it written and handed over, the
Oral Torah provides the wife with important points of participation
in the process of ordinary divorce, even when man initiates that
process. And the woman's stake in the process correspondingly gains
enormous consequence. She has the right to dictate the conditions of
delivery. She has the right to be correctly informed, to participate in
the transaction as an active player, determining how her half of the

matter will be conducted by dictating the circumstances under which she will receive the document. And, above all, because the Oral Torah also imposes the most severe and long-lasting penalties upon a woman whose writ of divorce turns out to be impaired and so invalid, and who on the strength of such a document remarries, the woman must thoughtfully exercise her power within the transaction. So the woman not only is given a role in the process but is assigned also a very heavy responsibility in the correct implementation of the transaction. For that reason, she takes anything but a passive role in the matter.

For man's part in the matter, as with the documentary requirement in effecting the relationship of sanctification, culminating in the marriage agreement, everything depends upon a document, which on earth properly done, is ratified in Heaven as an act consequential in the sight of God. A woman enters the relationship of sanctification to a given man through the media specified at tractates *Qiddushin* and *Ketubot*. The former identifies as the media of sanctification the willing exchange of money, a writ, or sexual relations with betrothal the intent. The consummation of the union depends, further, on the provision of the marriage contract, which protects the woman in the event of divorce or the husband's death by providing for alimony. In these transactions, the woman's former status is removed by the provision of a document that nullifies the token of betrothal and the relationship it represents and that brings about the enforcement of the marriage contract and its provisions. So the document at the end—for which Scripture makes provision—completes the document at the outset, of which Scripture knows nothing, but for which the logic of the transaction, matching beginning to end, surely calls.

Then what brings about the deconsecration of the woman takes on heavy significance, since Heaven, as much as man and woman, takes a keen interest in the process. The counterpart to the process of the disposition of the beast sanctified to the altar for a given purpose by a designated sacrifier differs at one fundamental point. The man's act of will in consecrating the beast cannot be nullified by a corresponding act of will to deconsecrate it. Scripture is very clear on that point, when it forbids even an act of substitution of one beast for another (Lev. 27:10). Once the beast has been consecrated, therefore, it leaves the status of consecration only with Heaven's assent, meaning, by following the procedures that the Halakhah deems appropriate.

Heaven has a different relationship to the marriage, and other parties enter in. When the husband determines that he wishes to deconsecrate the wife, he has the power to do so only in such a manner that the wife is fully informed and takes an active role in the transaction, receiving the writ of divorce—initiated solely on the husband's volition to be sure—on terms that she has the power to dictate. The Halakhah states eloquently that she must play a fully conscious role in the transaction when it says she may not be asleep when the writ is handed over to her, and she may not be misinformed as to its character. Thus she must know that the document is a writ of divorce; she must be awake; if she sets conditions for the reception of the document, these must be met. In these fundamental ways, then, she accedes to the process of deconsecration, to the secularization of her status within the Israelite household.

Does Heaven take an equivalent role to its engagement in the disposition of the sanctified beast, and if so, where and how does that engagement take effect? The answer is, predictably, that Heaven, not only the husband and wife, concerns itself with the change in the woman's status as holy. Where, in the repertoire of the Halakhah, does that concern express itself? It is in the valid preparation of the document itself. That document—properly written, properly witnessed, properly handed over—serves to deconsecrate the woman, as surely as the rites of disposition of the consecrated animal not used for its correct purpose deal with the change in status of that beast. So it is the document that is the medium of effecting, or of annulling, the status of consecration. And what gives the document effect? The answer is in two parts.

First, we know that the witnesses are the key element in the process; the document is validated by valid witnesses, and, lacking valid witnesses, even though it is correctly written and delivered, it has no effect at all. In the end the particular witnesses attest not only to the facts of what is incised in the writing but also to the specificity of the writing: this man, this woman, this document. Then what is to be said about the witnesses to the preparation of the document, for whom do they stand? Given Heaven's stake in the transaction and the witnesses' status as nonparticipants, we may offer only one answer: the witnesses validate the document and give it effect because they stand as Heaven's surrogates. Israelite males not related to the parties, the witnesses accord cognizance on earth in behalf of Heaven to that change in intentionality and status that the document attests. When the witnesses to the validity of the writ prepared overseas say, "Before us it was written and before us it was signed" (that is, by the witnesses to the document itself), they confirm what is at stake in the entire transaction: Heaven has been informed of the change of intention on the part of the husband, releasing the wife from her status of sanctification to him. So the change in intentionality must be attested on earth in behalf of Heaven. And that which is certified by the witnesses is not only the validity of the writing of the document but the explicit transaction that has brought about the writing: the husband has instructed the scribe to write the writ of divorce, that particular writ of divorce, for his wife, for the named wife and no other woman (even of the same name). When he has done that, pronouncing his intent to nullify the relationship of sanctification that he proffered and the woman accepted, then all else follows.

But, second, Heaven wants something else as well. Not only must the intention be articulated, and explicitly in the transaction at hand and no other. The document itself must give evidence of counterpart specificity. What makes all the difference? The Halakhah specifies irregularities of two classes, first, those that do not fundamentally invalidate the transaction, second, those that so completely invalidate the transaction that the original status of sanctification retains effect, despite what the husband has said, despite what the wife has correctly received by way of documentary confirmation of the change of intentionality and therefore status, his and hers, respectively. That represents a most weighty result, with long-term consequences.

The Halakhah before us rests on profound reflection about the character of intentionality and its effects. What the law ascertains encompasses not only the intentionality and will of the husband, not only the conscious, explicit cognizance of the wife, but the facts of the case. Specifically, the Halakhah insists that the husband's act of will carries effect only when confirmed by valid action. Intention on its own is null. The full realization of the intention, involving valid provision for all required actions, alone carries effect. Not only so, but a third party, the scribe, intervenes in the realization of the husband's will. That means, facts beyond the husband's control and the wife's power to secure a right to supervise and review matters take over—with truly dreadful and permanent results.

So the wife, having acted on the writ invalidated by the scribe's, not her or her husband's actions or intentionality, emerges as the victim of circumstances quite in contradiction to anybody's will. The upshot is, by the rule of the Halakhah, she may not then claim that her intention—in this case, the acquiescence in a successive relationship of consecration—has been thwarted by the actions or errors of a third party and so ought to be honored in the breach. The Halakhah rejects that claim. She acted in accord with the rules of intentionality and in good faith—and it makes no difference. And the first husband, with all good will, cannot confirm that he intended to divorce the woman, and her actions fully accord with his initiatory intentionality. The Halakhah dismisses that allegation as well. Neither bears material consequence in the validation of what is, by reason of the facts of the case, an invalid transaction.

But the scribe possesses no intentionality in the transaction (other than the will we assume motivates his practice of his profession, that is, professionalism). The very role accorded to the scribe, not to the contracting parties, underscores the position of the Halakhah. It is that intentionality not confirmed by the correct deeds in the end does not suffice. The scribe's errors stand athwart the realization of the intentionality of the husband and the participation (where possible) of the wife; but the scribe obviously did not intend to make mistakes. So what stands in judgment of intentionality and its effect are the facts of the case: the objective actions taken by third parties. In a legal system that has made a heavy investment in the priority of intentionality and the power of will, the statement made by the Halakhah of *Gittin* sounds a much-needed note of warning. Good will and proper intentionality do not govern when facts intervene.

G. *Yebamot*

So much for man's power to bring about the deconsecration of the marital bed. What about God's? He has his own stake in the consecration or deconsecration of the conjugal bond, as we shall now see.

The most important datum of the Halakhah is that the levirate marriage, Dt. 25:5–10, brought about by Heaven's intervention—death without offspring—is fully comparable to the marriage brought about by a man with a woman of his choice. The counterpart of the act of betrothal of a secular union is the act of "bespeaking" (my translation for the Hebrew word *ma'amar*, act of speech) by which a surviving brother indicates his intention of entering into levirate marriage. Just as the act of sanctification effects acquisition in the case of a woman only when both of them are agreed, so a statement of bespeaking effects acquisition of a sister-in-law only when both of them are agreed. The act of bespeaking sustains the original act of sanctification. The surviving brother confirms the intentionality of the deceased brother and quite properly proposes to realize the deceased's original act of will in consecrating that particular woman: to produce children.

The woman, remaining under the original bond of sanctification, can, to begin with, have rejected the now-deceased husband, but she cannot reject the surviving brother. She remains in the status of sanctification, *because the original intentionality, confirmed by deed, has not yet been realized.* That explains why sexual relations in any circumstance—even inadvertence, even rape—now consummate the marriage. By contrast, had the now-deceased husband originally raped the woman, she would not have automatically become his wife merely by reason of sexual relations performed without her consent. Party to the ongoing relationship of sanctification, by contrast, she now continues the relationship with the surviving brother. And the surviving brother, too, has no choice once the matter of sexual relations, rather than the rite of removing the shoe, enters the picture. He, too, may be forced into having sex with the childless widow.

Now we make no distinctions as to intentionality—constraint, deliberation, consciousness, or inadvertence. Why not? Because no one in the transaction possesses the power of intentionality. The widow has consented, to begin with, in the process of producing offspring for her husband's household. The surviving brother is subject to the deceased's act of will and can only accede or decline, but not redirect the course of the original transaction. He is given the right to decide only one matter: not whether he is to enter into a relationship with the widow, but how he is to dictate the course of the already-existing relationship that Heaven has imposed upon him. Only when the original act of sanctification, to which the woman did consent, has accomplished its purpose does the transaction conclude.

But, it goes without saying, when the woman has produced a child by the surviving brother, carrying forward the deceased, childless brother's intentionality, she remains wed to the levir; no one imagines that at that point the marriage concludes. No marriage contract pertains, since the original one, covering the deceased's union with the woman now widowed, remains in effect. The levirate marriage, made in Heaven, once consummated, cannot be differentiated from a secular marriage, brought about by man. Property relationships are the same. Only the marriage contract is charged against the estate of the original husband.

The bed is sanctified by the man's intention, together with the woman's acquiescence, ratified by a deed. It is desanctified by [1] the man's intention, communicated to a fully-sentient woman, ratified by the deed of drawing up and delivering the properly witnessed document of divorce. It also is desanctified [2] by the death of the husband, his intention having been realized in offspring. So intentionality may be nullified by contradictory intentionality or by the full accomplishment of the original intention—the one or the other.

But death on its own does not always desanctify the relationship. Where there are surviving brothers, the relationship brought about by the generative intentionality and initial confirming deed overspreads the surviving brothers. Then the status of sanctification persists until resolved through levirate marriage or the rite of removing the shoe, counterparts to the original betrothal and marriage, on the one side, and to the writ of divorce, on the other. So the principal way in which what is sanctified may by man's action be desacralized is the realization of the intentionality, confirmed by deed, that motivated the original act of sanctification. The principal way by which Heaven may intervene and desacralize a relationship is through the death of the one who to begin with imparted the status of sanctification to that which has been made holy: the woman.

IV. Sacralization and Intentionality

To what is the public life of Israel comparable? It is, in the villages, to be compared to its counterpart in the temple. The Israelite couple, the Adam and Eve of Israel, defines one of the two loci of sanctification—where the language of sanctification predominates—and the other is the temple in Jerusalem. In both places considerations of sanctification come to concrete realization in the media for the sustenance of life: food rules for the table, rules governing procreation for the bed. What exactly defines the status and substance of sanctification? In the Torah, to be holy is to be like God, to act like God. Scripture is explicit on that point at Lev. 19:2: "You shall be holy, for I the Lord your God am holy."

Then to sanctify means to act like God, to do a deed such as God does. And in sages' view, what God does above all else, which man and woman emulate, is sustain life now and restore the dead to life at the end of days. How God creates and sustains life defines the model by which man and woman do the same. The Torah through its law consecrates life in its critical aspects: propagation and maintenance. Accordingly, God created all life, with man and woman the climax of creation. Man and woman, like God, create life. In so doing, they are, they act, like God—in our image, after our likeness. It is no wonder, then, that God engages with man and woman at the critical foci of the life processes, the bed for the propagation of life, and (as we shall see in due course) the table for its maintenance.

When we deal with the conjugal bond and its dissolution through divorce or death, what we find is where and how God engages with, ratifies, the processes of deconsecration, as much as he confirms those of sanctification. That engagement with deconsecration takes place, as Scripture makes explicit, in the temple. It also comes to localization, as the Oral Torah insists, in the Israelite household, the other, and corresponding, locus of sanctification. As sages read the Written Torah, the critical moment of sanctification takes place where life begins or is sustained, at the confluence of intentionality and deed modeled after God's intentionality and deed. "Let us make man in our image, after our likeness" (Gen. 1:26), states the intention. "So God created man in his own image, in the image of God he created him; male and female he created them" (Gen. 1:27) formulates the deed. "And God saw everything that he had made, and behold it was very good" states the judgment. When, as I said, man and woman act like God and create man, that action, like God's to begin with, realizes the intentionality of sanctification of the woman by the man, with the same result as in the beginning: the act of creation of life. The man's sanctification of the woman, then, forms a detail in the larger work of sanctifying the world, meaning, carrying forward God's work of creation that came to its climax in the repose of the Sabbath, sanctified at the conclusion of creation.

That accounts for the focus upon the Israelite household, represented as the natural continuation of the labor of creation at Eden.

The purpose of marriage is procreation, and the sanctification of the woman to the man comes about for that reason: man and woman, like God, create life. In the setting of the household, that means, not life in general, but the life of the very next generation of the family of the husband in particular. It is for that purpose that the husband betroths the wife, and that purpose by its nature suffices to sanctify the union. The husband's intention and confirming action, confirmed by the wife's acquiescence, constitute the pertinent act of sanctification.

Now how is such a transaction completed? And at what point is the process of sanctification brought to fruition? When we considered the Halakhah of betrothals, we realized that the woman enters the status of sanctification as does an animal, the one for the marital bed, the other for the altar. So the Halakhah of the altar and that of the bed have to be drawn into juxtaposition for purposes of analogy. In the analogy of the cult, the answer to the question, When is sanctification fully realized and so no longer effective? is, when the intention has been fully realized. Let me make the point very concrete. A householder takes a secular beast and declares it to be sanctified for the altar for a particular purpose, e.g., "Lo, that animal is my sin offering" (with a very particular sin in mind). Is there any point at which the animal or extant parts thereof is no longer sanctified? Indeed there is. It is when the initial act of sanctification has come to its realization, when the beast has accomplished the purpose for which it has been sanctified. And, when a beast is sanctified to the altar, at what point is the act of sanctification realized? It is when the priest has collected the blood and tossed it onto the appropriate part of the altar, doing so with the correct intention (e.g., an animal designated as a sin offering being prepared and presented in the classification and by the rites of the sin offering, and so throughout).

What then happens to the remainder of the beast? Part or all of the meat may be burned up on the altar, depending on the classification of the offering; certain organs will be burned up on the altar; and so on. But what about the rest of the blood that has been collected in the act of slaughter? That blood is poured out as null, no longer being treated as consecrated; it flows downward into the gutters and is sold to farmers for fertilizer. The Halakhah is explicit on that matter. That indicates the besought fact: *when the purpose of the act of sanctification has been fully realized, the initial status of sanctification*

*that has taken over the beast in question no longer affects the beast, the pertinent
remnants being treated as secular.*

So as a general rule, we may posit, the intentionality to sanctify the
beast lapses in the actuality of the rite at the altar, the parts of the
beast not subjected to ongoing sanctification, having served their part
in the event, now becoming secular.

Now—to find the upshot of the theological reading of these components of the Halakhic system—we may return to the Halakhah of
the desacralization of the bed—*Gittin* and *Yebamot.* We already realize
that man on his own may declare secular or common, available to
anyone, the woman that he has consecrated. He does so with a writ
of divorce, which Heaven ratifies, as Heaven has ratified the initial
act of sanctification. When the man declared the woman sanctified
to himself and the woman acceded to his declaration, Heaven recognized the transaction, just as much as Heaven recognizes the
sanctification for the altar of a beast that the farmer has declared holy
for that purpose. Then if the woman violates her status of sanctification, she is punished. But when the man forms the intention of
removing from her the status of sanctification (with her full knowledge, if not with her consent), and when that intention is realized in
an appropriately prepared and delivered document, particular to the
woman at hand, then the status of sanctification is removed from the
woman. So one medium of desacralization of the marital relationship is the formal nullification of the initial intentionality and act of
sanctification.

But Heaven on its own, not only in partnership with man, may
desacralize the marital union, and, further, Heaven on its own may
arrange for the propagation of life through a particular woman. If the
husband dies having accomplished his goal of producing children, the
union, now irrelevant to the propagation of life, is severed, desanctified. The woman is free to marry anyone she chooses, within
the limitations of the Torah (e.g., as a widow, she cannot marry a
high priest). But should Heaven intervene, the husband die childless,
the union need not lose its sanctification, for life may yet be propa-
gated in accord with the deceased's initial intentionality and act of
sanctification. That provision, made by Heaven to realize the original intentionality and deed, carries us to the levirate marriage. In
such a marriage, the originally-sanctified woman remains subject to
the initial act of consecration by the particular man she married, and

his intentionality—to propagate life in his household—may yet be realized. That is through continuation of the sanctified relationship, now with a surviving brother of the childless deceased.

That fact forms an appropriate conclusion to the Halakhic account of the process of sanctification of life in propagation. Like God, man intends to create life and so acts to realize his intentionality. But, unlike God, man dies. If his intentionality has been accomplished, the status of sanctification falls away from that which has been made holy. If not, as we realize, steps to accomplish that original plan are to be taken. Then, like divorce, when the intentionality is declared dead and so nullified, death marks the abrogation of the original act of will, resulting in the nullification of the status of sanctification. What man's intentionality has brought into being is either concluded when the intentionality is realized or is abrogated by the willful cessation of that same intentionality. Or the status of sanctification of the bed ceases with death.

And death marks the point at which we turn from the bed to the table, which through death and things analogous to death also loses its status of sanctification, signified by purity, meaning, freedom from the effects of the sources of cultic impurity specified in the Written Torah. And principal and generative among these is corpse-uncleanness. So sanctification of the bed or the table sustains life and finds its counterpart and opposition in death, just as we noted at the outset. The difference between life and death should not be missed. Man's intentionality confirmed by deed brings about life. But death comes about willy-nilly. Made "in our image," to be "like God," is not to be God, immortal. But that is not wholly so, as we shall see in due course: when man rises from the grave and stands in judgment, he and she enter upon life eternal. Then what of the interim—the everyday life in the workaday world?

CHAPTER TWELVE

ISRAEL AND ADAM, THE LAND AND EDEN, SIN AND ATONEMENT

I. Corporate Israel: The New Moral Entity

For Adam and Eve the fall brooked no looking back; sin marked the end of Eden. But for corporate Israel, the community between that forms the new moral entity man and God, sin is not indelible. That is because, for Israel viewed whole, the Halakhah provides for the means of washing sin away and overcoming the propensity to rebel. The entire system of the Halakhah embodies that means for confronting the inclination to rebel, as we have seen many times. The media of atonement encompass sacrifices that atone for inadvertent sin, confession and the Day of Atonement, reconciliation with the wronged party, and associated acts of repentance. These constitute public transactions, deeds sponsored by Israel's social order, involving God and Israel, viewed whole. They therefore represent communal, not familial, let alone private or personal, categories alone. The category-formations involving corporate atonement, then, represent the formation of a new moral entity, Israel, the entire community, responsible for what its constituent members do: atonement defines the social order that has sinned.

That is why, when we turn to questions of sin and atonement, we revert to the precipitating motif of mythic monotheism, the origin of man at Eden. To this point we have treated "Eden" as a circumstance, e.g., to be recapitulated on the Sabbath. But "Eden" stands for not only a situation but a story. That story captures a theme and embodies it in narrative. So, as we shall see in this account of the Halakhah of Israel's sacrificial system examined within the framework of the situation and story of Eden, the Halakhah relates to its starting point in three ways.

First, the Halakhah translates into social norms critical details of the story itself. That we have seen in Chapter Eleven. Second, the Halakhah explores the continuation of the story, in the present case, the entry, into the narrative, of Adam's and Eve's successors, the moral entity, Israel. That is subject to presentation via the generative category-formations in the present chapter. And third, the Halakhah then addresses what is implicit in the story, the theme that the stories turn into narrative, which is the conflict of intentionalities, God's and man's, in the context of Eden, the clash of man's and God's will, also treated in the present chapter.

The Halakhah finds urgent the question, How is man, subject to God's rule, to atone for the sin that, by his rebellious nature, man is likely to commit? The Torah's answer to that question formulates the rules that govern man both [1] when under God's dominion and [2] when in rebellion against God's will. These represent the two aspects of the one story that commences with Eden, leads to the formation of Israel through Abraham, Isaac, and Jacob, God's antidotes to Adam, and climaxes at Sinai. But Israel also is man, so that story accommodates both Adam's fall and Israel's worship of the golden calf, and, as the denouement, Adam and Eve's exile from Eden and Israel's ultimate exile from the Land. The question that remains for the story to answer: What now, what next? And the answer enters in with the account of how God proposes to repair the world he has made, to take account both of man's character and Israel's own proclivity. It is through the Halakhah, which then formulates in norms of everyday conduct the rules consequent upon the tale of how God undertook to rehabilitate the human condition. And as intentionality takes a primary position in the negotiation of Israel's and God's transactions in the Land that is Eden, so intentionality plays a principal part in the story of sin and atonement, on the one side, and the conduct of the civil order of Israel's society, on the other.

These fall into two sets, the one on atonement for sin, the other on the regulations of life in God's kingdom. We follow the Halakhah that pertains to the shift from the condition of Eden to the long-term consequences of what happened there: [1] sin but also atonement and [2] Israel's resolve to live by God's will, not one commandment but many, revealed to Moses at Sinai in the Torah.

The first of the two critical passages of the Halakhah—sin but also atonement—reveals the effort not only to restore Eden but also to recapitulate, with a different result, what took place there. The Halakhah registers that sin is not permanent: man can atone and attain reconciliation with God.

The second then sets forth how life is to be lived in God's king-dom, subject to God's dominion. In both passages, Israel, like Adam but for the Torah, takes over the tasks of Adam. That defines the task of the enterprise to provide for a new moral entity, that is, Israel as counterpart to Adam: [1] how to accommodate its character, [2] how to educate its conscience, respectively. So we explore how the Halakhah provides for the story of atonement for Israel's sin, on the one side, and for the cultivation of Israel's commitment to obey and carry out God's will, on the other.

What took place in Eden at the very instant of perfection hardly requires elaborate retelling, except as the Oral Torah's restatement pinpoints the task that the Halakhah would undertake for itself. Man's innate trait—the power of will, which makes man like God—transformed Eden from the circumstance of bliss into the setting of sinfulness. That is to say, what lent uncertainty, hence the critical movement to Eden, provoking the story to be told, was man's pos-session of freedom of will and his action in consequence of freedom not to freely acquiesce in, but rather to rebel against, God's will. Then the task of restoring Eden must focus upon the regeneration of man, the nurture, in man, of the capacity not only to rebel but also to atone and, in entire freedom, to accept, submit, obey. That is what the Talmud means when it says that the commandments were given only to purify the heart of man. Here is how the sages tell the tale of man's tragedy.

The Fathers According to Rabbi Nathan I:XII.1

A. What was the order of the creation of the first Man? [The entire sequence of events of the creation and fall of Man and Woman took place on a single day, illustrating a series of verses of Psalms that are liturgically utilized on the several days of the week.]

B. In the first hour [of the sixth day, on which Man was made] the dirt for making him was gathered, in the second, his form was shaped, in the third, he was turned into a mass of dough, in the fourth, his limbs were made, in the fifth, his various apertures were opened up, in the sixth, breath was put into him, in the seventh, he stood on his feet, in the eighth, Eve was made as his match, in the ninth, he was put into the Garden of Eden, in the tenth, he was given the commandment, in the eleventh, he turned rotten, in the twelfth, he was driven out and went his way.

C. This carries out the verse: "But Man does not lodge overnight in honor" (Ps. 49:13).

A different version of the same thought is worth attention:

The Fathers According to Rabbi Nathan I:XIV.1

   A. On the very same day Man was formed, on the very same day man
       was made, on the very same day his form was shaped, on the very
       same day he was turned into a mass of dough, on the very same
       day his limbs were made and his various apertures were opened up,
       on the very same day breath was put into him, on the very same
       day he stood on his feet, on the very same day Eve was matched
       for him, on the very same day he was put into the Garden of Eden,
       on the very same day he was given the commandment, on the very
       same day he went bad, on the very same day he was driven out and
       went his way,
   B. thereby illustrating the verse, "Man does not lodge overnight in
       honor" (Ps. 49:24).

So within the logic of the Rabbinic system and structure,—Adam,
sinful at the end, was flawed from the outset—Adam and Eve did not
spend even the first Sabbath, the Sabbath of creation, in Eden! That
theological fact places in a new light the provision for restoring Eden
laid out in the Halakhah considered in Chapter Eleven. Now we see
the full challenge set by the Sabbath, the Sabbatical Year, and the
other Halakhic statements concerning the recovery of the condition
of Eden: *to bring man back into an Eden that in fact man never enjoyed.* It is
not only to restore the occasion meant as Eden's climax, the moment
of its perfection and ultimate repose. It is to realize that perfection for
the first time, but in the here and now of Israel's quotidian life.

     Israel, the new moral entity, is meant to accomplish what Adam
and Eve, creatures of the sixth day, missed, which is, for all that it
represents, the Sabbath day. Then their successor, Israel, on the
Sabbath day makes up for the original failure of man. The story of
Sinai recapitulates the events of Eden. For just as the fall of man, the
act of rebellion, took place within a brief spell before the Sabbath of
creation, so Israel's rebellion erupted while Moses was yet on the
mount. Israel at the foot of Sinai then retraces the steps of man, conducting its rebellion in the very shadow of Sinai as had man at the
instant of the perfection of creation.

     So what is to be done, if, as the Torah insists time and again, Israel
itself embodies the innate flaws of man as it does? Deliberately or
otherwise, Israel is going to sin; that fact defines the human condition. The task of the Halakhah, then, is to provide the remedy for the

natural condition of Israelite man, to afford media for reconciliation. These encompass atonement for sin and regeneration, an act of divine grace not accorded to the original man but consequent upon the formation of Israel through the giving of the Torah. If, as the Torah underscores, "the wickedness of man was great in the earth and every imagination of the thoughts of his heart was only evil continually, so that the Lord was sorry that he had made man on the earth," (Gen. 6:5–6), the Torah also tells the tale of God's search for a successor to the original, ultimately incorrigible man. That succession runs via Noah through Abraham to Israel at Sinai.

The Halakhah recognizes the frailty of Israel: still merely man. The new moral entity, Israel, too would write a record of rebellion and sin. But responding to Noah's offering of every clean animal and bird as burnt (or peace) offerings on the altar, God, determined "in his heart never again to curse the ground because of man, for the imagination of man's heart is evil from his youth, nor ever again to destroy every living creature" (Gen. 8:21). That is the context in which atonement finds its place: God's response to the offering of man represented by Noah, an offering presented in good faith. Israel's corporate existence takes place within God's resolve, in response to Noah, to bear with man and not to destroy him. Just as the story of Noah proves integral to the tale commencing with man, so the provision of media of atonement proves essential to the logic defined by man's disobedience, now in the form of Israel's relationship to the Torah.

But we cannot leave matters at just that point. For, as is clear, God could not rest with the provision of atonement but would have to accord man exercises of transcendence, possibilities of changing his nature. And it is in that context that God provided a relationship for Israel, this new moral entity, that he had not accorded to the original man. That relationship, embodied by the Torah, encompassed two dimensions. On the negative side, if and when Israel sinned, it could achieve atonement through sacrifice. On the positive side, Israel would be accorded numerous opportunities to engage with God as God had always wanted, that is, to carry out God's instructions, or commandments, thus showing itself regenerate. As for Israel at Sinai, then Israel in the Land, and Israel at the loss of the Land, the entire narrative of Scripture would set forth to tell the tale of Israel's exile and return to the Land, parallel to man's loss of Eden but with a different outcome. Abundant Torah and numerous commandments would form the remedy to man's innate capacity to rebel and sin.

The tale of the Torah accordingly falls into two parts, the one complementing the other. First, Israel is given the Torah and commandments, so afforded the occasion to show itself obedient, loyal to God's will. Then Israel overcomes Adam's heritage. But, second, Israel also sins, whether willingly or inadvertently.

So, unlike Adam, Israel is allowed the opportunity to atone. The Halakhah devotes a principal chapter of its statement to the medium of atonement and reconciliation, the temple offering, especially its blood rite. To the Halakhic nurture of a long-term, stable relationship between God and Israel despite Israel's sinfulness we devote the present chapter. Then comes the Halakhah governing the life of Israel under the Torah, meaning Israel living in accord with God's rule, within the dominion of God and in accord with the commandments of God.

A. *Sheqalim*

If the generative and encompassing myth of the Halakhah retells the story of man and woman in Eden and their counterpart Israel in the Land, then the logic of the tale that equates Israel to Adam requires the *incorporation* of Israel in a very precise sense: the formulation of Israel as a single responsible body, counterpart to Adam. Israel must be portrayed as collectivity culpable as a whole, and not solely by reason of the activities of the individual parts. Only in that way is Israel able to form Adam's and Eve's counterpart. Israel then emerges not merely as the sum of the parts—numerous individual Israelites all together—but on its own a whole moral entity, viewed, by God, in its own terms and framework, culpable but capable of atonement. By analogy, the Torah, Written and Oral, will view other principal players in world history as collectively capable of guilt: Babylonia, Media, Greece, Rome, for instance.

But what, then, makes Israel unique among nations? It is that corporate Israel, alone possessed of the Torah, is obligated to, and can, carry out atonement all together. It is the temple and its cult that set the stage for the embodiment of entire Israel and that mediate between Israel and God, and now we know precisely why that is so and how corporate Israel, confronting the God of all creation, comes about. To Israel alone has God given not solely the possibility but as a matter of obligation, the very power to carry out an act of sanctification of the goods of this world, things of value, translated whether into produce designated for God's purposes, whether coins for the purchase of what God requires. And these worldly goods purchase beasts to be sanctified, that is, designated for atonement rites.

To spell this out: Adam was one man, Eve one woman, but Israel formed man incorporate, the entity of an entire society contemplated by God all together and all at once, each responsible for all, all to each. And just as the new moral entity, Israel, responded in one voice at Sinai to obey and do what God commands, so that same moral entity was accorded a second chance, such as Adam and Eve never had, through the rites of atonement. Specifically, what Adam did not have that Israel did possess was the possibility of atonement, which God announced in the Torah. Israelites become "all Israel" for the purpose of presenting the daily whole offering for atonement for sin. This they accomplish when they contribute, in equal measure, a small sum to sustain the sacrifice, morning and night. Scripture describes the half shekel in the following language, the key words being italicized.

Exodus 30:11–16, RSV

The Lord said to Moses, "When you take the census of the people of Israel, then each shall give a ransom for himself to the Lord when you number them, that there be no plague among them when you number them. Each who is numbered in the census shall give this: half a shekel, according to the shekel of the sanctuary . . . half a shekel as an offering to the LORD. Every one who is numbered in the census, from twenty years old and upward, shall give the LORD's offering. The rich shall not give more, and the poor shall not give less, than the half-shekel, *when you give the LORD's offering to make atonement for yourselves.* And you shall take the atonement money from the people of Israel and shall appoint it for the service of the tent of meeting; *that it may bring the people of Israel to remembrance before the LORD, so as to make atonement for yourselves.*"

The collection of the half shekel as a ransom "that there be no plague . . . when you number them" plays no role in the Halakhah of the Oral Torah. There the conception that through the half shekel, everyone acquires a share in the atonement offering predominates. And the stress on the public offerings as atonement offerings, which the Halakhah picks up, clearly begins in the Written Torah. Then what is at issue in the half shekel offering, collected annually from every male Israelite? For the Oral Torah and its Halakhah the Tosefta makes explicit what is at stake in the matter, which is atonement.

Tosefta Sheqalim 1:6

They exact pledges from Israelites for their sheqels, so that the public offerings might be made of their funds. This is like a man who got a sore on his foot, and the doctor had to force it and cut off his flesh so as to heal him. Thus did the Holy One, blessed be he, exact a pledge from Israelites for the payment of their sheqels, so that the public offerings might be made of their funds. For public offerings appease and effect atonement between Israel and their father in heaven. Likewise we find of the heave-offering of sheqels which the Israelites paid in the wilderness, as it is said, "And you shall take the atonement money from the people of Israel, and shall appoint it for the service of the tent of meeting; that it may bring the people of Israel to remembrance before the Lord, so as to make atonement for yourselves" (Exodus 30:16).

And here is the point at which the new moral entity finds recognition. For what the shekel accomplishes is to form of all Israel a single entity before God: all have sinned, all atone, *all together*. Collective sin, collective atonement—these categories of the relationship with God, defined by Scripture from the story of the golden calf forward—transcend class, genealogy, and location.

The key to the Halakhic category-formation lies in the purpose of the shekel, which is to afford all male Israelites a portion in the daily whole offerings of atonement for Israel's corporate sin. The recognition of Israel as a new moral entity comes about not for the merely adventitious consideration that Israel encompasses vast populations beyond the limits of the Land, on the one side, and vast social diversity within, as much as beyond, the limits of the Land, on the other. To be Israel, wherever one is situated geographically and socially, is to participate in the collective character of Israel, its capacity to sin, its vocation of atonement. God views Israel as a mutually responsible social entity, not as a collection of individuals of shared convictions and origins, but as a collectivity that encompasses individuals and forms of them something else, something other than what, as individuals, they are. Among the innumerable statements of that view, Amos 3:2 suffices in its use of you-all, the you-plural: "Only you [all] have I known of all the families of man, therefore I will visit on you [all] all your iniquities." The half shekel provides for that collective guilt and collective atonement that makes Israel Israel.

That is why the Halakhah makes provision for all Israel's equal participation in the daily whole offering presented in atonement for sin. How does every Israelite gain a share in the rite? The half shekel, annually paid by all Israelites wherever located, serves as a principal medium by which all adult males are obligated, and women permitted, to effect an act of sanctification of something of worth to make possible the collective atonement offering to God. In the model of second tithe, produce translated into specie for transportation to Jerusalem, then reconverted to produce, we may say that the coin bears and embodies the sanctification of abstract value that the Israelites effect in paying the half shekel. All Israel, everywhere, relate to God through support of the public offerings in expiation of collective guilt. Here the entirety of (male) Israel, the holy people, participate. That is, all have a share, and—more important—the share is exactly the same for everyone. Not only so, but in the obligation to provide that support all are equal, rich and poor, priest and convert, resident of the Land and of the exile alike. The half shekel that is paid itself is sanctified in the way in which the heave offering or tithe is sanctified, and the analogy to second tithe, on the one side, and the heave offering paid to the priests, on the other, is Halakhically explicit. The half shekel moreover is taken up in the consecrated manner—randomly, through an act of raising up—and then is used for the purchase of animals in behalf of all Israel and for certain other purposes connected with the cult and the building where it was located.

The upshot is that the new moral entity in succession to Adam, Israel, unlike Adam and Eve, relates to God not only one by one, but, by analogy to Adam, all together. That principle, implicit throughout, is made explicit in the following rule: If people volunteered the funds on their own, they are valid, on condition that they, to begin with, explicitly donate the funds to the community for public use. And, it follows, not only do Israelites sin and atone one by one, but Israel as a whole sins and requires atonement. That is the purpose of the daily whole offerings, as Scripture makes explicit. The public offerings— the daily whole offerings—atone for Israel's sin. Public offerings appease and effect atonement between Israel and their father in heaven, just as is stated in the Written Torah and as the Oral Torah, in the Tosefta, makes equally explicit. It is the collectivity of Israel that is embodied in the half shekel offering. And that statement of the corporate character of Israel comes to expression in the half shekel in particular.

B. *Tamid and Yoma*

Not only does the daily whole offering bring about atonement for sin, so too does the advent of a particular span of time, the Day of Atonement. The Oral Torah provides the text of the high priest's confession on that occasion:

Mishnah Yoma 3:7

> O Lord, I have committed iniquity, transgressed, and sinned before you, I and my house. O Lord, forgive the iniquities, transgressions, and sins, which I have done by committing iniquity, transgression, and sin before you, I and my house. As it is written in the Torah of Moses, your servant, 'For on this day shall atonement be made for you to clean you. From all your sins shall you be clean before the Lord.'

So the Day of Atonement, the offerings of the day of atonement, and the daily whole offering, all mark the occasion on which Israel atones for sin. God responds to acts of atonement, both those involving repentance and reparation and the ones requiring cultic actions as well, such as the Torah specifies. The Halakhah at no point diverges from the spirit, let alone the letter, of the narrative of Lev. 16. That the high priest declaims the pertinent passages of the Torah, as specified at M. *Yoma* 7:1, underscores the intent of the narrative that conveys the Halakhah in place of the usual apodictic instructions: to portray precisely what the Written Torah has specified. And even the opening unit of the Halakhic norms for conduct on the Day of Atonement, dealing with "afflicting the soul," remains well within the framework of Scripture. All that is set forth is a definition of that affliction.

But the entire process of atonement underscores what is new in the new moral entity constituted by Israel, which is the capacity to repent. What Adam does is blame Eve, and Eve, the snake. By contrast, Israel blames itself and repents of sin and resolves not to repeat it, and God responds to the act of repentance, essential as it is to atonement and reconciliation. We look in vain for a counterpart transaction made available to Adam and Eve and their successors. The presentation of the Halakhah tells us what is at stake in the transaction of atonement, even on the Day of Atonement, which is the prophetic reading of the cult: it cannot suffice without the heart of man. Stated otherwise: there is no such thing as preemptive atonement.

Mishnah Yoma 8:7

He who says, "I shall sin and repent, sin and repent"—they give him no chance to do repentance. "I will sin and the Day of Atonement will atone"—the Day of Atonement does not atone.

For transgressions done between man and the Omnipresent, the Day of Atonement atones.

For transgressions between man and man, the Day of Atonement atones, only if the man will regain the good will of his friend.

This exegesis did R. Eleazar b. Azariah state: "'From all your sins shall you be clean before the Lord' (Lev. 16:30)—for transgressions between man and the Omnipresent does the Day of Atonement atone. For transgressions between man and his fellow, the Day of Atonement atones, only if the man will regain the good will of his friend."

Said R. Aqiba, "Happy are you, O Israel. Before whom are you made clean, and who makes you clean? It is your Father who is in heaven, as it says, 'And I will sprinkle clean water on you, and you will be clean' (Ezek. 36:25). And it says, 'O Lord, the hope [Miqweh = immersion pool] of Israel' (Jer. 17:13)—Just as the immersion pool cleans the unclean, so the Holy One, blessed be he, cleans Israel."

Jeremiah's call to repentance, Isaiah's reflections on the role of death in the penitential process, God's infinite mercy, Ezekiel's insistence on purity of spirit—these flow into the exposition of the Halakhah. Above all, sages underscore God's explicit promise to purify Israel, the promise set forth in Ezekiel's and Jeremiah's prophecies. So the Halakhah recasts the entire category of the Day of Atonement, taking the theme of atonement to require an account of repentance, on the one side, and God's power to forgive and purify from sin, on the other. The main point is, the rites of atonement do not work *ex opere operato* but only conditionally. And it is the attitude and intention of the Israelite that sets that condition.

Two fundamental messages then register. First, the rites atone and so does death—but only when joined with repentance, and repentance reaches its climax in the cleansing effect of the occasion, the Day of Atonement itself. A sin offering and an unconditional guilt offering atone. Death and the Day of Atonement atone when joined with repentance. Repentance atones for minor transgressions of positive and negative commandments. And as to serious transgressions, repentance suspends the punishment until the Day of Atonement comes along and atones.

But the entire system realizes its promise of reconciliation with God only on one condition: *the Israelite to begin with must frame the right attitude.* Repentance, by definition, forms a transaction concerning intentionality: there is no such thing as preemptive atonement. And that is the mark of original sincerity and initial integrity:

> He who says, "I shall sin and repent, sin and repent"—they
> give him no chance to do repentance. "I will sin and the Day of
> Atonement will atone"—the Day of Atonement does not atone.

These statements, we realize, involve attitude and intentionality. They pertain not to the Day of Atonement nor even to the rites of penitence, but to the spirit in which the person acts when he commits a sin. If in the commission of the sin he declares his conviction that his attitude makes no difference—I shall do what I want, and then repent in impunity—that attitude nullifies the possibility of repentance and the Day of Atonement to do their part in the work of reconciliation. And the Halakhah carries the matter still further when it insists that, in the end, the attitude of the repentant sinner does not complete the transaction; the sinner depends also upon the attitude of the sinned-against.

I cannot think of a more eloquent way of saying that the entire condition of Israel depends upon the inner integrity of Israel: the intentionality that motivates its actions, whether with God or with man. When we consider the matter of the daily whole offering, we find slight interest in issues of intentionality. But we shall now see that the attitude, plan, will of the sacrifier—the one in behalf of whom the offering is made, who benefits from the expiation accomplished therein—governs alongside that of the sacrificer, the priest who presents the blood rite.

C. *Zebahim and Menahot*

When we reach the Halakhah of the matching native categories, animal offerings and meal offerings, *Zebahim* and *Menahot*, we come to the very heart of the process of atonement for sin. The tossing of the blood, the taking of the handful of meal—these mark the moment of expiation, as Scripture states in so many words. And, as we shall now see, the Halakhah exquisitely articulates the conception of the centrality of attitude in the attainment of atonement. But let us start with first things: how the temple and its everyday rites recapitulate creation, only now with a different ending. That brings us to the very heart of the matter of atonement through sacrifice, which is the issue of intentionality. In one category after another, the Halakhah makes provision for the Israelite to show God the very innermost secrets of the heart, to atone for rebellion through acts of sincere obedience. What we now see, in the general rules of animal and cereal offerings, is a systematic essay on the priority of proper intentionality in the atoning encounter with God. Adam went one way, Israel the other, and here we see the evidence. The Halakhah of the Oral Torah, constructed as it is in a detailed and systematic dialogue with that of the Written Torah, in connection with animal and meal offerings makes its most explicit statement on the issues that inhere when Israel meets God. That is where, as the Written Torah plainly says, the encounter takes place: at the tent of meeting become the temple. There through offerings of meat, grain, wine, oil, and incense, Israel atones for sin and seeks to win God's favor as God in the Torah declared he may be propitiated.

Where Israel atones for sin and presents itself as ready for the meeting, there God and Israel would found their Eden. No wonder, therefore, that the offerings at the temple altar commemorate and celebrate creation—the new beginning of God's and man's transaction. And that explains why the sacrificial cult is celebrated as a memorial to creation, and the Psalms that the Levites sing identify the particular aspect of creation that took place on a given day of the week. The entire rhythm of the relationship of Israel with God—and of humanity through Israel—then was to be recapitulated in the weekly celebration of creation. Then how does Israel figure? The key motif, as we should anticipate, concerns sin and atonement. In the conflict of God's word and man's will, the drama of the cult takes its cue in the particular role of Israel, sinful but, possessed of the Torah, Israel repentant and seeking to atone. If Israel represents humanity at large, the regenerate part thereof, then the priesthood stands for Israel. They serve as bearers of the sin and embodiment of the atonement of Israel, as we shall see again and again. The priesthood in the cult takes on the garments of Israel's atonement, to offer the atoning sacrifices. That proposition is made entirely particular and concrete in this account of how the garments that the priest wears atone for particular sins that Israel commits:

Song of Songs Rabbah 48.5 *to Song of Songs* 4:4

3. A. And what is that which I tore away [spoil]?
   B. It is "Your teeth are like a flock of shorn ewes."
   C. That is to say, things that are subject to a definite and fixed number, specifically, the garments of the high priesthood.
4. A. For we have learned in the Mishnah:
   B. The high priest serves in eight garments, and an ordinary priest in four:
   C. tunic, underpants, head-covering, and girdle.
   D. The high priest in addition wears the breastplate, apron, upper garment, and frontlet [Mishnah *Yoma* 7:5A–C].
   E. The tunic would atone for bloodshed: "And they dipped the coat in the blood" (Gen. 37:31).
   F. Some say, "It atoned for those who wear mixed varieties: 'And he made him a coat of many colors' (Gen. 37:3)."
   G. The underpants atone for fornication: "And you shall make them linen underpants to cover the flesh of their nakedness" (Ex. 27:42).
   H. The head-covering atones for arrogance: "And he set the head-covering on his head" (Lev. 8:9).
   I. For what did the girdle atone?
   J. For double-dealers.
   K. Others say, "For thieves."
   L. The one who says that it was for thieves maintains that view because the garment was hollow, standing for thieves, who work in hiding.
   M. The one who says that it was for the double-dealers is in accord with that which R. Levi said, "It was thirty-two cubits long, and he would twist it on either side."
   N. The breastplate would atone for those who pervert justice: "And you shall put in the breastplate of judgment the Urim and the Thummim" (Ex. 28:30).
   O. The apron [ephod] would atone for idolatry: "And without ephod or teraphim" (Hos. 3:4).
   P. The upper garment [robe] would atone for slander.
5. A. R. Simon in the name of R. Jonathan of Bet Gubrin: "For two matters there was no atonement, but the Torah has provided atonement for them, and these are they:
   B. "Gossip and involuntary manslaughter.
   C. "For gossip there was no atonement, but the Torah has provided atonement for it, specifically through the bell of the robe: 'And

it shall be upon Aaron to minister, and the sound thereof shall be heard' (Ex. 28:35).

D. "Let the sound that this makes come and atone for the sound of slander.

E. "For involuntary manslaughter there was no atonement, but the Torah has provided atonement for it, specifically through the death of the high priest: 'And he shall dwell therein until the death of the high priest' (Num. 35:25)."

6. A. [Resuming 4.P:] The frontlet would atone for impudence.

B. Some say, "It was for blasphemy."

C. The one who says it was for impudence cites the following verse of Scripture: "And it shall be upon Aaron's forehead" (Ex. 28:38), and also, "Yet you had a harlot's forehead" (Jer. 3:3).

D. The one who says it was for blasphemy cites the following verse of Scripture: "And it shall always be upon his forehead" (Ex. 28:38) along side, "And the stone sank into his forehead" (1 Sam. 17:49).

Accordingly, God abides in Israel, and, within the Land of Israel, at the temple. There his presence came to rest, thence his presence departed when Israel's sin yielded the temple's destruction—and there he will return, to the Land, for the resurrection of the dead and restoration of life eternal, at the end of time. Where heaven and earth intersect, at the altar, whence the flames rising from burning meat, grain, oil, wine, and, above all, blood, from fires burning day and night ascend toward heaven, there in the fragrance of the incense and in clouds of smoke, Israel encounters God. The parties to the transcendent transaction are God, the priest as mediator, and any Israelite or even (for some offerings) a gentile. The priests act in behalf of Israelites individually and severally.

Here is a profusion of contradictions or paradoxes. God is one but ubiquitous, universal but localized. The Land defines the arena of encounter, but the tent of meeting is situated, to begin with, in no-man's-land, the wilderness possessed by none and all, the temple reaches toward heaven from earth, and Jerusalem is distinct from the rest of the Land. Not only so, but God dwells among the whole people of Israel, but the priesthood is singled out. How then to mediate between the special position of the genealogical caste and the paramount standing of the people of Israel, among all of whom God dwells? The priests do not act on their own. For the most part, they work solely in behalf of all Israel in carrying out the liturgy for the public offerings or of individuals subject to obligation for the personal

ones. In this negotiation between the presence of the entire holy people and the priority of the priesthood we find the model for other
negotiations that are required: the God of all creation, ubiquitous and
omnipotent, declaring that he will dwell among the people of Israel,
the God of all humanity identifying himself as "their God."

The altar marks the center, the point of intersection, the mode
and focus of mediation. In a rite that is acutely locative—here and
nowhere else—but essentially utopian—from here to heaven. The
rites in general are timely, restricted to the occasion, but the service
is meant to go on through time. Then and there three parties intersect. These are God, the priesthood, and Israel one by one and also
en masse. They come together spatially, but the encounter takes
place—can only take place—when all three concur about the purpose
of the exchange. So shared space does not suffice, nor even the correct time of a particular occasion, though both matter much. In the
wrong space, at the wrong time, nothing happens to affect Israel's
relationship with God. Then what precipitates the transaction of
meeting? What brings about the intersection is concurrence: God, the
Israelite, the officiating priest agree on the intentionality that pertains.
The Israelite designates the beast for the correct, sacred purpose, so
sanctifies it. He then delivers the beast to the priest. The priest for
the correct purpose takes the beast, cuts the neck organs and veins,
catches the blood, and sprinkles some of it at the appropriate part of
the altar, then places the animal or entrails of the animal on the altar.
And God, responding to the appropriate intentionalities, validating
the offering, receives the scent of the sacrificial parts as they are
burned on the altar. So much for the sequence of actions, just as the
Written Torah prescribes.

What of the Halakhah itself? Let us focus upon details—spread out
in Mishnah tractate *Zebahim*, chs. 1–4, with its companions in Tosefta
and Bavli *Zebahim*—of the matter of intentionality in the sacrificial
system: The link between Israel and God is effected by the attitude
or intentionality of the Israelite and of the priest, each in his position
in the transaction. God responds to the Israelite's and the priest's feelings and plans, and the offering is acceptable to him only so far as
these are correct in a particular, specific way. At what points, in connection with what specific actions, does the intentionality of the donor
and the priest register? The Halakhah makes its statement solely
through its cases, and here, by what it says, it also eliminates many

possibilities. The offering is offered for six purposes, and the priest acting in behalf of the donor must have in mind the proper attitude concerning all six. The attitude of the officiating priest governs, and if the priest expresses no improper attitude, that suffices to validate the offering on these points. For the sake of six things is the animal offering sacrificed: (1) for the sake of the animal offering, (2) for the sake of the one who sacrifices it, (3) for the sake of the Lord, (4) for the sake of the altar fires, (5) for the sake of the odor, (6) for the sake of the pleasing smell. And as to the sin offering and the guilt offering, for the sake the sin expiated thereby. That is to say, the officiating priest has to have in mind the particular offering at hand, offering a burnt offering as a burnt offering and not as peace offerings. The one who sacrifices it is the donor of the animal, who benefits, e.g., from the expiation. The intent must be for God, not for an idol(!). The intent must be to roast the meat on the fire of the altar, not at any other location. One must intend an odor to ascend from the roast. And in the case of the sin or guilt offering, the particular sin that is expiated must be in mind. As to the particular actions at which these six aspects of intentionality must conform, they involve these deeds: cutting the pertinent organs, collecting the blood in a bowl, conveying the blood to the altar, and tossing the blood on the altar.

The priest is required for preparation of an offering; a non-priest cannot carry out the critical procedures of the blood rite. An invalid priest likewise spoils the rite by his participation, e.g., one who was unclean, improperly dressed, and the like. But if the status of the priest weighs heavily on the rite, the attitude of the priest carries still greater consequence. Specifically, as just now noted, four processes integral to the rite, killing the beast, collecting the blood, conveying the blood to the altar, and tossing the blood on the altar, must be carried out by the officiating priest in accord with the intentionality of the *sacrifier*—the person who benefits from the offering, as distinct from the sacrificer, the priest who carries out the offering. There must be an accord between the will of the sacrifier in designating the beast and the will of the sacrificer in carrying out the rite. Should the priest declare that he carries out the action for some purpose other than the designated one, e.g., conveying the blood of a lamb for the purpose of peace offerings when it is the fourteenth of Nisan and the beast has been designated for a Passover, the rite is spoiled.

Why does the attitude of the officiating priest bear so heavily on the matter? To find the answer, we take the classic case of how intentionality invalidates a deed. What we see is that what one intends before the fact governs the status of the act itself, and even though one performs the act correctly and ultimately acts in accord with the law, the initial intentionality still dictates the outcome. I can think of no more powerful way of stating that what one intends in advance, and not what one does in fact, dictates the outcome of a transaction. Before us then is an extreme position, one that imposes its own perspective upon all else: the intentionality that motivates an action, not what is really done, governs. The way this is said is not complicated. It involves a rule about the priest's consuming the meat of the offering that he presents and how, at the moment of slaughter (encompassing the other phases of the blood rite) he intends to eat that meat, when and where.

Specifically, the meat of the offerings that the priests receive must be eaten by them within a specific span of time, two nights and the intervening day. If the priest when slaughtering the beast (or wringing the neck of a bird) says that he will eat the meat later on, that very act of intentionality suffices to render the act of slaughter one of abomination, and the status of the offering is determined—without any action whatsoever on the priest's part. Now we see what it means to evaluate what happens solely by reference to what one intends to make happen: not what one actually does after the fact, but what one is thinking in advance of it. The rule is framed in terms of not what the priest does but what he is thinking of doing later on. If he slaughters the animal offering intending to toss its blood outside of the temple court, to burn its sacrificial portions outside, to eat its meat outside, or to eat an olive's bulk of the skin of the fat tail outside—it is invalid. If he slaughters the animal offering, intending to toss its blood on the next day, to burn its sacrificial portions on the next day, to eat its meat on the next day, or an olive's bulk of the skin of the fat tail on the next day—it is refuse. And that is without regard to the actual deed of the priest. If after the fact of the declared intention he did the deed at the correct time or place, it changes nothing. With such remarkable power over the status of the beast that the mere intention to eat the meat outside of its proper time or to dispose of it outside of the proper place suffices to ruin the offering, the priest's intentionality in connection with immediate, concrete actions in other aspects of the offering will make a massive difference as well.

What about the transaction of the priest in behalf of the sacrifier? Here too, the action is evaluated by the intention, so that even if all the rites are correctly carried out, if the priest does not do them with the right attitude, the sacrifier loses out. This is expressed in the formulation that follows. If a beast, designated as sanctified by its owner for a particular classification of offering, is actually slaughtered for a purpose other than that for which it was originally designated, what is the result? If the officiating priest does not carry out the intention of the Israelite who purchased and sanctified the beast, the offering remains valid; the blood is collected, conveyed to the altar, and tossed there. So far as the beast is concerned, the act of sanctification is irrevocable. So far as the householder is concerned, his obligation has not yet been carried out; he must present another animal to accomplish his purpose, e.g., to present a sin offering or carry out a vow. There are two exceptions to this rule. If on the afternoon of the fourteenth of Nisan an Israelite's animal, designated to serve as a Passover offering, is offered for some other purpose, e.g., as peace offerings, it is null. So too an animal designated as a sin offering must be presented for that purpose and for no other. In both cases, the specificity of the occasion—the Passover, the sin—takes over; the animal that has been misclassified by the priest is lost.

Here the initial designation is indelible and the animal that has been destined for the specified purpose may then serve no other. If an animal sanctified as a Passover or sin offering is slaughtered for some other purpose, it too is unfit. This principle of specificity is broadened by the generalization that follows: If one slaughtered them for the sake of that which is higher than they, they are valid. If one slaughtered them for the sake of that which is lower than they, they are invalid. How so? Most holy things which one slaughtered for the sake of lesser holy things are invalid. Lesser holy things which one slaughtered for the sake of most holy things are valid. The firstling and tithe which one slaughtered for the sake of peace offerings are valid, and peace offerings which one slaughtered for the sake of a firstling, or for the sake of tithe, are invalid.

What—apart from the shared project, the activity itself and its outcome—links the one party to the other two and about what do the three parties concur? What the Israelite desires, what the priest intends, and what God requires—these three acts of will must coincide. Sages here translate into rites their deepest convictions about

what joins God to men, which is, God's will and man's corresponding will, each capable of free, uncoerced choice. Here, at the points
at which the Written Torah falls silent, the Halakhah in the particular idiom chosen for its statement turns eloquent. Setting forth in the
context of the transcendent transaction of the altar and its rites and
offerings, the Halakhah patiently lays out, through sharply-etched
cases, the thickest layers of thought of the entire Halakhic structure
and system. Most of the facts that are invoked and systematized, e.g.,
definitions of the classification of offerings and their hierarchy, derive
from the Written Torah. What the Halakhah contributes are layers
of construction upon deep foundations of reflection. What rises up is
a towering account of the role of Israel's and the priests' and God's
will in the blood rite conducted to propitiate God and win his good
will. The Land transcended, Israel transformed, in silence but for the
Levites' singing, in smoke and blood and fire God is approached, propitiated, pleased, as in the Torah he said he could and would be.

That account of the climactic encounter, in the cult, between Israel
and God does not exhaust the accomplishment of the Halakhah.
Scripture sets forth a variety of facts. The Halakhah identifies what
is implicit in those facts, picking out the indicative traits that open
the way to generalization, to identification of the principle embodied
by the case. Then the Halakhah regularizes, orders, systematizes,
classifies, and above all, hierarchizes, the discrete facts. These the
Halakhah shapes into a single, utterly cogent structure. And then the
Halakhah shows how the structure sustains a working system. Much
as any thoughtful person will find much to admire in the acumen and
perspicacity of the Halakhah throughout, its power to construct data
into coherent and logical order, here (and at the corresponding
Halakhah of cultic cleanness) we encounter the acme of Halakhic
thinking: what it can accomplish, through applied reason and practical law, in the translation of theology into concrete conduct.

The blood rite—that is, the rite that actually atones for sin—forms
the center of the transaction between Israel and God at the altar.
That is shown in the answer to the question, At what point is the
offering validated, so that the disposition of the animal bears consequences? It is when the blood has been properly sprinkled or tossed.
Then the offering is "permissible," meaning, the blood is burned on
the altar and so the meat is eaten by the priest and (where appropriate) by the Israelite sacrifier too. The proper sprinkling or tossing

of the blood therefore marks the turning point. Then the sacrifice comes within the category of being subject to the rule of refuse and extirpation. But if what permits the meat to be eaten is not properly offered, the blood not having been properly tossed so that the sacrificial portions of the animal may be burned up and the edible portions eaten, the sacrifice is not subject to the rule of refuse. If the blood rite is improperly performed, therefore, issues of attitude and intention prove null. The decisive deed dictates the disposition of the initial intention.

The basic conception is, when the rite is performed properly with the correct intentionality, it accomplishes its goals (it is "valid"). When the rite is performed properly but classified incorrectly, it is invalid. The Halakhah bears no messages concerning the meaning of the blood rite, only the conditions that are required for its effective accomplishment. The attitude or intention takes priority in the validation of the rite over the actualities of deed. This is expressed in the following way. A bird that one designated to serve as sin offering of fowl which one prepared below the red line, (1) that is to say, properly, in accord with the rites of the sin offering, (2) in the classification "name" of the sin offering, obviously is valid. What does it take to invalidate the rite? If one did the actions correctly but classified the transaction improperly, that is, had the wrong intention, it is invalid. If one prepared a bird designated to serve as a sin offering of fowl (1) in accord with the rites of the sin offering, (2) but in the classification "for the name" of a burnt offering—(1) or in accord with the rites of the burnt offering below the line, (2) but in the classification "for the name" of a sin offering—(1) or in accord with the rites of the burnt offering, but in the classification "for the name" of a burnt offering, it is invalid. If one prepared it above the red line instead of below, but, otherwise in accord with the rites of either of them, it in all events is invalid. It would be difficult to state more forcefully that the right attitude governs, taking priority even over right action, so that if things are done correctly but with improper intentionality, the rite is null.

Why the stress on intentionality? The Israelite has the power to change the status of a beast from secular to sacred, and this he does by an act of will. He designates a beast as sacred, specifying the purpose of the act of sanctification. So the entire process of presenting personal offerings (as distinct from the public ones considered at

Sheqalim) depends upon the act of will effected by the individual Israelite. And since the rites are carried out at the critical turnings by the priest, the attitude that governs his activities likewise must register. Neither the Israelite nor the priest is portrayed as an automaton, nor do the actions of the two parties emerge as coerced or automatic. What the Israelite does realizes his will, which is why the deed makes a difference, and, the Halakhah takes for granted, the priest too engages through an act of will. Both are deemed to have, and to make, choices, and these choices respond to the intentionality that motivates the entire transaction, start to finish. So the Halakhah portrays the cult as the stage on which Israel—priest and Israelite alike—work out in concrete actions the results of their interior reflections.

Since, as with the daily whole offerings of all Israel all together, the entire rite is time and again represented as an exercise in expiation of sin, even though a variety of offerings serves another purpose altogether (e.g., celebration, service, and the like), we do well to recall the principal (but not sole) occasion for individual participation:

Mishnah Keritot 1:2

> For those [thirty-six classes of transgressions] are people liable, for deliberately doing them, to the punishment of extirpation, and for accidentally doing them, to the bringing of a sin offering, and for not being certain of whether or not one has done them, to a suspensive guilt offering [Lev. 5:17]—[except for] the one who blasphemes, as it is said, "You shall have one law for him that does anything unwittingly" (Num. 15:29)—excluding the blasphemer, who does no concrete deed.

The sin offering expiates sin only when the sin is inadvertent; deliberate sin is expiated through the sacrifice of years of life ("extirpation"). Then the transaction at the altar, so far as the expiation of sin forms the center, so far as individuals are involved principally concerns those actions that one did not intend to carry out but nonetheless has done. The intentionality governing the deed therefore proves decisive, and we may not find surprising the focus upon attitude accompanying the action of sacrifice. The right attitude is confirmed by the offering done in the right spirit.

Just as the offering expiates an inadvertent sin, so the attitude that motivates the sacrifier (and, correspondingly, the priest too) will define matters: it is for this particular sin, that I did not mean to do, that I have deliberately designated as holy that particular beast. An unintentional, sinful act then provokes an intentional act of expiation. Then what God follows with close anticipation is how this act of will is realized—confirmed in actuality; that occasion of acute advertence is what concludes the transaction begun inadvertently. And that means, in the concrete arrangements of the cult, how the actions of the priest conform in the priest's intentionality to the original act of sanctification brought about by the Israelite's intentionality. The entire relationship between Israel and God works itself out as a match of the intentions of the several parties, each of them qualified to form an independent act of will, all of them conforming to bring about the successful result, the expiation of sin or the fulfillment of commitment.

Accordingly, in the offerings of the altar, the Israelite relates to God by an act of will in designating as sacred for a specific purpose, defined as acceptable by God for purposes of propitiation, an animal and related materials. The priest then mediates this act of will by realizing, in actions resulting in the tossing of the animal's blood on the altar, the intentionality of the Israelite. And God relates to the Israelite, in that same transaction, by paying closest possible attention to the interplay of the Israelite's initial intentionality in the act of sanctification and the concrete outcome, in the priest's realization of that same intentionality, in the act of offering.

We should not miss the negative, for it yields a positive result. It is not enough that the Israelite designate the animal; God must know that the priest has prepared it in accord with the definition of the sanctification that has taken hold of that animal by reason of the Israelite's act of sanctification. The priest must carry out the action within the same framework of purpose established by the Israelite for the beast. So it does not suffice for the priest to impose his judgment upon the disposition of the beast; the initial act of sanctification has imposed limits upon his purpose. The Israelite requires priestly conformity to his, the Israelite's, act of will in designating the beast. The priest effects the correct offering only when he subordinates his will to that of the Israelite. The Israelite attains atonement and reconciliation with God only when, after an unintended violation of the Torah, he demonstrates that, in giving something back (whether a costly beast, whether a bird of no account), he subordinates his will to that of God. We find matched acts of willful and deliberate subordination—the priest's to the Israelite's, the Israelite's to God's.

The sequence of acts in conformity with the will of another having been worked out, God then accepts the actions that come about by reason of right thought and responds by accepting the blood offering as an act of propitiation and atonement, on the one side, or of fulfillment of obligation, on the other. What is required in a valid act of fulfillment of the Israelite's act of consecration is uniform conformity of deed to will. When it comes to characterizing Israel's relationship with God, what counts, then, is that God follows this sequence of steps, this process leading the beast from the secular herd to the sacred altar, its blood turned into the reagent to wash away the inadvertent sin of the sacrifier. Everyone must concur in sequence, the sacrifier, the sacrificer, and God in confirmation to the correct intention of both. It is as though God wished to set up a system carefully to monitor the will of successive participants in the process, each exposing for God's inspection the contents of his hearts. God closely attends to the match of deliberation and deed, and only when the Israelite's intent and the priest's intent coincide does God confirm his gracious acceptance of the result, propitiation resulting.

So while the presentation of offerings superficially places the human side of the transaction at the center—it is the Israelite's, then the priest's parts that effect the relationship—in fact, it is God's engagement with the same transaction, his close and careful surveillance of the match of intent and action, word and deed, that makes all the difference. In the cult Israel relates to God intimately and concretely. Once the Israelite undertakes by an act of will to engage in a deed of sanctification, God's participation in the process, step by step, his close attention to the interior of the activities consequence upon the undertaking—these responses embody God's intense interest in the Israelite's attitude, to which God responds.

That is why intentionality takes on very concrete and specific meanings in the setting of the offering to God of the gifts of the Land—meat, wine, oil, grain and the like. When an Israelite expresses his intentionality to sanctify a particular animal for a specified offering, that consecrates the beast for God's service at the altar. But the intentionality of the Israelite then requires a corresponding attitude on the part of, with a confirming action by, the officiating priest. If he does the deeds of the sacrifice for some purpose other than the announced one of the Israelite, he denies the Israelite the benefit of confirmation of his intentionality by a cultic action. What is the result of the priest's misconceiving of matters? Where the beast can serve for some appropriate cultic purpose, it does so. That is to say, the original action of the Israelite in sanctifying the beast is not nullified by the contradictory intentionality of the priest. But where the beast is designated for a very particular purpose and can then serve no other, the sacrificial act is lost.

Then when is a beast sanctified with such specificity as to be lost by the priest's contradictory intentionality? It is when either the time or the circumstance intervenes and so defines the status as to sanctification of the beast as to render the beast useless for all other purposes. For the Passover offering in particular, the time is the eve of the Passover, when the lamb designated for the Passover offering must be offered up under that designation and no other. Any other time, the same lamb may serve as peace offerings. So the time makes all the difference in avoiding confusion as to the intent of the sacrifier.

The other consideration—the circumstance—appeals to much weightier concerns, confirming what has already been said about why intentionality registers in so weighty a way. The circumstance is the inadvertent commission of a particular sin. The beast designated as the sin offering for a given sin can serve to expiate no other. It is the demonstration of correct intention—the good will, not the rebellious will—that the offering embodies. The correlation of the sin offering with the inadvertent sin is expressed in the following way:

Tosefta Keritot 2:4

[If] it is a matter of doubt whether or not one has sinned, he brings a suspensive guilt-offering [M. Ker. 4:1, 2A–B]. [If] he has sinned, but is not certain what particular sin he has committed, he brings a sin-offering. [If] he has sinned and is informed of the character of his sin but he has forgotten what sin he has committed, lo, this one brings a sin-offering [M. Ker. 4:2C–D], and it is slaughtered for the sake of whichever [sin he has committed] and it is eaten. Then he goes and brings a sin-offering for that sin of which he is informed, and it is slaughtered for the sake of whatever [particular sin he has done] and it [too] is eaten.

A very particular occasion then has precipitated the act of will involved in designating the beast as a sin offering, and that same purpose must govern throughout.

In both cases, then, the act of sanctification takes on a particularity that drastically limits options in case of priestly error. The reason for the latter—the sin offering—is self-evident. God permits the man who has inadvertently sinned to atone for the sin he did not mean to commit or even know that he committed. Once he finds out what he has done, he wishes to show the true state of his will, and that is through the sin offering. The offering then is linked to that action and no other. Sin is particular, concrete, and delimited—an action, not a condition. And so is the intention to be made manifest: that act I did not intend to commit, shown by this act, which I fully will.

That negative rule—the sin offering and Passover are invalidated if the priest's intentionality does not conform to the occasion (the will of the sacrifier) or the time (the afternoon of the fourteenth of Nisan)—yields a striking, positive result: God pays exceedingly close attention to the act of will exercised by both the sacrifier and the sacrificer, responding to what is in the heart of each in assessing the effect of the act viewed whole. Then the activity that yields the event—the sacrifier's selection of the beast, designation of its purpose in an act of consecration, his presentation to the priest with the sacrifier's laying on of hands, then the priest's cutting of the beast's throat and collection of its blood, conveyance of its blood to the altar and the splattering of its blood thereon—all of these activities must be uniformly animated by the initial intention of the Israelite, and the continuation of the program by the priest is at issue. It would be difficult to formulate a more concrete and far-reaching statement that God pays the closest possible attention to the Israelite's will than the rule at hand. The offerings at the altar accomplish their goal because God attentively engages with, responds to, the Israelite's and the priest's intentionality. God will respond, the Halakhah takes for granted, and accord atonement, register the fulfillment of an obligation for example, only when these coincide: the will of the sacrifier, the will of the sacrificer.

But an important qualification enters here, in two parts. First, if a person may validly perform an action within the sacrificial rite, e.g., slaughter the animal, then his or her intentionality registers. But if an unfit person collects the blood, the action is null, and so too the intention of such a person in connection with that action is null. So we discern a close correspondence of opposites, a tight logic that governs the whole. What matters—intentionality at the critical points—is all that matters. Second, going over the same ground in a different way, intentionality must concern what is legitimate to begin with. If he who slaughters the animal sacrifice intends to eat something which is not usually eaten, to burn something which is not usually burned—the offering nonetheless is valid. God monitors the normal and legitimate; there improper intentionality proves effective. But God does not take account of attitudes in procedures that to begin with are null. And there is a third point not to be missed: when it comes to actions, God takes the lenient view that an act improperly performed can and should be corrected. If properly performed at the end, the rite is not ruined. The entire construction of the law reinforces the centrality of intentionality in relationship to legitimacy: an improper attitude toward that which one may properly do makes its mark. The act must match the intention, but if the intention is correct, the improper act, brought into line, cannot spoil the procedure.

What about the Halakhah's rules for the regulation of the altar? The altar sanctifies what is appropriate to it but has no effect upon what is not appropriate to it. Sanctification does not inhere in the altar, such that mere contact with the altar transforms what touches the altar into something permanently sacred. And along these same lines, perfectly rational considerations govern questions of precedence. In all three instances of the disposition of "the sacred," we find sanctity not an inherent trait but one that depends upon circumstance and suitability. The full meaning of these important components of the Halakhah emerges only when we consider the Written Torah's judgment of the same matter, which is stated at Ex. 29:37: "the altar shall be most holy; whatever touches the altar shall become holy." That Halakhah significantly qualifies that statement, adding the language "that is appropriate" to the phrase, "whatever touches. . . ." The issue is whether sanctification is indelible or stipulative. Schismatic opinion holds that what is sanctified in the sanctuary is indelibly sanctified so is not removed from the altar. If, then, the cause of invalidation for the altar took place in the sanctuary, the sanctuary accepts the thing in any event and it is not removed from the altar. If its invalidity did not take place in the sanctuary, the sanctuary does not accept it and it should be removed from the altar. But that position concerning sanctification by being assigned to a named sage as against "sages" is labeled as not normative, and consequently the Halakhah underscores the logic of its generative position, which is, sanctification affects status, not substance.

Then we must ask, does not the Land sanctify? Does not the city

sanctify? Does not the altar sanctify? We know that all three do have
that power. To take one case, produce designated as second tithe is
sanctified upon entry within the walls of Jerusalem. So introducing
the principle of appropriateness qualifies what we should have
anticipated would represent an absolute condition. Since Scripture
explicitly declares the altar itself to be not only holy but capable of
imparting holiness to whatever touches it, we cannot miss the drastic
way in which the Halakhah mediates the meaning of sanctification.
It is now not a condition but a transaction, subject to variables and
stipulations. It is no longer locative and place-bound, nor, indeed, is
it utopian (the altar is unique and singular, where it is and nowhere
else, as Deuteronomy has made the fact).

What the altar represents, rather, is merely the place at which a
given transaction can take place, the only place where, under proper
conditions and stipulations, God and Israel meet for the purpose at
hand. It is holy because of what takes place there, not because of
intrinsic quality or character. We recall that it is the intersection of
Israel, the people, with the Land of Israel that brings about the activation of processes of sanctification that inhere therein. When the
Israelite farmer, who possesses the Land, expresses his intentionality
to make use of the produce, then God's interest is aroused in the produce of the Land that he, God, owns. A gentile farmer of the Land
of Israel does not produce the same effect. The altar then corresponds
to the Land, each in its context setting the stage for an encounter that
can take place only there and nowhere else. But neither the altar nor
the Land plays a part in the meeting; the Land requires the presence
of Israel, the altar of the priest. The walls of the city encompass
second tithe; entry within them means the produce cannot then be
removed from the city. But the walls do not impart the status of
sanctification to the produce; the farmer has done so by designating
it as second tithe. These and numerous other details of the law make
the same point as to what takes place in the transaction of
sanctification, when Israel relates to God: it is the realization of what
is potentially present by reason of forces extrinsic to the setting, but
intrinsic to God's and Israel's very being. And that, I hardly need
specify, is what is common to them: the freedom to choose, the
autonomy of the will, in Israel's case, obedience freely proffered.

What is at stake is the insistence of the normative Halakhah that,
while the altar alone serves as the nexus of Heaven and earth, not

even the altar embodies, let alone transmits, what is intrinsically holy. What can become holy realizes its potential upon the altar: the right place, the right time, confirmed by the right intentionality. Then some things are relative to others, and location, time, and attitude all together coincide. Then the potential sanctity becomes actual, then alone. We cannot speak in the Halakhic framework of "the Holy," only the status of holiness, which depends upon meeting specified conditions and turns out to be relative and stipulative.

If sanctification represents a transaction, not a condition, then we should anticipate other indications of that same fact. And so we find in the unfolding of the Halakhah of our present category. Raising the question of priority or precedence among classes of holy things presupposes that "the sacred" is not uniform and inherent, homogenizing whatever is affected thereby. It differentiates and itself is differentiated. But throughout the Halakhah, start to finish, no supernatural intervention is required to determine priority among differentiated holy things. Again we cannot speak of "the sacred," but only the status of sanctification, with its appropriate consequences. The entire transaction underscores the relative and stipulative character of sanctification and denies its absoluteness. Here too, precedence is assigned for fundamentally neutral and extrinsic reasons, not by appeal to the substantive and intrinsic character of what is sanctified. But when we identify the governing criteria for priority among holy things, we find our way deep into conceptions of Israel's relationship to God.

So we return to our starting point. The Halakhah of *Zebahim* focuses upon atonement for sin, just as Scripture says time and again. The blood rite and all the elaborate arrangements of a spatial character round about it are represented, time and again, as essentially a medium for atoning for sin. That is explicitly why the daily whole offerings are required, and, as we have seen time and again, whatever other motivations animate God's commandments concerning the sacrificial cult, the main one, the governing one, repeatedly is, atonement for sin. And here, in the Halakhic recapitulation of Scripture's norms and narratives, it is the *only* variable that transcends fixed rules, meaning, it is the only authentic variable. Atonement for sin alone appeals to other than established procedures, hence the distinction that makes the significant difference. It is not only the Halakhah, but also the Aggadah, that takes the view of the blood rite: it is principally an act of atonement for sin, and when the rite was brought to an end, another medium of atonement had to be identified:

The Fathers According to Rabbi Nathan IV.V.2

A. One time after the destruction of the Temple Rabban Yohanan ben Zakkai was going forth from Jerusalem, with R. Joshua following after him. He saw the house of the sanctuary lying in ruins.
B. R. Joshua said, "Woe is us for this place which lies in ruins, the place in which the sins of Israel used to come to atonement."
C. He said to him, "My son, do not be distressed. We have another mode of atonement, which is like atonement through sacrifice, and what is that? It is deeds of loving kindness.
D. "For so it is said, 'For I desire mercy and not sacrifice, and the knowledge of God rather than burnt offerings' (Hos. 6:6)."

In this context, we find that the Halakhah and Aggadah match in finding the governing variable in hierarchizing cultic activities not only the formal but also the substantive, not only the ordering by the strict character of the rules pertinent to one but not so much to another act of service, but also the ordering by appeal to the purpose of the entire exercise. With its recapitulation of the Written Torah's presentation of matters, the Halakhah, with the Aggadah, makes explicit the critical factor that will bring about the restoration, which turns out to be the same power that in the offerings on the altar brings about expiation and reconciliation: the realization in actuality of the required intention, which only Israel has the power to bring into being. Presented with the Halakhah alone, we should have postulated a generative story involving intentionality. Taking account of what is at stake, we should have readily supposed a transaction of conflict, between God's and Israel's will. And a story very like the one of Eden would have accommodated the facts of the law and explained their generative tensions and their recurrent points of insistence.

The meal offering for the poor accomplishes what the animal offering achieves for those wealthy enough to present an entire beast: the atonement for sin. That fact, explicit in Scripture, defines the question facing the sages of the Halakhah. For the Halakhah of *Menahot* addresses a particular problem: how more than a single category of creation accomplishes one and the same task. Scripture is clear that animal offerings atone. It is equally explicit that, where necessitated by reason of poverty, so do vegetable offerings, meal offerings in particular. Now Scripture carefully delineates and distinguishes the product of the herd and flock from the produce of the orchard and field, for example, prohibiting the wearing of garments made from wool together with those made from linen, in the theory that what derives from beasts should not be mixed with what derives from the field. And yet, when it comes to atonement, Scripture is equally clear that an offering of the one serves equally well with an offering of the other. The way in which the Halakhah sorts out matters defines the critical focus of the analysis here, and the solution, the specification of rules that apply to both distinct categories of offering such as to yield a common result, proves characteristic of the Halakhic system throughout. So what is achieved through the ordering of facts, most of them provided by Scripture, vastly transcends the mere recapitulation, within an encompassing and rational framework, of familiar data. Through the very work of regularization and rationalization, imposing upon meal offerings the rules that govern animal offerings, the Halakhah solves a critical problem of what we might classify as an ontological character: how animal and vegetable, distinct categories of creation, yield the same consequence.

So far as the Halakhah of *Menahot* makes a statement on how Israel relates to God at the altar, it consists of a single proposition: those who bear full responsibility for their actions by reason of enjoying full command of their own will stand as equals before God. All, rich and poor, sin.

Mishnah Menahot 13:11

> It is said of the burnt offering of a beast, "An offering by fire, a smell of sweet savor" (Lev. 1:9) and of the bird offering, "An offering by fire, a smell of sweet savor" (Lev. 1:17) and [even] of the meal offering, "An offering by fire, a smell of sweet savor" (Lev. 2:9)—to teach that all the same are the one who offers much and the one who offers little, on condition that a man will direct his intention to Heaven.

To all accorded responsibility for their actions God affords the possibility of atonement and reconciliation. That striking fact then underscores that it is not the blood rite that makes the difference, for the meal offering accomplishes exactly the same thing. Just as sanctification constitutes a status, not a substantive quality, so the altar carries out its task only when man's attitude and activity warrant: what is appropriate for the altar, not what is not appropriate for it, is what ascends. The Halakhah in its norms for actualities then characterizes man's relationship with God: man is responsible for his own will, and God responds to man's will. But knowing who and what man is, God gives man ample occasion to manifest the character of his conscience, the quality of his conviction. It is when man discerns the inadvertent sin that he has committed and atones therefor that man makes his will conform with God's will, freely to love, freely to obey. That is why the Halakhah in such an elaborate manner equates the hugely costly ox with the paltry handful of flour: on condition that a man will direct his intention to Heaven. Once more, we find in the Halakhah of holy things a sustained essay on the primacy of man's will and on the power of man through an act of subordination to God to change God's mind about man. That is by revealing an attitude to God, to which God responds, just as God responded in Eden when man rebelled.

D. 'Arakhin

What place then for the individual Israelite, apart from corporate Israel? To answer that question we cross the boundaries set by the story of Eden and man, the Land and Israel—but explore what is implicit in that story, which is, the primacy of the encounter between God's and man's wills. Here intentionality encompasses another transaction altogether, different from the one of atonement. For to understand the meaning of the Halakhah of 'Arakhin, we have to move beyond the limits of atonement and to consider what it means for an individual to donate to God through the temple on his own something subject to his will and possession, whether his own worth, whether the worth of a material good. For we now take up the way in which the Halakhah makes provision for individuals to single themselves out in devotion to God through the temple: What may they do, and what meaning does the deed possess?

Israel not only constitutes a corporate moral entity but also encompasses private persons, all of them capable of independent volition and action. How to hold together the public and the personal dimensions of the relationship of Israel with God? For Israel forms a moral entity comprising moral entities, collectivity and individuality alike. Israel looks to God in its entirety. Israelites also turn to God in their individuality. All Israelites bear equally the obligation to support the public offerings of atonement. No Israelite is assigned a counterpart, obligatory offering, except in cases of uncleanness and purification or of inadvertent sin, in which case he or she may present a sin offering to atone for the unintended act. Other individual offerings are votive and supererogatory, not obligatory. So while embodied Israel is required to present the half shekel, forming the parts into the whole for purposes of cultic atonement, no counterpart obligation is imposed on individuals.

Reinforcing the lesson of *Sheqalim*, the main point of *'Arakhin* is negative. The Halakhah by its silence stresses that *only* corporate Israel carries out God's commandments concerning public atonement offerings; individuals may not on their own initiative provide them. One person may not atone for another person's sin, but all Israel may atone for the sin for which all equally bear responsibility. The community alone acts in behalf of entire Israel. Not only so, but corporate Israel acts not on its own volition but only when instructed to by God's explicit commandment. And God does not respect persons or provide for individuals an occasion for self-aggrandizement through acts of obligatory piety. That is why—a triumph for the Halakhah!— no one may contribute more than the half shekel for the public atonement offerings. Recognizing neither wealth nor poverty, neither utter purity nor total corruption of a given person, God permits no distinctions when it comes to atonement. All Israel equally bear guilt, having sinned collectively, not merely individually, for example with the golden calf, which set the stage for the provision of the cult. At God's word Israel formed itself into a collectivity, a moral entity, at Sinai. The Torah, once accepted voluntarily by the entirety of Israel, explicitly dictated commandments pertaining to the whole community, not only to persons one by one (or, more to the point, by families, as at Ex. 12).

Principally as a matter of personal initiative, individuals consecrate something of value. Such supererogatory acts of sanctification may pertain either to persons or to real estate, and both are covered within the Halakhic category of *'Arakhin*, Valuations. That is, specifically, the value of persons or real estate is estimated, and the cash paid to redeem from the sanctuary the pledged value, whether personal or landed, goes to the temple for its upkeep. Scripture explicitly makes provision for such votive offerings of personal worth, specifying the requisite number of shekels that measure the worth of a person of a given classification. For an adult male, it is one hundred times the half shekel paid annually, for an adult female sixty, and so on down. But those who sanctify their own value and cannot pay the fixed sum may be subjected to an individual evaluation. When it comes to real estate, the Halakhah focuses upon the disposition of real estate received by inheritance, that is, real estate assigned in the original, perfect division of the Land to one or another specific party to the entry into the Land. Both personal valuations and dedications of real property—fields and houses under specified circumstances—represent donations to God through the temple and the priesthood.

Leviticus 27:1–8

> The Lord said to Moses, "Say to the people of Israel, When a man makes a special vow of persons to the Lord at your valuation, then your valuation of a male from twenty years old up to sixty years old shall be fifty sheqels of silver according to the shekel of the sanctuary. If the person is a female, your valuation shall be thirty sheqels. If the person is from five years old up to twenty years old, your valuation shall be for a male twenty sheqels and for a female ten sheqels. If the person is from a month old up to five years old, your valuation shall be for a male five sheqels of silver and for a female your valuation shall be three sheqels of silver. And if the person is sixty years old and upward, then your valuation for a male shall be fifteen sheqels, and for a female ten sheqels. And if a man is too poor to pay your valuation, then he shall bring the person before the priest and the priest shall value him; according to the ability of him who vowed the priest shall value him."

Scripture supplies the main components of the Halakhah, but not all of them. The Halakhah explores the question, what place do individuals find for themselves, for the natural and concrete expression of their personal devotion to God? Whatever derives from individuals, by reason of personal initiative and idiosyncratic motivation to contribute to the public interest goes to the upkeep of the temple, not to the altar except in special circumstances to which the Halakhah just now surveyed has made reference.

Individuals, accordingly, contribute their own scarce resources, whether property, personalty, or realty, to the public space that is consecrated to God. That they have the right to do, because they possess and may dispose of goods and land and—in a world that countenanced slavery (the buying and selling of persons)—also themselves, their own market value. Of this they may dispose in accord with their own will; they make his will their will, their property his. So they give what they command, in proportion to what they hold. And that to which they give then corresponds to what is given: individual worth to the worth of the temple building, individually possessed land to the sacred space that sustains the temple. In that they really are distinguished from one another; in that they willfully distinguish themselves in godly dedication.

But here once more God's perspective differs from man's. When it comes to God's valuation of persons as of atonement offerings whether meat, whether grain, all are equal; when it comes to man's, the beautiful are worth and give more, the ugly less. That underscores the fact: when the Halakhah takes the measure of individuals within entire Israel, all weigh equally and give appropriately. When the Halakhah accords to individuals the right to distinguish themselves, it carefully defines that by which they take their own measure and restricts to appropriately corresponding loci and foci that to which they then may donate. That is why, when moved to volunteer to God something of personal value, individuals have every right to pledge the value of their persons or property. In line with the Written Torah, the Halakhah deemed it entirely rational to devote scarce resources to the upkeep of the temple, entirely proper for individuals to do so on their own. And—a point we should not miss—also in line with the provisions of Leviticus, supererogatory donations to the priesthood, either immediately, through the *herem*, or in the course of nature at the end of the Jubilee cycle, certainly had their place.

That fact brings us to a second answer to the question, Why is it that individuals have the right voluntarily to contribute to enhance public space in the holy place, on the one side, and to sustain the priesthood, on the other? To answer that question out of the Halakhah, but now another, if kindred, sector of the Halakhah, we ask another: Under ordinary circumstances, who must support the priesthood and its activities? The answer is, the householder, out of the produce of his land. Then in permitting individuals to pledge personal valuations of themselves for the support of the temple, the Halakhah treats the population without land, including the population without the Land, as equal in all ways to the enlandised householder. The entire population of Israel, at home and in the exile, finds itself in a position of equality vis-à-vis the holy place and its staff. The stress on the equalization of all Israel in the matter of personal valuations is explicit: wealth and poverty, beauty and its opposite—these play no role in assessing the worth of a person who pledges his, or another's, valuation to the upkeep of the temple and its priesthood. And just as the householder may contribute more than the prescribed minimum, may decorate his firstfruits and contribute the supplementary decorations, for example, so every individual enjoys the same option. He or she has every right to pledge not the fixed valuation—the *price fixe*—but the actual worth, and the Halakhah takes pains to differentiate the fixed valuation from the actual worth and dictate how the latter is assessed.

E. *Bekhorot*

Man—the householder—by his act of intentionality sanctifies most offerings for the altar. Whether beast or bird, the offering is the Israelite's choice. But, identifying his selection among animals and man, God effects acts of consecration as well. The best comes first. Specifically, he selects the firstlings, the firstfruits of the life-processes of Israel itself—counterpart to the firstfruits of the Land taken by the householder to the priest. These are God's designation of the firstborn males among animals, of Israel among the nations, and of the priesthood among Israel. The class of animals that end up on the altar that God chooses correspond to a class of mankind linked to the altar and a class of Israel also chosen by God. The first therefore is comprised by firstborn animals, the second by firstborn male Israelites, redeemed from the altar, and the third by the priesthood, fed from the altar and accorded special rights over the firstborn of animals and of Israel. What these three classes bear in common, then, is that all are sanctified by God's, not man's, selection.

But among the three, the firstborn among beasts belonging to Israel, when brought into juxtaposition with the firstfruits of the soil of the Land of Israel, conveys the message that the Halakhah wishes to set forth through this particular category. What is conveyed is the equivalency of Israel to the priesthood. While the Halakhah of firstlings encompasses the firstborn of man, the firstborn of a clean beast, and the firstborn of an unclean beast, the exposition of the Halakhah explicitly treats the priesthood, within Israel, as equivalent to the firstborn among clean beasts, meaning, blemishes that disqualify beasts from the altar disqualify priests from serving at the altar. So the equivalency of the firstborn of any Israelite couple (here the woman's condition is essential to the transaction) and the priests is established.

Firstlings and the tithe of the herd and flock compare to firstfruits and the tithe of the field and orchard and express the same conception. God claims his share out of the best of the produce. But here God's claim takes effect not when man determines to make use of the produce of the Land, as in the case of tithes and heave offerings of crops of the Land of Israel. Rather, God's claim on the fruit of the womb comes into view as soon as the offspring, human or animal, emerges. Upon birth, then, the firstling is holy, belonging to God, hence the priesthood, and has to be redeemed in the case of man or otherwise disposed of in the case of animals.

Firstlings derive only from the Land, while overseas herds and flocks are supposed to be tithed. Since both are destined to the priesthood, the difference lies in provenience. The fact that they are owned by Israelites makes them eligible for tithing, and that is without regard to where they are raised. And that underscores the main point I discern in the Halakhah, which is the genealogical link of Israel to the altar. When it comes to first born, whether among animals or people, derivation from Israel, not localization in the Land of Israel, governs. The pointedness of that principle emerges most sharply when we compare firstlings to firstfruits.

By contrast to firstfruits, obligatory only for Israelite landholders, firstlings must be presented by all Israelites, not only in the Land of Israel but wherever they are located, who own herds and flocks. And all Israelites' firstborn male children, wherever they are born, must be redeemed. So the source of sanctification is personal, therefore utopian, not enlandised, and here we find ourselves within a realm of sanctification that derives from genealogy, not geography. Birth to an Israelite father and mother (within the qualifications the Halakhah sets forth) imposes the liability of redemption upon the father, and birth to an Israelite owner imposes liability to tithing the herd or flock. Note the contrast to the obligation for firstfruits: what is required is firstfruits of those species in which the Land specializes. Who is obligated is the Israelite who not only possesses a share in the Land but also derives from the Israel to whom the Land was initially handed over. A more striking contrast would be difficult to locate than the one that differentiates firstfruits from the firstborn of man and beast, on the one side, and the obligation to tithe the herd and flock, on the other.

Presenting firstfruits and reciting the declaration characterize one who is wholly Israel, possessing both the Land by inheritance and the genealogy that mark one as such. But firstlings, also presented to the priesthood, require no such declaration. God possesses them from the womb, and, if unblemished, they are offered up to him or redeemed from him, with reference to beast and man respectively. So firstfruits testify to enlandised Israel, firstlings to genealogical Israel. When it comes to genealogical Israel, as distinct from enlandised Israel, everyone participates—from the womb. That is the critical point. Converts, on the one side, and non-householders (landowners) on the other, fall outside of the rite of firstfruits. Those who cannot state that the Land is theirs find themselves excluded from the Israel, possessed of the Land, who celebrate their relationship with God in the rite at hand. But all Israel, wherever they are located, tithe their herds and flocks, and all Israel, men and women, may potentially produce firstborn.

Firstlings and firstfruits celebrate the procreation of life, the one by animate Israel (encompassing its herds and flocks), the other by the Land of Israel. Firstfruits focus upon the Land as the particular medium for the celebration of life, the Land as the womb for the seed planted by the householder and nurtured by God and taken over by the priesthood. The laws of the firstborn and of tithing the flock and the herd celebrate life in a different way, now, life formed in the womb of the seed planted by animate Israel (including, once more, Israel's flocks and herds). So the Halakhah celebrates Israel in the Land and Israel detached from the Land.

In this context we recall the contrast between ordinary offerings and firstfruits. Anyone may buy a beast or bird or cereal and designate it for a personal purpose. Only the householder presents firstfruits. Anyone may declare the classification of a beast or bird or cereal, e.g., a sin offering, a guilt offering, a freewill offering, a peace offering. Only the householder may classify the produce as firstfruits by an explicit designation. When it comes to the firstling and the tithe of the herd and flock, any Israelite participates through ownership, but only God designates what or who qualifies—which beast, which son. That the firstborn son must be redeemed from God contains the entire statement. The rite of firstfruits defines the relationship of Israel and God in acutely personal terms, invoking the "I" and the "my," in giving back to God the first testimonies to God's ongoing benevolence. Firstfruits makes the relationship between God and Israel personal and immediate, familial and genealogical—wholly through the nexus of the holy Land.

Firstlings, by contrast, represent God's giving back to Israel the fruit of the womb of herd or flock or woman. Whoever owns animals, wherever he lives, like any husband and wife in the appropriate circumstance, is a candidate for entry into that relationship, for receiving that gift of a future and a hope, and for giving back to God the first of what God has given to him. So the Halakhah wishes to state that Israel in its fleshly embodiment of families through genealogical ties relates to God at the temple through the gifts of grace presented by the Land. Then the Halakhah can make no more particular and concrete statement than it does through the laws of the firstfruits. So too, the Halakhah wishes to state that God shows grace to Israel in the fleshly embodiment of families by giving firstborn sons to their mothers and fathers, and by giving firstborn offspring to herds and flocks. And it finds in the Written Torah's laws of firstlings the ideal medium for that statement. I cannot imagine a more just and exact match between the medium and the message.

F. *Me'ilah*

Israel's relationship with God requires clear lines of distinction between what belongs to God and what belongs to the Israelite. But the distinction between secular and sacred proves complex, the gradations are several, and the nuances such that Scripture's admonitions against trespassing on the territory of the sacred are considerably complicated. An animal, originally secular, when identified to serve as an offering passes through four stages: it is consecrated, therefore susceptible to sacrilege; it is susceptible to invalidation by a person not wholly in a state of cleanness but also not unclean; it is susceptible to the prohibitions of refuse, remnant, and uncleanness; and it is no longer susceptible to sacrilege.

The act of sanctification on its own commences a process, it does not transform what has been sanctified. The fact that what is sanctified may be resecularized underscores the Halakhic principle that directs attention to matters of attitude and negotiation and away from issues of the working of the sacred *ex opere operato*. For, time and again, we have seen that sanctification is a matter of status, not a matter of substance. And that forms the main point of the law, which is the variable status of that which has been sanctified. The principal problem that occupies the Halakhah is, What is the status of a holy thing that has been subjected to sacrilege? The governing theory is, if we punish a person for inadvertently committing sacrilege, we treat as secular what has been subjected to sacrilege.

That principle places narrow limits on the matter of sacrilege. For, the Halakhah holds, once anyone may legitimately use what is God's, then the status of sanctification—what belongs uniquely to God—is suspended. If any person may legitimately utilize for his own benefit a holy thing, even a priest, the holy thing is no longer subject to sacrilege. So an ordinary Israelite who inadvertently eats meat of an offering that the priests have every right to consume is not guilty of sacrilege. Once the meat of a meat offering has been permitted to the priesthood, the blood having been sprinkled on the altar, then the meat that is left for the priests is no longer subject to sacrilege. Since some persons are permitted to enjoy them, anyone who enjoys them is not guilty of sacrilege. So long as there has been a time at which the holy thing was permitted, sacrilege is no issue. What belongs wholly to God, by contrast, as a burnt offering, is subject to sacrilege. If this is done inadvertently, one pays the value of what he has used plus an added fifth of the value and also offers a ram of a specified price as a guilt offering; that effects atonement.

The definition of sacrilege as an act of inadvertence bears implications for assigning responsibility. Take the matter of agency, for example. If an agent carried out his errand and thereby inadvertently committed an act of sacrilege, the householder who appointed the agent is responsible and inadvertently has committed the act of sacrilege. If the agent did not carry out his errand in committing an act of sacrilege, the agent is responsible and inadvertently has committed the act of sacrilege. If the householder sent an agent who was a deaf-mute, an imbecile, or a minor to purchase goods with money which unbeknownst to the sender, was consecrated, if the agent carried out the errand, the householder has committed the act of sacrilege. If he did not carry out the errand, the storekeeper has committed the act of sacrilege. If he sent something by means of a person of sound senses, and realized before he reached the storekeeper that the coins are consecrated and therefore regretted having sent those coins, the storekeeper will have committed the act of sacrilege when he pays out the coins.

The premise of the Halakhah then rests on a reading of Israel's proper intentionality. The Halakhah of *Me'ilah* rests on the assumption that Israel maintains the correct intentionality for holy things. Israelites are assumed *not* to wish to appropriate for their own use what belongs to God and will not do so. If they do so and realize it, they make amends. In this way they make manifest their correct attitude, they realize and embody what the sacrificial process is meant to nurture: acceptance in full freedom of will of God's dominion. And for his part, God responds to the manifest right thought with its counterpart. That is why he readily gives up what is his; once the priest has a right to part of an offering, God's claim to the offering is set aside, and sacrilege no longer pertains. The upshot is, the act of sanctification effects a change in the status of what is sanctified, but only for a limited period and for a highly restricted purpose. In imposing such a narrow construction to the matter of sacrilege—inadvertent misuse of what God alone may use—the Halakhah underscores a now-familiar principle. It is that sanctification is relative to Israel's condition, not intrinsic to the condition of what is consecrated. How better say so than by treating as secular what has one time only been subjected to sacrilege or what has to someone, if not the right one, been permitted for personal benefit? The occasion of unintended sacrilege, its discovery and atonement, match the moment of sanctification: the Halakhah's disposition of both transactions underscore what the Halakhah finds important in the meeting of God and Israel at the altar: Israel's exemplary love and loyalty to God.

G. *Temurah*

With *Temurah* we reach an appropriate conclusion to the protracted account of the Halakhah that defines Israel's corporate and individual relationship with God at the intersection of heaven and earth: Jerusalem's temple and its altar. At issue is the use of language to classify, and for once at stake is not the disposition of one's intentionality but the concrete results of actual speech. What we learn concerns the last detail of how heaven and earth intersect through acts of speech unnuanced by considerations of attitude or will; in the present case, what one says on its own makes all the difference. The Halakhah that frames Israel's relationship with God completes its work here, with a small corpus that makes an important point, one dealing with the finality of speech. It is that the Israelite's act of sanctification through speech irrevocably transforms the status of that which is sanctified, without regard to any further act of sanctification or deconsecration that the Israelite then may undertake in connection with that same beast. As we see, in concrete terms, one may not substitute a secular beast for an already-consecrated beast. If he proposes to do so, then the initial act of sanctification is unaffected, but the further act of sanctification is valid in its own terms. It is Scripture that establishes both principles—the indelibility of the original act, the effect of the second act, of consecration. The Oral Torah amplifies and extends Scripture's rule within Scripture's frame of reference.

We find ourselves dealing with a familiar principle, the one encountered at M. *Zeb.* 10:1, that the altar sanctifies what is appropriate for it, but does not sanctify what is not appropriate for it. Then, it must follow, once an Israelite has sanctified to the altar what belongs there, the act is irrevocable, even though its consequences may vary according to circumstance and procedure. There is, then, no possibility of changing one's mind, only the requirement of sorting out the results of one's initial decision and act of intentionality. And that same conception governs here: once one has sanctified a beast, he cannot deconsecrate it by replacing it with another. The initial act is valid, assuming that the beast is one that appropriately serves in the classification for which it has been designated. True, one may redeem from the status of sanctification an animal that he has consecrated, as Lev. 27:15 makes explicit: "And if he that sanctified it will redeem his house, then he shall add the fifth part of the money of thy valuation." But redeeming what has been sanctified is not the same thing as nullifying the original act, e.g., by an act of substitution of one thing for something else, specifically, the substitution of a secular beast for one already sanctified.

The law of substitution encompasses an anomaly: an act contrary to the Torah produces effects of which the Torah takes account. One is not permitted to substitute one beast for another. If one does so, however, consequences follow. That anomaly hardly presents a surprise, given the purpose of the cult, which is to atone for sin. Even in the very heart of the cultic process, the consecration of the beast by the Israelite as a medium of reconciliation with God, a violation of God's instructions will be accommodated. One may say, just as the altar sanctifies what is appropriate to it but does not sanctify what is not appropriate to it, so the act of consecration of a beast sanctifies not only the beast that is appropriately classified, but any beast that is declared comparable thereto—that is appropriately sanctified like the originally-consecrated animal. The violation of the Torah having taken place, the transaction then is accommodated by the encompassing power of the altar itself.

The basic issue of the Halakhah of *Temurah* is whether or not the status, as to sanctification, of that which is sanctified is subject to revision. And the position of the law is that once something has been sanctified, not only is the sanctification indelible (except through the Halakhah's own media of secularization) but it is permanent in its character. That is to say, one may not change the status of an already sanctified beast from consecrated to secular, and one also may not change the level of sanctification, e.g., declaring most holy things to lesser holy things or vice versa. This is stated in the following language: All the same are most holy things and lesser holy things: one is not permitted to effect a substitution, whether on a weekday or on the Sabbath. They do not change them from their status as to sanctification, even from a lesser status of sanctification to a greater status of sanctification, and it is hardly necessary to say, from a greater status to a lesser status of sanctification. If one said concerning a firstling or concerning peace offerings, "Lo, these are a burnt offering," he has said nothing. And it is not necessary to say, if he said concerning a burnt offering, "Lo, this is a firstling," "Lo, this is peace offering."

Because the act of substitution is null, the categories of offerings play no role in the working of the Halakhah. They substitute one animal for others different from it. And why not, since the originally-sanctified beast is unaffected by the declaration of substitution. The only trait of that beast that pertains is its sanctification, not the category as to sanctification that applies.

Here the Halakhah takes account of an act that is illegitimate but that produces effects. One may not substitute a beast for an already-consecrated one, but if he does so, his act takes effect—not that a person in any event is permitted to effect a substitution. For it is forbidden to make such a statement of substitution of a now-secular beast for one already consecrated. But if one has effected a substitution, that which is designated instead of the beast already consecrated is deemed a substitute and also consecrated. And—as we have already noted—the person who does so also incurs the penalty of forty stripes. Not only so, but while on the Sabbath one may not effect an act of consecration, an act of substitution produces the anticipated result.

I find two considerable points that the Oral Torah sets forth in its amplification of the logic of the Halakhah of the Written Torah, both of them consistent with the Halakhah elsewhere.

The first is that language is not magical, because God is not coerced. The formula that transforms a secular beast into a sacred one accomplishes its act of transformation only when the prior condition is met, that the one who uses the language has the right to use it. The language, on its own, bears no coercive quality, is not a formula that works without regard to circumstance. That is a point clarified by the Oral Torah and consistent with counterpart rulings in parallel contexts. It follows that the first important contribution of the Oral Torah to the religious system at hand involves the conditional character of the power of language. Scripture at Lev. 27:10 is mute on that point. The Oral Torah makes explicit that the language of substitution works only when spoken by one who has the right to use it (just as the altar takes over what is appropriate to it but not what is not). Who carries out a valid act of substitution? One who owns the beast. Then the language on its own does not suffice; the right person must use it, and he or she must have the power to effect it. Now, as we know, the Halakhah does not regard the act of sanctification as operative *ex opere operato* but only as conditional. Language constitutes an act of substance, not of status. It follows that, in connection with a beast belonging to someone else, one may use the language of substitution and produce no result at all.

The Halakhah, second, insists that the actualities of the originally-consecrated offering play no role whatsoever. The beast declared a substitute need not belong to the same category as the beast that has already been sanctified; the analogy—"this in place of that"—focuses upon the "this," not the "that." The trait of the initially-sanctified beast that registers is only its classification as holy, not the particularity of that for which it has been sanctified. And that violates the rule that one may not change the status, as to sanctification, of a designated beast. If it has been declared most holy things, it cannot be reclassified as lesser holy things, and so throughout. When it comes to the transformation of the substitute, by contrast, we ignore considerations of classification—specificities and particularities—and invoke only a single criterion: the classification of sanctification per se. God responds to the language and circumstance but need not take account of irrelevant details in the transaction at hand. So one may substitute an animal for others different from it—an amazing point that fits entirely within the present rationality.

The upshot is, the entire system of matching intentionality to actuality, the will of the sacrifier to the deed of the priest and the intentionality as to the offering expressed by the priest, here is suspended. Why should that be the case? Because at issue here is not the utilization of the substituted beast, only its status as to sanctification. The effective statement concerns only gross classification, not detailed disposition. The only limitation is that of comparability: limbs or fetuses do not compare with one another or with whole beasts. A statement of substitution then violates the rules of the governing metaphor: something must be like something else in the ways that count, but need not be like something else in the ways that do not count. And that theory of matters, while surely congruent with the facts set forth by Scripture, makes distinctions important in the prevailing system of the Oral Torah. As in numerous other settings, so here as well, in order to make the statement that it wished to make, the Oral Torah could accomplish its goals better through the category at hand, *temurah*, than through any other category. To say what they wished in general to say, the sages could have found no more effective medium for their message than the exposition of the Halakhah of substitution for the altar.

II. INTENTIONALITY AND THE COSMIC ORDER

Given the Halakhic definition of sin as rebellion against God, we hardly find surprising the emphasis, through the processes of sin and atonement, on the proper intentionality of both parties to the transaction. These are the (inadvertent) sinner and the mediating priest. So even the jarring statement that offering a handful of meal offering accomplishes atonement as well as presenting an expensive beast, so long as the heart is directed to Heaven, repeats the single message that permeates the atonement theology and the law that expresses that theology for the conduct of the sacrificial cult. But that is what atonement removes: the consequences of an unintended act of rebellion. What about this world and its affairs? How does the paradigm of Eden impinge?

In a well-crafted system for the social order, whether in the form of law or in the form of theology, the same thing is said about many things. So a small and coherent body of principles ought to make their impact on diverse details. Having identified the principal message of Eden—the situation, the story, the implicit statement—with the centrality of intentionality, I have now to show how the same paramount consideration plays itself out in the far reaches of the Halakhic system. This I have now done for the rites of sin and atonement.

I turn to face the challenge of showing that what the Halakhic theology says about the intangibilities of God's relationship with man recapitulates what it says about the concrete transactions between and among Israelites themselves. Only then may I fairly claim that the Halakhic theology of Eden finds in the principal parts of Israel's social order as much as in those of the cosmic order evidence for its basic thesis. To accomplish that demonstration I move from the realm of what we should deem sacred to the domain of what we should regard as secular matters, to the practicalities of the social order. What animates the Halakhah of the encounter with God at the altar will now be seen to prove paramount for the workaday world of civil transactions in politics and the marketplace. All depends upon the righteous will.

III. INTENTIONALITY AND THE CIVIL ORDER: LEGITIMATE VIOLENCE. WHO DOES WHAT TO WHOM?

The Halakhah dictates the character of (its particular) Israel's civil order, its political institutions and system of criminal justice, so setting forth the theme of legitimate violence. The Halakhah that addresses the civil order of Israel specifically undertakes a labor of differentiation of power, indicating what agency or person has the power to precipitate the working of politics as legitimate violence at all. When we understand the differentiating force that imparts to politics its activity and dynamism, we shall grasp the theology that animates the structures of the politics and propels the system. The details of the Halakhah, in particular the sanctions assigned to various infractions, affects the taxonomy of power. Chapter Eight has shown us that that forms an implicit exegesis of the story of Eden, translated into reflection on the power of intentionality. The encompassing framework of rules, institutions, and sanctions is explained and validated by appeal to the forms of God's shared rule. Portrayed by the Halakhah, that dominion, exercised by God and his surrogates on earth, is focused partly in the royal palace, partly in the temple, and partly in the sages' court. The issue then is the differentiation of power, which is to say, which part falls where and why? Through its cases, the Halakhah explains who exercises legitimate violence and under what conditions, and furthermore specifies the source for differentiation. And that is, in line with the Halakhic theory of what man is, the quality of intentionality that has entered into a deed. That is the upshot of my systematic discussion of the classification of sins and crimes by the criterion of the quality of intentionality that has accompanied the deed. I need not say more, since this proposition has been amply treated in Chapter Eight, section I, "What Disrupts Eden?"

What we saw in that discussion may be briefly summarized. The theology of politics derives from that same narrative of origins its points of differentiation. It explains, by reference to the principal components of that myth—God's and humanity's will and power—the dynamics of the political system at hand. God commands, but humanity docs what it then chooses, and in the interplay of those two protean forces, each power in its own right, the sanctions and penalties of the system apply. Power comes from two conflicting forces, the commanding will of God and the free will of the human being. Power expressed in immediate sanctions is also mediated through these same forces, heaven above, human beings below, with the temple mediating between the two. Power works its way in the interplay between what God has set forth in the law of the Torah and what human beings do, whether intentionally, whether inadvertently, whether obediently, whether defiantly. Now to the constructions that sustain that judgment of how to decode the details of the Halakhah.

A. *Keritot*

Sinners and criminals have to answer not only to man but also to God. Man's penalties are spelled out in *Sanhedrin-Makkot*, and those inflicted by, or involving engagement with, God, are worked out in *Keritot*. Like *Sanhedrin* and *Makkot*, *Keritot* concerns atonement for sin or punishment for crime. But here, instead of fines, capital punishment, or flogging, what is required is either a sin offering or a suspensive guilt offering or extirpation. What is the difference between the sin offering and extirpation? Man bears responsibility for what he does, and the Halakhah provides the opportunity to atone for doing what God has commanded is not to be done. The Written Torah explicitly imputes guilt even for actions committed inadvertently and not with the intention of violating the Torah. It follows that the Halakhah has to provide for penalties to expiate sin or crime, whether deliberate or otherwise. Here making its statement concerning the taxonomic power of intentionality, the Halakhah distinguishes deliberate from inadvertent sin or crime. A sin offering is required in the case of an action, the deliberate commission of which is penalized by extirpation (early death, before the age of 60), and a suspensive guilt offering in the case of doubt. The principal interest then is in animal offerings that expiate sin. The Written Torah contributes to the topic the following statement at Lev. 5:17–19:

> If any one sins, doing any of the things that the Lord has commanded not to be done, though he does not know it, yet he is guilty and shall bear his iniquity. He shall bring to the priest a ram without blemish out of the flock, valued by you at the price for a guilt offering, and the priest shall make atonement for him for the error that he committed unwittingly, and he shall be forgiven. It is a guilt offering; he is guilty before the Lord.

Three divisions make up the topical presentation, occasions on which the sin offering or extirpation, as the case may be, is required, a single sin offering and multiple sins, and the suspensive guilt offering, required where one inadvertently may or may not have committed a sin. The order is logically necessary, since the suspensive guilt offering cannot come before the sin or guilt offering for what one is certain he has done.

The Halakhah of *Keritot* eloquently makes the distinction, critical to the Halakhic system overall, between an act that is deliberate and one that is inadvertent. In its principal divisions—the sin offering as against extirpation, the suspensive guilt offering as against the unconditional guilt offering—the Halakhah treats in concrete terms the distinction between deliberate, intentional sin and unintentional law violation. Except at the difference between manslaughter and murder, nowhere else in the Halakhah of either Torah, Written or Oral, do we find so sharp a line distinguishing the unintentional sin, penalized by an offering, and the intentional one, penalized by extirpation. The reason that that critical distinction concerns us in the particular Halakhah at hand is self-evident. Here—with premature death—is where God intervenes, and it is God above all who knows what is in man's heart and can differentiate intentional from unintentional actions. And it also is God who has the heaviest stake in the matter of intentional sin, for intentional sin represents rebellion against the Torah and God's rule through the Torah.

Offerings expiate those sins that are not committed as an explicit act of rebellion against God. These God accepts, graciously, as an appropriate act of atonement for an act for which one bears responsibility but which was not meant as defiance of God. The ones that embody an attitude of rebellion, by contrast, can be expiated not through the surrogate, the blood of the beast, but through the sinner himself, who is put to death by the court here on earth, or is flogged by the court's agents, or is cut off in the prime of life. So the religious principle that pervades *Keritot* is simple: God sees into man's heart. That is why the same act produces diverse consequences, based upon the intentionality with which the act is done. Indeed, in its own way that same conception animates the exercises on how many sin offerings are owing for a single action or how many actions may be subsumed under, and expiated by, a single sin offering. Beyond *Keritot*, the matter is expressed best in the Halakhah of *Shabbat*. There it is made explicit: A sin is atoned for by a sin offering only when the act is inadvertent. A deliberate action is not covered, so M. *Shab.* 11:6J–K: "This is the general principle: All those who may be liable to sin offerings in fact are not liable unless at the beginning and the end, their sin is done inadvertently. But if the beginning of their sin is inadvertent and the end is deliberate, or the beginning deliberate and the end inadvertent, they are exempt—unless at the beginning and at the end their sin is inadvertent."

When it comes to the specification of the penalty for sin or crime,

Keritot remains the principal point at which the Halakhah makes its statement of the prevailing distinction. Why here in particular? Because of the sanction for inadvertent sin, which is an offering. Hence, in the present context, it is in the temple, God's abode, that man meets God; there the offering is brought that expiates inadvertent sins or crimes. God is party to the transaction, for reasons already spelled out. And, corresponding to the temple, it is in the course of the Israelite's life that God intervenes, shortening the years of the deliberate sinner in response to the offense against life represented by deliberate sin or crime of the specified character. And that brings us back to the classes of transgressions that God punishes and man does not punish: sins involving sex, the temple, and the violation of negative commandments (e.g., not to eat forbidden fat, not to work on the Day of Atonement and the like). None of these represents a social sin, and none endangers the social order. All involve God and principally God, and none encompasses a victim other than God.

So where else, if not in the activities subject to extirpation or the sin offering (and so too with the other offerings treated here) will God's power to know precisely what man intends be better brought to bear? Sins or crimes that affect the social order, that endanger the health of the commonwealth, come to trial in the court conducted by sages and are penalized in palpable and material ways: death, flogging, and the like. Here God does not intervene, because man bears responsibility for this-worldly transactions. But just as man shortens the life of the criminal or sinner in the matters specified in *Sanhedrin* and exacts physical penalty in the matters covered by *Makkot* (not to mention *Shebuot*, where specified), so God shortens the life of the criminal or sinner in matters of particular concern to God. These are matters that, strictly speaking, concern only God and not the Israelite commonwealth at large: sex, food, the temple and its cult, the laws of proper conduct on specified occasions. Where the community does not and cannot supervise, God takes over. Israel does Israel's business, God does God's. For both the upshot is the same: sin or crime is not indelible. An act of rebellion is expiated through life's breath, an act of inadvertent transgression through the blood of the sacrificial beast, with the same result: all Israel, however they have conducted themselves in their span of time on earth, will enjoy a portion in the world to come. All but the specified handful enter eternal life beyond the grave.

B. *Sanhedrin-Makkot*

Here we find ourselves, then, at the heart of the Halakhah's system of criminal justice. The topic is sanctions for the protection of the social order, that is treated in the category-formation defined at tractate *Sanhedrin*. What captures sages' interest in the topic is a hierarchization of sins or crimes as indicated by the severity of the penalties that are imposed, matched also by the formality and procedural punctiliousness of the courts' process. Stated simply, we may say that sages find important in the category-formation criminal justice, the issue, Which sin is more severe than the other, and how does the penalty fit the crime in a set of hierarchized sins with matching sanctions? That is the center of the matter. Once that question is asked of this topic—the problematics of hierarchization as that pertains to criminal justice—the order of presentation is set, the sequence dictated, start to finish. For tractate *Sanhedrin*, we move from property cases to capital cases, and, within capital cases, through the penalties for catalogued crimes from the heaviest to the lightest in context. Then, at the end, we turn to the most severe penalty of all—one that the earthly court cannot inflict but only the Heavenly court can impose. The auxiliary tractate that follows then proceeds from capital to corporal punishment. So the order of the whole is [1] the earthly court and property cases; [2] the earthly court and capital punishment; [3] the heavenly court; and, appended, [4] corporal punishment. That manner of exposition then identifies for us what is at issue when the topic at hand is addressed. To this we turn.

Eden concerns man, but criminal justice—like the Halakhah of sin and atonement—addresses the rehabilitation of Israelite man—that new moral entity of which we spoke, who has the promise and possibility of redemption. So the venue radically has shifted. But the basic issue of Eden governs, and that is in two parts.

First, as we noted earlier, while Adam and Eve found no medium for atonement for the radical evil of rebellion, Israelite man enjoys the grace of atonement; second and, acutely present here, the principle that man is made in God's image. The criminal justice system set forth in the Halakhah of the categories *Sanhedrin* and *Makkot* works out yet another medium of atonement for sin.

Second, and more important, *Sanhedrin-Makkot* also explores the implications of that similitude, with the focus upon Israelite man.

Given their conviction that all Israel possesses a share in the world to
come, meaning that nearly everybody will rise from the grave, the
sages took as their task the specification of how, in this world, crim-
inals-sinners would receive appropriate punishment in a proper procedure, so expiating sin or crime that, in the world to come, they
would take their place along with everyone else in the resurrection
and eternal life.

It follows that the religious principle that comes to expression
in *Sanhedrin-Makkot* concerns the meaning of man's being in God's
image. That means, as God lives forever, so it is in man's nature to
surpass the grave. And how, God's being just, does the sinner or
criminal survive his sin or crime? It is by atonement, specifically, paying with his life in the here and now, so that at the resurrection he
may regain life, along with all Israel. That is why the climactic
moment in the Halakhah comes at the end of the long catalogue of
those sins and crimes penalized with capital punishment. It is with
ample reason that the Bavli places at the conclusion and climax of its
version the ringing declaration, "all Israel has a portion in the world
to come, except. . . ." And the exceptions pointedly do not include
any of those listed in the long catalogues of persons executed for sins
or crimes.

When, accordingly, we come to the heart of the matter, the criminal justice system, we take up an entirely abstract theological problem, the fate of man after death. Here we move to the limits of Eden,
viewed as a situation and a story, focusing upon what is explicit in
Eden, the governing simile for man. And that is God, which is to say,
man is in God's image, after God's likeness, possessed of an autonomous, and free, will. That is what accounts for man's fall from the
paradise of repose by reason of rebellion. In the setting of the civil
order, then, the issue of man's rebellion plays itself out, for in the
criminal justice system we turn to the outcome of it all. Now we consider what happens to the sinful or criminal Israelite, the one who
willfully does what God forbids, or deliberately refrains from doing
what God commands, the fate of the sinner or criminal who acts in
the manner of Adam and Eve. If we broaden the matter, we see that
the most profound question facing Israelite thinkers concerns the fate
of the Israelite at the hands of the perfectly just and merciful God.
Since essential to their thought is the conviction that all creatures are
answerable to their Creator, and absolutely critical to their system is

the fact that at the end of days the dead are raised for eternal life, the criminal justice system encompasses deep thought on the interplay of God's justice and God's mercy: How are these reconciled in the case of the sinner or criminal?

Within Israel's social order the Halakhah addresses from a theological perspective the profound question of social justice: What shall we make of the Israelite sinner or criminal? Specifically, does the sin or crime, which has estranged him from God, close the door to life eternal? If it does, then justice is implacable and perfect. If it does not, then God shows his mercy—but what of justice? We can understand the answer only if we keep in mind that the Halakhah takes for granted the resurrection of the dead, the final judgment, and the life of the world to come beyond the grave. So this world's justice and consequent penalties do not complete the transaction of God with the sinner or criminal. Eden restored at the end of days awaits. From that perspective, death becomes an event in life but not the end of life. And, it must follow, the death penalty does not mark the utter annihilation of the person of the sinner or criminal. On the contrary, because he pays for his crime or sin in this life, he situates himself with all of the rest of supernatural Israel, ready for the final judgment. Having been judged, he will "stand in judgment," meaning, he will find his way to the life of the world to come along with everyone else. Within the dialectics formed by those two facts—punishment now, eternal life later on—we identify as the two critical passages in the Halakhah of Sanhedrin-Makkot M. *Sanhedrin* 6:2 and 10:1.

As to the former: the rite of stoning involves an admonition that explicitly declares the death penalty the means of atoning for all crimes and sins, leaving the criminal blameless and welcome into the kingdom of Heaven; I italicize the key language.

Mishnah Sanhedrin 6:2

A. [When] he was ten cubits from the place of stoning, they say to him, "Confess," for it is usual for those about to be put to death to confess.

B. For whoever confesses has a share in the world to come.

C. For so we find concerning Achan, to whom Joshua said, "My son, I pray you, give glory to the Lord, the God of Israel, and confess to him, [and tell me now what you have done; hide it not from me.]" And Achan answered Joshua and said, "Truly have I sinned against the Lord, the God of Israel, and thus and thus I have done"

(Josh. 7:19). And how do we know that his confession achieved atonement for him? For it is said, "And Joshua said, Why have you troubled us? The Lord will trouble you this day" (Josh. 7:25)—*This day you will be troubled, but you will not be troubled in the world to come.*

D. And if he does not know how to confess, they say to him, "Say as follows: 'Let my death be atonement for all of my transgressions.'"

So within the very center of the Halakhic exposition comes the theological principle that the death penalty opens the way for life eternal. Achan pays the supreme penalty but secures his place in the world to come. All Israel, with only a few exceptions, is going to stand in judgment and enter the world to come, explicitly including all manner of criminals and sinners. And the latter passage states explicitly that all Israel, with specified exceptions, inherit the world to come:

Mishnah Sanhedrin 11:1

A. All Israelites have a share in the world to come, as it is said, "your people also shall be all righteous, they shall inherit the land forever; the branch of my planting, the work of my hands, that I may be glorified" (Is. 60:21).

B. And these are the ones who have no portion in the world to come: He who says, the resurrection of the dead is a teaching which does not derive from the Torah, and the Torah does not come from Heaven; and an Epicurean.

The executed criminal does not figure among these exceptions, only those who willfully defy God in matters of eternity.

What the Halakhah wishes to explore then is, How is the Israelite sinner or criminal rehabilitated, through the criminal justice system, so as to rejoin Israel in all its eternity? The answer is, The criminal or sinner remains Israelite, no matter what he does—even though he sins—and the death penalty exacted by the earthly court. So the Halakhah of *Sanhedrin* embodies these religious principles: [1] Israel—man "in our image"—endures forever, encompassing (nearly) all Israelites; [2] sinners or criminals are able to retain their position within that eternal Israel by reason of the penalties that expiate the specific sins or crimes spelled out by the Halakhah; [3] it is an act of merciful justice that is done when the sinner or criminal is put to death, for at that point he is assured of eternity along with everyone else. God's justice comes to full expression in the penalty, which is instrumental and contingent; God's mercy endures forever in the forgiveness that follows expiation of guilt through the imposition of the penalty. *Sanhedrin-Makkot*, devoted to the exposition of crime and just punishment, turns out to form an encompassing exercise in showing God's mercy, even, or especially, for the sinner or criminal who expiates the sin or crime. That concludes the transaction, but a great deal will follow it—and from it. In the context of the Torah I cannot think of any other way of making that statement stick than through the Halakhah of *Sanhedrin-Makkot*: this sin, this punishment—and no more.

C. *Baba Qamma-Baba Mesi'a-Baba Batra*

We come to the tractates that govern secular transactions in the civil order, the three "gates" (*babas*) of the law as conventionally defined. The Halakhah of these most critical tractates coheres with the larger logic characteristic of the entire system and fully realizes that logic. How so? Stability, stasis, equity in exchange, and restoration of what is inequitable—these mark perfection of the social order that the Halakhah proposes to bring about in Israel's inner existence. The goal of the system of civil law set forth in the three *Babas* is the recovery of the just order that characterized Israel upon entry into the Land, recalling the goal of the Sabbatical Year (*Shebi'it*) and of the Halakhah that governs land ownership and utilization in general. Here too, the Halakhah aims at the preservation of the established wholeness, balance, proportion, and stability of the social economy realized at that moment. This idea is powerfully expressed in the organization of the three tractates that comprise the civil law, which, divided down the middle, fifteen chapters fore and aft, treat first abnormal and then normal transactions. The framers deal with damages done by chattels and by human beings, thefts and other sorts of malfeasance against the persons and the property of others. The civil law in both aspects pays closest attention to how the property and person of the injured party, so far as possible, are restored to their prior condition, that is, the state of normality disrupted by the damage done to property or injury done to a person. So attention to torts focuses upon penalties paid by the malefactor to the victim, rather than upon penalties inflicted by the court on the malefactor for what he has done.

Most of the Halakhah that Rabbinic canon sets forth on Israel's civil society makes its appearance in the Mishnah, Tosefta, Yerushalmi, or Bavli tractates of the *Babas*. Here is where restorationist theology makes its deepest impact upon the Halakhah, with its stress on preserving the status quo, securing for all parties to a transaction a proper exchange so that value remains constant, designing and sustaining a social order aimed at an equitable structure and secured by ancient custom. The purpose of the Halakhah that we have examined is simply stated. The first half of the tractates, which, as we shall see in just a moment, break in the middle of *Baba Mesi'a*, focuses upon repairing damage that is done to the social order, the second half, upon preserving the balance and perfection of that same social order. Israel on its own, in its interior relationships, is governed by Halakhah that establishes and maintains stasis, which signifies perfection, all things in their place, all persons possessing appropriate value in property, security in person. That goal the Halakhah accomplishes, as is clear, by righting imbalances and preserving them.

That dual purpose explains why the three tractates form a single, unfolding, and coherent statement, half (*Baba Qamma*'s ten chapters and the first five chapters of *Baba Mesi'a*) devoted to repairing damages done to the political economy of society by chattel and persons, the other half (the second five chapters of *Baba Mesi'a* and *Baba Batra*'s ten chapters) to maintaining the perfection of equitable relationships. To interpret that statement, we have to stand back and see the three tractates whole. Then the several dimensions of discourse will emerge. When we survey the entire construction of the three *Babas*, what we see is a simple set of eight units. They move from abnormal to normal events, I–IV, then V–VIII. The whole begins with damages done by chattels or by persons, thefts and other sorts of conversion of the property of others, with special attention to how we restore to a state of normality the property and person of the injured party. Numbers I–IV run through the whole of *Baba Qamma* and half way through *Baba Mesi'a*, to M. *B.M.* 5:11. The second half of the three tractates then shifts to normal transactions, not those involving torts and damages: labor relationships, rentals and bailments, real estate transactions, inheritances and estates, units V–VIII. Then the whole produces two complementary constructions, first abnormal or illicit, then normal or licit transactions. That is shown by the correspondence of unit IV, illicit commercial transactions (overcharge and usury) and unit VII, licit commercial transactions, the legal transfer of goods, unstipulated conditions and how they are enforced. This plan furthermore explains why we treat bailments twice, at III.C, damages to bailments, and then at V,C,E, responsibilities of the bailee. The former fits into the larger structure of law on the restoration of the balance of the social order (here, the value possessed by parties to the transaction at the outset, equitably distributed at the end), the latter, that on the preservation of the same order. Here, in brief is the picture of the whole:

I. ILLICIT TRANSACTIONS; RESTORING ORDER

Baba Qamma
   i.   Damage by Chattels 1:1–6:6
   ii. Damages Done by Persons 7:1–10:10

Baba Mesi'a
   iii. The Disposition of Other Peoples' Possessions; Bailments 1:1–3:12
   iv. Illicit Commercial Transactions. Overcharge, misrepresentation, usury 4:1–5:11

II. LICIT TRANSACTIONS; PRESERVING ORDER

   v.   Hiring Workers. Rentals and Bailments 6:1–8:3

Baba Mesi'a, Baba Batra
   vi. Real Estate B.M. 8:4–10:6, B.B. 1:1–5:5

Baba Batra
   vii. Licit Commercial Transactions 5:6–7:4
   viii. Inheritances and Wills. Other Commercial and Legal Documents 8:1–10–8

The whole of *Baba Qamma* takes up the results of wicked intentionality, an act of will that takes the form of malice, on the one side, or flagrant neglect of one's duties, on the other. The rules of *Baba Mesi'a* address the situations in which intentionality plays a role, is excluded as irrelevant, and may or may not enter into the adjudication of a situation of conflict. And, as we have seen, the topics treated in *Baba Batra* in common take account of the idiosyncrasy of intentionality and exclude private interest from intervening in customary arrangements.

So we may say that the entire repertoire of topics lays itself out as a huge essay on the role of man's intentionality—his will, his private plans—in the ordering of Israel's inner life. All topics grouped by me as illicit transactions involve righting the wrongs done by people on their own account. When free will is taken into account, encompassing negligence and malice, the social order requires forceful intervention to right the balance upset by individual aggression. Some licit transactions permit individual intentionality to register, specifically, those freely entered into and fairly balanced among contracting parties. And some licit transactions leave no space for the will of the participants and their idiosyncratic plans. Considerations of fairness take over and exclude any engagement with the private and the personal. So Israel's social order takes account of intentionality, especially controlling for the damage that ill will brings about.

The first fifteen chapters then treat intentionality as a critical factor in assessing damages, negligence representing a chapter therein. But normal licit transactions are carried forward in accord with those rules of balance, proportion, and coherence that yield a society that is stable and enduring, fair and trustworthy. In the second fifteen chapters, intentionality forms only one consideration in the process of preserving the status, as to value, of parties to transactions and exchanges; it may make all the difference, no difference, some difference; it may not enter into consideration at all. That underscores the judgment of the Halakhah that, when it comes to righting wrongs against chattels and persons, the malefactor has acted willfully and has therefore to be penalized in an equitable manner. By his act of will, he has diminished the property or person of the victim. He must then restore the property or person to its prior value, so far as this is possible, and may not benefit from what he has done.

That goal the Halakhah accomplishes, as is clear, by righting imbalances and preserving them. The whole begins with damages done by chattels or by persons, thefts, and other sorts of conversion of the property of others, with special attention to how we restore to a state of normality the property and person of the injured party. The second half of the three tractates then shifts to normal transactions, not those involving torts and damages: labor relationships, rentals and bailments, real estate transactions, inheritances and estates. The whole of *Baba Qamma*, with its focus on damages and torts, takes up the results of wicked intentionality, an act of will that takes the form of malice, on the one side, or flagrant neglect of one's duties, on the other. The rules of *Baba Mesi'a*, the mediating tractate, address the situations in which intentionality plays a role, is excluded as irrelevant, and may or may not enter into the adjudication of a situation of conflict. And the topics treated in *Baba Batra* in common take account of the idiosyncrasy of intentionality and exclude private interest from intervening in customary arrangements.

In accord with the Halakhah of *Baba Qamma*, man undertakes to assume responsibility for what he does, always in just proportion to causation. Within Israel's social order what God wants a man to do is take responsibility for his own actions, for the results of what he or his chattel has done—no more, no less. And that pervasive point of insistence transforms our view of the Halakhic category before us. True, it forms an exercise in restoration and stasis of the just society. But in the details of the law is worked out a chapter of theological anthropology, an answer to the question, What, in the formation of the just society, can a man do? And the answer is, A man can and must take responsibility for not only what he does but also—and especially—what he brings about, the things he may not do but does cause to happen. Viewed in this way, the laws of *Baba Qamma* form a massive essay upon the interplay of causation and responsibility: what one can have prevented but through negligence (in varying measure depending on context) has allowed to take place, he is deemed in that same measure to have caused. And for that, he is held in that same measure to make amends.

Responsibility begins in right attitude. Man must form the intentionality of taking responsibility for his actions. This he must do by an act of will. That is why the whole of *Baba Qamma* plays itself out as an exercise in the definition of the valid intentionality in transactions involving damage and conflict. Where one has diminished another, he must willingly take responsibility for his deed of omission or commission. The message of the Halakhah on man's taking responsibility cannot be missed in the ringing opening words of the Mishnah tractate, which link causality and responsibility:

Mishnah *Baba Qamma* 1:4

> What they [generative causes of damages] have in common is that they customarily do damage and taking care of them is your responsibility. And when one of them has caused damage, the [owner] of that which causes the damage is liable to pay compensation. . . . In the case of anything of which I am liable to take care, I am deemed to render possible whatever damage it may do. If I am deemed to have rendered possible part of the damage it may do, I am liable for compensation as if [I have] made possible all of the damage it may do.

That remarkably eloquent, decisive formulation contains the entire message of *Baba Qamma* and the first half of *Baba Mesi'a*.

It follows that man in all of his dignity is portrayed through the Halakhah of *Baba Qamma* as possessed [1] of free will to assume responsibility, on the one side, and [2] of the power to take action in consequence of responsibility, on the other. And that principle assumes religious status in two steps. First, in the words of the Written Torah, God himself has framed the laws that link causation and responsibility—negligence and culpability, for instance. In the very portrayal of the holy society that Israel at Sinai is commanded to realize, God's stake in man's framing of the social order is made explicit. And consequently, second, Israel in the workaday transactions of one person with another acts out in this-worldly terms its governing principle of transactions with heaven. The one in palpable terms shows the character of the other in intangible ways.

Consider the topical program of the Halakhah, and see how, start to finish, the details define a statement concerning the data of the category at hand. Here is the repertoire: how compensation is to be paid; the variation in compensation by reason of Scripture's distinctions, e.g., between cases of mere accident and those of culpable negligence (attested dangers), where people should have known to take care; man's responsibility for the public interest and the general welfare of the public domain; variables in liability for oneself and one's chattels; attenuated forms of responsibility ("He who causes a fire to break out through the action of a deaf-mute, idiot, or minor, is exempt from punishment under the laws of man, but liable to punishment under the laws of heaven"); penalties for causing damages done in the three dimensions of social concern: damages done to the Land (public property, encompassing ecological considerations), damages done to persons, and damages done to private property.

And the statement that is made, and that can best be made in connection with the topics of injury and misappropriation, emerges in sages' sorting out of details and nuances of responsibility and consequent liability for compensation. If someone set out to teach through a concrete example the variation of responsibility by reason of variables of what is willful and foreseeable and preventable, how better to deliver the message than by distinguishing between what is (formerly) deemed harmless and what is (formerly) an attested danger? Once the Torah makes that distinction, the message emerges: we are responsible for all damages that we could have foreseen, but our responsibility is mitigated when the damages cannot have been foreseen, prevented, let alone wanted. And, further, responsibility is to be accepted, damages compensated—the whole in a forthright transaction among honorable men.

The Halakhah holds that we are responsible for what we do and what we cause, but we are not responsible (or not responsible in the same degree) for what we cannot control. So the law asks, how does our action or lack of action relate to the consequence of what we do or not do? If we do not know that an act has caused a result, we cannot hold responsible the person who has done the act for the consequences he has brought about. The law works out these gradations between total culpability or blame, by reason of one's forming the efficient cause without mitigating considerations, and total absolution from culpability and blame, by reason of one's bearing no responsibility whatsoever for what has happened:

[1] responsibility for all damages done, because the event that has caused loss and damage is voluntary and foreseeable, not the result of overwhelming external force; preventable; brought about by willful action; the result of culpable knowledge; deliberate choice, not mere negligence;

[2] responsibility for the greater part of the damages that are done, because the damage is foreseeable; not the result of overwhelming external force; preventable; thus in the event the ignorance is classified as culpable; but not voluntary;

[3] responsibility for the lesser part of the damages that are done, because the damage is foreseeable; but the result of overwhelming external force and not preventable, thus involuntary, but the result of culpable ignorance and negligence;

[4] no responsibility at all, the event being involuntary, the result of overwhelming external force, not foreseeable, hence, inculpable ignorance; e.g., pure chance.

We therefore identify in the working out of the Halakhah three operative criteria—points of differentiation in the analysis of events and the actions that produce them—which form a cubic grid, with, in theory, nine gradations of blame and responsibility and consequent culpability:

[1] an event produced by an action that is voluntary vs. involuntary;
[2] an event that is foreseeable vs. not foreseeable, or an action the consequences of which are foreseeable vs. not;
[3] an event that is preventable vs. not preventable; or an action that is necessary and therefore blameless, or one that is not.

Thus we may construct a grid of three layers or dimensions, one grid formed of considerations of what is voluntary vs. involuntary, the second, of what is foreseeable vs. not foreseeable, the third, of what is preventable vs. not preventable. That permits us to identify an efficient cause that is voluntary, foreseeable, and preventable; voluntary, foreseeable, and not preventable; involuntary, foreseeable, and preventable; involuntary, not foreseeable, and not preventable; and so on.

The social order then forms an exercise in man's accepting responsibility for what he does or causes. What, in Israelite context, marks that statement as critical to the theology of the Halakhah? To answer that question, we revert to the initial point at which the world order of justice was disrupted by an act of man. Israel relates to God in one way above all, and that is, by exercising in ways that show love for God and acceptance of God's dominion the power of free will that God has given man. Correct the error of Eden—that time and again turns out to form the religious statement of the Halakhah, just as we noted in connection with the Halakhah of 'Orlah. The story of man's disobedience in Eden (Gen. 3:11–13) tells why man's accepting responsibility for what he causes forms the center of the Halakhah of damages and misappropriation. Here is the original version of man's denial of responsibility, already cited but worth a reprise:

> God: *Did you eat of the tree from which I had forbidden you to eat?*
> Man: *The woman you put at my side—she gave me of the tree and I ate.*
> God: *What is this you have done?*
> Woman: *The serpent duped me and I ate.*

At the center of the story of the human condition in the tragedy of Eden is man's and woman's denial of responsibility for the deed each did, and, implicitly, rejection of responsibility for the consequent loss of Eden that is coming. At the heart of the Halakhah of damages and misappropriation is the opposite: Israelite man's explicit acceptance of responsibility for what he causes. If Israel wants to show God that it is regenerate, how better to do so than act out in cases of damages and injury the requirement to bear responsibility for what one does and causes to happen (Adam, Eve, respectively)? Here in its everyday conduct of the inner affairs of the community, Israel shows how, unlike Adam and Eve, through the instruction of the Torah, Israel has learned what it means to take responsibility for injury and damage to others.

Within Israel's workaday life, in the very practicalities of conflict and its resolution aimed at restoring and preserving the perfection of the status quo, is conducted an ongoing exercise. It is one of making explicit one's responsibility for what one has caused, then apportioning damages in proportion to one's negligence or malfeasance. What is voluntary, foreseeable, and preventable imposes maximum liability for restoration. Man cannot blame his ox, nor in the public way impose upon bypassers the responsibility to accommodate the obstacles he has set up. The premise of the exercise is that Israel's inner affairs, the transactions between and among Israelites, in the most practical terms, are conducted as a test of whether regenerate man— Israelite man—can bear responsibility for his own actions, now viewed in the broadest context of causation, and, if so, what it means to match levels of compensation to degrees of responsibility. No excuses ("the woman you put at my side," "the snake duped me") exculpate when one has caused damage, because Israelite man assumes the burden of his actions and takes responsibility so far as possible to restore the world to its original condition, before, in the here and now, some deed or act of negligence of his has disrupted it. I can think of no more direct response to "the woman . . . the snake . . ." than the language, "In the case of anything of which I am liable to take care, I am deemed to render possible whatever damage it may do."

In the myriad of individual transactions for which the law provides, Israel shows it has learned the lesson of Eden and applied that lesson to the social order of the Land. Why in the interiorities of relationships at home? Because it is not among strangers but within the community that workaday actions matter most. In intimacy, responsibility registers. In Eden it was before God that man was ashamed, and, in Israel, it is with one's fellow Israelite that man shows he has learned the lesson of Adam's denial. That is what is at stake in those eloquent, implacable words, which Adam should have said but Israel now does say: In the case of anything of which I am liable to take care, I am deemed to render possible whatever damage it may do. And, in the language of the Mishnah itself: Man is perpetually an attested danger whether what is done is done inadvertently or deliberately, whether man is awake or asleep. If he blinded the eye of his fellow or broke his utensils, he pays the full value of the damage he has caused. Would that Adam had said of himself to God what Israel affirms day by day and, as we see in the spinning out of the Halakhah, in every way as well.

Sin, crime, torts, and damages—these carry forward bad attitudes; differentiating types and degrees of intentionality when addressing how the social order is disrupted yields nothing of interest. By contrast, in treating ordinary exchanges and transactions, the Halakhah turns out to form an essay on when intentionality matters and when it does not. How is this the case? When it comes to restoring the perfection of society, specifically, where do we take account of intentionality and where not? Intentionality or attitude matters in situations of conflict. Then the attitude of both parties makes all the difference, since to resolve conflicting claims, we have in the end to conciliate all parties to a common outcome; there, intentionality or attitude forms the critical medium for restoring and sustaining balance and order. Parties to an exchange are now responsible to one another, and they must intend the outcome to be a proportionate and equal exchange of value. Both parties must accept the outcome, that is, form at the end the same attitude toward the transaction. A claim of ownership ends in an act of despair. Responsibility is proportionate to the attitude of the bailee, that is, to the degree of accountability that he has accepted to begin with. So much for the uses of intentionality in the restoration and maintenance of the social order.

But then where do we dismiss as null all considerations of intentionality or attitude, even when parties to an exchange concur? In market transactions, by contrast, true value overrides the attitude of the players, who cannot agree to an exchange that in objective terms is deemed null. Even where all parties agree, the Torah too must approve. And, we noted, we impute to all parties the same attitude and deny the pertinence of idiosyncratic or private meanings. Broadly-held expectations govern, whether those of custom or of the written Torah's own law. In these two ways—the Torah's law, which is not relative to the will of man, and established custom, which defines the norm for man—intentionality possesses no power, because it serves no purpose in restoring or sustaining the balances of a well-ordered society.

So the thirty chapters, through the exposition of the law, set forth a massive exercise in the applied reason and practical logic of the abstract categories, responsibility and intentionality. What message emerges when we move from the illicit to the licit, the abnormal to the normal? The transactions that all together form the ordinary life of inner Israel, Israel on its own, yield two matching propositions. First, when it comes to acts that disrupt the social order, man is responsible for what he does. But, second, when we turn to transactions that sustain the ordinary relationships within Israel, man's proper intentionality takes over. Then man's will forms only one element in a complex transaction. Where wills clash, compromise takes over. Where the Torah imposes its own rule, intentionality is null. Publicly accepted custom and procedure take the paramount position. In cases of negligence or malfeasance, man takes responsibility for what he has done—so much for the first half of the *Babas*.

And that brings us to the everyday conduct of affairs in ordinary Israelite society, as in the world of perfect order and stasis of Eden at the outset and the Land of Israel at the end. Social order restored, the status quo as to value regained, what forces hold the whole together? Where responsibility prevails, man's own will and intentionality, God's will in the Torah, and the customary arrangements of a stable, just society—all these variables come into play and are to be sorted out. That is why, while a single message addresses the abnormal and the illicit, the realm of torts and damages: take responsibility to attain Eden, a much more complex message states the requirements of maintaining matters. That message responds to the realities of the ideal society that the Halakhah makes possible.

Specifically, Israel in its interior arrangements is to hold in the balance [1] personal will, [2] the Torah's law, and [3] the long-standing customary requirements of enduring order. In the *Babas*, as this survey of the Halakhah has shown, these distinct and interrelated forces—man's will, God's law, and accepted public practice—are far from abstractions. In the interplay of individual will, God's absolute law, and ancient, enduring custom, Eden endures in the realization of Israel in the here and now. No wonder the great teacher, Samuel, took the view, "There is no difference between the world to come and the days of the messiah, except the end of the subjugation of the exilic communities of Israel" (B. 11:12 I.24/91B). That is to say, in context, the Messiah will restore Israel to the Land (one of his two principal missions, raising the dead the other), the Torah to the government of Israel in the Land. Then, for all eternity marked by "the world to come," Eden once recovered will endure forever. But Eden is an occasion, a situation, a mode of organization, as much as a location. In the statement of the Halakhah, Eden is a condition that prevails in the here and now of inheritances and wills, real estate and market transactions, a circumstance that comes about in the compromise of conflict and through the fair and just arrangements brought about among the householder and laboring craftsman and farm worker. With the proper intentionality, in full responsibility, maintaining the ancient order and arrangements of the Torah, Israel in the Land will realize Eden—this time around forever.

D. *Horayot*

At *Horayot* we deal with collective expiation for the corporate sin brought upon individuals by erroneous instruction on the part of the government, the head of the community, the priest, or the sage, as the case requires. What links the individual to the community, so assigning to the collectivity the consequence of private behavior? Here we turn to the matter of where and how the public bears responsibility for private, individual conduct—collective guilt for individual action. The individual is subsumed within the community when his action results from a common misconception fostered by the community's representative agencies. What triggers the application of the collective penalty provided by the Halakhah of *Horayot* is reliance upon the community's court. He who relies on himself is liable, and he who relies on the court is exempt. When, then, does the person who does a deed validly assign guilt to a third party?

It is when the court speaks in the name of the Torah—erroneously; but even here, the conditions under which such a claim may register are narrowly defined. The only case in which the community at large does not deliberately violate the Torah, and incur the penalty of death now and the loss of eternity at the last judgment, involves erroneous instruction on the part of the court. Then, when an individual sins in ignorance, he is exempt from penalty, having relied on the court. Even though an individual knows the law, if he relies upon the court, he is exempt. The court is liable. But the error of the court must pertain to details, not to the basic rule, which the court is expected to know. The individual, as much as the community, bears responsibility to know the Torah's explicit laws. Inadvertent errors in detail based on court instruction alone allow the individual to assign guilt to the community at large. And then Scripture then provides for a means of expiating the collective sin. But inadvertence affects both the community and the court, so a range of possibilities comes under consideration, e.g., if the court gave an incorrect decision inadvertently, and the entire community followed their instruction and did the thing in error; if the court gave an incorrect decision deliberately, but the community, following their instruction, did the thing in error inadvertently; if the court gave incorrect instruction inadvertently; and the community followed their instruction and did the thing in error deliberately, and so on. So much for the court and community.

What about unwitting sin carried out by the two other institutions of politics and public policy, the high priest and the ruler? These two also fall into the class of the community at large. Here too, inadvertent sin is wiped away by an appropriate offering, the bullock in the present case. Then the issue concerns whether the priest or ruler erroneously decided and acted by himself or did so with the community. Then the same rules that govern a mistaken decision taken by the court come into play. As to the ruler or high priest, a sequence of situations is worked out: What offering pertains to an anointed priest who sinned upon leaving office? So too a ruler; What do we do with one who sinned before appointment and then was appointed?

What we address in the Halakhah of *Horayot* is the problem of sorting out obligations involving the individual and the community, private sin and collective guilt. As we have seen, the Halakhah addresses the individual and his crime, punishment, and rehabilitation before God. Ofttimes the court, sometimes the temple, and occasionally God all collaborate to secure expiation of sin in this life, so that the individual will rise from the grave and stand in judgment and enter the eternal life. The system moreover works out the distinction between deliberate and inadvertent sin or crime, so a complete picture of the process by which rebellion against God is punished in its way, inadvertent sin in its manner. When it comes to the community at large, deliberate sin is dealt with, too. But what of the interstices between public and personal sin or crime? There the Halakhah sets forth a systematic and cogent statement, entirely coherent with the larger systemic message.

The logic of the Halakhah dictates that Israel, not only individual Israelites, answer for sins or crimes committed by the holy people as a whole. That logic is expressed in the key statement, "All Israel has a portion in the world to come," so that being part of holy Israel carries the promise of resurrection and eternal life. Individuals secure their position in Israel by atoning for sin, paying the penalties that are specified in *Sanhedrin-Makkot, Shebuot,* and *Keritot.* But when the Halakhah thinks of Israel, it addresses not only individuals but the entirety of the community. Israel, not merely Israelites, forms that community that God called to Sinai to constitute the kingdom of priests and the holy people. And all Israel is subject to judgment. The Written Torah leaves no doubt about the penalties inflicted upon deliberately sinful Israel: loss of the Land and exile. The narrative from Genesis through Kings—the authorized history—fully spells out the meaning of national sin and exile. To that set of facts, the Oral Torah, for its part, contributes a separate consideration: the disposition of a sinful (idolatrous) community.

E. *Shebuot*

The story of creation assigns to words the power to make worlds. But that defines the medium of God's relationship with man and with Israel as represented through Scripture. The Halakhah, in its exploration of how man is like God, now investigates the complementary question, how does man's word compare to God's, in whose image man is made? If the sages wished to make the statement that man's word is comparable to God's and that, for man as for God, words properly formulated form media of sanctification, they could find no more suitable occasion for doing so than in their discussion of the oath (as distinct from the vow, classified as an act of temper and not one of deliberation, such as the oath is) And if, further, they wanted to say, God is everywhere present, a sentient being who pays close attention to everyone all the time, to what people say, not only to what they do, and, especially, to what they say upon the invocation of God's presence in particular—if that is what they wanted to say, then *Shebuot*—the Halakhah of the oath—provides not the ideal occasion but the only really appropriate one. That is for two reasons.

First, the oath by definition calls God to witness the transaction (and the vow does not); the person who takes the oath invokes God's name and calls upon God to confirm his allegation. So the consequence of asking God to join in one's claims and certify them, the conviction that God is everywhere, all the time, when he is called upon, forms the foundation of all else. Second, the oath represents a purely verbal transaction, not ordinarily confirmed by concrete action, not commonly subjected to the supervision of all parties. It is the transaction that in the end depends upon the integrity of the person who makes the statement in God's name, "By an oath, I shall not eat," for who is going to keep watch to see that the man does not eat?

The theological premise of oath-taking accordingly involves an assessment of man's and of God's character. God oversees all things; he will know when his name has been taken in vain. Man is possessed of character and conscience; he does not need to be subjected to supervision by a this-worldly force outside of himself, when, having invoked God's name, he has subjected himself to God's oversight. So to language sages impute remarkable power, specifically the capacity to change a transaction, through intangible but powerful formulations, by the introduction of an interest on God's part into an arrangement otherwise between men alone. These convictions come to full expression in the Halakhah at hand, stating in concrete language and norms that—like man—God responds when his name is invoked and is not to be deceived—ever. That conviction provides ample motivation for a detailed definition, in norms of speech, of the circumstances and formulas that engage God's interest and participation, respectively.

The oath represents the use of words for an inviolable and utterly dependable result: if I take an oath, I invoke God's name, and in doing so, I declare myself completely truthful—"so help me God." But God not only enforces the oath, having a personal stake therein. God himself takes oaths and binds himself thereby, Scripture being rich in divine oath-takings, e.g., Gen. 22:15, "By myself I have sworn an oath, says the Lord, because you have done this and have not withheld your son, your only son, I will indeed bless you. . . ." In formulating matters in that way, God undertakes a perpetual blessing for Abraham's heirs, the taking of the oath securing credence from Abraham and imposing an ironclad obligation upon God. The upshot is, the oath possesses an integrity, an autonomy of power, such that

God as much as man is bound. Words properly formulated therefore exert extraordinary power, and that is why, from deeds that represent sins or crimes, the Halakhah now turns to words. It follows that the Halakhah will carefully define the formula by which words take on the power to bind or loose, by which God himself is engaged in the transaction among men. But, as we already realize, the Halakhah also focuses its attention upon the power of the oath here at home, within Israel's interior transactions, in relationships between one Israelite and another.

In taking the oath, man is like God; God binds himself by an oath, so does man. There is one difference between God and man. God supervises man. God needs no supervision; he is truth. The Halakhah then bears the message that the language Israelites use among themselves in the engagement with God's name affects not only the intangibles of transcendent faith but the palpable results of ordinary activities: acts of faith and faithlessness, acts of honesty and dishonesty, acts of integrity and deceit—all of them measured by the criterion of truth established in what is said and in the way it is formulated. Using God's name in certain contexts brings God into the here and now, and that represents a power that language, rightly used, possesses. No wonder sages find the topic so richly engaging.

What is at stake in the Halakhah of oath-taking is trustworthy relationships, effected through verbal formulas, between man and man. The upshot is, God's relationship with man, defined and regulated by the use of language to impose an oath, forms the model of man's relationship to man. If God is bound by the oath that he takes by his own name, man all the more so is bound by the oath that he takes in God's name; man is like God, and man's words matter just as God's words matter; the same formulas pertain.

The power imputed to the oath, the context in which the oath exercises its controlling authority, the cogency of the details of the types of oaths—all work together to say in concrete and detailed ways precisely what the sages wish to express, God's intimate, eternal, and ongoing engagement with what Israelites say to one another within Israel's interior social order. If sages wanted to say, God listens carefully to what people say and pays attention to the details of what they do, God knows what you promise and observes how you carry out your promise, God oversees what no man witnesses, God lives among us and abides with us—if sages wished to underscore the perpetual presence of God within Israel's everyday life, they could have accomplished their goal no more effectively than by setting forth the laws of *Shebuot* in the way that they have. And, it goes without saying, no more explicit a statement of intentionality can be made than the oath, which links man's intention to God's witness—and personal engagement.

IV. In Defense of Israel's Authentic Eden: The Struggle in the Household between Life and Death

So much for the world of interior Israel, engaged in constructing a social order in accord with the principles of integrity and responsibility, on the one side, and appropriate attitude and intentionality, on the other. It is a world animated by the memory and hope of Eden.

But that is not the ultimate stage of the struggle between life and death. That contest takes places in the household, at the points at which life is created and nurtured. The household, comparable to the temple at the occasion of Eden, the Sabbath, as we have seen, forms the smallest whole unit of the Israelite social order for which the Halakhah legislates. Our question is now, how does the Halakhah embody principles that protect Israel's authentic Eden, the household that compares to the temple, from enemies visible and tangible and otherwise? And in what ways does the Halakhah secure for the house-hold—the house of Israel—the possibility of overcoming death? To that matter, central to the Halakhah, we now turn.

CHAPTER THIRTEEN

ENEMIES OF EDEN, TANGIBLE AND INVISIBLE

You may freely eat of every tree of the garden; but of the tree of the knowledge of good and evil you shall not eat, for in the day that you eat of it, you shall die.

—Genesis 2:16

In the sweat of your face you shall eat bread until you return to the ground, for out of it you were taken; you are dust and to dust you shall return.

—Genesis 3:19

I. The Contest between Death and Life, Uncleanness and Sanctification: [1] The Sources of Uncleanness

Death is the outcome of the tragedy of Eden. In invisible form death effects uncleanness, which brings about exclusion from what is sacred. In the context of the temple and household, that means removal of person or object from what is to be kept cultically clean and ready (in the temple) to be sanctified. In tangible form, death is represented by such principal sources of uncleanness as the corpse, on the one side, and the gentile, on the other. The elaborate system of cultic cleanness put forth by the Halakhah of the Mishnah-Tosefta (not much amplified by the Yerushalmi or the Bavli) contrasts life with death, cleanness or sanctification with uncleanness, represented at the apex of sources of uncleanness by the corpse.

That is just as the narrative of Genesis would lead us to anticipate. Eden stands for eternal life with God, so the loss of Eden brought death in its place; that is the very meaning of the action. And it is articulated by mythic monotheism: Adam will work until he dies. Not surprisingly, then, the principal source of uncleanness is the corpse. The enemies of Eden, the sources of uncleanness, which pollute the Israelite table and bed, are formed in the model of death or in hierarchical relationship to death. From these Israel in its household, like the priests in the temple, is to be protected. Perpetual alertness is required to stand against the sources of uncleanness, representing death. To be alert is to take care, to act out an attitude of responsibility—the opposite of that inattention and sloth that brought about the loss of Eden and eternal life of bliss.

In the theological system of the Rabbinic canon, that death comes about by reason of sin is stated in so many words, in a great many passages, of which the following is representative:

Pesiqta deRab Kahana XIV:V.1

J. "So too all the generations came to the first Man, saying to him, 'Is it possible that the Holy One, blessed be He, is imposing the attribute of justice on you?'

L. "He said to them, 'God forbid. I am the one who has brought about my own death. Thus did he command me, saying to me, "Of all the trees of the garden you may eat, but of the tree of the knowledge of good and evil you may not eat" (Gen. 2:17). When I violated his instructions, I brought about my own death, for it is written, "On the day on which you eat it, you will surely die" (Gen. 2:17).

Death does not define God's purpose for the life of Adam and Eve but violates the teleology that governed God's making of them. No wonder, then, that death should constitute the paramount intangible enemy of Eden, the corpse, of cleanness for temple and household alike. But we begin with the tangible enemy of Eden, the idolaters, who reject God outright, willfully.

That temple and the Israelite household in the Land of Israel, on a hierarchical continuum with the temple, form the arena for the contest between life and death forms no mere abstraction. That has concrete reasons: what takes place in the temple sustains the life of Israel in the Land of Israel, and so too, what happens in the household procreates and nurtures life. The principal activities of the household—creating, sustaining life—also involve acts of sanctification (in creating life) and the maintenance of the model of sanctity (in sustaining life by eating food in the home prepared in conditions of cultic cleanness that pertain to the temple offerings). The whole mirrors the space (in alertness against uncleanness effected by the presence of what is analogous to death), time (as at the Sabbath), and activity (in the mirror image of that of the temple (as we saw in Chapter Eleven).

That is why holy Israel, confronting round about the sources of contamination, takes as its task constantly to remain alert and watchful. That is lest those sources of cultic contamination that signify death affect Israel in the home or temple, situated as they are in the Land that is comparable to Eden (but there alone). And that means, Israel must watch not only what it eats and drinks, and wears, and where it stands and sits and lies. Israel also must pay attention to what the food that Israel eats itself may have earlier touched, who may have earlier stood or sat upon the clothing that the Israelite wears and the beds on which he takes a rest. So not only the present condition but the past story of utensils, food, drink, clothing, and furniture comes into account. That consideration of an infinite regress is expressed in the language of "removes from a source of uncleanness." What has touched what has touched what has touched a corpse may itself be positioned on a continuum of contamination and impart uncleanness, or at least render unfit, food that it touches.

To preserve the condition it ought always to enjoy, which is, the state of sanctification, Israel has then to maintain a constant surveillance of the present and past of the world in which it lives and the people among whom it makes its life. Just as marrying without carefully investigating the genealogy of the Israelite family into which one marries can produce as offspring *mamzerim*, excluded from Israel for a thousand generations, so sitting on a bench without finding out who has sat there before can produce uncleanness that can contaminate much else. Along these same lines, eating a piece of bread without knowing where it has been and who has touched it can diminish one's standing in the hierarchy of sanctification, as spelled out in Mishnah-tractate *Hagigah* chs. 2 and 3 and Mishnah tractate *Tohorot* ch. 2, with their Tosefta supplements (and in the case of *Hagigah*, Yerushalmi and Bavli analyses as well).

The Israelite household, the space occupied by it for the sacred occasions (each man in "his place"), and the property in the full sense of the word—realty, personalty, and movables, all three—furthermore are treated as analogous to the sacred space. That is comprised by the temple, occupied by the consecrated caste, the priesthood and their staff, and what is kept therein. What establishes the analogy? Both are subject to the same dangers in the metaphor of death. The sources of change and disruption that threaten the cleanness, hence the sanctification, of the temple are the very same sources that threaten the norm of cleanness of the household. What follows is that, if the same uncleanness affects the temple and the table, then the only

difference is one of degree, not of kind, as the Halakhah states explicitly. And the rest flows.

The web of relationships between sanctification and uncleanness,
accordingly, spins itself out into every corner of the Israelite household, where the system makes a difference. The source of the system's
movement, its dynamism, in light of the character of its generative
analogy, is readily predicted. Given the story the Halakhic system
tells, it is—and it can only be—the will of the householder. That is
what determines the difference that the distinction between clean and
unclean is going to make. Everything is relative to the householder's
will. He has it in his power, through acts of perpetual alertness
depending on his, and his household's, will to draw the household
table into alignment with the altar in the temple. That is to say, if he
wills it always, he by his own intentionality can place the table and
the food set thereon into relationship, onto a continuum, with the
altar and the holy things of the cult. How so? Let me state with heavy
emphasis: *This act of will motivates an attitude of constant watchfulness for
those very sources of contamination that Scripture identifies as danger to the Lord's
altar in the Jerusalem Temple—death above all.*

So, in the cosmology of the system, the struggle for life and against
death, lost in Eden, is recapitulated—with results Israel can bring
about—in the temple, mirroring below the condition of heaven
above, the place on earth opposite God's residence above, and in the
household, conducted as an analogy thereto. Such an attitude of
watchfulness then comes to realization in actions that confirm the
attitude and embody the intentionality: take note, avoid, watch out
for this, that, and the other thing. That is because the faithful of the
Halakhah think of themselves as subject to the disciplines of
sanctification like temple priests but nonetheless situate themselves in
the ordinary world.

But there is a massive difference, according to the ordinary Israelite
a cosmic challenge, an extraordinary importance in the sight of
Heaven. In the actual temple, avoiding sources of uncleanness, e.g.,
corpses, menstruating women, people suffering a flux, posed no enormous problems, for most of the virulent sources of uncleanness were
walled out to begin with. Corpses were kept out, unclean persons
(including priests) were removed and by elaborate rites readmitted.
But in the household and in the marketplace who knows what can

happen—and commonly does? And who can control for the unto-
ward or the unnoticed? But there is more. Bumping into someone
quite inadvertently, who can trace the history of each person, his or
her encounter with a corpse, her period, for instance, or with someone who has had such an encounter or sat on a chair on whom a
menstruating woman or a man with flux has sat? The possibilities for
cultic contamination, controlled in the cult, prove limitless outside—
so too the responsibilities, above all, the requirement for constant willful attention to what happens. But then, the Halakhah aims at
imposing order and a certain rationality, a well-construed assessment
of probabilities, upon that chaos of death embodied in the unclean
and the profane.

So much for the construction of a world of sanctification and
desacralization in response to the householder's will and intention.
Now we turn to what lies beyond his power, to matters upon which
his attitude and plan have no bearing. These are the sources of
uncleanness that do function *ex opere operato* and that, when they do,
take what is sacred and render it unclean, inaccessible to its ordinary
purpose and task, sustaining the life of holy Israel.

On the side of life eternal, Israel abides within God's kingdom,
both unseen and seen, tangible, visible, and temporal. To aspire to
live in God's kingdom bears a variety of meanings, but the simplest
and most explicit calls upon Israel to be holy like God: "You shall be
holy, because I the Lord your God am holy" (Lev. 19:2). Just as the
holiness of the temple, where God abides and Israel meets him, is to
be defended from the sources of uncleanness that represent death, so
the Israelite household, its table, utensils and food, as much the bed,
are to be protected against those same enemies. In the model of
Eden, man bears responsibility for his part in the confrontation.
Where exactly does the will of man enter into the contest between
life and death? That question occupies us in our inquiry into how
Israel takes its position within the kingdom of God, choosing life.
And, by now predictably, the answer will be, by an act of will Israel
enters the contest.

A. *Tangible Enemies: 'Abodah Zarah*

Idolatry represents the tangible enemy of God. When the Halakhah
takes up the world beyond Eden, it invokes its own metaphors for

death: the gentiles in the tangible world outside the genealogical frontier of Israel, corpse-uncleanness in the invisible, if equally tangible, world beyond the locative limits of the altar, the temple, and Jerusalem. And that fact precipitates its opposite: the status of the world of the gentiles. The world beyond the bounds of Israel—the people in its household walls, the Land within its frontiers—forms an undifferentiated realm of idolatry and uncleanness. In the Halakhah, the idol has contaminating power comparable to the corpse, e.g., by overshadowing (by analogy to the corpse at Num. 19). The gentile, too, contaminates on a continuum with the corpse, and clumps of dirt beyond the limits of the holy land are deemed permeated with corpse-matter.

Then how is Israel to negotiate life with the world of gentiles and their idolatry, corpses and their contamination? The Halakhah constructs, indeed defines, the interiority of an Israel sustaining God's service in a world of idolatry: life against death in the two concrete and tangible dimensions by which life is sustained—trade and the production of food. No wonder Israel must refrain from engaging with idolatry on days of the festivals for idols that the great fairs embody—then especially.

I cannot overstress the power of analogy in shaping the Halakhic structure. Among the sources of uncleanness, tangible and invisible, we begin with the gentiles and proceed to corpse- and comparable kinds of uncleanness. The two—gentiles, corpses—form a single domain. The former bears the same uncleanness as the latter. And corpse-uncleanness is not further differentiated, in the way in which the sources of uncleanness affecting Israel in the household are. A picture in cartographic form of the theological anthropology of the Halakhah, indeed, would portray a many-colored and much-differentiated Israel at the center of the circle, with the perimeter comprised by all-white gentiles. For white is the color of death, how the unclean graves are marked off to warn priests and others concerned with cleanness. If, as I claim, gentiles, like their idols, constitute a source of uncleanness of the virulence of corpse-uncleanness, how is this expressed? What detail of the Halakhah embodies the principle that Israel stands for life, the gentiles like their idols for death? An asherah tree, like a corpse, conveys uncleanness to those who pass underneath it, so M. 'Abodah Zarah 3:8: "And he should not pass underneath it, but if he passed underneath it, he is unclean."

Not only so, but gentiles, always meaning idolaters, and Israelites, defined as worshippers of the one and only God, part company at death. Only for the moment do Israelites die, for later on, at a determinate time known to God, they are to rise from the grave. Gentiles die for eternity. The roads intersect at the grave, each component of humanity taking its own path beyond. Israelites—meaning those possessed of right conviction—will rise from the grave, stand in judgment, but then enter upon eternal life, to which no idolater will enjoy access. So, in substance, humanity viewed whole is divided between those who get a share in the world to come and who will stand when subject to divine judgment and those who will not. And humanity also is divided between Israel, acutely susceptible to a broad variety of sources of uncleanness but also capable of attaining purity, and the gentiles, uniformly unclean always. That is the meaning of the fact that all gentiles—even righteous ones—are sources of the undifferentiated uncleanness of the corpse.

When a gentile abandons idolatry and accepts the dominion of God exercised through his self-manifestation in the Torah, he loses the corpse-uncleanness that afflicted him, is immersed and transformed, as if newly born in the rite of immersion. Nothing in his past affects his new status as part of Israel (though his status within Israel is subject to those same criteria of hierarchization and differentiation that govern all others within Israel in one way or another). Then the Halakhah, distinguishing those who love from those who hate God, takes as its religious problem the concretization of that distinction, the demonstration of where and how the distinction in theory makes a huge difference in the practice, the conduct, of everyday affairs. And, as we shall see, invisible, though tangible, sources of uncleanness also form analogues to death.

Idolatry—rebellious arrogance against God—encompasses rejection of the entire Torah. The religious duty to avoid idolatry is primary; if one violates the religious duties, he breaks the yoke of commandments, and if he violates that single religious duty, he violates the entire Torah. Violating the prohibition against idolatry is equivalent to transgressing all Ten Commandments. Differentiated by genealogy and other indicators, all Israelites are defined by submission to God and acceptance of the Torah as God's will. That conclusion is sustained by a simple inversion of subject and predicate in the Halakhic definition of Israel, which we have already encountered.

The Halakhah states, "All Israelites have a share in the world to come. And these are the ones who have no portion in the world to come: He who says, the resurrection of the dead is a teaching that does not derive from the Torah, and the Torah does not come from Heaven; and an Epicurean" (M. *San.* 11:1). Then we may say, those who have a share in the world to come are those who affirm God, self-manifest in the Torah.

What accounts for the identification of idolatry with death? The transaction of Eden lies at the foundation: rebellion. Idolatry forms a deliberate act of rebellion against God. Gentiles are deniers, their status imposed by their own act of will. That is why, in full deliberation, they are unreconstructed man, destined for the grave and classified as corpses even while alive. So the Halakhah maintains that Israel encompasses those who will enjoy eternal life, but gentiles are those who perish at the grave. The contrast between life and Israel, death and gentiles, is concrete and practical, for the spit and urine of the gentile are unclean, since a gentile is classified as a *zab* (Lev. 15). That means that even a Gentile who accepted the seven commandments that pertain to the children of Noah falls outside of the system of differentiated contamination that pertains to Israel, e.g., is not subject to the uncleanness described at Lev. 13–14, and Israel itself prior to the giving of the Torah was not subject to that uncleanness. If Eden stands for life with God, then beyond the limits lies the realm of death, tangible in gentiles, invisible in corpse- and other sources of uncleanness, including the idol. In this world, death is to be held at a distance, uncleanness is to be kept away, from the temple altar, and, by analogy, from the table of the Israelite household, and, in the world to come, gentiles, idolaters, molder in the grave and death itself will die.

How does the Halakhah respond in practical terms to these convictions? The Halakhah takes as its task the negotiation between Israelites and the pagan world in which they live, how they are to conduct themselves in accord with the Torah so that at no point and in no way do they give support to idolatry and so betray the one and only God. In its basic exposition of the theme of idolatry, the Halakhah rests squarely on the foundations of Scripture, supplying rules and regulations that carry out the fundamental Scriptural commandments about destroying idols and everything that has to do with idolatry. But the Halakhah so formulates matters as to transform the entire topic of idolatry into an essay on Israel's relationships with the gentiles, who, as I said, are idolaters by definition. The Halakhah addresses the condition of individuals, the ordinary life of common folk, rather than concentrating on the situation of all Israel, viewed as a collective entity. The Halakhah therefore tends to find its problem in the condition of the private person and in the interiorities of his life in the Israelite community.

For the Torah, the community at large forms the focus of the law, and idolatry is not to be negotiated with by the collectivity of holy Israel. In its Land, Israel is to wipe out idolatry, even as a memory. Scripture is clear that Israel is to obliterate all mention of idols (Ex. 23:13), not bow down to gentiles' gods or serve them but overthrow them and break them into pieces (Ex. 23:24): "You shall break down their altars and dash in pieces their pillars and hew down their Asherim and burn their graven images with fire" (Dt. 7:5). Accordingly, so far as the Written Torah supplies the foundations for the treatment of the matter by the Rabbinic exegetes, the focus of discourse concerning the gentiles is idolatry. Scripture's Halakhah does not contemplate Israel's coexisting, in the Land, with gentiles and their idolatry.

But the Halakhah of the Mishnah-Tosefta-Yerushalmi-Bavli speaks to a world that is not so simple. The Land belongs to Israel, but gentiles live there too—and run things. The Halakhah of the Rabbinic canon commences with the premise that gentiles live side by side (whether or not in the Land of Israel) with Israelites. Then Israelites have to sort out the complex problems of coexistence with idolatry. And that coexistence involves not whole communities, corporate Israel, and the peoples, whoever they may be, but individuals, this Israelite living side by side with that gentile. The Halakhah deals first with commercial relationships, second, matters pertaining to idols, and finally to the particular prohibition of wine, part of which has served as a libation to an idol. The whole is regularized and ordered. There are relationships with gentiles that are absolutely prohibited, particularly occasions of idol-worship; the Halakhah recognizes that these are major commercial events. When it comes to commerce with idolaters, Israelites may not sell or in any way benefit from certain things, may sell but may not utilize certain others, and may sell and utilize yet others. Here, we see immediately, the complex and systematic mode of thought that governs the Oral Torah's treatment of the topic vastly transcends the rather simple conception that animates Scripture's discussion of the same matter. There are these unstated premises within the Halakhah:

[1] what a Gentile is not likely to use for the worship of an idol is not prohibited;

[2] what may serve not as part of an idol but as an appurtenance thereto is prohibited for Israelite use but permitted for Israelite commerce;

[3] what serves idolatry is prohibited for use and for benefit.

In reflecting upon relationships with the gentiles, meaning idolaters, the Oral Torah moreover takes for granted a number of facts. These turn out to yield a single generalization: gentiles are assumed routinely to practice bestiality, murder, and fornication. Further negative stereotypes concerning idolaters occur.

The Halakhah then serves as the means for the translation of theological conviction into social policy. Gentiles are assumed to be ready to murder any Israelite they can get their hands on, rape any Israelite women, commit bestiality with any Israelite cow. The Oral Torah cites few cases to indicate that that conviction responds to ordinary, everyday events. The hostility to gentiles flows from a theory of idolatry, not the facts of everyday social intercourse, which, as we have seen, sages recognize is full of neighborly cordiality. Then why take for granted that gentiles routinely commit the mortal sins of not merely idolatry but bestiality, fornication, and murder? That is because the Halakhah takes as its task the realization of the theological principle that those who hate Israel hate God, those who hate God hate Israel, and God will ultimately vanquish Israel's enemies as his own.

In line with its focus upon issues of intentionality, the Halakhah insists that, just as gentiles make choices willfully, so in dealing with idolatry and the gentiles, Israel too may exercise its own will. Under all conditions, the Halakhah assumes, Israelites possess freedom of will: they are always man, "in our image." The Halakhah presupposes not gentile hegemony but only gentile power. It further takes for granted that Israelites may make choices, may specifically refrain from trading in what gentiles value in the service of their gods, and may hold back from gentiles what gentiles require for that service. Israelites may live in a world governed by gentiles, but they form intentions and carry them out. They may decide what to sell and what not to sell, whom to hire for what particular act of labor and to whom not to sell their own labor, and, above all, Israelite traders may determine to give up opportunities denied them by the circumstance of gentile idolatry.

The Halakhah therefore makes a formidable statement of Israel's freedom to make choices, its opportunity within the context of everyday life to preserve a territory free of idolatrous contamination, much as Israel in entering the Land was to create a territory free of the worship of idols and their presence. In the setting of world order, Israel may find itself subject to the will of others, but in the house of Israel, Israelites can and should establish a realm for God's rule and presence, free of idolatry. And if to establish a domain for God Israelites must practice self-abnegation, refrain from actions of considerable weight and consequence, well, much of the Torah concerns itself with what people are not supposed to do, and God's rule comes to realization in acts of restraint. So much for the life of Israel under the commandments.

B. *Invisible Enemies: Death. Ohalot*

While gentiles bear responsibility for their own condition, willfully worshipping idols instead of God, uncleanness ordinarily comes willy-nilly and does not bespeak an act of deliberation. Uncleanness functions inexorably, *ex opere operato*, once the conditions for susceptibility to uncleanness have been met. Uncleanness, though invisible and in some forms intangible, bears its own substantive and material character. A critical characteristic comes first: human intentionality cannot dictate the definition or character of uncleanness, only that *upon which* uncleanness works, where it makes a difference.

That the corpse constitutes the apex of the hierarchy of sources of uncleanness is stated in so many words at the beginning of the tractate that commences the division of Purities, *Kelim*. Here is the operative language of hierarchical classification:

Mishnah Kelim 1:1–4

M. 1:1 The [generative, principal] Fathers of Uncleanness [which on their own impart the status of uncleanness] [are] (1) the creeping thing, and (2) semen [of an adult Israelite], and (3) one who has contracted corpse uncleanness, and (4) the leper in the days of his counting, and (5) sin offering water of insufficient quantity to be sprinkled. Lo, these render man and vessels unclean by contact, and earthenware vessels by [presence within the vessels' contained] airspace. But they do not render unclean by carrying.

M. 1:2 Above them: (6) carrion, and (7) sin offering water of sufficient quantity to be sprinkled. For they render man unclean through carrying, to make [his] clothing unclean. But clothing is not made unclean through contact.

M. 1:3 Above them: (8) he who has intercourse with a menstruating woman, for he conveys uncleanness to what lies [far] beneath him [in like degree as he conveys uncleanness to what lies] above. Above them: (9) the flux of the Zab, and (10) his spittle and (11) his semen and (12) his urine, and (13) the blood of the menstruating woman, for they render unclean through contact and carrying. Above them: (14) the saddle, for it [the saddle] is unclean under a heavy stone. Above the saddle: (15) the couch, for touching it is equivalent to carrying it. Above the couch: (16) the Zab, for the Zab conveys uncleanness to the couch, but the couch does not [convey equivalent uncleanness to] the couch.

M. 1:4 Above the Zab: (17) the Zabah, for she renders him that has intercourse with her unclean [for seven days]. Above the Zabah: (18) the leper, for he renders unclean by his coming [into a house]. Above the leper: (19) a bone about the size of a barley corn, for it renders unclean for a seven [days'] uncleanness. Weightiest of them all: (20) the corpse, for it renders unclean by overshadowing [a mode of rendering uncleanness by] which none of the rest conveys uncleanness.

The bases for hierarchization, the sources of uncleanness, need not detain us. The important side is the result of the hierarchical classification, which is the presentation of the corpse as the climax, together with the reason therefor: he contaminates the household by his very presence, to which we now turn.

Every source of uncleanness imposes one and the same status, that of uncleanness. That is with the uniform result of the prohibition of certain activities in consequence of entry into that single status. When it comes to what the person may or may not actually do, someone made unclean by corpse-uncleanness differs from someone made unclean by a dead creeping thing in not a single detail. His status in consequence of contamination by the one source is the same as that brought about by contamination of the other source, and so throughout. So the hierarchization of uncleanness as to virulence finds no correspondence in the ordering of consequences of contamination for the person, food, or clothing in its own terms and framework. That fact comes to expression in a remarkable uniformity that characterizes the predicate of discourse concerning uncleanness: *it is/is not unclean.* That predicate may bear modifiers, e.g., "unclean for seven days," but (controlling for removes of uncleanness, as at M. *Hag.* 2:5ff. and M. *Toh.* 2:3ff.) the net effect remains the same. The uniform consequence then yields a single result: what I cannot do by reason of contamination by corpse-uncleanness I cannot do by reason of uncleanness deriving from a dead frog. The system of taxonomic hierarchization stops short, and the language that encapsulates the Halakhah underscores that point in nearly every line of the law. The homogenization of consequences of contamination bears its own message.

To discern that message, we turn to the Halakhic category at hand. We begin with the conception of uncleanness deriving from the corpse and ask, What, exactly, does that abstraction, "uncleanness," stand for or refer to? Can we explain why what is unclean is unclean, and what would represent the antonymic relationship to that uncleanness? I think that we can, and therefore we may find in the explanation of the religious meaning inhering in corpse-uncleanness a key to what is at stake in the entire system of cultic uncleanness, viewed not as a social but as a metaphysical statement.

The Halakhah contains within itself a profound conception that we may uncover by identifying the following governing principle repeatedly invoked by the law of the transmission of corpse-uncleanness in a contained space (in line with Num. 19:14–19): corpse-uncleanness passes through a handbreadth of open space; its passage is impeded by a handbreadth of closed space. The specified dimension is a trait of corpse-uncleanness that Scripture does not indicate. The handbreadth in breadth, depth, and height, sufficient to contain the corpse-uncleanness that exudes from a corpse or corpse-matter, has no relationship with a tent except in abstract form and (equally abstract) function.

What exactly does the contained space of a cubic handbreadth contain? The details of the Halakhah, read inductively, answer the question. It contains a kind of thick liquid, which flows and dissipates in the airspace that is contained by the tent as defined in the pure abstraction, A cubic handbreadth introduces uncleanness and inter-poses before uncleanness. To that statement we need only add, re-versing predicate and subject as is our way: What is contained in the cubic handbreadth of contained space is the uncleanness of the corpse, which is to say, that invisible matter that flows like liquid from the body of the deceased. Then we refer to what leaves the body at death, having been contained therein through life. These simple facts lead us, inductively, to the generative conception of the Halakhah, which is, what exudes from the corpse at death, that viscous matter that is unseen but attaches itself to whatever in the contained space of the tent is not tightly sealed, is a fourth of the volume that a per-son occupies in the space of the world. That is, a human being is deemed to occupy three cubits for purposes of Sabbath rest, as we have seen in the Halakhah of 'Erubin. That is the physical dimension of the ordinary person. The body retains its physical dimensions in death, so the cubic handbreadth of viscous fluid that the body emits, that which animates the body in life, defines the uncleanness of the corpse. To state matters as bluntly as sages do, corpse-uncleanness stands for "the uncleanness of the soul."

The Written Torah speaks of a tent or house in which whole and healthy people live. The Oral Torah speaks of a tent as a space that is capable of containing that which exudes from the body at the moment of death, a tent that replaces the body and holds what the body held or transmits that portion of the person that exudes at death. The handbreadth that is at the foundation of dissemination or interposition is the space through which the effects of the corpse makes its way. A tent is not the same thing as a house or building in which people can live; it is the contained space that holds the gaseous effusion of the corpse. When we say that a tent must measure a hand-breadth squared, either to prevent uncleanness from entering an enclosed space or to keep uncleanness within an enclosed space, we speak of not what holds the body but what holds the part of the per-son that exudes at death, the soul. If corpse-uncleanness is something that can be contained by a tent, and a tent is something that can con-tain or interpose against corpse-uncleanness, then we deal, in a tent, with the functional equivalent of the body. The tent takes the place of the body, makes a place for that which, in the body, leaves at the point of death. It is to be understood then as a surrogate for the body, restoring the imbalance that has taken place with the leaving of the

body by that which exudes from it. Death has released this excretion
or effusion, and the tent can contain it. What exudes from the corpse
at such a viscosity as to pass through an open space of at least a handbreadth is the uncleanness of the corpse; it is the soul, the spirit surviving after death and requiring a new locus.

That notion represents more than mere surmise. It is expressed in
so many words by Philo, when he says (*Special Laws* 3:206–207, trans.
F. H. Colson, p. 605):

> Those who enter a house in which anyone has died are ordered not to
> touch anything until they have bathed themselves and also washed the
> clothes that they were wearing. And all the vessels and articles of fur-
> niture and anything else that happens to be inside, practically every-
> thing is held by him to be unclean. For a man's soul is a precious thing,
> and when it departs to seek another home, all that will be left behind
> is defiled, deprived as it is of the divine image. For it is the mind of
> man that has the form of God, being shaped in conformity with the
> ideal archetype, the Word that is above all.

Whether sages will have found Philo's explanation for the uncleanness of what the soul leaves behind I doubt, since in their view, it is
that effusion—that which leaves the corpse—that constitutes what is
unclean.

So let us dwell on that matter of Halakhah. It speaks in images and
invokes analogies of physics. A tent keeps back uncleanness if it is
merely covered, but a utensil has to be tightly sealed. A utensil, whole
and serviceable, compresses uncleanness; it does not scatter its effects
against its own cover. That is why corpse-matter in a pot spurts
upward or downward but not to the sides, while corpse-matter in a
tent spreads upward against the cover of the tent, but will not pass
through the roof and beyond. The language "breaks forth upward
and downward" expresses the conception. How do a tent, which
diffuses the corpse-matter's uncleanness against the roof and prevents
its passage beyond, and the utensil, which does not have that capacity, differ? The tent serves as a broken utensil. The utensil when
whole cannot hold back uncleanness, when broken it can. Then the
object is not susceptible to uncleanness and cannot be acted upon by
uncleanness. When the object is a utensil, it itself is subject to
uncleanness, so it squeezes out the viscous substance within and causes it to spurt forth upward or downward. When it is not a utensil but
a tent, insusceptible to uncleanness, it can contain that to which it is

neutral and insusceptible. The soul, having left its broken utensil, the corpse, finds a domicile only in another broken utensil.

So much for the poetry of the Halakhah. What of its theology? That emerges from a simple fact. When a person is alive, the soul that animates the body is sacred, because it is that part of the human being that corresponds to God, who creates man and woman "in our image, after our likeness." At death the soul no longer animates the body; that is what death means. Then the soul leaves the body, and, no longer sacred, leaves behind a Father of fathers of uncleanness and itself, in its viscosity and fluidity, likewise functions as a Father of fathers of uncleanness—unless, and until, it is contained in the grave, awaiting the resurrection of the dead.

So if I had to state what I find critical in the Halakhah, it is the intense engagement with the issue of how the uncleanness that exudes from the corpse, which we have shown corresponds to the soul leaving the body, is domiciled in the long interval between death and resurrection. The Halakhah of *Ohalot* affords to those concerned with uncleanness and sanctification—that is to say, to the heart of holy Israel—acute and intense reason—the extreme virulence of the uncleanness of the corpse and its excretions—to secure that which represents the soul, that viscous fluid. Why so? It is so as to give that which leaves the body a permanent home for the interim. And that explains, by the way, why the effects of uncleanness do not require differentiation but produce, whatever the source of uncleanness, a common result. Uncleanness, whatever its source or virulence, serves a single purpose and therefore is not classified or hierarchized as to consequence.

C. *Negaˁim*

Death embodied in the corpse supplies a generative analogy: what resembles a corpse is a source of uncleanness comparable to that of a corpse. We have already noted that gentiles are unclean like corpses. The uncleanness affecting them is otherwise undifferentiated. But when it comes to Israelites, uncleanness is extensively differentiated. So there are forms of uncleanness particular to not only the Israelite person and his clothing and covering (analogous to his skin) but the Israelite household. And these are so defined as to prove analogous to the corpse-uncleanness we have just examined.

The very building where Israelites live is subject to uncleanness, not only the persons of the Israelite residents. But the reason that the building and clothing are affected is explicit: when an Israelite possesses, dwells in the building, or purchases and makes use of the clothing, then his status as to sanctification extends to the house or the garment. So it is the Israelite that imparts the capacity to receive uncleanness, because it is the Israelite, dwelling in the land of Israel, that also imparts the status of sanctification.

Nega⁽-uncleanness, the source of the skin-ailment uncleanness described at Lev. 13–14, affects only a house in the Land of Israel in which Israelites live, and when the gentile sells the house, then and only then is it inspected afresh, and only from that point is nega⁽-uncleanness an issue. The same is so for garments. Only Israelites are subject to the uncleanness of plagues, just as only Israelite corpses emit corpse-uncleanness. Only the Israelite possesses a soul that, upon death, exudes and forms a principal source of uncleanness, and the same conclusion pertains to nega⁽-uncleanness and its signification.

The status as Israelite makes a person susceptible to uncleanness but also allows the Israelite to interpose against uncleanness, and in accord with susceptibility is the possibility of sanctification: Israelites receive uncleanness and afford protection for clothing in the house afflicted with plague. But the gentile and the beast do not receive uncleanness and do not afford protection for clothing in the house afflicted with plague. What is subject to a higher degree of sanctification also is susceptible to a longer sequence of removes from the original source of uncleanness.

The sages' definition of the irregularities in a person's skin or in the mould affecting garments or a house makes sense in the context of corpse-uncleanness. The Halakhah persists in insisting on a square shape for the marks of uncleanness. Why must the spot be square-shaped? The Halakhah of *Ohalot* has already supplied the answer. That is to say, the only possible answer presents itself when we invoke the analogy of corpse-uncleanness, which also passes through a square-shaped space. But here the space is much smaller, and it may well be diffused through the body. So too the raw flesh must be four-sided. The decisive issue is the size and shape of the sign, and whether it grows or diminishes. If the raw flesh loses its four-sided character, it ceases to signify uncleanness: the size and shape matter. That is the contribution of the Oral Torah.

So the key is the insistence of the Halakhah on the square shape of the indicator of uncleanness and whether, retaining its proportions, it grows or diminishes to nullity. The uncleanness of *nega'im* is as though the soul were leaking out of little square holes, rather than pouring forth from a large square hole affecting the entire corpse, such as takes place with the uncleanness of the soul that exudes at death. Two white hairs in the bright spot signify the same, and they must be equal in length. The signification of the raw flesh may derive from the decay that takes place after death; that is less certain in my view. What is clear is that the Torah insists that the markings endure for a period of time, a week, matching the week's uncleanness that the corpse causes, and the week of the purification rite—all correlated with the seven days in which the world was created. Here is a mark that the created world is not functioning in accord with its nature.

The analogy to corpse-uncleanness persists throughout. But while comparable to corpse-uncleanness, the condition of *nega'*-uncleanness differs, in that we deal with an interstitial condition. It is with someone who puts out the markings of a corpse but is not a corpse. If the person is wholly covered by a bright spot, his condition no longer is interstitial; he is now a breathing corpse and in no way unclean (Lev. 13:10 is then read to cover all markings of uncleanness). So a person may be classified in one of three ways: wholly a corpse, wholly natural and alive, and somewhere in between, and that is where uncleanness signifies abnormality. But entering the interstitial situation is only for the Israelite. Israelites alone contract uncleanness from the skin ailment (and related markings). The upshot is, if the bright spot flowered over the entire body, then, as Scripture says, the man is clean. The Halakhah then clarifies, since the spot that breaks forth when the man is unclean clears him, one that breaks forth when the man is clean certifies that he is unclean. If the spot recedes from the tips of the limbs, then the man reverts to uncleanness. So the interstitiality of the man's appearance, resolved in favor of his appearing entirely like a corpse, is resolved and the uncleanness ends; he obviously is not a corpse, so he is now clean.

Israelites enter into the system of uncleanness, purification, and sanctification. A gentile who has accepted the seven commandments that pertain to the children of Noah is not affected, any more than is a Gentile; they are perpetually unclean, becoming pure only when en route to sanctification, that is, in the immersion pool in the process of transformation to the status of Israelite. But, more to the point, Israelites become susceptible to *nega^c*-uncleanness only after the giving of the Torah, thus M. *Neg.* 7:1: "These are clean bright spots: Those which were on him before the giving of the Torah, on the Gentile, and he converted, on the child, and it was born." Birth into Israel after the giving of the Torah, or conversion to Judaism, or birth within Israel—these mark the point at which bright spots indicate uncleanness. I cannot imagine a more explicit way of making the point that the entire system concerns itself with the condition of Israel when subject to the Torah.

How do sages account for the uncleanness at hand, the situation of transient death, the death that is not permanent? The advent of *nega^c*-uncleanness in the Halakhic representation of matters signifies that the victim gossiped or behaved arrogantly. Here we encounter the only source of uncleanness that is explicitly held to signify moral failure. Sages in the Halakhah do not impute a negative moral judgment to the natural conditions of the *zab* and *zabah*, the menstruating woman, the woman after childbirth, all the more so the corpse. None of these sources of uncleanness involves repentance as a condition of purification, though a purification rite is involved for all persons that have served as animate sources of uncleanness. Here, by contrast, an explicit judgment is made, in the context of the Halakhic exposition:

Tosefta Nega^cim 6:7

> He would come to the priest, and the priest says to him, "My son, Go and examine yourself and return from your evil ways. For plagues come only because of gossip, and leprosy comes only to those who are arrogant. And the Omnipresent judges man only in mercy."
>
> If the plagues come on his house: if he repents, it requires dismantling; and if not, it requires demolishing.
>
> If, then they appear on his clothing: if he repents, it requires tearing; and if not, it requires burning. lo, they appear on his body: if he repents, he repents;
>
> and if not, "Solitary shall he dwell; outside of the camp is his dwelling" (Lev. 13:46).

Not only so, but the neighbor of a wicked man pays a price as well: he does not bring one stone to replace two, nor two for one, but he brings two for two, for three, for four. On this basis have they said, "Woe to an evil person. Woe to his neighbor." The two of them tear down the stones, the two of them scrape the walls, the two of them bring stones. But he alone brings the dirt. As it is said, "And he shall take other plaster and plaster the house" (Lev. 14:40). The upshot is, in cause and effect, *nega*ᶜ-uncleanness is a social disease. Here is how the cited passage of Tosefta on the matter is amplified in *Sifra*:

Sifra CLV:I.8

A. ". . . saying" (Lev. 14:35)—

B. The priest will say to him words of reproach: "My son, plagues come only because of gossip [T. 6:7], as it is said, 'Take heed of the plague of leprosy to keep very much and to do, remember what the Lord God did to Miriam' (Deut. 24:80.

C. "And what has one thing to do with the other?

D. "But this teaches that she was punished only because of gossip.

E. "And is it not an argument a fortiori?

F. "If Miriam, who did not speak before Moses' presence, suffered so, one who speaks ill of his fellow in his very presence, how much the more so?"

G. R. Simeon b. Eleazar says, "Also because of arrogance do plagues come, for so do we find concerning Uzziah,

H. "as it is said, 'And he rebelled against the Lord his God and he came to the Temple of the Lord to offer on the altar incense and Azariah the Priest came after him and with him priests of the Lord, eighty strong men, and they stood against Uzziah and said to him, It is not for you to do, Uzziah, to offer to the Lord, for only the priests the sons of Aaron who are sanctified do so. So forth from the sanctuary. And Uzziah was angry,' etc. (2 Chron. 26:16)" [T. *Neg.* 6:7H].

Gossip endangers the health of the household of Israel. All forms of wicked speech fall within that same category. In the principle of measure for measure, gossip, which disrupts community harmony, finds its penalty in ostracism, inflicted on the person who gossips through the medium of the skin ailment that is treated by excluding the afflicted person from the common life.

D. *Zabim and Niddah*

The forms of uncleanness set forth at Lev. 15, in the continuation of Lev. 13–14, uncleanness affecting the sexual organs—a flow of blood or semen at other than the natural occasions, on the one side, menstruation on the other—form the subject of the exposition of *Zabim* and *Niddah*, respectively. At issue is the character of a woman's vaginal secretions or blood: when does it appear, how is it classified? The distinction between menstrual or *niddah*-blood and *zibah*-blood, the former part of the procreative cycle, the latter not, yields very little difference in actuality, except at the point of purification. The one is vaginal blood that flows during the woman's established menstrual cycle. The other is vaginal blood that flows during the eleven clean days between one cycle and another; these are called *zibah*-days, in that blood that flows during the eleven days between menstrual cycles is deemed *zob*. In some ways—those that have to do with actualities— the two types of vaginal flow are comparable, in others, they contrast.

If we compare Scripture's presentation of the two forms of animate female sources of uncleanness, we see how they relate, starting with the menstruating woman. The first thing we notice is that, while the menstrual period is limited, the uncleanness attaching to the *zabah* is indeterminate. The woman who menstruates may before and afterward engage in sexual relations and become pregnant. The *zabah* may not engage in sexual relations and so may not become pregnant. She is removed from the entire procreative process so long as her excretions continue. The second thing we see is that while the *niddah* accomplishes purification through immersion and sunset, the *zabah* undergoes an elaborate cultic rite, comparable to the rite of purification after contracting corpse-uncleanness. So while the signification of the uncleanness—vaginal flux—is the same, the circumstances as to timing and longevity vastly distinguish the one from the other, and, as I shall suggest presently, the distinction makes a massive difference in our reading of what is at stake.

The menstruating woman and the *zabah* convey uncleanness through touch, and both serve as fathers of uncleanness, setting into the first remove of uncleanness whatever they touch. One who touches what they have lain upon or sat upon immerses, awaits sunset, and is then clean. As to sexual relations, the menstruating woman imparts her own status to the one with whom she has sexual relations, and he imparts pressure-uncleanness by sitting and lying as well. As to the *zabah*, touching produces the same result; no provision is made for sexual relations. A cultic purification rite is provided for her, but not for the menstruating woman, who, at the end of her period, simply immerses and waits for sunset. She is then in the first remove, her period having concluded.

Viewed together, the Halakhah of *Zabim* and of *Niddah* makes a single coherent statement. The contrast between blood in the *niddah*-days and blood in the *zibah*-days frames the issue at hand. We cannot understand the Halakhah of *Niddah* outside of the framework of the Halakhah of *Zabim*, and, in the nature of things, the contrary is also the case. The points of intersection—the consequences of uncleanness imparted by vaginal blood—and the points of differentiation—sexuality and the purification rite, respectively—leave no choice but to consider *Niddah* and *Zabim* as a single statement within the Halakhah, of which *Zabim* forms the main lines of thought, *Niddah* the subordinated and secondary results thereof.

The character of *zob* and of its flow guides us to the center of the religious world view at hand. It is genital discharge that by its nature cannot accomplish that for which it is created, its purpose or teleology. In a word, the physical world portrayed here finds its definitive traits in the teleology of things, which yields the meetings and the matchings that produce the Halakhah of *Zabim*. The uncleanness generated by sexual fluids that do not realize their teleology passes via pressure, analogous to that of the sexual relation, to objects that serve for sexuality. When the teleological physics of sexual fluids accomplish their goal, they bring about life. Then, consequently, a minor uncleanness is brought about by semen properly ejaculated, and so too with vaginal blood of an episodic character outside the regular period. When the teleology—the procreation of life—of the sexual parts, encompassing further the objects used for sexual intercourse, and extending even to the activities and exertions characteristic thereof—when that teleology is not realized, then severe uncleanness results. That uncleanness then overspreads each of the components of procreation that has not realized its purpose:

[1] the fluid itself, now source of uncleanness analogous to corpse-uncleanness;
[2] the activity, exerting pressure, now medium for disseminating not life but uncleanness, and
[3] the bed and analogous objects, now the focus of not procreative activity but contamination.

Now, not realizing their tasks within the teleological physics at hand:

[1] the fluid is unclean,

[2] the bed and analogous objects become the unique foci of the uncleanness of said fluid, and

[3] the activity—pressure—serves as the medium not of life but of anti-life, such as, we now realize, cultic uncleanness disseminated through Midras-uncleanness in particular represents.

How are we to compare and contrast the uncleanness of the soul, the seven-day uncleanness of the corpse and corpse-matter, with the uncleanness of *zob*? When we examine the uncleanness exuding from the *zab* or *zabah*, encompassing not only the flux itself, whether semen or blood, but the body fluids, e.g., the spit, the urine, of a person so afflicted, we find an interesting fact. *Zob* does not constitute a father of fathers of uncleanness as the corpse does. The *zabah* or *zab* is a father of uncleanness, contaminating the garments and utensils of someone who touches her or him, also those things that bear her or his weight. These are made unclean in the first remove. So the virulence of the escaping soul vastly exceeds that of the genital excretions that do not realize their purpose.

Different in degree, they form a common genus. The character of *zob* fluid and the uncleanness of the soul that we examined in the context of corpse-uncleanness share the common quality that, when touched, both sorts of viscous, invisible fluid impart uncleanness. If there is an object suitable to serve as a bed or chair or saddle that lies underneath a stone, and a *zab* or *zabah* bears down on the stone, e.g., stands, sits, lies, or leans on it or hangs from it, because he is supported by the stone, the bed or chair that bears the weight of the intervening stone is itself contaminated. But corpse-uncleanness—e.g., a receptacle containing a bone—not touched but nonetheless the weight of which is carried produces no effect, e.g., through an intervening layer of disconnected material, while *zob*-uncleanness that is not contacted but the weight of which is carried does produce its uncleanness. So corpse-uncleanness possesses a tangibility, a tactility, that *zob*-uncleanness lacks, and *zob*-uncleanness responds to forces that affect corpse-uncleanness little or not at all. What is the difference?

Using our imagination of the workings of the physics of liquids in this odd context, we may on that basis differentiate the uncleanness of the corpse from the uncleanness of flux. The one, while thick, diffuses into the air of a contained space. It is therefore comparable to a gaseous substance; but, as we noted, it flows like a viscous fluid, along fairly firm lines, within a sizable space, a squared handbreadth. So while comparable to a gaseous substance, it remains, if invisible, thick and tactile. *Zob*, by contrast, does not diffuse in the air. It permeates the objects that are congruent to its effects ("susceptible to *zob*-uncleanness," which is to say, objects used for lying and sitting, encompassing also carpets and benches and the like). Then, if a clean person bears down, the *zob* under pressure is excreted upward onto the clean person, even through intervening, disconnected layers of material; the transmission takes place by reason of pressure, not contact.

That conception comes to expression in many cases, e.g., the following: the *zab* and the clean person who sat in a ship or on a raft, or who rode together on a beast, even though their clothes do not touch, lo, these are unclean with Midras-uncleanness. If they sat on a plank, or on a bench, or on a bed frame, and on the beam, when they are infirm—if they climbed up on a tree which was shaky, on a branch which was shaky on a firm tree—if they climbed up on an Egyptian ladder when it is not fastened with a nail, on the bridge, and on the beam, and on the door, when they are not fastened with clay, they are unclean.

Now how are we to differentiate the gaseous corpse-uncleanness, which does not respond to pressure, from comparable *zob*-uncleanness, which does? A difference in (imagined) viscosity ought to explain matters. Corpse-uncleanness flows within a guiding framework (under pressure, spurts upward and downward, we recall). But it does not permeate and pass through intervening fabric ("tent") or other materials. *Zob*-uncleanness under pressure is not guided along the lines of that which conveys the pressure—the tent for example—but flows right into, and through, the fabric or other material that contains it. Hence, seen in physical terms, the former is dense, glutinous and semifluid, the latter attenuated, spare and light.

But those physical traits on their own do not suffice to explain the difference as to the modes of movement between the uncleanness exuding from the corpse and that emitted by the sexual organs, male or female. Specifically, why should the latter classification of uncleanness flow so as to pass through the stone on which the *zab* exerts pressure through direct contact, as well as weight, to the bed beneath, on which the *zab* exerts pressure not through contact but only through weight? Why should a receptacle contain corpse-uncleanness but not the uncleanness of *zob*, that is, why should a receptacle be unaffected by Midras- or pressure uncleanness of a *zab* or *zabah*? Asked in that way, the question bears its own answer. We deal in *zob* with a kind of uncleanness that matches, that responds to, its own origin, assignment, and character: origin in sexual organs, assignment, procreation, and character defined by a dysfunction in those organs. Sexually-generated fluid that, by (sages') definition cannot accomplish the purpose that, by nature, it is supposed to achieve—procreation of life—affects those sorts of objects that serve sexually, ones used for lying and the like, but not those sorts of objects that under normal circumstances do not serve sexually, receptacles, for example.

As with the corpse and the uncleanness of the person afflicted with the skin ailment described at Lev. 13—the uncleanness is transmitted through spatial relationships not involving direct physical contact: overshadowing the corpse or being overshadowed by it, so too the *zab* or *zabah* in relationship to a bed or chair, so too the person afflicted with the skin ailment within a contained space. In all three instances, location within a demarcated spatial relationship with the source of uncleanness, not only actual contact, direct or through pressure (as the case requires), serves as cause of dissemination of uncleanness from the source to the focus thereof. Let us address the particular rule of spatial relationship in the transmission of uncleanness of a *zab* or *zabah*, because there we shall see the inexorable operation of the principle of realized or unrealized teleology as the key to all else, affecting both the source and the subject of contamination.

That brings us to the paradoxical fact of the Halakhah that overshadowing serves corpse-uncleanness and *zob*-uncleanness, but with powerful distinctions, and each in its own way. What overshadows a corpse contracts corpse-uncleanness, and what a corpse overshadows is contaminated by corpse-uncleanness. That is without regard to the character of the objects. We do not, furthermore, differentiate between the two locations of the corpse relative to the object in relationship thereto. So locative relationship and substantive character play no role in the transmission of corpse-uncleanness through overshadowing. The corpse that overshadows or is overshadowed produces its effects without regard to what is affected. But that is not how matters are with *zob*-uncleanness. Here we do differentiate, in the situation of overshadowing, between the character of classes of objects. And, concomitantly, we also differentiate locatively, between the two locations that said classes of objects take up: above, below the *zab*. So we have two variables as to the character of objects, and two variables as to their location, and, further, these variables produce opposite results, the locative for the substantive, as the case requires.

Here are some of the exemplary facts. If a *zab* overshadows food and drink, unlike the corpse he has no effect upon them. But if food or drink is located above the *zab*, they are made unclean. Why the mirror relationships? What is located where the *zab* lies or sits but cannot serve for lying or sitting is unaffected by him; what is located where the *zab* cannot lie or sit and cannot serve for lying or sitting— thus what in relationship to the *zab* is in its natural location, not in its unnatural location—is affected by him. So he functions as does a corpse in conveying uncleanness, the medium is the same; but he does not impart uncleanness as does a corpse. What does not conform in relationship to the *zab* to its natural location is affected by him; what conforms is not.

Here again, a teleological logic comes into play through analogical-contrastive dialectics, then, with the things that enjoy their natural relationship to the *zab* subject to his effect, those not, not; and then the opposite comes into force: what the *zab* cannot use for lying that is located where the *zab* cannot lie down is affected by the *zab*! So considerations of fulfilling the physical purpose for which the thing is shaped take over, even here. To state matters simply: teleological physics dictates the course of contamination by *zob* and the results, for things affected by that contamination, as well. And it is a simple teleology, which we identified at the very outset: what serves for procreation is distinguished, in respect to *zob*-uncleanness, from what docs not. And the rest follows.

As with Aristotelian physics, therefore, what we confront is a physics permeated by teleology: the flow of fluids in response to the condition or purpose of that to which, or from which, they flow, and not in response only to their own character, e.g., to the density of the atoms that comprise the fluid and define its viscosity. That which matches the character of an object or its purpose flows to that object or its purpose, and the invisible flow itself conforms to the character of the activity conducted with said object. The bed, used for lying or sitting, then is affected by pressure, carried on in acts of lying or sitting; the particular uncleanness at hand, sexual excretions in a non-procreative framework, affects those objects that by their nature serve, through those actions that by their nature produce, procreation.

When sexual activity bearing the potential of procreation takes place, a transient uncleanness results—that of healthy semen, which passes upon immersion and sunset, as Scripture says. When sexual excretions lacking that potential take place, a virulent uncleanness takes over, life replaced by anti-life, by a form of death nearly as virulent as the death that takes over the life of a man and causes the excretion of the soul. The soul of the fully-realized man or woman is thick, the unrealized, proto-soul of *zob*, thin. But the former can be contained in physical limits, as it was in the body, while the latter flows teleologically, its character and therefore its purpose overriding the substantive, physical traits, or physical traits responding to teleological matches (whichever formulation better serves).

The goal of nature, its telos in procreation, pertains to Israel and the propagation of the holy people. Sages make that point explicitly, because their perfect mastery of the Written Torah so instructed them. Let me explain. With a system so permeated by the conviction that things bear a natural purpose and accomplish a goal that is set for them by their very nature, we must identify the central and generative focus of the teleology realized in uncleanness or sanctification. So we ask ourselves, Who matters, who makes a difference? The answer, repeated in one sector of the Halakhah after another, is, only the Israelite. It is his or her life force that comes under scrutiny. It is that life force, that blood, that accomplishing its teleology procreates life and yields a minor form of uncleanness, but, not accomplishing its teleology, is deemed analogous to the departing soul. What does it take to constitute an animate source of uncleanness, affecting the Israelite household, when it comes to the sexual organs? The first and most important consideration is, only Israelites produce flux capable of effecting contamination under the laws of *Zabim*.

And this returns us to our starting point: *gentiles do not*. The Halakhah of *Niddah* makes that point explicit. Their body fluids contaminate under other rubrics of uncleanness, but in general they contaminate like corpses and not like animate beings. They, their persons, their body fluids, their land—all represent a realm of undifferentiated death, contrasting with the highly differentiated life attaching to holy Israel. In the articulation of the Halakhah of animate sources of uncleanness, therefore, we see the consequence of the basic problem, the generative tension of the Oral Torah, with its conviction about the sanctification and sanctity of the Israelite household in the model of the holy temple. Once issues of sanctification encompass not only the family and genealogy, but also the bed and the table, procreation and sustenance of life, then those who keep the entire Torah, Oral and Written, have to work out those governing patterns of behavior that will guide toward the realization of sanctification and the preservation of sanctity. Such patterns then order and regularize relationships between the cultically clean and the cultically unclean, specifying the causes and consequences of contamination.

Through the laws of animate sources of uncleanness covering *Niddah*, *Zabim*, and *Nega'im*, the Oral Torah explicitly declares its focus, the point of attentiveness: the conduct of the observant living among non-observant Israel. All Israel is holy, but only part of Israel maintains its condition of cleanness in preservation of sanctification. All Israel may contract uncleanness. Then that part of Israel that, at a given moment, is cultically clean must take heed of that part that is not—and so too, the cultically unclean Israelite has to protect the contrary condition of the clean one. What the Oral Torah then brings about is a state of perpetual awareness between and among Israelites—who alone contract cultic uncleanness and who alone enter the condition of cultic cleanness. To state matters simply, within the Oral Torah, while Israel is vastly differentiated, everybody else falls into an undifferentiated state, one that is altogether beyond the limits of sanctification.

Intentionality plays no role in the capacity to transmit uncleanness imputed to the animate beings; the corpse transmits uncleanness *ex opere operato*, from the moment of death, about which the deceased was not consulted, and so too the menstruating woman, man afflicted with flux or the *zab*, and the woman or the *zabah* afflicted with flux outside of her regular period, effect uncleanness willy-nilly. The woman's period does not depend upon her intentionality. And, equally probatively, the Oral Torah lays great stress that the flux of the *zab* and the *zabah* that bears the power to contaminate—semen from the one, blood from the other—make its appearance on its own. The blood or semen must come about without the connivance of the afflicted party. The teleological principle that permeates the whole underscores the exclusion of man's or woman's will.

And that leads us to the very heart of the Halakhah of *Zabim*: the analogy to death. Why does the Halakhah defining sources of uncleanness exclude all consideration of the attitude or intentionality of the animate being, the man or woman, who becomes a source of uncleanness? Because of the governing analogy, death. We die willy-nilly, neither by intention nor by plan, and to death our attitude is null. What by its nature compares with death also contaminates like death, which comes whether or not it is wanted. Then the details of the law flow from the natural teleology that governs: excretions of the sexual organs that by their nature cannot procreate life affect objects used in that process, and that is accomplished by means of activities analogous to the sexual act or integral thereto: *zob* or semen from a flaccid penis affect beds and like objects through pressure.

The entire system of cultic cleanness in the household envelops the table and the bed for one and the same reason. Uncleanness attended to, cleanness attained, all media of restoration of cleanness, Israel's natural condition, set the household of Israel en route to sancti-fication. That is a condition localized in the temple down below, matched by heaven up above, realized by the household here and now, actualized in Eden then and there. And these terms invoke no ineffable abstractions, but, we must constantly recall, where life and death contend. That is within the concrete activities of procreating and nourishing life that routinely take place in bed and at table, respectively.

II. The Contest between Death and Life, Uncleanness and Sanctification: [2] The Locus of the Struggle for Life

When Scripture defines sources of uncleanness, it is to protect from death and for life the camp of Israel, which sages understand to refer to the temple and its altar, and the Israelite household by analogy thereto. In the temple what is at stake is nourishing God through the offerings, and nourishing the priesthood through their share of the offerings to God. Any analogy built upon the temple will therefore focus upon how nourishment is carried on, and within that govern-ing analogy, the temple's rules of how food is preserved for the altar and the priests and how it is rendered unsuitable for them will take center stage.

But the altar is not the only locus of life against death. Just as God's altar is to be kept free of uncleanness, so too is the Israelite table. And so too the bed, for the act of procreation is explicitly identified as one to be protected from uncleanness and also a source of uncleanness, so Lev. 15. In that way the Halakhah places the household upon a continuum of sanctification with the temple. In light of the character of the forces of uncleanness, choosing nourishment alongside procreation as the principal occasion for acting out the sanctification of the household in the model of the temple presents no surprise.

How does the Halakhah place the household of holy Israel in the holy land upon the same continuum as the temple? This it does by providing rules for cultic cleanness and uncleanness in the temple and among the priests—in connection with preparation of secular food for the household at home. Food, together with the pots and pans and other utensils used in connection with preparing and eating it, and, by extension, the other domestic furniture of the household, is explicitly placed upon that continuum when the food is prepared in accord with the rules of cleanness that pertain to the altar and the temple in Jerusalem. Food and its appurtenances, broadly construed, then may be removed from the status of cleanness, within the hierarchical framework of sanctification, and plunged into the status of uncleanness, by exactly those same sources of uncleanness that render a priest or an offering unclean and unfit for the sanctity of the temple altar and courtyard. So along with the desacralization of the bed, more broadly, of the household, at the point of sanctification of the union of husband and wife, food for the domestic table may lose its position on the continuum of cleanness and holiness that observance of the rules of cultic cleanness may accord to it.

That continuum that accommodates the household in the Land of Israel in relationship, as to sanctification and uncleanness, with Jerusalem, the temple, and the courtyard with its altar, is established in an explicit way, with particular reference to the effects of sources of uncleanness. For, while sources of uncleanness affecting household and temple are not differentiated, their effects are. What is higher in the hierarchy of sanctification also is more subject to contamination in the hierarchy of sources of uncleanness. Uncleanness has a deeper effect upon the temple and its holy things than upon the priesthood and their rations, and what affects the priesthood and their rations is more virulent than what affects the household and its everyday food.

Holy Things, heave offering, ordinary food prepared in accord with the rules of sanctification of temple food—these form the descending steps of a single progression, a unitary continuum. The constant is uncleanness, the variable, the level of sanctification that is required. The more holy, the more susceptible to uncleanness—that principle is stated not only implicitly in ladders of sanctification matched by sensitivity to uncleanness, but explicitly as well.

Among the passages that differentiate the levels of uncleanness and corresponding ones of sanctification, the following proves readily accessible. It differentiates food of three levels of sanctification: ordinary ("unconsecrated") food (which the household wishes to preserve in conditions of cultic cleanness and to eat in those same conditions), food that has been designated as tithe, and food that has been designated as priestly rations or "heave offering." The first is the least holy, the third the most. Beyond that is the level of cultic cleanness required in the preparation of purification water, which does not concern us here. The basic point of importance to us is, there is a category of cleanness that pertains to unconsecrated food, not to food in the status of tithe or that in the status of heave offering (priestly rations), let alone that in the status of holy things, deriving from the Lord's altar. What that means is, people not involved in the priesthood or in eating priestly rations may prepare their food as though they were priests eating their rations.

The notion that unconsecrated food—food not set aside as priestly rations, not deriving from temple offerings (thus not heave offering, not holy things)—may be prepared in accord with the rules governing holy things, even for use at home, is expressed in so many words at M. *Toh.* 2:8B in the following language: "Unconsecrated food which is prepared in accord with the rules pertaining to Holy Things— lo, this is like consecrated food." In that matter, opinion differs: R. Eleazar b. R. Sadoq says, "Lo, it is like heave offering, conveying uncleanness at two removes and rendering unfit at one [further] remove [from the original source of uncleanness]." This is a matter to which we return when we consider the Halakhah of *Tohorot.* The point, for the present context, is self-evident. First, the Israelite may by an act of intentionality observe the rules of cultic cleanness even outside of the temple. When he does so, that attitude toward secular food affects the status of said food. Food that is in the status of what is unconsecrated but preserved in conditions of cultic cleanness, or of tithe, or of heave offering or of holy things, all classes of food take a position on a single continuum of sanctification. So food prepared as if it were holy things, even though it is not, fits into the hierarchy of the holy. Here is one way in which that continuum is portrayed:

Mishnah *Hagigah* 2:5

A. [For purposes of cultic purification, it is sufficient if] they wash the hands for eating [1] unconsecrated food, [2] tithe, and [3] heave offering;

B. and for eating food in the status of [4] Holy Things [that is, food deriving from animals offered on the altar and handed over to the priest and to the sacrifier for their consumption, e.g., portions of the sin-offering assigned to the priest, portions of the peace offering reserved for the farmer and his household], it is sufficient only if they immerse;

C. and as to [5] [the preparation of] purification water [through the burning of the red cow], if one's hands are made unclean, his entire body is deemed to be unclean as well.

But the normal sequence of levels of sanctification are three: unconsecrated food, tithe, and heave offering. In the present case, if one has contracted uncleanness and immerses to rise once more to the status of cleanness, his intent in the act will govern the result. If the intent is to immerse so as to rise to the level of cleanness for eating unconsecrated food, the result serves for that but for nothing higher; if for tithe, he may eat unconsecrated food or tithe but not heave offering, and so on upward.

Mishnah *Hagigah* 2:6

A. He who immerses for the eating of unconsecrated food and is thereby confirmed as suitably clean for eating unconsecrated food is prohibited from eating tithe.

B. [If] he immersed for eating tithe and is thereby confirmed as suitable for eating tithe, he is prohibited from eating heave offering.

C. [If] he immersed for eating heave offering and is thereby confirmed as suitable for eating heave offering, he is prohibited from eating food in the status of Holy Things.

D. [If] he immersed for eating food in the status of Holy Things and is thereby confirmed as suitable for eating food in the status of Holy Things, he is prohibited from engaging in the preparation of purification water.

E. [If, however], one immersed for the matter requiring the more stringent rule, he is permitted to engage in the matter requiring the less stringent rule.

F. [If] he immersed but was not confirmed, it is as though he did not immerse.

Now we move down the ladder of uncleanness. So far as those who eat their ordinary food in a state of cleanness, the clothing of ordinary people, who do not enter the state of cultic cleanness except when they go to the temple, is deemed unclean with that form of uncleanness described at Lev. 15. For priests, the clothing of those who eat their ordinary food in a state of cleanness is equivalently unclean. For officiating priests (who eat holy things), the clothing of priests clean enough to eat heave offering is equivalently unclean.

Mishnah *Hagigah* 2:7

A. The clothing of ordinary folk is in the status of Midras uncleanness for abstainers [a.k.a., Pharisees, more generally, persons who eat unconsecrated food in a state of cultic cleanness].
B. The clothing of abstainers is in the status of Midras uncleanness for those who eat heave offering [priests].
C. The clothing of those who eat heave offering is in the status of Midras uncleanness for those who eat Holy Things [officiating priests].
D. The clothing of those who eat Holy Things is in the status of Midras uncleanness for those engaged in the preparation of purification water.

Along these same lines, the rites of purification follow an ascending sequence of points of stringency, most for holy things, less for heave offering, still less for the rest, and these are specified and will be dealt with in context:

Mishnah *Hagigah* 3:1

A. A more stringent rule applies to Holy Things than applies to heave offering,
B. for: They immerse utensils inside of other utensils for purification for use with [food in the status of] heave offering,
C. but not for purification for use with [food in the status of] Holy Things.

What is clear from this brief passage, which has a far weightier counterpart at M. *Toh.* 2:3–7, to be considered presently, is that the rules of cultic cleanness are assumed, by the Halakhah, to pertain not only to the temple and to the priests when engaged in their temple duties, but to priests outside of the temple, as Scripture specifies in connection with priestly rations, eaten by the priests' families, and, still more important, to Israelites in the households of the Land of Israel.

But in the household, what difference does cultic cleanness or uncleanness make? The Torah takes for granted that what one may not do when unclean that he may do when clean is [1] enter the temple courtyard and beyond, on the one side, and [2] eat priestly rations and holy things, on the other. One further activity is forbidden by reason of uncleanness, affecting priest and layman alike, and that is sexual relations during a woman's period and comparable times, such as is described in Lev. 15. To that given, the Oral Torah clearly adds the further expectation that people in a state of cultic uncleanness will not eat ordinary meals in the household. So, as we see, at stake throughout is the cultic cleanness in the domestic setting of the person, the food, and the utensils in which the food is prepared and served. Wherein does the Halakhah identify man's responsibility? Man cannot create uncleanness, but man by his intentionality inaugurates the processes by which what is insusceptible to uncleanness becomes susceptible; that is so both for food and for utensils. We focus first (sections A, B, C) upon food, then (section D) upon domestic objects of utility.

A. *Makhshirin*

Nature alone can produce that which contaminates, and natural action alone purifies that which is subject to purification. But man by action made consequential through his *intention renders susceptible to uncleanness* that which he values, finds useful, deems worthwhile, whether utensils or food. Specifically, human agency inaugurates the processes of contamination, so the system is activated by the work of thinking man. Man's attitude, joined to requisite action where pertinent, renders susceptible to uncleanness that which man values. Natural sources of uncleanness, natural media of purification—when it comes to food these await the pleasure of man to do their work.

We begin with susceptibility to uncleanness, the Halakhah that concerns the point at which produce becomes susceptible to uncleanness. (In due course we shall examine the counterpart, when utensils become susceptible.) Lev. 11:34, 37 are read by sages to mean that produce that is dry is insusceptible to uncleanness, but produce that has been deliberately wet down is susceptible. By contrast *Ohalot* (not to mention *Zabim* and its companions) excludes purposive man from any part in the formation of a source of uncleanness. Uncleanness comes about willy-nilly. That is by definition: the corpse is unclean because the person has died, and that is by God's will alone. So too, contaminating flux comes about only in the complete exclusion of human intentionality in the production of said flux. Now, that extreme statement of the irrelevance of human will to the generation of the most virulent forms of uncleanness finds its counterpart and opposite in the Halakhah of *Makhshirin*. That body of Halakhah forms an essay on the centrality of human intentionality in inaugurating the process by which the sources of contamination take effect upon the foci and loci of contamination: the persons, things, and locations that can be affected by uncleanness.

The notion that food that is dry is insusceptible to uncleanness, but food that is wet is susceptible, cannot puzzle sages. They understand corpse-uncleanness as a viscous liquid that flows in the dimensions of a square handbreadth. If corpse-uncleanness is the model of other uncleanness, then sages will deem quite routine the notion that uncleanness of other classifications, e.g., that which exudes from the dead creeping thing, will correspond. Now, it is to what is wet that that same viscous liquid flows, so it would seem. We recall the concrete matter of the preparation of dough for bread, with special attention to the point at which the dough becomes liable to dough offering (*Hallah*). It is in particular when the householder adds water to the mixture of flour and yeast that the dough becomes liable. Why is that the case? When the householder adds water, the process of kneading dough to bake bread commences. With the irrigation of the yeast and the dough, the moment at which the dough congeals and the yeast buds and ferments, producing its sugar, its carbon dioxide, and its ethanol—at that exact moment, the instant of animation, at which the bread begins to live, the householder goes on the alert for dangers to the bread—and so throughout. So the case of the point of susceptibility of dough to dough offering captures the governing theory: when man takes what is inert and imposes upon it his will for nourishment, when he acts purposefully to begin the process of creating food, then he must alert himself to protecting his food from the effects of death, however attenuated (e.g., from dead creeping things, representing metaphorizations of the serpent as corpse).

So quite understandably in a cuisine based on bread (not potatoes, not rice, for example) what is at stake in "wetting down seed," based on the analogy of adding water to dry flour and yeast, is the point at which vegetation begins the process by which it becomes maximally edible and useful to the householder. That explains why the householder goes on the alert at the point at which he intentionally puts water on the dough. Then—life bubbling up in the process of fermentation, deliberately inaugurated—the state of sanctification comes under threat from the source of uncleanness, such as corpse-uncleanness and its analogues, that the Torah has identified.

But what has all this to do with man's intentionality? Sages take as fact that if produce is wet down by man's deliberate action, that is, by an informed intentionality confirmed by a concrete deed, then it is susceptible to uncleanness. At that point man's active engagement with the food is, or should be, precipitated. It is unthinkable, in the Halakhic system, that man should produce food without concern for its cleanness. But what if produce is wet down naturally, on the one side, or by some action not initiated by man, on the other? Then the produce is not rendered susceptible to uncleanness—even though it is wet. For its physical condition on its own does not classify it as to status (unclean/clean), only its condition relative to man's will, permeating and transforming the material world as it does.

Then the Halakhah of *Makhshirin* will find its problematics in the nature and meaning of intentionality, and problem after problem will explore the concrete implications of conflicting positions on one issue: is intentionality without action effective, or do we require a deed to confirm the attitude that we impute to a person? Then the state of sanctification, which inheres and is normal for the Israelite household, comes under threat from the source of uncleanness, such as corpse-uncleanness and its analogues, that the Torah has identified. The moment of wetting grain down defines the hour of conflict between life and death—and this in concrete ways. No wonder that, at the very time, the act done with deliberation precipitates the conflict. But that is only if the householder cares. If the householder does not intend the dough to congeal and the yeast to rise, nothing of consequence happens. It is the Israelite's will and intention and the act that realizes them that endow with consequence what by nature happens willy-nilly.

The really critical and generative question asks about the relationship of action to intentionality. At issue is the relationship between what one has brought about and how one bears responsibility for the consequences of one's actions—the paramount issue of the civil law and its politics too. Do we decide on the basis of what one has done the character of his prior intention, that is, of what he intended to do? If I take up water in order to pour it out, does my ultimate action in pouring out the water govern the interpretation of my original plan for the water? If it does, then even though for a time I might have wanted the water in its present location, by my final disposition of the water, I have defined that original intention and determined that the water never was wanted; therefore, retrospectively it does not impart susceptibility to uncleanness. We have a variety of positions. The first is [1] intention without action is null; [2] action is retrospectively determinative of the character of intention—we judge the intention by the result. A further view is that prior intention plays a balancing role in the interpretation of the status of the water. We do not decide solely by what one has done, by the ultimate disposition of the water. So if one's action never was intended to bring down water, the water is not utilized intentionally and does not impart susceptibility to uncleanness. Or the deed dictates the character of the intent, and the result is paramount in interpreting the means. Or what one wanted has to be balanced against what has happened. If one wants the water to fall, that is not the end of the matter; he wants it to fall in a particular place, and it falls both there and elsewhere; then what has served his purpose imparts susceptibility, and what does not serve one's purpose does not. What is incidental to one's main purpose is not taken into account, and that is without regard to the ultimate consequence of one's deeds. And then there is the possibility of distinguishing immediate from ultimate result, primary from subordinate outcome, and so on. The upshot of the Halakhah may be stated very simply:

[1] Liquids impart susceptibility to uncleanness only if they are useful to man, drawn with approval, subject to human deliberation and intention.

[2] Liquids that can impart susceptibility to uncleanness do so only if they serve a person's purpose, are deliberately applied to produce, irrigate something through human deliberation and intention.

What then does the Halakhah say about the sacralization and desacralization of the household? It introduces the notion that the householder bears responsibility in a realm of reality other than the interpersonal, the concrete, and the material. The household finds its definition, also, in the formation of an intangible world, an impalpable reality of analogies and metaphors, to which the householder and every person in his ménage must remain sentient. The issue is not righteousness and goodness, as the written Torah commands, but sanctification and aspiration to form a sanctuary. Moral acts of restraint—self-abnegation, abstinence, not of aggression through murder or overreaching—these find their counterpart in cultic acts of perpetual alertness for what can contaminate the holy. Preserving the cultic purity of food, including clothing and utensils, so that the household may take its place upon that continuum that the indelible sanctification of holy Israel establishes by its very presence, defines what is at stake. Remembering what one has done and what has happened, remaining ever alert to the dangers of pollution and the opportunities of sanctification represented by one's own restraint— these underscore one's obligation and shape one's attitude. Noting well one's own intentions and acting in full responsibility therefore— these constitute the counterpart to the moral imperatives.

When life renews itself through the deliberate, life-precipitating touch of water, that is the point that precipitates concern with the forces of death. Then, to preserve purity, Israel goes on the alert for the danger of pollution—at the moment when yeast, flour, and water ignite the processes of animation. So, too, for all of their counterparts: if water be put on the seed, take care. The dough congeals, the yeast ferments and yields gas, and so, life-processes having commenced, death and its surrogates threaten. Then the householder goes on the alert—if he cares, if by an act of deliberation he has made life happen. But that consideration—that the householder care—makes all the difference. Only then does the Eternal intersect with the temporal, the finite, and the transient, the life of man in the ongoing processes of sustenance.

B. *Tohorot*

Called "purities," generically, the Halakhah of *Tohorot* covers four topics that correlate:

[1] fathers and offspring of uncleanness;

[2] removes of uncleanness, from the original source, and the affect of what is made unclean at one or more removes upon food in various degrees of sanctification;

[3] matters of doubt in connection with the uncleanness of food and utensils, and principles for their resolution;

[4] relationships between those who keep the purity laws within the domestic household and those who do not, and how ambiguities are resolved in that connection.

The Halakhah of *Tohorot* addresses the topic of the uncleanness affecting food and drink, offering some large-scale generalizations and—for the shank of the topic—a set of guidelines on how to resolve cases in which the status of food as to uncleanness is subject to doubt. The matter of doubt further encompasses relationships between those who at home for the domestic table keep the cleanness laws and Israelites who do not keep those laws and hence are subject to cultic uncleanness. Since day-to-day relationships are assumed to be close and constant, the issue arises: how to sort out cases in which such an outsider—called in Hebrew *'am ha'ares*, someone who does not tithe meticulously or eat his household meals in a state of cultic cleanness (M. *Dem.* 2:2–3)—has had access to the things belonging to an observant person and, in the status of a person afflicted with flux (*zab*), imparts uncleanness to what he touches, called in Hebrew *haber* (variously defined, but at a minimum, one who tithes meticulously and preserves cultic cleanness in household meals), and therefore may or may not have imparted cultic uncleanness.

Sages contemplate an intangible world of confusion between and among classes of things and persons that are both alike and not alike: things that may contract uncleanness but also attain sanctification; sources of uncleanness; things that may be unclean or clean; persons who are Israelites all together, but who may or may not keep certain laws of the Torah. What the Halakhah accomplishes in each case is to identify things that are to begin with alike—that stand along a single continuum, that bear traits in common—but that also exhibit differentiating qualities. Extrapolating from cases, the Halakhah then offers the governing rules that sort out these mixtures of things that are both alike and unlike. The Halakhah tells us how to differentiate the unlike among the like, so to sort out confusion and clarify the categories that pertain. Take the categories one by one. Sources of uncleanness form a single classification; but we differentiate between the primary source and removes therefrom. That is, we follow successive contacts: the source, what has touched the source, what has touched what has touched the source, and so on into the outer reaches of imagination. Thus, in philosophical terms, we distinguish what is primary from what is secondary and derivative, that is, between efficient and proximate causes.

And again, sources of uncleanness form one category, but some sources are more virulent than others, that is to say, some sources of uncleanness produce powerful and long-lasting effects, others limited and transient ones; some affect many things, others only a few; some transmit uncleanness only if touched, others when overshadowed, or when carried even though not touched, and so on. The two points of engagement—removes, fathers/offspring—clearly correspond, as we move from the source of uncleanness through the successive removes, and from the father of uncleanness through the diminishing effects of the offspring thereof. So much for differentiating between sources of uncleanness and among their effects, a labor of identifying the lines of order and structure that separate uncleanness from uncleanness and differentiate their effects upon food and drink and clothing at various levels of sanctification: this affects that, but not the other thing; this is affected by that, but not the other thing.

What about what is affected by sources of uncleanness? That question carries us from corpses, spit, and blood of certain origin to food, drink, and human beings. The third subdivision of the Halakhah involves food and drink, the fourth, persons. In both cases we confront the same problem: how to deal with doubt as to the status, in respect to uncleanness, of food and drink, on the one side, and persons, on the other. What persons, food, and utensils have in common is that all may be made unclean, but, from the perspective of the Halakhah, they also may attain cultic cleanness, and, in the setting of the household as much as the temple, ought to. That with which we have to reckon, then, is whether in an unguarded moment they have contracted uncleanness.

Now to consider in more general terms the matter of resolving doubt. We resolve doubt as to the classification of food and drink by appeal to a variety of probabilities. It is more probable that the status quo has prevailed than that it has not; it is more probable that what is dragged, and so can touch something, has touched the thing than that what is tossed, and so cannot touch, has made contact. Common sense about the more or the less probable, however, is joined to certain principles that appear to be arbitrary. Because we want the householder to maintain a high state of alertness concerning sources of uncleanness, we declare that cases of doubt in private property are treated as unclean. Because the public domain contains many imponderables and cannot be closed off to the faithful, we declare cases of doubt in public property to be treated as clean.

Now that position is counter-intuitive, since in the public domain circulate gentiles, whose persons and secretions are by definition unclean, as well as Israelites who do not keep this aspect of the Halakhah. And, given the distractions of crowds, one is more likely there than in private domain to step on unclean spit or urine deriving from gentiles. And who is to know the "history" of an object— what the one who touched it has touched, and what that has touched, backward for however many removes from the initial source of uncleanness? Reason therefore suggests that a case of doubt in public domain should be resolved in favor of uncleanness, and in private, cleanness. So here the system concerns itself with its larger goal— sanctifying the household and its table—and mitigates its more extreme possibilities. Where people can and should take care, they are held to a high standard. Where circumstances make difficult a constant state of alertness amid a barrage of occasions for contamination, they are not.

So much for food, drink, and utensils. What about persons? Here we classify the category of Israelites, differentiating the *haber* from the *'am ha'ares*, that is, those who prepare their ordinary food as though it were heave offering or holy things from those who do not. The former take care either not to contract uncleanness or to remove its effects through immersion. The latter do not. Then how do the two classes of Israelites interact, and, more to the point, how do the ones who keep the purity laws determine the status of their persons and property that has been subject to the disposition of those who do not keep those laws? Here again, as we have seen, a few comprehensive principles accommodate the cases and problems at hand; these have already been specified.

What is at issue? Viewed from one perspective, the philosophical, it is how to differentiate the species of a given genus: on the side of contamination, source of uncleanness from removes, father from offspring; on the side of sanctification, what is subject to uncleanness of one virulence, what to another; what food or drink may or may not have contracted uncleanness; what Israelites may or may not have imparted uncleanness under specified circumstances of indeterminacy. Viewed from another perspective, the theological, we deal with a variety of persons and objects that have had each its own "history." Each must tell its own story, but the chapters are the same: is the person or object, food or drink, to be classified as unclean or clean? To answer that question, I need to know the following:

[1] the level of sanctification for which the cleanness is required (how the person, object, food, or drink has been subject to surveillance over time);

[2] the character of the uncleanness to which the person or food may or may not have been exposed, primary or secondary, and the number of removes from exposure to that source at which the person or food stands: immediate contact, once-removed, and so on outward;

[3] in what location (public, private domain), in what season (dry or rainy), and within what sort of transaction the exposure is supposed to have taken place or not taken place;

[4] what sort of instructions, conditions, and rules were articulated to the parties who may or may not have imparted uncleanness by touching the food or drink or utensils that are subject to doubt.

In reaching a decision on how to classify a person, object, food, or drink, each of these questions requires an answer, and at every stage in the process of interrogation, we have to reconstruct the story of what has happened to this person, object, food, or drink in the context established by the inquiry into the status that pertains. And, having come this far, we realize what holds the whole together: the four principal parts of the Halakhah before us contribute to the single, sustained narrative that encompasses the person or object, the food or drink, and that determines the taxonomic outcome of the process. The narrative tells us what things the person or object has touched, what things those things have touched, and so on through a sequence of removes; and it further tells us the status imputed to the food or drink (or, as we noted just now, in line with Halakhah of *Hagigah*, the person) by the attitude and intentionality of the principal player in the drama, the person affected by the considerations at hand: uncleanness at the one side, sanctification at the other. All of this, amplified by the consideration of removes, forms a small narrative of a cosmic transaction.

So much for the unfolding of a single coherent account, a sequence of facts concerning intangibles to make sense of which we have invoked the metaphor of history: the tale of sequential and coherent events, each of which causes the next in the chain of happenings that leads to the final decision. But the components of the Halakhah hold together in a more intimate connection as well. Each component turns out to appeal, in the end, to a consideration that operates for them all, and, by this point in the exposition it is scarcely necessary to say, that is intentionality. In this unseen world the impalpable force of the attitude of responsible actors makes its impact everywhere. Uncleanness is relative to that which it affects, and the sensitivity to uncleanness of that which is affected by uncleanness depends upon the status imputed by man's will.

Stated simply: if man assigns food or drink to the status of holy things and so acts as to preserve the cleanness of what is sanctified in that status, then the sources of uncleanness affect the food or drink through successive removes, as many as three (*Parah* will add yet another, as we shall see later on). If man's intentionality does not impart to the food or drink the standing of holy things but of ordinary, secular food or drink, then fewer removes from the source of uncleanness produce effects. It is the initial decision and attitude of man that make the difference. If man is alert and capable of forming intentionality, if man can be interrogated in the assumption that he cares about contamination, then the rules of contamination are strictly enforced; if not, then they are null. A child cannot form an intention to preserve cleanness and, therefore, in a case of doubt, he also cannot be assumed to have imparted uncleanness. The *'am ha'ares* is assumed to touch whatever he can reach—unless he is instructed not to. Then his intentionality, to respect the wishes of the householder, is assumed to pertain and therefore to protect from uncleanness what the *'am ha'ares* can have touched but probably did not contaminate at all. At the critical turnings in the decision-making process, the taxonomic question finds its answer in the relativities of attitude and intention.

But one matter is not subject to the decision-making process of man, and one component of the system, one chapter of the narrative, does not find its dynamics in human will. That is the sources of uncleanness. These do function *ex opere operato* and do not depend upon man's will for them to bring about contamination. On the contrary, the corpse contaminates whatever is in the tent that overshadows it, and the contaminating power of flux (*zob*) depends upon its emerging naturally and not by artificial stimulus. That same insistence on the inexorability of the workings of sources of contamination emerges in the consideration of the distinction between fathers and offspring of uncleanness; at no point in that corpus of Halakhah do considerations of attitude intervene.

So when we contemplate the Israelite household as the Halakhah portrays it, we see a space marked off in three ways:

by [1] the family sanctified by reason of its descent from the holy seed of the patriarchs and by its avoidance of the improper marital relationships spelled out in the Written Torah,

which acts [2] on specified occasions of sacred time to sanctify the household by words and deeds and acts of restraint from deeds,

and which further acts [3] to preserve the cultic cleanness, therefore the potential sanctification, of the food and drink consumed in the household, and, consequently, to avoid cultic contamination of the clothing and utensils of those that live there.

Then what is the given and what marks change? The Halakhah rests on the foundations of a single condition: Israel is holy, wherever located. That is its natural condition. What removes Israel from its status as sanctified is unnatural to Israel, but a given of the world. Sanctification is the established condition for family and property (food, drink, clothing, utensils). What removes the family, its food, drink, clothing, and utensils from the status of sanctification interferes with what ought to be natural. Sources of uncleanness also come about by nature; sages adhere rigidly to the definition of those sources that Scripture establishes and do not add a single new source or extend an existing source in any consequential way.

Now we see the context in which the texts that invoke intentionality find their place, the reason that the entire system treats cleanness and sanctification, or uncleanness and desacralization, as relative to the Israelite's attitude and will. What the Israelite values as food receives or conveys uncleanness as food. What he does not value does not contract or transmit uncleanness. Only that to which an Israelite to begin with pays attention counts for anything in the system of watchfulness with which we deal. What the Israelite values as a useful utensil may contract uncleanness. What the Israelite deems an essential part of a piece of fruit or vegetable is integral to the fruit or vegetable, adds to its volume, contracts from, or transmits to, the fruit or vegetable such uncleanness as takes effect. What the Israelite holds inedible or disgusting even for dog food does not contract uncleanness as food. When the Israelite subjects to the cleanness regulations of consecrated food what is merely everyday edibles, the rules of consecrated food pertain—even though the substance of the food is unchanged. In these and numerous other details the relativity of all things to intentionality comes to full and rich instantiation. So the Halakhah manages to say the same thing about many things.

C. *'Uqsin*

The primacy of intentionality over material actualities in the status of the components of produce—are they integral or extrinsic, connected or deemed distinct?—comes to expression not only in detail but also explicitly. Here is one such statement: Olives which one pickled with their leaves—the leaves are insusceptible to uncleanness, for one pickled them only for appearance sake. If one changes the physical form of produce, chopping it up for cooking, it is deemed not connected; its form has changed. But if one had the intention not to cook the produce but to pickle or seethe or place it on the table, it remains connected. The form is the same; the intention is what changes the matter. But intentionality can change, and, as with documents, so here too, sages want an action to confirm the intention. If one wants the marrow of a bone, that does not change the status of the marrow—it is connected to the bone. Only when one has crushed the bone to get at the marrow has the intention of taking the marrow been confirmed; then it is not connected.

Certainly the most fecund statement of intentionality comes at the end. To understand the statement, we recall that what requires intention is food not usually consumed by human beings, and what does not is food people naturally eat. Now, there are things which require preparation to be made susceptible to uncleanness but do not require intention, intention and preparation, intention and no preparation, neither intention nor preparation. That familiar mode of schematization of matters yields profound judgments. First comes the main one: All edible foods which are designated for use by man require preparation but do not require intention. "Do not require intention" means, these are foods that the generality of humanity deems edible. They therefore fall into the class of food for purposes of contracting uncleanness, whatever a given individual may have in mind. But they have to be prepared as food for the generality of intentionality to take effect. By contrast to what? Meat. To be classified as food, meat must be prepared for eating. Not only so, but whatever its source, whatever its status, for it to be deemed food man must intend that it serve as food; we do not take for granted that meat is food unless man means to eat it (and then by deed confirms that intentionality). Placing perfectly valid meat, from a beast or fowl, in the same class with meat that Israelites cannot eat, e.g., carrion, fat that may be forbidden, and the like makes a striking statement. It is that eating meat is not done by nature, in the way in which eating fruits and vegetables is—there, intentionality is not required—but always subject to a particular decision on man's part. We recall that the matter of intentionality carries with it the ongoing reflection on when action is required to confirm intention. Here are the contending views:

Mishnah 'Uqsin 3:12

A. Honeycombs—from what point are they [is the honey-liquid] susceptible to uncleanness as liquid?
B. The House of Shammai say, "When one will smoke out [the bees therefrom]."
C. And the House of Hillel say, "When one will have broken [the honeycombs to remove the honey]."

Liquid is susceptible to uncleanness when it is wanted, that is, when it serves man's purposes, and it is not susceptible to uncleanness when man does not regard it as bearing consequence.

What is at stake here? The important question is, is liquid deliberately applied to produce? Then dry produce, insusceptible to uncleanness, has been deliberately wet down, and because of man's deliberate action has been brought into the system of uncleanness and rendered susceptible. The subsidiary point that is clarified here concerns when man's intentionality takes effect. When the beekeeper smokes out the bees from the honeycombs, he exhibits his intentionality of taking and using the honey. So that is the point at which susceptibility to receive uncleanness affects the liquid honey, or, in the correct context, it is the point at which the honey, if applied to dry produce, imparts to the produce that puissant moisture that imparts susceptibility—that is to say, liquid deliberately put onto the produce. So far as the house of Shammai are concerned, therefore, a secondary cause (smoking out the bees) serves as readily as a primary cause (actually breaking the honeycombs). But the house of Hillel insists, and the Halakhah with them, that one actually must have carried out an action that directly confirms the intentionality. Secondary causation does not suffice; primary causation is required. Here the religious issue—how do we sort out the intentions of man as Heaven responds to those intentions— joins together with the Aristotelian-philosophical one—how do we classify types of causality, efficient versus secondary and derivative— to produce the Halakhah at hand. The position of the Halakhah about the character of man cannot be missed: whatever they intend or say, wait to see what they do—as in Eden, before and after the fall.

D. *Kelim*

The Halakhah of *Kelim* affirms the centrality of human intentionality: only deliberate action by man renders a utensil or food susceptible to uncleanness. As to *kelim*, susceptibility to uncleanness by human agency is imparted to what is whole, complete, and useful. Not only is the space demarcated by the household sanctified, and so too are objects used for domestic purposes. These are subject to considerations of uncleanness. But what is susceptible to becoming unclean by reason of the Levitical sources of uncleanness specified at Lev. 11–15 and Num. 19 also serves for sacred purposes. That point is explicit in Scripture—contracting uncleanness makes a difference because what is unclean cannot be utilized in the temple and its offerings or by the priests when they consume priestly rations. So we deal with the paired opposites, uncleanness and sanctification. Since what is susceptible forms the topic of the Halakhah of *Kelim*, at stake here too is uncleanness and sanctification—but now not in the temple or among the priests in their sacerdotal role and rite, but in the household, at the domestic table.

The topical program of the Halakhah leaves no doubt whatsoever of the household venue of the laws. Here we deal in rich detail with what domestic utensils are susceptible to uncleanness—when, in the process of making them, they enter the status of susceptibility, and when, in the process of breaking them, they leave that same status. Through the principles at hand, the Halakhah will make a profound statement on the power of man's intentionality, a statement no less explicit and decisive than the one affecting the status of sanctification of a woman to a man. Here the governing criterion is the use to which a given utensil is put, and man's assessment of the utensil's functionality. Constant reference, therefore, invokes the attitude, plan, program or intention, that man forms with regard to the object under discussion.

Whether or not sanctity inheres, uncleanness is relative, contextual, dependent upon matters of will and attitude. Perhaps matters begin with the principle of Scripture that what is useless is insusceptible or clean (as the case may be), which the Halakhah then amplifies: Who defines usefulness, and how do we know? And from that humble question a path is opened for the entry of the entire matter of intentionality, how one proposes to use an object, whether the attitude of one is the same as that of the other, or whether we take account only of individual preference. How the form of a utensil governs its usefulness, without respect to the plans of the user of the vessel? and on and on. The Halakhah explicitly and repeatedly insists that uncleanness does not inhere in things and is not an absolute and intrinsic, material trait, but rather a matter of status imputed by man himself.

The status of utensils as to whether or not they can receive uncleanness is relative to the form of materials imparted by man and the use of materials decided by man; the attitude and intentionality of man, confirmed by his actions. Time and again masses of details make a single point: what man finds useful, what serves man's principal purpose and carries out his generative initiative, marks the materials, that is, the object that they form, as susceptible to uncleanness. So if the materials are located in a tent of a corpse, they can receive and retain the uncleanness exuding from the corpse. And what man deems negligible and of no account is useless and insusceptible. Materials located in a tent of a corpse that man has not formed into something of which he takes do not receive uncleanness.

So it is man who decides whether the entire system of cultic cleanness pertains or does not pertain. Because the householder has chosen to treat his food at home as though it were holy things on the altar—

thus to conduct his household as though it were the temple, imposing the laws of cultic cleanness of the altar on his table, the entire system of uncleanness *and its counterpart structure of sanctification* comes into
play. The householder immerses to remove such uncleanness as he
has contracted—then eats unconsecrated food. The Halakhah we
have noted at M. *Hag.* 2:6 explicitly states that then he is suitably
clean for eating unconsecrated food. But that does not place him into
that higher level of sanctification required for eating priestly rations.
If he is a priest and permitted to eat heave offering, he still has to
immerse with the intention of eating heave offering, and so on
upward. The intentionality as to immersion then takes over and
determines the status, as to sanctification, of the man who has
immersed on account of uncleanness. The rules that determine
sources of uncleanness, the things affected by uncleanness, and the
mode of sanctification do not shift; the utensils that are susceptible
are susceptible to uncleanness without differentiation as to the use to
which those utensils are to be put. Immersion for cleanness, en route
to sanctification, is done in the same way for the eating of unconsecrated food, heave offering, and holy things. What differentiates, so
far as cleanness is concerned? Not the action but the attitude.

If I had to identify the single emblematic detail of the Halakhah
concerning utensils, it is the stress on usefulness and functionality as
criteria for entry into, or leaving, the system that leads from profound
uncleanness and distance from the holy of holies to the highest level
of sanctification at the altar itself. The broken secular utensil that has
contracted uncleanness is clean, meaning, it has lost the uncleanness
that afflicted it and is no longer party to the system of contamination
at all. The whole utensil, which serves its normal function, is party to
the same system. The broken holy utensil likewise leaves the system
of sanctification, as we have noted. And when we realize that, in so
many words, the Halakhah states that the system of uncleanness corresponds to, and matches, the system of sanctification, so that what is
more sensitive to uncleanness also is more susceptible of sanctification, we recognize what is at stake. What can attain a higher level of
sanctification also is more susceptible to uncleanness, more sensitive
at more removes from the original source, than what attains only a
lower level of sanctification.

Intentionality expressed in an assessment of what is useful and what is not useful is not the only variable. We further distinguish among various materials, each possessing its own indicative characteristics. We also differentiate parts of utensils, primary and secondary. And, finally, we do not depend upon individual whim in classifying objects as to their status of uncleanness or cleanness; we also introduce two further considerations. First, we impose the governing expectation, the general and broadly held attitude, upon the idiosyncrasy of the individual. Second, we recognize that people may change their minds, so when a person deems an object useless, we want some evidence in actuality that he has so treated the object as to render it what he holds it to be. Actuality must confirm intentionality. Within these few considerations that pervade the law and define the character of the details, everything is made to set forth a single coherent statement.

A motif throughout concerns man's intentionality for a given object. As we often note, the Tosefta states matters with power: All utensils descend to their uncleanness with mere intention, but do not ascend from their uncleanness without an act that changes them. But the Mishnah competes in clarity: In any situation involving leather in which no part of the work is lacking, intention renders unclean. And in any situation in which there is work lacking, intention does not render unclean. That is to say, when man deems the object useful, even if he has not made use of it, his intentionality suffices to impart to the object the status of susceptibility to uncleanness. But if an object is deemed useful, then the determination no longer to use it must be confirmed by a concrete action, e.g., breaking off a part, or unlacing a laced bag or removing the laces altogether, and the like. Time and again the Halakhah deems the point at which an object enters or leaves the status of susceptibility to be dictated by the point at which an object becomes or ceases to be useful. But functionality in the end depends upon man's attitude, the purpose for which he makes and values an object. When an object accomplishes man's primary purpose for it, it is susceptible. When it ceases to accomplish his principal goal, it loses susceptibility. And a subsidiary or subordinate use does not affect matters.

Not only so, but time and again the point at which an object accomplishes, or ceases to accomplish, man's intentionality for it marks the shift. And that may mean, man himself has to express the intentionality to use an otherwise-undistinguished object; when he deems the formless block to serve as a chair, that may or may not suffice. Some opinion wants an action to confirm the intentionality, some suffice with the transformation effected by attitude alone. The language that is used is "will give thought." *'Uqsin* has shown us the identical conception, that a natural substance that is not ordinarily used for food may or may not serve as food, depending upon the attitude of man; that is what affects the classification of the natural subject, one way or the other. If man regards the natural substance as food, then his intentionality classifies the substance as susceptible to uncleanness affecting food.

The upshot is simple. Intentionality governs where man's attitude makes a difference. But what comes about naturally, by God's arrangement of matters, does not enter the purview of man's intentionality or attitude. The lesson of *Kelim* is clear. What man values can be sanctified and therefore also can be made unclean by sources of contamination that otherwise affect only the cult. It is by an act of will that holy Israel, living in the Land of Israel, transforms itself into a kingdom of priests and a holy people, and its food into priestly rations. All that ordinary Israel has to undertake to sanctify the household and its table is to pay attention to those matters that, to begin with, God has identified as matters of cultic concern. Since the written Torah makes explicit that these do constitute matters of concern to God, the point is simple: when Israel cares what God cares for, Israel under the specified conditions and in the indicated circumstances acts like God, because Israel shares God's attitudes, as God is represented in the Aggadah as sharing Israel's emotions.

So much for the contest between death and life. How are matters to be resolved, meaning, how is the status of cleanness to be restored to that which is reparable and subject to restoration to its natural condition as God made it in creation? To the media for overcoming death—which prove to be in large measure precisely the media that impart susceptibility thereto—we now turn.

III. OVERCOMING DEATH: RITES OF PURIFICATION

From death and its affect upon food and drink, that is, the uncleanness caused by, and analogous to, death, we turn to the media for the restoration of cleanness, that is, to life. Water of various classifications removes uncleanness of diverse kinds from liquids, persons, and utensils, subject to a range of conditions. The role that the deliberate application of water plays in inaugurating the process of susceptibility to uncleanness finds its counterpart in the Halakhic program for the removal of uncleanness, which requires the use of water unaffected by human will. In general, the rule that the water must be subject to human will, intention, and activity, so that liquid must be deliberately put on produce to render it susceptible to uncleanness is matched by the opposite. For water effectively to remove uncleanness, it must collect naturally and not through human intervention. That, as we shall see, defines the kind of water collected in an immersion pool, immersion in which serves to inaugurate the process of purification from uncleanness.

But that same process of analogical-contrastive reasoning, producing a dialectic of opposites—deliberate imposition of susceptibility to uncleanness by human will matched by the removal of uncleanness by water unaffected by human intervention—also registers in the exceptional case of water that serves to remove corpse-uncleanness itself. To understand what is different, we have to know that most other classifications of uncleanness are overcome by still water, naturally collected, as we shall see in part three of this chapter. By contrast, the water that removes corpse-uncleanness must be gathered deliberately, in a useful vessel, the whole subject to a high level of intentionality. Preparation of that water requires the highest degree of human alertness and intervention. Corpse-uncleanness comes about willy-nilly, but removal of the same demands the exact opposite, total engagement in the process. That ultimate act of purification of the ultimate source of uncleanness defines our starting point.

A. *Parah*

Acute intentionality alone will make possible the preparation of purification water for the removal of corpse-uncleanness. Why should that be so? The reason is that man by an act of rebellion brought death to the world. Man by an act of high consciousness creates the purification water that removes the uncleanness he has caused by his willfulness. That is why we begin with the archetypal uncleanness, that of the corpse. In line with Scripture (Num. 19:1ff.), the uncleanness of the soul—corpse-uncleanness—is removed in a unique way. Scripture defines a distinctive process of purification from corpse-uncleanness in particular. This it does by providing for the preparation of purification water, a mixture of the ashes of a red cow and water, and for the application of that water upon a person or object that has suffered corpse-uncleanness. The mixture is applied on the third and seventh days after contamination, and on the seventh day the unclean person immerses and regains cleanness with the sunset.

The Halakhah recapitulates the Torah's account of the purification rite. But Scripture says little, and the Halakhah says much, about the procedures for collecting and mixing water and ash, the protection of both from uncleanness, the role of intentionality in the procedure, and the like. Moreover, Scripture's rules leave open the generative question that the Halakhah takes as the center of its program: how does a rite conducted outside of the temple courtyard ("the camp") relate to the rules governing rites conducted inside? And, at a still deeper level, the problem awaits attention: how can the mixture of ash and water that purifies derive from a rite that contaminates all of its participants, and how can that same purification water both purify the person that is made unclean by a corpse and also contaminate the person that applies the water? It should be noted that the condition of uncleanness that the rite and the utilization of its results brings about is not corpse-uncleanness, but that uncleanness that can be removed through immersion and sunset, that is, an uncleanness in the first remove from the father of uncleanness that contamination by the corpse—the father of fathers of uncleanness—imparts.

The rite of burning the red cow to produce ashes for purification water to remove corpse-uncleanness, as set forth in Scripture and amplified in the Halakhah, encompasses two paradoxes, involving the creation of cleanness out of uncleanness, and uncleanness out of cleanness. The first paradox is that it is possible to create a realm of cultic cleanness in the unclean world that lies outside the boundaries of the temple—the world of death. This is expressed in the proposition that the cow is burned outside of the camp, that is to say, outside of the temple, in an unclean place. Its blood is tossed not on the altar but in the direction of the altar, toward the front of the tent of meeting. Then the cow is burned outside of the temple, the ashes are gathered and mixed with water, and the purification water is then prepared. So the Halakhah underscores that, in the condition of uncleanness, media for achieving cleanness from the most virulent source of uncleanness, the corpse, are to be brought into being. And the Halakhah is explicit in identifying the threat as that of corpse-uncleanness.

So in the very realm of death, media for overcoming the contamination of death are brought into being. The lesson for Israel contained within that paradox will come to our attention presently. Here it suffices to note that the highest level of cleanness is required—higher than that demanded even for eating holy things off the Lord's altar in the temple itself—from all those who are engaged in the rite. The most perfect sentience is demanded from them. Everything they see that can become unclean is deemed (for the present purpose) to be unclean. It would be difficult to state more eloquently the simple proposition that, faced with the most extreme challenges to attaining uncleanness, Israel can become cultically clean. Nor does the implicit lesson require articulation, what Israel must do to overcome death is self-evident.

The second paradox is that, even encompassing those who have gained the highest level of purification, uncleanness envelops the world, for all death is ever present. Thus those who have attained and maintained the extraordinary level of consciousness required to participate in the rite of burning the cow, collecting the ashes, gathering and transporting water, and mixing the ash and the water, as well as those who propose to utilize the purification water so brought into being—all, by virtue of their very activity in creating media of purification, are deemed unclean. They have defied death in the realm of death and overcome—but have contracted uncleanness nonetheless, indeed a paradox. They are decreed to be unclean in the remove that suffices for affecting their clothing as well, therefore requiring immersion and the setting of the sun to return to the ordinary condition of cleanness that they (presumably) enjoyed prior to entering into the work of the rite itself. So it is not corpse-uncleanness that they suffer, but uncleanness nonetheless. That is Scripture's decree, and it sets forth the paradox that out of cleanness comes the cause of uncleanness. So the upshot is, the high priest, who performs the rite involving the cow, is unclean, so too the one who burns the cow. A clean man (a priest is not specified) gathers the ashes and keeps them in a clean place outside of the temple; he too is made unclean by participation in the rite.

So, paradoxically, out of a contaminating rite comes water for purification, and, still, the one who sprinkles the purification water also becomes unclean. Now sages explore the requirements of an offering conducted outside of the temple, in a condition of uncleanness, in a place that is unclean by definition, by priests who contract uncleanness (but not corpse-uncleanness) by participating in the rite. Does that mean we impose more stringent purification rules, to create a circle of cleanness in the unclean world? Or do we impose diminished rules, taking account of the givens of the circumstance? Along these same lines, do we perform the rite exactly as we should in the temple at the altar, or do we perform the rite in exactly the opposite way, that is, as a mirror image of how it would be done in the temple? These parallel questions provoked by the twin paradoxes of Scripture's and the Halakhah's rules for the rite, respectively, define the problem addressed by the Halakhah, which contains the Oral Torah's deepest thinking upon the meaning of sanctifying the secular, ordinary world.

The Halakhah decisively answers the generative question: the highest level of alertness, the keenest exercise of caution against uncleanness—these alone will create that circle of cleanness in the world beyond the temple courtyard that, by definition, is unclean. So the Halakhah recapitulates its insistence that man attain the highest level of consciousness and concentration to enter into, and remain in, a state of cleanness preparatory to that of sanctification. That accounts for the bizarre arrangements for transporting the youngsters with the stone—therefore insusceptible—cups from the temple, where they have been born and brought up, to the Siloam pool and thence to the Mount of Olives—all to avoid corpse matter buried at great depths. And still more to the point, the Halakhah suspends the strict purity rules protecting from contamination not only common food or priestly rations but even holy things and imposes much more stringent ones.

This it does in a variety of ways, three of which represent the rest. First, while hand-washing suffices for eating in a state of cleanness food in the familiar classifications, to purify oneself for participating in preparing the purification water, total immersion is required; the familiar distinction between hands and body falls away. Second and more decisive, purification water contracts uncleanness (and so is rendered useless) at any number of removes from the original source of

uncleanness, even one hundred; that is to say, we do not count removes. Everything is unclean by reason of its history—a history of
which we may well be ignorant. Third, persons involved in preparing the mixture—collecting the ashes, gathering the water, mixing the
two—must remain not only constantly alert but perpetually active.
From the beginning to the end of their work, they may do only what
concerns the task.

With the model of *Makhshirin* in mind, with its emphasis upon alertness from the point at which water is applied to flour and so susceptibility commences, we find no difficulty in understanding the extreme
character of the rules governing the activity and intentionality of
those involved in the rite. These rules form the paradigm of what it
means, of what is required, to attain cultic cleanness: the most
intense, best focussed, concentration on the matter at hand. But what
lessons does the Halakhah set forth in its context through those rules?
The key to the entire construction, so remarkably cogent as it is, presents itself in the paradox noted just now. Scripture is clear that those
who participate in preparing the water or in using it in a purification
process later on contract uncleanness through their activity. So, as the
medieval commentaries to Num. 19 underscore, we have the paradox
of uncleanness produced by what is clean, matching that of cleanness
produced from a rite involving uncleanness. Now, in the setting of a
system that concerns itself with establishing a domain of cleanness in
the world beyond the temple, matching the situation of holy Israel
among the gentiles, what message may we discern from the stringent
Halakhah at hand, and what is the household to learn in particular?

The lesson is in two parts: [1] cleanness is possible, but [2] death
omnipresent. The first is that even on the Mount of Olives, outside
of the temple, proper effort, sufficient energy, appropriate intentionality serve to establish a domain of cultic cleanness. In the world outside the holy place, there killing and burning the red cow will
produce ashes for mixing with properly-gathered water, the mixture
then serving to remove the most virulent uncleanness that the Torah
knows, the uncleanness of the corpse. The second is that that domain
of cleanness that man creates beyond the temple retains its essential
character as the realm of death. And that is why (so the Halakhah
might propose) all parties to the preparation and use of purification
water, from the high priest who kills the red cow to the person who
tosses the water on an unclean person or object, are classified as

unclean, must immerse and await sunset to return to a condition of cleanness. The encounter with death overcomes even the most pure level of intentionality and its realization—but Israel can overcome death and its effects.

So cultic cleanness beyond the cult is possible only through the exercise of enormous resources of will and concentration, such as Adam and Eve had lacked but that Israel is educated to nurture. But, however devotedly Israel undertakes the work, the perpetual prevalence of uncleanness persists: the person who has attained an astonishing level of cleanness to participate in the rite and who has concentrated all his energies and attention upon the rite and succeeded—that person, Scripture itself decrees, emerges unclean from his labor in perfect cleanness to prepare purification water. The one proposition—to participate, the highest, most extraordinary level of cleanness is required—requires the other—one emerges unclean from the labor. Thus cultic cleanness beyond the cult is possible, but the world beyond the temple remains what it is—no matter what. Having created the instruments for removing corpse-uncleanness, the parties to the rite immerse just as they ordinarily would, and wait for sunset—a matter to which we return at *Tebul Yom*. Only then, at sunset, do they eat their evening meal in the condition of cultic purity that the Halakhah makes possible: the ordinary immersion pool, the quotidian sunset suffice, but only provisionally. Tomorrow is another day, and it already has begun, if in the state of cleanness that is, or ought to be, the norm for Israel.

Accordingly, if Israel wishes to attain that status of cleanness that marks the way-station en route to sanctification, enormous efforts alone will make possible the realization of such an aspiration. Perfect concentration on the task at hand, pure intentionality to accomplish the goal to the exclusion of all extrinsic considerations and activities— these alone will make attainable the accomplishment of such purity as is possible, that transient kind that is all for now. To accomplish the extraordinary deed of preparing purification water to overcome death, the Halakhah prohibits participants in the rite from sitting or lying or even touching receptacles of any kind, other than actions of sitting or lying intrinsic to the labor at hand and utensils required therefor.

And why all this? I see two intended statements. The first is to underscore that death is always with us, so too the contamination effected thereby—but the Torah sets forth the provisions by which the effects of death can be removed from the living. The principal medium of removing death is living water, flowing or spring water, which serves only for the corpse and counterpart-uncleanness, those of the *zab* and *zabah* and the person afflicted with the skin ailment. Nature itself supplies the medium, then, for recovering cleanness from death, which is the kind of water that exhibits the traits of vitality—but only that kind. So nature contains within itself the power of renewal, the source of regeneration.

The second is to serve as a reminder that the uncleanness that stands for the departing soul is *sui generis*; to contain that uncleanness appropriate consideration is required—and never suffices. Death leaves its mark, which no protracted counting of removes from the original source serves to delimit. But the mixture of living water and ash, prepared with due deliberation beyond death's grasp, may wipe away, may dissolve, the uncleanness of the soul: acute alertness, intentionality beyond all disruption—these produce the Torah's final solution, the mixture of living water and ash of the red cow, applied with hyssop, however sparsely, to the person or object that has come under the shadow of death, the departing soul, en route to its sojourn until the resurrection.

B. *Miqvaot*

The principal medium for removing uncleanness of other classifications than corpse-uncleanness is immersion in a pool of forty seahs of still water that has collected naturally, beyond the intervention and intentionality of man. Under some conditions, in correct volume, deriving from the appropriate source, water, which can contract uncleanness, also has the power to diminish or even remove uncleanness, still water the former, flowing water the latter. The immersion pool in particular is comprised by collected raindrops. That water must accumulate naturally, deriving from the runoff of rain and equivalent, natural sources, e.g., seawater. It may not be drawn by human action. But by the indirect action of man it may be led into the pool on its own, e.g., in a duct.

So the main point is that it must not be drawn water or in any way collected through human intentionality and intervention. In volume, the immersion pool must have sufficient water to cover the entire body of a human being. Insufficient pools may be intermingled through a whole of a given size. One may further pipe valid water, e.g., a higher pool may be emptied into a lower pool to form the requisite volume. But one may not carry or draw the water. As we noted, what validates water for the purification rite invalidates it for the immersion pool. Drawn water may be used to augment the volume of a valid pool, meaning, a small quantity of drawn water is neutralized by, and fully integrated with, valid water. If water collects in jugs, one may break the jugs or turn them upside down, with the water flowing naturally into the cistern. But he may not pick up the jugs and empty them into the cistern. Mud of an appropriate character may serve. Any sort of man-made utensil serving as a catchment for gathering rain water is ruled out.

Drawn water absolutely may not be used for the immersion pool; a person on the greater part of whose body drawn water is poured in the volume of three logs is unclean. The Tosefta's formulation is clear: A clean person on whose head and the greater part of whose body three *logs* of drawn water have fallen is unclean. If they fell on his head but not on the greater part of his body, on the greater part of his body but not on his head if they fell on his head and on the greater part of his body whether from above or whether from the side—he is clean—until they fall on his head and the greater part of his body in the usual way. Accordingly, water that is subject to human action and intent not only does not purify but contaminates.

Now to generalize upon these facts of the Halakhah. Just as uncleanness comes about by nature—as we noted in the setting of *Zabim-Niddah, nature's failing to realize its teleology and not by human activity or intentionality*—so nature serves to remove uncleanness and naturally to restore the normal condition of persons and objects, which is cleanness. This is accomplished by purifying water, falling from heaven and naturally collected without human intervention, and then, in sequence, by the movement of the sun to sunset. Nature with rain and with sunset then restores what nature has disrupted, the celestial removing the chthonic, so to speak. That is in two stages, still water marks the cessation of uncleanness, sunset the beginning of the new cycle of Israel in conformity with the purposive character of nature, as we shall see in the following unit in connection with the status of *tebul yom.*

Still water therefore defines the problematic of the Halakhah, in these aspects: [1] it must not be subjected to human intervention or intentionality [2] it must not be collected in utensils; [3] but it must flow naturally (with the flow permissibly directed by man) to its collection point in the pool. And, conversely, drawn water imparts uncleanness and, if poured into a collection of rainwater of a volume insufficient to constitute a valid immersion pool, spoils the water into which it is poured. And these facts yield the answer to the question, What is it that turns water from a source of uncleanness (if drawn) or a facilitator for the transmission of uncleanness (if poured upon seed through an act of will) to the medium for removing uncleanness? The matter may be expressed positively and negatively. It is the negative fact that water has not served human purposes or been subjected to human activity. Water left in its natural condition, in sufficient volume, pouring down from heaven in the form of rain and collecting on its own upon the earth—that is Heaven's medium for removing uncleanness. Required to preserve passivity, man may only dig a hole into which rainwater will naturally flow. But that is how uncleanness takes place, ordinarily by nature, rarely by an act of human intentionality. Now to turn to a matter critical to the purification process, the activity of the sun in the heavens, specifically, the setting sun that marks the movement from uncleanness to cleanness for objects that have been immersed and now await the end of the cycle of uncleanness.

C. *Tebul Yom*

Immersion in the immersion pool does not complete the transaction of purification. Scripture leaves no doubt that what has been washed in water is unclean until the evening, then, when the sun has set, it is clean. Here are some pertinent statements to that effect:

> Lev. 11:31-2: Any anything upon which any of them [dead creeping things] falls when they are dead shall be unclean . . . it must be put into water and it shall be unclean until evening, then it shall be clean.
> Lev. 15:13: And when he who has a discharge is cleansed of his discharge, then he shall count for himself seven clean days for his cleansing and wash his clothes and he shall bathe his body in running water and shall be clean.

That interval between immersion and sunset on the same day defines the status of the person or object called *"tebul yom,"* what or who has been immersed on the same day and now awaits sunset for the completion of the process of purification.

The Halakhah further registers that the *tebul yom* is in the second remove of uncleanness, e.g., imparting unfitness to heave offering. The logical next question is, What is the affect of sunset? Does the residual uncleanness of what has been immersed mean that what has been immersed is really unclean until evening, therefore falling into the same status as all other sources of uncleanness? Or is what has been immersed really clean, therefore imparting unfitness to heave offering in accord with the distinction between what is primary and what is secondary? The issue of classification is addressed at the point of acute interstitiality, which is connection. There (at *'Uqsin*) we wanted to know whether the object affects the status of what is attached to it, whether the attachment (the stem to the fruit) is deemed detached therefrom. So we shift the analysis of the intermediate status of the *tebul yom* to the status of what is intermediate in the object of uncleanness. And there we further ask other relativizing questions: What is primary and what is subordinate in a mixture? What is essential and what is peripheral in a composite? And, we note at the very outset, for the first and only time in considering the sources of cultic uncleanness that contaminate the Israelite household, we even introduce the variable of intentionality. For an essay on interstitiality and mixture, the Halakhah of *tebul yom* provides an ideal setting.

Concerning the character of cultic uncleanness in the household, the Halakhah could not have made a more vivid statement than it does here. What it stresses is the negative, that uncleanness is not intrinsic but imputed, and the positive, that the attitudes and arrangements of the householder vis-à-vis sources of uncleanness directly affects the effects of those sources, which is to say, the power of a source of uncleanness to contaminate is mediated by, even vitiated within, the circumstances that govern. The person has immersed but the sun has not set, so now, but not before, the person's intentionality plays a role, on the one side, and issues of connection resolved in terms of primary and subsidiary utilization of parts of a composite require resolution, on the other. Then what difference does sunset make? How the Written Torah responds to that question—whether sunset is deemed palpably and tangibly to change the character of the object that has been wet down and thus dries in the sun's heat, or whether it serves merely to mark a formal span of time—hardly puzzles: the Written Torah explicitly calls the person or garment unclean until sunset. But for its part the Oral Torah makes the unmistakable statement that sunset constitutes a formality, it does not measure a substantive change in the character of things.

Then what does the sun do in setting? It marks time, which is to say, it indicates the status of a given interval of the day divided by light from darkness and by the character of light at one point from that at some other, all in sequence. The Halakhah of the status, not condition, of the *tebul yom* alerts the householder that if he wishes to know the condition of his property and possessions, he must pay attention to sunset. That is in two aspects. Until sunset he not only is not to use for purposes of preparation of food in conditions of cleanness what has just been immersed, he has also to notice the relationships between what has just been immersed and what not. The matter of connection brings about the same heightened consciousness as the matter of removal from uncleanness on the inner side of immersion, before the rinsing. Just as removes from the source of uncleanness require us to know not only the condition of an unclean object but also the subsequent history, from the moment of contamination, of that same object, so connection in the differentiation by reason of immersion imposes alertness not only as to the primary but also the secondary and peripheral contacts of the object that has been immersed.

Sunset triggers a whole new moment of alertness, a fresh start. At sunset the system of cultic cleanness in the home renews itself, marking the commencement of a new span of time in the ongoing process, the beginning of a new day. In the moment marked by sunset, then, the religious meaning of the Halakhah inheres: that is the point at which ambiguities are clarified, interstitialities resolved.

Sunset marks the creation of the new day, hence the commencement of a new span of time that tells the story of the struggle of Israel, naturally clean, to remain clean from the sources of uncleanness round about. Uncleanness does not accumulate, but, when the householder determines by the act of immersion to bring uncleanness to closure, terminates at sunset, the end of the old day. That same consideration comes to mind at M. *Niddah* 1:1, where the passage of twenty-four hours forms the measure of one cycle of uncleanness, the last prior inspection, the other. The woman is held to have been unclean only during the preceding twenty-four-hours when this lessens the period from the examination to the [last] examination, and she is held to have been unclean only during the period from examination to examination when this lessens the period of twenty-four hours.

But the relativities of twenty-four-hour periods give way to the determinate time of sunset, a decisive indicator of the end of one cycle and commencement of another. And herein we find the meaning of the matter: what sunset indicates is that Israel returns to its natural condition of cleanness—if Israel has so acted as to accord with its nature by immersing, earlier in the day, to that end. Whatever the condition of persons or objects as to uncleanness, once the process of cleanness has properly commenced with the act of immersion, the result is inexorable: Israel becomes clean as surely, as reliably, as the sun sets. No wonder, archaeology now shows, people wanted immersion pools in their houses, signaling as they do the authentic condition of Israel.

Perhaps sages grasped that Moses had had that very thing in mind when he specified, "it must be put into water and it shall be unclean until evening, then it shall be clean." For, in line with the creation of the world, the new day starts at sunset: "and there was evening, and there was morning, one day." Then the line demarcated by sunset in the history of the passage from uncleanness to cleanness is indeed one of classification: the spell of uncleanness has ended not with the immersion, which changes the condition but not the status of the contaminated person or object, but with sunset. Then what marks the condition is not natural to Israel. Only what indicates the status speaks of Israel by nature. So time, not circumstance, makes all the difference. When the priests of M. *Ber.* 1:1 complete the restoration of their proper condition of cleanness, Israel notes the sunset by proclaiming God's unity and accepting his dominion, then eats supper in the condition of the priests eating their priestly rations—all Israel en route to sanctification. That is how life is to be sustained, and why cleanness makes a difference—at sunset.

D. *Yadayim*

The hands form a special realm of uncleanness, for they are deemed perpetually unclean. That is for a reason coherent with the working of the rest of the system: the hands are not subject to the rigors of human attention and intentionality; they have their own life, moving and touching even when the person is unaware. That is why the area from fingertips to wrist forms a distinct domain. There, the hands contract uncleanness and are rid of uncleanness in a process that operates distinct from the rest of the body. In addition to immersion for known encounters with uncleanness that have taken place during the day, accordingly, handwashing is required for cultic cleanness prior to eating a meal; and that has no bearing on whether or not the sun has set or when the meal takes place.

The hands are deemed constantly active, whether or not the person pays attention, and so are assigned a permanent position in the second remove of uncleanness. That is to say, even though the person may know what he or she may or may not have touched, the person cannot know with what the things the hands have touched themselves have had contact—thus the second remove. Accordingly, the hands form a distinct realm of uncleanness and require their own rite of purification.

The required handwashing in the Halakhah has no bearing on hygienic cleanliness. To state matters simply, it is performed in accord with cultic rules. It constitutes an act of cultic purification of a demarcated part of the body. The hands, up to the wrist, are restored to cleanness not through immersion in an immersion pool but through rinsing. The water that hits the hands affects but is affected by them, and that water too requires a rinsing—hence a cultic purification through a repeated act of rinsing. Further, how the water is collected and administered defines a rite of purification for a component of the person that bears its own traits of cultic uncleanness. The human being's hands then constitute an animate source of uncleanness.

Like persons or objects in the status of the *tebul yom*, the hands are in the second remove of uncleanness. Sages maintain that, even though a person does not contract uncleanness from an offspring, but only from a father of uncleanness, the hands are in a different category. If the hands have touched something unclean in the first remove of uncleanness, even though the person's body is not made unclean, his hands are deemed in the second remove. They then spoil priestly rations that they touch, even though they do not make it unclean. Along these same lines, sacred Scriptures impart uncleanness to the hands that touch them. Finally, even if someone does not know whether or not his hands have touched an offspring of uncleanness, they are deemed by definition to be unclean in the second remove: "the hands keep themselves busy." Then, if someone wishes to protect the cleanness of priestly rations or to eat his ordinary food in a state of cultic cleanness, he must properly, cultically wash the hands.

To wash hands one must make use of a utensil, just as for the purification rite one draws water with a utensil. For immersion pools one must not make use of water drawn in a utensil. To wash hands, one must make use of water that has never been used before. Further, an act of labor extraneous to the rite itself spoils the water used for washing hands. The same rule applies to the water for use in preparing purification water. An act of labor extraneous to the rite spoils that water that is to be mixed with the ashes of the red cow in the making of purification water. But the water of an immersion pool may be used again and again, and that is not so for the water used for washing hands. Thus the rules of washing hands clearly depend on the analogy drawn to rules of water used for purification water. The rite of the red cow depends upon cleanness established and attained outside of the temple, and the rite of washing hands leads to cleanness for eating food outside of the cult, so in both cases, human agency, guided by an alert human being, is required, by contrast to rainwater, which is collected naturally upon the ground and would be spoiled for an immersion pool if human action intrudes.

The difference between the uncleanness of the hands and of the rest of the body and removing that uncleanness through a process guided by its own distinctive rules derives from the Written Torah, which identifies the hands (and feet) as a realm of uncleanness unto themselves and specifies a process of removing that uncleanness distinct from the process that pertains to the rest of the body. And it uses its own language for the one and for the other. The key language derives from Scripture, using the word "sanctify" to refer to the cultic rinsing of hands and feet. Take, for instance, the very vocabulary at hand. The word for wash for purposes of cultic cleanness used in the Halakhah of *Yadayim* is "sanctify," as at T. *Yadayim* 1:7: Priests sanctify in the sanctuary only with a utensil.

The analogous actions then involve the purification rite, sprinkling purification water, pouring water for handwashing. The uncleanness of hands and the purification thereof carry us deep into the Halakhic theory of the interpenetration of household and sanctuary. Here the model of the cult, for both uncleanness and cleanness in the home, is most explicit. The language of Scripture for rinsing persons and objects from uncleanness for purpose of restoring cleanness is "rinse" or "wash," and Scripture is always explicit that after such dunking in an immersion pool, the object remains unclean until sunset. So matters could not have been made more explicit.

And that difference between "sanctifying" hands and "rinsing/ washing" persons or garments leads to the question, What about the contrast between uncleanness and sanctification? That too is drawn explicitly. The Halakhah expresses the contrast between death and sanctification, but it makes its statement of the match of opposites in its own way. That way appears in a variety of details, but the most important concern the character of the utensil used in connection with water for sanctifying hands as against water for rinsing, and the preparation of the water used for sanctification as against that used for removing uncleanness.

A utensil that cannot be used for drawing water for hand-washing does not require a tightly sealed cover to serve to interpose against uncleanness, and one that does also requires a tightly sealed cover in the tent of a corpse. So the areas of Halakhah are deemed corresponding and opposite. The contrastive force of death and sanctification renews itself in the present matter.

But there is a still more blatant expression of the same contrast. The immersion pool water, naturally collected, without human intervention, cannot serve for the sanctification of the hands. The gathering of the water used for sanctifying the hands conforms in the definition of the required attitudes and actions to the requirements for collecting the water used for mixing with the ashes of the red cow (Num. 19:1ff.) in preparing purification water for the removal of corpse-uncleanness. As with the Halakhah of *Parah*, the collection of the water for combining with the ashes, not just the appropriate utensil for use in that connection, involves strict and rigid rules. These same rules govern here as well, so far as sages can apply them. The act must be purposive, the water gathered deliberately, by human action, in a valid utensil. Water for the immersion pool must collect naturally, unaffected by human action, and may not be collected in a utensil. The same rules govern water for mixing with ashes to make purification water for the removal of corpse-uncleanness and water for use in sanctifying the hands.

It follows that uncleanness of hands is removed by water, and preparation of the water accords with the rules pertinent to purification water utilized for mixing with the ashes of the red cow, Num. 19:14ff. That governing analogy is made explicit, e.g., they draw, and they mix water with the ash of the red cow, and they sprinkle purification water, and they pour water for hands only with a utensil. The analogy of the immersion pool and its water is rejected. Deliberate human action effected through a whole, useful utensil is required. I do not know how the Halakhah could have stated more blatantly than it does the contrast between death and sanctification, and the identification of the hands as the principal media, the arena where that contrast is acted out.

And to underline the difference between the sanctification of the hands and the purification of utensils or the greater part of persons, intentionality is insisted upon: the collection of water by intention for sanctifying hands would invalidate water for immersing persons and utensils in an immersion pool. That is to say, by contrast, deliberate human action that collects water in a utensil spoils water for use in an immersion pool. So the special standing of the hands and their sanctification comes to expression in the Halakhic invocation of the metaphor of the rite for removing corpse-uncleanness rather than the rite for moving uncleanness in general. So sanctification and corpse-uncleanness are explicitly juxtaposed as opposites in the details of the Halakhah.

Water used for sanctification involves human agency and intentionality, and water used for purification from uncleanness (but not sanctification) does not—a huge difference signaled by a small distinction. Since the hands are not immersed in water but rather water is poured out onto the hands, human agency is required in the use, not only the preparation, of the water. Human agency, by contrast, would spoil the water for the immersion pool, which must be collected naturally; human agency is demanded for water used for the purification rite. Hence, as we see when we examine the preparation of purification water as set forth in the Halakhah of *Parah* and the collection of water for the immersion pool in the Halakhah of *Miqvaot*, we find ourselves drawing upon the analogy supplied by *Parah*.

What emerges from the facts now adduced is that

[1] the hands are deemed always just one remove away from corpse-contamination, and

[2] it is through water analogous to that used for preparing purification water for the removal of corpse-uncleanness that the hands are sanctified (not merely cleansed of uncleanness, with sunset required to complete the process of purification) even for eating food in the status of priestly rations.

What I hear from the Halakhah is the statement that death is ever present, if not in what is touched, then in what has touched what is touched. So the hands are always in the second remove of uncleanness, meaning, death is always just a step or two away from contact with what is meant to be kept holy, clear of death. And that is—in the context of the hands and when they are sanctified—food for the nourishment of Israel. But death and all that death overspreads can be kept beyond the boundary of the household table by deliberate action defined by perpetual concern: the right intention, especially for the meal. So with that first bite of bread at the meal, the stakes are very high indeed.

E. *Where the Contest is Resolved: Home and Temple in Hierarchical Formation: Hagigah*

The focus on domestic meals ought not obscure the fact that in the temple, not only at home, Israelites, not only priests, eat God's meat, not only secular food outside the realm of sanctification. That is in certain offerings presented on festivals, which yield not only parts to be burned on the altar but also parts to be eaten by the officiating priest and also the pilgrim and his family. An account of the working of the purity laws in their domestic context must then take account of how the Halakhah places cultic cleanness at the temple upon a single continuum with cultic cleanness at the domestic table. And that is in connection with pilgrimages, when ordinary folk are assumed to attain the requisite status of cleanness to participate in the temple rites as the Torah provides, specifically, as I said, to eat meat in the status of holy things, right off the altar of God. If uncleanness stands for death and sorrow, then here cleanness stands for joy in God's presence, in God's sight.

Rejoicing on the festival means eating meat at God's place, in the condition in which God eats his meals as well: cultic cleanness. It is then that the Israelite appears before God and is seen by God. The nexus of the encounter is the meal, in which the Israelite accepts the rules of cleanness that pertain to God's table, the altar. With the Halakhah of *Hagigah* we come to the rules of cleanness as these pertain to the cult. The main point is, whatever is done at home serves in the household, but the cult is clearly differentiated from the household, with special reference for those that preserve cultic cleanness even within the household.

That is expressed in connection with persons and utensils alike. One may immerse a utensil for purposes of cultic cleanness, but, when it comes to use in the cult, a utensil has to be processed to begin with in a state of insusceptibility to uncleanness and so must be cultically clean when it becomes susceptible, and still it must be immersed for use in the cult, that is, in connection with holy things. So too, for the cult one must wash hands even if the food that the hands will touch is insusceptible to uncleanness, which is not the case with heave offering. With unclean hands they eat food which has not been wet down in the case of heave offering, but not in the case of holy things. The same theory that animates the institution of the *ma'amadot*, the priestly delegations with their counterparts among Levites and Israelites that participate in the temple cult over the year, explains the institution of the pilgrimage offerings.

The attitude of the pilgrim governs. The effect of his act of purification through immersion is dictated by the attitude with which he immerses. If one was unclean and immersed with the intention of becoming clean, that serves. He who immerses in order to rise up from uncleanness to cleanness, lo, this person is clean for all purposes. He who immerses—if he had the intention of becoming clean, he becomes clean. And if not, he remains unclean. If he immersed for eating food in the status of holy things and is thereby confirmed as suitable for eating food in the status of holy things, he is prohibited from engaging in the preparation of purification water. If, however, one immersed for the matter requiring the more stringent rule, he is permitted to engage in the matter requiring the less stringent rule. If he immersed but was not confirmed, it is as though he did not immerse. But there are realms to which the attitude of the Israelite gains no access. The area within the veil excludes all but the priesthood, so the intentionality of Israelites is null therein, thus, just as that which is within the veil is exceptional, in that it is not subject to the knowledge and consent of the Israelites, so are excluded heave offering, heave offering of tithe, and dough offering, which are subject to the knowledge and consent of the Israelites.

Then the problematic of the Halakhah, when it comes to its consideration of the laws of cultic cleanness in connection with the pilgrimage, is clear. It concerns the hierarchization of the rules that govern the sanctity and sanctification of Israel, from the household upward to the temple courtyard and the altar in Jerusalem. It is, in particular, for the occasion of the ascent to the city and the temple that the hierarchization of sanctity and uncleanness is required. Then the Halakhah has to answer the question, Is cleanness at home equivalent to cleanness in the cult? Is the cult differentiated from the household, even while both are deemed sanctified?

And the Halakhah answers that question in an explicit way: attitude has its limits, and the facts of sanctification override the attitude of the pious person. However much one wishes to attain cultic cleanness and actually does so in the household, still, the cult preserves its own rules and requirements. The recognition that levels of cleanness, depending on circumstance and attitude, differentiate one's suitability for eating food at various levels of sanctification, yields a broader judgment. It is that there is a match between levels of sanctification and levels of uncleanness, with the hierarchy of the one matched by the hierarchy of the other, ascending, descending, respectively.

It is in connection with the pilgrimage for which *Hagigah* provides that these matters become urgent. And, we note, on that occasion, the limits of intentionality and its power are reached. The intentionality to attain cleanness in the domestic household now does not suffice, nor do the rules and regulations that pertain when ordinary folk in their homes eat their food as though they were in the temple in Jerusalem. The Halakhah embodies the difference between imagination and intention, on the one side, and actuality, on the other. What suffices in the pretense that one's table forms the altar, the members of the household form the priesthood and its ménage, the home forms the temple, now does not serve. Actuality intervenes: the real temple imposes its own very strict rules, and all of the proper intentions in the world will not serve now. The table compares to the temple, the household to the priesthood, the boundaries of the home to the temple—but in a hierarchical structure, encompassing rules of

both sanctification and uncleanness. How more eloquently and vigorously to make that statement than through the Halakhah of *Hagigah*
I cannot begin to imagine. But we ought not to miss the power of the
conception of Israel in relationship to God that animates the
Halakhah. Here the occasion, the location, and the participants intersect, here Israel meets God. The condition of Eden is replicated, the
experience recapitulated—but with a different outcome.

IV. Cause and Effect: Where and Why Man's Will Matters

Man's will makes no difference when it comes to producing sources
of uncleanness, which come about naturally and not by human intervention. What about the matter of purification? Let us return to our
starting point and interpret the opposed rules of water for immersion
pools and water for the purification of corpse-uncleanness. The question is, Why does still water unaffected by human agency restore the
natural condition disrupted by uncleanness other than that of the
corpse and its analogues, while by contrast purification water systematically subjected to human intervention—constant attention, deliberate action, start to finish—alone removes corpse-uncleanness? We
have then to account for the exclusion of man from the one process,
the radical insistence upon his inclusion, in full deliberation, within
the other. The reason is, we deal with two essentially distinct types of
uncleanness, one ordinary and natural, the other extraordinary and
in violation of nature.

The facts must carry their own message. Uncleanness that comes
about by reason of any cause but death and its analogues is removed
by Heaven's own dispensation, not by man's intervention: rainfall and
in sequence sunset suffice. Ordinary purification is done by nature,
resulting from natural processes. Water that falls from heaven and,
unimpeded by man, collects in sufficient volume restores the natural
condition of persons and objects that have contracted uncleanness at
second hand or by reason of minor sources of contamination. Still
water serves for the moment, until sunset marks the new, now-clean
spell in the story of the person or the object. But as to persons and
objects that have contracted uncleanness from death, nature on its

own cannot produce the kind of water that bears the power to remove that uncleanness and restore the condition of nature. Only man can. And man can do this, as *Parah* has shown us, only by the highest level of concentration, the most deliberate and focussed action. The water is not still, but flowing water, living water overcoming death. And the water is kept alive, in constant motion until it is stirred with the ash. Any extrinsic action spoils the water; stopping to rest on a bench, doing any deed other than required for the rite itself—these disrupt the circle of sanctification within the world of uncleanness that the burning of the cow has required.

Life overcomes death through the working of the human will in collaboration with natural processes. So the facts lead us to the critical question at the heart of matters: Why does the state of human intentionality govern in the confrontation with corpse-uncleanness? Man's supreme act of will, embodying intentionality in highly purposive activity, can overcome even the effects of death. If the Halakhah wished to say that man can overcome death through the correct and deliberate attitude, it could not have embodied that message in more powerful language than the activities required for the formulation of purification water.

Man's act of will overcomes the uncleanness of death, just as man's act of deliberate rebellion brought about death to begin with. Man restores what man has disrupted. As to the rest, man refrains from deliberate action, and nature, providing purifying water from heaven, accomplishes the restoration. That is because the other forms of uncleanness come about by nature's own failure to realize itself, so nature provides the medium of the removal of the consequence: water that Heaven supplies naturally matches nature's condition. But since death comes about by reason of Adam's and Eve's original act of will, their heirs' supreme act of concentration and deliberation is required to bring about the preparation of the medium of purification.

The Rabbinic sages explicitly maintain that God is not at fault for Adam's fall; Adam brought about his own death: "When I violated his instructions, I brought about my own death." It was through an act of deliberation and will. So let an act of deliberation and will remove the consequence corpse-uncleanness. Had the Halakhah wished in its terms and categories to accomplish a reprise of the story of man's fall, it could not have made a more eloquent statement than it does in the contrast between the Halakhah of *Miqvaot* and that of *Parah*. To what man has caused man must pay full mind, and nature—the rain, the sun—restoring itself to its own purposive condition takes care of the rest. By an act of will, man regains the Kingdom of God.

CHAPTER FOURTEEN

CHOOSING LIFE IN THE KINGDOM OF GOD

I. From Eden to the Kingdom of God: Accepting the Yoke of the Commandments

The final chapter in the theology of the Halakhah carries us to those components of the theological structure that realize God's rule in Israel. That is a suitable conclusion. For the theology of the Halakhah recapitulates the story of humanity from Eden onward, with Israel bearing the divine imperative that Adam and Eve had violated. To recover Eden, Israel is meant, then, to accept God's dominion and the yoke of the commandments, as in the Halakhah. As much as man by his nature rebels against God, man tutored by the commandments willingly accepts God's will and therefore his rule. Morning and night, in reciting the Shema, Israel does just that.

The normative theology therefore raises the question at the end, What are the Halakhah's media for the reformation, regeneration, and renewal, of man? The Halakhah, acutely present tense in time, legislates for not Eden but the Kingdom of God, in the here and now—and therefore in the future. For Sinai's answer to Eden's question both encompasses and transcends the matter of sin and atonement. After the reconciliation, what? That is the question that the Halakhic structure addresses: the conduct of the ordinary, everyday life lived under God's rule. That is because the normative deals with the normal, not just the exceptional: the life made up of not only sinful, but also obedient, moments.

So the final solution to God's dilemma with man—how to accord man free will such as God enjoys but to nurture in man freely-given love for God ("You will love the Lord your God . . .")—lies in the Torah. In its Halakhah for the common condition of man in the workaday world, the Torah provides not only for sin and the antidote to sin, but the rules of the ordinary life under God's dominion. That formulation of matters states in abstract language the clear message of the Shema in two parts: [1] acceptance of the yoke of the

Kingdom of Heaven in the words, "Hear, Israel, the Lord our God is the one God," and [2] acceptance of the yoke of the commandments.

That way of life in accord with God's rule means to form the *paideia*, the character-building education to transform man (idolater) into Israelite (one who knows God) by making Israelite man's freely-given obedience *to* God as natural as was the first man's contumacious rebellion *against* God. That is why the Halakhic provision for life in God's kingdom moves from the day and its duties to the table and its everyday nourishment, then to the meeting with God that is seasonal and temporal, and finally to the climax of the system, confrontation with routine crisis. The answer to Eden and its tragedy that is set forth in the Halakhah of the Kingdom of God begins, therefore, where it must, with the Shema.

A. *Berakhot*

The Halakhah governing the recitation of the Shema, the principal theological statement of Rabbinic Judaism, extends to the entire discipline of daily obligatory prayer. The category-formation of the theological structure, *Berakhot*, follows the natural sequence of the day, from formal recitation of the creed, the Shema, and the petitionary prayers, at dusk, evening, and morning, to conduct in connection with eating, to other occasions of worship:

[1] recitation of the creed, the Shema, to which reference has just been made;
[2] the Prayer (the Eighteen Benedictions);
[3] blessings said before and after eating food;
[4] other rules for public worship at the table;
[5] blessings said on other occasions.

In providing for these topics, the Halakhah takes up the conditions of ordinary life and defines in detail where and how Israel meets God in its everyday existence: locating the Kingdom of God temporally, by time of day and circumstance. The Land now figures only in detail, for God's Kingdom is not limited thereto: Eden serves, but, as the system reaches its climactic statements, falls away, as the governing metaphor, when God's Kingdom comes into view.

A massive theology is encompassed within the prayers that are

treated. The Shema, the Prayer, the Grace after Meals—these obligatory prayers contain the creedal principles of the faith: God's unity
and dominion, the Torah as God's plan, the categories, creation, revelation, redemption, as these organize holy Israel's existence. From
the recitation of the creed, the Halakhah turns to the direct address
to God conducted in the concrete presence of God. Finally in the
Halakhic repertoire comes equally direct address to God when, in
the center of Israel's ordinary life, Israel sustains itself with food. At
issue now is not the cultic metaphor that defines how holy Israel
nourishes itself in the model of God's food, but the attitude that
accompanies the act of nourishment, of sustaining life. God's beneficence and benevolence are declared, and as Israel encounters
evidences of God's intervention in the everyday, his activity is acknowledged with thanks. So the creed, prayers, and blessings that are
encased in a web of rules and regulations recapitulate principal elements of the theology of the dual Torah. But the substance of that
theology—here merely alluded to—is spelled out only in the Aggadic
counterpart to the Halakhah.

The issue is, what should we not know about the interiorities of
Israel's relationship with God if we did not consult the Halakhah?
Asking the question in that way, we find the answer blatant. If in the
liturgy we learn the principles of the theology of God's and Israel's
relationships, by the Halakhah we are given the practical and concrete means by which those principles are made substantive, how
they are not only declared but acted out, imposed upon, discerned
within, the everyday life of holy Israel, encompassing the ordinary
Israelite. Here is where being Israel is defined most fully and comprehensively. Within the details of the laws is embedded a major
statement about what is between God and Israel. And while the law
makes that statement in a prolix manner and forever only through
details, never stating the point in general terms, in fact its principles
are few and accessible of economical formulation.

It is a simple statement. God is forever and everywhere present
within Israel and holds in his hand the life and soul of every Israelite.
The law then spells out the consequences of God's ubiquity within
and intense engagement with Israel: how ought people behave who
live out their days in God's presence, under God's gaze? Here are the
two dimensions of the theology of God's presence, the one God's

view, the other Israel's, both of them fully exposed in the details of the law, only there, but always repeated in every particular detail.

1. God takes a constant and intense interest in the condition of Israelite attitudes and opinions. He cares that Israel affirm his unity and declare his dominion, through the recitation of the Shema and related acts of prayer. He responds. He waits for the expression of love, he hears, he feels, not only thinks. That is why he pays close attention to the manner in which the obligation to do so is carried out, noting that it is done in a correct and respectful way. How else is a merely formal gesture to be distinguished from a truly sincere, intentional one? What is important is that when the correct words are spoken, they are spoken with the attitude of acknowledging God's dominion, as an explicit act of accepting the government of Heaven and the discipline ("yoke") of the commandments. That is what is meant in the laws covering reciting the blessings, for instance, *Blessed are you . . . who . . .*, or *Blessed are you, who has sanctified us by his commandments and commanded us to. . . .* God values these words of acknowledgement and thanks. God further hears and responds to the praise, supplication, and thanks of Israel, as these are set forth in the Prayer. Reciting the Prayer while facing Jerusalem's temple and the holy of holies, the Israelite directs the Prayer to the place in which God's Presence once came and one day will again come to rest. The attitude of the Israelite in reciting the Prayer acutely concerns God, and that must be an attitude of solemnity; the one who says the Prayer must conduct himself or herself as in the very presence of God, in the model of the rules of conduct before the emperor.

How does God respond to Israel's acknowledgement, thanks, and above all, acceptance of his dominion? God sees to it that life is sustained, with special reference to food, and prayers that acknowledge the gift of life through food must respond with precision to the specificities of the gift: what particular class of food is involved? Finally, when Israel is embodied in a quorum of Israelites, God's presence, not only his gifts, is to be noted properly in a call to attend upon the shared rite. Finally, God intervenes at all times, past, present, future, and in all circumstances, however humble and personal, and God's intervention is to be watched for and acknowledged. So when the Halakhah insists that all Israel—meaning everyone who accepts the rule of the one and only God and enters into his dominion by accepting "the yoke of the commandments"—will rise from the grave to eternal life, while the gentiles, defined by their idolatry and rejection of God, are destined to death, that point of insistence bears more than abstract interest. It is a conviction acted upon every day, every hour, in every circumstance of the workaday life. God is intimately involved in the ongoing life of Israel, sustaining that life in the here and now, not only at judgment and in the world to come. At man's every act of breathing, on every occasion of nourishment (as of procreation, in the ontological context established by *Zabim-Niddah*), God renews the promise of the creation of life and confirms the promise of restoration at the end. No wonder sanctification is forever at stake, salvation merely implicit. Sanctification is salvation, the Sabbath a foretaste of Eden but a recapitulation of its condition.

2. Through the life of prayer and fulfillment of commandments, Israel wraps itself before God in a cloak made up of the fabric of actions that sanctify—thread by thread. From Israel's perspective, all Israel and individual Israelites conduct life under the perpetual rule of that just and merciful God who made the world, and that rule is personal, immediate, and penetrating. If God immediately engages with Israel, for its part Israel, all together and one by one, seeks that engagement. That is because Israel lives and acts under God's perpetual gaze. In the morning the Israelite accepts God's dominion in an act of personal submission, then explicitly undertakes to carry out God's commandments, in all their concrete specificity. In exchange, the Israelite recognizes that whatever happens expresses a chapter in God's plan for creation, a paragraph—perhaps only a sentence, a word, a mere letter—of God's intention for that particular person.

That fact forms the premise of the Prayer, with its systematic, personal program of praise, supplication, and thanks. More broadly still, the very fact that the individual lives attests to God's will, by which every man lives or dies that very moment through the course of life. Life depends on food, the point of intersection, then, between man and God, the moment of special and appropriate acknowledgement of the gift of life: nourishment by this means provokes these words, by that means, those words. Since God pays such close and continuing attention to what each person says and how he says it, what he does and why he does it, none need find surprising God's intervention or man's specific and appropriate response. That is why the correct formula of acknowledgement guides response, also, to all miracles, both the routine and the extraordinary, that embody God's intervention. Throughout, there is no distinguishing Israel from the Israelite; what affects the whole obligates the one, what happens to the one forms the destiny of all.

As between the generalities of the liturgy and the Aggadah, wherein theology states the governing principles, the logic, of world order established by the only and all-powerful God, who is just, and the specificities of the Halakhah, with their concrete details of religious actions and attitudes in the here and now, there can be no doubt where God lives. It is in the four ells of the law. There God becomes immediate, concrete, and tangible. At issue in Eden was not attitude but action embodying attitude: a particular tree, a particular deed with reference to that tree. Here, in the Halakhah, the relationship between Israel and God shapes interiorities of attitude and emotion, identifying the noteworthy and guiding response thereto. The Halakhah defines the how of the relationship of Israel to God. There is the point of immediate contact. That is where, through word and deed, speech and silence, there is realized Israel's intimate and everyday quest to live in eternal relationship with the Creator. No wonder then, that what matters in meeting the Creator is the act of intimacy involved when he gives life and takes life, to this one, to that one. That is why the Halakhah of *Berakhot* requires ample attention to the rules of the table as much as those governing the recitation of the Shema and the Prayer. In these tangible details God takes his place and establishes his presence—there, and nowhere else.

No wonder, then, that not only what one says but how he recites the Shema—e.g., when working in a tree or standing on the ground—makes a difference, so too the direction one faces when silently reciting the Prayer. The concern for inner dimension of existence explains why humble details covering when, in what stance, and with what inner feelings and attitudes, one recites the Prayer matter as they do. And if the sages wanted to make the statement that God's rule extends to the food man eats, because God creates and sustains life one by one and breath by breath, how better say so than in the language of rules and regulations such as set forth for thanking God for food? And since, at issue in sustaining life is restoring life at the end of days in the resurrection of the dead, how more explicitly to link the act of eating to death and resurrection than to say so in the Grace after Meals, Israel having declared itself in being by formally invoking the quorum of Israel there present. In the Halakhah of *Berakhot* sages instruct Israel on what it means to take God personally.

B. *Hullin*

What does it mean for the Israelite to aspire to a life of holiness, to be "holy like God," as Lev. 19:3 commands? In one massive exercise on that issue, transcending the rather diffuse laws of domestic cleanness rules, the Halakhah investigates the relationship of God's table in the temple to the Israelite's table in the household. The Halakhah of *Hullin*—unconsecrated food and how it is rendered suitable for the domestic table of Israel—takes as its problem the comparison and contrast of the same act—in itself governed by rules of sanctification—performed in different circumstances. It deals with, specifically, the preparation of food with special reference to the spilling of blood for the nourishment of man, meat-eating.

The Torah repeatedly asserts that "the blood is the life," making provision for the disposition of blood produced in slaughtering an animal. If killed for God, that is to say, in the temple courtyard, the animal yields blood for the altar, to be sprinkled at the corners in an act of expiation; it further produces the sacrificial parts to be burned up in smoke on the altar fires and thence to ascend to God's nostrils; and the beast may also yield meat for the priests and their families to eat. If killed for man's needs, the animal yields blood to be covered with dust, returned to the earth. God and man therefore stand in alignment with one another. It is that alignment, expressed in the language of man's being created "in our image, after our likeness," that defines the generative logic of the Halakhah before us, because at issue is the hierarchization of the realms of sanctification that ascend from earth to heaven, through Israel.

But the governing metaphor—household like temple, or, in another context, Land like Eden—serves the situation in which the temple stands, Israel locates itself in the Land of Israel, and both consecrated and unconsecrated beasts are subject to the rite. What happens when the blood rite has ceased, beasts are no longer sanctified for the altar, the temple has fallen, and Israel is no longer possessed of the Land? Then the balance, the perfect match of slaughter for the altar and slaughter for everyday food, is lost. If we read as a set of

interdependent, categorical actions the requirements of the Written
Torah in connection with taking the life of an animal for God's and
man's use, then what law persists in this time? That is the question
answered in the depths of the law of *Hullin*.

The subject is the proper modes of killing and dividing the animals
that are used for meat at home. The first four chapters of the normative Halakhic statement in the Mishnah deal with that subject. What
is important here is that most of the rules for slaughtering an animal
for God's table apply also to slaughtering one for the Israelite's. The
same blemishes that invalidate a beast for the altar invalidate one
for the Israelite table. If we control for the fixed differences—the
infinitely more elevated level of sanctification that applies to the holy
space of the temple and the holy caste of the priests—we can account
for the few consequential differences. But the story does not end with
the legal narrative that requires beasts for ordinary Israel to be
slaughtered, and evaluated as to use, as though for service on the
altar. But here the context of the Halakhah intervenes, for a very
specific problem confronts the Halakhah, namely, the relationship of
the three realms of sanctification, the Land, the Temple, and Israel,
each in its own position in the hierarchy of realms of sanctity that rise
from earth to heaven. Here is how the Halakhah states the matter
over and over again:

Mishnah *Hullin* 5:1

M. 5:1   [The prohibition against slaughtering on the same day] "it and
          its young" (Lev. 22:28) applies (1) in the Land and outside the
          Land, (2) in the time of the Temple and not in the time of the
          Temple, (3) in the case of unconsecrated beasts and in the case
          of consecrated beasts. How so? He who slaughters it and its
          offspring, (1) which are unconsecrated, (2) outside [the Temple
          courtyard]—both of them are valid. And [for slaughtering] the
          second he incurs forty stripes. [He who slaughters] (1) Holy
          Things (2) outside—[for] the first is he liable to extirpation,
          and both of them are invalid, and [for] both of them he incurs
          forty stripes. [He who slaughters] (1) unconsecrated beasts (2)
          inside [the Temple courtyard]—both of them are invalid, and
          [for] the second he incurs forty stripes. [He who slaughters] (1)
          Holy Things (2) inside—the first is valid, and he is exempt
          [from any punishment], and [for] the second he incurs forty
          stripes, and it is invalid.

The same formulation characterizes other Halakhic subdivisions, which I abbreviate, since the same provisions repeat themselves:

M. 6:1   [The requirement to] cover up the blood applies in the Land and abroad.

M. 7:1   [The prohibition of] the sinew of the hip [sciatic nerve, Gen. 32:32] applies (1) in the Land [of Israel] and outside of the Land

M. 8:1   Every [kind of] flesh [i.e., meat, of cattle, wild beast, and fowl] it is prohibited to cook in milk, except for the flesh of fish and locusts. And it is prohibited to serve it up onto the table with cheese, except for the flesh of fish and locusts. He who vows [to abstain] from flesh is permitted [to make use of] the flesh of fish and locusts.

M. 10:1   [The requirement to give to the priests] the shoulder, the two cheeks, and the maw (Deut. 18:3) applies (1) in the Land and outside of the Land.

M. 11:1–2   [The laws concerning the obligation to donate to the priest] the first shearings [of wool from the sheep of one's flock (Deut. 18:4)] apply both inside the Land of Israel and outside the Land of Israel

M. 12:1   [The requirement to] let [the dam] go from the nest [Deut. 22:6–7] applies (1) in the Land and outside of the Land.

What is the issue and how is it provoked? The Halakhah (as usual) is explicit on that matter and does not leave to later exegetes the discovery of what provokes the question concerning the hierarchical classification of the three components of the domain of the sacred upon which we focus here. The Halakhah states in so many words what it wants to know, which is whether [1] the destruction of the temple and cessation of the offerings, [2] the degradation of the Land of Israel, and [3] the exile of the holy people, Israel, from the Holy Land, affect the rules of sustenance in the model of the nourishment of God in the temple, in the Land, among the holy people.

Stated with the eloquence of the Halakhah, with its powerful rhetoric, the answer is, whatever the condition of the temple and its altar, whatever the source—the Holy Land or unclean gentile lands— of animals, and whatever the location of Israel, whether enlandised or not, one thing persists. The sanctification of Israel, the people, endures [1] in the absence of the cult, and [2] in alien, unclean territory, and [3] whatever the source of the food that Israel eats. Israel's sanctity is eternal, uncontingent, absolute. The sanctification that inheres in Israel, the people, transcends the Land and outlives the temple and its cult. Since the sanctity of Israel, the people, persists beyond the temple and outside of the Land, that sanctity stands at a higher point in the hierarchy of domains of the holy that ascend from earth to heaven and from man to God.

The Halakhah, to make its statement about the eternal sanctification of the people, Israel, explicitly responds to three facts:

[1] Israelites live not only in the holy land but abroad, in unclean land;
[2] the temple has been destroyed;
[3] and, consequently, animals are slaughtered not only in the temple in the Land but in unconsecrated space and abroad, and the meat is eaten not only in a cultic but in a profane circumstance.

Anyone who wonders whether the Halakhah that applied to the temple and the home when the temple was standing and Israel was in the Land of Israel continues to apply with the temple in ruins and Israel in exile here finds his answer. Although the sanctity of the temple stands in abeyance, the sanctity of the Israelite table persists; although Israel is in exile from the Holy Land, Israel remains holy; although in the temple rules of uncleanness are not now kept, they continue in force where they can be. Birds and animals that flourish outside of the Land when prepared for the Israelite table are regulated by the same rules that apply in the Land and even (where relevant) at the altar. So Israel, the people, not only retains sanctity but preserves it outside of the Land, and the sanctity of Israel transcends that of the temple and its altar.

When it comes to the preparation of meat, the Halakhah deals with three settings: the temple, the Land of Israel, and foreign land. And for all three, it insists, the same rules pertain, even despite the considerable differences that apply. Since all territory outside of the Land of Israel is by definition unclean, the premise of the Halakhah is that, despite that fact, Israel is to consume its secular meat in accord with those rules of sanctification that pertain to food and its preparation. The laws of cultic cleanness may apply to the household in the Land of Israel but cannot pertain abroad; nonetheless, the other principal admonitions apply overseas. The existence of the temple or its destruction makes no difference.

Then with the classifications established, how do we accomplish the work of hierarchization? Affirming the unique holiness of the temple and the Land of Israel, the Halakhah of *Hullin* wants to show how the holiness of the people Israel retains its own integrity, wherever the people is located, whatever the condition of the temple and its altar. And that demonstration accomplished, the Halakhah establishes that the sanctity of Israel is higher in the hierarchy than the sanctity of the Land and of the temple and its altar. Israel remains holy even outside of the Land, even in the age without the temple. That is why meat prepared for Israel, wherever it has itself been nourished, even on gentile ground, must be prepared as though for the altar in Jerusalem. Then Israel's sanctity persists, even when that continuum in which it stood, the chain of continuity with the temple altar in Jerusalem (as the formulation of Dt. 12:20–24 framed matters), has been disrupted, and Israel's sanctity endows with sanctity even animals raised in unclean ground, so powerful is the sanctification that transforms Israel. The liturgy, stating in its way what the Halakhah sets forth in its manner, explains why, in the afternoon worship for the Sabbath: "You are unique and your name is unique, and who is like your people, Israel, a unique people on earth?"

Why turn in particular to the Halakhah of *Hullin* to make that statement that Israel is holier than the Land and than the temple and endows with sanctity the animals slaughtered to nourish the people? Because the Written Torah supplies a law that contains the entire message, when it imposes the same requirements that pertain to the slaughter of an animal sacrifice for the altar in Jerusalem to killing an animal for the use of Israel at home. That means that meat Israel eats is subject to the same regulations that apply to meat God receives on the altar fires. The same law is explicit that meat for those who are not holy, that is, gentile idolaters, is not subject to the same rules (Ex. 22:30, Dt. 14:21). So the point cannot be missed: food for God and for Israel must be prepared in comparable manner, which does not apply to food for gentiles.

C. *Megillah*

Not only does Israel, the people, transcend the temple and the Land in its sanctification, so too Israel marks time in God's way wherever

Israel is located. And that leads us to the temporal manifestations of God's Kingdom, treated both locatively, here, and temporally, in the next units, to the end of this chapter.

The first of these temporal manifestations is the formation of an Israelite quorum for worship: *when* that takes place, there God is present. *Where* that takes place makes no difference. To understand the matter, we have to take a step back and see from a distance where and when God and Israel meet. Viewed as a whole, the Halakhah identifies two locations for the encounter of God and Israel, the altar at the center, the households and villages arrayed round about. The field or orchard present occasions for the encounter with God in possessing the Land, and the household provides for meeting with God at meal time, to take two obvious cases. And that leads us to ask, where and how does the Halakhah find for the synagogue a place in its structure and system? Since sages explicitly state that study of the Torah may take place anywhere, and since, we know full well, not only votive but obligatory prayer is offered wherever one is located at the time (excepting inappropriate places such as privies), what is left for the synagogue as a location, or, more to the point, the synagogue as an occasion for meeting God? And what, within the framework of the Halakhah, can we possibly mean by "synagogue"? The answer is implicit in the Halakhah of *Megillah*.

The Halakhic answer is that the synagogue represents the occasion at which ten or more Israelite males assemble and so embody Israel, and in particular the synagogue provides for the declamation of the Torah to Israel: it is Sinai, nowhere in particular, to whom it may concern. It is a place made holy by Israel's presence and activity, anywhere Israel assembles, and the presence is for the activity of hearing the Torah proclaimed. It is, specifically, in reference to the synagogue that the Halakhah provides its category-formation accommodating the rules for declaiming the Torah and—more to the point—it is in that context, and there alone, that the Halakhah further specifies *other* rules that govern the sanctity of the synagogue. The other rules, in addition to the Shema and the Prayer, that are set forth in the setting of obligatory prayer concern conduct at the meal, the blessings recited before eating, the Grace after Meals, rules of cultic cleanness at the meal, and, at the end, other obligatory prayers, or blessings, and the occasions that entail them. *Berakhot*, the category-formation for prayer in the conventional sense of the word, scarcely hints that the synagogue is the particular venue for that activity, though the

Halakhah accommodates prayer in the synagogue, as much as in the house of study or the fields, streets, marketplaces, and households.

The Halakhah combines rules for declaiming the *Megillah*, the Scroll of Esther that must be recited at Purim, with rules for declaiming other obligatory passages of Scripture. These Israel must hear not only in community—that is, with other Israelites, e.g., in the marketplace of the village—but in the framework of a particular location, the synagogue and there alone. That is the premise of the Halakhah and accounts for its presentation first of the case, that is, the public recitation in the synagogue of the *Megillah*. What follows is the rule, the public declamation of other passages of the Torah. And that order of discourse raises its own predictable question.

How does the Halakhah of the *Megillah*-reading accomplish sages' goals in the present setting, sustaining the proposition they wish to set forth concerning the synagogue? Since Scripture knows two foci of sanctification, meeting points for God and Israel, altar and village comprised by households or "tents," the Written Torah is able to contribute to the exposition of the laws and life of the synagogue only the single fact that there lections of the written Torah are declaimed. The juxtaposition of what is explicitly required in Scripture—the reading of the Scroll of Esther—with synagogue rules yields the besought conclusion. It is that the declamation of Scripture takes place most suitably in the congregation gathered in a particular building erected and set aside for that purpose—not for prayer, not for sacrifice, not for study, but for Torah declamation. That purpose defines within the Halakhah what the synagogue serves—that alone. And the synagogue is not at the apex of the ladder of sanctification, either of location or of activity.

What then defines the synagogue? It is not contained space of a particular character but the presence of the quorum of male Israelites assembled for the conduct of certain specific activities. Strictly speaking, were the Halakhah to describe how things were, not only how sages wished them to be, archaeology should identify as synagogues in particular remarkably few contained spaces, e.g., buildings of a distinctive character. The Halakhah after all does not specify the traits that a building must exhibit to qualify for use as a synagogue, though it does recognize that a building certainly may be consecrated for synagogue activities alone. But the Halakhah does indicate what is necessary for the conduct of the activities particular to a synagogue, and that is in terms of the presence of holy Israel, embodied in ten males.

Among fewer than ten [1] one does not conduct the recitation of the Shema; [2] and one does not pass before the ark to lead public worship; [3] and one does not raise his hands in the priestly benediction; [4] and one does not read in the Torah; [5] and one does not conclude from a Prophet; [6] and one does not stop and sit after attending a funeral; [7] and one does not recite the blessing for mourners or [8] consolations for mourners, or [9] the groom's blessing; [10] and one does not invite people to say the grace after a meal in God's name. Of the items on the list, some may be performed in private by an individual, e.g., nos. 1 and 10; the others are conducted only within the required quorum. Some of the items on the list—the funeral cortège, for instance—clearly do not involve a particular contained space, a synagogue building, others may. But, we realize, since a quorum may assemble in any suitable space, a synagogue finds its definition in terms not of space but of circumstance. The synagogue, even when required for a particular holy deed, is embodied in the quorum, not in the building. But the building, once sanctified, is deemed holier than a contained (or open) space that has not been sanctified, a fairly minor concession that we shall see in a moment.

So the synagogue finds its definition in its function; it is not a place to which Israelites go to meet God, as the temple is. Rather, it is utopian in the simplest sense: anywhere ten Israelite males conduct a specified activity, the function of the synagogue is carried out, and that is without regard to the location of the Israelites or the character of the space, if any, that contains them. Now, as a matter of fact, that is explicitly *not* the case when we define the two other venues where Israel and God meet, the temple and the enlandised household, extending to the village, that is, the household in the Land of Israel possessed of a plot of land in the Land.

To state matters negatively, the temple cannot be defined as the place where ten Israelites come together to kill a cow. The enlandised household cannot be set forth as a location where ten Israelites produce crops, only a plot of ground owned by an Israelite in the Land of Israel that produces crops. The temple is locative in that it can be only where it is and nowhere else, in Jerusalem, on the Temple Mount.

And, in positive terms, it is there and only there that the activities characteristic of the temple can be carried out. Israelites may say their prayers anywhere, may gather to hear the Torah declaimed in any location. But to slaughter an animal designated for God, to collect its blood and toss the blood upon a stone altar, to burn up parts (or all) of the animal as an offering made by fire to God—these activities can take place only in one place.

The Halakhah assigns to the provenience of the synagogue as consecrated space few critical activities of the life with God. The rhetoric of the Halakhah takes for granted that study of the Torah *may* take place anywhere, but *does* take place in the *beth hammidrash* or house of study. The synagogue is not identified with the house of study or with the activity of study in sages' sense; declaiming the Torah and reciting prayers in public do not compare. While the Halakhah treats as established fact the provision (by sages) of an order of prayer, prayer takes place as much in the household and in the temple as in the local synagogue. The Halakhah of *Berakhot*, as we have already seen, speaks of the Shema, and the Prayer, and the Grace after Meals, all the while taking for granted that the context for reciting these prayers is the household (and equivalent places, e.g., the fields and orchards where workers are at work). Individual obligatory prayers, the Shema and the Prayer, therefore take place wherever the Israelite is located; he need not enter sacred space. The Festivals of Tabernacles and Passover, we recall, encompass home celebration and temple activity, but what takes place in the synagogue on those occasions scarcely registers, and it goes without saying, the same is the case for Pentecost.

Third, when it comes to public prayer, the Halakhah in its classical formulation in the Mishnah assigns that activity to the venue of the temple in the context of the Daily whole offering, so insists the Halakhah of *Tamid*. The account of prayer recited in public—as distinct from the preparation of the daily whole offering at the altar or prayer recited in private or in some other venue than the temple—begins with the priests' recitation of the Shema after they have completed their labor of preparing and presenting the offering:

Mishnah Tamid 4:3Q–T

Q. All of them turned out to be standing in a row, and the limbs in their hands. . . .

R. They went and put them on the lower half of the ramp, on the west side of it.

S. And they salted them the limbs and meal offering.

T. Then they came down and came to the office of hewn stone to recite the *Shema*ᶜ.

Then the priests recite blessings and prayers:

Mishnah Tamid 5:1

A. The superintendent said to them, "Say one blessing."
B. They said a blessing, pronounced the Ten Commandments, the *Shema*ᶜ ("Hear O Israel," Dt. 6:4–9)), "And it shall come to pass if you shall hearken' (Dt. 11:13–21), and "And the Lord spoke to Moses" (Num. 15:37–41).
C. They blessed the people with three blessings: "True and sure," "Abodah," and "the blessing of priests."
D. And on the Sabbath they add a blessing for the outgoing priestly watch.

The upshot is, prayer—public or personal—in no way is linked by the Halakhah to the synagogue in particular, and the synagogue enjoys only a subordinate role in the everyday meeting with God that Israel undertakes. In the synagogue Israel encounters the publicly declaimed Torah, and, in the words that are proclaimed, Israel hears God. In that aspect, the synagogue actualizes the Kingdom of God, not as a place but as an event. Rabbinic Judaism in the Halakhah states that what counts is not localization and enlandisement but attitude and action: Eden is not where but when.

D. *Rosh Hashanah*

Within the Halakhic system, the celebration of the New Year at the first of the lunar month of Tishré—when the full moon of the autumnal equinox will make its appearance, fifteen nights later—marks one of the few occasions at which utopian Israel along with the temple defines the venue for Israel's meeting with God. In most other temporal encounters the altar, alone or in contrastive analogy to the household, sets the stage of the meeting, and in only the declamation of the Torah does the utopian Israel, the synagogue, form the principal location for the meeting. Perspective on the Halakhah of *Rosh Hashanah*, accordingly, is gained only in the setting of the Halakhah of *Megillah*. The shofar, the detail of Rosh Hashanah upon which, within the logic of its system, the Halakhah chooses to concentrate, is sounded in the temple—so Scripture states explicitly—but also in the synagogue, as the Halakhah knows as fact. Yet, in line with the issue of the Halakhah of *Hullin*, the decision is reached that when the temple rite is suspended, as it has been from 70 forward, the shofar is not sounded when Rosh Hashanah coincides with the Sabbath day.

The Halakhah deems the shofar rite particular to the occasion of judgment upon the New Year marked by the first of Tishré and, it follows, legislates for the synagogue as much as for the temple. The formal (if not substantive) key to the Halakhah, the apparent center-piece of its interest, lies in the opening point of the Halakhic state-ment: the judgment that is carried out at the four seasons—at Passover through grain; at Pentecost through fruit of the tree; at the New Year all who enter the world pass before Him like troops, and on the Festival of Tabernacles they are judged through water. But of these four occasions, the only one that registers is the first of Tishré, the New Year. The shape and structure of the Halakhah work out two matters: the sounding of the shofar, the character of synagogue liturgy. Scripture knows that the shofar is integral to the temple rite. But the presentation of the synagogue liturgy insists upon the shofar rite as integral to synagogue worship, and, it follows, the Halakhah centers upon the synagogue service in connection with divine judg-ment of mankind.

Here is a case in which there is no understanding of the Halakhah without constant reference to the Aggadah (generated by Gen. 22) that accounts for, imparts sense to, the rites of the occasion. Divine judgment—God as king—is signaled at the sounding of the shofar in the additional service coincident with the recitation of the pro-nouncements of God's dominion, remembrance, and redemption (the sovereignty, remembrance, and shofar verses). God rules, so God judges. But God remembers, so God judges with mercy. And, finally, God redeems—at the sound of the shofar. In selecting the shofar as the critical rite of the first of Tishré—parallel to the identification of the character of the sukkah as the centerpiece of the Halakhah of Tabernacles—the Halakhah invokes God's mercy in response to Abraham's faith and Isaac's forbearance at Moriah. The Halakhah at hand makes sense only in light of the Aggadic exposition of the ram's horn, well embodied in the following, which carries us even to the matter of substitution, *temurah*, with which this part of the exposition commences:

Genesis Rabbah LVI:IX.1

A. "And Abraham lifted up his eyes and looked, and behold, behind him was a ram, [caught in a thicket by his horns. And Abraham went and took the ram and offered it up as a burnt offering instead of his son]" (Gen. 22:13):

B. What is the meaning of the word for "behind"?

C. Said R. Yudan, "'Behind' in the sense of 'after,' that is, after all that happens, Israel nonetheless will be embroiled in transgressions and perplexed by sorrows. But in the end, they will be redeemed by the horns of a ram: 'And the Lord will blow the horn' (Zech. 9:14)."

D. Said R. Judah bar Simon, "'After' all generations Israel nonetheless will be embroiled in transgressions and perplexed by sorrows. But in the end, they will be redeemed by the horns of a ram: 'And the Lord God will blow the horn' (Zech. 9:14)."

E. Said R. Hinena bar Isaac, "All through the days of the year Israelites are embroiled in transgressions and perplexed by sorrows. But on the New Year they take the ram's horn and sound it, so in the end, they will be redeemed by the horns of a ram: 'And the Lord God will blow the horn' (Zech. 9:14)."

Genesis Rabbah LVI:X.1

A. "So Abraham called the name of that place 'The Lord will provide,' [as it is said to this day, 'On the mount of the Lord it shall be provided']" (Gen. 22:14):

B. R. Bibi the Elder in the name of R. Yohanan: "He said before him, 'Lord of all ages, from the time that you said to me, "Take your son, your only son" (Gen. 22:2), I could have replied to you, "Yesterday you said to me, 'For in Isaac shall seed be called to you' (Gen. 21:12), and now you say, 'Take your son, your only son' (Gen. 22:2)." God forbid, did I not do it? But I suppressed my love so as to carry out your will. May it always please you, Lord our God, that, when the children of Isaac will come into trouble, you remember in their behalf that act of binding and be filled with mercy for them.'"

Now we understand why what is important is the exposition of the law of the shofar, on the one side, and the rites of the synagogue, on the other—the shank of the Halakhah.

The Halakhah then forms a coherent statement. When God meets all Israel, all together and all at once, it is at the temple. There Israel atones, the entire holy people sharing in the daily whole offerings and the other public offerings. When God meets Israel in its parts, the house of Israel assembles within the walls of the household. There Israel celebrates, the households and families of Israel commemorating freedom from slavery, on the one side, celebrating the repose of creation, on the other. When—as we see at the end of this chapter—Israel encounters God in God's inflicting the penalty of drought in response to social sin, it is in the streets of the village, where all assemble out in the open, exposed to the elements, and when Israel remembers God's act of deliverance, it is in the synagogue of the village, under the roof and its protection. But when God judges Israel, it is one by one, and no particular place—not the temple as against the synagogue, nor vice versa—is required, for the encounter is entirely personal—as God's act of judgment of Israel one by one requires.

E. *Pesahim*

For the Halakhah as for the Aggadah, Passover marks the advent of Israel's freedom, which is to say, the beginning of Israel, en route to Sinai. The liturgy for the occasion makes that matter explicit, and that represents a Halakhic statement of a norm: "Passover . . . the season of our freedom." But that only focuses the question of the Halakhah: What is that freedom that Israel gained at Passover, freedom from what? And to what, in the Halakhic framework, had Israel been enslaved? Alas, on the surface the Halakhah in its classical formulation is not only remarkably reticent on that question but lays its emphasis elsewhere altogether.

What makes Israel into Israel, and what defines its trait as Israel, so far as the Halakhah is concerned, is twofold: [1] the preparation of the home for the festival through the removal of leaven, which may not be consumed or seen at that time; and [2] the preparation and presentation of the Passover offering and the consumption of its meat in the household. These define the topics of Halakhic interest—and no others pertinent to the festival register. So the celebration of Israel's freedom turns into the transformation of Israel into a kingdom of priests and a holy people, celebrating its birth by recapitulating the blood rite that marked the separation of Israel from Egypt and the redemption of Israel for life out of death, Israel's firstborn being saved from the judgment visited upon Egypt's. That defines the focus of the Halakhah: the act of sanctification unto life that marks, and re-marks every year, the advent of Israel out of the nations. The freedom that is celebrated is freedom from death.

Its message for the occasion of Israel's beginning as a free people focuses upon Israel's sanctification, and that message comes to the fore in the stress in the Halakhah upon the analogy of the Israelite

household and the temple in Jerusalem, an analogy that takes effect
on Passover in particular. The upshot is, Passover marks the celebration of Israel's redemption, meaning, its separation from Egypt—*the
separation being marked off by blood rites on both sides*—and its entry into
the condition of cleanness so that a temple offering may be eaten in
the very household of the Israelite. True enough, the temple offering
is one of the very few—the offering of the red cow for the preparation of ashes for the purification water (Num. 19:1–20) is another—
that may be conducted in a state of uncleanness. The second
Passover, in the month of Iyyar, explicitly provides for that circumstance. But the point of the Halakhah should not be lost: conforming
with God's explicit instructions in the written Torah, on Passover
Israel differentiates itself from the nations (Egypt) and chooses as the
signification of its identity the attainment of the condition of cleanness in the household, such that, as I said, temple meat may be eaten
there.

Like the Halakhah of *Yoma*, most of which is devoted to the temple rite on that occasion, the Halakhah of *Pesahim* therefore stresses
the cultic aspect of the occasion: the disposition of the Passover
offering. In volume, nearly half of the Halakhah is devoted to that
one theme—Mishnah tractate *Pesahim* 5:1–9:11—and in complexity,
by far the best articulated and most searching Halakhic problems
derive from that same theme. But the Halakhah of *Pesahim* also
belongs to the realm of the Israelite household and even yields a statement on the character of that household that the Halakhah of *Yoma*
does not even contemplate. The household is made ready to serve as
part of the cult by the removal of leaven and all marks of fermentation; now man eats only that same unleavened bread that is God's
portion through the year. The household is further made the locus of
a rite of consuming other specified foods (bitter herbs, for example).
But the main point is, the offering sacrificed in the temple yields
meat to be eaten in the household, at home, not only in the temple
courtyard.

That rule pertains only to lesser holy things, the peace offerings
and the festal offering, for example—and to the Passover, so M. *Zeb.*
9:14: most holy things were eaten within the veils (of the temple),
lesser holy things and second tithe within the wall (of Jerusalem).
Among offerings eaten in Jerusalem in the household but outside of
the temple walls, the Passover offering is the only one precipitated by

the advent of a particular occasion (as distinct from peace and festal offerings pertinent to any festival). The festivals of Tabernacles and Pentecost, by contrast, do not entail a home offering of a similar character, nor does the celebration of the New Month. For its part, the Halakhah of *Yoma* describes an occasion that is celebrated at the temple or in relationship to the temple. In this context, then, the Halakhah of *Pesahim* alone sets forth an occasion in the life of all Israel that commences in the temple but concludes at home. Its message, then, is that for Passover in particular—"season of our freedom"—the home and the temple form a single continuum. That is why I characterize the advent of Israel's freedom from Egypt as an occasion of sanctification: the differentiation through a blood rite in particular of Israel from the nations, represented by Egypt.

On what basis, then, does the Halakhah before us pertain to the world within the walls of the Israelite household in a way in which the Halakhah of *Yoma*, the counterpart, does not? Why have sages treated in a single tractate so distinct a set of venues as the home and the temple, rather than leaving the exposition of the Passover offering to take its place in tractate *Zebahim*, the general rules of the cult, where the Passover makes its appearance in context? Once the question is framed in that way, the obvious answer emerges. Sages through their emphases transformed the festival of freedom into the celebration of Israel's sanctification, embodied here and now in the act of eating the Passover offering at home, in a family, natural or fabricated, that stands for the Israelite household. So as God abides in the temple, so on this occasion God's abode extends to the household. That is why the Passover offering takes place in two locations, the temple for the blood rite, the home for the consumption of the meat assigned to the sacrifiers—those who benefit from the expiation of sin accomplished by the offering.

The law is explicit that people bring the animals to the temple, where the beasts are sacrificed, the blood collected, and the sacrificial portions placed on the altar fires. Then the people take the remaining meat home and roast it. So Passover is represented as a pilgrim festival alone; the home ritual hardly rates a single penetrating Halakhic inquiry, being presented as a set of inert facts. It follows that, on the occasion at hand, the household (at least in Jerusalem) relates to the temple. That means, also, that the Passover sacrifice then stands in an intermediate situation, not an offering that takes place in a state of uncleanness, like the offering of the red cow, which takes place outside of the temple (Num. 19:1–20), nor an offering that is presented and eaten in the temple in a state of cleanness, with the meat eaten by the priests in the temple itself, like the sin offering and other most holy things. As to where the sacrifier eats his share of the Passover offering (and its comparable ones), the Halakhah takes for granted it is in a state of cleanness. So far as the Passover is concerned, it is not eaten in the temple but at home or in a banquet hall, which by definition must be in Jerusalem. That consideration gains weight when we take account of the unleavened character of the bread with which the meat is eaten, in the model of nearly all meal offerings: "All meal offerings are brought unleavened [Lev. 2:4–5, 6:7–9], except for the leavened cakes in the thank offerings [M. 7:1] and the two loaves of bread [of Shabuot], which are brought leavened [Lev. 7:13, 23:17]" (Mishnah tractate *Menahot* 5:1).

By treating the sacrifice in that intermediate realm—the sacrifice in the temple, the meat eaten at home—the Halakhah takes account of the requirement of the Written Torah, which, read as a harmonious statement, dictates that the Passover take place in two locations, the home and the temple. Deuteronomy 16:1–8 places the rite in the temple in Jerusalem. It is explicit that only in the temple is the Passover offering to be sacrificed, and nowhere else. It is to be boiled and eaten in the same place, not at home, and in the morning the people are to go home. With that statement in hand, we should treat the Passover offering as a temple rite, as much as the sacrifice for the Day of Atonement is a temple rite.

Then where is the altar in the home? Exodus 12:1–28 treats the offering as a rite for the home, with the blood tossed on the lintel of the house as a mark of an Israelite dwelling. The lintel then serves as the counterpart to the altar. That is where the blood rite takes place, where the blood of the sacrifice is tossed. Here we find as clear a statement as is possible that the Israelite home compares to the temple, the lintel to the altar, the abode of Israel to the abode of God. Why the lintel? It is the gateway, marking the household apart from the world beyond. Inside the walls of the Israelite household conditions of genealogical and cultic cleanness pertain, in a way comparable to the space inside the contained space of the temple courtyard.

How exactly are the enclosed spaces of household and temple comparable? It is temporal and occasional, not permanent and spatial.

True, the Oral Torah treats the lintel of the Israelite home to the altar, the contained space of the Israelite household as comparable to the temple courtyard, the household serving as the venue for an offering comparable to the sin offering. But that analogy takes effect only at a very specific moment, just as the household compares to Eden only at the specific moment of the Sabbath day, the invisible wall descending to mark off the temporal Eden in the particular space consecrated by the Israelite abode. The advent of the first new moon after the vernal equinox—the fifteenth of Nisan—then compares with the advent of sunset on the sixth day, the beginning of the Sabbath comparing, then, to the beginning of the lunar calendar marked by the first new moon of spring. The Sabbath places Israel in Eden. The fifteenth of Nisan places the Israelite household into a continuum with the temple, the lintel with the altar (in the Written Torah's reading).

With Passover the Israelite, in the Halakhic theory, carries his offering to the temple and brings home the sacrificial parts to be consumed by himself and his family (or the surrogate family formed by an association organized for that particular purpose), so treating the household as an extension of the temple for the purpose at hand. That same conception extends to other lesser holy things, eaten in Jerusalem but not in the temple; but Passover among festivals is unique in having its own offering, celebrating its own specific event in the natural year and in the rhythm of Israel's paradigmatic existence as well.

While the Passover, moreover, may be subject to the rules of lesser holy things, still, it bears its own very particular signification. Some of the lesser holy things are interchangeable, in that if an animal is designated for one purpose but offered for another, it may serve, e.g., as a freewill offering. But in the case of the Passover in particular, we deal with a lesser holy thing that is not interchangeable. The Oral Torah stresses that the rite is analogous to the sin offering, in that the animal that is designated for the rite must be offered for that purpose—and for that particular sacrifier. If it is designated for the benefit of a given party (sacrifier) and offered for some other sacrifier and it is not possible to clarify the situation, the animal is simply disposed of, so we recall M. *Pesahim* 9:9 for example: "An association, the Passover offering of which was lost, and which said to someone, 'Go and find and slaughter another one for us,' and that one went and found and slaughtered [another], but they, too, went and bought and slaughtered [one for themselves]—if his was slaughtered first, he eats his, and they eat with him of his. But if theirs was slaughtered first, they eat of theirs, and he eats of his. And if it is not known which of them was slaughtered first, or if both of them were slaughtered simultaneously, then he eats of his, and they do not eat with him, and theirs goes forth to the place of burning, but they are exempt from having to observe the second Passover." The stress on the specificity of identification of the beast and sacrifier aligns the Passover offering with the sin offering, not with peace or free will offerings.

That analogy is stated explicitly at M. *Zeb.* 1:1: "All animal offerings that were slaughtered not for their own name are valid (so that the blood is tossed, the entrails burned), but they do not go to the owner's credit in fulfillment of an obligation, except for the Passover and the sin offering—the Passover at its appointed time (the afternoon of the fourteenth of Nisan), and the sin offering of any time." The theory of the matter is explained in the argument of Eliezer that the guilt offering should be subject to the same rule: "The sin offering comes on account of sin, and the guilt offering comes on account of sin. Just as the sin offering is unfit (if it is offered) not for its own name, so the guilt offering is unfit (if offered) not for its own name." Eliezer's statement takes for granted that the sin offering is brought in expiation of (inadvertent) sin, and it must follow, the Halakhah in general must concur that the same category encompasses also the Passover offering. That matches the story of the blood on the lintel, an offering that expiates sins of Israel and atones for those sins for which, on the same moment, Egypt will atone through the offering of the firstborn among men and cattle alike. Within that theory, how shall we find in the account of the offering the basis for treating it as comparable to the sin offering, which is offered to expiate inadvertent sin? Since the Passover offering signals that Israel is to be spared the judgment of the Lord executed against the firstborn of Egypt, it is reasonable to suppose that the blood of the Passover lamb, placed on the lintel, not only marks the household as Israelite but also expiates inadvertent sin carried out in that household.

True, the Written Torah itself imposed the requirement of celebrating Passover in two places, Deuteronomy in the temple, the meat consumed in Jerusalem, exodus at home, the meat consumed there.

But in joining the two conceptions, with its rules for the household wherever it is located, the Halakhah has made a statement of its own out of the facts received from Scripture. That statement is in two parts. First, the Israelite abode is treated as comparable to the temple not merely in the aspect of cultic cleanness, but in the aspect of cultic activity: the place where the sacrificial meat was consumed, within the unfolding of the rite of expiation of inadvertent sin itself. It is that analogy, between the Passover on the fourteenth of Nisan and the sin offering at any time, that forms the critical nexus between the Israelite abode and the temple altar. So the question arises, why that particular analogy, and to what effect? Or to state matters differently, what statement do we make when we say, as the Halakhah explicitly says, the Passover offering is comparable to the sin offering?

The answer derives from the occasion itself, Israel on the eve of the exodus from Egypt, at the threshold of its formation into a kingdom of priests and a holy people. When God executed judgment of Egypt, exacting the firstborn of man and beast as the sanction, he saw the blood, which—the Oral Torah now tells us—compared with the blood of the sin offering. Israel then had expiated its inadvertent sin and attained a state of atonement, so entering a right relationship with God. On the eve of Israel's formation, the Passover offered at home, with the blood on the lintel, marked Israel as having expiated its sin. The sinless people were kept alive at the time of judgment— just as, at the end of days, nearly all Israel will stand in judgment and pass on to life eternal.

Sin and atonement, death and life—these form the foci of Passover. If sages had wished to make the theological statement that Israel differs from the Egyptians as does life from death, and that what makes the difference is that Israel is sanctified even—or especially— within its household walls, not only within the temple veils, how better to say so than through the Halakhah of Passover? Eat unleavened bread as God does in the meal offerings, consume the meat left over from the blood rite of the Passover offering, analogous to the sin offering in its very particular identification with a given family unit, and the actions speak for themselves. These are the two facts out of the repertoire of the data of Passover that the Halakhic statement from the Mishnah through the Bavli chooses to explore and articulate. It is the Written Torah that sets forth the facts, the Oral Torah that explores their implications for the norms of conduct, while, in doing so, imparting its sense for the proportion, therefore the meaning and significance, of the whole.

Why these two topics in particular? The sages will assuredly have maintained they said no more than the Written Torah implied, and, as we have seen, that claim enjoys powerful support in the content of the Halakhah. But sages are the ones who framed the law, chose among its points those for proportion and emphasis. In doing so, they shaped the law into a statement congruent with the stresses of their system as a whole. The Halakhah's—so I have argued from the outset—was a theology of restoration, Israel to the Land standing for mankind to Eden—all to God's dominion. Sages knew full well that all Israel was resident outside of Jerusalem; in the time that the Halakhic statement was being formulated, Israel could not enter Jerusalem, let alone sacrifice on the ruined, ploughed-over temple mount. But to the realities of the moment sages chose to make no statement at all; these meant nothing of enduring consequence to them. For the situation of Israel in the here and now did not define the focus of the Halakhah, only its venue.

For sages, at stake in the Halakhah is the transformation of Israel by time and circumstance, the reconciliation of Israel and God by rites of atonement for sin, and the location of Israel and God into a single abode: the household now, Eden then. What is at stake in the Halakhah of innermost Israel, the Israel embodied in the abode of the household? It is what takes place in the holy of holies on the Day of Atonement: the encounter of Israel, its sins atoned for, its reconciliation in the aftermath of the fall from Eden complete—the encounter of Israel with God, the occasion of eternity, the moment at which, for now, death is transcended.

Scripture said no less, sages no more: "It is the Lord's Passover. For I will pass through the land of Egypt that night, and I will smite all the firstborn in the land of Egypt, both man and beast; and on all the gods of Egypt I will execute judgments; I am the Lord. The blood shall be a sign for you, upon the houses where you are; and when I see the blood I will pass over you, and no plague shall fall upon you to destroy you, when I smite the land of Egypt." The Halakhah makes the statement that the freedom that Passover celebrates is Israel's freedom from death. Where Israel lives, there life is lived that transcends the grave. When, as is the custom, some people at the Passover Seder wear their burial garment, the gesture says no less than that.

F. *Sukkah*

The Halakhah of the festival of Tabernacles focuses upon the sukkah, an abode that cannot serve in the season that is coming, announced by the new moon that occasions the festival. Israel is to take shelter, in reverting to the wilderness, in any random, ramshackle hut, covered with what nature has provided but in form and in purpose what man otherwise does not value. Israel's dwelling in the sukkah is fragile, random, and transient—like Israel in the wilderness. Out of Egypt Israel atoned and lived, now, after the season of repentance, Israel has atoned and lived—but only in the condition of the wilderness, like the generation that, after all, had to die out before Israel could enter the Land and its intended eternal life.

The temporary abode of the Israelite, suspended between heaven and earth, the sukkah in its transience matches Israel's condition in the wilderness, wandering between Egypt and the Land, death and eternal life. Just as Passover marks the differentiation of Israel, expiating sin through the Passover offering and so attaining life, from Egypt, expiating sin through the death of the firstborn, so Sukkot addresses the condition of Israel. It is, we must remind ourselves, the generation of the wilderness with which we deal, that is, the generation that must die out before Israel can enter the Land. So entering the sukkah reminds Israel not only of the fragility of its condition but also —in the aftermath of the penitential season—of its actuality: yet sinful, yet awaiting death, so that a new generation will be ready for the Land. So it is that interstitial circumstance, between death in Egypt and eternal life in the Land, that the festival recapitulates. Sages maintain that had Israel not sinned, the Torah would have contained only the Pentateuch and the book of Joshua, a neat way of stating in a few words the conviction that permeates the Halakhic reading of the Land as counterpart to Eden, Israel as counterpart to Adam. It is on that basis that I see the wilderness as I do: the interval between death in Egypt and eternal life in the Land. The sukkah, the now-abode of Israel-in-between is the house that is not a house, protected by a roof that is open to the elements but serves somewhat: Israel en route to death (for those here now) and then eternal life (for everyone then).

It is at the sukkah itself that I find the center of the Halakhic repertoire concerning the festival of Tabernacles. Israel in the wilderness, replicated annually from the first new moon after the autumnal equinox, lived in houses open to the rain and affording protection only from the harsh sunlight, shade if not continuous shadow such as a roof provides. Their abode was constructed of what was otherwise useless, bits and pieces of this and that, and hence useless and so insusceptible to uncleanness. And, we note, that is the abode in which Israel is directed to take up residence. The odd timing should not be missed. It is not with the coming of the spring and the dry season, when the booth serves a useful purpose against the sun, but at the advent of the autumn and the rainy one, when it does not protect against the rain. And it is for rain that Israel now beseeches God.

Reminding Israel annually by putting the Israelites into booths, that Israel now lives like the generation of the wilderness then, sinful and meant to die, the Halakhah underscores not only transience. It emphasizes the contemporaneity of the wilderness condition: the sukkah is constructed fresh, every year. Israel annually is directed to replicate the wilderness generation—Scripture says no less. The dual message is not to be missed: Israel is en route to the Land that stands for Eden, but Israel, even beyond the penitential season, bears its sin and must, on the near term, die—but in death enjoys the certainty of resurrection, judgment, and eternal life to come. What we are dealing with here is a redefinition of the meaning of Israel's abode and its definition. All seven days a person treats his sukkah as his regular dwelling and his house as his sometime dwelling. On the occasion of the festival, Israel regains the wilderness and its message of death but also transcendence over death in the entry into the Land. Only in the context of the New Year and the Day of Atonement, only as the final act in the penitential season and its intense drama, does Sukkot make sense. It is the Halakhah that draws out that sense, in the provisions that define the valid sukkah upon which I have laid such heavy emphasis.

True, the Written Torah tells more about the observance of the festival of Sukkot than about the occasion for the festival. And the Halakhah follows suit, with a systematic account of the temple

offerings for the same occasion. But viewed from the perspective of
this study, what it does say—"that your generations may know that I
made the people of Israel dwell in booths when I brought them out
of the land of Egypt"—suffices. The reversion to the wilderness, the
recapitulation of the wandering, the return to Israel's condition outside of the Land and before access to the Land, the remembrance of
the character of that generation, its feet scarcely dry after passing
through the mud of the Reed Sea when it has already built the
golden calf—that is the other half of the cycle that commences at
Passover and concludes at Sukkot. Who can have missed the point of
the festival, with Scripture's words in hand, "that I made the people
of Israel dwell in booths"? The rabbis of the Halakhah certainly
did not.

Let us compare the provisions for the principal Halakhic moments,
Pesahim and *Sukkah*. Viewing the festival of Tabernacles in the model
of the festival of Passover, we find that three elements require attention, in two divisions: what happens in the home, what happens in
the temple, and what happens in the home that connects the home
to the temple? Passover has the home cleansed of leaven, with the
result that the bread of the holiday corresponds to the bread served
to God in (most of) the meal offerings. What happens in the temple
is the sacrifice of the Passover offering. What happens in the home
that connects the home to the temple is the eating of the portions of
the Passover offering that the ordinary Israelite on Passover eats, just
as the priest in the temple eats portions of the sin offering (among
other most holy things). So, as we have seen, Passover marks the
moment at which the home and the temple are made to correspond,
the whole taking place within the walls of Jerusalem. That perspective turns out to clarify the divisions of the Halakhah of *Sukkah* as well:
what happens in the temple is a celebratory rite involving the utilization of certain objects (lulab, etrog) and the recitation of the Hallel
Psalms.

What happens in the home? The home is abandoned altogether, a
new house being constructed for the occasion. During the festival,
the Israelite moves out of his home altogether, eating meals and
(where possible) sleeping in the sukkah, making the sukkah into his
regular home, and the home into the random shelter. Just as, in the
wilderness, God's abode shifted along with Israel from place to place,
the tabernacle being taken down and reconstructed time and again,

so, in recapitulating the life of the wilderness, Israel's abode shifts, losing that permanence that it ordinarily possesses. What happens in the home that connects the home to the temple? At first glance, nothing, there being no counterpart to the Passover Seder. But a second look shows something more striking. To see the connection we must recall that during the festival a huge volume of offerings is presented day by day. There he will consume the festal offering (*Hagigah*) and other sacrificial meat, e.g., from the freewill offering. Israel removes to the housing of the wilderness to eat the festival meat, doing in the sukkah what God did in the tabernacle in that epoch.

At the new moon following the Day of Atonement, having atoned and been forgiven, Israel takes up residence as if it were in the wilderness. Why so? Because in the wilderness, en route to the Land, still-sinful Israel depended wholly and completely on God's mercy and good will and infinite capacity to forgive in response to repentance and atonement. Israel depends for all things on God, eating food he sends down from heaven, drinking water he divines in rocks—and living in fragile booths constructed of worthless shards and remnants. Even Israel's very household in the mundane sense, its shelter, now is made to depend upon divine grace: the wind can blow it down, the rain prevent its very use. Returning to these booths, built specifically for the occasion (not last year's), manipulating the sacred objects owned in particular by the Israelite who utilizes them, as the rainy season impends, the particular Israelite here and now recapitulates his total dependence upon God's mercy.

Accordingly, requiring that everything be renewed for the present occasion and the particular person, the Halakhah transforms commemoration of the story of the wandering into recapitulation of the condition of the wilderness. The sukkah makes the statement that Israel of the here and now, sinful like the Israel that dwelt in the wilderness, depends wholly upon, looks only to, God, lives not only in God's dominion but wholly by God's mercy. Israelites turn their eyes to that God whose just-now forgiveness of last year's sins and acts of rebellion and whose acceptance of Israel's immediate act of repentance will recapitulate God's ongoing nurture that kept Israel alive in the wilderness. The Halakhah's provisions for the sukkah underscore not so much the transience of Israel's present life in general as Israel's particular condition. The Halakhah renders Israel in the sukkah as the people that is en route to the Land, which is Eden.

Yes, Israel is en route, but it is not there. A generation comes, a generation goes, but Israel will get there, all together at the end. So in defining the sukkah as it does, the Halakhah also underscores the given of God's providence and remarkable forbearance. In a negative way the Halakhah says exactly that at M. *Sukkah* 2:9: "[If] it began to rain, at what point is it permitted to empty out [the sukkah]? From the point at which the porridge will spoil. They made a parable: To what is the matter comparable? To a slave who came to mix a cup of wine for his master, and his master threw the flagon into his face." No wonder, then, that in the Aggadah Sukkot is supposed to mark the opportunity for the Messiah to present himself and raise the dead.

G. *Mo'ed Qatan*

In this context it is not surprising that, presenting the Halakhah of the intermediate days of the festivals of Tabernacles and Passover, the Mishnah, the Tosefta, Yerushalmi, and Bavli focus a sizable proportion of the Halakhah upon the rules of burial. What connection does the Halakhah discern between rites of mourning and the rules governing conduct on the intermediate days of the festival? What made sages conceive that the latter should find a comfortable and capacious place amid the former—even to the extent of extensively and promiscuously interspersing rules of mourning in expositions of intermediate days of the two protracted, week-long festivals of first full moon after the autumnal and vernal equinoxes, respectively?

What has death to do with the intermediate days of the festival? To answer that question we remind ourselves how the Halakhic founders, the framers of the Mishnah, conducted their speculative thought. The principal mode of thought of the Mishnah is that of comparison and contrast. Something is like something else, therefore follows its rule; or it is unlike the other, therefore follows the opposite of the rule governing the something else. So as a matter of hypothesis, let us assume that the framers of the Halakhah of *Mo'ed Qatan* found self-evidently valid the modes of thought that they learned from the Mishnah and so made connections between things that were alike, on the one side, or things that were opposite, on the other. How do death and mourning compare to the intermediate days of the festival? The point of opposition—the contrastive part of the equation—then proves blatant. Death is the opposite of the celebration of the festival. The one brings mourning, the other, joy. And the Mishnah's inclusion of the mourner on its list of those whose special situation must be taken into account then precipitates thought about the item on the list—the mourner—that most clearly embodies the special circumstance of all items on the list.

But if the contrast proves obvious, the point of comparison—how are these things similar, and what rule pertains to both—emerges with equal facility. Extremes of emotion—mourning, rejoicing—come together in the normal cycle of life and the passage of time. Each takes its place on a continuum with the other, whether from the perspective of the passage of time in nature or the passage of life, also in nature; whether from the perspective of the sacred or from the standpoint of uncleanness. The natural rhythm of the year brings Passover and Tabernacles, the celebration of the first full moon after the vernal and autumnal equinoxes, respectively. The natural rhythm of life brings its moments of intense emotion, too. But death and the festival also form moments of a single continuum, one of uncleanness yielding to its polar opposite, sanctification, sanctification yielding to uncleanness. Death, we must not forget, also serves as a principal source of uncleanness, the festival, the occasion for sanctification beginning with the removal of cultic uncleanness and the entry into a state of cultic cleanness. These opposites also take their place on a single continuum of being. And, as a matter of fact, death takes place on festivals and on Sabbaths as much as on secular days.

So in establishing the connection, through treating the categories as equivalent and counterpart to one another, between death and the festival's intermediate days, what does the Halakhah say? Dealing with the inevitable, death, in the setting of its opposite, the festival, the sages make the connection between the one and the other—death and the festival's intermediate days—so as to yield a conclusion concerning the everyday and the here and now. These are neither permanently sanctified nor definitively unclean, neither wholly the occasion for rejoicing without restriction as to acts of labor nor entirely the occasion of common ventures without restriction as to attitudes of exaltation. The days between festivals, like ordinary life, after birth but before death—these are to be seen as sanctified but not wholly so, just as life forms the realm of the angel of death, but only for a while. The festival comes—and so does the resurrection of the dead and the life of the world to come, of which the festival, like the

Sabbath, gives us a foretaste. The Halakhah has addressed the necessities of everyday life—death on the intermediate days of the festival—and encompassed those opposites, mourning and rejoicing, in a single statement of how things are. It would be difficult to point to a more intimate, a more mundane, or a more exalted conception than the Halakhic one at hand, the one that dictates the consideration of seasons of rejoicing and seasons of mourning as these intersect. In life they do.

H. *Besah*

One may prepare food on the festival days of Passover, Pentecost, and Tabernacles. Scripture is explicit on that point. But the Halakhah of *Besah* wishes to raise searching questions. If I had to select the single most pervasive principle of Halakhah, it is the insistence on designating food before the festival for use on the festival, on the one side, and linking the status of the householder to the status (e.g., as to location) of his possessions, on the other. In advance the householder must designate for use on the festival what he is going to prepare on the festival. That represents an act of particularization, this batch of food for this festival in particular, and it is entirely familiar to us in another context altogether. The temple and its offerings define that context, where, we recall, e.g., from the Halakhah of *Pesahim*, the animal to be used for a Passover offering must be designated for that purpose. Once the animal is designated, without appropriate rite it cannot then be used for some secular purpose or some other sacred purpose. An animal for use as a sin offering must be linked to that particular sin; the farmer who presents it must have in mind the inadvertent transgression that the animal expiates. A general statement that the animal expiates generic sin will not serve. Insisting on that same procedure in connection with the bulk of food and utensils for food preparation used for the festival treats the food for the table as comparable to the food for the altar. The same rule governs the identification and particularization of both, each for its respective purpose.

The first and most profound case to yield an abstract issue, the famous one about the utilization of an egg laid on the festival day—can it be said to be prepared in advance for use on that day, because it existed in potential form, or not prepared and forbidden for use, because it did not exist in actual form—raises a philosophical question and shades over into reflection upon a theological issue. The philosophical question is, how do we classify what is potential? Do we deem it as actual, in that the acorn contains within itself the potentiality of the oak, so the acorn is classified as an oak *in nuce*? Or do we deem what is potential as distinct from what is actual? Readers familiar with Aristotle's deep thought about the classes of causation will find themselves right at home here. The Halakhah takes the position that the egg may not be eaten, meaning, we differentiate the potential from the actual.

Embedded in the same case, especially in Tosefta's rich amplification of it, is the Halakhah's recurrent stress on the particularity of intentionality. Here the principle is, one must in advance of the festival designate for use on the festival whatever one is going to utilize on that day. What about food? We impute to the householder the intent to prepare certain food that comes to hand, therefore a calf born on the festival may be slaughtered and eaten on that same day. At the same time, in the language of the Mishnah, nets for trapping a wild beast, fowl, or fish, which one set on the eve of the festival day—one should not take [what is caught therein] out of them on the festival day, unless one knows for certain that [creatures caught in them] were trapped prior to the eve of the festival day. It follows that while, as we see later on in the Halakhic exposition, an act of prior designation is required for using on the festival various things, that does not pertain to food of every origin itself; there we simply stipulate that food available *in nuce* is designated for use. On the other hand, Tosefta adds, the owner has to have known in advance that what he will eat on the festival in fact was available as food; even though the egg is edible, since the owner did not know, in advance, that the egg would be available, he did not designate it for eating on the festival, and so it is not available for that purpose.

The theological question concerns the divisibility of the sacred, which is to say, do we differentiate what is sacred for one reason from what is sacred for another, the time that is sacred as the festival from that which is sacred as the Sabbath, in the present case? Or does the festival flow naturally into the Sabbath? At issue is whether what is legitimate on the festival may be done on the festival for utilization on the Sabbath, a deeply reflected-on question indeed? The answer carries us into the conception of commingling. We recall that space may be commingled, so that on the Sabbath ownership may be shared to a common courtyard or alleyway. Owners relinquish their private ownership for the common good of establishing a shared domain, and a fictive, symbolic meal of commingling accomplishes that task. In the case of commingling time, the Halakhah both differentiates the holiness of the festival from the holiness of the Sabbath and also commingles them. It does so by treating them as not continuous but subject to melding. That yields a number of concrete rules, all of them based on the differentiation of contiguous spells of consecrated time.

First, one may prepare food on the festival, and what is left over may be used on the Sabbath, on which one of course does not prepare food. So the Halakhah is explicit. On a festival day one is permitted only to prepare food for that same day while he may not prepare food for use after the festival; on the festival he may prepare food for the festival itself, and if he leaves something over, he has left it over for the Sabbath.

Second, one may not prepare on the festival food specifically for use on the Sabbath that follows immediately. Thus the rule states: As for a festival that began on Thursday night, such that its conclusion coincided with the eve of the Sabbath on Friday night—a person should not do cooking to begin with on the festival day that is, Friday for the purposes of the Sabbath. That is the point where the two spells of sacred time are kept distinct, each following its own rule.

Third, if one starts preparing food on Thursday for the festival that falls on Friday, he may continue adding food to the mixture on Friday, leaving over more food for the Sabbath. And before the eve of the festival day, that is, on Thursday, he may prepare a cooked dish and rely on it to prepare food on Friday for the Sabbath. The preparation of this dish marks the beginning of the individual's cooking of food for the Sabbath. Once he has begun, on Thursday, to prepare food for the Sabbath, he may continue that preparation, even on the festival day itself. And for that purpose a single dish is sufficient. That represents a commingling of time effected through a meal, comparable to the commingling of space effected through the meal.

Through these closely linked rules, the Halakhah states that we respond both to the unity and to the diversity of sacred time. All consecrated time bears the same traits, e.g., the prohibition of labor. But within that genus, we speciate sacred time on which one may prepare food from that on which one may not. Just as we noted in connection with the intermediate days of the festival, we move from the concrete to the abstract, so here too we do the same. That is, from the fact that on the intermediate days, festival offerings are presented, we proceed to the abstract conception that, in some ways, these days on which it is permitted to work are differentiated from other days on which it is permitted to work, because on these days offerings respond to the level of sanctification accorded to those intermediate days.

That is to say, the differentiation at the one point is generalized into elements of differentiation elsewhere. Here too we both treat as continuous and differentiate the sacred time marked by the festival, on the one side, and the Sabbath, on the other. Just as on the one occasion we may cook and on the other we may not—cooking then representing the indicator in the household, comparable to the offering in the temple—so on the one occasion we may not prepare food for the other occasion. But we may both use on the Sabbath food left over from the festival and also prepare in advance a single stew or broth that will serve both. Preparation in advance of the festival for both the festival and, en passant, the Sabbath, is certainly permitted. In sum, we both differentiate and homogenize.

That leads us to a further Halakhic case that embodies a profound issue: doing actions connected with preparing food on a festival day in a different manner from on ordinary days. That is an issue familiar from the principle, in connection with the Sabbath, that if on the Sabbath one carries something from one domain to another in an other-than-ordinary manner, he is not culpable. Now, when it comes to food preparation, encompassing bringing food from place to place, one brings jars of wine not in a basket but on his shoulder. And so too, he who takes straw should not hang the hamper over his back. But he brings it carrying it in his hand. What is at issue here? If we say that on the festival, those acts that are permitted may be carried out in a routine way, as they are done in ordinary time, then we maintain that the secular breaks into sacred time, the act of cooking on the festival (encompassing also secondary and tertiary stages in the process) is comparable to the act of cooking on a weekday. In this aspect the festival is distinguished from the Sabbath and therefore in this aspect is secular.

What position does the Halakhah take? If we say that on the festival those acts that are permitted must be done in a manner different from the way they are done in ordinary time, we are saying that the sacred time of the festival is different from the sacred time of the Sabbath, but remains sacred time, subject to restrictions upon secular behavior even when actions in the category of the secular are permitted to be carried out. The law takes the latter view. It recognizes the genus, sacred time, and its species, Sabbath distinct from festival. That explains why many of the acts that are permitted in connection with food preparation must be carried out in a manner that distinguishes the same action from the way it is done on an ordinary day. We deal, then, with two subdivisions of sacred time, each sharing traits with the other, while distinguished from the other; we distinguish the sacred from the sacred.

The difference between the holiness of the festival and the Sabbath is intrinsic and substantive. The difference between the intermediate days of the festival and utterly profane time is notional and circumstantial: hard work versus routine work—but work if done, then done in the usual way. The issue, then, is, How do we differentiate secular time that is distinguished at the cult from secular time that is not, hence the intermediate days of the festival from ordinary days? Here, by contrast, we differentiate the sacred from the sacred, and that explains why what work is permitted is done in a manner that registers the difference between the holy day on which it is performed and the manner of doing the same work on an ordinary day. When the Sabbath concludes, followed by a festival day, the liturgy that marks the distinction between the Sabbath and other time—the rite of differentiation or habdalah—states the matter very simply. At the end of the Sabbath prior to a weekday, the prayer praises God for distinguishing the holy from the ordinary. At the end of the Sabbath prior to a festival day, the same prayer praises God for distinguishing the holy from the holy. The Halakhah says no less, but spells out the meaning of the distinction, which is shown in rich detail to make a huge difference.

I. Ta'anit

So far as the Halakhah is concerned, Israel lives in God's Kingdom in three ways: through performing deeds of sanctification, through the provision of regular offerings, and through worship. Israel, wherever located, engages in an endless conversation with God, a dialogue in which, as, in the Aggadic representation of matters, God talks to Israel through the Torah, so in the Halakhic portrayal, Israel talks to God through prayer. And God communicates his will in what happens, as Israel responds to God's will by appropriate words and deeds. So much for the public relationship of ongoing, perpetual, daily dialogue of word and deed. It goes without saying that private persons furthermore express prayer as a matter of option and also as a matter of Halakhic duty. The everyday and ordinary public relationship effected through words comes to expression in acts of worship, with stress on the profession of acceptance of God's dominion and thanksgiving for God's beneficence and benevolence.

What happens when events bear the message that Israel has sinned, which is to say, when rain fails or when gentiles threaten? The answer to that question concludes the theology of the Halakhah by completing the circle of the system. The Halakhic statement of *Ta'anit* spells out how Israel relates to God through prayerful statements to him on both ordinary, natural and extraordinary, historical occasions. That is why regular prayers for rain, for example, are supplemented by extraordinary prayers and related activities, as the case requires. When the rhythm of nature is disrupted, so that rain does not come in its season, then the orderly gives way, the everyday prayer not having sufficed. Then Israel responds to the admonition carried by events by reconsidering its relationship with God and identifying the flaws in its part of that relationship that have provoked divine punishment in the form of drought. Accordingly, in the setting of the transcendent transaction at hand, Israel relates to God not only in the temple and through the possessions and goods and persons of the holy people, but also in everyday encounters. Everywhere and all the time, God hears and answers prayer. And when Israel prays and does not attain its goal, e.g., for rain that does not fall, then Israel responds by showing its humility and remorse for sin.

The premise of the Halakhah is that if times of trouble punish Israel for sin, then the correct response is penitence. Fasting alerts God to the penitential attitude of Israel. But Israel relates to God also by invoking God's long record of saving Israel from calamity. So Israel presents itself to God as both worthy of compassion and bearer of a heritage of divine favor. The present situation—outcry for salvation from drought—then recapitulates the long record of a trustworthy relationship. The key to the relationship of God and Israel is located in the formal prayer recited in behalf of the community on seven successive fasts. The realized theology of the Halakhah is contained in the liturgy of the fast day, as much as it is embodied in the liturgy of daily worship:

Mishnah Ta'anit 2:1

The manner of fasting: how [was it done]? They bring forth the ark into the street of the town and put wood ashes on the ark, on the head of the patriarch, and on the head of the head of the court. And each person puts ashes] on his head. The eldest among them makes a speech of admonition: "Our brothers, concerning the people of Nineveh it is not said, 'And God saw their sackcloth and their fasting,' but, 'And God saw their deeds, for they repented from their evil way' (Jonah 3:10). "And in prophetic tradition it is said, 'Rend your heart and not your garments'" (Joel 2:13).

Mishnah Ta'anit 2:2

They arise for prayer. They bring down before the ark an experienced elder, who has children, and whose cupboard [house] is empty, so that his heart should be wholly in the prayer. And he says before them twenty-four blessings: the eighteen said every day, and he adds six more to them. And these are they: Remembrance verses, Shofar verses, "In my distress I cried to the Lord and he answered me . . ." (Ps. 120), and, "I will lift up my eyes to the hills . . ." (Ps. 121), and, "Out of the depths I have cried to you, O Lord . . ." (Ps. 130), and "A prayer of the afflicted when he is overwhelmed" (Ps. 102).

Mishnah Ta'anit 2:4

For the first [ending] he says, "He who answered Abraham on Mount Moriah will answer you and hear the sound of your cry this day. Blessed are you, O Lord, redeemer of Israel."

Mishnah Ta'anit 2:5

For the second he says, "He who answered our fathers at the Red Sea will answer you and hear the sound of your cry this day. Blessed are you, O Lord, who remembers forgotten things."

Mishnah Ta'anit 2:6

For the third he says, "He who answered Joshua at Gilgal will answer you and hear the sound of your cry thus day. Blessed are you, O Lord who hears the sound of the Shofar."

Mishnah *Ta'anit* 2:7

For the fourth he says, "He who answered Samuel at Mizpeh will answer you and hear the sound of your cry this day. Blessed are you, O Lord, who hears a cry."

Mishnah *Ta'anit* 2:8

For the fifth he says, "He who answered Elijah at Mount Carmel will answer you and hear the sound of your cry this day. Blessed are you, O Lord, who hears prayer."

Mishnah *Ta'anit* 2:9

For the sixth he says, "He who answered Jonah in the belly of the fish will answer you and hear the sound of your cry this day. Blessed are you, O Lord, who answers prayer in a time of trouble." For the seventh he says, "He who answered David and Solomon, his son, in Jerusalem, will answer you and hear the sound of your cry this day. Blessed are you, O Lord, who has mercy on the land."

The list takes shape around no clear point in common other than the predicate, ". . . will answer you." Some of the items involve a time of crisis, e.g., Jonah; some pertain to times of drought, e.g. Elijah; but Abraham on Moriah obeyed God's will and issued no prayer for salvation, and quite how David and Solomon in Jerusalem fit is not easy to say. So it is the long-term relationship, not the specificities of the incidents or persons that are invoked, that registers.

The Halakhah provides for the individual and for all Israel, for the exile and for the Land. At the outset of what appears to be a drought, individuals take action, fasting in daytime, eating at night. They, and the community at large, conduct themselves in the normal way. When the drought deepens, then the community as a whole responds, and all renounce normal life, giving up working, bathing and washing, ordinary garments, and sexual relations. If the crisis turns into an emergency, then the community goes into massive public mourning. The Halakhah underscores that the Israel of the here and now participates in that enduring present framed by the figures of Abraham, Jonah, and the rest.

The Halakhah of *Ta'anit* encompasses a second topic. When the priests of a given village go up to Jerusalem to undertake their work at the altar of the temple, the entire community of Israel, priests, Levites, and Israelites, participates. Outside of Jerusalem, Israelite delegations at home gather, give up labor, and in worship and Torah-study recapitulate the six days of creation in the village, as their neighbors and representatives conduct the celebration and commemoration and recapitulation in the Jerusalem temple, day by day. Here, too, as at *Mo'ed Qatan*, the Halakhic statement introduces two distinct topics and treats them as intersecting. How to interpret the jarring juxtaposition of public fasting for sin and public celebration of creation? The answer to that question encapsulates the entire theology of the Halakhah.

The creation of the world, the salvation of Israel in times of trouble—these two topics of the Halakhah of *Ta'anit* embody those transactions that override the bounds of time and locale. Then Israel plays out its life in an eternal present and celebrates in the here and now the very beginnings of the world, on the one side, the tale of God's reliable salvation, on the other. What affords Israel entry into a world beyond time—Abraham at Moriah—and before time—God in creation—is Israel's own invocation: calling on God here and now to repeat the response to Abraham at Moriah and Israel at the sea; repeating day by day the record of the first six days of the natural world—but rewriting the end of the story of what happened on that awful sixth day.

So looking backward, we see in perspective how the path from Eden to the Kingdom of God passes through the realm of death and emerges in eternal life. The Halakhah serves as the guideposts along the path of Israel within the interior spaces of the heart.

EPILOGUE

THE HALAKHIC STRUCTURE SEEN WHOLE

I. The Problem and the Halakhic Solution

The theological narrative of the Halakhah may be briefly summarized as a whole in a few sentences, in two paragraphs, the one describing the problem facing God in the encounter with man, the other the solution put forth at Sinai through the Halakhic account of the regenerate social order Israel is to realize.

A. *The Problem*

God created nature as the setting for his encounter with humanity. Creation was meant as God's Kingdom for man's bliss. But with the sin of man committed in rebellion against God's will, the loss of Eden, and the advent of death began the long quest for the regeneration of man. In the unfolding of generations, ten from Adam to Noah, ten from Noah to Abraham and thence to Sinai, it was only Israel that presented itself for the encounter. But then Israel too showed itself man. For on the other side of Sinai came the celebration of the golden calf.

B. *The Halakhic Solution*

What to do now? It is to rebuild God's Kingdom among that sector of mankind that undertakes to respond to God's self-manifestation in the Torah and to realize God's dominion and imperatives: the Torah, the commandments. God provided for Israel, surrogate of humanity, the commandments as a medium of sanctification for the reconciliation with God and renewal of Eden, the triumph over the grave. Freed of sin through offerings that signified obedience to God's will, by reason of repentance and atonement, signifying man's acceptance of God's will over his own, which to begin with had brought about the fall from Eden, man might meet God, the two in mutual and reciprocal commitment. Where Israel atoned for sin and presented itself as ready for the meeting, there God and Israel would found their Eden, not a place but an occasion. In overcoming the forces of death and affirming life through purity, Israel brings into being such an occasion. The Halakhah then serves as the medium of sanctification of Israel in the here and now, in preparation for the salvation of Israel and its restoration to Eden.

II. The Halakhic Reconstruction of the Human Condition

The Halakhah sets forth a systematic and coherent response to the Torah's account of the human condition, set forth in the Pentateuch, Genesis through Deuteronomy, and in the Prophetic Books, Joshua through Kings and Isaiah, Jeremiah, Ezekiel, and the Twelve. That account portrays the tragic situation of man from Eden onward, the hopeful situation of Israel from Sinai onward. The Halakhah lays out how Israel's entire social order may be constructed to cope with the situation precipitated by the loss of Eden now and to restore Eden as originally intended. Israel, educated by the Torah, undertakes the task, counterpart to the first Adam. But this time it would be through the willing realization of God's rule, both in the present hour and at the end of days. That actualization takes place within Israel.

How will it happen? Tutored by the Torah to want by nature what God wants but will not coerce Israel to want—"the commandments were given only to purify the heart of man"—Israel makes itself able to realize God's will and to form his kingdom within its holy community. Through examining the Halakhah in its native categories or tractates, these propositions are shown to animate the entire Halakhic corpus, which is thus proved to embody a theological system, one that rests firmly upon the foundations of Scripture whole and in detail.

III. Reprise: The Halakhic Structure Epitomized

To transcend the mass of detail set forth in Chapters Eleven through Fourteen, let us now see the Halakhic structure whole. I briefly recapitulate the main findings derived from the specific category-formations/tractates that we have systematically set forth.

CHAPTER ELEVEN

WHERE AND WHEN IS EDEN?

i. *Shebi'it*
ii. *'Orlah*
iii. *Kilayim*
iv. *Shabbat-'Erubin*

By "Eden" Scripture means that place whole and at rest that God sanctified; "Eden" stands for creation in perfect repose. In the Halakhah, Eden stands for not a particular place but nature in a defined condition, at a particular moment: creation in Sabbath repose, sanctified. Then a place in repose at the climax of creation, at sunset at the start of the seventh day, whole and at rest, embodies, realizes Eden. The Halakhah means to systematize the condition of Eden, to define Eden in its normative traits, and also to localize Eden within Israel, the people. How so? Eden is the place to the perfection of which God responded in the act of sanctification at the advent of the seventh day. While the Land, in the Written Torah's explicit account of matters, claims the right to repose on the seventh day and in the seventh year of the septennial cycle, it is the location of Israel wherever that may be at the advent of sunset on the eve of the seventh day of the week of creation that recapitulates Eden.

WHO OWNS EDEN?

i. *Ma'aserot*
ii. *Terumot*
iii. *Hallah*
iv. *Ma'aser Sheni*
v. *Bikkurim*
vi. *Pe'ah*
vii. *Dema'i*

The story, within the motif of Eden, expands to the matter of ownership and possession as media for the expression of the relationship between man and God. God accorded to Adam and Eve possession of nearly everything in Eden, retaining ownership—the right to govern according to his will—for himself. The key to the entire system of interaction between God and Israel through the Land and its gifts emerges in the Halakhah of *Ma'aserot* and its companions, which deal—along the lines of *Shebi'it* and *'Erubin*—with the difference between possession and ownership. God owns the world, which he made. But God has accorded to man the right of possession of the earth and its produce. This he did twice, once to man—Adam and Eve—in Eden, the second time to Israel in the Land of Israel. And to learn the lesson that man did not master, that possession is not ownership but custody and stewardship, Israel has to acknowledge the claims of the creator to the glory of all creation, which is the Land. This Israel does by giving back God's share of the produce of the Land at the time, and in the manner, that God defines. The enlandised components of the Halakhah therefore form a single, cogent statement of matters.

ADAM AND EVE

i.   *Qiddushin*
ii. *Ketubot*
iii. *Nedarim*
iv. *Nazir*
v.   *Sotah*
vi. *Gittin*
vii. *Yebamot*
viii. Sacralization and Intentionality

The Halakhah of the family, covering the act of sanctification of a woman by a man (*Qiddushin*), the marriage agreement (*Ketubah*), vows and special vows, the disposition of a charge of unfaithfulness against a woman, and the severance of the marital bond of sanctification through a writ of divorce or death, does not ubiquitously invoke the metaphor of Adam and Eve in Eden. Our task, then, is to identify the principal foci of that Halakhah and to investigate the appropriate context in which it is to be interpreted. How here does Eden figure? The connection is made articulate by the (possibly later) liturgical framework in which the Halakhah plays itself out. There, in the liturgy of the marriage canopy, the act of creation of man is recapitulated, the bride and groom explicitly compared to Adam and Eve. Not only so, but the theme of the Land and Israel intervenes as well—two motifs dominant in the Halakhic theology examined to this point.

CHAPTER TWELVE

SIN AND ATONEMENT

i.   The New Moral Entity
ii. *Sheqalim*
iii. *Tamid* and *Yoma*

iv. *Zebahim* and *Menahot*
v.   *'Arakhin*
vi. *Bekhorot*
vii. *Me'ilah*
viii. *Temurah*

The Halakhah takes account of the tragedy of Eden and provides for a new moral entity, a reformed transaction accorded that entity, one not available to Adam and Eve. For God at Eden made no provision for atonement for sin, but, in the unfolding of man's story, God grasped the full measure of man's character and drew the necessary conclusion and acted on it. Endowed with autonomous will, man has the power to rebel against God's will. Therefore the Halakhah finds urgent the question, How is man, subject to God's rule, to atone for the sin that, by his rebellious nature, man is likely to commit? The Torah, to answer that question, formulates the rules that govern man both [1] when under God's dominion and [2] when in rebellion against God's will. These represent the two aspects of the one story that commences with Eden, leads to the formation of Israel through Abraham, Isaac, and Jacob, God's antidotes to Adam, and climaxes at Sinai. But Israel also is man, so that story accommodates both Adam's fall and Israel's worship of the golden calf, and, as the denouement, Adam and Eve's exile from Eden and Israel's ultimate exile from the Land. How, then does God propose to repair the world he has made to take account of man's character and Israel's own proclivity?

INTENTIONALITY AND THE CIVIL ORDER

i.   Legitimate Violence: Who Does What to Whom
ii. *Keritot*
iii. *Sanhedrin-Makkot*
iv. *Baba Qamma-Baba Mesi'a-Baba Batra*
v.   *Horayot*
vi. *Shebuot*

The Halakhah dictates the character of Israel's civil order—its political institutions and system of criminal justice. It undertakes a labor of differentiation of power, indicating what agency or person has the power to precipitate the working of politics as legitimate violence. When we understand the differentiating force that imparts to politics its activity and dynamism, we grasp the theology that animates the structures of the politics and propels the system. The details of the Halakhah, in particular the sanctions assigned to various infractions, effect the taxonomy of power, which forms an implicit exegesis of the story of Eden, translated into reflection on the power of intentionality.

CHAPTER THIRTEEN

ENEMIES OF EDEN, TANGIBLE AND INVISIBLE

THE CONTEST BETWEEN DEATH AND LIFE, UNCLEANNESS AND SANCTIFICATION: THE SOURCES OF UNCLEANNESS

i.   Tangible Enemies: *'Abodah Zarah*
ii. Invisible Enemies: Death. *Ohalot*
iii. *Nega'im*
iv. *Zabim* and *Niddah*

The enemies of Eden take shape around the grand struggle between life and death, in the here and now meaning Israel and the gentiles, at the end of days meaning those who will stand in judgment and go onward to the world to come and eternal life, and those who will perish in the grave. Specifically, the world beyond the limits of Israel forms an undifferentiated realm of idolatry and uncleanness. Then how is Israel to negotiate life with the world of gentiles and their idolatry, corpses and their contamination? Among the sources of uncleanness, tangible and invisible, we begin with the gentiles and proceed to corpse- and comparable kinds of uncleanness. But the two—gentiles, corpses—form a single domain. The former bears exactly the same uncleanness as the latter. Gentiles, defined as idolaters, and Israelites, defined as worshippers of the one and only God, part company at death. For the moment Israelites die—only to rise from the grave. Gentiles die for eternity. The roads intersect at the grave, each component of humanity taking its own path beyond. Israelites— meaning those possessed of right conviction—will rise from the grave, stand in judgment, but then enter upon eternal life, to which no one else will enjoy access.

THE CONTEST BETWEEN DEATH AND LIFE, UNCLEANNESS AND SANCTIFICATION: THE LOCUS OF THE STRUGGLE FOR LIFE

i.   Uncleanness and Sanctification
ii. *Makhshirin*
iii. *Tohorot*
iv. *'Uqsin*
v.   *Kelim*

The sources of change and disruption that threaten the cleanness, hence the sanctification, of the temple are the same sources that threaten the norm of cleanness of the household. If the same uncleanness affects the temple and the table, then the only difference is one of degree, not of kind, as the Halakhah states explicitly. And the rest follows. The web of relationships between sanctification and uncleanness spins itself out into every corner of the Israelite household, where the system makes a difference. And it is the will of the householder that determines the difference that the distinction between clean and unclean is going to make. Everything is relative to the householder's will; he has it in his power to draw the household table into alignment with the altar in the temple, that is to say, to place the table and the food set thereon into relationship, onto a continuum, with the altar and the holy things of the cult. This he can accomplish through an act of will that motivates an attitude of constant watchfulness in the household for those very sources of contamination that Scripture identifies as danger to the Lord's altar in the Jerusalem temple.

OVERCOMING DEATH: RITES OF PURIFICATION

i. *Parah*
ii. *Miqvaot*
iii. *Tebul Yom*
iv. *Yadayim*
v. Home and Temple in Hierarchical Formation: *Hagigah*
vi. Cause and Effect: Where and Why Man's Will Matters

From death and its affect upon food and drink, that is, the uncleanness caused by, and analogous to, death, we turn to the media for the restoration of life. Still water unaffected by human agency restores the natural condition disrupted by uncleanness other than that of the corpse and its analogues, while by contrast purification water systematically subjected to human intervention—constant attention, deliberate action, start to finish—alone removes corpse-uncleanness. We have then to account for the exclusion of man from the one process, the radical insistence upon his inclusion, in full deliberation, within the other. Uncleanness that comes about by reason of any cause but death and its analogues is removed by Heaven's own dispensation, not by man's intervention: rainfall, sunset suffice. Ordinary purification is done by nature, resulting from natural processes. But as to persons and objects that have contracted uncleanness from death, nature on its own cannot produce the kind of water that bears the power to remove that uncleanness and restore the condition of nature. Only man can. And man can do this only by the highest level of concentration, the most deliberate and focussed action. Man's act of will overcomes the uncleanness of death, just as man's act of deliberate rebellion brought about death to begin with. Man restores what man has disrupted. Had the Halakhah wished in its terms and categories to accomplish a reprise of the story of man's fall, it could not have made a more eloquent statement than it does in the contrast between the Halakhah of *Miqvaot* and that of *Parah*.

CHAPTER FOURTEEN

THE KINGDOM OF GOD

i.   From Eden to the Kingdom of God: Accepting the Yoke of the Commandments
ii. *Berakhot*
iii. *Hullin*
iv. *Megillah*
v.   *Rosh Hashanah*
vi. *Pesahim*
vii. *Sukkah*
viii. *Mo'ed Qatan*
ix. *Besah*
x.   *Ta'anit*

As much as man by his nature rebels against God, man tutored by the commandments willingly accepts God's will and therefore his rule. What are the Halakhah's media for the reformation, regeneration, and renewal of man? The Halakhah here legislates for not Eden but the kingdom of God. For Sinai's answer to Eden's question transcends the matter of sin and atonement and encompasses the conduct of the ordinary, everyday life lived under God's rule. The normative deals with the normal, so the final solution to God's dilemma with man—how to accord man free will but to nurture in man freely-given love for God—lies in the Torah. That way of life in accord with God's rule means to form the *paideia*, the character-building education to transform man by making Israelite man's freely-given obedience to God as natural as was the first man's contumacious rebellion against God. That is why the Halakhic provision for life in God's kingdom moves from the ordinary day and its duties to the table and its everyday nourishment, then to the meeting with God that is seasonal and temporal, and finally to the climax of the system, confrontation with routine crisis.

IV. System and Structure: How the Aggadah and the Halakhah Intersect

In fact, we have in the Halakhah a reworking of two parallel stories, the story of the creation and fall of Adam and Eve from Eden, then the story of the regeneration of humanity through the Torah's formation of Israel. The two stories then are linked in the encounter of Israel and the nations, represented by the uncleanness of death that, through the disciplines of purity, Israel is to overcome. The tension between them comes to its resolution in the resurrection of Israel from death, those who know God being destined for eternal life. The two stories, adumbrated in the heads of the outline that follows, represent the native category-formations of the Aggadah. Now, the native category-formations of the Halakhah as expounded in these pages are folded into the Aggadic framework:

I. The story of man and rebellion, sin and atonement, exile and restoration

   Where and When Is Eden?
   Who Owns Eden?

II. The parallel story: Israel and God, sin and just punishment, repentance and atonement, forgiveness and restoration

   Israel's Adam and Eve
   Sin and Atonement
   Intentionality and the Civil Order

III. The story of Israel and the nations, specifically, Israel formed by the Torah, the gentiles lacking the Torah

   Enemies of Eden, Tangible and Invisible
   The Contest between Death and Life
   Overcoming Death
   The Kingdom of God

The sages' philosophical reading of Scripture—its Halakhah and its Aggadah alike—leads to the transformation of the Torah's account of humanity's story into the design for Israel's social order: God's kingdom, Eden realized now, restored at the end.

V. The Theology of Rabbinic Judaism

This brief précis of the results shows how a few large motifs form of the details of the Halakhah a single coherent system, one that tells a story. Rabbinic Judaism sets forth a massive, detailed, concrete actualization of Scripture's imperatives, both those implicit in narrative and articulated by the Aggadic system, and those explicit in Scriptural law and logically expounded by the Halakhic structure. Clearly, the Halakhah works from Scripture forward. But, being theologians, systematic thinkers, intent on a philosophical reading of religion in quest of a coherent, proportionate, and rigorously argued statement, the Rabbinic sages do not randomly rework this detail or that. Rather, the sages' philosophical reading of Scripture—its Halakhah *and* its Aggadah alike—produces a coherent theology. It tells a coherent story. That continuous narrative leads to the transformation of the Torah's account of humanity's story into the detailed design for Israel's social order. The details all find their place within the structure of the whole, and in its workings, the system that sages have constructed animates the whole, the parts working well together to make a simple statement.

That is easily set forth. In its actualities Israel embodies—or is meant to embody—God's plan for mankind, not individual, but as a social entity: God's kingdom, Eden both realized in the here and now and restored at the end. The Rabbinic Judaism embodied, actualized, and realized in the Halakhah is the religion that publicly, in the sight of all humanity, realizes now and for eternity the imperatives of God, made manifest at Sinai, in the Torah, and that thereby shows the way to eternal life with God.

So we have followed the interior architectonics of Israel's being that the Halakhah tells through concrete action-symbols. The Halakhah brings about the transformation of the here and the now, of the particular occasion (thus: place and time and event, mostly in nature) into the embodiment, the exemplification, of the abstract ground of being. Involved is relationship of realms of the sacred: the rules of engagement between and among God, Land, Israel, time, place, circumstance. Through the fabric of everyday life of the Land lived out in the household, village, and the holy metropolis, Jerusalem (the three dimensions of the social order of which the Halakhah takes account), Eden is read as not historical moment but situation and occasion. That then precipitates thought about the human condition. But Eden does not impose narrow limits on the amplification of that thought. It is not the only condition.

There is also the situation brought about by the second great theme, besides Eden, that is implicit in the Halakhah. It is God's self-manifestation in the Torah, the occasion for the reform and renewal of man through Israel, the counterpart and opposite of man. The Halakhah therefore will be shown to begin with Eden but to progress to the realization of God's kingdom within holy Israel's social order, conceiving of Israel both enlandised (defined within the Land) and utopian (located anywhere), as the category of the Halakhah requires.

A third massive motif involves Eden once more, this time under God's rule, and it too engages with the Torah's account of Israel at Sinai. It concerns the re-embodiment of Israel, the restoration that comes about not alone in the end of days when the Messiah comes, but in the here and now of the workaday world. It is there that Israelite man formed by the discipline of the Torah learns both to atone for and to overcome, his natural propensity willfully to rebel against God. Within the social order of an enlandised Israel moral man constructs a godly society. That reading of the Written Torah and translation of its law into the canons of ordinary life speaks in the acutely present tense to portray for man a worthy future well within man's own capacities to realize: "the commandments were given only to purify the heart of man," and "All-Merciful wants the heart," as the Talmud frames matters. Therein I identify the theology of the Halakhah: massive, closed system that, in dialogue with the Aggadah and wholly coherent with its system, but in its own category-formations and language, says the same thing about many things.